# Let's Do It

# Let's Do It

## The Authorised Biography of Victoria Wood

Jasper Rees

TRAPEZE

First published in Great Britain in 2020 by Trapeze,
an imprint of The Orion Publishing Group Ltd
Carmelite House, 50 Victoria Embankment,
London EC4Y 0DZ

An Hachette UK company

1 3 5 7 9 10 8 6 4 2

© Jasper Rees 2020

A CIP catalogue record for this book is
available from the British Library.

HB 978 1 4091 8409 6
TPB 978 1 4091 8410 2
eBook 978 1 4091 8412 6

Typeset by Input Data Services Ltd, Somerset

Printed and bound in Great Britain by Clays Ltd, Elcograf S.p.A.

www.orionbooks.co.uk

To Emily

# Contents

'Have just made myself laugh so much. I was sitting at my desk, and looked over at my tall shelf that my awards are on. I wondered idly what the nearest one was, a bronze round one, I couldn't recall . . . I got up to look; it was a brass ceiling light the electrician had left there . . . I think I will just leave it there and tell people it's my prize for best new sitcom from the Oslo television festival.'

Victoria Wood, fax to Richenda Carey, 13 April 2001

# INTRODUCTION

# VICTORIA WOODS

'My mother sent a note to say you must excuse me . . .'
'The Ballad of Barry and Freda', 1986

'I feel like the luckiest person in the world to be able to do this job, to be able to live this life and just work in a job with other people who want to be there.' It was the middle of the night when Victoria Wood spoke these words into a cassette recorder. 'And not just write,' she went on, 'but to be able to sell what I write and be on television with what I do. I mean God, I couldn't ask for more and I don't. I don't ask for more.'[1]

This was in July 1998. Having spent the previous six months alone in her office writing the first series of *dinnerladies*, now she was doing the bit she loved best: joining up with talented friends to generate laughter. Uniquely for a British sitcom, every episode of *dinnerladies* was recorded in front of an audience twice: once on Friday night then, incorporating yet more rewrites from Victoria, again on Saturday night. It made for a gruelling schedule and she was living on adrenalin.

At the age of forty-five, she had made barely any television in four years; indeed, her previous series – a set of half-hour comedies collected under the title *Victoria Wood* – was nearly a decade in the past. In the interim, in a succession of national tours each spanning the best part of a year, Victoria had established herself as the preeminent live comic of her generation. In between she had given birth to two children. The joy she felt at making *dinnerladies*, she confided to the tape, was her reward for taking the painful decision not to have a third.

As Victoria returned to the BBC, it came to her that this might be the moment to prepare for a memoir. The audio diary is a patchwork in which reflections on the day's work intermingle with stories from long ago – the time she first encountered Julie Walters, or competed on *New Faces* in dungarees she loathed. She would record her thoughts and memories early in the morning before she went to work, or late at night after an exhausting day in the rehearsal room or the studio. Often she makes herself laugh. In this particular entry, done so late on a Friday it was already Saturday, Victoria speaks intimately, seeming to let herself into her own secrets as she gives thanks for her good fortune: 'I feel I've been given and given and given so much. I feel I've been given so much talent and I've somehow struggled to acquire the discipline to use it and it's not been wasted.'

At a quarter past one, she pressed stop and went off to tidy the house. In the morning she got up at seven to do a food shop, before heading to Television Centre. The tapes are punctuated with deep, shuddering yawns. They would not be heard by anyone until after her death.

In the closing credits of *Acorn Antiques*, wobbling diagonally across the screen, it says the part of Berta is played by 'Victoria Woods'. Has there ever been a truer typo? More than anyone on your television, Victoria Wood seemed to be plural. In her passport she listed her profession as 'entertainer'. She was, more accurately, an entertainment industry in the body of one woman. She first appeared on national television winning a heat of a talent show. In her last appearance as herself, baking cakes for Comic Relief, she was still winning. The forty-one years between those two victories brought four stage musicals, four West End residencies, five major national tours, incorporating forty sold-out nights at the Royal Albert Hall, three sketch series, four Christmas specials, eight television dramas plus one short, thirteen documentaries and three appeals shot in fifteen countries, ten original contributions to Comic Relief, eight hours of sitcom, half a dozen half-hour plays, two scripts for children's TV, more than 180 songs, countless awards, and innumerable gags. She wrote, acted, composed, sang, directed, produced, presented, joked. She played the piano, the trumpet and the ukulele. Once upon a time she even did magic tricks.

Until Victoria, no comedian had attempted to tell a British audience how women really think and feel. She was the first to talk frankly about the disappointment they were liable to encounter in the bedroom, and the complex relationship they might have with their own bodies. In the early 1980s, as she began in stand-up, she was free to monopolise a field of human experience that was out of bounds to men. 'They're terrible things, bras,' she said in her first solo tour. 'I read this thing once in a magazine and it was a test to see whether you needed to wear one or not. And the test was if you could hold a pencil underneath. It was very depressing for me. I could hold a small branch of WH Smith.' This was new. It had always been men who joked about breasts, but Victoria repossessed them. Over the years, onstage on her own, she would describe the journey of the female body as she had progressively experienced it – puberty and periods, conception, pregnancy, childbirth and breast-feeding to menopause and, finally, hysterectomy. The other subject she majored in was television. She spent a lifetime watching it then, with a savage love, surgically deconstructing it.

And then there was northernness. 'We'd like to apologise to viewers in the north,' said her snooty southern continuity announcer. 'It must be awful for them.' Her ear for the gradations of class grew out of jostling tensions in her Mancunian family tree. The sensibility she inherited was Lancastrian, which conferred linguistic riches but also relentless stoicism. 'They have a really good way of expressing themselves,' she explained. 'It's very unemotional. You'd never say, "Oh darling, you were marvellous." People in Lancashire would say, "Oh that's not bad," or "I didn't mind it."'[2] Her innate aversion to gush was such that co-workers were often deprived of the praise some of them craved.

These were her themes. Her turns of phrase were uniquely her own. She wallpapered her world with a vocabulary that made her laugh – macaroon and minestrone, balaclava and raffia, grouting and guttering and vinyl flooring. She adored and frequently used the surname Mottershead, deemed the letter K the alphabet's funniest – hence Kidderminster, Kiri Te Kanawa, Kirkcudbright, Knutsford. Every word she selected had a weight and a value and a role, even when sometimes her dialogue amounted to a set of Dalíesque non-sequiturs: 'My daughter born Christmas Eve, so we called her Brenda.'

'The lady's credits gang up on you in a way that was once reserved for Orson Welles,' wrote Clive James in 1980, when she'd barely begun.[3] Years before the eruption of all-round brilliance she titled *Victoria Wood As Seen on TV*, one reviewer was referring to a type of comedy known as 'Victoria Woodland',[4] another to 'modern Victoriana'.[5] Victoria could compress an essence of who she was through the lens of a television camera and telegraph it out to a theatre seating thousands. She would make audiences laugh till it hurt and could choke them up with sorrow. The widest pendulum swings between joy and pathos were to be found in her songs. They could be merry and oh-so-clever with rat-a-tat triple rhymes to rival the wit of Cole Porter and Noël Coward. Alternatively, they'd rip hearts in two.

Thus Victoria Woods. The misnomer was a coded joke. One night in May 1974, the month she turned twenty-one, Victoria in her Birmingham student bedsit watched till the closedown of the day's broadcasting in the hope of hearing her name spoken on television for the first time. 'Also appearing,' advised the regional announcer, 'Virginia Wood.' Later that year a nervous compère on *New Faces* announced her as 'Joanna Wood', and, after she won her heat, her first ever newspaper interview referred to her as 'Christine Wood'. Once, doing a play in Sheffield, she was introduced to Hayley Mills, who called her 'Veronica Wood'. In her act she enjoyed mixing herself up with two Virginias, Woolf and Wade.

There were two Victorias in another sense. When they met her, people were looking for their friend Victoria, the one who always seemed to be bouncing for joy on the piano stool of life. One after another they were surprised to find her shy and guarded, not laughing and larking and yanking her sleeves up to unleash yet more jokes. That Victoria Wood, who bounded on stage to greet an audience with a glittering smile and a cheery hello, was an optical illusion, conjured up with the assistance of an actual conjuror who happened to be her husband Geoffrey Durham, better known to the public as the Great Soprendo. It was this mirage whom readers of the *Independent* voted the Briton they'd most like to have as a neighbour, over and above the Queen Mum.

'People think I'm nice,' she once told the *Radio Times*.[6] People were right. Many friends and colleagues testify to Victoria's kindness, her generosity, her loyalty. She was a good and wise person to know in a crisis. But an ambitious woman coming to light entertainment in the all-male 1970s required something else. Victoria knew with absolute conviction how she wished things to be done, and she would say so. She wanted her lines to be spoken as written, with the stress correctly placed to land the gag. Some of the cast of *dinnerladies*, recalling the strain of learning and relearning her dialogue, still appear to suffer from a sort of post-traumatic sitcom disorder. Later, when Victoria began to direct her own work for the stage, she deployed none of the coaxing diplomacy that traditionally goes with the role. It was a culture shock for her casts. But all concur that, in the matter of selling her comedy to an audience, she was always *always* right. On rare occasions when she found herself not in charge, she could grow frustrated. She was nearly sixty when, in Kolkata to front a documentary about tea, she vented to a friend back home: 'Am writing this in hotel loo escaping from production meeting where I am repressing the cry "you are all fuckwits please just do as I say . . ."'[7]

When the distance between the two Victorias became apparent, it could be a shock. A couple of months before *dinnerladies* was filmed, she went to a party hosted by the actress Richenda Carey, whom Victoria knew via her husband Geoffrey's regular attendance at Quaker meetings. She cut an isolated figure among socially confident actors. Her hostess was so troubled to discover Victoria was no mingler that she rose in the night to fax an apology: 'It was only after, when you left, that I thought, no, I've just been really thick about what it must be like to be you . . . I think it's because you are in people's sitting rooms, and being very Down Home and sort of Ordinary and Friendly, that it gives a weird impression of intimacy which is completely unfounded.'[8] People felt that they knew Victoria, but this was because she knew them. She knew all about ordinary people living ordinary lives in ordinary bodies, and she used her knowledge to make extraordinary comedy.

Her education in such things began when she was a teenager who watched and listened from the wings. She prowled guiltlessly, even ruthlessly, among her friends too. Celia Imrie accepted that the price of being in Victoria's gang was to have her life and even her appearance mined for comedy. Julie Walters was warier. 'It would be hard to be weak with her,' she says. 'Very hard. Early on it was a very immature jokey relationship, so there was no place for that. But generally to be weak with her was not a good idea. Because she would possibly use it.' Mostly, though, Victoria scavenged for material in the rich seam of her own memories.

She started a diary in her late twenties – coincidentally or not, the same sort of age as her father began his – and stuck to it for more than three decades. As for the idea of a biography, such a book was first proposed in 1986 by Geoffrey Strachan, her publisher at Methuen, soon after he'd brought out her first collection of sketches. Victoria herself mentioned it in the form of a joke on tour in 1993. 'Maybe I should start having an affair,' she would say onstage, 'because somebody will want to write a biography of me one day and there'll be nothing to put in it . . . Perhaps I'll just settle for a very, very thin biography. Was born, lived, told a few jokes, knackered a few bras in the tumble drier, died.' In 1997, by which time Victoria was so famous that the Post Office could deliver fanmail addressed 'Victoria Wood, London' to her door in Highgate, she was approached by a fellow old girl of Bury Grammar School about collaborating on such a project. She politely declined, but it helped prompt her to start keeping the audio diary. Then, when *dinnerladies* was being broadcast to millions, she was asked again by a leading publisher. 'I keep thinking I could write a good book too!' she replied.[9] The arrival of an unauthorised biography in 2002 – she asked everyone she could think of not to talk to its author – focused her mind once again. She was an enthusiastic devourer of biographies and memoirs, including no fewer than three by the Scottish actress Molly Weir. But somehow, while publishers

kept tempting her with ever-increasing offers, she always had something else that wanted doing more. Instead Victoria's instinct was to
pass personal truths through the prism of her imagination. She told
her story by other means, filtering her childhood, her marriage and
the loneliness that came after her divorce into songs, sketches and
dramas. Meanwhile, on the walls of her home, framed covers of the
*Radio Times* and *TV Times* measured out her life in carbon-dating
haircuts. She once even had the idea of chopping up all the costumes
she'd worn onstage and, with her sewing machine, fashioning them
into a quilt: her CV would be draped across her bed in electric blue,
canary yellow, rainbow Lycra and of course Kimberley orange, in
and among the elegant crease-free suits and coats that Betty Jackson
designed for her.

I first met Victoria in 1999 when she was making the second series
of *dinnerladies*. For the next decade we had many conversations in
which she would talk of her current work but also offer detailed
answers about her childhood and her earlier years. What was striking
in someone so very famous, aside from her seriousness, was her honesty. Usually there's a formality to such encounters – a consciousness
that on some level an interview is a transaction. With Victoria I could
detect no such distancing membrane. In 2007 I asked her if she might
one day write an autobiography. 'I could write a memoir,' she said.
'I've been offered a ton of money. I'm sort of interested. I just hate
going into a bookshop and seeing all those books by people who can't
write with their big fat photograph on the cover, people who've done
nothing and can't string a sentence together, and I just think it deval-
ues people who can put a sentence together and can write a book. I
would like to write one about my first few years in show business.'[10]

While that memoir was never written, our hours and hours of
interviews have allowed me to place Victoria's voice at the heart of her
own story. I have also been able to draw on her archive of correspondence, notebooks, scrapbooks, scripts, tapes, cuttings and photograph
albums, as well as letters, faxes and emails which have been generously
shared by many, above all a correspondence spanning more than forty
years with Jane Wymark, whom she met at Birmingham University in
1971. Victoria, it goes without saying, was an inimitable letter writer.

She could be dazzlingly witty and then frankly confessional or, in the best of times and the worst, both at once.

The earliest sample of her handwriting is from a postcard written to her sister Rosalind in 1957, when she was four. 'LOVE VICKI', she inscribed above a couple of crosses, one vertical as a crucifix.[11] The last letter written in her name was in fact composed by Cathy Edis, her personal assistant for nearly twenty years. Victoria had returned home after three months in hospital when yet another offer to write a memoir came in. Cathy ventriloquised a reply: 'I have too many other things to work at and have not yet found the time or energy to devote to my memoirs! I shall let you know when that moment arrives.'[12] Two weeks later the nation was mourning Victoria's loss.

While I have pieced together the jigsaw of Victoria's life wherever possible using her own words, her story could not have been told without the guidance of many others: her children Grace Durham and Henry Durham, their father Geoffrey Durham, her sisters Rosalind Watson and Penelope Wood, her assistant Cathy Edis, her so-called 'lady bodyguards' Lucy Ansbro and Adele Fowler of Phil McIntyre Entertainment, her original gang Julie Walters, Celia Imrie and Duncan Preston, her long-standing enabler Geoff Posner, her directors and producers, tour managers and promoters, musical collaborators, friends from school and university and beyond, a large support network of women friends, Piers Wenger and the younger gang she gathered around her in later years as she tilted from comedy to drama, documentary and musicals.

One of those newer friends was Daniel Rigby. In 2010 they played mother and son in *Eric & Ernie*, the BBC drama about the young Morecambe and Wise. After the shoot, Victoria invited him to be her lodger, and together on the sofa they became obsessive about *MasterChef*. Long after he'd moved out, he turned to her for advice when struggling with some writing. 'If it was easy everyone would do it,' she counselled by email. 'And you are bothering because although it may not feel like it, you are happier bothering than not bothering.'[13] Victoria was happier bothering. While the resulting work occupies the foreground of her story, in the background there are other constants: exercising, watching TV, reading, donating blood, doing charity fundraisers, baking spectacular birthday cakes, sticking snaps in albums, walking up and down fells, sorting cupboards and taking stuff to Oxfam, eating egg and chips in cafés, shopping in Brent Cross, going to films and shows, renovating homes, collecting teapots, hosting Christmas parties, curating her friendships.

Above all, from 1988 onwards, motherhood became the galvanising pulse of each and every day. Put simply, if a child of hers were to swim the channel, Victoria would have been in the support vessel. Where that drive to be a good mother came from is, perhaps, the defining theme of this book. Her fans must reckon with a bleak equation: that without the neglect of parents who left her to be brought up by the television set in her den, there would be no Victoria Wood as we know her. Her genius – and genius it was – came at a cost.

I had one precious experience of watching Victoria at close quarters as she worked an audience. A season of her work was being shown at the BFI Southbank in 2008, and I was to interview her in a packed cinema. Before we went on, she was quiet and self-contained. As we walked through the pass door onto the stage she seemed to blossom into her other self. Once the ecstatic applause had died down, I introduced her with a long respectful account of a distinguished career containing countless reinventions. The longer I went on, the more I could see cogs whirring mischievously. Eventually I finished. She looked at me with those twinkling blue eyes, measured out an immaculately timed pause and said, 'Please could you repeat the question?'

Let's do it – while the mood is right.

# I

# FACES

**'I've wanted to be famous since I was tiny.'**
*The South Bank Show*, 1996

She had an adoring female audience long before she drew her first breath. 'The baby's kicking,' her expectant mother would say. 'Come and put your hand on my tummy.' Penelope, then seven, and Rosalind, two and three quarters, would feel their unborn sibling beating out a rhythm with her feet. Their brother Christopher, who was twelve, may have been less engrossed by another arrival. When the time came, Helen Wood entered a nursing home in Prestwich on the northerly outskirts of Manchester. Stanley Wood's diary entry recorded the birth of 'VICTORIA WOOD, 7 lbs 12 ozs born @ 8. P.M.'[1] A proud father pronounced her 'a lovely baby in every way'.

The date was 19 May 1953. A quarter of a century on, the day of her birth would have a bearing on what Victoria Wood always considered her first properly constructed joke. In a sketch she called 'Sex', a confused young woman played by Julie Walters thinks she might be pregnant. 'Where are you in the menstrual cycle?' she is asked. 'Taurus.'

When mother and child were brought home in Stanley's Austin 7 to 98 Tottington Road in Bury, they were met by paper bunting draped in zigzags across the yard at the back, fashioned by Penelope with Rosalind's help. A message greeted the baby: 'Welcome home, little Victoria'. For the next twenty years she would be known as Vicky

– sometimes spelled Vicki – which is how, deep into her twenties, she signed herself in letters to her family.

The baby's name gave expression to her mother's passionate interest in the Victorian age – its literature, its social history and, despite her republican leanings, its queen. Before Victoria was two weeks old Elizabeth II was crowned, and for the first time the Woods hired a television. Friends were invited round. Helen imagined the words running through the monarch's head as the carriage processed across the screen: 'I bet she's saying, "I could do with a cup of tea."' Such family stories lodged in Victoria's imagination and, decades later, would bubble up to the surface. 'Oh, but I shall never forget the Coronation,' says a gnarled washerwoman played by Victoria in *Victoria Wood As Seen on TV*. '1953. We all crammed into the one front room and stared at this tiny grey picture. Somebody had cut it out of the paper – nobody got television till the year after.' Later, on a tour of the nation, the queen's cavalcade passed through Bury. Helen, with Rosalind in tow, pushed the big coach pram down the hill to see it pass. They found themselves standing by a lorry, whose driver invited them into his cab so they could get a better view.

In the beginning she was simply 'the baby'. The baby cried a great deal in the early months, and only after she was weaned did she start to sleep. There was help from Penelope, who now had a second little sister to mother. When Helen went into Bury to shop, the baby with her big blue eyes was much admired. As soon as Vicky was old enough to walk, Rosalind would take her up the road to loiter at the nearby factory gates around lunchtime when the workers were streaming out: 'Because she had these amazing ringlets, they would stop and say, "Oh she looks like Diana Dors!" And I could get sixpence.' The money, which she shared, brought Victoria her first earnings.

The house was a red-brick end-of-terrace to the north of the town centre. Its acquisition was, like the car, another mark of the Woods' post-war progress. Helen and Stanley met at a Communist Youth League event on Boxing Day in 1937 when she was eighteen and he twenty-five. They had almost nothing in common. Stanley's father worked for the Post Office in Manchester, which allowed the family to live in relative comfort in respectable Chorlton-cum-Hardy. He was an only child both indulged and neglected by his mother Eleanor, who was keen on golf and bridge and farming her son out for long periods to relatives. He grew up inured to solitude. From his mother he inherited tapering cheeks that hinted at smirking amusement; he would pass them down to Victoria. Stanley had a cheerful, even childlike, temperament and a tendency to slip out of confrontations. A gifted musician, he played the piano in big jazz orchestras and a piano accordion in his own trio, and would boast that he could play stride piano so fast you couldn't see his hands. He wrote songs with waggish lyrics. One went, 'I'm Carmen Miranda / I need a veranda.'

Helen Mape, initially known as Ellen, was one of six surviving children who grew up in poverty. Her father, injured in the Great War, was unable to work, obliging her mother to make ends meet as a cotton spinner in the mill opposite their terrace, while he did the cooking and the childcare. She was a strong-willed girl who earned a reputation for bossiness. In a memoir she began writing before Victoria's birth, she described herself as good at the written word but argumentative with teachers and inclined to wander the streets reading a book. Despite her intelligence, there was no question of staying on at school beyond the age of fourteen, and she found a job as a runner in a steelworks, where she was the only female among hundreds of men. Although of Irish Catholic stock, she had from infancy been a junior member of the Independent Order of Rechabites, founded by Manchester Methodists in 1835 to promote temperance. She took part in Rechabite essay competitions – entrants roamed as freely as they might around the subject of abstinence from alcohol. In the year she was to meet Stanley she won first prize and was chief guest in a Manchester meeting where she was awarded £1. She read out her essay titled 'Alcohol – Health and Citizenship' in which she fearlessly denounced the Rechabite leadership as 'old fossils'. Her photograph appeared in an edition of the Rechabite paper: aged seventeen her dark hair is pulled back from a round and beaming face. The caption refers to her as 'Sis. Nellie Mape'. She disliked Nellie intensely enough to change her name to Helen – though Stanley furtively called her Nellie Mape in his diaries. He had similar misgivings about his own name and urged her to call him Stan. With typical contrariness, for the next fifty years she addressed him as Wood.

Helen's other interest was politics. She joined the Young Communist League, a provocation too far for her father, who exiled her from the family home. Social sniffiness penetrated even this supposedly egalitarian body. The Young Communists set out on regular rambles from Manchester, and Helen would tag along in her only shoes. 'Next week wear some proper shoes,' a woman once told her. One night aged eighteen she decided to tramp across the moors in Derbyshire on her own. The hiking story resurfaced as a boast by Kitty, the Cheadle battleaxe played by Patricia Routledge in *As Seen on TV*: 'I'm something of a celebrity since I walked the Pennine Way in slingbacks in an attempt to publicise Mental Health.'

Stanley was much taken by Helen's forthright personality and physical amplitude. Victoria would inherit these from her mother, while her father handed down a talent for music. A year into their courtship, he took Helen to a studio to record a couple of his own compositions, with him jaunty at the piano and her smartly keeping time with brush drumsticks. In 'If I Were a Lad', Stanley comically flattens his Lancashire vowels, then Helen joins in, warbling confidently as she dreams of changing gender: 'An' I'd play a boop-a-doop / And moan an' groan an' shriek / An' I'd join a blooming jazz band at hundred quid a week.'

In Helen, Stanley found an antidote to his mother's snobbery, but they were so poor that at the cinema they couldn't afford sweets and would munch on chopped carrot squares they brought in a paper bag. The memory would reappear half a century later in *Wood and Walters*. 'In my day there was rarely money for sweets,' says Dotty, a middle-aged agony aunt played by Julie Walters. 'But we didn't care. Quite happy sucking a twig or a ball bearing.'

Stanley's mother was not amused when he brought home a working-class communist who had a job and wore neither heels nor make-up. The two women were thrust upon each other when Helen fell pregnant. She and Stanley married in 1940 when she was four months from full term, and had no choice but to move in with his parents. Eleanor did not spurn the chance to undermine her daughter-in-law.

Once when Helen was going out for a social occasion, she carped, 'Oh look, she's wearing a skirt and a top instead of a suit.'

Stanley entered the insurance industry as a claims inspector before trying his hand at journalism. Then in 1941 he joined the navy and was stationed in Hampshire. Helen escaped with the baby Christopher into lodgings. From then on, says Penelope, Eleanor and Helen 'had nothing whatsoever to do with each other'. In 1943 Stanley was transferred to Devonport, and Helen moved to Plymouth to be nearby. Victoria's knowledge of Stanley's war record was sketchy: 'My father only ever said that he'd been in the navy and he had his teeth taken out, and he did sketches and songs and played the piano and was in a band and did naval revues.'[2] Later, when he put on entertainments at jumble sales to raise money for charity, she remembered 'something he did where men came on in army boots and tutus, so that's probably a thing that people used to do in the war and think was funny'.[3] He also edited the naval paper *Guzz*. Victoria put a fleeting tribute to his war record into the mouth of Kitty: 'Where were you when they bombed Plymouth?'

In 1945 Penelope was born. To feed his growing family, Stanley had a go at writing fiction. In 1947 he had a novel published called *Death on a Smoke Boat*, for which he took the pseudonym Ross Graham. Set in the south-west in 1944, it told of the hunt for a fifth columnist sabotaging the estuary barges which sent up smokescreens to confuse German bombers. By now he was working as an agent for the Liberal Party in Bury, where he and Helen rented two rooms before moving to a modest semi in Ramsay Grove. With the birth of Rosalind in 1950 Stanley returned to insurance, joining Manufacturers Life of Canada, and the growing family moved up the hill to Tottington Road.

The new home was large enough to accommodate Victoria when she arrived three years later. The sitting room was co-opted as a playroom where Stanley would spin music from his collection of 78rpm records on a wind-up gramophone. The furniture was pushed aside and, once she could walk, Victoria would dance like mad with her sisters to Harry Roy's 'Tiger Rag' and the ragtime of Trinidadian pianist Winifred Atwell. Upstairs in her tiny box bedroom, Penelope devised games for her little sisters, who shared a bigger bedroom. The Three

Boys, inspired by Dickens, cast the girls as maltreated boarding-school orphans who stole bread from the kitchen. With Helen having embarked on a secretarial course, Penelope would make her sisters' tea, bathe them in front of the fire and tell them stories: 'They were so sweet when they put on their little Winceyette nighties and had damp hair. I just loved them; they were like big dollies.'

Behind a row of gardens around the back a gate gave access to stone steps which plummeted down through dense jungle-like vegetation towards a brook. Penelope led the way and mucked in with the rough boys who mustered under a low-hanging canopy of branches, fashioning weapons from Japanese knotweed. Rosalind and little Vicky nervously held back and watched. Just upstream was a paper mill which spilled its coloured dyes into the water, so their clothes came back with tidemarks of orange or blue or yellow or green until eventually Helen forbade the girls to paddle. In winter, when it was too cold and dark to play outside, a television was hired. Victoria's earliest viewing consisted of *Muffin the Mule* and *The Woodentops*.

Helen was not sociable and kept her distance from the Mapes. As a result, Victoria met few children of her own age. When her big sisters, whom she called Leppy and Lollind, left for school every morning she yearned to follow them. She would hurl herself at the front door and holler, 'Lollind and Leppy, me go cool!' When she was three, Victoria devised a strategy for being noticed. She would hide in the pantry and pop out wearing a comic face and weirdly contorting her body. 'She must have done it when she was just with Mummy,' says Rosalind, 'and she said, "You must show everybody when they come home from school." So we all lined up and she came out and we all applauded.' The routine became formal enough to be known as 'Faces'. 'Do another!' they'd all yell, and she'd run back into the kitchen. 'She really made us wait before she came out.' This was Victoria's earliest memory of performance and her first intoxicating taste of audience appreciation: 'It just gave me a good feeling. It was just something very, very deeply rooted and instinctive. I didn't feel I had any choice in the matter.'[4]

Victoria dated her craving for fame to this formative age. She remembered 'sitting in our garden in Tottington Road and wanting be famous'.[5] Her other goal was to be a man: 'When I was about three, I didn't know that if you were a girl you had to grow up to be a woman . . . I thought you could choose at eighteen which you wanted to be, and I wanted to be a man. I didn't want to be a girl at all . . . I never liked girly things; I never liked frilly frocks.'[6] Her songs and stand-up would burst with mannish schoolgirls and men who wear dresses or go under the knife.

In early photographs the blonde curls soon straightened and darkened. Her hair was cropped into a bob or trained into bunches. Aged one she sits on Stanley's knee at the beach in a bright dress, white socks and sandals, laughing. Wearing a smart coat with a bonnet she looks shyly away from the lens as Helen leans down and clutches her shoulders from behind. A year or so older, the little girl who dreams of celebrity stands to attention in a striped jumper, tartan skirt and zip-up ankle boots. She never made faces for the camera, unlike the extroverted Rosalind.

Rosalind kept a diary. A snapshot from the first months of 1958 glimpses the four-year-old Victoria taking part wherever she could and looking on when she couldn't:

> Vicky brought us a biscuit each instead of breakfast . . . I came home and peeping out of the window was Vicky . . . Vicky and I danced. Mummy and Daddy are going to a party, so I went to bed and Vicky too and Penelope began to twizz us . . . We played at giants and me and Vicky were children . . . took Vicky for a walk . . . went to Brownies with Vicky . . . We had dinner and went to the pictures to see Bambi and went home and had tea and went outside and played with our jewels and Vicky had a jewel box and Mummy gave her some and we went to bed . . . I was a girl baby and Vicky was a boy baby . . . VICKY'S BIRTHDAY.

On 13 April 1958, the month before she turned five, Victoria was finally able to follow her sisters out of the door in the morning to attend Elton Primary nearby. Her previously narrow world expanded vastly from one day to the next: 'You stood by the front gate till you were five and suddenly you had a quick spit wash and you were in a brick building with forty-seven other children. "How has this happened? Who are these? I've never seen any people of my height." I thought I was the only child in Bury. I didn't realise there were others. It was a terrible shock.'[7] After two days at school she reported back to her parents that she had acquired three boyfriends and was 'in a quandary as to which one to marry'.[8]

The decision was taken out of her hands as she was there for only a term. The Woods were leaving Tottington Road. On the youngest member of the family the move was to have an immeasurable impact.

# 2

# HOUSE ON THE EDGE

'At the top of Castle Hill Rd you turn left and just follow the road for about a mile, it becomes more of a track as it goes on, and my house is opposite the Golf Course and is (or was) a double fronted bungalow in a very big garden with fields behind.'

Directions to television researcher, 1996

When she entered her teens, Victoria was given a handsome photograph album. 'Vicky Wood,' she wrote on the opening page. 'May 19th 1966. aged 13'. Below is a snap of Birtle Edge House, where she had lived for the previous eight years. 'OUR HOUSE,' she captioned it in red capitals. And above she added a parenthesis: '(WHERE IT ALL HAPPENED.)'

What exactly did happen at Birtle? On the one hand, almost everything that went into forming her. On the other, almost nothing. Victoria would characterise it as 'a prefab on steroids'.[1] Helen first spotted an advertisement in the *Bury Times* for a former children's holiday home overlooking the Rossendale valley. Stanley did not share her enthusiasm, put off by the price but also its poor state of repair. It was built in 1908 as a rural bolthole for Bury's disadvantaged children. Among the more recent occupants had been Polish refugees during the war. A handsome red-brick exterior with elegant original features had long since been protected from the elements by cement render. The house had no electricity or running water, and no sewage system, and being a bungalow its expanse of roof was in constant need of fixing. The same went for the wind-buffeted windows. The courtyard had a delicately canopied colonnade, inserted by an architect who took an optimistic view of the house's situation.

Stanley succumbed and secured a private mortgage from a member of the Liberal Party. For several months the Woods took on the project of renovating their next home. They would all troop up at weekends, occasionally staying overnight. Stanley donned overalls, in which he would be seen for years to come, to clamber up a ladder and apply another layer of cheap waterproof cement paint. Inside, every light had to be drawn down on a chain and lit, a fiddly process because the delicate gas mantles broke to the touch. The water was pumped from the farm half a mile away. The septic tank, which smelled in summer, meant they had to be careful about what they flushed into the system. Walls were often being knocked down or windows boarded up. 'It was a wreck,' says Rosalind. 'It put a terrific strain on them. They didn't have the money to do it up properly. They tried to do it piecemeal as they went along, and neither of them had the temperament or the know-how to pull it off. It was too big and too isolated and cold and damp and uncomfortable and draughty.'

Into this house the Woods moved over the summer of 1958. The isolation was what appealed to Helen. 'My mother couldn't be doing with neighbours and gossip and suburban life,' said Victoria.[2] According to Penelope, Helen was 'a bit sociopathic'. Her dream for her children was an idyllic expanse of countryside in which they could spread out. Although the front of the property bordered a golf course, behind it there were fields full of sheep. When snow arrived, they tobogganed. As Penelope entered her teens, she gradually stopped initiating games, leaving her sisters to make house in the rhododendrons or climb the trees to watch the golfers.

The view, enfolding Manchester and the moors, was panoramic, but there was a cost. The nearest bus stop was a half-hour walk down a rough unmetalled farm track, and to get to Bury by car took fifteen minutes. Victoria started at Fairfield County Primary at the bottom of the hill, and after school she and Rosalind sometimes had to walk back up it. The house had a certain local notoriety – 'Ooh, you live int' holiday home,' people would say to the girls – but they didn't come to see it for themselves. 'Nobody came to tea at all,' Victoria recalled. 'We had to bribe people to come and visit because it was a mile and a half walk from school.'[3] Once Helen did organise a charity picnic in the adjoining field, but no one entered the premises. If they had, they would have found an unconventional household. To accommodate a family of six, the building had to be converted from its previous incarnation, in which the rooms were the size of dormitories. Victoria extracted comic mileage from the image of her mother 'dragging bits of plywood off bombsites and lashing them to the top of a minivan and driving them home and making rooms out of them'.[4] The truth was slightly more prosaic. The partitions were created from plasterboard fitted into wooden frames; a builder installed them to Helen's plans to save on the cost of an architect. The bungalow was H shaped and along one side were the girls' bedrooms. The other side included a sewing room for Helen, where she made all her daughters' clothes. She'd build a fire in the Victorian hearth and would summon the girls to try things on. They were required to knock first. When he returned from work, Stanley retreated into an office, where he pursued his second career writing radio scripts and composing entertainments for annual jamborees in the insurance industry. Their half of the house rattled to the percussive clack of the sewing machine and the typewriter. Christopher's bedroom was vacated when he left for university in 1959. Victoria, who was six, would barely see him again till she herself went to university.

The Wood family started to lead cellular lives: they were isolated not only from the town, but also from one another. Victoria compared it to living 'like battery hens'.[5] Imposing isolation on their children may not have seemed unnatural to parents who had, for different reasons, known it themselves when young. In her room Victoria embarked on a lifelong passion for reading. Her weekly diet included *Bunty* and later *Jackie*. She would fondly namecheck both in her songs and sketches, and kept her back editions of *Bunty* for the rest of her life. Later she moved on to *Punch*, which were bound into volumes. But books were the thing. There was no shortage of titles to choose from as Helen crammed the house with literature:

'My mother was an obsessive collector of second-hand books. I only ever had a new book bought for me at Christmas – I'd get a new paperback. The rest of our books were second-hand, and there were tons and tons of them. There were lots and lots of those Boots library books that were circulating from the mid-Thirties onwards. I was an absolutely obsessive reader.'[6] Bookshelves sprouted everywhere, many constructed by Helen from planks propped on bricks. When these filled up, the books were pushed back to the wall and a new row started. Shelving even invaded the loo. Victoria's early preference was for children's classics such as A.A. Milne, Just William, Billy Bunter and Jennings 'where they just live in their own mad world'.[7] It's a measure of her precocity that at seven she picked up a copy of *Gentlemen Prefer Blondes*, thinking, 'This is quite a nice story about these two nice girls that go round Europe. I didn't realise they were sleeping with men for money.'[8] Some books would have a more lasting influence. She feasted on Noel Streatfeild's *Ballet Shoes* (1936) in which three penniless orphan girls make ends meet in Cromwell Road: 'I was attracted by the London aspect of it – these big houses and iron railings and the V&A. It was very different from where I lived.'[9] *Ballet Shoes*, she said, 'had a big effect on me later when I was deciding what to do'.[10] She also feasted on a volume found around the house called *Modern Masters of Wit and Humour*: 'It was full of A.A. Milne-type pieces, and I found it absolutely hysterical.'[11]

But nothing would have as deep an impact as *The Swish of the Curtain*, Pamela Brown's 1931 novel about a group of children who create their own theatre in a disused chapel. Victoria's enthusiasm was such that she was commissioned to write the entry on it for *The Cambridge Guide to Children's Books*. 'The descriptions of the preparations for the shows are convincing and absorbing,' she wrote. 'Parents are satisfyingly absent from most of the action, and readers can lose themselves in a lost innocent world of exercise-book scripts, raspberry-juice wine and home-made costumes.'[12] The freedom to put on plays was an attractive fantasy, but it was the lack of adults that went to the core of the book's appeal for Victoria. 'I don't like authority figures,' she said. 'I only really liked books where there weren't any parents.'[13] In particular she 'madly identified' with Maddy. 'She is supposed to be slightly fat, and I was slightly fat. She's cheeky and a bit anarchic, and I identified with her completely. I just liked the idea that they all sit there with pencils. It said, "By the end of the evening they'd written the first act." I drank it all in, and I didn't think of it as a fantasy.'[14]

When family members did meet they would do so on a provisional basis, standing in a group to talk and josh, but never sitting. Stanley's habit was to natter in doorways, as if always keeping open the option of a getaway. 'My father was lovely in a way,' Victoria would say, 'but not easy to talk to, he didn't hurt one, he just didn't connect.'[15] He also loitered impermanently when Victoria watched television: 'He would only watch it standing up, as if about to leave, and so you would spend the whole time thinking, is he going?'[16] Victoria would watch anything comic: 'I think I laughed at everything. I can remember Lucille Ball and Phil Silvers, but I don't remember anything particular that I liked about them. I liked the fact that it was comedy.'[17] The rental television was not a permanent fixture – it went back to the shop over the summer: 'If anything happened in the summer, I never saw it. "Did Ken and Deirdre get married?" "Oh yeah." "When was that?" "July." "Oh well, that's why I didn't see it."'[18] Helen never watched television.

The Woods would meet in the dining room round an oval mahogany table covered in a tablecloth. There was a connecting hatch to the kitchen, in which a black ring of grease gradually bloomed on the ceiling above the stove. Helen's repertoire included Irish stew, cottage pie and corned beef curry. Rosalind was outgoing and enjoyed these gatherings. Stanley might comically embellish an encounter from the world of insurance. 'If somebody had a good story to tell, they'd talk,' says Penelope. 'Otherwise it was a bit grim. We were either full of tension or hilarity. There was nothing in between. At mealtimes we'd be sitting round, and nobody would dare to speak.' Victoria would bring a book to the table, though reading while eating was discouraged. Once she was asked if the family had rows. 'Didn't talk enough to have rows!'[19]

The family was together in a more concentrated way when they crammed into whatever new or hired car Stanley was driving. An enthusiastic motorist, he would queue up to test a new section of the motorway, and would happily give anyone a lift anywhere, or dash down to the shop two miles away. He changed cars often – the various makes of Morris would fetch up in Victoria's sketches and monologues. The three girls squashed into the back, with Victoria always in the middle. 'If we got a bit quarrelsome,' says Penelope, 'Mum used to lean over and arbitrarily just whack with her hand.' There were weekly trips to the Saturday matinee to see whatever was showing – cartoons, musicals, westerns. Or they went further afield to stately homes, galleries, museums, parks, the Dales, where the thrifty Helen would encourage the girls to bag wool snagged on barbed-wire fences. She planned to knit jumpers. The muddy wool was soaked in the kitchen, then hung out to dry, but it stayed soggy and was always thrown away. Once they visited Haworth Parsonage – Helen was a Brontë fan – and then strode up onto the moors to breathe the air that inspired *Wuthering Heights*.

Several times a year they went further afield, often with a caravan in tow – to the seaside, to various corners of the UK, including London, where they stayed in small hotels, visited the sights and caught shows: *The Sound of Music* with Petula Clark and *My Fair Lady*, *Oliver!* and *Anne of Green Gables* 'which I remember even then as being dreadful,' said Victoria.[20] They drove up one coast of Scotland and down the other, and took the ferry to France. Stanley's longest drive was to Vienna: 'It took us about five days, towing a Sprite Musketeer four-berth caravan behind him. He went everywhere with his caravan, because my father didn't really like to go away without his own chip pan.'[21] Penelope shared a double with Rosalind, and Victoria took the bunk on top. The beds were hidden behind curtains. In the mornings the smell of toast would permeate the caravan. 'Dad would say, "Toast, anyone?"' says Penelope. 'And this hand would come through the curtain with a plate of buttered toast.' Victoria kept a visual record of these trips in a photograph album. It was perhaps the Musketeer caravan that inspired Victoria's earliest recorded joke, jotted by Stanley in his diary when she was eight in the summer of 1961: 'Me: "D'Artagnan was one of the Three Musketeers." Vicki: 'I suppose he was deaf (Must-get-ears)."'[22] Her technical knowledge of caravanning enabled her to write a double entendre in *dinnerladies* that was both technically correct and filthy: 'Can I winch my legs down onto your hardstanding?'

Hugger-mugger in the car, the Woods would sing songs, or look out of the window and observe. There was a culture of commentary in the family as other people came under the microscope. The practice extended to cafés. Helen was the more disparaging critic – 'She's not going to be able to go very far in those shoes,' she might say – while Stanley would silently lean back and cock an ear to a conversation at a table behind him.

Victoria's father was a source of good cheer. Family snaps show him balancing a ball on his head or smiling in a collapsed deckchair. His gregarious nature suited him to his job. 'He always seemed to enjoy his work,' said Victoria. 'I can remember when I was little him coming home and saying, "I've done three sales today." And my mother would say, "Oh, that's good."'[23] All the girls loved having lifts by him on their own, when he gave them his undivided attention. 'He was a silly man,' says Rosalind. 'He could clown around. He wasn't an authoritarian at all. He stepped back from that side of parenting. If Mother was telling us off, he'd give you a little look. I think he saw himself as another child.' Sometimes he was told off himself. 'Oh, Stanley Wood!' Helen would bark, perhaps adding a thump for emphasis. Their to-and-fro was a game both were in on – according to Penelope it was 'like being with Morecambe and Wise'. Once Stanley boasted about his father having fought with Lawrence of Arabia, prompting mockery from his wife: 'I suppose he saluted him when he went past on his camel, did he?' 'She always claimed very proudly to have no sense of humour,' said Victoria. 'And she had no sense of humour, but she could be quite witty, and she was very, very observant. She was always coming back and telling us what she'd seen, so she had a good eye.'[24]

The sense of isolation in the family was intensified by the absence of other relatives. Both Victoria's grandfathers had died before she was born, and Helen had little contact with her own mother, who died in 1961. That left Stanley's mother Eleanor, who they knew as Nana (pronounced Nanaah). She never came to Birtle, so Penelope took her sisters on the bus to Chorlton-cum-Hardy. Nana offered a glimpse of a different world. Her house had proper furniture, she wore fur coats and scarves, smelled of lavender, and poshly dropped the H when she said 'otel, where she would take afternoon tea. She went to gatherings of the Women's Institute and made up a bridge four with friends who in 1960 would join the original cast of *Coronation Street* – Violet Carson, better known as Ena Sharples, and Doris Speed, who played Annie Walker. She introduced the girls to the more child-friendly whist and rummy, and used card games and word games to help coax Victoria out of her shyness. 'It allowed Vic to join in – and win,' says Rosalind. 'She was very patient and encouraging with her.' The other treat of visiting Nana was the television lurking in a mahogany case. 'Shall we look in?' she would say, and open the doors. Once a year she booked tickets for the three girls to go to a pantomime at the Palace Theatre or the Opera House in Manchester, and insisted they scrub up for the occasion. Rosalind and Victoria were put into new dresses.

This was another field of battle between Helen and her mother-in-law. Unusually for the era, Helen often dressed her daughters in trousers, deeming them more practical. It would excite comment in the street. Victoria's lifelong aversion to dresses started here. For all Helen's enthusiasm for clothes-making, she struggled to keep her daughters looking neat and clean. She was summoned for a chat with the headmaster about the girls' appearance. 'We were both very dirty and obviously looked neglected,' says Rosalind. 'I remember standing in the dinner queue and saw my mum's van come into the car park. She had had her hair done and was wearing lipstick and a skirt and stockings. He greeted her like she was Princess Margaret.' Both girls were soon smartened up.

Her daughters' neglected appearance was a product of Helen's struggles with depression, during bouts of which she would give up on cooking and washing. 'Sometimes you'd go through the sitting room and she'd be sitting in a slump,' says Penelope. According to Victoria, the root of her depression was Birtle: 'She had moved from a normal busy street to this rather windswept bleak house, and I think she couldn't quite extricate herself; she couldn't say, "Actually we made a mistake." . . . I think she was depressed for a lot of the time when I was a child.'[25] Her hoarding was another manifestation. The house gradually filled not just with row upon row of books, but other bulkier and less practical items. From salvage yards Helen scavenged Victorian wardrobes which would fill the hall and corridors, into which she'd stuff other things she'd rescued from junk shops. 'I lived in a house that never had anything new in it,' said Victoria. 'Everything was second-hand. My mother was a believer in economy.'[26] The seamstress in her was moved to buy the costumes from a production of *The Merry Widow* which sat untouched for fifteen years. Her most eccentric acquisition was a sack of shoe lasts, retrieved from outside a shop or factory with the intention of burning them as fuel in the basement furnace, but they were found to contain metal and stayed in the sack for decades.

One household item which served a practical function was the grand piano next to Stanley's office, where he would play after work to unwind. When she was seven Victoria showed an interest in the instrument, and Stanley gave her an induction, pencilling the names of the notes on the keys and on the sheet music for 'Polly Wolly Doodle': 'And then he left the room, typically.'[27] The piano swiftly developed into her new obsession, and the notes on the keys had to be refreshed more than once. 'This morning I found Vicki in her pyjamas in the playroom,' he wrote a week before Christmas in 1960, 'engaged at the New Chronicle Song Book, reading every word and note bar by bar. Rather like the infant Mozart.'[28] Helen arranged for her to have lessons with a male teacher, but the new pupil's shyness soon asserted itself: 'I couldn't cope with the embarrassment of being alone in a room with a man. It used to make me sweat and I'd have to go and wash my hands. I stopped going in the end because I didn't have enough social skills to handle it.'[29] But she had enough confidence to play in front of her class when her teacher heard she was learning, while back at home Victoria continued furtively to explore the piano when no one else was listening: 'I was so ashamed of not being able to go that I thought my parents would be cross if I played the piano, so I used to play it when they were out, and then when I used to see the car headlights coming up the drive I used to jump off and shut the lid.'[30] Her secret was soon discovered, and she started to play duets with her father.

Helen's depression did not impact on Victoria's progress at school.

By the end of her first year her reading was deemed 'good' and her writing had 'improved a great deal', while 'her illustrated work is colourful and shows promise'.[31] At the end of 1960, she finished second in a class of forty-two, gaining full marks in nearly every subject. 'She puts a great deal of effort into everything she does,' said her teacher.[32] Victoria looked back on this period as one of quiet confidence and emotional calm rooted in her status as one of the clever pupils – she was even deemed bright enough to read stories to younger children, much as her mother once had as a child. Many years later it would dawn on her that attainment was somehow connected to class: 'One row had all these poor little children with eczema and impetigo and the ones who'd weed on the floor. They didn't do terribly well in tests. There was the middle one with people who were stupid but were clean. And then there was the top row, which was these girls with very, very good plaits. I had plaits, but I couldn't do a centre parting, so I had one big plait. Then there was a row of boys with dickie bows and sleeveless pullovers like tiny antique dealers.'[33]

Consistent with her early desire to end up male, in the playground she looked on enviously as the boys played while the girls talked about playing, 'with their raincoats tied round their waists by the sleeve to make themselves into ladies . . . I thought I was trapped with forty-seven middle-aged women. I didn't want to be a woman at all.'[34] She could certainly hold her own with roughhousing boys. One day after school she was walking up the path towards the Bury Road when the class buffoon took her by surprise and leaped on her back. Her classmate Graham Howarth witnessed it: 'I remember her grabbing both his arms and just hoisting him right over her head on his back on the floor in front of her. Needless to say, he didn't do anything like that again. She didn't suffer fools.'

Graham Howarth was the only classmate ever to see the inside of Birtle Edge House. The occasion was Victoria's eighth birthday, which she said she'd like to celebrate. An arrangement was made for Stanley to collect half a dozen children from the bottom of Castle Hill Road: 'Only one boy came. It was like nobody thought it was a real place because they'd never seen where I lived because it was so far away. And I remember going with my father, who was driving round to all these people's houses saying, "Is your child coming to my child's birthday party?" And they're going, "No, don't know anything about it." And my mother coming out to greet everybody, and there's just me and the school swot. The balloons and a cake and just this one boy.'[35] After playing hide and seek in the house's many rooms – Graham Howarth found it much bigger and messier than his own – they tucked into the spread of sandwiches, ice cream and jellies. 'She made the best of it, and we had a good time,' he says. Victoria refused to dwell on the apparent snub as some kind of formative trauma: 'I blanked it. I wouldn't see that it had any significance. I can see that it's sad, but I didn't feel it as sad at the time.'[36]

If the world of her home felt contracted, Victoria's knowledge of the outside world expanded with every book, every visit to the cinema. But there was one outing in particular that she would cite as life-changing when, a month shy of her ninth birthday, the family went to see Joyce Grenfell perform to a half-empty Buxton Opera House. One line in particular sank in: 'I'll give you a minute to decide if my dress is leaf green or lettuce green.' Victoria was entranced by her conversational style, her command of the stage and the fact that, unlike every other comic performer, she was a woman: 'I just thought she was so funny. It all made sense to me. I could picture everything she was doing. It really stayed with me . . . I didn't know you could be onstage just all by yourself. And that was what set me off.'[37]

There was a coda to the evening which helped cement it in her memory. Penelope had a habit of going to the stage door to meet the stars, and on this occasion she and Rosalind made it into the dressing room. As recorded in Stanley's diary, Victoria wanted to go too and 'complained bitterly to her mother – in getting lost backstage and being scared of stagehands'.[38] She stayed outside with Helen. 'Joyce Grenfell had these full-body pink corsets hanging up on the wall,' says Rosalind. 'She or a member of staff thought Victoria was too young to see ladies' underwear. She said, "There are just the two of you?" And we said, "No, we've got a sister." And she said, "Oh, I must meet her." She came out and said, "So you're Vicky, are you?" So she was made a bit of a fuss of.'

As she approached and passed her tenth birthday, Victoria's progress in class was praised – 'particularly in English'.[39] 'especially in English'.[40] In early 1964 she sat the eleven-plus. Fairfield County Primary had a good record in the exam, and Victoria didn't let the school down. Where most children set their sights on the Derby School, Bury's state grammar, Victoria's parents aimed for a place at the more middle-class Bury Grammar School, which two of her three siblings had attended (Rosalind, being dyslexic, failed her eleven-plus and went to a Catholic school in Rochdale). 'The work of your daughter, Victoria Wood, in the recent examination qualifies her for a fee-paying place in the school,' wrote the headmistress Miss L.D. Lester. The place was accepted in May, though Helen, who took charge of all educational matters, did not give up hope of avoiding the fees. The Lancashire Education Committee offered a free place at Bacup & Rawtenstall Grammar, but that would have entailed a far longer journey and a separate trip down to the bus stop. So the decision was taken to pay. In her final term at primary school Victoria finished fourth out of forty-one. Out of a possible 450 marks in her final term, she scored 424. Almost all of the dropped marks were in arithmetic: 'Vicky has worked exceptionally well and produced a first class result.'[41] There was every chance that at Bury Grammar she would thrive.

# 3

# BURIED

**'I wouldn't be an adolescent again if you bumped my pocket money up to three and six.'**
*Victoria Wood As Seen on TV*, 1985

'I wanted to catch up with what I had missed when I was younger. When our youngest child was fixed up with the 11-plus examinations, I decided to start.'[1] In the autumn of 1964, Helen Wood resumed the schooling she had been obliged to abandon at the age of fourteen. She spent two years studying for five O levels at Bolton Technical College, where she returned to complete her A levels after a year studying drama at Manchester College of Further Education. In 1968, at the age of forty-nine, she moved on to a general degree in history, English and drama at Manchester University. 'I intend to participate in the university's social life,' she told a local newspaper. 'I shouldn't think there will be any domestic problems – everyone will rally round to help.'[2]

At the same time as Helen accelerated through her secondary education, her youngest daughter stumbled into hers at Bury Grammar School for Girls. The problem, as Victoria came to perceive it, was the shock of no longer standing out. Everyone else had passed the eleven-plus too: 'Instead of saying, "Well, I will be more clever," I just sank underneath. I thought, well, I won't compete, I won't do my homework, and I won't wear clean shirts and I won't wash my hair. I just sank below the surface.'[3]

Her descent is recorded in her school reports. Suddenly praise no longer rang in her ears. 'Victoria must extend the effort she makes in English and French to include every subject,' said her form mistress at the end of her first term.[4] Her bluntest report was reserved for music: 'Victoria could do much better.'[5] The slump wasn't as chronic or dramatic as she sometimes, when eyeing a laugh, liked to suggest – 'I just dug holes in my desk with a pair of compasses for seven years'.[6] But she was deemed 'capable of making a much better effort generally'.[7] Her dismal reports for needlework suggest rebellion against her mother's domestic passion. By the end of her second year her work was 'still very variable'.[8] Her indifference showed in her appearance: her blue jumper would be too baggy, her grey skirt lopsided and one knee-length woollen sock would be down round an ankle.

Bury Grammar School had offered education to both sexes since the late eighteenth century when £5 was bequeathed for the schooling of ten poor girls. Girls were still in the minority by 1903 when the new school building, a solid presence built in red Accrington brick in the neo-Renaissance style, was completed to the west of the town centre. The girls were in possession by the time Victoria arrived, the boys having moved to newer premises. It meant the hundred pupils in Victoria's year were free to file through a door whose carved inscription identified it as the Boys' Entrance. Above it the school's early Victorian crest depicted a swan with a key in its beak. '*Sanctas clavis fores aperit*' went the motto: the key opens sacred doors. The centrepiece of the school was the assembly hall, tall and imposing with high stained-glass windows, a raised stage at one end, and a Steinway grand piano along one flank. There were heavy stone staircases, and the corridors were tiled and painted in washable gloss. If girls were caught dawdling in them between classes, they were hurried on by teachers, who seemed yet more stern when they donned gowns for assembly.

In 1964 Dorothy Lester, who was short and round, had been headmistress for ten years and was known to the girls as Lettice Leefe, after the heroine of a popular Fifties comic strip. Her legacy in the oeuvre of Bury Grammar's most famous pupil is a line in *Good Fun*, the play Victoria wrote in 1980: a schoolboy nicknamed Lettuce 'always maintained he was going into show business'. Many other teachers were also of a certain age. Victoria wrote out a list of the twelve mistresses who taught her in the Upper Third. In brackets Victoria's mother added annotations against two: 'red hair, young' for her English teacher; 'blonde + young' for her history teacher. Youth was a rare and distinguishing feature, and an *aide-mémoire* for Helen whenever she attended parents' meetings. Not that she was a regular sight at the school. Lesley Schatzberger became one of Victoria's closest friends from the start, but not even once did she meet Helen or Stanley, who, in her memory, 'never came to school'.

The first impression Victoria made on Lesley was that she was withdrawn: 'She tended to have her head a little bit down in a shy way and hide behind her curly hair.' The two girls shared a sense that they were misfits – Lesley was the child of Jewish refugees from Vienna and preferred ballet and classical to pop. They bonded as musicians. At the start of their second year the school offered pupils the chance to take up an instrument. Victoria opted for the trumpet, while Lesley chose the clarinet. Victoria got an A for technique in her first year, and the girls were soon playing duets. 'She seemed to come to life somewhat playing the trumpet,' says Janet Davies (née Eastwood), a young music teacher who conducted the school orchestra.

After school Victoria regularly went to Lesley's home on the train a few miles to the north of Bury. Decades later Victoria still fondly recalled Mrs Schatzberger's Austrian mincemeat loaf. Her own home remained out of bounds to others – when Lesley's father took her back to Birtle, Victoria insisted on being dropped at the edge of her drive. 'It felt as though she was ashamed of us getting any nearer to the house,' says Lesley. Miss Eastwood had a similar experience when, taking girls back late one night after an outing to the opera in Manchester, Victoria asked to be dropped right at the bottom of the hill rather than driven up the rutted track.

Victoria would joke that she 'had all the lame friends that you didn't really want to be friends with but were just available because they had calipers or plasters over their glasses. And I was fat, so I was in the losers group.'[9] She was aware that her body was changing faster than the girls around her. 'She developed quite big boobs quite early on,' says Lesley. 'She seemed self-conscious a lot of the time anyway.

She always walked in that way [as if to say] "I shouldn't be here. I don't want people to see me very much."' On the hockey field her body would be cocooned inside the goalkeeper's comical padding. 'I couldn't play games,' she said. 'I was in the hockey team for about twenty minutes and I let in thirteen goals.'[10]

At the same time there was the ordinary jauntiness of a girl on the cusp of her teens. At the end of her second year, in July 1965, Victoria went on a summer trip to Selsey on the West Sussex coast, where she slept in a school dorm with five other girls. 'Dear Mother and Father,' she wrote. 'The food so far is not too bad (spaghetti and chips for tea).'[11] She approved of the number of televisions on site (three) but not what could be seen on them. 'Excuse my writing,' she added, 'but I did not have enough money to buy a proper fountain-pen (HINT-HINT).'[12] She went into more detail reporting to Rosalind, noting the mods 'whizzing past on lovely scooters' and two nice German boys, both well over six feet:[13] 'The short (HAR-HAR) one has taught me to play table-tennis (which is the only decent game), but I do not see him much as he has to go around with his friend who likes a tarty girl who is in our room.'[14] She drew a picture of her lumpy lower bunk. 'On top of me,' she concluded, 'is a very fat girl who creaks all night.'[15]

Her burgeoning wit was apparent to her classmates. At twelve, inspired by the squibs she read in *Modern Masters of Wit and Humour*, Victoria wrote a comic account of a school trip and read it out. Getting the laugh became a vital prop, she discovered, 'because I didn't have a huge amount of confidence in other areas at all. It was my way of getting in with people . . . My way of being in was to act a bit strange. I felt they were normal, and I wasn't quite normal, so I exaggerated my oddness. I was always desperate for attention.'[16] This craving ran in parallel with a contradictory instinct to keep others out. 'She usually acted as though she was very sulky,' says Lesley Schatzberger, 'and reticent to reveal anything.' Here, in embryonic form, was the split between Victoria's public and private faces.

In the third year at Bury Grammar streaming was introduced, and Victoria met a kindred wit in Anne Sweeney, who was intrigued by her new classmate's attitude: 'She was very self-contained and not bothered about pleasing. It was as if she didn't care about getting approval.' They first bonded when their maths teacher was talking about a trapezium. 'He flies through the air with the greatest of easium,' muttered Anne, and Victoria completed the rhyme: 'The daring young man of the flying trapezium.' They were sent out to stand in the corridor.

At the Sweeneys' house in Prestwich, Victoria politely accepted square meals in a spick-and-span kitchen. 'She thought my home was comical, being so conventional,' says Anne. 'We'd find things hilarious – my mum insisting on coasters. We had a disdain for what we saw then as stuffy, suburban, old-fashioned things.' Whenever Victoria visited friends' homes, she professed herself 'amazed that the house wasn't full of junk'.[17] Anne became the first friend regularly to break into the inner sanctum of Birtle Edge House, which she found 'rambling and neglected' but 'thrillingly bohemian'. What was most unusual of all was that 'there didn't seem to be anybody there saying, "Do this, do that." She never used to talk about her parents at all. They just seemed shadowy presences.'

The house was emptier with Penelope having left for Leeds University, while Rosalind was at school in Rochdale and, if not sewing, Helen was studying. Meals were not cooked as often, and no one sat around the dining table any more. Victoria catered for herself and, says Anne, ended up 'eating quite badly'. When she was twelve, Helen took her to the GP and asked for a prescription for pills to suppress both their appetites: 'I wasn't that big, but of course once you start dieting you upset the whole thing. I used to have a slimming tablet instead of a meal and then go [to my room] for the good bit – four Curly Wurlys.'[18] When her mother did lay on meals they might be found to feature Energen, crispy low-calorie rolls which mainly consisted of air. According to Penelope, this neglect seems to have been rooted in impatience. 'Mum wasn't very nice to Vicky really,' she says. 'I think she found it hard that she was so scruffy and lazy and sleeping and reading all the time. I think Vicky might have been hard going for Mum somehow.' When Penelope came back in the holidays, the three sisters would convene in the kitchen at ten each night to make cocoa with toast and bananas. 'Occasionally,' says Penelope, 'Father would poke his face into the kitchen and say, "It's about time people were in bed." We had no proper rules at all. We grew up despite our parents, not because of our parents.'

It was made harder for Victoria that her sisters were tall, thin mods: 'I felt they were better at everything, and they were very glamorous . . . I thought if you were thin you were happy, if you had a boyfriend you'd be happy, if you had a different family and lived in a nice, clean semi, you'd be happy.'[19] The contrast between Victoria and her sisters is memorialised in her photograph album. Where Rosalind wears eye liner and glad rags, Victoria is usually in a duffel coat. She was also found to have defective eyesight and started wearing National Health specs: 'I wasn't very prepossessing to look at. I was fat. I had very fat spots, like Dick Whittington's hanky. I had glasses. We only used to wash our hair once a week, so by Thursday afternoon it had gone; it was like chip-pan fat.'[20] It was an effort to keep her hair clean at Birtle, as there was no shower and she had to take a basin of hot water from the kitchen to her bedroom: 'The rest of the time you fannied about with dry shampoo and lemon juice and vinegar. The amount of time I spent combing talcum powder through my hair and trying to brush it out, I could have washed it in half the time.'[21]

Victoria's private territory expanded across the house. She still had her bedroom, dominated by a Paul Newman poster onto which she daubed red lipstick. Now she also took over her brother's former bedroom beyond Helen's sewing room, where Stanley installed an upright piano for her. Here, alone and unsupervised, she could pursue what she identified as her four obsessions: piano, books, TV and eating: 'I don't know if I was obsessive because I had nothing else to do, or whether I was just like that anyway. Certainly it was a way of filling up time as much as anything.'[22] The arrival of the piano coincided with the resumption at thirteen of piano lessons. 'Victoria undoubtedly has a talent for the piano,' wrote her new teacher Rosamund Collins. 'She practices [sic] new pieces <u>too quickly</u> though.'[23] She was glued to the instrument, and was soon experimenting on it, making up tunes, consulting a book in her father's collection called *Orchestration for the Modern Jazz Band*. At thirteen she wrote her first ever lyrics, about a girl of her age whose flat chest enlarges miraculously when she takes some pills: the ambition to be funny was rooted, from the first, in personal experience. She played these early compositions to Rosalind, who didn't see the point of them: 'My sister said, "Why don't you write proper songs instead of these stupid jokes?" I said, "But I *like* stupid jokes."'[24] As for improving on the piano, when Victoria missed her last lesson of the academic year in 1967 no summer holiday work could be set, 'but I am sure she will learn several new pieces on her own without my telling her what to do. We will do Grade II in November.'[25] By the following summer she was working on Grade IV.

One of the things Victoria didn't do at home much was homework. She would come up with ruses to explain its absence: 'When we used to give our essays in, I used to steal the last eight from about Sutcliffe through to Wilson and throw them away. The teacher would say, "Oh, I see there are a few missing." I'd say, "Mine was in there." It wasn't.'[26] (In truth she pulled off this stunt only once.) There was other chaotic behaviour. She pocketed money raised from a charity walk, pinched books from Bury Library, tied a girl in a cupboard. More innocently she rejoiced in mischief. In one lunch hour, when it was strictly out of bounds, she lured two girls into the main hall and played them 'The Stripper' on the Steinway. The deputy head appeared and asked Victoria to identify the tune. She fobbed her off with a made-up composer and opus number.

Her rebellious instincts meant she was not an easy girl to teach. 'She'd sit at the back in the Lower Fifth,' says Janet Davies, who taught Victoria music for O level, 'and she'd be very quietly disruptive. But nice. I couldn't help laughing when she said things you were sort of not meant to hear. She had something about her; there was a bit of spark. Some teachers would simply find her annoying for not fulfilling her potential because she was lazy and didn't get on with anything she'd been told to do.' She certainly didn't knuckle down in music O level: 'She didn't shine because she found it a bit boring. You had to follow rules. That was the way to be able to get good marks. She liked to write as she wanted to write.' Her English teacher Leonie Welch found her compositions 'were always strikingly original – although not necessarily what I asked for. On one occasion

I asked for a one-minute talk on any subject, and Victoria proceeded to speak for two minutes about elastic bands. It was quite brilliant.'[27]

Victoria took the chance to write what she wanted in *Cygnus*, the school magazine whose editorial committee she joined in the Upper Fifth. As the only trumpeter, she reported on the activities of the school orchestra, signing her name Vicky Wood. Unusually for *Cygnus*, another piece of hers had no byline. She titled it 'Pardon?' and into its few unpunctuated lines condensed a prophecy of her future path:

> I was born with a warped sense of humour and when I was car-
> ried home from being born it was Coronation Day and so I was
> called Victoria but you are not supposed to know who wrote this
> anyway it is about time I unleashed my pent-up emotions in a
> bitter comment on the state of our society but it's not quite me so
> I think I shall write a heart-warming story with laughter behind
> the tears and tears behind the laughter which means hysterics to
> you Philistines . . .'[28]

She had just turned fourteen. Her facility with words prompted her to write to Willie Rushton, the satirical humourist who co-founded *Private Eye*: 'I wrote what I thought was the funniest letter imagina-ble. I never got a reply. I hated him for that.'[29]

Bursting with a desire to be noticed, Victoria did not yet have access to the means. Her best opportunities for self-expression came outside the school. At thirteen she joined the Bury Military Brass Band, which also had room for woodwind, so the repertoire expand-ed beyond marches to the likes of Duke Ellington, a taste for which she had inherited from Stanley. She loved her time in the band, which rehearsed in Tottington Road: 'I would be in the middle – and if I got there a bit late I'd have to squeeze along the row with my trumpet case and music stands are never very stable and I would knock them over with my breasts as I went past.'[30] Even in jest she was conscious, for the first time, of being a young woman in a masculine environment – there were forty males and three girls, who had to wear knee-high socks: 'I wasn't bad at playing, but I wasn't good at marching. I couldn't get the two together. You've got a little card stuck on your trumpet. If you play second trumpet, all the notes are the same because it's a harmony part. It all looks the same; you lose your place because you're wobbling along the cobbles. And my socks used to fall down. They used to shout at me from the back, "Tell that bloody girl to pull her socks up."'[31] She reported one exchange at rehearsal to Penelope: 'I was sitting next to these two old blokes. One said, "Do you like my new tie?" And his friend said, "Oh, I thought it was your tongue hanging out."' 'Older men were attracted to her,' says Lesley Fitton, another lifelong friend she made at school, 'and she had a horrible fascination with them. She used to snog unsuitable bandists behind the UCP in Bury.' (The UCP was a restaurant run by United Cattle Products.) There was less desirable attention from older strangers in the cinema, or at the bus stop: 'Even if you looked like the back of a pickle factory if you'd got breasts . . . you'd be in a bus queue and you'd think, is that somebody's briefcase? Oh no it's not. Somebody would give you a lift home and go, "Shall we just pull in for bit?" "No, get off!"'[32]

But she didn't seem to be interested in boys of her own age and, perhaps fearful that it wouldn't be reciprocated, made no effort to flirt with them. In her mid-teens she was 'a slightly awkward person phys-ically,' says Lesley Fitton, 'slightly gawky, a bit shy and self-conscious. She wasn't actually a fat schoolgirl, but she was a bit top-heavy, but always had really good legs and also uncompromisingly straight hair cut like a paintbrush.' Lesley once persuaded Victoria to come along to a school disco at Gigg Lane, Bury FC's ground. The girl who by now always wore jeans and was fixated on baseball boots was lent a little green dress: 'She completely hated it. She was just completely like a fish out of water. The rest of us were typical teenage Sixties girls in pastel short things and frosted pink lipstick. That was absolutely not her scene.' Only later would she come to regard these agonies as an advantage. By staying outside of things, and not making herself available for any form of social interaction, she was able to watch instead. 'If I'd been thin as a teenager and gone out with boys,' she reasoned, 'I wouldn't have had anything to write about.'[33] But then she did meet a boy.

# 4

# WORKSHOP

'Rochdale was hugely liberal compared with Bury. Rochdale had the sculpture festival, it had sculpture in the streets, it had the poetry festival, it had public speaking. Bury had an abattoir.'

*Parkinson*, 2000

Victoria was fifteen when an opportunity came up to take part in an enlightened experiment in arts education in Rochdale. The previous year Rosalind was invited to join a new initiative called the Rochdale Youth Theatre Workshop. It was founded by David Morton, a graduate of Central School of Speech and Drama. The council's education committee, chaired by the (posthumously disgraced) Liberal MP Cyril Smith, briefed him to set up a youth theatre. Morton was a visionary who developed the workshop into a pioneering forum where young people were encouraged to explore, experiment and create. Local teenagers would attend two or three evenings a week, and there were daily workshops during the summer holidays. In September 1967 Rosalind was in the cast of the inaugural production, Thornton Wilder's *Our Town*, for which she also designed the set. Morton was, in her estimation, 'a uniquely inspiring man who was able to get the balance between being your mate and showing leadership. And he was ahead of his time in treating girls and women as equals.'

Rosalind's previous efforts to lure Victoria to group activities – the Brownies, Girl Guides, ballroom dancing, rambling – had all failed:

'She had an absolute horror of anything organised. I took her along and she didn't like it. She didn't like being bossed about. Anything that was like school she didn't like. She didn't do things where she was part of a tcam. She could be very stubborn.' In an unguarded moment she admitted she couldn't see herself ever getting a boyfriend: 'I said, "You should come to the theatre workshop."' It took a while to overcome her usual objections, but she caved in the third time Rosalind mentioned it, agreeing 'on the grounds that she could meet boys'.

Victoria started attending the evening sessions in 1968, joining a group of forty teenagers. By then Morton had taken over the top storey of a large Victorian school building at the far end of Rochdale, where he installed lighting, sound rigs and tiered flexible seating. Barring a lone physics teacher, Victoria had barely ever encountered a male authority figure before. Morton was a tall, bearded, smartly dressed man with a resonant baritone voice who gently exuded authority. He diligently corresponded with each and every participant, advising them by letter of rehearsal times and summer schedules. The ethos of the youth theatre workshop was based on improvisation and experiment, and designed to empower the creative instincts of young performers. It could not have been better tailored to Victoria's needs. Yet even now her social awkwardness imposed a barrier. 'Outside the impro sessions she was incredibly shy in the early days,' says Joe Dawson, who was a couple of years older. 'She was often to be seen sitting in a corner nursing her trumpet. During the impro work she would come alive, often throwing inspired curve balls of observed northern life into the mix. She flourished and was soon an integral and popular member.'

At first Victoria travelled on the bus to Rochdale with her sister but, once working on different productions, she started going on her own. 'So she made her own friends,' says Rosalind. 'Shortly after I introduced her, I didn't see much of her.' (One of her new friends was Mary Jo Randle, who would play Kelly Marie Tunstall's friend at the bus stop in *Victoria Wood As Seen on TV*.) The sisters also had quite different interests. Rosalind was drawn to the mind-and-body sessions, featuring much meditative lying on the floor or stretching and strengthening, while Victoria, wary of leotards, preferred the music, poetry, design and script workshops.

That summer she had a small role in Ann Jellicoe's *The Rising Generation*, premiered at the Royal Court only the year before, and painted the set. She was credited as Vikki Wood. In November she looked after the props on Arnold Wesker's *Chips with Everything*. Both plays, requiring big casts and shaking a fist at the status quo, were a Rochdale Youth Theatre Workshop signature. In a vacuum, with no template to go on, Morton laid on a remarkably complete introduction to drama in all its forms. In Victoria's first summer school there were three resident tutors, one from Columbia University, and a dozen guest tutors, experts who covered every aspect of theatre craft – stage fights and masks, lighting and costume design, voice and speech. There was even advice on dramatic criticism, plus a session with the Olympic fencing coach. Free performances were laid on. 'I hope for excellent attendance,' Morton said of one entertainment he'd brought in, 'in order to justify the expense involved. Bring your friends.' One of them was a reading by the poets Adrian Henri and Adrian Mitchell. Peter James, who co-founded the Everyman Theatre in Liverpool, came to Rochdale to give a three-day course in directing in 1969. When an outing took Victoria to Liverpool nine months later to see Beckett's *Endgame*, she looked him up and he gave her a tour of the theatre. James remembers her 'with her school uniform and satchel, looking extremely inquisitive'.

What Victoria thrived on was taking part: 'It was my complete transformation. I found there was something I could do. After being told constantly I had terrible handwriting and I was grubby and no good at hockey, always being told you're no good at this, suddenly there were things I could do. And I was good at them and I got laughs. I thought, oh yeah. And that feeds you if you feel that you've not been quite adequate up until then.'[1] Whenever she talked about the Workshop in later life, she spoke of it in similar terms: it was her 'salvation',[2] the moment she was 'for the first time feeling comfortable about doing anything'.[3] Morton offered pupils four levels of participation, ranging from casual attendance to full time. Victoria followed her sister and chose full time. The three three-hour sessions a day started at ten o'clock and ended twelve hours later, and people had to keep an eye on which they were required to attend. Punctuality and reliability, not hitherto Victoria's forte, were insisted upon.

During breaks she and Joe Dawson would sometimes slip off to play piano duets. By the late 1960s, having spent so much time at home practising, Victoria had developed into a highly competent sight reader. Her own taste was for the rich harmonies of the American songbook and the English wit of Coward or Flanders and Swann, but she also loved to customise classical repertoire – when they played Grieg's *Norwegian Dances* together, she would scat along over the top. She was also writing songs for the Workshop, playing the trumpet and, back at home, composing a duet for piano and flute in the style of an English pastoral, to be performed with Lesley Fitton. Asked for a title by her music teacher, at the last minute she called it 'Serenade to a Cuckoo'.

Victoria's witty persona and zest for participation caught the eye of the Theatre Workshop's rising star. Bob Mason was two years older. In the year they met he won first prize in the *Daily Mirror*'s national verse-writing competition with a poem called 'Loughrigg Autumn', which traded in doomy romance ('I touch the sodden rug of her life / And kiss the tears of love / From her cold face'). He was a serious young man but also, according to Joe Dawson, 'a strong character with a Bohemian offbeat view of the world and a great sense of humour'. Victoria later joked that, being a poet, 'he would have his photograph taken in front of mill chimneys'.[4] His writing was encouraged by Morton. He had already had two plays staged at the Workshop when, the month Victoria turned sixteen, his third appeared in a trilogy alongside Beckett and Ionesco. That summer Rosalind played his daughter in *Hobson's Choice*, which Morton chose as a vehicle for his performing talent, while Victoria acted with him in a programme of short plays by the likes of Pinter and Albee. 'He wasn't a *great* actor,' says Rosalind. 'He was adequate. He was a bit fat and had a wry northern humour.' He was just right for Victoria and soon joined the minuscule inner circle of people she trusted enough to bring home to Birtle. They would canoodle, and doodle on the piano. 'She was in her very awkward, not very forthcoming way obviously deeply fond of him,' says Lesley Fitton. He became an important prop in Victoria's life, although their relationship was, she conceded, 'full of rows and screaming and him leaving me at the bus stop and him coming back because I had his cigarettes in my pocket'.[5] His main gripe about her was her addiction to reading. 'You shouldn't read in polite company!' he'd tell her. She ignored him.

In September 1969 Rosalind left for university, making Victoria even more isolated at home. She started on her A levels (in English, music and religious knowledge) on the back of disappointed sighs from her teachers after indifferent O levels. And yet thanks to 'Workshop', as she called it, she entered the sixth form with a greater sense of self-worth. She imported her new-found knowledge of acting and improvisation to run a lunchtime drama club – 'a most helpful member of the group,' purred her form tutor. 'Victoria deserves this generally pleasing report,' concurred Miss Lester. She even earned a 'quite good' for PE. 'In the sixth form we were treated in a different way,' says Anne Sweeney, 'which suited Vic much more.'

In this more relaxed atmosphere, some teachers admired Victoria's rapier wit and took to her, especially those who taught her English and could see how widely read she was. Others saw her as maverick with the potential to disrupt. One even warned Lesley Fitton that Victoria might be a bad influence. Lesley passed this on: 'I thought she would find it funny – but she was actually very hurt. I was quite as capable as everyone else of falling for her adopted persona as the funny and slightly naughty one. That was far from the whole story. She really didn't like the teachers, and at the time I wasn't completely aware of that.'

In their final year Lesley became head girl, and Victoria showed what she thought of her badge of office by making an imprint of it in the mashed potatoes at lunch. They were both thrown out of the dining hall. Her insurrection took on a subtler form in school assembly. Victoria was one of the very few girls deemed good enough to play the Steinway as girls filed in. Her party trick was to impart a twist of swing to Bach or, when the heavy-set Miss Lester approached, breaking into the 'Dance of the Sugar Plum Fairy' from the *Nutcracker*. She also mimicked the headmistress with merciless accuracy, and the brisk manly stride of the scripture teacher who whisked off her cardigan and hung it on the back of her chair. The deputy head spoke with a quavery, lamb-like bleat which, after she complained of a homosexual subtext in a production of *Coriolanus*, became a standing joke for years. Not all teachers were targeted. When the very young Miss Eastwood left at the end of 1969 to become Mrs Davies, her music class gave her a present with an inscription written by Victoria, who had somehow discovered the name of her teacher's fiancé. 'To Miss Eastwood and Steve,' she wrote, 'with love and kisses from the A-level group.' She added the first four notes of Mendelssohn's Wedding March.

Victoria was at her happiest contributing in music and drama. 'She already showed that huge verbal facility,' says Lesley Fitton, 'and because of that she was liked and admired and famous within that circle. That's how she made friends.' The circle of friends would find themselves written into the songs which Victoria had started to compose and would play in the sixth-form common room. One girl, who wore a lot of lip gloss, exuded a world-weariness that often sounded like plain moaning, resulting in a song which went, 'She has been sitting there all day whining / Poking out her bottom lip, it's shining'.

From writing songs, Victoria graduated to writing an entire show to be performed by the Lower Sixth. She titled it *Pearl: A Melodrama*. Inspired by the fact that soap operas were originally sponsored by soap manufacturers, she invented a sponsor called Cupid's Kiss Cornplasters, and during the performance the action was suspended while the cast sang advertisements hymning the product:

We're the Cupid's Kiss Cornplaster,
You can run much faster,
You can live a life of bliss
With a Cupid's Kiss.
With Cupid's Kiss Cornplaster,
You'll have feet of alabaster.
Be a missus, not a miss
With a Cupid's Kiss.

She also wrote a short play to raise money for charity which she called *Malice in Sunderland*. It came by its title at the last minute when Victoria scrawled an M on the poster as it was being designed. There was a larger audience for the school pantomime, a subversive *Cinderella* written and composed by Victoria in which she made winking references to the sexuality of Prince Charming – he has the hots for Dandini in a pink bikini. The censorious deputy head was horrified all over again, but the production was allowed to proceed uncut, with Victoria dashing between the stage and the Steinway. 'It was quite good actually,' she allowed. 'It was all in rhyming couplets. We only had about four people, so we made big cardboard figures on sticks and poked them in and out like a threepenny theatre.'[6] Victoria was so much in her element that she assumed everyone else would love acting too. Anne Sweeney, who played Buttons, surprised her by not relishing the prospect: 'She didn't seem to understand that would be a nightmare to me.' 'As usual,' reported *Cygnus*, 'Victoria Wood rallied support for the Upper VI's hilarious version of "Cinderella".'[7]

These opportunities fed Victoria's craving, formed as a small child, for celebrity and acclaim. She even switched her allegiance from one character to another in *The Swish of the Curtain*. Lesley Fitton asked her friend if she identified with Maddy, the funny and much-loved young character in Pamela Brown's story. The answer would once have been yes. 'No,' Victoria replied, 'I identify with Lynette, who ends up with her dream of kissing her hand to the box while the audience all applauds.' In an instant Lesley saw her friend with new clarity. 'I thought, of course that's who you are.'

Increasingly, Victoria was aware that this was who she wished to be: 'Everything was going fine for me. I was very happy. I had a boyfriend and I had all the things you would ever want.'[8] In the privacy of a school exercise book she made a note of this satisfactory state of affairs. '1970 is a good year for Victoria Wood,' she wrote in her very tidiest handwriting. 'Only a few things make me laugh. Not true,' she added on the same page. In the rest of the exercise book she jotted cartoons in blue biro, bits and pieces of maths, and gags she was trying on for size: 'he wears a leather jacket in his hair'; 'I haven't laughed so much since Ma caught her tits in the mangle'. Like the girls in *The Swish of the Curtain*, Victoria used the first half of the book to write out her earliest surviving script, an untitled short play in two acts. Her dramatis personae, as she listed them at the start, include Mr and Mrs Bacon and Mr and Mrs Bones, but also 'Jack (of Beanstalk fame)'. Their seemingly humdrum existence is spiced up by a mail-order catalogue which enables fantasies. Mrs Bones awaits the delivery of the crown jewels, while Mr Bacon hankers for Miss Bognor Regis 1953 (the year of Victoria's birth). There are cameos for Dracula pushing a coffin on a trolley, and Noddy, who becomes a wary object of lust. 'You might rust my bells,' he cautions. Victoria sprinkled the dialogue with references to the poet Gerard Manley Hopkins and 'Ramsbottom's answer to the Tiller Girls'. And she had fun deconstructing the mechanics of theatre. 'Unproductive pause,' says one stage direction. The offstage prompter goes on strike. A policeman cuts two pages of dialogue, before being ejected for being in the wrong play. The mashup of kitchen-sink drama and capering surrealism was 'nicked,' she later suggested, 'off Joe Orton. He was about the only person I'd ever read.'[9] But already she was playing with words and images in a way that would come to be characteristic. Mrs Bones is 'expecting two new clichés for the kitchen this afternoon', but worries about unreliable delivery men: 'last time we had something new (an apostrophe for the back bedroom, it was) they clumped about dropping their aitches all over the carpet and they split two of my best infinitives'.[10]

Nineteen seventy was indeed a very good year. Victoria passed Grade VII piano, with much stress on Bach, for which she had an aptitude. 'Her playing is quite musicianly at times,' trilled Miss Collins. But she was ever the rebel. Lesley Fitton felt 'vaguely aware of it being "daring", and faintly disapproved of, to go off and hang round with Vic". Victoria later remembered a four-day school trip to Stratford-upon-Avon because 'someone bet me 50p I wouldn't kiss the coach driver, which of course I promptly did'.[11]

It was audacity which fuelled Victoria's growing desire to be a comic performer. She had heard about Libby Morris, an actress from Canada, performing at the Liverpool Everyman. 'She had a thing called a one-woman show and I thought, what on earth is that?'[12] Whatever it was, she knew that she 'wanted to go on stage and be incredibly funny. I didn't think of it beyond that.'[13] There was a chance to hone her comic abilities when she was cast as Autolycus, the clown in *The Winter's Tale*, which she remembered for 'these really horrible brown tights that hadn't been washed for about a million years and looked like Ryvita'.[14] Her entertaining turn as the play's only comic relief stunned Anne Sweeney: 'It was a great surprise, as she normally disliked being the centre of attention. She just threw herself into it. It was a very physical performance – she rolled and cavorted around the stage and enjoyed herself. Everybody else was standing there like a piece of wood.' She also wrote some of the music. Then in the summer of 1970 came the big production at Rochdale Theatre Youth Workshop. In Brecht's *The Caucasian Chalk Circle*, Victoria played the vulnerable servant girl Grusha, a non-comic role which 'she played with convincing pathos and touching poignancy,' says Joe Dawson. Thus, as her final year loomed, Victoria was emboldened to dream of becoming an actress despite opposition from Miss Lester, while the careers adviser suggested she harness her writing skills in journalism or advertising. At a Bury careers fair the drama desk was run by 'just a very miserable man with dandruff. I said I wanted to be an actress and he just said, "Don't, that's my advice."'[15]

Emboldened by Workshop, Victoria could not be dissuaded, though her confidence went only so far, and she avoided applying to the prestigious schools: 'I didn't feel worthy. I thought you can't go to Central if you're fat. You can't go to RADA if you're fat.'[16] In fact, she sent off to only two places because 'it was five quid every time you applied to drama school and I only had about ten quid'.[17] She went down to London to try for New College, a teacher-training establishment in Swiss Cottage, where she delivered Juliet's deathbed speech. 'The trouble with you,' she was told, 'is you've got a deformed jaw. You can't say S properly.'[18] She didn't get in. She also applied to Manchester Polytechnic, which had a drama course: 'My mother, not knowing me terribly well, knowing that I never wear green, had bought me a green cardigan. I had a flowery blouse that she'd made me and a long midi-skirt of all the unflattering things to give anybody with milk bottle legs.'[19] A debilitating attack of nerves caused her to vomit: 'We'd do a bit of an audition and then I'd have to go away and throw up and then I'd come back again. And at one point I had to do a mirror exercise with somebody else and the room started to go black and I just started to lose it altogether and I had to go out. And then about halfway through the afternoon I suddenly felt OK.'

Her recovery coincided with the presence of an English and drama student who was showing everyone around and reminiscing about her time as a nurse wheeling a commode around the ward. She was a small young woman with 'lots and lots of shoulder-length brown hair but very, very thick with a great big fringe and lots of eye make-up, very small eyes and lots of blue liner underneath. And just keeping the whole room completely entertained walking around the room. She said, "I used to go around the wards at night with this trolley." And I didn't know her name, but I used to wonder.'[20] This was Victoria Wood's first encounter with Julie Walters. Julie remembers that Victoria 'was very frightened and shy, and she had glasses and was shrinking from everyone else in the room'. The image of Victoria lodged in her memory thanks partly to the wastepaper bin she was clutching. Her application was unsuccessful.

Victoria was vouchsafed a quirky glimpse of life in professional theatre when she visited Bob Mason, who had a job with Century Theatre, a mobile company performing in the Lake District during the summer of 1971. He rented a flat in an eccentric house with purple clapperboards in a remote valley five miles from Keswick. Victoria was still working towards her A levels when she first visited, and afterwards came up for weeks at a time throughout the summer. 'They laughed a lot,' says Jack Chissick, an actor who was also renting in the house. 'Bob was a blunt northerner and very bright. Victoria was a ray of light who was quite shy but interesting when you got talking to her.' They were back in Lancashire by early September. 'They are much together,' Stanley recorded in his diary, 'and observed through windows and in the garden, V shrieking as she rides on B's shoulder down side path. In other words, much canoodling, snogging, or spooning.'[21]

In her A levels, Victoria secured an A in English, a C in religious knowledge and general studies, and – because of her aversion to theory – a D in music. Lesley Schatzberger won the music prize.

Lesley Fitton won three awards. Victoria won nothing. Six years later, reflecting on her years at school, Victoria wrote a song imagining a headmistress under the stained-glass windows at her leavers' last school prayers 'with tears running over her wart'. The song foretold disappointment for her fellow schoolgirls; they were destined to be sad, hairy-legged teachers, or teenage mothers, or mistaken for men. Victoria ended the song with a triumphant self-portrait:

But I backed the girl in the filthy blazer,
The one who's burned her school report.

# 5

# THE GREEN ROOM

'I was at Birmingham University, but I feel better now.'
Interview, 1980

There is a spoof documentary in *Victoria Wood As Seen on TV* called 'On Campus'. In it Victoria cast herself as a gawky fresher who is studying religious knowledge, learns the guitar and is self-conscious about her weight. Bullied and ostracised, she attempts suicide. 'I think going away to university for the first time puts a strain on anybody,' reasons her thin friend. 'If you're fat and ugly with a hopeless personality you're probably better off taking an overdose or something.'

Having failed to get into a drama college, Victoria made a successful application to study drama and theatre arts at Birmingham. While the course purported to be academic, it also offered practical training for aspiring actors. 'It was the only university that offered me a place,' she said, 'because I only had two O levels and a diving certificate so you can't really blame them.'[1] Lancashire Education Committee made her a county award of £320 for the academic year.

It soon seemed she'd chosen to study in some hermetic underworld. The drama department was in a basement reached via a spiral staircase. The main area where students milled was a glorified corridor filled with sofas and chairs, with a hatch for a coffee bar at one end. The students called it the green room, which, in defiance of theatrical superstition, had been painted green. On one of the sofas Victoria sat in silence and, quite often, sucked her thumb. Her fellow drama students had no idea what to make of her. 'She sat in a heap in the corner for weeks,' says Bill Lloyd, who was in the year above. 'It was all Afghan coats and loons and she was literally wearing a crumply old jumper or cardigan and huge baggy trousers. She looked like a fifteen-year-old unpopular girl in the class. A weird oddball. She used to roll her eyes a lot.' According to John Carnegie, a third-year student, she 'stuck out like a sore thumb. I hadn't seen anybody who wasn't a three-year-old child wear dungarees.' Other students began to worry about this voiceless girl in the corner and deputed George Irving, a Geordie in the year above, to coax her out of her shell: 'I said, "She'll speak to people in her own time."'

Her silence was the product of shyness, but also a kind of toxic shock: 'I felt everybody was taller, blonder, better-looking, thinner, more southern,' she recalled, 'and I thought I can't be bothered with this.'² Two of the first people she met were Catherine Ashmore and Jane Wymark, who knew each other from Camden School for Girls and were both the daughters of famous actors. This underpinned Victoria's dread that everyone else had some kind of coded connection with one another. 'My first memory was in that green room,' says Jane. 'She was wearing a sweater decorated with pixies collaged on, made by one of her sisters, with very bright colours. Her hair was shoulder length, with red circular barrettes. And she demonstrated how to do a forward roll. She was a deeply shy person, but she was always a performer.' To those she did dare to address she introduced herself as Vic.

The drama department was housed in the Allardyce Nicoll Tower, a brutalist new building named after the founder of the Shakespeare Institute in Stratford-upon-Avon. (In 'On Campus' there's a tower which, according to the university prospectus, 'is where everyone commits suicide'.) The department acted as a sealed environment, caused partly by the geography of Birmingham. The campus fanned out across a hilly redoubt in Edgbaston. Victoria, who chose not to live in a hall of residence, had rented a bedsit at the top of a three-storey house in Harborne, a forty-minute walk from campus. There was little choice but to stick around all day with everyone else.

With no more than a dozen students in each intake, there was much interaction between the years. The small group was overseen by a quartet of male lecturers occupying glass-fronted offices on the floor above. Clive Barker, who had a dark beard, rangy hair and horn-rimmed glasses, had a strong association with Joan Littlewood's Theatre Workshop in east London and also taught at the Drama Centre in London, whose reputation as a psychological torture chamber for vulnerable students earned it the moniker the Trauma Centre. Barker imported its tenets to Birmingham. 'It was all about intense finding yourself, and somewhat confrontational criticism of whatever you did,' says Jane Wymark. 'Clive didn't keep that divide clear enough, so a lot of criticism felt very personal.' Before lectures began at ten o'clock, he instituted the daily morning workout, featuring Laban technique and modern dance, to which Victoria gave a wide berth. 'You have to wear a leotard,' she told Bill Lloyd. 'I'm not going to wear a leotard.' Barker belonged to that generation of male directors who allowed their hands to wander and had a reputation for taking young women into his office for private study after hours, 'which we all suspected was sex of some kind,' says Fidelis Morgan, a charismatic figure from Liverpool who was in the year above. Some years later when Victoria joined a keep-fit class she described the exercises as easy 'for anybody who has had their groin felt by C. Barker'.[3] In retaliation to his unkind comments about her physique, she'd pepper his seminars with sarky one-liners and loud undermining sighs. Victoria much preferred the laissez-faire approach of Jocelyn Powell, a towering intellectual who lectured in Renaissance and Greek theatre.

The first-year reading list featured canonical text books: *World Theatre*, *The Development of Theatre*, *Seven Ages of the Theatre*. Lectures reverberated with the names of Slavic eminences such as Jerzy Grotowski and Konstantin Stanislavski. 'It was like hearing people sneeze,' Victoria would joke, although she had certainly come across these theatrical thinkers at Rochdale Youth Theatre Workshop.

In this bewildering environment Victoria could think of only one way to make her mark. About four weeks into the course she chose her moment and approached George Irving in an empty green room: 'Suddenly she was standing next to me. She said, "You're George, aren't you?" I said, "Yeah." She said, "They say that you're the one that's got it all taped." She looked at me over her National Health glasses and there was a little twinkle and I thought, you're not quite as shy as you think you are.' She told him she'd found a piano in the students' union building and wondered if he wanted to hear her play a couple of songs. 'When?' he said. 'Could we go now?' she replied. They trooped across campus and Victoria led him to the top of the building where behind high stacks of chairs was an upright piano with the front missing: 'It was falling apart and out of tune. She played me three songs. I didn't go, "Whoopee! A star is born." But they were very plaintive. They had an "Eleanor Rigby" quality about them, a northern melancholy.' She used the same confronting tactic on his girlfriend Fidelis Morgan. 'Another student said you were a zany madcap,' Victoria told her, 'so I am avoiding you.' They were soon sloping off to play their songs to one another. A deeper bond was cemented when they discovered that, unlike everyone else in the department, they were allergic to Monty Python.

Uncomfortable in groups, Victoria would isolate individuals in order to befriend them. Another student she played her songs to was Steve Trow, who was from West Bromwich and the first in his family to study at university. They'd go to the union and eat a lunch of bangers, beans and chips. One untitled song she played him was in the voice of a girl with low self-esteem writing to *Jackie* magazine's agony aunt.

> They say I ought to smile at him and ask him round to tea
> They don't know how difficult a simple thing can be
> And if I did I know what he'd do sure as eggs is eggs
> He'd ask my sister out cos she's got sexy legs.

In due course Victoria found a common bond with the southerners too. She and Jane Wymark discovered they were both avid readers. Slowly Victoria overcame her shyness in the green room to make witty observations that drew an audience. She sat at the piano and sang songs about her fellow students. Catherine Ashmore's ears pricked up at the phrase 'stomping past with flat feet': 'She would just be playing away and singing and suddenly you'd walk past and think, 'that's me she's singing about. She would sum everybody up in a flash.' Alison Sabourin, in the year above, even asked for a song: 'Two days later she came up with it. It was very perceptive.' Its raucous chorus correctly predicted a rural future for her friend: 'Ali's got her wellies on, Ali's got her mac / Ali's gone out farming and she ain't coming back'. Victoria impishly rhymed Sabourin with 'so boring'. She was sufficiently proud of the composition to play it to another second-year student. Jane Wynn Owen was an aspiring opera singer from Rhyl in north Wales. They met one day by the soundproofed practice booths at the back of the Elgar concert room in the Department of Music. Victoria offered to be her accompanist, and so found herself playing along to Italian arias and German lieder. One day she played her 'Alison's Song': 'It was not only very well observed, it was musically so deft. I thought, blimey, you're a dark horse. She wanted people to know that she could do this.'

Music, like reading, could be a place of refuge for Victoria. Sometimes she combined the two – Bill Lloyd once found her devouring a novel while practising her scales. Her other refuge was Bob Mason, who was studying at Central School of Speech and Drama. Victoria took the coach to London to stay with him in Finsbury Park, where he shared a bedroom with his brother: 'If we wanted to sleep together, we had to pay him to sleep on the living room floor.'⁴ She was so unfamiliar with London that when Bob didn't meet her off the coach once at Victoria Station she fled straight back to Birmingham. On another visit at the end of her first term he informed her that he had fallen for a student at Central. Victoria returned distraught and, not wanting to be alone all weekend in her bedsit, latched onto George Irving, who had a rehearsal but gave her a key to his flat in Kings Heath. When he got back there that evening she was sitting on the floor of the bathroom, drinking his Scotch: 'She was obviously very unhappy. I put her into my bed and slept next door. I got up the following morning and she was sitting up with the curtains open and reading a paperback. There was one by the side of the bed that she'd already finished. She said, "Do you mind if I just stay here for a bit?" She was there for three days altogether and by the time she left there were eight paperbacks by the side of the bed. At the end of it she was fine. She was still very sad, but she dealt with it.' Despite being dumped, Victoria was midway through sewing a triangle of cloth into the ankles of Bob Mason's loonpants to turn them into flares. She finished the job and sent them in the post: 'I thought, well, he'll be so touched and moved that he'll chuck old actress-face out the window and come back to me.' When he next wrote to her he said, 'Jeans v. poor.'[5]

Romantic sorrow soon inspired her to write a song called 'It's Not Easy' in which self-pity was leavened by her urge to see the funny side:

> What will the man in the next flat think?
> He used to hear us making love
> What will he do when we've stopped it?
> He'll have to listen to the flat above.

The earliest surviving recording of a Victoria Wood composition is from her second term. In January 1972 the drama department staged *All's Well That Ends Well*. A series of alarums and fanfares for a pair of trumpets were written by Victoria, who well knew how the instrument worked. Mixed in among the traditional bugle calls were some striking blasts of mournful dissonance. But academically the year was a failure. Offered barely any opportunities to act, as early as her second term she confided to Steve Trow that she was depressed and was thinking she should try for drama school instead. For her practical exam piece at the end of the year, Victoria wrote and performed three monologues. Her lecturers were unimpressed. David Hirst, who was one of them, said as much to Steve Trow: 'She was just the same person in all three . . . and what on earth did it have to do with the course?' Victoria was one of a trio of students who decided to break into a lecturer's office to rummage through the assessments. Clive Barker had written one line about her: 'How do you teach a Christmas pudding?'

She got her own back more than a decade later in *As Seen on TV*. 'To Be an Actress' was another mock documentary featuring Sarah Wells, a naive actress who auditions to join a new company. Victoria hid autobiographical clues in the script, naming the other actors after her drama department friends – Bill, Steve, Jane. The pretentious director asks one of them to improvise in the character of Marie Lloyd – the Edwardian music hall star's real name was Victoria Wood. He doesn't want Sarah to do Juliet's death scene, which had been so fruitless for Victoria, instead asking her to improvise as Lady Godiva. As she prepares to strip, the older goateed actor leering at her looks uncannily like Clive Barker.

Victoria went home in the summer to resume friendly relations with Bob Mason as David Morton encouraged old protégés to return and help out with the Rochdale Theatre Workshop. Together they supplied the songs for an improvised piece about a cotton mill town, which they composed at Birtle Edge House. 'The evening air along the passage between the den and my office is filled with harmonious howling hour after hour,'[6] recorded Stanley Wood. The on-off relationship would rumble on. (Stanley was also being productive. While he continued in insurance, his first script for *Coronation Street* was aired in October 1972.)

Back in Birmingham, Victoria moved into a terraced house in Witton far on the other side of the city from the university. The arrangement didn't last long, as she was too dependent on housemates for lifts. She spent much of the year kipping at the two-up two-down terraced house in Selly Oak which Fidelis Morgan had bought with a small windfall and named Harrods. Bedecked with mattresses, Harrods became a stopover for drama students who had missed the last bus. Victoria dropped in during the day to watch daytime television, an obsession she shared with the landlady. A favourite drama of theirs was *Kate*, about an agony aunt in which Penelope Keith supplied them with a highly adaptable catchphrase: 'I'm absolutely fuming, Kate!' One programme above all they devoured with religious fervour at half past five every afternoon in vacations. 'We heard gales of laughter coming up the stairs,' says George Irving. 'One of us said, "What possible good can come out of Victoria coming round here and watching *Crossroads*?"'

There was also a musical connection with Fidelis Morgan. In

November 1972 drama students were invited by Jocelyn Powell to take part in what he called 'an environmental sound spectacular': the British premiere at the Great Hall on the university campus of John Cage's *Musicircus*, a democratic epic in which all musical styles and sounds were performed at once. It was a prestigious event to be part of. Victoria on piano and Fidelis on drums were to perform songs by Noël Coward, only for Victoria not to turn up. Days later Fidelis discovered she had been ill. 'Vic got rather cross with me for making a fuss,' she says.

In her second year Victoria's status as a misfit solidified. Later she characterised the syllabus as a BA in 'groping' for students who 'feel each other up with the lights out';[7] alternatively, it was 'a course in lounging about drinking coffee'[8] with a training in tying ropes onto cleats and operating a revolve. For all the degree's apparent breadth, the faculty seemed to find no means of accommodating her talents. 'They didn't know what do with Vic,' says Jane Wymark. 'They handled her really, really badly. Vic was always totally herself; she was not really malleable. The staff could only keep trying to force her into something that she didn't want to be.' She found herself confined to backstage roles in which she proved negligent. As stage manager for a play in which George Irving had to suck food through a tube stored in a fish tank, for one performance she didn't change the food and he nearly vomited mid-performance. 'She was sort of on strike,' says Fidelis.

Theoretically the second year was meant to provide students with the chance to act in front of paying audiences and even local critics. There was a majority of women on the course, but a minority of roles for them. They would wait nervously in the green room for casts to be announced. 'I never got to do the acting,' Victoria said. 'That was all done by the very tall blonde girls.'[9] Her best shot was a production of Joe Orton's *Loot*, to be staged in February 1973. The play has only one female part and Victoria was ideal for it. She learned before Christmas that she hadn't got it, which plunged her in gloom. 'Everyone was outraged,' says Steve Trow, 'so we went to Fid's house for some sympathy and commiseration, and the general opinion was that it must have been other senior staff sticking their oar in again.'

Fidelis, whose mother was a professional reader of Tarot cards, did a reading for Victoria. It told her that she had 'great talent' and would one day be 'very famous'. The next day was a reprise of the *Musicircus* performance at the Roundhouse in London. Fidelis drove down and remembers 'a vague sense of inevitability when, once again, Victoria didn't turn up'.

The director of *Loot* offered Victoria an olive branch in the shape of an invitation to top and tail the production with music. The brief was to play hymns, but Victoria ignored it and seized the chance to parade her own growing repertoire of songs. One, called 'Going Home Again', was a pointed commentary on middle-class students pretending to be proletarian:

In the lies about your father
I think that you have rather
Strayed from the path
He's not a crippled miner
He's a winer and diner
More at home in a sauna than an old zinc bath.

There was no egress other than through an upstage door, so she sat stage left at an upright piano, somewhat pulling focus in red and blue boots with silver sprayed in her hair. She had also just started wearing contacts, so the National Health glasses had gone. To top off her act she ate a salad sandwich onstage and ad-libbed the odd gag: of the Coke bottle on the piano top she said, 'People sniff this stuff, you know. I don't know how they get the bottle up their noses.' At the end, as the audience got up to leave, Victoria asked them to hang on and sang a song which pointedly referred to the fact that she should have been in the play.

Did you like the play?
Time to get your coats on
We know we'd like to see you again some day
You never know it might be me.

'I have just been a great success starring in the Department's production of *Loot*,' Victoria reported to Rosalind. 'They should have cast
me in it, but they didn't. So I played the piano before, in the interval
and after. I stole the show.'[10]

News of her performance reached the ears of an influential student
on campus who organised concerts. 'More than one friend came up
to me,' says Sahlan Diver, 'and said they'd heard this fantastic girl
singing a medley of songs with piano. I was warned she was extremely
shy.' One morning they met in the student union and then moved
on to a soundproofed piano room in his hall of residence: 'And I was
treated to a fifteen-minute private concert of pure genius. The sheer
musicality and inventiveness of her piano playing was immediately
clear to me. She told me she'd written her first song to cope with
the trauma of a boyfriend leaving her. She sang me the very song.'
Another was a protest song called 'We're Having a Party for the End
of the World'. Channelling anxiety about the prospect of a nuclear
doomsday, Victoria gloomily depicted the downbeat celebrations
('We'll stand in the cold / And say at least we'll never grow old'). They
agreed to put together a concert that would take place at the end of
the academic year.

By now Victoria had moved closer to the university, to the garret
flat of a detached Victorian house on Richmond Hill Road in a leafy
part of well-heeled Edgbaston. She slept in the sitting room on a put-
me-up while ceding the double bed to her flatmate Jane Wynn Owen:
'Her idea of a put-me-up bed was one of those garden loungers that
folds up in three. So in the night you'd suddenly hear, bang, "Fuck!",
and silence. I'd have to unfold her.' Sahlan Diver was round at the flat
when the BBC announced Princess Anne's engagement to Captain
Mark Phillips. Victoria looked forward to sending the horse-mad
couple a card 'congratulating them on the birth of their first foal'.

Victoria turned twenty on 19 May 1973. Inviting friends to a
children's afternoon tea party, she asked them to suggest a favourite
sandwich. While assembling these she drank a couple of glasses of
wine and muddled the ingredients. A notice for the guests cited the
famous Morecambe and Wise sketch with André Previn: 'Dear folks,
here are the sandwiches you asked for but not necessarily in that order.

PS do not eat the grey sandwich.' There were children's party games. As requested, her flatmate gave her roller skates. She strapped on her new second-hand pair. 'Meals on wheels,' she quipped as she ate jelly and custard.

Victoria was not a habitual drinker. When alcohol got the better of her, it would loosen her tongue. 'She would get completely paralytic and then she would start telling people home truths and it was quite frightening,' says Alison Sabourin, who was once advised by Victoria that she was far too good for her boyfriend Bill Lloyd and should forget about him. Yet her fondness for both was not in doubt. That term she composed 'A Song for Bill Ill' after he was hospitalised with stress before finals. It concluded, 'Don't be forlorn / The day will dawn / On a less sick William Lloyd'. It was written in a 'tempo di convalesco', and she signed it 'affec rgds VW'. She wrote a solo speech for Alison to perform in her final assessment. It was a despondent piece with barely a joke, channelling her own feelings about Bob Mason, in which a young woman in a bedsit explains how her boyfriend has abandoned her for a student with platform shoes and uncombed hair. In the end Alison felt more comfortable doing something with other actors.

Bluntness was a side of Victoria that all her friends had to get used to. She thrived on gossip, which is partly why she favoured the intimate exchange of one-on-one conversation. 'When you got her on your own, that's when she blossomed,' says Robert Howie, who was in the year below and for several years would become an intimate friend with whom she caught ropey matinees at the Alexandra Theatre. On these outings Victoria would insist on going to Woolworths for egg and chips, and often they'd slip into a passport photo booth and gurn for the camera.

At the end of June the concert took place in the common room of University House, a hall of residence. Also on the bill was Hettie Pipe & Her Jug Band Experience, featuring Bill Lloyd and Sahlan Diver and an array of cider jugs which produced a boomy bass sound. To promote the gig they did a photoshoot: Victoria, wearing flared jeans and sneakers, brandished a ukulele which she was attempting to learn. Tickets cost 20p. For the concert itself she sewed the letters

VW onto the back of her denim jacket in plastic mother-of-pearl stars
which flashed under the lights. She sang three sets of songs, two on
her own and one with a scratch band led by Sahlan Diver. Opening
with 'Alison's Song', she treated it as a showcase for the songs she had
amassed. The strongest composition, that would have the longest life,
she introduced as 'Sad Salad Sunday' 'because it's about those three
things'. With a wistful verse and a sprightly chorus, she pictured a
couple sagging into the emptiness of middle age while their teenage
daughter rolls her eyes.

> Children be nice to your father
> He is still alive at thirty-five
> While your eyes get brighter
> His trousers get tighter
> His wife's hair is as hard as her voice
> And his freedom of choice is blown out through the window
> That cost him so much to put in.

Punctuating her songs were tunes from between the wars, including
an obscurity called 'When a Woman Loves a Man', which she introduced as the work of 'a male chauvinist pig'. Her drummer smugly
whistled the tune in an instrumental break as if he was the chauvinist,
while Victoria cast disdainful looks that brought the house down.

Sahlan Diver arranged for the concert to be recorded, thus capturing on tape Victoria's first gig. In twelve songs she exuded a confidence
which undermines her later claims that at this stage she had no idea
how to perform to an audience. The songs, even those tinged with
sadness, provoked explosions of laughter. It 'went v. well,' she reported
to Rosalind. So buoyed did she feel by the performance that she sent
off a tape of demos to Dick James Music in Oxford Street. 'Dick
James is the one that does Elton John,' she unflappably added.[11] The
swift reply was discouraging. 'I am afraid that there is nothing on the
tape that really interests me as songs,' wrote the music publisher Leslie
Lowe, who recommended she stick to 'known standard material as
does Blossom Dearie . . . rather than trying to sell yourself as an artist
and a composer'.[12] Victoria pasted the letter into the first page of her

scrapbook and under it wrote 'thank you Leslie'. There was better news from BBC Radio Birmingham, who had someone in the University House audience among her throng of friends. 'Radio Brum asked me to do 15 mins in their half-hour student programme,' she proudly announced.[13] Two weeks later, Victoria stayed in, turned on the radio and listened on her own to her broadcasting debut. 'It is 6pm and I'm waiting to hear myself in an hour,' she told Robert Howie. 'At the moment there's a Jamaican steel band playing the Hallelujah Chorus & an announcer who keeps saying Ooops . . . sorry.'[14]

Victoria spent the summer in Birmingham. Though she feared being lonely, she decided to move into a single room in the same building in Edgbaston. She got a summer job as a barmaid in the Sportsman, a pub in Harborne where, as she pulled pints for 30p an hour, she cocked an ear to the conversation. 'The pub is v. interesting as far as listening to the people and writing about them is concerned,' she told Bill Lloyd, although she was demoralised that the men talked about 'cars, booze and "chicks"' and the women about 'getting engaged, drinks and clothes'.[15] She later reckoned that it helped her deal with her shyness – 'it's a very theatrical job: you're on stage, on show' – and towards the end of one night she overcame her diffidence enough to sit at the piano and perform some of her songs.[16] A BBC producer called Gerry Hynes who regularly drank there heard her and the next day told John Clarke, an established director at Pebble Mill, the BBC's studios in Birmingham, who was always on the hunt for new young performers: 'Gerry came in and said, "I've seen a girl performing at the Sportman and I think she's a knockout. I'll get her to come in if you like." He got a contact number for her and we arranged a time for her to come in.'

When Victoria reconstructed this event in later years, she mined it for comedy. In one version she was invited to a party 'and I was such a show-off I played the piano and sang'.[17] In another, she laughed at the BBC producer and said, 'Ha ha ha, get yer 'and off my bosoms, will you please?'[18] At Pebble Mill she was met by Clarke, Hynes and another producer, who led her into a storeroom where they kept a grand piano: 'She seemed to be perfectly at ease the moment she sat down at the piano and started to play. A light went on in all our minds. This girl has got it. She had the spark; she had the talent. We've got to have her. It's rare to get a BBC producer to laugh out loud at an audition but certain turns of phrase made us fall about laughing.' The song that had this effect was 'Lorraine', a deftly worded postcard about young female anxiety in which Lorraine has 'gone and got engaged again' and dreads sex with her looming husband Dick.

> He must have some good points
> Hang on a minute I'll check
> I don't think I've seen a cleaner Cortina
> He washes it more than his neck.

She sang half a dozen songs, including 'You're Going Home Again'. 'I was sold after the first one,' says Clarke. 'I wanted to know how long it took her to cook up a new song. She said, "How long have you got?" "Can you write a song by this evening?" She said, "No problem." She had an extraordinary sense of her own ability, which was strange because her manner was of a very shy person.'

'They quite liked me at the BBC,' Victoria neutrally told Rosalind, 'so I'll see what comes of that.'[19] To friends who had now left Birmingham, she mentioned that she was in contact with a BBC television producer. 'I've got a feeling you're destined for fame ducks, but you'll cope,' wrote Jane Wymark.[20] She was soon on the radio again, introduced as 'a young lady trying to make a name for herself'. When she listened back to the interview, she thought she 'sounded like a depressed clog'.[21]

These successes ignited a desire to prove to Bob Mason what he was missing, so that summer Victoria entered a cabaret contest: 'I wanted to show him that I could get on without him . . . I'll win and he'll come and see me being terribly famous and be hurt and wounded.'[22] She passed an audition and met the drummer who was to play with all the contestants. 'He says they'll all be awful,' she told Bill Lloyd hopefully, 'so I might win.'[23] In August she sang in a late-night heat at a club called Barbarella's. The piano was bolted to the floor, which meant she had to play with her back to the audience. Judgement was said to be by clapometer. Though she never heard it in operation, she was back for the semi-final two weeks later, where she finished runner-up: 'They wanted men with wobbly voices too near the mike singing 'By the Time I Get to Phoenix' so I wasn't too disappointed.'[24] By now she was optimistic that a career path was opening up. She told Rosalind, whose artwork she admired enough to decorate her walls with it, that she'd like her to design her LP covers 'when I get that going'.[25]

Victoria spent one week back at Birtle in September. Given how infrequently her parents now saw her, it may have been during this week – years later she recalled that she was twenty at the time – that she had an awkward exchange with Stanley in his car: 'My dad said there was a lady he would like me to meet. I knew instantly this was someone he was having an affair with and with huge sophistication stared out of the window and didn't reply. He never mentioned her again.'[26]

Over the summer Victoria had a commission from the drama department to come up with music for a production of John Arden's play *The Island of the Mighty*. The Arthurian epic had been in the news the year before when the playwright picketed the RSC's stage door. Victoria dubbed it 'Island of the Boring'.[27] Her contribution resulted in another argument with a faculty member, this time the director Graham Woodruff, who had to pester her for the music. Her ego bolstered by her summer triumphs, she played hard to get: 'Saw Graham the bum on Thurs. Told him I could only spare 10 minutes and kept glancing at my watch in an executive manner which annoyed him.'[28] When the music did finally arrive Woodruff dismissed it as not good enough. During rehearsals Victoria sat 'on a bandstand pinging on triangles and banging on drums for tedious dramatic effect'.[29] When it was performed in October she defiantly added 'Louisville Lou', a sultry, swinging Tin Pan Alley song from the 1920s in praise of a vamp – 'the most heart-breakin'est, shimmy shakin'est that the world ever knew'. She noted that 'endless people have told me how bad the music was except for the last song. So I've determined never to do my worst on anything like that again.'[30]

Victoria would come to view her final year at Birmingham as a period in which she 'ducked out of the system again completely. I didn't go to lectures and I didn't do any of the work.'[31] Rather than sleep in her bedsit, Victoria half-moved into Harrods, and only went back to her digs once a week to collect her post. Fidelis Morgan was her one friend from the year above not to be have left the city. They spent their spare time boning up on cheap television – *Crown Court*, *General Hospital*, *Emmerdale Farm* and the Welsh-language soap *Pobol y Cwm*, which they renamed 'Pobbly Quim'. The other lure of Harrods was the presence of a piano, which she and Fidelis found next to a skip and wheeled back along the main road, enlisting help from passers-by. 'Life in the Dept. is v. strange,' she told Bill Lloyd, 'not at all as it used to be. The 1st year fill the green room playing guitars singing, and talking about awareness (probably singing about it too) . . . BRIGHT SIDE THOUGH [and here she drew a smiling self-portrait] – Words are pounding thro' my head so some plays should be forthcoming.'[32]

Fidelis encouraged her to enter a *Radio Times* competition for writers with a prize of £2,000. Instead she aimed higher, submitting a short untitled play to Pebble Mill, which was becoming a source of powerful television drama. Drawing on her experiences of school, this was the first of her many scripts to explore the dynamic between two young women, one an extrovert, the other an introvert. The main protagonists were two sixth-form girls. Barney is socially successful and popular; Christine is slovenly, chaotic and a loner. Victoria clearly identified with Christine, while putting something of herself into Barney, who steals essays from the teacher's pile to conceal the absence of her own. 'I'll put them in her locker and take away the bottom seven,' she says, 'that's me, Stevenson, Taylor, Turtem, you, Wilkinson and Wood.' The play also expressed conflicted feelings of longing and embarrassment about the attentions of older men. It was rejected in October, but Victoria was undaunted. 'I am trying to write a play about Cabaret,' she revealed later the same term, 'because a woman at the BBC said I was good.'[33]

In her final year Victoria enrolled on a newly created course in television. It was taught by a producer called Paul Morby whose most recent credit had been for a single episode of *Gardener's World* in 1968.

She enjoyed it. 'TV is v good,' she told Bill Lloyd.[34] One assignment was to write a song to accompany Catherine Ashmore's experimental film about a huge statue of King Kong, which had been commissioned by Birmingham city council to stand in the Bull Ring. When they rejected it, the statue was sold to a second-hand car dealership. Sticking to a formula she developed on other songs in this period, Victoria favoured a melancholy verse and a hectic chorus: 'Ding dong King Kong / Loved you from the minute I saw you / You caught my eye, I don't know why / I thought everybody would adore you'. She was genuinely surprised to fail the course after getting a low grade for a five-minute script filleted from her rejected BBC play.

Victoria was sufficiently disillusioned by her final year to apply to E15, the influential drama school which was seen as a radical working-class alternative to RADA and Central, and she travelled to east London for more than one callback. It's unclear whether she or the school eventually decided they were not a good fit but a decade later, after a grim evening watching third years do performance pieces, she would refer to it as 'E.15 School of Wanking and Ejected Semen'.[35] 'I'm not a very good actress,' she rationalised in an early interview. 'I think if I'd wanted to do it, I could've done it but there are about a million people that are as good as me so it didn't seem worth it.'[36] On a deeper level she suspected that she didn't look like an actress: 'I thought I'll have to do so many things to change. If I want to get into rep, I'll have to lose my accent and look more normal, and I thought this isn't going to work, so it did put me off the idea . . . at the time it was rather depressing.'[37]

Another lure in London was still Bob Mason – she went down to see him in a play. They were definitely not together any more – Christmas 1973 was 'my 1st Bobless Christmas in 4 years' – but she seemed unable to flush him out of her system. Meanwhile she could not get excited about the romantic attentions of other men who, she wearily explained to Bill Lloyd, 'expect a running comedy act before during and after – or they expect to find the "real me".'[38] She complained that 'there are very few people here that I like and sometimes I get slumped in an armchair in my pink cardy staring at my blue fluffy slippers with a little smile on my face, and then it means I am feeling a bit unattached and surrounded by people who think I am funny bless their boring old sox'.[39] Balancing out this introspective streak was a growing awareness that to be an entertainer she had to look the part. She experimented with fake tan and tried making her own clothes but more often offered to pay Rosalind to do it for her. 'I've lost weight again,' she wrote, requesting 'a pair of zoomy jeans'.[40] The following term she reported that she hadn't 'eaten anything for 3 days except lemon juice with saccharin in it. I go about with a permanently crinkled mouth.'[41]

This new focus coincided with her television debut in March 1974 on a folk programme called *Springs to Mind*. 'I hit the headlines at last,' she wrote alongside a TV listing glued into her scrapbook. 'Not a very good title,' she later suggested, 'and the show went downhill from there.'[42] But it earned her an elusive Equity card, conferring membership of the actors' union and enabling her to work – it arrived in the month she turned twenty-one. There was soon more exposure on a four-part series, for which she had a black velvet jacket made. 'V flash. I hate it really but it looked OK on TV.'[43] The cheaply assembled show she appeared in was broadcast in the opt-out slot for regional programming. *St John on . . .* was presented by St John Howell, who introduced items on various themes (food, money, etc.) to do with life in the Midlands. John Clarke, who directed it, asked Victoria to submit four songs to fit the theme, and advised that the perfect length was exactly two minutes and ten seconds. The edict was absorbed to the point that she 'found it very difficult to write a longer song than that for years'.[44] Victoria behaved like a practised entertainer from the start. 'There was never any problem with her,' says Clarke. 'I would cue her and it was like starting a musical box. She'd play it note and word perfect every time, totally professional.' As for the first show, Victoria was not a fan: 'It was the worst thing I've ever seen. All the items were stupid, like a kid's essay . . . I didn't know when I was on and was cringing for half an hour.'[45] It didn't stop her staying up one night before to see if an episode would be plugged at the closedown by BBC Birmingham's continuity announcer. She was rewarded: 'Also appearing Virginia Wood.'[46] In a couple of the programmes she sang alongside cartoons by 'Larry', whose work had been appearing in

*Punch* since Victoria was a small girl. She was chuffed to meet him. 'He's v nice,' she intimated to Rosalind.[47] He gave her an original cartoon which she proudly hung on the wall. Another consolation was her first review, which savaged the programme but exempted her: 'There was one saving grace. Victoria Wood is a remarkable lady vocalist and piano-player who sounds like a cross between Jake Thackray and Blossom Dearie. More please.'[48] She would have to get used to these comparisons – in particular to Thackray, an observational singer-songwriter from Yorkshire. The series, for which she was paid '£33.75 per programme, less 71p insurance,' she told Lesley Fitton, was recorded as she revised.[49] One even fell in the middle of four days of exams: 'Whoopee that's going to be a great week.'[50]

Years later, reminiscing onstage about these early appearances in regional television, she would joke about how few people saw them: 'I might as well have been playing in the snug of the Bermuda Triangle for all the good it did me.'[51] In fact, Victoria had no idea of the big break that awaited. The pilot of an ATV talent show produced in Birmingham called *New Faces* had aired the previous summer, followed by an autumn series and another in the new year. The show positioned itself as the professional alternative to the BBC's more established *Opportunity Knocks*. 'Artistes new to network television are cordially invited to write for an audition at one of the centres covering their area,' went the announcement. The first person to urge Victoria to try for the show was Louise Fisher, a make-up artist working at ATV who helped on drama department productions: 'I told her, "There's this new show and you've really got to do it, Vic." I told her I would help sort her costume and look after her coming into the world of TV. I was shy too, so I understood how the TV experience would be intimidating for her. I had to persuade her quite heavily.' Victoria dragged her heels for so long that eventually Fidelis Morgan put her up for *New Faces* without her knowing. She did it for the same reason she simultaneously entered her sister in an ATV beauty contest – 'both of them were so depressed!'

In April Victoria showed up to an all-day open audition at La Dolce Vita nightclub and found a long line of hopefuls that looked, in her colourful recollection, 'like something by Fellini – naked people playing the spoons, dogs with hats on'.[52] Louise Fisher went along with her as, in effect, her chaperone. 'I knew the floor manager and I had to go back to work by a certain time and I just said, "Can I put Victoria's name at the top?"' Victoria would credit this intervention as the stroke of luck that would land her on national television: 'Otherwise I'd have been at the back of the queue and not been seen.'[53] The audition was not filmed, but there was an audience. When silver-maned producer Les Cocks wanted to cut off an audition he'd theatrically slash his hand across his neck. Victoria's song impressed him. As she told Rosalind, 'He came in, sat down, and said, "Right, make me laugh." So I did.'[54] He even planned to rush her straight into the spring series which was still running. She wrote to all her friends. 'Do you get lots of money for doing TV things? If not why not?' replied Lesley Fitton.[55] 'Is this the Break Vicki was always waiting for?' asked Alison Sabourin. 'Will V Wood soar to stardom?'[56] 'I would wish you luck,' said Anne Sweeney, 'but it seems stars don't need it.'[57] It was then decided to hold Victoria back for the autumn series.

Meanwhile, her student years were about to end. 'No one ever gets a first,' she predicted before her exams, 'so it's no use trying for that.'[58] She was right to arm herself against disappointment. In part thanks to her fail in the television course, Victoria was awarded a pass degree without honours. Her name was listed at the very bottom of the page in the *Birmingham Post* on 13 July 1974. On the same day there was a graduation ceremony. Victoria did not attend.

# 6

# NEW FACE

**'I think it was the only TV talent show to have its own stomach pump.'**

*Lucky Bag*, 1983

Victoria's plan upon graduating was to make a living as an entertainer, but the first thing she did in the summer of 1974 was to start claiming the dole. Resolving to stay on in Birmingham, she packed up in Richmond Hill Road and moved less than a mile down the hill to a ground-floor bedsit in a mid-Victorian mansion in Priory Road, close to the main road into the city. At last she had room for a piano, bought on the cheap. It was in such poor nick that eventually she invested in a second upright. Birtle-style, she fashioned shelves from bricks stacked on planks. At the side was a kitchen conservatory which was bitterly cold in winter. She heated food on a Baby Belling and warmed the place up with bold blues and purples. On a chair she kept a stack of women's magazines – 'where I get my ideas from,' she told Louise Fisher. To get around she bought a second-hand bicycle for a tenner.

At her *New Faces* audition, Victoria found herself drawn to half a dozen middle-aged men competing as the Eagle Jazz Band. Scenting her interest in traditional jazz, the clarinettist Bob Smith invited her to his home in Walsall to sift through his collection of sheet music from the 1920s. 'She was fascinated by it and went through it piece by piece,' he says. 'She played a bit on the piano. She could not believe there was a tune called "I Fell Down and Went Ow".' Over the summer she made the twenty-five-mile round trip several times, and also turned up at the Eagle Jazz Band's pub gigs – the Wheatsheaf in Walsall, the Old Crown in Digbeth, the Golden Eagle in the city centre. One night the band suggested she play during an interval: 'She wasn't in the slightest bit pushy. We invited her. We saw it as an addition to the entertainment of the evening.' She didn't always persuade the audience to stop talking as she played.

At one pub Bob Smith was surprised to spot her at the bar with John Clarke, whom he'd known since school, and who now invited Victoria and the Eagle Jazz Band to perform on a one-off regional show called *Mother Muffin's Music Stand*. Although it wouldn't be broadcast until early December, it was recorded in September, giving Victoria some practice in performing to an audience and a camera at the same time. Over a plaid shirt, she wore a Wrangler jacket with rainbow colours which she had chain-stitched along the shoulders and round the wrists. She would embroider further embellishments: richly coloured panels on the front and back, flowers in pots, her name and initials. The Eagle Jazz Band were local television regulars, whereas Victoria was so nervous beforehand that she could be clearly seen by the audience lying flat on her back stage right. She played two new compositions. In 'Fashion' she described a young typist called Dorothy who yearns to break free of her controlling mother and dress according to magazine style tips.

> She sees herself in black satin
> With no back and no sides and no top
> The sort sexy ladies pop out of
> 'Cept Dorothy's got nothing to pop.

She explored similar territory in 'Nice Girl', which told of a polite young wife who plots breakout fantasies of nailing her father to the railings and escaping her marriage to become a stripper ('I'll be introduced as Sadie / A rather evil lady'). For this stomper the Eagle Jazz Band provided Dixieland backing, while she peppered the camera with beaming grins.

Her heat of *New Faces* beckoned in October, and Victoria encouraged Rosalind, who was expecting a baby, to tune in: 'Maybe you'll have your own "new face" by then hee hee.'[1] While excited to be making her debut on national television, she watchfully guarded against failure: 'I bet I get hammered on "New Faces" – they award points for "Star Quality". Won't win. Never mind.'[2] She prepared by putting herself on a lemon-juice diet ('I'm back on the PLJ shrivel shrivel'), while Louise Fisher introduced her to a designer friend called Pru McEwen who created flamboyant outfits.[3] For Victoria she made denim dungarees and a wide-lapelled blue satin blouse, and gave her a necklace of multicoloured beads.

Her heat was filmed at the ATV studios on a weekday before the Saturday night broadcast. Beforehand there were rehearsals when she and the other contestants spent most of the day doing soundchecks and a dress rehearsal. 'I can remember her in my make-up chair,' says Louise, 'trying out what we should do for hair and make-up and then testing how it looked on camera. She was in unknown territory. I'd get her on, get her off. I stuck with her the whole time like glue.' The staff in the control room were so taken by her that the set designer took it upon himself to tell her how they all felt. For support Victoria took along Robert Howie, who sensed his friend needed morale-boosting compliments and 'kept telling her how marvellous she was that evening'. She also had a claque in the audience whom she supplied with huge VW badges, prompting the compère Derek Hobson to joke about a Volkswagen owners' club. Backstage Victoria stayed quietly within her shell until the moment came for her to perform.

The other contestants, including a unicycling ventriloquist known as Davy Wanda, would all sink without trace. Career death was also predicted for Victoria. The show had a rotating cast of male judges in velvet tuxedos and floppy bow ties – Les Cocks had decided that female viewers didn't warm to female judges. On that episode's panel were venerable comedian Ted Ray, the prolific record producer Mickie Most, Birmingham nightclub owner John Smith and the *Daily Mirror* television critic Clifford Davis, the show's pantomime villain whose damning verdicts provoked boos. When she performed 'Fashion', they awarded her very high marks for presentation, content and star quality, but Davis added a caveat that her act belonged to a bygone age, which he attempted to clarify with her in post-show drinks. The message Victoria took away was that, while she had won the episode and would go through to the next round, 'she'll never work because she's a sophisticated cabaret act and there's no places for her to work'.[4] While downcast at the suggestion she was in a stylistic cul-de-sac, she felt validated by the praise: 'I was very excited that people like Ted Ray and Mickie Most said, "She's fantastic." I thought, ooh-eh! I am good. I am good.'[5] And she enjoyed observing these celebrities backstage. She told Rosalind about meeting Ted Ray: 'I've never seen anyone that pissed before that was still standing. He kept saying, "Wouldn't mind a bit of that" gesturing drunkenly towards me, while everyone smiled indulgently.'[6]

That week she was showered with enquiries from potential agents. 'I just cannot believe all this is happening to me,' she told the *Birmingham Evening Mail*, who sent a photographer to Priory Road to snap her at her piano. 'This is my major breakthrough.' The reporter referred to her as Christine, but there was no misrepresenting her sunny enthusiasm. 'My eventual ambition,' she said, 'is to do a one-woman show on television or on the stage. I have a trunkful of songs I have written for when the time comes. I am just keeping my fingers crossed that my luck holds.'[7]

At the recording there was one agent in particular, a thickset man in his middle years, who pledged to make her a star. Later in life Victoria avoided identifying her manager, whom she took to describing as 'certifiably insane'.[8] His real name was Handel Huckridge, but he was better known as the bandleader Jack Dorsey, who had also worked in A&R. He swiftly typed up a contract in front of her and naively she signed it. 'Am having v exciting time signing my life away to a big band leader (the band's big, he's quite small),' she told Rosalind, adding anxiously, 'I wish I could understand contracts.'[9] Later she claimed never to have read the contract: 'I thought, it'll look so rude; it'll look like I don't trust him. God knows what it said. "I give all my money to Jack Dorsey."'[10] The contract, she soon discovered, meant that he took 50 per cent of her royalties. He also signed London Management to act as her agents.

During these developments, Victoria prepared to go forward to a winners' final a month later. The prize was a place in the grand final at the London Palladium, where the victor would earn a gig in Las Vegas. For this episode Victoria wore a fresh pair of dungarees by Pru McEwen: 'I'd asked for them to be made in red, yellow and blue patchwork corduroy. When she brought them, she said, "Oh, I couldn't face making them in red, yellow and blue so I made them in green and brown." Absolutely loathed them. And also either she'd made them too small or more likely I'd done a lot of nervous over-eating the weeks preceding the show and I couldn't get into them.'[11]

As the contestants were introduced on camera, Victoria sat nonchalantly smoking next to an eight-year-old contestant called Malandra Newman. The other finalists included two hirsute all-male bands, a light soprano and a couple of mimics. One of them was Les Dennis, to whom Victoria introduced herself as a university friend of his school friend Jude Kelly. They bonded throughout the day while sizing each other up: 'After the rehearsal Victoria came up to me and said, "It's either going to be me or you." I said, "I think you're going to win."'

For one night only Derek Hobson joined the judging panel and handed presenting duties to Nicky Martyn, a Lancashire stand-up who had been a runner-up in a previous programme. He puffed Victoria up as the owner of an honours degree whom viewers might imagine better suited to the Old Vic or 'somewhere very Shakespearean'. He then introduced her as 'Joanna Wood', twice. Victoria sang 'Lorraine'; in her own estimation it was not as accomplished as 'Fashion', though it too was a cleverly worded snapshot of young womanhood.

I don't think his mother likes me,
I can tell by the look in her eyes
As she sips her port and lemon
Says 'I've got a little premon-
ition you're in for a surprise.'
I know what she's trying to tell me
I've heard about marital rites
It sounds like 'ell so it's just as well
It only happens on Saturday nights.

The audience laughed cheerfully at this grim portent. When Hobson urged her not to think of losing two stone as Lorraine does in the song – 'You're lovely the way you are,' he said – Victoria blew him a kiss which turned into a sardonic side-eye as he likened her to Jake Thackray. She finished sixth out of eight. 'I think she was gutted,' says Les Dennis, who was fourth. The other mimic won.

Victoria's consolation as a heat winner was to be named Midlands Musical Entertainer of the Year, the prize for which was a residency at the New Cresta Club in Solihull owned by the *New Faces* judge John Smith. It was a demoralising week: 'I had to wear a dress and the audience were eating scampi in a basket and that was just terrible. The only laugh I knew how to get was "I've got to go now because I've got to have a wee". And I used to say that earlier and earlier.'[12] To amuse himself the emcee used to hold the curtains together to prevent her coming off.

Such experiences suggested Clifford Davis's prophecy might have been right after all. Jack Dorsey had no idea what to do with her, and it didn't help that he lived in Hove. If she wanted to see him, she had to pay for her own travel. His default tendency was to reject gig bookings. 'My girl doesn't do anything like that,' he'd say. 'I don't know why he wanted to sign me. He had no interest really in doing any work for me at all. It was just weird and I was so stupid to do it.'[13] At the time, she submitted to Dorsey's plan, telling a local reporter that her manager rationed her bookings to those that he felt were right for her. 'If you're confident you're going to make it anyway,' she said, 'you can afford to take time.'[14] His strategy, such as it was, was to hold out for television offers and secure a recording contract. 'I'll speak for Fatty,' he'd say as he took her to meetings: 'I should have said "Don't call me Fatty, Baldy" but I didn't, I just took it – I suppose because I thought it was my fault that I was overweight.'[15] An album, notionally titled *Cameos*, never came to pass.

Victoria's own contacts were a steadier source of employment. Steve Trow formed a strolling theatre company called Jubilee Arts who introduced themselves with a pub entertainment called *The Tipton Slasher Show* about a Black Country prize fighter which toured West Bromwich pubs in late 1974. Victoria wrote the songs and joined the band. Her introductory number included a dig at greedy agents, and perhaps at her own credulity: 'This boy is heaven sent, / He's so bloody stupid, / I'm on 99 per cent.' The rambunctious show was performed on tiny cramped stages with everyone mucking in – Victoria even turned her hand to drumming. Her pay was not forthcoming and she had to write, crossly, to demand her £5 fee.

Meanwhile she continued to rely on John Clarke. In early December he brought her in to Pebble Mill to record songs for a programme he called *Good Heavens, Look at This!* Not for broadcast, it was a training day for BBC staff learning to call the shots in a television studio. There were twelve trainees and so twelve short programmes to film. Cued in at the same place each time, Victoria recorded a dozen songs from her repertoire built up over the previous two years. ('I had one good song and eleven hopeless songs,' she would later say, 'and I used to do that in my act.')[16] This mix of jolly patter songs, wistful ballads and bluesy torch songs reflected the preoccupations which would be with her for the next forty years: love, sex, class and body image. In the determinedly unfunny 'Nobody Loves You When You're Down and Fat' she explored the psychology of comfort eating:

> People can be very cruel
> There's no use denying
> Inside every jolly fat girl
> Is another one crying
> So get thin or keeping smiling
> And that's that.

Twenty years her senior, John Clarke was a significant figure in Victoria's life as she stepped onto the lowest rungs as a professional entertainer. She dropped in for coffee or a drink at Pebble Mill, introduced him to a clutch of her friends and would invite him to Priory Road. A snap of a thickset middle-aged figure with dark curly hair and a leather jacket survives in an early photo album. 'John Clark', she captioned it, misspelling his surname. It was in her bedsit that he told her there was only so much he could do to help her career. 'We had a conversation in Priory Road about what she was going to do,' he says. 'I wasn't going to be able to provide her with work from here on in. She said, "That's all right, I'm going to be a star anyway." I said, "What makes you think that?" She said, "I know it, I don't think it.""

The last time John Clarke put Victoria's face on television was to have a domino effect. He asked her to write a song for a regional review of 1974. One of the other contributors was Roger McGough, the Mersey poet who had known fleeting pop fame singing 'Lily the Pink' with the Scaffold. As part of the all-male performance collective known as GRIMMS, he was working on a film for a BBC Two series called *The Camera and the Song*, which married quirky filmmaking and folkish songwriting. Impressed and amused by Victoria, McGough recommended this unusual young singing wordsmith to the producer John Bird. She was commissioned instantly.

'We have found our last performer,' wrote Bird in an internal BBC memo, recommending she be paid £60.[17] London Management negotiated the fee up to £100. All Victoria had to do was propose a topic to Bird. 'I hope I'm awake before he rings,' she told Roger McGough, 'or I might say something embarrassing that I don't mean like "Ramsbottom in Winter" or "What Men are Really Like."'[18] In fact, she suggested a song cycle about the dullness of suburbia. Thus she shivered in her bedsit and worked on threading together half a dozen songs on the same theme – she dubbed the show 'The Camera and too much work'.[19] 'When I've written all these bloody songs I'll let you know,' she told Robert Howie, 'and you can come round for tea and laugh at my new lampshade.'[20]

The songs emerged quickly and were handed over to an arranger. After recording, they were given to a cinematographer who had free rein to produce the images to match them. It wasn't conventional for the composer to appear in the films, but Victoria had a cameo as a barmaid clearing tankards during a song about men in pubs, inspired by her time at the Sportsman. There would be a frustrating wait before *The Camera and the Song* was broadcast.

In the meantime, the new songs entered her repertoire. A couple of them – one called 'Marriage', the other 'Divorce' – had an airing in

March at the Teddington Hockey Club Dance in south-west London, where Victoria was paired on the bill with Beetles and Buckman, a comedy duo who had met as junior doctors. Before the booking she visited Rob Buckman's house in Islington and, with Chris Beetles, had a go at sketch-writing. 'We were relentlessly extrovert and ridiculous and she very quickly got over her shyness,' says Beetles. In the end the doctors did their own material and Victoria performed her songs. Her sad, fine-grained observations weren't really hockey-club fare. 'People in backless dresses and powder over their acne kept saying they'd seen me on the box,' she told Rosalind, 'and did I write those little songs myself?'[21]

A month later Beetles and Buckman's management booked them to perform a showcase at the Mermaid Theatre in London, and they asked Victoria to join them. The idea of the evening was to introduce the performers to a packed house of producers and impresarios. Chris Beetles noticed a competitive streak in Victoria: 'If we were getting good jokes, then she would sulk. She was a bit of sulker. There had to be a winner.' Bernard Miles, who ran the theatre, enthused to Beetles and Buckman: 'You gave great pleasure last evening. It was also an inspiration to plant a plump and more leisurely figure at the grand piano to set off your vigorous tempi.'[22] Victoria pasted the letter into her scrapbook with the words 'Thank you Bernard'.[23] In her estimation, the only exposure the evening brought was that she was 'exposed for being a talentless prat'.[24] In fact, she did earn a commission to write a song for *Woman's Week*, a new show fronted by Joan Bakewell about how women are featured in the media.

A bigger commission came from Thames TV, whose magazine programme *Today* sought songs on local places – Kew Gardens, London Zoo. 'The silly provincial looks at London,' she snorted.[25] She wrote one on Soho which involved poking around a sex shop for inspiration 'and they wouldn't let me do it because it was too rude'.[26] She made no great claims for their artistic merit and had no intention of watching them when they were broadcast in May. 'I was really diabolical,' she would say later. 'No one could grind out any words of praise at all for that.'[27]

Through all this, funds remained scarce. 'I keep signing contracts and not getting any money,' Victoria told Roger McGough. 'Is all show business like this?'[28] Back in Birmingham, she spent a great deal of time scrimping and scavenging with Fidelis Morgan. Once they dug for spuds in Harrods' abandoned vegetable patch and made mashed potatoes with butter bought from the butter tokens they were given with their dole money. If unable to pay Fidelis petrol money for taxiing her to hotel gigs in her orange Beetle, Victoria would pinch teapots and towels as payment in kind. These ended up with Oxfam.

Having both stayed on in Birmingham, the two spent a lot of time together. In the front row at the Alexandra Theatre they saw the vast cue cards held up for Marlene Dietrich in the wings. At another play they got the giggles which were transmitted to the cast and the show ground to a halt for five minutes. Back at Harrods they consumed vast quantities of radio and television. They were obsessed with Julie Dawn, who in a curdling voice broadcast late-night inanities with a right-wing Christian tinge on Radio 2. Attempting to capitalise on their lack of work, they started writing a sitcom about two girls on the dole, inspired by their experience standing in the queue with alcoholics and addicts. They called it *Take Two Nutters* and mapped out a series. One episode was based on an incident when Fidelis was teaching Victoria to drive and a wasp flew in causing havoc. But they never submitted it to a broadcaster.

With Victoria's career as a cabaret performer refusing to ignite, ATV offered salvation. To maintain interest in *New Faces*, and parade its newly discovered talents, they created a vehicle called *The Summer Show* and asked Victoria to join the cast of seven. Rehearsals at Elstree Studios began in June. Vaguely modelled on the US revue *Tune In*, the concept was to race through sketches and songs, each episode organised around a theme. Victoria found herself working for men from an older generation. The producer Colin Clews was a dour-faced veteran of television vehicles for Tom Jones and Engelbert Humperdinck who came to work in a blue safari suit. The writers included the American-born comedy trooper Dick Vosburgh, who had scripted material for David Frost, Tommy Cooper and *The Two Ronnies*. None had come across anyone like Victoria before. During every week's rehearsals the same question was asked, says Trevor Chance, a crooner in his thirties who won the pilot episode of *New Faces*: 'What shall we do with Victoria? Stick her in the corner on the piano? Make her a waitress? They were always stuck as to how to use her. The writers and directors couldn't quite see where she was coming from.'

The first show, on the theme of holidays, was compèred by the suave all-round entertainer Leslie Crowther, with whom Victoria sang a duet. The scripts, dashed off at speed, stuck firmly to the middle of the road. 'It was all very bog-standard sketch material,' says Lenny Henry, then a gangly sixteen year old. 'You were very much within their structure and it was very strict. They didn't like us pissing about.' But piss about they did. The director tasked with keeping an excitable ensemble under control was Peter Harris, who would go on to direct *The Muppet Show*. The ringleader testing his patience was Marti Caine, the singing goofball from Sheffield who was lanky and manic with a voluminous shock of bright red hair. One day Harris, gentle by nature, got so frustrated he strategically hurled a chair across the rehearsal room. Victoria was deeply shocked, though she did a funny impression of him losing his cool and queenily snapping a pencil in two.

Her status as a reclusive outsider was cemented at the Spider's Web Motel in Watford, where the cast was put up for five weeks. 'She'd have a laugh, but she was very private,' says Lenny Henry. 'There were no high jinks. You never saw Vic in the bar.' The mimic Aiden J. Harvey, who gave her lifts to and from Elstree, found her assertive enough to ask him not to smoke in his own car. She could be forceful in rehearsals too. When Colin Clews wanted her to wear a pastel-lemon frock exploding with frills for one item, she threw a tantrum and burst into tears. In the opening episode, with everyone else togged up in boas and tuxedos, Victoria wore denim. She was less fussy about costumes if a sketch called for it. For her duet with Crowther she consented to a voluminous dress and flowers in her hair. In other episodes she'd be got up as Maid Marion or a nurse or in heels and tights.

Victoria would describe *The Summer Show* as 'one of those really bad variety shows where they got the scripts out of other people's dustbins. It was just dreadful.'[29] But at the time, she 'felt sort of an affirmation to be picked to be on a proper telly show. You got proper money, which for somebody who was on the dole at something like eleven quid a week was quite a hike.'[30] The pay was an astronomical £125 a week and, unlike the others, she had the weekly freedom to perform her own work. One song took a swipe at the health industry. With the piano setting a frantic pace, she advised viewers to 'Never spend a fortnight on a health farm / You'll end up with fourteen days of health'. A couplet promised a salty rhyme for 'mist' then, after a gossamer-thin pause, opted for 'drunk' – this would become a regular trick in her skill set. For the 'mystery and crime' episode she wrote 'If Only the Blood Matched My Dress'. Singing in a posh voice, she imagined reading a murder story set in a country house where the sudden death of each occupant is treated with frivolity. It concluded with the narrator's own demise:

> I say, someone is cutting my head orf
> I'm halfway through my vodka and lime
> Good heavens it's Mummy, how perfectly crummy
> Did you guess it was her all the time?

'She was under major pressure to produce all these songs,' says Lenny Henry. 'It wasn't just something that fell out of her. She was really working hard to find the right rhymes, the right structure, the right melodies. It wasn't a full flaring, but you had an inkling this is something special.' It was only once the series was ready for broadcast that Victoria started to suspect *The Summer Show* was a vehicle for Marti Caine: 'We all had our photographs taken for the cover of the *TV Times* and her photograph was the only one that was used. People started to catch on.'[31] Caine was the one member of the ensemble to take a pay cut – 'The money's rubbish, in't it?' she said to Victoria, who did not resent her higher status. There was even talk of her writing lyrics for Caine to sing in the *New Faces* grand final at the Palladium. Perhaps it was her competitive streak which pumped her full of bravado in interviews during rehearsals. 'I would like my own television show,' she declared, 'and it's only a matter of time before I get it.' She was aware this might sound conceited. 'No one sings like me,' she informed the *TV Times*. 'I'm unique. I think I'm wonderful, but I suppose I'll have to wait a while until everyone else thinks so, too . . .'[32]

Victoria later claimed never to have met anyone who had ever seen *The Summer Show*. She missed it too, as well as the ten songs she recorded for *Music Through Midnight* on Radio 2 ('for which I received the grand total of £22') because she was busy making her debut at the Edinburgh Fringe.[33] The invitation came from Roger McGough, who was mounting a revue called *Wordplay*, alongside GRIMMS collaborators, the zany John Gorman and songwriter Andy Roberts. The company prepared at the latter's home in north-west London, where Victoria cadged a bed. She threw herself into ensemble work. McGough saw her as 'someone confident in her own work who fitted in with what we were trying to do'. Away from rehearsals she struck Andy Roberts as 'a deeply unhappy individual. When the day's work was done, she was pretty shy and withdrawn, even awkward.' She never sat down to eat with her hosts, instead disappearing upstairs with a packet of biscuits.

The sketches McGough had written on the theme of verbal mis-communication were much more to Victoria's taste than the dross in *The Summer Show*. So were the white coats the cast all wore, as if in a language lab. In Edinburgh a newspaper rang to ask if there was a female cast member they could photograph. McGough put Victoria on the phone. 'Imagine a cross between a schoolgirl and a lorry,' she said. They didn't send a photographer. During the run Victoria met the jazz-singing *flâneur* George Melly, who informed her that her taller, thinner co-star Lindsay Ingram 'gave him an instant erection' while he 'told me to lose 2 stone'.[34] In Edinburgh she bonded over weight worries with Nina Myskow, with whom she had a long con-versation comparing notes on food addiction and anxieties about size. 'She is v. jolly and fat and talks all the time about it so you won't think it was your own idea,' she told Rosalind.

The atmosphere of *Wordplay* was 'v boozey and rock-band-ish,' she told Lesley Fitton. 'It all felt like being an early Beatle,' but it gave Victoria access to the wisdom of experienced performers.[35] Andy Roberts introduced her to the songs of Randy Newman and encour-aged her in the idea that she could be his English equivalent. He was impressed by 'We're Having a Party for the End of the World', the doomsday song she performed in the show, and urged her to steer away from whimsy. She took up his suggestion and worked on 'some songs that I think you might like better than my other ones – nicer music and no funny words'.[36]

Back in Birmingham she found herself 'suffering from a rash of Being Recognised'.[37] 'It's that pianist,' she overheard someone say in the laundrette. Nascent fame had its uses. Her university friend Claire Horrocks drove Victoria to Mansfield to see Aiden J. Harvey perform in a nightclub. 'It was all very glam low-cut frocks and frilly shirts, and Vic and I rolled up in denim. However, because Vic was known from television and we had come to see Aiden backstage we were excused and treated like minor royalty.' But there were grim rites of passage too. One was at Catterick army camp. 'As far as unrewarding creative experiences go,' she reported to Roger McGough, 'I nominate singing for 50 16-year-old recruits on Pernod for the first time who'd been deflected from the Disco by the Military Police.'[38]

Much greater recognition beckoned. Although it had yet to be broadcast, Victoria's edition of *The Camera and the Song* was circulated internally within the BBC, where it caught the eye of the makers of *That's Life!*, the consumer-affairs juggernaut fronted by Esther Rantzen, watched at its peak by eighteen million viewers. The show had a slot for a topical songwriter – its most recent occupant had been Jake Thackray. The director Pieter Morpurgo and editor John Morrell went up to see Victoria perform in Birmingham. After she was summoned to audition for Rantzen, Victoria was incensed to learn that Jack Dorsey had somehow turned the job down for her. 'When I found out I rang up and said it was all a dreadful mistake.'[39] She eventually heard in December that she'd been hired for four episodes.

Dorsey's unhelpful influence was evident when, the same month, *Wordplay* was booked for a three-week run at Hampstead Theatre Club and Victoria had to persuade him it was worth doing. 'I sorted out my manager,' she assured Roger McGough.[40] As a result, for the first time Victoria found herself performing before serious London critics such as Irving Wardle of *The Times* and B.A. Young of the *Financial Times*, who found her 'particularly adept at socially-pointed songs at the piano'.[41] 'I got very good reviews for that,' she later said, 'and only had little bits to do, which was much better than trying to do a whole half hour on my own.'[42] (The *Evening Standard* identified her as 'Victoria Woods', a misnomer she would gleefully exhume for the closing credits of *Acorn Antiques*.) She was offered £30 a week, although it proved difficult to extract her royalty, especially as her association with London Management had now fizzled out. 'I guess I'll get it in the end,' she sighed.[43] Meanwhile Hampstead Theatre Club commissioned her to write a show for her and John Gorman to take to Edinburgh in the summer. She was soon fretting as she made her first solo stab at sketch comedy. 'I keep thinking I must have a serious bit here, and then a song etc which is stupid,' she told Roger McGough. 'Isn't writing HARD? I can't tell whether things are funny or not.'[44]

At the very start of 1976, Victoria was phoned by Esther Rantzen, who asked her to write a song about the end of sexual discrimination, suggested by an advertisement in the *Sunday Times*. A few days later, one Sunday lunchtime, Victoria reported to the BBC Television Theatre on Shepherd's Bush Green to make her first appearance on *That's Life!* She was rewarded with gales of laughter from the audience as she imagined a man explaining that women were now free to fondle their thighs on the bus: 'We'll know we are winning if you pass a shop window / Denis gives massage and lessons in French'. She was worried the song was too saucy: 'I thought after that my number'd be up, but they gave me a fortnight spot.'[45]

Victoria's topical songs made an impact. 'And that's the rather clever Victoria Wood who's singing her own stuff,'[46] purred the *Sunday Times* listing before her third appearance. Good news followed the episode. 'Esther (Dentures) Rantzen has asked me to stay on for the rest of the series,' she informed Roger McGough. 'It's nice to have a regular job.'[47] The song that clinched her contract extension was 'More Sex Please, We're British', inspired by a report that the UK was turning to the bedroom to combat the financial slump. Granted a national platform to mine the bedroom for comedy, Victoria looked impishly into the camera and sang, 'You have to admire us, the great British nation /

All popping upstairs just to combat inflation'. As these fortnightly appearances accrued, she had to fend off the suspicions of the people at Social Security, who couldn't work out what someone on national television was doing claiming the dole. She was paid £35 per episode. 'Television is nice,' she said the following year, 'but it doesn't give you very much money. It meant I was quite well known, but I was sitting on my bottom for most of the time.'[48] She did attempt to capitalise on her visibility. 'Direct from That's Life' blared an ad for a gig in a Liverpool folk club after her third appearance.

Her main point of contact on the show was Pieter Morpurgo, who noticed that 'on camera she had this great spark which somehow wasn't there when you just spoke to her about sorting out what we were going to do'. But it was Esther Rantzen who called to discuss topical issues that might provoke a song. According to Victoria, she 'used to ring up on a Friday night and say, "Go and get Wednesday's *Guardian* and look at page thirty-two and write something about that." And I used to go round and borrow it from a friend because I don't buy the papers.'[49] Thanks to Victoria's shyness, Esther Rantzen says she 'always felt a bit concerned that I was talking too much. The best songs came out of her own experience and what she wanted to talk about so it was a two-way conversation.' One was inspired by Victoria's (possibly made up) experience of turning the clock back instead of forwards. She knocked off a song about the centenary of the first General Post Office telephone call ('no heavy breather ever used a pigeon', she sang, 'as far as I know'). Among these impersonal commissions Victoria was able to smuggle in crafty references. She evoked memories of the school playing field in 'the blushes on the shiny face / Of the girl who lumps in last on a skipping race'. One song she called 'Thank Heavens I'm Taurus'. In general, the slot gave her an instant high more than long-term satisfaction: 'It's very easy to think you've written something brilliant in the heat of the moment. You rush in with great bags under your eyes and red rims and say, "Look, look, hot off the sticky old typewriter." And then eight weeks later you find it's no use to you at all.'[50]

As usual much of Victoria's discomfort was to do with her appearance: 'I was still suffering from "fat equals frock" brainwashing. I went to Laura Ashley and poked about among all the size 16s with the fervent interest of someone unblocking a toilet and ended up with a huge blue thing that made me look like the unhappy victim of a fertility drug overdose.'[51] Needing more than one dress, in a panic she asked Rosalind to knock up something at speed. 'It suddenly struck me that even tho' I've lost weight I won't be able to get a decent size 16 cos nobody makes any.'[52] Fans wrote in to praise her. 'PS you're not bad looking,' said one. Another correspondent complimented her on her dresses before adding, 'Victoria my only real problem is I wet my bed – every night my sheets are soaking and my pyjamas.'[53] As it had a Liverpool postmark, she worried it might be a prank. 'I'll kill you if it was you,' she told Roger McGough.[54]

One dress was loaned by Celia Imrie, a new friend who lived in Hammersmith not far from the theatre. 'It was rather a beautiful rust-coloured dress with a V neck,' says Celia. 'Actually not a good idea for people with big bosoms, as it had a sash that went underneath and emphasised it even more. It was quite a prized possession of mine and I was rather thrilled that she wanted to wear it.' Celia had become fast friends with Fidelis Morgan on a world tour of *Hedda Gabler* starring Glenda Jackson and met Victoria when Fidelis brought her to Derby Playhouse, where she was hoofing in a pantomime: 'I knew that Victoria was coming and I got so nervous – she'd been on telly and she was a winner – that I fell over. She thought that was hilarious.' Over the following year Celia was subsumed into the Birmingham gang in which Fidelis was the leader and Victoria the intimidating court jester: 'I had this rather childlike thing of feeling a bit stupid in their company. It occurred to me that they were very critical of everything. It made me a bit jumpy because I didn't know what they were on about. I found it rather alarming. And Victoria was very witty.'

The fortnightly routine of *That's Life!* brought Victoria down to London on Saturdays. Because she composed at night – 'I used to sit there writing, as white as a sheet' – she would get little sleep before the trip south.[55] She stayed with her former flatmate Jane Wynn Owen, who had a place in Highgate with two grand pianos, on one of which Victoria would finetune the latest song. She strove to get them right partly because she was backed by a seasoned trio of leading session musicians. 'We were more than capable of picking up a simple sequence,' says Dave Richmond, who had played bass on '5-4-3-2-1', 'Je t'aime' and 'Your Song'. 'And some of them were quite simple songs harmonically. There were no surprises within the music because everything was coming from the lyrics.' Victoria saw the band as her allies. 'We spend all day (me and the lads – the musicians) talking about tits and smoking,' she reported, 'and occasionally playing a bit of music. It's great.'[56] Their intimacy bore fruit musically. In one song she slipped in a cheeky bit of Haydn; another had a lively ragtime solo. Pastiching George Formby, she tapped into the guitarist Judd Proctor's status as a prince of the ukulele with 'You Don't Need a Degree to Play the Ukulele'. In a lumberjack shirt and jeans, accentuating her Lancashire vowels and pulling doubtful faces, Victoria gave the fullest expression to her personality yet seen on television. With the band hollering refrains, she ended on another of her saucy non-rhymes:

> Forget the fancy piano bits!
> Just a banjo jammed against my . . .
> If George Formby can do it, why not me?

Before her run in *That's Life!* ended, viewers saw a more reflective side to Victoria when her episode of *The Camera and the Song* was finally broadcast in May 1976. It had been so delayed that she 'got to the point where I kept writing to the BBC to ask them when, if ever, they were going to put the programme on'.[57] Previewing it in the *Radio Times*, Sheridan Morley pronounced Victoria 'our first genuinely funny female singer since Joyce Grenfell', although humour was not the dominant mood in a barely veiled self-portrait which she titled *As She Sees It*.[58] Into the cycle of half a dozen songs Victoria loaded everything she'd ever wanted to say about the constrictions she had endured as a teenager: a young girl's eagerness to escape her parents, drab days and nights alone in her bedroom, the dread pall of body-consciousness. The strongest composition was 'Sad Salad Sunday', written in her second year at Birmingham. The cinematographer John Baker illustrated her songs by filming a party, a pub, a keep-fit class, a teenager's bedroom, but the coup was getting permission to capture Radio 1's Tony Blackburn at work, trading banal chat with expectant brides and elderly housewives. The film closed with an image of Victoria puffing moodily on a cigarette. 'The plump, aggressively untrendy girl-composer is undoubtedly a major talent in a minor area,' wrote a *Sunday Times* previewer, 'disguising her sharp lyrics with sweet melodies. Would Tony Blackburn have larked about so co-operatively if he had realised she was cutting him into little strips?'[59]

For her final turn on *That's Life!* a fortnight later, Victoria (back in denim) and the boys teamed up with Five Penny Piece, a folk band with whom she'd alternated on the show, to sing 'That's Life Is Over Now, My Friend'. In the middle section she mourned the prospect of returning to social security, where she'd be listed as 'singer, slightly used' with 'three musicians and a piano to feed'. Perhaps her degree would help her to find work. 'I've got one, it's just a bit small,' she confessed.

> Think of me when you turn off your TV
> It's me you fade down to a dot.
> My job ends at the end of this programme
> I bet you're all thinking, so what?

She would come to regard her run on the show as a missed chance: 'I was very unenterprising. I could have used that as a launching pad but sadly didn't have the nous to really capitalise on it.'[60] After eight appearances in front of many millions of viewers – she cut out the ratings figures, ringing every mention of *That's Life!* – Victoria was close to fulfilling that vision she'd had as a tot in the garden at Tottington Road. She was nearly famous. Yet she felt no further on or better off. The series wrapped with a party at a hotel. 'Victoria had lots of friends there,' says the show's bassist Dave Richmond, who went along too. 'At one point she came over and said, "Dave, can you lend me two quid?" I never got it back. Whenever I saw her on the television, I felt it quite an honour that she still owed me two quid.'

# 7

# SOPRENDO

'I don't know if I would have done what I did without Geoff.'

*Desert Island Discs*, 2007

In the week her run in *That's Life!* ended, Victoria turned twenty-three. The long heatwave of 1976 lay ahead. One sunny afternoon Fidelis Morgan threw a party in the back garden of Harrods. The theme, inspired by a rationing cookbook found in a second-hand bookshop, was wartime austerity. Taking the role of a land girl, the hostess cast her guests. Robert Howie came as a shirtless injured soldier, tended by Celia Imrie's nurse. Victoria wore overalls and a top-knotted head-scarf in the guise of a factory worker, with a ration card wedged in her top pocket.

She barely needed to imagine austerity. Her summer schedule included almost no bookings aside from a benefit gig for Birmingham Youth Theatre with an eccentric avant-garde local comedian billed as Mr John Dowie. But there was no cheque for that, even if a plan was formed to get a few dates together in the near future. With not much else on, one weekend in June Victoria visited her university friends Steve Trow and Jude Kelly. The latter was rehearsing for a show for the Phoenix Theatre Company in Leicester. *Gunslinger* was a goof-ball western romp with songs, commissioned by the artistic director Michael Bogdanov to mark the bicentenary of American independ-ence. It starred a then unknown Alan Rickman as a character based on

Sitting Bull. Victoria's fame as Esther Rantzen's songbird went before her and the rehearsal room was abuzz. The only person who drew a blank was an actor cast as the whip-cracking Buffalo Bill. 'Everyone recognised her and I didn't know why because I never watched telly,' says Geoffrey Durham. 'Her fame was lost on me. I said, "I'm ever so sorry, I don't know who you are." She said, "That's all right." She told me who she was and we started talking. And we got on very well.'

Victoria and her future husband might never have met again, but at short notice a week of performances in Southampton was announced for which the musical director was not available. At the suggestion of her friends in the company, Victoria was offered the job. It represented quite a comedown, but she was grateful for the income: 'I said, "Well, yeah," because it was twenty quid a week or something.'[1] Once the show was in performance, she returned to Leicester to start learning a sophisticated accompaniment that tested her mettle as a pianist. One weekend she and Geoffrey spent a day and then a night together and didn't tell a soul. The company moved to the Nuffield Theatre in Southampton where, dressed in a cowboy hat and checked shirt, Victoria performed as Wild Wilhelmina Fifty Fingers. 'All theatrical fun and games here – wigs falling off, corpsing etc,' she told Robert Howie.[2] Before the show the cast wandered through the audience saying 'howdee'. Victoria was far too embarrassed to join them.

Since the final break with Bob Mason, Victoria's patchy romantic history had mainly consisted of liaisons with older men – one of them affectionately nicknamed Nobby – as she tended to reject advances from those her own age. 'I met someone who fancied me last week,' she told Roger McGough. She thought him 'quite reasonable considering what emotional cripples are usually after me' and invited him back to Priory Road only to be subjected to hours of boasting about his countless conquests. He had 'more knots in his string than Hywel Bennett. Big deal. He then asked me if I wished to sample his irresistible technique but the thought of all those knots was making me cringe so I refrained.'[3]

When news of her relationship with Geoffrey seeped out, the person best acquainted with them both was puzzled. 'I was quite surprised they got together knowing both of them so well,' says Steve Trow. 'She always was a very private person. Geoff was very extrovert and very much took centre stage socially. Vic would never do that. I couldn't quite work out how this chemistry worked.'

Geoffrey Durham was four years older than Victoria and pleasingly steeped in theatre. He had been a flyman wielding curtains and scenery at the City Varieties Theatre in Leeds, worked in youth theatre at Glasgow Citizens, run a roadshow company in Liverpool and along the way he became an actor and director. He developed a street act in which he ate fire and swallowed razor blades, and read minds in art galleries at lunchtimes. In the autumn of 1975 he fetched up in Leicester where, for a forthcoming roadshow, he swiftly worked up an act lampooning conjurors. He called himself the Great Sorprendo, from the Spanish for 'to astonish', then for ease of pronunciation changed it to Soprendo.

Marking the end of a bleak romantic phase in her life, Victoria wrote a valedictory dirge called 'No More Old Men' – 'No more old men, no more affairs / On my brown pillow case no more grey hairs' – and included it in a dozen songs she recorded at Zella Records in Birmingham. It was among the songs she played to her new boyfriend to introduce him to her work. As far as Victoria was concerned it was 'a fantastic stroke of luck' meeting Geoffrey. 'I couldn't have met a better person for me.'[4] His role in her career would evolve but initially it was to boost her morale. For the previous two years this job had fallen to Fidelis Morgan. There was a kind of handover in early August when she invited Victoria to join a group jaunt to the Isle of Wight. The rendezvous point on the Saturday night was the Old Vic. 'You've got to meet Geoff,' Victoria said, and brought him to the stage door before joining the small convoy heading south to catch the 2 a.m. ferry. 'As I was driving,' says Fidelis, 'I thought she wants my approval and she's passing the baton. He's now the person who gets her out of bed.'

Getting Victoria out of bed in the early phase of their relationship was not always easy. 'She just completely went into a depression,' says Geoffrey. 'I don't think I recognised it as depression; I think I recognised it as laziness. That's how she talked about it too. She used to lie in the dark most of the day. I wondered what I'd got into.' The

depression was triggered by the fear that she may never wrestle free
of her chrysalis: 'I was really anxious. I remember meeting him and
saying, "I'm twenty-three and this is all over." I had had about four
lucky breaks and nothing had happened out of any of them.'[5]

Most of those breaks had been in television. Happily, as if on cue,
another now presented itself, but in theatre: a commission to write a
play. Jude Kelly had only just taken over the Solent People's Theatre, a
community company touring around Southampton and Portsmouth,
and Victoria was an obvious port of call. Kelly requested a cheerful
Christmas entertainment with songs, and Victoria set to work. She
called it *Sunny Intervals* and drew on a scenario familiar from *Cinderella* which also echoed her own experience. The Wilkins family
consist of Dad, a former ping-pong champ, and his three daughters.
Two are trendy glamour pusses who boast of leaving school 'with CSE
knitting and O Level Sex'. The youngest, Gail, is 'dopy, plain, insig-
nificant'. Victoria gave her all her own anxieties.

My dad says that I'm just a shy girl
I don't know what life's all about
He says 'Gail come out of your shell more'
But it seems safer in than out.

For the first time Victoria approached the theme of parental neglect.
Gail is so invisible her parents left her at the hospital after she was
born and 'didn't think twice till she came knocking on the door five
years later'. Her sisters think she looks like the back of a bus and sit
on her as if she's a sofa. Wondering what job she can possibly do, she
sings, 'I suppose being funny is all I've got'. And she knows that one
day she will meet 'someone who's going to need me'. Sure enough, a
swashbuckling former film star, who lives in a magic castle on the hill,
needs a young female co-star for his comeback and announces a talent
contest in the village hall. Everything ends to everyone's satisfaction
and the company all sing the final chorus: 'Just remember to remember / Even in December / You can have a funny sunny day'.

There wasn't much else on, and little job satisfaction to be had when
in early August Victoria made a brief return to national television to

write and perform a song on BBC One's early evening current affairs show *Nationwide* – she dismissed it as 'just a list set to rhyme'.⁶ Then a job cropped up at the Edinburgh Festival Fringe. John Gorman had booked GRIMMS in for a fortnight at the festival and invited the singing Brummie comic Jasper Carrott to join the gang. But across the week of rehearsal GRIMMS somehow evaporated. Victoria, who a few months earlier had been writing a show for her and Gorman to perform, answered his summons to come and pad out the booking. A day before the trio were due to debut the act they'd hurriedly lashed together, Gorman disappeared, leaving the two non-members of GRIMMS to perform under that banner twice daily for a fortnight.

'We just thought, we're up here, we'll just do the show between us and see what happens,' says Jasper Carrott. 'We cancelled the afternoon shows and we made a good fist of it.' Each did their own thing, Victoria singing songs, Carrott flitting between observational humour and comedy folk songs that were modish thanks to the rise of Mike Harding and Billy Connolly. 'J. Gorman has gone home to sort out his personal problems,' Victoria reported, 'and J. Carrott and I are gamely holding the fort – alternately he pooters, making announcements, offering money back, even smiling at the bloody audience.'⁷ She was also invited to join the bill of a late-night café show with Quentin Crisp, newly famous after the recent television version of his memoir *The Naked Civil Servant*. 'Should be good for a laugh,' she said.⁸ Victoria wasn't always so buoyant at the festival. Depressed in a pub after one show, she broke down in front of Carrott: 'I gave her a good talking to. I told her to have confidence in herself, along the lines of "you're much better than you think you are and you might be a bit too concerned about your weight. You don't have to worry. People will take you as you are."'

The worry that she was stalling professionally was connected to the situation with Jack Dorsey. When Victoria returned from Edinburgh, she still hadn't received her fee of £40 for the *Nationwide* song. The song was called 'Since Last We Met'. She hadn't met Dorsey in a while and wrote to the BBC to check that the money 'has not been sent to Jack Dorsey, or London Management, neither of whom now represent me'.⁹ The BBC copyright department advised that she should apply to Dorsey, to whom the fee had indeed been sent. Jasper Carrott's manager helpfully perused her contract with Dorsey, which still had a year to run. 'He said, "I don't think this contract is worth anything,"' Victoria recalled. '"I don't think you have to abide by its terms. I don't think it's a legal contract." So after about two years he sort of faded away.'[10]

Carrott was sufficiently impressed in Edinburgh to invite Victoria to support him on his coming tour. His manager was not so generous when Victoria negotiated her modest fee directly – 'a very measly sum,' she grumbled.[11] She mentioned too late that she'd need a piano, only to be advised that she would have to supply her own. She bought a second-hand Roland electric, which as a devotee of grand pianos she hated. It was 'like a little typewriter. I sat there sort of typing away in front of all these people.'[12] The cost, upwards of £350, ensured she made a loss across the autumn tour, though she sold the piano soon afterwards.

Before the tour began Victoria had a morale-boosting invitation. It came from Glenda Jackson via Fidelis Morgan, who had promoted her talented friend: 'I was handing out the tape and saying she's wonderful. Glenda said, "You know this friend that you go on and on about? Would she like to come and sing a song? We've got a two-minute slot."' Thus Victoria made her West End debut on a Sunday night in September 1976. The gala supported women's right to choose, which brought a bevy of anti-abortionists to the pavement outside the Cambridge Theatre.

Then she set off with Carrott. 'I did OK,' Victoria reported after the first date in Worcester. She performed in leather boots and a dark sparkly blue jumper with rainbows hand-knitted in that she'd spotted in Leicester. It was so expensive Geoffrey paid for half of it: 'The tour promoter informed me I looked like I'd just got out of the bloody car.'[13] Her introduction as 'a girl from Ramsbottom' came at her behest because it sounded funnier than Bury. She soon began to feel sidelined. 'Jasper's manager, sound crew etc think he's the funniest thing since Graham Woodruff [one of her Birmingham tutors],' she wrote, 'and they ignore me accordingly as befits my status as a humble support.'[14] She grew increasingly despondent as the tour continued. Carrott was the main draw, especially in the Midlands, although further north 'we were both on level footing,' he says. 'We had a good rapport. She was happy to get the work. I don't know what she thought of me.' 'He is the most puerile of the New Wave of raconteur / folk singers / comedians,' Victoria informed Rosalind, who was out of the loop having moved to the Bahamas.[15] Often in the safe space of her letters, she allowed her competitive streak and frustration with her lot to be directed externally. Her unhappiness was vented less at Carrott, who gave her lifts to and from some gigs in his Daimler, than his audience, whom she described as 'beer-swilling football fans, so any attempt to take the piss out of men was met with either blank stares or drunk heckling'.[16] The repertoire of heckles at a late-night booking in Leeds included 'Fuck off you cunt, we've come to see the Carrott etc etc.'[17] Twenty minutes of subtle songs, some about overweight girls in failed relationships, coyly performed without any audience rapport, were not calculated to win them over. At a working men's club in Leamington Spa she had support from her personal claque in the shape of Fidelis Morgan and Celia Imrie, who remembers 'thinking this is clearly not what they want. They were talking behind us. I realised this wasn't their humour, possibly because she was a woman. It wasn't comfortable.' Victoria moaned in the car on the way back to Birmingham.

Her parents drove the few miles from Bury to sit near the front of an audience of 800 in Middleton Civic Theatre. 'She was very good,' her mother told Rosalind.[18] Her father agreed: 'Vicky was super. Wonderful music and chords underneath and the usual wily lyrics.'[19] Victoria couldn't fall in with their supportive assessment. 'I died on my arse,' she told Robert Howie.[20] Stanley Wood felt Carrott's manager was exploiting her by making her pay her own travel expenses to promote the show on BBC Radio Leeds. The booking was a disaster – the train came in late and she arrived five minutes before the end of the programme: 'The DJ insisted on playing a very long and tedious Swingle Singers record before welcoming me to the studio and bidding me farewell all in the same breath.'[21] This humiliation would later be put to good use.

The last and most prestigious date on the tour was at the Shakespeare

Memorial Theatre in Stratford-upon-Avon, where Victoria had often sat in the audience as a student. The night was a career-changing triumph for Carrott: Michael Grade signed him to do a pilot for LWT that became *An Audience with Jasper Carrott*. She was just as eager to impress such an influential figure, but Grade told Carrott that 'she didn't register at all'. This happened to be the only night on the tour that Geoffrey was able to catch: 'She was glad to be working, but she knew it wasn't what she wanted to do, and she wasn't making any money. The worst thing was that she didn't have an act. Jasper was storming the place every night, and she just felt like an amateur, sitting at the piano singing song after song after song.' She didn't receive her fee until three months after the end of the tour. 'It was supposed to be my big break, but it was terrible,' she reflected four years later. 'I died on my arse wherever we went and people just sat tapping their watches and thinking "Uuuuhh . . . when's Jasper coming on?"'[22]

Victoria's confidence took a further blow while she was on tour. Jude Kelly's Solent People's Theatre had already embarked on their first tour of pubs and clubs, and in the *Stage* announced a Christmas musical 'which is being written by Victoria Wood for the company'.[23] The autumn season leaflet went into some detail about the plot: 'This riotous adaption of that age-old fable "Beauty and the Beast" combines ludicrous situations with lively entertainment.' The script which Victoria submitted, typed out by Geoffrey with a cassette of song demos enclosed, didn't quite adhere to this blurb. She heard nothing back for a nerve-racking fortnight until the deafening silence was broken. 'Jude turned my script down on the grounds that it was badly written, unfunny, too short, unsubtle etc etc,' she told Robert Howie. 'She asked me to go down and write them another scenario for the actors to improvise on, and I could write down what they improvised. She said it would be stimulating for me. I declined. I wasn't really in the mood for stimulation.'[24] Her first attempt to broaden her professional portfolio had ended in rejection.

'It could not have come at a worse time,' says Geoffrey. 'She was going through this desperate uncertainty and not sure if anything she did was any good or not.' One person who could still be relied upon was John Clarke. In October he commissioned Victoria to write music for a studio discussion in which six guests criticised one element of Midland life. He titled it *Knockers*. On top of £35, Victoria got two more quid when it was repeated in January. It was her last commission from him, and their connection fizzled out. 'She kept reappearing on Pebble Mill,' says Clarke, 'and every time she called my office and I was out. So I wasn't able to renew our acquaintance.'

Victoria's precarious position communicated itself to her father when she stayed at Birtle Edge House while recording a pilot for Radio 2 in Manchester with Beetles and Buckman in mid November. He drove her to the recording and sat in the audience wishing it was for television: 'All very good. Let's hope it comes off. (But only radio.)'[25] The next month her parents motored down to Leicester to be introduced to Geoffrey, who was appearing in *The Tempest*. 'Vicky was cussing surphuriously [sic] under her breath all the time in the theatre,' wrote Stanley, 'because the M.D. was hopeless, the lighting appalling, the direction putrid, and Geoffrey did not get a square deal at all.'[26] Of her new boyfriend they greatly approved. Stanley described him to Rosalind as 'a big rather moon-faced lad with specs and a gentle amiable manner'.[27] 'He is the cuddly type. (Didn't say so, of course),' added Helen.[28] Geoffrey for his part was shocked by Helen's volcanic bossiness in the passenger seat: 'Whatever he said, she would say, "OH WOOD. YOU SILLY MAN! OH WOOD, YOU DO ANNOY ME! WHAT ARE YOU TALKING ABOUT, WOOD, YOU FOOL!" I've never heard anyone speak so loudly in a car.' When they visited Birtle Edge House, he was able to observe for himself the tendency of everyone to keep to separate rooms; this status quo extended to him and Victoria, who were expected to sleep apart. He pronounced the kitchen the filthiest he had ever seen.

Geoffrey was appearing in his third Shakespeare that autumn and was close to the end of his tether. 'Poor old Geoffrey is practically at screaming point at the Phoenix,' Victoria wrote. In rehearsal the company would lie on their backs and share the previous night's dreams: 'Geoff always denies having dreamt anything, which always launches a full discussion about how interesting and they wonder why that is.'[29] His actual dream was to become a full-time magician. After commuting throughout the autumn between Leicester and Birmingham, practising tricks on trains and in waiting rooms, he handed in his notice and moved permanently to Priory Road in early 1977.

Everything was changing in Birmingham, where the last of Victoria's friendship group had graduated the previous summer. The romantic agonies of the ones who stayed on provided comic fodder in her gleeful letters but were also an exhausting source of tension. Victoria even fantasised about 'attempting to break off diplomatic relations' with a particularly trying friend.[30] 'When/if I get an agent and jobs,' she added, 'I'll be able to nip around a bit more and see my real friends.' She'd heard that an agent was interested in her, but nothing came of it. That January she sold two jumpers to a friend 'to boost my finances'. In February she found herself down to her last 10p 'so I can either go somewhere on the bus and walk back or have a bath'.[31] That winter she and Geoffrey shivered under a duvet lent to them by Rosalind. The only warm place in the flat was the bathroom, to which Geoffrey retired to read in the bath whenever Victoria was writing. As she found she worked best in the owlish hours of the night, theirs was an unconventional bedsit romance.

Victoria still had enough self-belief to acquire her first personalised stationery, an off-the-shelf set of cards with a V printed in two solid black blocks. Later she would frame her ambitions for this period as modest: 'to get off the dole . . . to have enough income to get a mortgage and to get a car'.[32] But the distance from her true goal, to achieve stardom through performing her compositions, was the cause of much anguish. The reality was that the stage persona she communicated through her songs, some funny but others downbeat, was simply not outgoing enough to make it happen. One night she was booked as the second half of a concert at the Centre for the Arts in Birmingham, the first half consisting of orchestral Vivaldi and Mozart. 'Victoria Wood entertains,' said the flyer. '(DIDN'T)' she added in her scrapbook.

At least she and Geoffrey were in the same boat. She pictured the pair of them as the Start-Rite kids, after the advertisement for children's shoes featuring an animation of a boy and a girl walking optimistically along a path towards the horizon. 'We are both writing off to agents etc, hoping to blossom into professionalism and prosperity soon,' she told Robert Howie, who was appearing in panto in Swansea.[33] In February, when they took their first holiday together to visit him, he recommended Victoria to the manager of the Swansea Grand: 'He'd seen her on *New Faces*. I said, "Why on earth wouldn't you book her?" He said, "Oh no, people don't think that sort of thing is funny."'

So when they came in the spring, the piecemeal dates organised by John Dowie through his contacts were 'like the sun coming out,' says Geoffrey. 'John was like a ray of sunshine for her. He was completely new.' Like Jasper Carrott, Dowie had a halo of ringlets and a thick Brummie accent, but his act swivelled away from the mainstream towards what would later be identified as alternative comedy. Waif-thin, barefooted and decked out in zany costumes, he chased laughs down dark alleys. Singing in a neurotic punkish drone, he twitted English xenophobia in 'British Tourist (I Hate the Dutch)'; 'I Don't Want to Be Your Amputee' was his taste-free rant about romance gone wrong ('the day you cut my left leg off you caught me on the hop'). Victoria's songs followed her own preoccupations. Her opening contribution was 'Nobody Loves You When You're Down and Fat', written in 1974 to challenge the myth of the cheerfully overweight person. It was pronounced the 'high spot of the evening'[34] at their sparsely attended first performance at the Birmingham Rep Studio by a critic from the *Birmingham Post*, who didn't see the irony of describing Victoria as 'plump and jolly'.[35] Another critic applauded her 'better-than-Jake-Thackeray [sic] songs'.[36] That night Victoria rang home 'sounding very pleased,' said Helen, 'and hurrying off to be interviewed on the radio'.[37]

'I'm definitely not a song machine,' she told a journalist before they performed in Sunderland, admitting her dissatisfaction with the process of writing topical songs to order.[38] Working with Dowie released her from that treadmill. 'The show I'm doing now is more my thing,' she told Rosalind. 'It's with a guy called John Dowie who does songs about amputees and cripples and halibut.'[39] There was some truth in one of their cheerful promo images, which had them perched on a stepladder with Victoria seemingly propped on her co-star's shoulders. In another she climbed up a stepladder and planted a foot on his head.

John Dowie had checked up on Victoria in performance before they started to write together and, noticing that she rushed from one song to the next, gave her notes about developing some patter. 'But she had very little chance to develop that,' he says. 'It was ad-libbed.' They assembled the show over a couple of months in Birmingham. There was a session or two at Priory Road, where Victoria's co-writer sampled her catering: 'She made a disgusting meal once. I don't think in those days her cooking skills were very pronounced.' He brought his own repertoire of sketches. One was a script from *The Archers* with, to save time, all the vowels removed. They wrote material together, including the set-up in which Victoria played a Women's Institute secretary in a tweed suit and slingbacks. 'The original idea was that we'd do a whole show based around some kind of a theme,' says Dowie. 'We had the beginning of it and thought, oh, that's all we need.' In another sketch he played a husband leafing through a sex manual. 'I was saying, "Let's try this to liven up the marriage. Let's start with foreplay. There's only two of us. Oh well, never mind." I think she probably wrote the punchline, which was "Oh sod this, I'm going off for a fuck." Our humour was a little broad.'

Mostly they performed alone – another song in Victoria's set was her murder-mystery parody 'If Only the Blood Matched My Dress'. They soon found that, their acts being so far apart in style, only one of them stood a chance of being to the taste of any given audience. If he got laughs, she wouldn't, and vice versa. Thus every night one of them died. When performing in Cardiff they imagined the final tantrum of a dying comic. 'We decided that the ultimate route for that kind of comedian was to go "fuck shit tit wank bollocks!" and then stalk off,' says Dowie. 'So every time we crossed over, the one who did badly would always go to the other one, "fuck shit tit wank bollocks".' Not that audiences were ever substantial. It prompted Dowie to wonder out loud whether a veteran of *New Faces* and *That's Life!* might have drawn more of a crowd. 'She was a bit miffed.'

That spring another avenue opened up when the publicist at the Phoenix Theatre suggested Geoffrey and Victoria do consecutive late nights in Leicester. To prepare she sat in Leicester Library and wrote her first ever comic monologue. Expanding on the incomplete idea hatched with Dowie, she chose the voice of a patronising Women's Institute president who outlines forthcoming events such as a talk titled 'Life has a lot to offer even if you've got no bowels'. Using the character's voice Victoria took on a subject she had often addressed in her songs – the joylessness of sex in the marital bed. Reporting the results of a questionnaire on 'the bedroom aspect', she announced that '63 per cent said the best excuse was a headache – in fact most of them had had continuous migraines since the Coronation'. In search of something else to pad out the songs, she learned a couple of tricks which Geoffrey had bought and no longer had use for. She flagged one of them with a joke: 'And now I'm going to get a man up.' The trick involved putting a card unseen in an envelope, pretending to identify it wrongly and then getting it right. 'She hated doing it,' says Geoffrey, 'because she hated talking to the member of the audience.' The other was a decapitation trick involving a head-chopper device and a Black & Decker saw. The two nights were attended, she reported, by 'the proverbial 2 lesbians and an Afghan' on the first night and then 'screaming hecklers who'd come mainly for the late bar'.[40]

The low point of the tour with John Dowie was at a pub in the West Midlands, where in the back row there was someone with a portable iron lung which emitted distracting clunks and whirs. There was an uneasy silence when Dowie asked for the noise source to be switched off. The culmination of the tour was a week at the ICA in the Mall. Previewing the show, the *Sunday Times* described Victoria as 'a rose with several thorns'.[41] On their first night a band of teenage punks asked if they could perform in the interval, having been booted out of the coffee bar for making too much noise. Dowie agreed. Victoria appeared in her WI tweed two-piece with the skirt undone due to a broken zip. 'Does anybody have a safety pin?' she asked. Sundry punks extracted pins from lips and lobes and brows. Thus Victoria was present at the performance debut of Adam and the Ants. 'We had a good review in *Time Out*,' she told Robert Howie.[42] It proclaimed Victoria 'the evening's revelation with her musical soliloquies on fat girls, convent schools, ante-college families, double talk, who-dunnits, and who didn'ts'.[43]

Victoria would come to regard her dates with John Dowie as her first break into comedy, when she could feel herself edge in the right direction: 'We never played to more than about seventeen people, and that was good experience because there was no pressure. The pressure was on him and I was just the support.'[44] It coincided with a gravitational pull away from Birmingham, her home for the previous six years. The same month as the ICA dates, Geoffrey was asked up to the Duke's Playhouse in Lancaster to act. When he told them he was a magician he was offered, sight unseen, a slot in their Victorian music-hall show at the theatre at the end of Morecambe pier. He barely had fifteen minutes of material, but it was enough to put him top of the bill: 'I learnt how to be a magician in that show. It gave me a lifeline. Vic didn't have that lifeline – she was sitting in a bedsit being the girlfriend. It was a really, really tough time.' The gales and the rain also got to her. Geoffrey had to do a matinee a week outdoors from a bandstand on the promenade with the audience watching from deckchairs. The wind blew his cards away. 'It was just next to the Aquarium,' Victoria would recall. 'I'd hear all this applause and it turned out they were clapping the bloody dolphins.'[45]

More work came in, but none she found fulfilling. There was 'an awful pilot for Thames which will never get on but I'm glad of the money'.[46] Another client asking for topical songs was *Start the Week*, the Radio 4 flagship presented by the patrician BBC TV newsreader Richard Baker. She was booked by the producer Ian Gardhouse, who had seen her showcase with Beetles and Buckman at the Mermaid Theatre. 'I have to be at the studio at 7.30 am,' she told Rosalind. 'Thank God it's not television and no one will care about red piggy eyes and crumply hair.'[47] The programme was often built around a topical theme. Victoria wrote a spiky attack on magazines which tell readers how to live their lives, based on advice its writers don't follow themselves:

On wobbly tables in seedy flats
With fibreglass curtains that smell of cats

Tiny minds type for a tiny fee
Those jolly articles full of fun
Crammed with sense and the occasional pun
Are actually written by ratty old bags like me.

She called it 'Just Believe What You Like' and was paid £30.

Then came a call from Granada in Manchester. 'I've just been writing songs for a programme called "Pandora's Box" (puke),' she told Roger McGough.[48] The series, broadcast in late summer, featured Joan Bakewell as host discussing topical feminist issues with guests Victoria characterised as 'people from "Spare Rib" magazine with dirty jeans'.[49] She privately expressed unsisterly contempt for the format: 'they all sit around for 6 interminable programmes whining about their ovaries'.[50] The show began with Victoria at an upright piano playing a short feisty theme tune, then she sat through the talk 'trying to keep awake long enough to sing my song (which of course comes at the end by which time the only people left listening are not the people I care to sing to)'.[51]

*Pandora's Box* was as close as she would ever stray to an overtly feminist project. At least in public, she made the right noises about equality, but she was wary of being a mouthpiece. 'I mean I know I've got 'em,' she would say of her own ovaries, 'but I don't want to sing about 'em.'[52] Later in the year she did two nights at a women's festival in London 'and they were terribly boring'.[53] She came to regard *Pandora's Box* as a nadir. 'I knew it was the end,' she said. 'I went into a decline and just sat at home moaning and whining. It's all a bit of blank but for six months I couldn't force myself to do anything. It was depressing and I was very unhappy.'[54]

In September 1977 the Start-Rite kids moved to Morecambe. Thus ended Victoria's time in Birmingham. She still only had a provisional licence, and Geoffrey didn't drive at all, so Celia Imrie drove the rented van with their effects up from Priory Road. The tailgate didn't work so they had to lower everything up and then down via a three-foot ladder. The biggest problem was presented by Victoria's blue upright piano. 'Geoffrey and I are both Cancerians,' says Celia, 'and get into a terrible panic. He and I tried to lift this piano up the stairs. We were both shouting and screaming and sweating. It was pretty hellish actually. We had fish and chips afterwards.'

Their new home was a rented maisonette in Oxford Street, a sloping terrace not far from the sea front. Freshly renovated, it was all floorboards and naked bulbs. The new tenants set to painting and putting up shelves which they filled with her vast library of paperbacks and his magic manuals. 'As we are quite poor it is hard to get the things we'd like to furnish it,' Victoria reported – they looked for bargains in an auction room round the corner.[55] The homemaking process took a while. Months later her parents visited and Stanley found 'Vicky slumped in a chair – with paste brush in her hand utterly exhausted'.[56] He declared it 'a smashing flat, very Bohemian/Chelsea/Habitat'. Spread over two floors, their new home provided room enough for two people with incompatible rhythms. Geoffrey could now sleep while Victoria, with a deadline looming, composed on the piano until six or seven in the morning.

Geoffrey often heard her argue that moving to Morecambe 'was a bad decision because we should have moved to London'. At the time her judgement had been clouded by Alan Bennett. *Sunset Across the Bay*, his tragicomedy for *Play for Today* directed by Stephen Frears about a couple from Leeds retiring to Morecambe, was broadcast in 1975: 'I thought it would be funny to live there. Well it's not funny to live somewhere just because you've seen it on the television. I mean it was mad.'[57] They soon developed a love-hate relationship with the town. On national television the Mancunian stand-up Colin Crompton had characterised Morecambe as a 'cemetery with lights' where 'they don't bury their dead, they stand them up in bus shelters'. Victoria took up the theme of Morecambe as a living mortuary when she observed the bunting that lingered long after the celebrations for the Queen's Silver Jubilee. 'I don't think anybody's told them it over,' she said. 'They probably don't know the war is over in Morecambe.'[58] The agedness of the population struck her when making a first foray into a local exercise class. 'The women are all 83 yrs old (pretty young for Morecambe),' she informed Robert Howie, 'and have huge stomachs and spindly legs. They wear leotards covered with beige bouclé crimplene cardis, and ordinary tights. I created quite a stir in my bright red footless tights.'[59]

As she got to know the rhythms of life and language in Morecambe, she was inspired to write a radio sitcom about putting on a summer show there, drawing on local characters she'd encountered and riffing on the fun she and Geoffrey had playing bingo and slot machines in Snappyland and Bermudiana on the sea front. The commission came from Bob Oliver Rogers, a young radio producer she'd worked with on *Beetles and Buckman's Open Window*. 'I'm writing a radio comedy,' she told her university friend Chrissie Poulter. 'At least it's supposed to be a comedy – hard to tell.'[60] She called it *Sunny Side Up*. The opening episode, titled 'All Quiet on Pigwood Front', introduced Audrey Coakley, a girl in her twenties who has been left a coach ticket to Pigwood on Sea in her late aunt's will. Various people bemoan the decrepitude of the town and its inhabitants, who 'only wear their hearing aids at the weekend'. Audrey wonders how long it is since anybody won anything on the pier's ancient fruit machine. 'I can't remember,' she's told, 'but whoever it was left their gas mask behind.' The pier looks 'like a council house on a stick'. The script included Victoria's first ever use of one of her favourite words. Audrey's aunt got on her nerves because 'she was always leaving macaroons in the toilet'. Rogers sent the script back, complaining that it had too many jokes: 'I thought, how can there be too many jokes in something?'[61] Sadly he died aged only twenty-nine and *Sunny Side Up* fell by the wayside.

That winter Victoria acquired her first car, a clapped-out Mini Van in which she drove herself and Geoffrey to gigs. It was so unreliable they had to factor in extra journey time in case it broke down. While there were not many gigs to drive to, at least Victoria and Geoffrey had each other. 'We came together as two people who wanted to be soloists,' he says. 'Vic and I gave each other the nerve to be what we had always thought we might be.' His quest to become a magician gave Victoria something to think about besides her own career. 'We spend many happy evenings with me tying his thumbs together,' she told Rosalind, 'or picking a card out of a trick pack.'[62] Her live show had become a patchy source of income and a reliable cause of depression. At the heart of the problem was her lack of technique, brought

on by paralysing shyness: 'I would get a live gig and die on my arse
'cause I was so dreadful. I just sat there with my back to the audience, mumbled my way through twelve songs without any patter and
they were bored stiff after three minutes. I was never booked to come
back.'[63] One performance at a student ball, when she was unable to
hold the attention of a wildly drunk young audience, typified her
experiences: 'I felt so embarrassed when the social secretary came up
and gave me the money and said, "Of course it's not your fault. You
were terrific." And you know they don't mean it. And they grudgingly
count out 150 quid and you think, I haven't done anything to deserve
this money.'[64]

There was a cautious boost for her confidence as a writer when
Geoffrey encouraged Victoria to send *Sunny Intervals* to the Young
Vic in London, which specialised in children's entertainment. Denise
Coffey, a director at the theatre, applauded the quality of the script
while regretting that they couldn't stage it, but she did invite them
both to do a Saturday morning children's entertainment in November.
The Mini Van broke down three times on the M1 on the way south to
perform 'a play with music and magic' that they wrote together and
called *Abracawhat?* In a send-up of a standard magic show, Victoria
played a woman who applies to become the assistant of the Great
Soprendo:

GS:   I'm the Great Soprendo, Spanish man of mystery.
VW:  I'm Maureen, I'm not really mysterious, am I?
GS:   Don't worry, I can be mysterious enough for both of us.
VW:  What will I do?
GS:   You can walk behind me explaining.

Victoria sprinkled the script with references to Morecambe and her
grandmother's home town Chorlton-cum-Hardy, and did the two
tricks she had learned. 'The whole thing is a complete ego trip,' she
said soon afterwards in her oldest surviving radio interview. 'I've certainly never got a grip of cabaret, so it seems the theatre is the safest
place to put me. I don't get heckled so much. It doesn't mean you land
in the scampi and chips at least.'[65]

The interview was recorded late in 1977 for *Sounds Local* on Radio Blackburn. Victoria performed seven songs as part of a half-hour broadcast, among them staples written for *Wordplay* or *The Summer Show*. A new song expressed an aversion to the jubilee ('Dear Queen, I cannot have a party in my street / Because I live between a mental home / And a workshop that makes artificial feet'). A perky song inhabited the mind of a *Bunty*-reading eleven-year-old convent girl asking favours of God such as 'I'd either like to be a star / Or first in the class to wear a bra'. Her interviewer Wendy Howard shrewdly picked up on the stark contrast between the introvert who timidly mumbled her answers and the extrovert who sang boldly opinionated lyrics. 'You seem to be very much an anti-person, a loner,' she suggested. 'I don't like joining in things very much,' Victoria agreed. 'I tend to sit back and watch. I don't like to compete with other people because I think I won't win so I don't join in and then I can't lose, which may not be a very sensible way to live your life, I suppose.'[66]

*Sounds Local* was broadcast on the first day of 1978 during a desperate period for Victoria with no income aside from a welcome repeat fee for *The Camera and the Song*. She had no work ethic to speak of: 'I would do anything rather than sit down and work. Even when I had sat down at the table I would look up all my friends' addresses in the A to Z, I would eat wine gums in a certain order, I'd plait my hair, I would work out different eye make-ups. But it sort of counted because I was sitting at the desk.'[67]

Victoria was fearful of rejection after sending out tapes that came straight back. 'They hear me and the piano and they think how boring,' she told Wendy Howard. 'I don't really blame them.'[68] Without an agent she had no easy means of putting herself in the public eye. She made an overture to Richard Stone, who represented Benny Hill and various sitcom actors. Lynda Ronan, who looked after cabaret for the agency, was sent to watch her at a small club off Tottenham Court Road: 'She was painfully shy and raucously funny. I told her that I was bowled over but didn't know what I was going to do with her because she was such a one-off.' Victoria was all too familiar with this verdict.

She spent the first half of the year drawing the dole and waiting for the phone to ring. 'It's v easy to sign on,' she told Robert Howie. 'I had a bit of trouble with them offering me jobs – 18 weeks on the beach as a kind of red coat.'[69] While she waited she read up to three books a day, played bingo, enjoyed walking around town and went to keep-fit. The woman running the class, who used to be on the stage, loftily told her 'it's only luck anyway' and mentioned friends 'who "write very funny songs" but haven't had the breaks'.[70] Victoria hoped there was more to it than blind luck but, as she turned twenty-five in May, she did badly need a stroke of good fortune.

# 8

# TALENTS

'Julie – on a rainy day,
You're the girl that sings the clouds away.'

*Talent*, 1978

When the break came, it came quickly. The Bush, a tiny boxlike theatre above a pub in west London, was planning a topical revue for the summer of 1978. The show, titled *In at the Death*, was being created at short notice after another production had fallen through. More than a year after their previous appearances together, Victoria and John Dowie had three dates in early June at the Battersea Arts Centre. The Bush's artistic director Dusty Hughes spotted something that nobody had yet remarked on: 'She had a lovely warm relationship with the audience, who took to her straight away. I wasn't sure that she would be interested but we needed music in the show.' Victoria, who had to decide fast, as work was to begin in days, accepted but turned down his offer to be in it. 'I just wanted to write the songs,' she said, 'because it was on for three weeks and I thought that was a terribly long time to be in anything and I didn't like Shepherd's Bush.'[1]

Victoria's first encounter with the five other older male writers was not encouraging. They met in Clapham at the home of the playwright Snoo Wilson, who had recently installed a vintage guard's van in his garden – the roof needed putting on and he enlisted the writers to help him. 'It's where I first heard the word "macho",' she would recall. 'Oh God, I don't like these people.'[2]

'Victoria was a bit overwhelmed by the high bohemian large house,' says Dusty Hughes. 'Although she was good-natured about it, there was the feeling of "you London trendies putting something together and I'm going to be the antidote to that".' She gave vent to that anarchic spirit when meeting Ron Hutchinson, another of the writers, at the National Theatre. Spotting a poster advertising a play of his, she jumped up, disassembled the frame, rolled up the poster and handed to him. 'You'd better have that,' she said.

The material for the new show at the Bush was to be drawn from events covered in that week's news. Unpromisingly for a comic song-writer, it had to be about death. Yet Victoria felt liberated: 'For the first time I wasn't being told exactly what to do. I was able to look through the papers, and write about things I actually cared about.'[3] She came up with a song inspired by London Zoo's most famous inhabitant, a gorilla who died in an operation on his teeth after the public fed him too many sweets. She treated the chorus as a rhyming challenge: 'Guy the Gorilla, Guy the Gorilla / Died of chocolate / Not usually a killer / In cottage flat and villa / They're crying on their piller . . .' More seriously, she wrote about a girl having an abortion and a teenage motorcyclist killed in a police chase. Her most endur-ing song was prompted by the acquittal of a man who had helped his dying wife commit suicide. Victoria took the story as a springboard to imagine a widower who, through embarrassment, missed his chance to tell his wife he loved her. With a simple delicate accompaniment and barely any rhymes, 'Love Song' was freighted with melancholy:

Made your breakfast this morning like any old day
And then I remembered, and I threw it away.

For the first time Victoria was 'trying not to be clever, or put in com-plicated rhymes to show off, but to say what I wanted to say as simply as possible'.[4]

When the cast assembled, she played her songs and was elated by the reaction but still felt no incentive to be in the show: 'I sat on Shepherd's Bush Green with my boyfriend. I said, "This is really horrible round here." Three weeks seemed like an awfully long time.

I only did about three jobs a year so the idea of doing eighteen consecutive shows was like being in *The Mousetrap* for ten years.'[5] Her
view changed when she heard one of the actresses telling stories about
nursing: 'She was very attractive, and she had this sleeveless waistcoat
on and these jeans tucked into cowboy boots. I just thought she was
a really friendly person.'[6] Her name was Julie Walters, and Victoria
dredged up a memory of her audition for Manchester Polytechnic:
'Vic said, "We've met before," and I said, "No we haven't. What do
you mean? When?" She said, "I auditioned." Then I remembered in
my first year I was used as an usher, which I loved. An image of this
little girl flashed up. "Oh my God, I do remember you being sick
in a bucket."' That evening Victoria took the news to Jane Wynn
Owen's flat in Highgate, where she and Geoffrey were staying. 'Oh, I
know Julie Walters!' said Geoffrey, having lived in the flat beneath her
and Pete Postlethwaite in 1974 when they were all with the Liverpool
Everyman.

Julie's presence made it easier for Victoria to join the company: 'I
thought, oh well, maybe if she's going to be in this it actually could
be quite fun to be in.'[7] They were soon peeling off from the cast to
lunch on liver boil and peas at the Café Rest in Goldhawk Road. On
one occasion, they got stuck down a cul-de-sac in Victoria's Mini Van,
necessitating a three-point turn in which she dented a garden wall.
'Don't listen to me,' her new friend advised her. 'I don't know what
I'm saying half the time.'[8] Instead Victoria listened as she had never
listened to anyone before. 'We made one another laugh straight away,'
says Julie. 'It was cruel taking the piss out of other people. Awful we
were, but it made us really laugh. God help someone if they were
snobbish or silly. There was a chap in the cast. He had very stretchy
Y-fronts. Probably needed a bit of a rinse. And we used to be in fits
about this.' One day they were looking down into Shepherd's Bush
Green and spotted Harold Pinter on the pavement below. Through
the bay window Julie hollered, 'Hey, Harold, you write plays, don't
you?' 'He looked rather bemused,' says Julie. 'Slightly cross at being
shouted at.'

In fact, there was a fresh source of material in-house. When
Snoo Wilson failed to submit one of his pieces, Victoria sniffed an

opportunity and asked if she could write something. Practised at composing songs to order, one lunchbreak she repaired to the ladies and, with Julie's voice in her head, wrote at speed. The sketch she tentatively presented was titled 'Sex' and was set in a northern library. Julie was to play a naive librarian dumped by a man called Brett after a one-night stand. Victoria was a housewife who is scathing about sex and, in particular, the absurdity of male genitalia:

> I mean the basic equipment's so ridiculous – how's he expected to take you to the brink of ecstasy with something that looks like a school dinner without the custard?

Victoria's housewife is planning to send off for a test-tube baby (topically, the first baby ever conceived by this method was born in Manchester during the show's run). Julie's librarian, by contrast, thinks she may be pregnant and worries about the cost of an abortion:

> J:  I'm only on 23 pounds 50 and I'm still paying my fine for
>       shop lifting.
> V:  What happened?
> J:  A duvet fell into my shopping bag.

Every night the line caused a detonation of laughter. In walks a hippie (played by Alison Fiske), who regards lentils as a contraceptive:

> A:  What exactly is the problem?
> J:  My period's late.
> A:  How late?
> J:  Five minutes.
> A:  When did intercourse take place?
> J:  Beg pardon?
> A:  Where are you in the menstrual cycle?
> J:  Taurus.

Victoria came to consider the sketch, and specifically this set-up and pay-off, as a life-changing revelation: 'It was after four years of trying to be funny and being nearly funny, which is awful, I was funny. And then I knew how you wrote a joke.'[9] She likened the discovery to striking a gong. Integral to this new sensation was an instinctive knowledge that she should not hoard the best lines when, in Julie, she had found someone she could be funny with: 'When we stood on stage doing that sketch – and we both loved doing it – it gave me such a boost. You think, ah, now I know – now I know what I'm doing.'[10] Julie had the same sense of a tectonic plate shifting: 'The first night we did it, the audience had been quite muted. Her sketch just brought the house down. I'll never forget "Taurus". It was fabulous every night. I couldn't wait to do that sketch. That really bonded us. I remember thinking the heavens had sent her to me, that she knew me. In my arrogance as a young person I thought no one else could do this but me. It was "she's written this specially, uniquely for me".'

*In at the Death* opened in July. To the amusement of the cast, before every performance Victoria washed her hair in the basin and prepared her face with make-up she carried around in an art box: 'It was important to me because I thought I was an act. I wasn't an actress, I was a turn and I had to have a proper turn's box. I'd do this great elaborate sketch by make-up and used to look like the back of the bus.'[11] While Victoria enjoyed working with professional actors, she didn't think highly of the show, nor the backstage facilities: 'If you wanted a wee, you had to go down into Goldhawk Road and mingle with the audience in your costume, which, if you were dressed as I was, in grey flannel shorts and ankle socks, was a bit dodgy. So the ladies of the cast tended to rely for short-term relief on handy beer glasses, which from indolence we would leave on the windowsill of Dusty's office. This led to the often-heard cry, "Don't drink that lager!"'[12] One night Victoria had an accident. 'We were all onstage except her,' says Julie. 'There was a great crash backstage and she'd knocked one of them down the stairs. There was all this bloody wee all over people's costumes.'

It wasn't difficult for the national critics to pick Victoria out. She spent most of the play upstage at the keyboard and when she first stood up to appear in a sketch by Ron Hutchinson about Northern Irish brickies she didn't speak – she joked that thanks to her inability

to do the accent she was cast as a deaf mute. So when she performed
'Sex', the impact was powerful. There was a cascade of praise: 'Victoria
Wood stands out in a vigorous company.'[13] 'Miss Wood is a real discovery, of whom much more is certain to be heard both as writer and
performer.'[14] 'An outstanding comic and *chanteuse*.'[15] 'She gets more
fun and more poetry out of Manchester speech than I have heard for
years.'[16] One reviewer issued a warning: 'I am going to be very very
angry if Ms Wood doesn't get discovered in a biggish way very soon.'[17]

In Victoria's modest explanation, 'I walked away with the reviews
because nobody had seen me before.' More precisely, nobody had seen
anyone like her before – a young woman who could glide with astonishing facility between melancholy and ribaldry. The raves helped her
finally to secure an agent. At Geoffrey's behest – she didn't dare ring
him herself – Richard Stone read the reviews, came to a performance
and promptly took her on. Nearing sixty, he was a larger-than-life
figure who wore silk suits and had a squint. 'I'm never really sure if
he's talking to you,' Victoria confided to Stone's assistant Vivienne
Clore. He wasted no time in asking her to write a sitcom for Barbara
Windsor and the bit-part comedian John Junkin. When Victoria
asked why those two, he replied, 'Because they're out of work, darling.' She had a stab at it but was soon waylaid by another job.

The Crucible Theatre in Sheffield was suddenly awash with money
from hosting the World Snooker Championship, and its artistic
director Peter James asked his associate David Leland to spend some
of the windfall on new writing. An inaugural season was rapidly
mounted in 1977. Leland was now scouting around for more new
plays and approached Ron Hutchinson, who recommended Victoria.
With time running out, Leland asked her for an idea by the following
morning: 'So I sat up all night in Highgate and come six o'clock in
the morning I had thought of this idea about a talent contest, seeing
as I had been in one. And I drove down to Tufnell Park . . . and put it
through his letter box.'[18] 'I heard the letterbox go,' says Leland. 'The
plot of *Talent* was written on the back of this brown envelope.'

David Leland never made it to *In at the Death*, so it was solely on
the basis of this synopsis that he commissioned Victoria to write a play
with songs. When she visited for further discussions, he stipulated

how many actors she must write for, gave her a deadline of only three weeks and asked for a title so they could print the posters: 'You could see it going in. I was pretty sure she would come up with something. She went away and I didn't hear a dicky bird from her.' There was no payment up front.

After the run at the Bush, Victoria drove straight back to More- cambe and fell into a rhythm of writing deep into the night. 'I've no idea whether it's any good or not but I'll keep struggling on,' she wrote to Robert Howie at half past five one morning.[19] She would ask Geoffrey, 'Is this a *play*?' He had a daily chance to consider the question, as once she went to bed he would type up the latest pages. This was a labour of love, his two-fingered typing skills being barely superior to hers. The result was that 'he was able to persuade me that *Talent* wasn't as bad as I thought it was'.[20] Victoria would think of the play's creation with sentimental fondness: 'It was like a real adventure that we were doing it together in this little flat in Morecambe.'[21]

The plot of *Talent* could easily fit onto the back of an envelope. Set in a sleazy northern cabaret club called Bunter's, it sprang from Victoria's knowledge of 'the creeps that hang around talent contests'.[22] Instead of writing directly about herself, Victoria created an aspiring singer who is desperate to escape a future of marital drudgery. She was so overwhelmingly inspired by Julie Walters that she couldn't imagine giving her any other name: 'It was very influenced by meeting her. She was a very extraordinary person. I was trying to capture things that she did when she acted that I knew only she would be able to do.'[23] The fictional Julie, as Victoria had discovered with the real one, could blast out a powerful impersonation of Shirley Bassey. The song written for her to sing in character was 'Fourteen Again', about a girl's bittersweet ache for her youth 'When sex was just called number ten / And I was up to seven and a half'. In fictional Julie's case, going back in time would wipe out her teenage pregnancy and the baby she had to give up for adoption. It was Victoria's most painterly composition yet, which conjured up a world of innocence in glinting detail:

I want to be fourteen again
Free rides on the waltzer off the fairground men

For a promise of a snog the last night of the fair
French kissing as the kiosks shut
Behind the generators with your coconut
The coloured lights reflected in the Brylcreem on his hair.

For moral support Julie brings along Maureen, a prudish sidekick who is 'on the chubby side' and still a virgin. 'I wouldn't know what to do,' she tells Julie. 'You don't do anything,' Julie assures her. 'Men do all the work.' Victoria didn't see these girls as a straight double portrait of herself and Julie, but she did draw on memories of being the shy girl who hated parties. 'There's the sort of person that lives under a stone until they're eighteen, which is me,' she explained, 'and the sort of person who is at it from the age of twelve, which is not me. But I knew those girls and I remember what they were like.'[24] Later she came to recognise that in each woman she was exploring aspects of herself: 'I was both. I put a lot of my own feelings of being uncomfortable in the world into Maureen and a lot of my excitement about being in show business into Julie.'[25]

She packed the dialogue with autobiographical references. Some were overt: bingo in Morecambe, addiction to chocolate, the clap-ometer, being in Shakespeare at school, Leslie Crowther, *New Faces*. Others were encrypted: Adam and the Ants, Pam Ayres, her mother's Irish roots. She channelled a recent memory of the Bush Theatre: the Bunter's loo doesn't lock or flush so Julie urinates (offstage) into a plastic straw boater then places it on the windowsill. Victoria even borrowed a joke from 'Sex'. 'I don't think I've got any hobbies, have I?' says Julie. 'Shoplifting,' says Maureen.

Victoria used her new knowledge of conjuring to create a retired factory worker called George who does comic magic. He was partly inspired by the Great Soprendo but also based on the pensioners she met when Geoffrey judged a magic competition in Lancaster. She gave George an assistant called Arthur, and for both gents she wrote a duet in the style of Flanagan and Allen and long speeches which proved her ear was as attuned to old men as to young women.

As for the younger men, the commission gave Victoria a chance to settle scores with bus-shelter pests and bedroom braggarts. The talent show organist turns out to be the callous ex-boyfriend who impregnated Julie. The compère offers Julie a place on a TV talent show in exchange for sex. 'Tonight's out, unfortunately,' he tells her. 'But my wife's away tomorrow, brass rubbing. I don't think you'll be disappointed . . . old John Thomas has put a smile on a lot of girls' faces.' He also tries his luck on Maureen, who is invited to his Cortina and instructed to remove her underwear in advance. 'And bring a tissue,' he adds. The line was greeted by shocked groans from women in the audience. The compère, Victoria revealed, was a 'conglomeration of a few nasty people'.[26] 'You've got a mediocre voice,' Julie is told, 'a terrible Lancashire accent, no experience and no act. On your own, you're going to get nowhere fast. But with me – I know more big producers than you've had hot dinners.' The girls scarper when they discover the talent contest is rigged.

Although the play was conceived as a vehicle for Julie, her friend was committed to a Shakespeare season at the Bristol Old Vic and, even if she had been free, David Leland already had a company under contract, although he did insist that Victoria play Maureen. 'I thought I could sit on my bum for a few weeks,' she said, 'so everybody else did the hard work and I got all the money, but they said, "Well, we won't do it unless you're in it. And you play the piano as well because that's a lot cheaper than getting somebody else in."'[27] The role of Julie was taken by Hazel Clyne, who needed a bit of coaxing from Victoria to capture the speech rhythms that played in her head. Geoffrey was hired as a magic consultant.

*Talent* was the final new play of the season. When the opening night in the studio theatre came round in November, from the moment Maureen and Julie fumbled onstage in the dark, the dialogue's zingers – 'My father says that girls with perms look like barmy sheep', 'she looks at me like I'm something spat out by their mynah bird', 'I thought coq au vin was a fuck in a lorry' – were met by waves of laughter. 'The first and last thing to be said about *Talent*,' enthused the *Guardian*, 'is that it is very funny – at times, too near the knicker-wetting degree.'[28] Because the play was only eighty minutes long, the audience was encouraged to come back at 10 p.m. for an hour-long double bill. First on was the Great Soprendo, announced as 'that Slick

Spick with the Spanish Vanish'. Then came Victoria in 'Tickling My Ivories, an evening of singing, talking, standing up, sitting down again and "possibly" one card trick'. The promise that she might stand up was more of an aspiration than a reality – her monologue about living in Morecambe was delivered from her piano stool. A new opening song called 'I Only Hope to God It Goes All Right' contained advice for anyone confusing her with anyone else:

> In case you're wondering I am not Pam Ayres
> She wears dresses and sits in chairs.
> (I like the chairs better.)
> And I am not Jake Thackray, he is taller
> He plays guitar and his tits are smaller.

(When Victoria eventually met Thackray, both had the same story to tell about each always being compared with the other.) *Talent* and its after-show continued into December. 'She absolutely loved every second,' says Geoffrey. 'It was what she'd always wanted to do.'

Victoria's mother, who after seven years had finished her master's dissertation on Victorian religious tract novels, found herself 'consenting to go having heard that Vicky has actually invited us'.[29] There was a more important visitor to the Crucible in the shape of Peter Eckersley, the head of drama at Granada. Victoria was chuffed to learn he was married to Anne Reid – the couple had met while he was writing for *Coronation Street* and she was playing Valerie Barlow. 'I've seen this amazing girl,' he told Anne when he went home. 'She's just hilarious.' Eckersley, a burly bald man with thick-rimmed glasses, was an erudite wit with an earthy northern sensibility who had a strong record of spotting writers such as Jack Rosenthal, Arthur Hopcraft and Brian Clark. He was excited enough by *Talent* to consider buying the television rights but informed Victoria that 'he couldn't make head nor tail of it' and sent Baz Taylor, a young director he knew, for a second opinion.[30] 'There are bits you can't have, like peeing in the pot,' he reported. 'But she is very funny. She's got something.'

The drama was duly commissioned. At a meeting in Manchester Victoria stipulated that she wanted Julie to play Julie. When Eckersley insisted she audition, Victoria joked to Julie that she'd play badly for the forty other actresses up for the role. Julie sang 'Isn't She Lovely?' 'because I knew I could hit the notes and I loved singing it in an echoey room' but what clinched it was 'Fourteen Again'. As she sang she undid a couple of buttons on her blouse and mimed popping acne on her chest. 'That's what sold us,' says Taylor. 'Pete said, "In for a penny in for a pound." It was clearly going to make Vic's day to do it and we took the risk. It stood or fell as a two-hander.' The fee was £2,500.

Peter Eckersley was to become Victoria's guiding light as she took her first steps as a writer for television. While acknowledging her talent, his skill was in urging her to pare down dialogue and not mourn the losses. 'I used really to enjoy coming to his office with a play I'd just finished,' she later said, 'and we'd whip through it together, and by the time we'd finished it was half an hour shorter and a lot funnier.'[31] Thus *Talent* lost twenty minutes in its transfer to television. As she adapted it in the first weeks of 1979, Victoria was conscious of learning a new craft. She joked to a friend, 'At the top of the script do I just write "turn the camera on"?'

There was little time to write it because suddenly, after years of drought, Victoria was deluged with work. After the Sheffield run *Talent* found a London home at the ICA in February, requiring further rehearsals. Victoria was also still notionally writing the sitcom suggested by her agent and had a commission to produce material for *The Marti Caine Show*, which she dashed off at pace – it was never used. Meanwhile, there was radio work. For *The Scenery Is So Much Better*, broadcast on Radio 4 on Boxing Day, Victoria wrote and performed two new songs. One of them, 'Music and Movement', was a charming comic ditty 'about the wireless programmes that little children used to listen to from the BBC in 1959,' she explained.[32] Sung in the character of a little boy in mixed infants, it was inspired by her memory of primary school:

And now we're in the hall with wireless on
With this woman saying what we have to do
Be as tall as a house, be as tiny as a mouse –
I'm knackered, it's only half past two.

*

As her name started to resonate Victoria received ever more frequent invitations from *Start the Week*. For the first nine months of 1979 she appeared roughly once a month, despite her deepening unease with topical songwriting. Its producer Ian Gardhouse would give her the list of guests and ask her to write something related. She would bring it in to be recorded at seven o'clock on Monday morning. Before breakfast television, *Start the Week* could have the pick of stars as grand as Lauren Bacall or Sophia Loren, supplemented by a pool of confident media performers – Kenneth Robinson, Esther Rantzen, Mavis Nicholson. 'She would sit at the piano, play the song, play it again,' says Gardhouse. 'She was a joy in that respect to work with. We then had a cup of tea and the guests would arrive. I invited Victoria to go into the studio and sit at the table and she never would. She was too shy. Sometimes she might leave before the piece came up.' The presenter Richard Baker, he adds, 'was always very pleased when I told him she'd been booked. I booked her as often as I could, but she wasn't always available.' Victoria took a different story home with her. 'Vic found Richard Baker deeply patronising,' says Geoffrey. 'She was very sensitive about the casual way women were ignored by men in the media, while the men who were doing the ignoring could see nothing wrong with their behaviour at all. That in turn made her defensive, angry, stand-offish and unwilling to participate. Hence the view that she was shy – which she often also was.' She compressed these frustrations into a single belittling gag: 'I suppose a little song in the middle gave Richard Baker a chance to nip out to the doings.'[33]

Such was the pressure on her time that Victoria started to take in songs she'd performed elsewhere – 'Guy the Gorilla', 'Leaning on a Convent Wall'. Her attitude to the show perked up in May when Russell Harty guested as a presenter. They bonded in an instant and he took her under his wing. 'She has a northern way with words, just like Alan,' Harty told Nicholas Barrett, his producer at LWT. By Alan he meant his friend Alan Bennett. Barrett, who would work with her years later, soon met Victoria himself when they all drove to a restaurant near Harty's home in the Dales: 'She was disturbingly taciturn until the music that had been playing softly on the car radio upped the tempo. Suddenly the headrest of my seat became a drum upon which she began to furiously accompany the unexpected rhythm. Head shaking and hair flying, Vic appeared to be in a self-induced trance.' Over the dinner she reverted to shy silence.

When *Talent* opened in London, the country was in the biting grip of a grim winter in early 1979. Victoria's parents were snowed in, and theatres were suffering. Not the ICA. 'Shows were closing because nobody was going out,' says David Leland, 'and we had queues of people trying to get in to see *Talent*. It had a phenomenal buzz about it.' The role of the compère was now taken by Jim Broadbent, a member of the Crucible company who brought extra sleaze to the moment he grabbed Julie's then Maureen's breasts. 'Curiously it wasn't the standout moment of the play,' he says. 'It was taken for granted – fringe-theatre nudity was almost de rigueur. It certainly wasn't a big hurdle that we felt we had to get over.' It was certainly a turn-off for *Kaleidoscope*'s male reviewer on Radio 4 – it 'gave an unpleasant taste to what, up until then, had been a very positive, warm, subtle evening'.[34] Theatregoers were drawn by more glowing reviews which homed in on Victoria's portrait of young women and their punctured dreams: 'the arrival of a natural writer';[35] 'she may have it in her to be our best female playwright'.[36] Richard Stone lured along Michael Codron, the preeminent West End impresario, who proved reluctant to transfer *Talent* partly because it was too short but instead encouraged Victoria to write a new play. But it would have to wait.

Soon after *Talent*'s short run at the ICA, Victoria reported to Granada, where ten days were earmarked to rehearse and record the television version. She did not regard the play as set in stone and accepted it when 'bring a tissue' was cut, as was one of the two breast gropes. 'The TV producer said we could only get away with it once on the telly,' she explained.[37] 'A fuck in a lorry' was toned down to 'love in a lorry'.

Julie, inheriting the lead role, recognised herself in her namesake. 'The girl was very like me in many ways in a parallel universe,' she says, 'except she was crueller. "You shouldn't eat so many chocolates" – I wouldn't say things like that to Vic ever!' Together she and Victoria made an impact at the studio. One day the boom operator, wearing his cans, overheard them on their radio mics in the ladies chatting about the clitoris and men with big long poles. 'They were pretending they didn't know the sound boys were listening in on it,' says Baz Taylor. 'It went round like wildfire that these girls were real rebels. They took Granada by storm. Nobody had seen anything like them in operation before.'

Work had to stop at ten o'clock, owing to union rules, and they would start drinking – in the Granada bar with Peter Eckersley, or the Midland Hotel on their own, where anything could happen. One night they both ended up falling asleep in Victoria's room when a fire alarm sounded. 'It went on for ages,' said Victoria, 'and we were dashing about putting on bras and contact lenses and didn't have time to get our shoes on. We were right at the top of the hotel and ran down, a bit dazed, and out into the street, to find it was broad daylight and they were testing the fire bells.'[38] Julie was in her pyjamas: 'Oh my God, we used to get pissed. We woke up on the floor [of the Midland bar] one time, just asleep, and someone hoovering around us.'[39]

'They were uncontrollable sometimes,' says Jim Parker, who arranged Victoria's songs for the drama. 'Once Peter was going to take us to an Indian restaurant and the waiters wore turbans. He said, "I don't think so with Vic and Jules."' Parker was hired at Victoria's behest – she knew his delicate and witty work on *Banana Blush*, the 1974 album of John Betjeman's poems set to music played by a quirky wind sextet. Victoria visited his house in Barnes to introduce him to the songs, and he set to arranging them. For the recording, Eckersley insisted on the best London session musicians, joined by Victoria on the piano. One guitarist arrived so blind drunk in a taxi he had to have his guitar attached to him. 'He gazed blankly at the music,' says Baz Taylor, 'then he nodded and did it in one take. Vic said, "How the hell did he do that?"'

While in Manchester Victoria had a visit from Robert Howie but felt the need to apologise for seeming to snub him. 'I was in a bit of a muddle as we were right in the middle of filming etc at Granada and there were lots of people around who wanted to talk about jobs. I didn't mean to be rude however . . .'[40] This was an early sign that her gathering success might make things awkward with friends in the business. She urged him and other pals to visit Morecambe, where guests were accommodated in the bedroom while the hosts slept with the piano and books downstairs. David Leland came but, according to Geoffrey, 'didn't get it. He said to Vic, "You have an insatiable appetite for the third rate." He meant bingo on the front.' John Dowie arrived with his wife. Looking round Morecambe's wax-work museum, the four of them tried to identify the exhibits without referring to the guide, only to discover that a label which formerly identified Muhammad Ali had been changed to Lenny Henry.

Though associated with Granada, Victoria now caught the attention of the BBC in the shape of David Rose, the esteemed producer who had nursed the talents of Mike Leigh and Alan Bleasdale. From English Regions Drama based in Pebble Mill, she accepted a commission to write a fifty-minute play with songs to be called *Amusements*. Inspired by Morecambe, it was to portray characters she'd met in the amusement arcades of a seaside town. Despite the fee of £1,750, a couple of months later Victoria asked for a postponement – it eventually became a cancellation – while she concentrated on the commission from Michael Codron. Stanley, jumping the gun, described this prospective play as 'a West End musical . . . I think the theatre is already fixed and the impresario wants her to act in it as well as write it.'[41] In fact, it was destined initially for the Crucible. Having mined her own experience for *Talent*, Victoria cast around for something else she could write about and alighted on the world of community arts, of which she claimed some hands-on knowledge, having joined her student friends on *The Tipton Slasher Show*. She called the play *Howard's Anorak*, then changed it to *Pals*, and set it in the flat of Liz, a well-meaning but disorganised community-arts administrator. Liz is mounting a festival which is to feature a Punch and Judy show presented as a feminist story about battered women and a women's group called Left Bosom, who perform in launderettes and are dramatising the repeal of the Corn Laws. A mass meeting of cystitis sufferers is also programmed. Victoria peopled the play with women – Liz's school friend Elsie, an Avon lady called Betty. There was a strong focus on women's hatred of their own bodies ('He can't always get an erection because of her stretch marks'), and crude gags about sexual organs and bodily functions. The only male character was Mike, a married geography teacher who takes advantage of the infatuated Liz. Victoria gave Elsie, whom she would play herself, a malfunctioning Mini Van, a strong knowledge of yesteryear's female comics and most of the best lines. 'Let's just say I prefer to go straight from the foreplay to the cigarette,' she says. Taurus was once again a punchline, and there were more jokes about lentils, punks, the *Crossroads* motel and macaroons.

She found it hard going. 'I've been writing a play for 20 years,' she told Lesley Fitton, 'and am envying that woman who only had to spin straw into gold.'[42] She even advised the *Mail* that 'it is a total disaster so far'.[43] *Pals* was typed up by Geoffrey and sent to Michael Codron, whose silence told its own story. Victoria itched to ask if his office had received it. Eventually he described it as 'very enjoyable' but said it needed surgery. 'I felt very pressured and anxious and rather too aware of the pitfalls of writing a second play (especially as *Talent* had been well reviewed),' Victoria admitted to Robert Howie, 'and it didn't turn out very well.'[44] She explained that, even though she 'based it' on a mutual university friend of theirs, she couldn't get to the bottom of Liz's motivation: 'I don't really understand her well enough to explain her to an audience. Anyway, after a few weeks' discussion, I decided not to patch it up here and there but to start again. I wrote a reasonably plotty scenario, sent it off to Codders and off we went again.'[45]

While she steeped herself in writing, over the summer of 1979 Victoria received what might have been a life-changing offer. John Lloyd and Sean Hardie were working on a topical news spoof destined for BBC Two called *Not the Nine O'Clock News*. 'We were complete nobodies and we thought she was an emerging superstar,' says Lloyd. 'I can see that it wasn't a very good idea. Vic was her own person and what we needed was a *tabula rasa*.' They eventually picked the unknown Pamela Stephenson. 'She knew it wasn't for her,' says Geoffrey, to whom she mentioned the offer only after rejecting it. 'She was very calculating and there were times when she didn't want any advice. Her reason was that she didn't read the papers and wasn't interested in the news. The thought that it could have been a golden opportunity never seemed to occur to her.'

Meanwhile the Start-Rite kids continued to struggle for money. In her letters Victoria often mentioned being broke. Geoffrey had even less income. The season he'd programmed in Morecambe was called off, while he was unable to accept some gigs as he couldn't afford the fare. One trick that required glue had to be put on hold because he didn't have the money for Copydex. Their landlord called them the Houdinis.

By the summer of 1979 Victoria had not appeared on television for two years, since *Pandora's Box*. Then, while in London to record *Start the Week*, she performed 'Fourteen Again' on a cheap BBC Two show called *It's a Great Life – If You Don't Weaken*, presented by Nicky Martyn, the Lancashire comic who got her name wrong on *New Faces*. Viewers were not informed that the song belonged to a drama to be shown on the other side, but there were enough opportunities to promote *Talent*. The week before broadcast Victoria nervously watched it in a roomful of journalists, after which her story was written up in every tabloid. Other interviewers made the pilgrimage to Morecambe. She got into trouble when one from *TV Times* referred to the sauce bottles in the window of the boarding house next door: 'The landlady was furious and refused to believe I hadn't written the piece myself to show her up.'[46] Her unguarded habit in these encounters was to talk up forthcoming projects – a revue for women for ATV, an album of songs from *Talent* – even if they were destined not to happen. One proposal she dismissed outright was a life swap with the journalist Vicki Woods. Victoria listened to the pitch over the phone then asked, 'Can you write songs?'[47]

*Talent* was shown in Granada's *Screenplay* slot. Victoria and Geoffrey watched the broadcast on a Sunday night in early August on their black-and-white portable. The next morning she took the phone off the hook in order to write, and, down to her last 40p, she didn't have money to buy the papers. So she was initially unaware of the overnight applause. 'Victoria Wood is exuberantly good on the façade of being female,' wrote Nancy Banks-Smith in the *Guardian*. '[Her] own talent . . . is a rising and a shining thing.'[48] 'The best television musical since *Pennies from Heaven*,' reckoned Sheridan Morley in the *Evening Standard*.[49] 'If she isn't immediately offered a series of her own,' said the *Listener*'s critic, 'television executives are even sillier than I thought them.'[50] On BBC Radio Blackburn there were complaints about the bad language. A woman wrote to Victoria to point out that 'Lancashire people never, never talk as fast as June Walters [sic] talked.'[51] Without correcting the name, Victoria wrote back that Julie was from Manchester.

Having craved fame from childhood, at first Victoria was alarmed that it had finally happened and for two weeks stayed indoors. She took to not answering the phone when Geoffrey was out 'cos so many funny people ring up, and it really puts me off my work,' she told Chrissie Poulter.[52] 'I don't even like being a little bit famous,' she confided to Robert Howie, 'and there are lots of shops I won't go into because they know I write plays.'[53] Her sudden celebrity was such that she was recognised by Eric Morecambe when they found themselves in a lift at the Midland Hotel. It was a brief encounter. 'Oh, it's Eric Morecambe,' she said. 'You're that girl from Morecambe,' he replied. 'I'm not, I'm from Bury,' she countered. He got out at the next floor and they never met again.

Michael Codron now took Victoria under his wing: 'I am his little pet writer and he is very nice to me – sends me funny letters and takes me to lunch et cetera.'[54] Giving her an October deadline, he forbade her from doing further interviews until her new play opened at the Crucible. She had September all to herself while Geoffrey did a bumpy month-long residency in Haifa. Before his departure she had attempted day shifts, 'having breakfast at 8.30 like real people but I couldn't do it, mornings are so dreary, especially with the blinds down and earplugs in',[55] so she reverted to writing in the small hours from '9.30 till God knows when'.[56] She nipped to London three weeks running to appear on *Start the Week*. Thanks to *Talent* she made a fan in Alan Plater, who included her in a Radio 3 documentary on musicals. Her final radio appearance of the autumn was a written piece for Radio 4 addressed 'to the people who hate her flat'. 'Our flat's a bit bright and jolly for some people's tastes, but I happen to like living in a tube of Smarties,' she started, before attacking the craze for technological kitchens where 'you don't know whether to have a cup of coffee or a hysterectomy'.[57]

Victoria called her play *Good Fun* and finished it in mid-November. Owing to a professional debacle Geoffrey had ample time to type it up. Fame was supposed to beckon for him too after he successfully auditioned for a new BBC talent show called *Rising Stars*. The *Daily Mail*, catching wind that the Great Soprendo was married to the author of *Talent*, asked to photograph them together. Neither fancied it and Victoria cited a back injury and a chest infection to get out of it: 'They said they would take photos of me in bed but I couldn't bear the thought – said no.'[58] Instead she agreed, as an expert on such contests, to write an article about it. When she turned up for the show in Blackpool, she was too shy to tell anyone who she was and was racked by nerves, justifiably, as Geoffrey finished last but one, and the next day his agent took a flow of calls cancelling several months' work.

Meanwhile Victoria raced to her next commission: 'I've just finished my play for M Codron and now have to start one for Granada straight away so I am broke and preoccupied.'[59] Thrilled by Victoria's screen chemistry with Julie Walters, Peter Eckersley had suggested two sequels and even proposed giving Julie and Maureen a series. 'I don't want them to end up like a rehash of *The Liver Birds*,' Victoria said warily.[60] She thought of sending them on a caravan holiday before deciding to keep them closer to home.

In *Nearly a Happy Ending* Julie is at a low ebb. Her mother is in psychiatric care, while her fiancé has been killed in a car crash alongside another woman. She's depressed enough to be listening to Radio 4 (Victoria had no qualms about biting the hand that fed her). As for Maureen, things are looking up. She arrives in her new Mini Van, having passed her driving test at the fifth go, and has shed more than three stone. Counting calories is now her main topic of conversation, but at least she can wear jeans without looking 'like something out of a biology textbook'.

The two women stop off at the slimmers' club, where Maureen hits her target weight and decides to celebrate by losing her virginity. So they head to a hotel where the bar is full of flirts in suits looking for extramarital fun. Maureen talks her way into the room of a tedious young divorcee called Tony, but he is turned off by her impersonal determination to skip the foreplay. 'We could always do it afterwards,' she says, 'if there's time.' Back downstairs Tony hits on Julie and they leave in Maureen's Mini Van while Maureen goes home drunk in a cab clutching a box of Black Magic. 'Hey, you'll get fat eating them,' warns the cabbie. 'I know!' she replies testily.

Victoria's decision to confront the issue of weight in ever greater depth coincided with her own weight loss through dieting and swimming. 'I didn't write the part in order that I would have to diet,' she clarified. 'I just wanted to write a part about somebody who was fat and boring and then became thinner and boring. So I had to lose weight for the part.'[61] She was goaded into action by ubiquitous references to her size in articles she pasted into her scrapbook. 'Victoria Wood plumply accompanies some dry rhymes of her own composition.'[62] She was 'plump and blonde',[63] 'more than plump'[64] and 'not unplump'.[65] 'Victoria plumps for quiet fame,' went one headline.[66] 'I was never anybody's plump chum,' she said defiantly, but the barrage got under her skin.[67] 'One of the things that I hate about being fat,' she told Mavis Nicholson, 'is . . . they look at you as if you're a criminal if you ask for anything above a fourteen.'[68] She vented her frustration in a letter to Rosalind when trying to make a pinafore she'd seen in *Woman's Own*. 'All the pattern books are either no bosom model or teacher's model,' she complained, biroing sketches by way of illustration.[69]

For *Nearly a Happy Ending* Victoria wrote no fewer than three songs which dwelled on body image. The catchiest was 'Don't Get Cocky', composed for the ladies of the slimmers' club to perform, complete with rough and ready choreography. The cheerful up tempo tune issued weight watchers with a motivational warning: 'We congratulate / You on losing weight / Don't get cocky, baby / You're gonna be back next month'. The verses ran through a list of women and their reasons for being there:

Just take Valerie, wouldn't know a calorie
If it came and bit her on the leg,

Starves all day and then gives way
Has eighty bacon butties and a large fried egg . . .

After it was broadcast, a slimming-club secretary asked the Granada press office for a copy of the song.

The 1980s began with morale-boosting endorsements from London theatreland. In January Victoria was named most promising new playwright at the Plays and Players Awards. At the start of February, in heels and a long smock-like gown she bought for the occasion, she was at the National Theatre for the *Evening Standard* Theatre Awards, where she was joint winner. Ian McKellen, who 'came up beforehand and said what he was going to say – no kissing or anything like that',[70] presented her with the award before Victoria nervously thanked the Crucible, the ICA and 'my director David Leland, who directed a play properly' – this was greeted with laughter and applause – 'and also let me write it. I just hope I get better at it.'

Having devoted nine months of 1979 to writing scripts, Victoria spent the first half of 1980 acting in them. She hadn't told anyone at Granada about her weight loss, so they were surprised when she turned up to make *Nearly a Happy Ending* in February. She continued to swim lengths of Salford baths every morning before filming – the publicity stills for the drama were even shot in the pool. The crew at Granada was queuing up to work with Victoria and Julie again. So was Peter Eckersley. 'He was like a big avuncular warm northern person you felt loved by,' says Julie. 'You never felt that he was tense about anything. Just he really appreciated you. Vic used to call him Peter Eckerslike.' His easy rapport with Victoria was captured in a memorandum sent on the last day of filming after some clothes were pinched from her car and she had to leave in her costume: 'In partial recompense for the stolen knickers Granada Television Limited would like you to take home and accept with their compliments the clothes are you currently standing up in.'[71]

The short shoot overran, requiring everyone to stay on for an extra day. Victoria told no one, but this thwarted a plan she and Geoffrey had hatched to get married on Friday 29 February. 'We kept it completely secret because Vic was secret about everything,' says Geoffrey, who had been asking her to marry him for a while. She had a wobble the night before, but on the morning of 1 March Victoria and Geoffrey made their vows at the registry office in Lancaster. The only witnesses were her drama department friends Bill and Alison Lloyd (née Sabourin), who drove down from the Lake District. They brought their newborn daughter, presented the newlyweds with a pair of kites and took photographs in a garden. Between neoclassical pillars Geoffrey grinned in a canary-yellow jersey, standing behind Victoria with a hand on her shoulder. She wore a double-breasted light-grey jacket, blue trousers and pink trainers in which she balanced coyly on the outsides of her feet. It was 'a laugh,' she told Chrissie Poulter. 'Five minute job then spaghetti on toast and knickerbocker glory.'[72] The press would not catch wind of the event for another three months. 'We've been married for some time now,' said a tight-lipped Victoria when the *Daily Mail* rang the flat.[73] She was disinclined to play the gushing bride: 'I think we had the 59th row about why we weren't married, and decided we might as well be.'[74] (Victoria's nonchalance about her marriage was nothing compared to her mother's. After they'd told their parents, Geoffrey's mother wrote to Helen Wood and didn't receive a reply. The two sets of parents would never meet.)

The honeymoon consisted of a day and a half in Wharfedale in the village of Grassington, which the newly-weds spent in bed eating sweets and watching television. Then on the Monday morning Victoria reported to the Crucible to reconvene with Julie, whom she'd last seen on the Friday in Manchester, and begin rehearsing *Good Fun*. The play which eventually reached the stage had much in common with *Pals*. It was still about community arts and featured a cystitis rally, a feminist Punch and Judy show and four women: drippy arts coordinator Liz, her sarky pal Elsie, gloomy pregnant teenager Lynne and batty cosmetics saleswoman Betty. Victoria added more male hangers-on. 'I couldn't bear the thought of rehearsing with just women,' she confessed to Robert Howie.[75] The action moved out of Liz's flat and into a community arts centre which, inspired by Rochdale Youth Theatre Workshop, Victoria stipulated should be 'the top floor of an old neglected building'. In a chaotic plot crammed with loopy twists and soapy revelations, the characters all find themselves somehow enlisted to run the weekend art festival.

At the recommendation of Peter James, the orchestration was put in the hands of David Firman, who had recently worked on *Chicago* and *Cabaret* at the Crucible and would be Victoria's main musical arranger for the next twenty years. He straight away found out who he was dealing with when sent to meet Victoria in Morecambe. After hearing what she'd composed he suggested some more sophisticated settings: 'Vic said, "No, I like them the way they are." When we got into rehearsal, I thought, she's dead right. This is her language.'

The theatre was abuzz. 'Vic had become our darling after *Talent*,' says André Ptaszynski, an associate producer at the Crucible. 'With this new play, it was an exciting time for everybody in the building.' She was invited to open a new independent bookshop and was the subject of no fewer than three television profiles. Brian Glover, the actor famous for *Kes*, interviewed her for Yorkshire TV arts programme *Calendar Carousel* as they walked arm in arm through the streets. Granada filmed her in her flat in Morecambe for a programme called *Celebration*; she energetically leapt from a wicker chair over to the piano to demonstrate songs, which she also performed to a studio audience in Manchester. Among the new songs from *Good Fun* was 'I've Had It Up to Here', a languid assault on the sexual demands of men who 'tend to feel a failure / If you don't love their genitalia / Though why you should, Christ only knows'. 'Nothing personal, boys,' she said to the audience. 'Just bitter experience.' *Celebration* was broadcast the same night in March as a report on Victoria for *Arena*, the BBC arts strand. In both, her confidence occluded her coyness, but when booked to promote the play live on Radio Hallam she was too shy to go alone and dragged the rest of the cast along; she and Julie got into trouble for boldly using language that was not yet acceptable even in a late-night broadcast.

There were two Victorias in the rehearsal room, inside which David Leland instigated a rule that she was to be seen as an actress, and only outside it could she be addressed as the writer. 'That was open to having the piss ripped out of it,' says Gregory Floy, who became her natural ally in the cast. 'She'd say, "I can't answer because I'm not

Veronica Wood the writer. Why don't you ask the writer?'" It was not immediately apparent that the show would get any laughs, especially when Leland asked for quiet in rehearsal. 'D. Leland is going off his nut,' she reported. 'We are not allowed to laugh at the jokes, which is a bit of a drag for me cos I am not convinced any of it is funny yet.'[76]

She need not have worried. On the opening night in April the audience roared at gags about sex, class and community arts. Victoria smuggled in more personal jokes about magicians, *That's Life!*, even her memories of being made by her mother to pick wool from hedge-rows as a child. The most reliable source of comedy was Betty, the first of Julie's many hunchbacks. She based her performance on a continuity woman they'd encountered at Granada, also called Betty. 'She had a bit of a lisp,' says Julie. 'She was quite bossy.' One day they wanted to visit the ladies and the lock wasn't working so Betty stood outside and flung her arms across the doorway: 'She said, "It's all right, it's all right, it's all right, Victoria. I'm guarding!" Every time we saw one another: "I'm guarding." "Are you guarding?" "Yes!" "We're guarding." Lots of my characters were her.' Betty had a paralysing power over audiences and even the cast. 'I had this speech – "never lay my hand on a strange knob". There was one night the laughter was so intense, the whole place was vibrating and everybody was trying to hold it together onstage and in the end we couldn't, it was just too infectious. Everybody roared.'

It was in *Good Fun* that Victoria first used Julie as a mouthpiece for flyaway speeches that mocked middle-class smugness: 'Today's young, they don't comprehend the meaning of home entertainment – they turn to each other's private parts out of sheer boredom. In my day, it wasn't remotely the same. I kept myself happy for years with a couple of bobbins and a crochet hook.'

This was the cue for a frenetic tango showstopper called 'Handi-crafts' in which a disco-dancing Betty sang of the joys of keeping yourself busy. Among those who had no choice but to laugh at *Good Fun* were the Birmingham University friends who had introduced Victoria to community arts. 'We were squirming in our seats,' says Steve Trow, who went with his wife. 'It punctured all of our preten-tions. The women against cystitis rally – that's exactly what we were doing, protests and marches and demos with women involved. And she was just taking the piss out of it all.' He duly told Chrissie Poulter than she was the model for Liz, prompting Victoria to write a long letter to her friend clarifying that 'they seem to have got the wrong end of the stick . . . and decided it was all about you which I swear by God, coke and the East Yorkshire school of driving – it isn't.'[77]

Yet something wasn't right about the play. At the recommendation of Michael Codron, the role of Liz went to Annabel Leventon, who had starred in the hippie musical *Hair* and formed the all-girl group Rock Bottom. She wasn't Victoria's type and they didn't click. In an ending that confused the audience, she was left alone on the stage to sing the defiant title song. Her role as the butt of the joke was made more uncomfortable by the fact that the character mainly kicking her in the shins was played by the playwright. 'Are these cloves?' asks Liz, planning parsnip wine. 'No,' says Elsie, 'they're carpet tacks.' When Richard Stone came up to see *Good Fun* with Michael Codron, he told his client, 'But, darling, you've written yourself the soubrette.' There was no dramatic function to Elsie. 'They asked me to be in this play,' Victoria told *Arena*, 'and I said, "No, I don't want to.' They said, "Well, if you're not in it, we're not going to do it." So I wrote myself a part which I thought I could manage, which is really me with all the horrible bits knocked out.'[78] (In her foreword to the published text she said Elsie 'is not really a part at all. It is some jokes and an anorak.'[79]) As for her performance, she was not quite a theatre animal. Sue Wallace, a fellow cast member, sensed that Victoria 'wasn't that confident as an actress. She tended to be slightly outside of it as well as inside. She was watching the reaction of the audience.'

The critics laughed along heartily – 'the conception of this anti-musical is monstrous and daring'[80] – but one argued that 'Miss Wood invents jokes better than situations, and *Good Fun* hasn't much dramatic coherence.'[81] Less attention had gone on structure and character. From his seat at the piano David Firman noticed that 'the play became much smaller than the big punchlines. The audience didn't really know how to take it.' Only Irving Wardle in *The Times* seemed to think *Good Fun* was about anything: 'Miss Wood's meaning is stonily clear: ask to be exploited and you will be . . . I hope we see it in London.'

Michael Codron was unpersuaded that *Good Fun* belonged in the West End, forcing the Crucible to rethink. One morning David Leland knocked on Peter James's door: 'I opened it and sitting in the office was Peter and Vic and whoever else. They all looked very sheepish and guilty. The upshot was that Vic was going to go away and rewrite.' Leland and the production parted company, and James appointed himself to restage the play. 'Play goes back to Sheffield in July to get it right,' Victoria told Robert Howie.[82]

When she returned to Sheffield in the summer she would have to do without Julie: 'I said to Vic, "I really don't want to be in the West End for a year – that's what Codron will want." She understood, though she was a bit deflated by it.' Besides, Julie had an alternative offer from the Royal Shakespeare Company: a short run in a new play called *Educating Rita*. After her own theatrical failure, Victoria was not in a generous mood when Julie showed her Willy Russell's two-hander: 'She went, "I don't think much of that. That's not going to do very well."'

# 9

# AND WALTERS

'I think they must have driven around in a bus saying, "If you don't like laughing, get on this bus and we'll go to Granada and we'll show you some sketches you're not going to enjoy!"'
Interview with BBC Additional Programmes Unit, 2009

As the 1970s came to a close, the *Observer* identified eighty people in public life to watch in the 1980s. Among the politicians and QCs was 'Victoria Wood, 27, actress, singer, pianist, playwright, composer and lyricist.'[1] There was another job description Victoria hankered to add to the list, and she expressed it in a song. While Maureen is upstairs on a mission to lose her virginity, downstairs Julie chats with an old-school northern comic. Finding her funny, he offers Julie the chance to assist him onstage, which prompts her to break into 'I've Always Fancied Being a Comedienne'. 'Imagine getting wages,' she drools, 'for taking the piss out of men.'

Through the character of Julie, Victoria gave voice to a fantasy. It's Maureen who pipes up as the voice of reason. 'You couldn't stand up and tell jokes,' she says. 'Girls don't.' But girls had. The casting for *Nearly a Happy Ending* hinted as much. Playing the attendant who cleans the ladies' loos was Jill Summers. Now a gravel-voiced septuagenarian, when she entertained troops during the war she was billed as a Lancashire comedienne. She was recommended to Victoria by Geoffrey, who marvelled at her outrageous antics when he worked as a flyman at City Varieties in Leeds.

Since the summer of 1978, Victoria's commitments had curtailed her opportunities to perform solo, and such bookings had not always gone well. One gig, organised through Geoffrey's new agent early in 1979, put them in front of a packed audience at York University. After doing his act Geoffrey watched hers from the back as she tried out some new material with no means of amplification: 'She struggled from the beginning. No one could hear properly and the show went downhill. I went for a walk round the building. As I came back two indignant guys were leaving. One said to the other, "That was awful. It was like watching *What the Papers Say*." I was mortified. It felt as if all the work we'd done was going down the pan. I never told Vic.' In the face of such calamities, Victoria was dauntless. 'I would much rather be out doing my own show,' she admitted when *Talent* was about to be shown.

Things started to shift when she secured a booking in January 1980 at a hundred-seat venue on the Lancaster University campus. 'Victoria Wood entertains' promised the poster. Under it, as if racked with self-doubt about such a lofty boast, she added further improbable claims in her own handwriting: 'chocolate's not fattening, sex cures cancer'. The *Observer*'s prediction was added in a diagonal strip: 'Stop press: Victoria Wood voted one of eighty for the Eighties'. Tickets cost £1.25.

At home in Morecambe, Victoria and Geoffrey devoted time to preparing for this one-off date. 'We started talking about how Vic might start being the first female stand-up comic,' he says. 'We were trying to find her style. What is a female comedian? Is she different from a male one? If so, how?' Victoria had just about graduated to giving a spoken introduction to each song from the piano stool and the odd short monologue. As for getting up on her feet, 'That was a very big deal and very scary,' says Geoffrey. 'If Vic stood up, she would be doing something unheard of. Men stood up; women stayed sitting.' Most venues she'd played up to that point had only one microphone, set up for her to sing into, which inhibited movement. At the Minor Hall in Lancaster she went and stood in the crook of the piano and picked up a handheld microphone hidden inside the instrument.

Because there were no female comedians, nor was there any template for how to dress. Other women who had made audiences laugh – Jill Summers, Suzette Tarri, Beryl Reid, Nellie Wallace – were all products of music hall who came on in character. Victoria proposed to come on as herself. She and Geoffrey established that she should not go back to the kind of dress she'd loathed wearing on *That's Life!* A skirt would cause men to look at her differently, so it had to be trousers. She decided she ought to wear a tie. 'This was for the audience's sake,' says Geoffrey. 'The audience expected jokes to come out of a masculine frame, and so in some way there needed to be something masculine about her.' (She would come to regret this as, aided by her feather cut, she was often assumed to be lesbian.) That night in Lancaster Victoria wore a square-cut grey tweed jacket and desert boots. She would admit to being 'not very fashion-conscious. As long as it's this year's gravy spilt down the front, I'm happy.'[2]

She opened with 'Comedienne' and added new songs from *Good Fun* and *Start the Week*. But the real innovation was Victoria's first foray into stand-up. The main setpiece was a monologue – written in an exercise book and tested on Geoffrey – about living in Morecambe, a subject she had already tackled in her unused radio comedy *Sunny Side Up*, from which she recycled the odd joke: the pier was 'a council house on a stick' and the residents wore 'kiss-me-quick hearing aids'. In the radio script she'd called it Pigwood on Sea, but this time she didn't shroud the town's identity. 'See Naples and die,' she said. 'See Morecambe and feel as if you already have.' She depicted pavements strewn with empty tins of denture cleaner and nosy neighbours so enfeebled they need Social Services 'to help twitch the lace curtains for them'. 'Morecambe' was mainly a twentysomething's ruthless assault on decrepit retirees, in which Victoria gave vent to conflicted feelings about her adopted home. It also found her bluntly scanning the female body for laughs. At a keep-fit class her head gets stuck between the legs of the leotard-clad instructor: 'I was thinking, I must trim our privet.' At the slimming club the girls 'are so enormous men have to have a heavy goods licence to ask them to dance'. Victoria also brought back her WI monologue, first performed in 1977, while in a shorter monologue about her schooldays she wasn't too proud to feminise patter nicked from Jasper Carrott: 'I went to a mixed school, all girls – half of them were really common and half of them were really posh.' During the laughs, or in the gaps where they were meant to be, she brandished a cigarette to give herself something to do.

Throughout the spring Victoria picked up further practice as part of a double bill with Geoffrey, who urgently needed the work. These were booked usually on a Sunday when venues were free and Victoria was not otherwise engaged with *Good Fun* – in a *Guardian* interview she cheekily touted for business at £400 per gig. The most successful was at Theatre Royal Stratford East in early May, trailed in the theatre listings: 'Sun. 8pm. Victoria Wood in Concert, with magician The Great Soprendo. Tkts £1–£3.' Victoria recorded her verdict on the performance in a notebook: 'Did two encores. They were in a good mood . . . Need a new encore.' In the same book Geoffrey jotted down thoughts for her consideration. 'Announce the Handicrafts song from the piano,' he advised. 'Careful of speeding up too much in the patter.' By the time she was asked back to close the Lancaster Literary Festival a few weeks later, Victoria was ready for an audience of hundreds. This was a prestigious booking: the week-long festival also lured John Updike, Lillian Hellman, Melvyn Bragg and Alan Plater. 'V good show,' she noted. 'Good enthusiastic audience. I was quite relaxed being a bit more familiar with the new material and having rehearsed the songs.'[3] It yielded the first ever review of Victoria as a solo performer, published in the *Lancashire Evening Post*, which praised her 'original wit and stunning professionalism' as well as her 'welcome departure from male-based jokes about sex . . . It must have been one of the happiest nights the Duke's Theatre has ever seen.'[4] She was learning the craft of stand-up comedy at pace. At a gig in Woolwich she was told by friends in the audience that she was talking too fast. 'But you often have to with a small house,' she reasoned, 'so they don't feel inhibited.'[5]

A week after Lancaster, *Nearly a Happy Ending* was broadcast. On the same day Radio 4 interviewed Victoria about her comic tastes for a show called *It Makes Me Laugh*. But the question of how to make others laugh now preoccupied her. 'I'm trying to be a stand-up comic,' she informed the *Radio Times*, 'but to do it in a new way, not to repeat the old pattern.'[6] Hers was a radical plan to reinvent not just herself, but the whole landscape of comedy. 'We don't really have that sort of comedienne in this country at the moment,' she argued, 'so why not me? I'm as well qualified as anyone.'[7]

At this point, very few people had seen Victoria tell a joke, which Russell Harty attempted to rectify by inviting her onto a pilot for a new literary review show called *All About Books*. Aside from her bashful appearances to promote *Good Fun*, this was the first time she had ever properly spoken on television as herself, and she treated it as an opportunity for display. In front of a studio audience, Harty introduced her as 'a lady commentator from Morecambe' who was 'very much flavour of the month'. On a serious panel including the Trinidadian writer C.L.R. James, she demolished four books about country living. One, which she refused to read because of its antique spelling, 'looked like a ransom note from Just William'.

Meanwhile, Victoria remained committed to *Good Fun*. After its first run ended, Michael Codron pointed out that none of the male characters spoke a single word to one another. She addressed this and added three new songs to a rewrite she submitted to Peter James, at whose insistence she stripped out some gags. Polly James, one of the original Liver Birds, replaced Annabel Leventon; Meg Johnson came in for Julie Walters. The day it reopened in June, a production of *Talent* began a run in North Hollywood. Victoria found herself fielding a barrage of queries from a baffled female director in Los Angeles such as 'Who is Eric Morecambe?' and 'Is Leslie Crowther a real person?' Back in Sheffield, she was falling out of love with *Good Fun*: 'It's terrible sitting there thinking, God this is boring and *I* wrote it *and* I'm acting in it.'[8] She asked Julie Walters if she might be free to rejoin the cast in a putative London transfer, but she was ever more tied to *Educating Rita*. 'It means we'll be in the W. End together,' Julie reassured her.[9] In fact, Michael Codron came up again and decided not to risk it on West End audiences. Victoria would always regard his decision as a disappointment but acknowledged the fault was hers. 'There was something terribly wrong with it,' she conceded. 'Why I just didn't end up on a huge laugh I don't know. People used to leave the theatre completely puzzled.'[10]

It wasn't quite the end of the line for the play. The King's Head, a small theatre above a pub in Islington, decided to mount a new production in the autumn. This soon brought about a second booking. Victoria had earlier sent some material to Dan Crawford, the theatre's impulsive director. He knew nothing about her, but, having heard about the Stratford East show with Geoffrey, Crawford booked them sight unseen to fill a vacant fortnight. When they came into the theatre, Geoffrey did all the talking. 'Vic was very shy and didn't say much,' says Crawford's colleague Jenny Bialek. 'She kept her head down and looked up under her fringe. It took her a while to feel at ease with us.'

Crawford proposed calling their double bill *Funny Turns*. They subtitled it *One Good Turn Deserves Another* and Victoria's half was trailed as 'A smile, a song and a lot of eye make-up'. 'As we started to do it together, we had a responsibility to make this a show,' says Geoffrey. 'I would be as camp as you like in the first half and she would walk on and her first line was 'Hello, chaps', the precise antithesis of what you'd just had. She would make friends with them. She developed a technique of watching latecomers and saying, "No, no, it's fine, you get that mac folded." It was new.' A friend told Victoria that 'our act was so good because Geoff wasn't totally masculine, and I wasn't totally feminine'.[11]

They approached the booking 'without any nerves at all,' says Geoffrey, 'because we were filling in, it wasn't full, and nobody knew what it was'. He had grown a steely carapace playing rowdy clubs in Yorkshire since his elimination from *Rising Stars* nearly a year earlier. 'Are you in show business?' he'd say in the Great Soprendo's Hispanic falsetto. 'Well, get your feet off the stage.' As for Victoria, she could confidently draw on a catalogue of songs in a variety of moods: she could be wistful singing 'Fourteen Again' from *Talent*, energetic with 'Handicrafts' from *Good Fun* and solemnly touching with 'Love Song' from *In at the Death*. First performed by others, they were now all reclaimed by her.

Dan Crawford didn't mention that the critics were coming. 'Neither of us had a clue,' says Geoffrey, whose most inflammatory trick involved ripping up a copy of the *Daily Telegraph*. 'If we'd known, it would have been a completely different story.' Victoria was variously praised as 'a cross between a plump and bashful schoolgirl and Joyce Grenfell with claws',[12] who delivered her turn 'as if serving a pound of crumbly Lancashire cheese across the counter of a corner shop'.[13] One review found her observations about sex and slimming 'crude and banal . . . shallow, and a bit patronising'.[14] Michael Billington in the *Guardian* felt she peppered the audience 'with gags like a one-woman firing-squad'.[15] For the lesser-known Great Soprendo there were unanimous raves. 'What splendid reviews Geoffrey got!' Stanley Wood beamed.[16] The capacity of the theatre was about 120, but most nights Crawford squeezed in thirty more. 'Standing room only unless they are left new chairs in will of old lady,' Victoria told Roger McGough.[17]

The intimacy suited her and she began to feel comfortable as a performer. 'I'm not hiding onstage,' she told Mavis Nicholson during the run. 'I'm not pretending to be anybody else onstage.'[18] Nicholson, interviewing her for Thames TV, alluded to her courage in daring as a woman to stand up and tell jokes. 'There's a lot of things that women thought they couldn't do,' replied Victoria. 'I just like to stick my neck out. I like to live dangerously.'[19] In acknowledgement of her pioneering role, Victoria was invited to the Women of the Year lunch at the Savoy. The event, to which she defiantly wore jeans, brought out all her social awkwardness. 'Hardly anybody spoke to me,' she blurted to an interviewer. 'I was sitting opposite a social editor of a glossy magazine and a woman rabbi and some old bat covered in diamonds.'[20] When someone asked her what she did, she mentioned she had a play opening that night, but the conversation closed down when she named the fringe venue.

*Good Fun* followed *Funny Turns* into the King's Head in October, and Victoria did her bit to promote the production. She sang two songs from the show on *On the Town*, a BBC arts programme introduced by Joan Bakewell. But she was ambivalent about the play's instant revival. According to Geoffrey, 'She was worried that it might not fit on the tiny stage and didn't especially relish the idea of watching someone else play Elsie.' That task fell to Nichola McAuliffe, while the thankless role of Liz was handed on to another sitcom refugee,

Paula Wilcox. The play proved beyond rescue. 'It wasn't a very good production,' she reflected later. 'They got their biggest laugh when a lighting bar broke loose and fell into the audience. They called out from the stage, "Don't panic, we'll carry on with the show." The audience were saying, "No honestly, we'd rather panic, please don't go on with the show."'[21] Some critics threw acid: 'A tiny disaster.'[22] 'Miss Wood has spread her wings too wide, and too frivolously. In attempting to do everything, she achieves almost nothing.'[23]

If he had been right to resist transferring *Good Fun*, Michael Codron was keen to bring *Funny Turns* to the West End. Frustratingly Victoria wasn't available, and the idea had to be deferred. Competition for her time came, as ever, from Peter Eckersley, who pressed for a third drama about Maureen and Julie. She was reluctant after the mixed reaction to *Nearly a Happy Ending*. Critics, male ones especially, were not persuaded by Maureen's sexual quest. Russell Davies wearied of 'great Clapham Junctions of one-liners . . . When we get over the novelty of Miss Wood, this is destined to be her biggest fault.'[24] That wormed its way under her skin, as did a barb from Herbert Kretzmer in the *Mail*, who suggested that she was 'stuck in a self-admiring rut . . . she should now be advised to stop giving interviews to every magazine and TV arts programme under the sun, and concentrate instead on perfecting her craft'.[25] 'She was really pissed off about that,' says Geoffrey.

While Victoria hated reading about herself, at this stage she was reliant on good press. 'If they say something bad, I always believe it,' she told one interviewer. 'If they say something good, I *can't* believe it.'[26] The critique that could not be avoided came from the proprietor of Preedy's, their newsagent in Morecambe. 'Not very good last night, Victoria!' he hollered at her. 'We expect more from you than that!" According to Geoffrey, 'That put the tin lid on it. It confirmed something we'd always known, which was that this little lovely funny old town was absolutely the wrong place to be if you were on the telly.' They walked over the road to an estate agent, spotted an end-of-terrace cottage in a picturesque village up the coast, viewed it the next day and, while the move itself took far longer than expected, they didn't look at any other property.

Victoria was adamant that she also needed to move on creatively. 'I turned down a few thousand pounds by refusing to write a third Julie and Maureen play,' she said. 'I thought it was a brave decision at the time. And then they offered me money to do what I wanted so I got my reward.'[27] What she wanted was to carry on with Julie Walters but to rediscover that extraordinary high they both felt when performing 'Sex' at the Bush Theatre. According to Baz Taylor, the idea crystallised during the shoot for *Nearly a Happy Ending*: 'Peter said, "These two girls are made for each other. I want to get the two of them just doing comedy sketches."' In Victoria's version, Eckersley 'asked me if I wanted to have my own show. I said, "I don't want to carry a whole show on my own. Can Julie be in it as well?" And we sat in a room for a day before anybody thought of the title *Wood and Walters*.'[28]

That autumn Victoria found time to script a pilot episode with four songs and four sketches. She eased her burden by borrowing from *Good Fun* and sent the results to her co-star. 'I just loved it instantly and couldn't wait,' says Julie. 'I thought, all of the stuff feels like mine, not something I've got to interpret.' After a week's rehearsal it was recorded in front of a receptive studio audience in Manchester. The two stars were dressed up to the nines in burgundy satin (Wood) and a plunging jumpsuit (Walters). 'Vic hated it because of her size,' says Julie. 'We both felt a bit pushed about in what we would wear. There was an uncomfortableness about it for both of us. She particularly didn't know what power she had then in being the writer and the performer.'

'Good evening, ladies and gentlemen,' said Victoria as they trotted onto a raised studio stage. 'Or for those of you with video recorders, where did you get the money?' They flagged the show as 'Two creatures great and small' or 'Wood is thicker than Walters', and introduced the band led by Jim Parker, which he filled with a quirky array of instruments to reflect Victoria's enjoyment of his Betjeman album *Banana Blush*. Unusually, it was only after the introductions that the title sequence rolled while Victoria sat at the piano and sang 'Turned Out Nice Again', a breezy song from *Good Fun*, comically shooing Julie away as if to establish her priority. Also lifted from the play was Betty, reincarnated as Dotty, a self-appointed agony aunt in a pink twin-set and blonde perm, who describes herself as the co-authoress of *Wuthering Womanhood*. 'This is my problem slot,' she announces, before realising it might sound like a bawdy reference to a nether region. 'I'm sorry, can we change that?' she calls off-camera. 'I've never liked it.' Dotty dispensed her tips on nookie before breaking into 'Handicrafts', in which she was joined by a lithe and nearly naked black male dancer.

Victoria would soon become the preeminent sketch-writer of her generation, and her very first foray was a promise of things to come. She played an unsophisticated woman sent by a computer on a blind date with a cultured but nervous man in pinstripes. Unlike him, she hasn't been to university. 'I was thinking of going,' she explains, 'but my mother thought I'd get better lunches in an office.' 'Do you like Manet?' he asks. 'Well, I spend it when I've got it obviously.'

The everyday preoccupations Victoria would make her own were all here: body image, sex and relationships, the specific minutiae of domestic life. She and Julie wore leotards and commented on other women in a fitness class. 'I'm bent over between her lower limbs,' said Victoria, borrowing from her Morecambe monologue, 'thinking I must trim our privet.' Julie played a Scouse hairdresser who yaks about sex: 'Oh, I do it, you know. Don't get me wrong. But I don't smile or nuttin'.' Together they sang 'Phone-In'. Composed for *Start the Week*, it was a melancholy portrait of a lonely single woman who from a phone box flirts with her favourite DJ on air before trudging back to her bedsit, 'short and stumpy up the stairs / Grey hair spread upon the pillow'. The show closed with a song in the bonkers style of GRIMMS, which experimented with self-referential jokes:

> But when you've got Victoria Wood completely mixed up with Pam Ayres
> We feel that you have come to the wrong place.

Two nights before *Wood and Walters* was broadcast, Victoria was herself in the wrong place, singing 'Fourteen Again' on Granada's *There Goes 1980*, a cheesily wholesome variety round-up co-presented by the middle-of-the-road Northern Irish comic Roy Walker. Her own show was to be the antidote to such fare. 'I've just recorded a TV show for New Year's (Wood and Walters),' Victoria nonchalantly informed Robert Howie. '10.20pm if you can stick Dr Zhivago first.'[29] In the event she was disappointed by the pilot when it was broadcast on 1 January 1981. 'She thought it wasn't up to her standard,' says Geoffrey. 'She just wanted to be Morecambe and Wise and realised that hadn't happened.' Two fan letters caught her attention: 'One advising me to wear crimplene dresses in dark colours, one saying I should be ashamed of myself, my mind is obsessed by intercourse. As if!'[30] Nonetheless Peter Eckersley was satisfied enough to commission seven more episodes.

First, she had to complete the third film in her Granada trilogy, to be directed once more by Baz Taylor. 'All over Xmas up to March I will be doing the writing,' she told Roger McGough. 'Nescafe and new biros.'[31] Having said all she needed to about female friendship, she was finished with Maureen and Julie ('in our minds they got killed in a car crash on the way home').[32] Instead she got the green light to write a love story with no role for her. The title she chose was *Bonkers About You*, later changed to *Living Together* and finally to *Happy Since I Met You*. Julie Walters was to play Frances, a drama teacher under pressure to tie the knot and have babies. One night she makes her escape from a toe-curling dinner party with a like-minded actor called Jim. They take a shine to each other, but she is nervous of commitment. 'I'm dead crabby,' she warns. They launch into a sexual relationship but then the mood sours. Frances comes home one day to find Jim's actor friends being pretentious. There is an outbreak of violence – Frances clouts Jim who shoves her back. Frances runs away on the train. Eventually Jim catches up with her and they reconcile in a greasy spoon. Jim was Victoria's first portrait of male decency, but this remained a woman's story, which Victoria made clear by giving monologues to her female protagonist.

She had some influence over casting. 'I made a list of all my favourite actresses and then tried to fit them to parts.'[33] They included Fidelis Morgan, Sue Wallace and Tracey Ullman, who had been in a revival of *Talent* at the Liverpool Everyman. The role of Jim was intended for Gregory Floy, but he was unavailable, so Peter Eckersley called in a gangly ginger-haired beanpole in his mid-thirties called Duncan Preston. When he arrived for his audition everyone was out to lunch. 'Julie and Vic came back a bit pissed,' he says. 'They were really, really noisy. Julie was taking the piss, kept saying, "God, he's tall! I'd have to jump up to hit him!" It was like being in front of a firing squad. The producer and director were trying to calm them down, but it wasn't very successful. I rang my agent and said, "I don't think for a minute that I would want to work with them. They were just out of order." He said, "They've just offered you the part." I was absolutely gobsmacked.'

Victoria was on set for the whole shoot in Manchester. 'I'm not in it so I just stand around on location in my anorak,' she grumbled to Rosalind. 'What I've seen so far isn't v. good but there's another two weeks yet.' Her frustration communicated itself to Duncan Preston: 'That was the first time she'd worked on film. She wasn't used to all the waiting. I got the sense that she wasn't happy with some of it.' Her sense of exclusion was exacerbated when the two stars enjoyed what Julie calls 'a bit of a romantic encounter' – Duncan backed Aldaniti in the Grand National and they blew his winnings on a weekend in a hotel. Once Victoria saw the first edit she was no happier. 'I was trying to do something different,' she confided to Robert Howie, 'and I should have had a different director really. It was all on film, which should have been great but just meant there was no time for rehearsal because they took so long to focus the camera. However, I am prepared to be hammered by the critics, tho this time I don't think I'm to blame.'[34]

To push the story along, Victoria wrote songs to be played over montages of Frances and Jim. Over the worst of their rows, the jolly title song plays. Another lilting song evoked the Beatles and the recent assassination of John Lennon:

Love was once an easy thing, I never disagreed
With Lennon and McCartney that love is all you need
But love just made me wash my hair and hover by the phone
And Lennon's dead and I'm bored with love, I'm happy on my
  own.

The script was rich with Victoria's signature wit, much of it about the reality of relationships with boring men who do DIY and bell-ringing. A colleague of Frances complains about a measly Christmas present from her fiancé: 'Last year I got Estée Lauder Youth Dew, a sapphire pendant, *Country Diary of an Edwardian Lady* and car seat covers.' In a health-food café Frances is served by a gloomy woman who is only there because her sister 'put her neck out unscrewing a jar of beetroot'. Two of Victoria's favourite words – raffia and guttering – took their first bow in a script of hers. Above all, in Frances she set out to create a frank portrait of a real woman who admits to farting, having 'breath like a car crash' and a history of bad relationships with men. 'When I lived on me own, and I got depressed,' says Frances, 'at least I didn't have to *explain* it or analyse it with somebody else.' Squalls and squabbles had been part of the fabric of their relationship from the start, according to Geoffrey: 'We found each other difficult to live with. There were frequent niggles, arguments and rows. The reasons were often trivial – usually pathetically so. We knew each other so well and were tuned in to each other's thoughts so acutely that a misplaced word or a frustrated glance could cause a minor explosion.' Doing press to promote the drama, Victoria suggested that 'Geoff's certainly a much nicer person than me'.[35] One source of tension was to be found in their contrasting rhythms in the tiny space they occupied in Morecambe, which didn't lend itself to creativity. 'We both work at home and it's a tiny flat with one bedroom,' Victoria told Rosalind. 'If people stay they have to sleep on the living room floor – which means I can't do any work . . . I work at nights and Geoff practises tricks all day – it's a bit odd.'[36]

One visit to the flat Victoria did sanction was by a documentary crew from Thames Television. *The English Programme* observed her working at her desk as she explained her process in composing a song for the Equal Opportunities Commission. Geoffrey worked on a rope trick in front of her. They both found the intrusion of the film crew intensely awkward, and it showed. When the programme was broadcast in March, the contrast between the downcast eyes of the interviewee and the bright commanding gaze of the performer was conspicuous.

Victoria's introverted side could act as a drag anchor on her career. When a researcher from *Parkinson* came up to Morecambe to audition her for the most prestigious chat show on television, she clammed up and reported to Geoffrey that 'the researcher had no idea who she was or what she might be able to offer and had annoyed her from the word go. So Vic's shyness – perhaps better described as ennui or simple lack of interest – started to kick in. When that happened, nothing could shift it.' She didn't get on *Parkinson* for another twenty years.

But there was plenty of other exposure to be had. In March, before an audience in Manchester, Victoria took part in the pilot episode of *The Little and Large Party*, to be broadcast on Radio 2. She sang 'Never Spend a Fortnight on a Health Farm' from all the way back in 1975. 'We'd never really heard of her,' says Eddie Large. 'She seemed really shy and introverted and we were thinking, why have they booked this girl? As soon as she gets on the piano she was a genius.' The rest of the songs, also from her back catalogue, were recorded and slotted in over the six-week series. She contributed songs to a Mother's Day anthology on Radio 4 called *The Price of Daffs Has Doubled* and sang on *Mid-Week: Russell Harty's People*. In April she made the first of many appearances on *Call My Bluff*, and formed a warm friendship with the avuncular wordsmith Arthur Marshall, whose passion for *Crossroads* matched her own.

Victoria and Geoffrey had always avoided travelling for fear they'd miss out on a career-changing break if out of the country. When they took a spring holiday in southern Spain it was Victoria's first time abroad since the Wood family caravan trips. Geoffrey assured her it would be hot. 'We're in Marbella watching the rain fall and English people being rude to the waiters,' she told Rosalind on a postcard.[37] They stayed in cheap B&Bs and got about in ancient trains. Among their holiday reading was Keith Waterhouse's satire *Office Life*, which they read aloud to each other. Back at home Victoria sent the author a fan letter which soon resulted in lunch. She felt a kindred spirit with him because 'like me he's a jolly person who writes about sad things'.[38]

In May Victoria embarked on a short northern tour of village community centres arranged by North West Arts. This was a way of staying in shape as a live comedian, but it was also an important step: at a time when this was still more or less unheard of, Victoria completed two halves of an evening's entertainment. She was wary of making such a bold step – 'I had to persuade her,' says Geoffrey. With audiences minuscule wherever she went, it was a chastening comedown after the high of *Funny Turns*. Then, for several months, Victoria was chained to her desk. 'Do come up and stay in the summer,' she urged Robert Howie. 'I'll be here on my own most of the time writing episodes 2-8 of "Wood and Walters". (I've just been paid for it all, which has made it all frighteningly definite.)'[39] To Rosalind she described herself 'chewing a biro every night trying to write sketches'.[40] Helpfully, Peter Eckersley remained happy for her to submit existing songs, and Jim Parker was set to work 'Music and Movement', 'Don't Get Cocky', 'Fourteen Again', 'Love Song', 'Comedienne' and 'If Only the Blood Matched My Dress'. There would also be guests, among them Jill Summers and John Dowie. To look for fiery young alternative talent, Eckersley took Victoria to one of the new comedy clubs in London. Rik Mayall was booked and alarmed Victoria when he mentioned a new comic pairing: 'He said, "Have you heard about these girls French and Saunders?" I thought, I don't like the sound of them. We don't need more girls in comedy, thank you. I kept well clear of them for years.'[41]

As she wrote, Victoria was encouraged by her producer. 'You did say keep the thoughts coming,' he wrote, proposing she be inspired by a Janet Reger underwear catalogue or an item from *National Lampoon* magazine about homosexual beekeepers. He envisaged a slow pan 'of girls in boob tubes. The first three look really like sisters, then the slow pan reveals mum, dad, suckling child . . . Can't think of a punchline. This is what is known as an ill-formed idea.'[42] Victoria worked it up into a parody of the clean-cut Irish girl group in gold-lamé tunics who include an alcoholic, a nymphomaniac and kleptomaniac, with a lead singer who would rather work a till at the Co-op. She called it 'The Reluctant Nolan' and on the lyric sheet specified that it should be sung by 'Vic and three genuine singers preferably a current sister act'. Eckersley's suggestions could be quite vague: 'two women in adjoining hospital beds'; 'two women on a coach-tour'.[43] He warmed to her Women's Institute character from

Victoria's parents Stanley and Helen Wood met at a Communist Youth League event in 1937.

'A lovely baby in every way' is welcomed home by her sisters Penelope (left) and Rosalind.

Victoria and her father having fun by the seaside in Whitby.

'Where it all happened': Birtle Edge House in the snow.

Helen coaxes a camera-shy young Vicky.

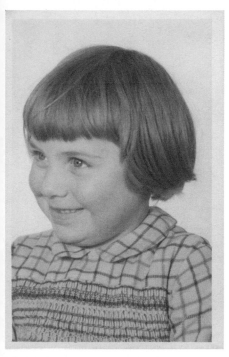

Victoria mugs for the photobooth camera with Rosalind.

Throughout primary school Victoria was near the top of the class.

'They were very glamorous': Victoria in her NHS glasses and duffel coat with her sisters Rosalind (left) and Penelope.

Playing Autolycus in *The Winter's Tale* at school, Victoria wore 'these really horrible brown tights that looked like Ryvita'.

Photobooth fun with schoolfriends Lesley Fitton (front) and Anne Sweeney.

Looking up to her first boyfriend Bob Mason in Rochdale Youth Theatre Workshop, where Victoria found that 'suddenly there were things I could do'.

With fellow drama student Steve Trow . . .                . . . and Robert Howie.

At the end of her second year in Birmingham, Victoria performed to a university audience, along with Sahlan Diver (kneeling) and Bill Lloyd (seated). Beforehand they posed for photographs in the basement.

At an early performance in Birmingham, Victoria learns to sing over her right shoulder.

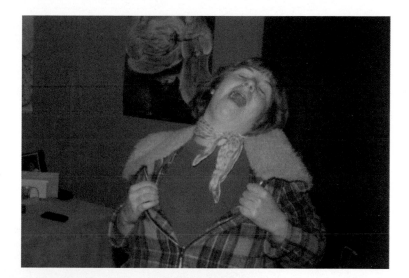

Larking in
Birmingham.

Victoria devoured
books whenever and
wherever.

'She'd been on the
telly and she was a
winner': Celia Imrie
was nervous the first
time she met Victoria
in 1975.

Austerity party at Harrods, 1976. Victoria wears factory overalls, Robert Howie is shirtless, Fidelis Morgan wears a tie, Chrissie Poulter is smoking and Celia Imrie is the nurse on the right.

'John Dowie does songs about amputees and cripples and halibut.'

*Funny Turns* and suggested a weekly monologue on training dogs or sex education or cosmetics. While Victoria did do her WI speech, the regular item became Dotty's Slot, in which Julie dispensed tips on a random variety of topics: burning bras, flatulence, insulating your loft with dog biscuits, culture ('I think Shakespeare did awfully well for a Brummie'). Victoria used Dotty as a way of savaging middle-class pretension: she receives one letter from a woman 'with all the trappings of success – a loft conversion, a ceramic hob and a daughter with anorexia'.

Eckersley couldn't let one old idea go without a fight: a pair of characters who discuss life and love in a weekly sketch. 'Could we make them two barmaids? (Called, perhaps, Julie and Maureen.)' He imagined them crushing the romantic approaches of 'various smooth-ies, oiks and dickheads'.[44] He would sign off affectionately: 'All the best, kid. P'; 'Love, Pete'.

His letters also covered the recording of the soundtrack for *Happy Since I Met You*, which took place in Manchester towards the end of July. Victoria's uncertainty about the drama lingered. 'The producer and I had another 15 minutes taken out of it,' she told Robert Howie, 'and that improved it a lot.'[45] Billed as 'a love story with songs', it was broadcast on 9 August. 'And hammered on Monday Aug 10,' she wrote on a clipping she cut out of a TV preview page.[46] In fact, although it was savaged in the *Guardian* (her admirer Nancy Banks-Smith was off duty), the other reviews were positive.

It was to be her last creative interaction with Peter Eckersley. That month he was taken ill; tests revealed that he had cancer and it was at an advanced stage. Victoria visited him in hospital and asked if there was anything she could get him. 'There's a very nice blouse in Lewis's window,' he said, a wag to the last. He died on 26 August 1981, aged forty-five. Among his achievements the obituary in *The Times* mentioned 'the first television plays of the dramatist, Victoria Wood'.[47] After the memorial in Manchester his widow Anne Reid presented Victoria with a photograph of her mentor, which she kept near her for the rest of her life. 'I will never forget him, nor will anyone else who ever worked with him,' she told his father James Eckersley. 'I'll never have another friend like him, because he wasn't just a brilliant producer, he was a friend and he used to make me laugh so much. I'm so glad I knew him.'[48]

While Eckersley's death devastated Victoria, only days later she had to fulfil a booking at the Theatre Royal Drury Lane in *The Secret Policeman's Other Ball*, one of a series of all-star entertainments to raise funds for Amnesty International. The only other woman on the bill was Pamela Stephenson. Victoria was too shy to appear in the opening line-up of gnarled comics and rock stars. Wearing a canary-yellow suit she had recently acquired, she performed 'I've Had It Up to Here' from *Good Fun*. 'This song is indicative of my deep interest in the act of physical lovemaking,' she announced. 'It's very short.' She got no laughs on the first night from an audience fed nothing but blue comedy by the male comedians. On the second night she decided to 'go filthy because that was the only way I could keep my head above water'.[49] When the publisher Methuen rushed out a book for Christmas to tie in with the Amnesty show, Victoria contributed a short defiant paragraph: 'Tampax. IUD. Pre-menstrual tension . . . That's the feminist part of the evening over with. I'm worn out. Pamela Stephenson and me are doing our best, but these boys are very demanding: "Suck that cock." "Mark that thesis." Fortunately they're getting on a bit.'

In the autumn Victoria joined her doctor pal Rob Buckman in a series of comic lectures about medicine for Radio 2 called *Get the Most Out of Your Body*. She was reluctant to write songs to order and, having first turned down the commission, squared it with Buckman that she could sing old ones instead. *The Times* critic spotted that her songs 'were not noticeably medical'.[50] Try as she might, she had less success negotiating with Granada, who despite Eckersley's death insisted she go ahead with *Wood and Walters*. Her new producer was Brian Armstrong, whose experience in comedy was with middle-of-the-road marital sitcoms with titles like *Can We Get on Now, Please?*, *Have I Got You . . . Where You Want Me* and *Chintz*. 'I'm having to shoot my mouth off,' Victoria grumbled during production. 'We have to explain so much. Somebody will say, "Why don't you have so-and-so as a guest?" and I have to waste time saying, "He's a boring old git and I don't want him." When I read now that somebody's supposed to be difficult to work with I just think ah, that's somebody else trying to get it right . . . Peter cared about every detail. He'd say, "I don't like your eye-shadow, you should say this or wear that' – but somebody has to fuss.'[51] Julie also felt exposed: 'There was a feeling for both of us that nobody really understood once Peter had gone, who was our mate. We were this little bubble of "nobody else gets it".' Roger Brierley, who had been in *Nearly a Happy Ending* and played authority figures in the show, later recalled Victoria and Julie 'slumped on the Granada rehearsal room floor, alternatively despondent and fucking furious at the inability of whatever that producer's name was who couldn't provide you with what you needed and who seemed to have little understanding of what you were trying to do'.[52]

There were other signs that comedy was not in Granada's DNA. To direct the pilot, and then the series, Eckersley selected Stuart Orme, partly because he was under contract. His experience of comedy was confined to working as a floor manager for Benny Hill and Tommy Cooper. At least he knew Victoria, having filmed her for the Granada profile *Celebration*. 'I didn't have any experience other than that one documentary of illustrating I knew how to deal with comedy,' he says. 'I suspect she realised that. She knew a hundred times more about comedy than I did. She seemed contained, confident and yet vulnerable. But definitely somebody who knew how it needed to be to make it work for the audience and for her.' Jim Parker also felt out of his depth: 'It was a mistake on my part. I'm not very good at being a musical director. I had to play the piano and I wasn't very happy with my own performances.' (In the pilot episode he was introduced as 'Jim Parker on antidepressants'.)

Each episode took a week to complete, comprising a read-through, rehearsal, tech run and taping, done on midweek afternoons, with the disastrous result that the audiences were drawn from the senior end of the demographic. Victoria reported to Geoffrey that it was like 'a jigsaw club for the recently bereaved'. 'We're missing *Brideshead* for this,' one audience member was heard to say. It proved so hard to get a reaction from them that Ted Robbins, a former Butlins redcoat hired to warm them up, resorted to desperate measures. 'Vic and Julie often laughed about this audience of retired ladies,' he says.

'In one of the pauses the floor manager said, "Get on and keep them amused." It was much bigger than anything I'd done before. There was a huge break for twenty minutes. I said, "I've nothing left to do." In desperation, the old rugby player in me came out and I dropped my trousers. It didn't get laughs but a terrible embarrassed silence.' At least Victoria found the disgusted reaction of one woman funny: 'She'd been through two World Wars and a Depression. It was going to take more than Ted's bum to make her crack a smile!'[53]

Victoria was going where no comedian had gone before: the burden of writing and starring in a mainstream sketch comedy had never fallen on a solitary individual. 'I didn't realise quite how much stuff you needed to write in order to be able to throw half of it away,' she later judged. 'I only literally wrote enough for six half hours and it wasn't enough. I should have written more. Some bits of it were good and some of it was deadly.'[54] Ted Robbins was aware she wasn't happy: 'The pressure to deliver got to her. If anything was a bit of a damp squib, you could see it hurt her.' Once, when he could sense her misery, he gave her a consoling hug in a lift: 'I suddenly saw this girl from Bury. She looked so fed up. She hugged me back.' Gregory Floy, who took on most of the younger male roles, encountered a different Victoria to the one he'd known in *Good Fun*. 'Vic was very much the perfectionist in control. I had not really seen her in that mode before. I did think, ooh God. I'd better be careful because she's not in gag mode at the moment.' She was aware of how she must come across: 'Rehearsals consist of lots of biscuits and me saying "You said nearly instead of almost." How they all love me.'[55]

Victoria and Julie were at least dressed as they wished to be in the first recording, with ties at half mast and in suits made for them in Soho, but even here there was angst. 'We spent the first few days buying lots of clothes,' Victoria told Lesley Fitton, 'which was lots of fun when they fitted and v. humiliating if not.'[56] They introduced the series as 'the comedy show with a difference: it's zany, it's offbeat, it doesn't get laughs'. Canned laughter, they promised, would be delivered before the end of the programme. Victoria came to regard the 'hello good evening' segment as misconceived: 'We used to go on together, which was a mistake, I think, because Julie never liked going on as herself. She liked to put a wig on or a false back on or something. So they were always a bit eggy, those bits.'⁵⁷ But the material bore Victoria's unique kitemark. As her schoolgirl practised the piano, she was heckled by Julie's tightly permed old char. 'Do you know "Dream of Olwen"?' she asks. 'It's lovely, that. That were on in women's surgical the night I had my cervix cauterised.' Victoria stood in the crook of the piano to recite her own rhyming verse about the waxwork museum in Morecambe, inspired by her visit there with John Dowie:

The dummies don't change year to year
They're Sabrina and Anthony Eden
And one that we think's Molly Weir
And the one that had been Muhammad Ali
They'd taken this towel off his head
They'd drawn a big line through his label
And put Lenny Henry instead.

One of the most innovative items, shot on film by a canal, was a documentary-style interview with two bored Scouse girls truanting from school ('they don't teach you anything important like how to inject yourself'). Victoria lent one of the girls a joke from *In at the Death* – 'a duvet fell into my shopping bag'.

The series brought Victoria's first assaults on the kind of television she found ridiculous: terrible advertisements, panel shows, game shows, a poncey classical-music quiz. She even attacked a literary talk show just like the one she'd been on presented by Russell Harty, although she redirected her fire towards another professional northerner: 'Next week I'll be talking to Melvyn Bragg about his twenty-ninth Cumbrian novel.' For the first time Victoria cast a celebrity. The sketch was about a star who gets a knock on his dressing-room door from two giggly teens. One name considered for the role was Trevor Chance, the singer who worked with Victoria on *The Summer Show*. 'No, he's not washed up enough,' as she said. In the end they cast Alan Lake, the third husband of Diana Dors, a sleazy seducer who gets more than he bargains for when the girls eagerly strip to their baggy undergarments.

'God love him, he did take it,' says Julie. 'There was something about him that was great fun to puncture, we both felt that.'

In one sketch a woman doesn't realise her husband is trying to get rid of her. 'It was actually his idea that I should swim the Channel,' she explains. The weirdest sketch, touching on the theme of parental neglect, featured Victoria as the mother of 740 babies. 'This is your problem not mine,' she said to Brian Armstrong when she handed in the script. An ad was put out for volunteers and eventually there were seventy tots on screen. 'I've never heard such a row,' said Victoria. 'I'd imagined doing it with dummies, never thought of doing it with real babies. It was awful.'[58] A press photocall harvested letters from cross mothers complaining of cruelty. The closing credits raced through all seventy names, including a baby from Rochdale called Victoria Wood.

Alongside existing songs, there were new numbers. After all those sad songs about dreary marriages that she wrote in the 1970s, Victoria produced a fist-shaking anti-matrimonial duet called 'Don't Do It'. 'Northerners' was a rollicking patter song about entertainers cashing in on the clichés of their roots, possibly a riposte to the *Guardian* review of *Happy Since I Met You*, which attacked Victoria for peddling 'vulgar speeches, which were supposed to reflect the great warm beating heart of the North':[59]

> You just go, tripe, clogs, going to the dogs,
> Wigan and Blackpool tram.
> Brass bands, butties in your hands,
> Whippets and next door's mam.
> Cloth cap, hankie full of snap,
> Shawls and scabby knees.
> Hot-pot, seven to a cot,
> Headscarves and mushy peas.

The song ended on a dark note: 'Dead at forty-five / From a back-street abortionist'. Victoria and Julie in headscarves were backed by a trio of male singers in flat caps. One was a well-disguised John Dowie.

Victoria's anxiety about the show was revealed in little items bookending each episode. She and Julie struggle to get into the studio without ID or wait for a compliment from the producer that never comes. Julie reads out an abusive letter from a viewer who turns out to be her mother – Victoria was perhaps thinking of her own. In one sketch, two actors agree that auditioning for *Wood and Walters* is a new low. It was as if Victoria was attacking herself as a form of defence. 'Usual ITV garbage.' 'I see this one's written by Victoria Wood.' 'Can't write for me.' 'Totally unconvincing when she writes for me.' They agree to rehearse their script, which turns out to consist of the lines they'd just been speaking.

There was the usual web of private and not so private references. As if putting a hex on other funny women of the moment, there were jokes about Marti Caine and Pamela Stephenson. Victoria could be ruthless about offending friends. A rip-off of talent shows called *Search for a Star* featured a 'young hopeful mezzosoprano from Rhuddlan in North Wales'. This sly nod to her former flatmate Jane Wynn Owen was more explicit in the original draft, which refers to 'Celia Wynn-Owen'. In a sketch expressing her disdain for beauty pageants, one of the contestants is named Marlena. Fidelis Morgan had entered her sister Marlena for Miss ATV, which she won, around the same time as she put Victoria's name up for *New Faces*.

*Wood and Walters* began filming in October. After it finished in November, the Houdinis finally managed to make their escape from Morecambe to 22 Stankelt Road in Silverdale. The house was on the edge of the village and stood on the crest of a deep slope with a view out the back down towards Morecambe Bay. Victoria emphasised the discomforts when her sister was due to stay: 'Am warning – it is v. primitive and dirty (everything covered in cement dust).'[60] Granada vouched for Victoria's income stream to help her to secure a mortgage.

The eighteen-month delay in taking possession had several causes. The elderly vendor's son took against the buyers as outsiders while work commitments meant Victoria and Geoffrey were rarely together long enough to make decisions. Then a surveyor discovered all sorts of faults, the worst a pervasive damp whose source was discovered only when a builder in a smart suit asked to see under a trapdoor in the kitchen and promptly sank up to his neck into an old water tank. 'The people who owned house – they really misled me,' Victoria wrote in an article about moving house. 'They disguised a damp cellar by putting in changing rooms and a diving board.' The article, titled 'Tile Though Your Heart Is Aching', was a litany of distress caused by nasty decor, clumsy builders and bone-shaking cold. 'There is ice all over the windows and I have to go into the garden to get warm . . . The pipes freeze so I cannot use the bath or the wash-basin. By this time I am crying a lot so my face is relatively dirt-free.'[61]

Victoria experienced these discomforts – and proudly put up her own bookshelves – alone that first winter while Geoffrey spent the pantomime season in Newcastle. They were reunited at Christmas as guests on *Russell Harty at Home*, hosted by the presenter in his own house on the edge of the Dales. The appearance was perfectly timed to remind viewers of Victoria's existence.

*Wood and Walters* began showing on ITV with a repeat of the pilot on the first day of 1982. Victoria started talking the series down while it was still running: 'Several actors who were wrong for the sketches were hired,' she said. 'I cut a lot out but some of it still makes me wince.'[62] Despite her claim to have cut, she did not produce enough material for the seven episodes originally planned, so Granada tacked a compilation of the best sketches and songs on at the end. The finale was more Walters than Wood, with many sketches powered by the same dynamic of Julie's character being comically foul to Victoria's. 'I would set myself up as a victim, and Julie would be the cruel one and I would be the one she was being cruel to. That was my own chip on my shoulder and my own insecurity about being fat or being northern or whatever that I felt insecure about I worked through in those sketches.'[63] She went about this process pitilessly. In one sketch Victoria seeks advice about make-up. 'It's up to you, Porky,' says Julie's beautician. 'I don't suppose you go out much being so ugly.' It was as if Victoria was using Julie as an instrument of self-harm. 'I thought of it as a character,' says Julie. 'I felt we're showing people what it's like to be Vic, what she's been through. And twats like this character say those kind of things: "What do you think this is, the elephant house?" That's how she felt about herself.'

While applauding Julie's abilities, reviewers acknowledged Victoria as the show's creative genius. 'Is there anything Victoria Wood cannot do?' asked *The Times*.[64] Only the *Financial Times* complained of 'derivative' or 'pointless' sketches, and songs that had all been heard before.[65] During the run of *Wood and Walters*, Victoria turned critic herself on the television review show *Did You See?* She was placed in the odd position of sitting in judgement over rival comedy *O.T.T.*, a late-night version of the rowdy kids' show *Tiswas*, starring, among others, Lenny Henry and John Gorman. 'I thought it was going to wipe *Wood and Walters* off the face of the earth,' she told guest host Mavis Nicholson. 'I thought it was going to be so good I'm going to look like a real fool. And then when it came on, I was quite relieved. I thought, well, it's not that good; it's a bit of mess.' She then conceded the show grew on her.

As for her own comedy, Victoria had a sense of anticlimax over *Wood and Walters*: 'I was very stressed about it all the time because I knew it wasn't really very good,' she recalled – yet the series was a rare achievement which established her as a unique writer-entertainer who could talk honestly about the lives of women, about the female body and the sexual revolution.[66] Above all, whether in sharp suits or babygrows, school uniform or poplin gowns, she and Julie cemented their reputation as a fresh and brilliant partnership.

Victoria's arrival as a new voice in television comedy was under-lined when, much to her surprise, the pilot shown a whole year earlier was nominated opposite Stanley Baker and the Two Ronnies in the light-entertainment category of the 1982 BAFTAs. 'Vic was convinced she wouldn't win, but the nomination was a nice compliment and she took it as such,' says Geoffrey, who went with her. 'In retrospect we reflected that the nomination was a gesture of encouragement to the first light entertainment show to feature a pair of women getting laughs.' (*The English Programme* profile of Victoria was also up in the so-called 'Flame of Knowledge' category.) Granada dangled a second series, but Victoria was unsure. 'I don't know if we can go through a series like this one again,' she said when the series was still running.[67]

At the same time, it was announced that Julie was to film *Educating Rita* alongside Michael Caine. Wood and Walters would barely be seen on TV together for nearly three years.

# IO

# FUNNY HOW THINGS TURN

'Anyway, this year, Victoria thought she'd do a show on her own. By herself. With nobody else there. Not even a fifty-piece orchestra. Not even a man with a mouth organ. I think she's flipped her boko, but she says it's going to be dead good. I suppose I wasn't a very good person to ask, because I don't find comedy funny.'

'Victoria Wood, by the woman across the road',
*Lucky Bag* programme, 1983

Victoria's dramas and sketches, written in the distinct and precise voice of the north, inevitably provoked comparisons with Alan Bennett. Although both were friends of Russell Harty, their initial encounter was accidental. 'I actually first met Victoria in Sainbury's in Lancaster sometime in the eighties,' says Bennett. 'It was, as she might have chosen herself, in the avocado section. I knew of her because Michael Codron who was always singing her praises. I was quite jealous.' It was Julie Walters who first worked with him, in 1982, in a *Play for Today* directed by Gavin Millar, but Bennett imagined collaborating with the pair of them. 'Alan Bennett sent his love,' wrote Julie – 'he wants us to perform his play Doris + Doreen, perhaps at Lancaster.'[1]

There may still have been talk of continuing their double act, but the stars of *Wood and Walters* now went their separate ways. Julie was propelled into a film career, while Victoria followed a twisting track towards an utterly new kind of stardom. The journey had to be made without any kind of map, because, until she decided to do it, no woman had ever walked onto a British stage alone as herself and laid on a whole evening of comedy.

Offers from beyond the world of television and theatre now began to come her way. Her high visibility on ITV had made her attractive to advertisers. Having mined her own weight issues for comedy, she was seen by one agency as the ideal face to front a campaign for a low-calorie drink called One-Cal. The approach initially required her to sing someone else's jingle, but she stood her ground and was allowed to compose her own thirty-second ditties. They displayed in miniature her mastery of wordplay:

> Yes dietin's disquietin'
> And that's exactly why a tin
> Of One-Cal cheers a slimming person up.

She had less control over the design. In one ad she wore white-and-pink togs at a white grand piano in a pink studio. A second ad took her to the Bahamas, where, after she sang her piece, she took a sip of One-Cal as the camera pulled away to reveal the piano on a floating island. There were so many takes that Victoria had to be ferried back to the shore to empty her bladder. 'It made us both sad that the ad industry saw her as a useful fatty,' says Geoffrey, 'but in the case of One-Cal at least, she enjoyed doing them and the money helped.'

Money was certainly needed. Victoria fretted about a popular misconception that because she was on television she must be rolling in it. 'By the time you travel from place to place and run the car,' she sighed, 'there doesn't seem to be anything left.'[2] Her professional partnership with Julie being on hold, she and Geoffrey started working together again. *Funny Turns* returned for the first time in eighteen months with such a long stretch of bookings in London that they decided to rent a garden flat in Maida Vale. Victoria was now describing herself as a 'new comic for girls'. Audiences in further-flung parts of the UK were not necessarily ready for such a conceptual innovation, yoked to a pretend-Spanish magician. In March there were two nights at the capacious Belfast Grand Opera House – a reviewer described their first-night audience as 'undeservedly small'.[3] The show was far better suited to the snug confines of the King's Head, where they returned for four weeks over Easter. Victoria knew her audience here. 'Don't worry about being mugged when leaving the theatre,' she reassured Islingtonians. 'You are much more likely to be subsidised.'

For her return to live performance, the tweed jacket was ditched in favour of her canary-yellow suit, which she also wore to promote *Funny Turns* on BBC Two's late-night variety show *Friday Night Saturday Morning*. This was not a happy booking. The show rotated guest hosts, and this misbegotten episode was presented by a supremely serious Diana Quick, fresh from *Brideshead Revisited*. After rope tricks from the Great Soprendo, Victoria performed 'What We Find', a richly allusive new song which recommended that women stop resisting the ageing process. To a chirpy, chuntering rhythm, she sang of bosoms falling, of anti-ageing cream 'made from bits of sheep', of 'this painful fight / Against grey hair and cellulite'. Singing in a television studio was old hat for Victoria. Talking was visibly a struggle. Having failed to get onto *Parkinson*, at least this time she made sure she had lines prepared. 'You can't make jokes about nice things,' she told Diana Quick. 'If I go onstage and say, "I have a marvellous relationship with my husband," then it's not going to get a laugh (a) because it's not true and (b) because it's not funny.'

The stars of *Funny Turns* had a fruitful creative partnership based on honesty and trust. 'It's all right to take criticism from somebody who understands how difficult it's been,' Victoria explained. 'If I've been up all night with a song, Geoff is the only person I could bear to show it to and have him say, "Well, I don't think it quite works."'[4] Another of her new songs was a protestation of love, containing many private references that only Geoffrey would spot: wearing striped pyjamas, eating Weetabix without milk, leaving 'books in the toilet so you can't close the door' and her tendency to lose her contact lenses. It was written from the heart:

I know I annoy you
And I make us have fights
But I love you.

At the same time something was shifting in their relationship. They were a pair of unknowns in their first run at the King's Head. By the second, eighteen months later, Victoria was a television star who won the stronger audience reaction and the more glowing reviews. 'That made her very happy,' says Geoffrey. The show sold out. 'You would run here for a year if you stayed,' Dan Crawford told them as he crammed audiences into the King's Head to perch on chairs, tables or any available flat surface. But *Funny Turns* had a much more prestigious booking: a year and a half on, Victoria was now free to take up Michael Codron's offer of a West End residency, and *Funny Turns* was duly booked in for a stint at the Duchess Theatre.

This was a genuine turning point. A female stand-up comedian had never headlined in the West End before. 'Women *are* just as funny as men,' Victoria asserted as she prepared to open, and served notice that her brand of humour would avoid the obvious: 'I want to go into stronger areas where the craft of the joke is more important than me saying knickers or Y-fronts just to get a laugh. I want to make it more original.'[5] To mark their promotion Victoria and Geoffrey had a plush new set by Roger Glossop, Sheffield Crucible's in-house designer who had become a friend. 'It was massive for both of us,' says Geoffrey, 'made more so by the fact that we'd waited so long for it to come through as a potential big break. We were both frantically nervous – Vic handled her nerves better than I did.' The audience on the press night in mid-May did not exactly teem with friendly faces. 'We are only allowed 4 tickets,' Victoria told Robert Howie, to whom she offered a lone ticket next to Celia Imrie.[6] Most of their supporters were in the back of the circle, while their most useful ally in the stalls was Russell Harty, who walked onstage to introduce the show. Geoffrey had to choose the volunteers for his act from row upon row of critics. Despite his nerves, the Great Soprendo's tricks and patter put the audience in a light-headed mood. 'My second trick is . . .' – and he paused slightly – 'impossible, so for my third trick I am going to do some mind-reading. I want you all to be as quiet as pins and hear a mouse dropping.' Victoria entered after the interval and proceeded to talk of cystitis and cellulite, hand-embroidered tampons and her Hollie Hobby vibrator. The raciest joke – the only gag that Victoria and Geoffrey ever constructed together – was about her attempts at sex with her first boyfriend: 'He was dyslexic and had lots of these sex manuals. He spent ages lying in bed looking for my vinegar.' Such talk made the *Guardian* opera critic's flesh creep ('this is all a tedious pose'), but everyone else applauded.[7] There were ever louder ovations for the songs, some of them ('Don't Do It' and, as a rousing encore, 'Northerners') imported from *Wood and Walters*. 'If we do not count *Guys and Dolls*, the best available on the London stage,' reckoned the *Financial Times*.[8] 'The best British lyricist (though emphatically not composer) since Noël Coward,' said the *Observer*.[9] The compliment which meant the most came from Jack Tinker in the *Mail*: 'Miss Wood . . . has the confidence of a seasoned stand-up comic at the microphone.'[10]

The raves did not translate into ticket sales, however, so while doing eight shows a week Victoria threw herself into promotion. Two weeks into the run she told Robert Howie, 'I don't have much spare time as yet – doing as much to publicise the show as possible.'[11] Most interviewers wanted to know about the advent of the funny woman, a phenomenon now sparking articles in newspapers. The competitor in Victoria did not particularly welcome being subsumed into a movement or trend. 'A lot of comediennes are just men with frocks on,' she snarled. 'They haven't written their own material, they're getting men to do it for them. The emphasis is on glamour.'[12]

The best chance to promote *Funny Turns* came when Geoffrey and Victoria appeared together on *Wogan*. The booking was set up through Greg Childs, a researcher on the show whose wife Jenny Bialek worked at the King's Head. Disastrously, Victoria clammed up. 'Terry expected performers to perform,' says Childs. 'She was not very forthcoming in the rehearsal, and Terry froze her out when it came to the recording of the show, to the point that it was almost embarrassing. She didn't fight her way back in. She just let it happen.' Viewers would not have been persuaded she was worth the price of a West End ticket. (Her resentment of Wogan simmered for a long time. 'He never pays much attention to what's being said,' she suggested years later, 'and he's patronising to the women.')[13]

Back at their flat in Maida Vale, Victoria and Geoffrey picked over reasons why the show was not selling. They fretted over Codron's decision to bill it as a revue, evoking his bygone triumphs with *Pieces of Eight* and *Beyond the Fringe*, and worried that *Wood and Walters* had made the idea of Victoria's equal partnership with someone else a harder sell. But the box office could not compete with a much more serious rival. 'There were lots of excuses for failing that summer apart from the usual ones of not being very good or famous,' Victoria recalled. 'It was the Falklands. Things closed like mad. The Strand was nearly dark by the end.'[14] Although Victoria and Geoffrey both grumbled about Codron's softly-softly approach to marketing, there was nothing any management could do to stop theatregoers staying in to watch the news. 'I ask my agent to get me a booking on "Newsnight",' Victoria joked in a diary column for *The Times*.[15] After three weeks, Codron requested that Victoria and Geoffrey forego their fee and two weeks later gave notice that the show was to close early. In all the run lasted seven weeks, for four of which they weren't paid. In her photograph album, over a snap of *Funny Turns* at the Duchess Theatre, Victoria scrawled, 'SO FUNNY NO ONE TURNED UP'.

The closure of *Funny Turns* was a blow, but there were other opportunities. In the summer she made her debut on *Just a Minute*. Her train was delayed, causing Derek Nimmo to castigate her on air for being late. Victoria fought back when he challenged her for repeating the word 'red' as she described her kitchen. 'They were different shades of red actually,' she replied, much to the audience's approval. She beat the three male contestants, including Kenneth Williams, to win the episode. In due course she accepted invitations from *Give Us a Clue*, *Password*, *The Pyramid Game* and *Tell the Truth*, on which she befriended Peter Cook. She was pragmatic about being a quiz regular. 'I took it for what it was. It was useful to the job and also it brought you in some more money.'[16] She also diversified, fronting a television documentary about pantomime dames for Channel 4 backed by the Arts Council.

In August *Funny Turns* went to Edinburgh, where Victoria also joined a panel of male comedians and writers debating taste in comedy. She earned a round of applause for the argument she'd formulated when filming *Talent* three years earlier: 'If something is good it couldn't be tasteless. If it is tasteless it couldn't be good.'[17] As for the show that brought her there, it was reaching the end of its natural life. A job guesting in *Crackerjack* had greatly raised Geoffrey's profile and he had become less available. To speed him on his way Victoria bought him a van for ferrying his props around the country. The time for Victoria to go solo had arrived.

In the autumn, therefore, a random run of dates was set up in small-scale venues dotted around England – from Maidstone and Horsham to Bowness and Tewkesbury. Her travels brought her to London in October to attend an award ceremony hosted by the British Clothing Industry Federation in the City of London. By dint of her penchant for wearing a tie in her act, she became the first woman to be nominated for Man of the Year.

Mainly, Victoria was at home attempting to write. The itch to return to the theatre grew out of the still recent memory of *Good Fun*. 'I start my PLAY in October,' she confidently informed Jane Wymark, but she had made no progress by Christmas, when the annual summons to appear on Russell Harty's seasonal special found Victoria and Julie Walters briefly back in tandem.[18]

At the start of 1983 Victoria was saved from her playwriting problem with an offer to adapt a novel into a film script. *The Natural Order*, published the previous year, would earn its author Ursula Bentley inclusion in *Granta* magazine's twenty Best of Young British Novelists alongside Martin Amis, Pat Barker, Julian Barnes, Ian McEwan and Salman Rushdie. The novel was a comic satire in which three young women from the south of England go to work in a Jesuit school in the north and all ending up sleeping with the charismatic head boy. Having agreed to adapt it, Victoria suddenly found herself in high-falutin company. The finance came from David Puttnam's company Goldcrest, which had won Oscars with *Chariots of Fire* and *Gandhi*. The producer was Leon Clore, whose most recent hit was *The French Lieutenant's Woman*. He and Victoria were not well matched. 'They lived utterly differing lives,' says Geoffrey, who accompanied her to 'a particularly toe-curling intimate dinner party at his house'. More intriguingly for Victoria, the director-in-waiting was Stephen Frears.

'I remembered reading about her first thing in Sheffield and think-ing she sounds really good news,' he says. When they met he was informed by Victoria that his film *Sunset Across the Bay* from Alan Bennett's script was the reason she'd moved to Morecambe.

In February she began on the script after three final dates for *Funny Turns* at the Theatre Royal Bath. 'I would like to do a Woody Allen,' she grandly told a local journalist in Bath.[19] The adaptation consumed her for several months, during which she turned thirty. For much of the time she was left alone, as Geoffrey was now touring with the other stars of *Crackerjack*. When he was away she fell back on the company of local friends. She had a stab at canoeing on Windermere with Roger Glossop and his partner Charlotte Scott, who owned a house by the lake. Closer to home she was finding friendships trickier because she felt she couldn't talk about work. One friend 'is not into it at all,' she told Jane Wymark; another was an actress who seemed to struggle with Victoria's high profile. 'Whenever I came back with tales of my own there would be a frosty silence, as if I was name-dropping or boasting, which I don't think I was.'[20] Nor could some older friends cope with her success. Over the summer she met one from university who 'managed to be incredibly jolly, insecure, rude and jealous which was entertaining if not pleasant'.[21]

Victoria handed in the first draft of the script in June and went down to London to hear the verdict. 'They told me what was wrong with it, in Stephen's case, helpfully, and in Leon's case, not ("can't we have this character in a few more scenes, I like her", "need a better joke here").'[22] She went home, cut it by forty minutes and resub-mitted it. On these trips to London she stayed with Frears at his home in Notting Hill. Frears's wife was heavily pregnant, so Victoria accompanied her on a shopping spree to Kensington High Street to buy baby clothes. Finding that 'S.F. appears unmoved by this coming event', she couldn't resist dropping hints about the imminent birth in the next rewrite.[23] 'There were lines in the script about little vests,' he says. With her contracted period for reworking the script set to expire in mid-July, she 'took it home and beat the hell out of it'.[24] Jim Broadbent was mentioned for the lead role, and Frears remained encouraging – 'he thought it was v.g. but had a few little last nitpicks'.[25] Having addressed these she gave the final draft a new title: *Gobsmacked!*, which reflected the reaction of Goldcrest upon reading it. 'They had no idea what to expect,' says Frears. 'When she handed it in everybody was very, very shocked. They just couldn't cope with it. They said, "We'll give it you back." They literally said, "It's all yours."' Thus Victoria's first adventure in the film world ended in disillusion. 'I don't think I will adapt another book I don't like,' she concluded. 'It's too restricting.'[26] While *The Natural Order* remained unfilmed, Victoria instead approached Deborah Moggach, whose fiction she had been reading since the novelist came to Morecambe to interview her in 1979. *Porky*, only just published, was a shocking depiction of an overweight young girl corrupted by her father's sexual abuse – Victoria wanted to adapt and star in it. 'We had this very stilted and rather wary lunch,' says Moggach, 'with this weird thought that she would play this incest victim. She didn't eat much quiche and when she left there was a funny smell. I saw I had accidentally melted this knife handle into it and nearly poisoned her. She didn't mention it and I never heard from her again.'

Meanwhile, Victoria itched to get back to stand-up comedy. The day after completing her script, she began working on a new solo set. 'I'm a bit nervous,' she told Jane Wymark, 'because I've never sat down and just written JOKES & PATTER before.'[27] In Stankelt Road she did intensive shifts conjuring up monologues in an exercise book and, whenever available, Geoffrey acted as her sounding board. In rehearsals at home he told her what worked and what wanted tightening or cutting. Once the text of a monologue was pinned down, Victoria would learn it by reading it over and over and once more perform it for Geoffrey, who checked her delivery against the script in the exercise book. If she deviated his task was to tell her which version worked best. These laborious sessions could last for a long time as the monologue was kneaded and chiselled. The contract of understanding between them was that she would trust him to tell her if something was funny, even if he grew so used to the punchlines he didn't physically laugh.

One thing they both thought about deeply was how to create variety. From his experience of northern clubs, Geoffrey argued against repeating an entry or an exit. 'If they've seen it once,' he told her, 'they don't want to see it twice.' So for the first half Victoria offered a simple welcome: 'Hi, chaps. Well done for picking your way through the brochure and getting here.' The idea was to acknowledge the effort entailed in leaving the house. 'You could have just stayed in and watched a video nasty. Like your wedding.' Her entry after the interval needed to be different, so she devised a costumed character whom she announced from the wings as 'the one and only Miss Paula du Val!' A salty northern pub entertainer with a tendency to overshare, she was the grotesque antithesis to Victoria's own act. She was based on Pauline Daniels, a groin-obsessed comic whose potty mouth Victoria aped with laser accuracy: 'Ooh, girls don't you just hate it when they gob in t'ashtray? I said, "If you must do it, do it in your bloody turn-ups."' Paula admits to having suffered her share of troubles: 'A dropped womb and two lads in Parkhurst.' 'She's the type of comedienne I can't bear,' Victoria explained. 'I can't bear the fact that they're reversing the role of the male comic. I don't think it rings true.'[28] With a ukulele Paula du Val sang a snarling ditty in the style of George Formby called 'Nasty Things' from her new album ('available in all good petrol stations'):

There's nasty things wherever you look
There's nasty things in every book
You're down and out, you've got no rent
Your leg's been mashed in an accident
There's nasty things wherever you look.

The next trick was to find a way of smoothly removing Paula's costume. Victoria hit on the idea of peeling off her long black wig and dress and revealing herself as a posh, nervous actress who has devised the previous act for auditions. 'I thought it would be nice for an audition, you know, sort of not to do Juliet or Lady Macbeth,' the character explains uncertainly.

As for getting off the stage, they chose to close the first half with a blackout. This freed Victoria from the requirement to work up to a climactic torrent of laughter. Geoffrey suggested she blindside the audience with one of her more sombre songs – 'Love Song', about a widower's unexpressed devotion composed five years earlier for *In at the Death*, proved the best fit. 'That would give her the opportunity to play to the gallery at the end and try for a standing ovation.' The songs she picked to close the second half made for a strategic contrast: 'Music and Movement', a cute comic ditty, was followed by the rambunctious 'Northerners'.

Victoria was aware that performing the show came with jeopardy. 'I wrote it myself, there's only me onstage, there's no script, which means if I go blank one night, I'm lumbered. No one can prompt me, or cover up for me – if I dry badly, and there's a silence, and you can hear the stage doorkeeper doing the *Daily Mirror* Quizword, I pretend to have a coughing fit.'[29] But from the moment the novel concept of a funny woman holding forth for a whole evening in stand-up and song was launched, Victoria was suddenly unique. 'That's where she turned into Victoria Wood,' says Geoffrey. 'It was completely impossible to compare her to anyone else.'

There was little time to assemble all of this. The deadline was imposed by a booking at the Coventry Festival in August, leaving less than three weeks to supplement existing material with twenty fresh minutes. On the way to Coventry they stopped in Birmingham, where Victoria plugged the gig on a TV show hosted by Chris Tarrant 'whom I know doesn't like me,' she wrote, 'but he managed to conceal his loathing'.[30]

Victoria generally enjoyed the relaxed atmosphere of festivals but not now as she unveiled her new solo show: 'I went blank, like an exam, and didn't think I could do it, but did in the end. The real problem was remembering the new opening – Geoff rehearsed with me over and over again and in the event I did remember most of it, tho' I was just operating on nervous energy and didn't really perform it v well the 1st night.'[31] Having written yet another song and a new monologue, Victoria then took the show to Edinburgh, where she was booked to perform in a converted church known as the Wildcat. For an hour and a half late at night, she played to sell-out houses whom she discouraged from excessive laughing 'because the Dutch juggler's in at midnight'. She officially titled the show *Victoria Wood on Her Own* and billed it as 'a one-man show with no men in it'. Audiences soon saw what she meant with references to the underwear she wore under her electric-blue suit: cheap pants from Safeway and a 'Playtex discontinued'.

After a swift resumé of her career so far – there were rich pickings in *New Faces* and *That's Life!* – she took the mickey out of the Arts Council for sponsoring depressed playwrights and alternative cabaret (including an act who 'juggles three copies of the *Guardian* and a wok'). She then sat at the piano perform a pacey new song called 'Even If', written specifically as a curtain-raiser. In it Victoria pledged to cheer her audience up:

> Even if you've not laughed since that Wednesday when
> Deirdre said she was leaving Ken
> Put it out of your mind.

The festival critics approved: 'She can make skeletons dance,' marvelled one.[32] The box office received a welcome leg-up from Channel 4, which repeated *Wood and Walters* in June to cash in on the celebrity of Julie Walters, who was now a film star after the royal gala premiere of *Educating Rita*. Feeling eclipsed by her friend at least gave Victoria a joke: she pretended to overhear a whine from the audience – 'It's the other one I like, the thin one.' Her competitive streak would only intensify when the Academy Award nominees were announced. 'Being a comedian takes a long time,' she explained. 'Julie was doing things like *Educating Rita* and being nominated for Oscars and I was playing Southport Theatre to 250 people. People would say, "Aren't you jealous?" Well, yeah, I was, but basically I was dedicated to learning that job.'[33]

After Edinburgh she went to Leeds to make a series of eighteen short programmes aimed at deaf children for Yorkshire Television. She played a so-called Wordwitch and wore a tiara, blonde ringlets and a pink tutu. There were sporadic live dates across England before she returned to the King's Head in late October with a new title. *Lucky Bag* suggested both a favoured collection of bits and pieces, and a woman who'd hit the jackpot.

Of the new numbers, there was a mock-sentimental northern love song she cheekily titled 'Skellern in Love', in which she crooned about 'You and me / And thirty-three / Big buggers from a big brass band'. In 'Funny How Things Turn Out', sung in the accent of a well-to-do southerner, Victoria imagined receiving news from old school friends. This was a dazzling improvement on a similar song she'd written in the mid-Seventies. Bobbie Fields ends up as a failed actress singing 'Lerner and Loewe to the mentally ill'. Jennifer Hill, once a sex-mad hippie, is now a stressed mother who 'moved to Tufnell Park / With a cat called Muriel Spark'. Then there's Brenda James, the captain of games:

I came out at a Lesbians Ball.
Didn't feel glad to be gay at all.
Whoever said that? Tom Robinson, was it?
I couldn't agree and got back in the closet.
Then saw the light and had no doubt.
I took all my savings and just disappeared
And found a nice doctor who said, 'You're not weird.'
Now I'm Jonathan James with a wonderful beard.
Funny how things turn out.

Meanwhile, each monologue was crafted to be distinctive. She hurled herself into a wild narrative rooted in the everyday but peopled by grotesques such as Hilda, who is six foot nine, has tattooed knuckles that spell 'anthrax' and lacquered hair 'like a 78 with a parting'. A man on release from a mental hospital owing to a strike wants to know what it feels like to be in a relationship so Victoria takes him home. 'What a night . . . We put up shelving.' One glorious story, about a disastrous radio interview, was inspired by just such a humiliation when she toured with Jasper Carrott.

These observational riffs were a means to dart from joke to dazzling joke, untethered by structure. If she was fond of gags first heard on *Wood and Walters*, she had no guilt about recycling them – one was about Shakespeare ('some of my best friends are Brummies'), another about Dutch caps ('If they're too small they make your ears itch'). But mostly *Lucky Bag* was an unstoppable volcano of invention: 'Sexual harassment at work – is it a problem for the self-employed? . . . I went to The Body Shop. I said have you got this in a size 8? . . . Last night I was in the library – I'd gone there for a new Shirley Conran book, *The Menopause and How to Make Money Out of It.*'

Each of Victoria's characters emerged from 'voices that lodge in my head . . . they are usually based on someone I've seen or someone I've met in a very vague form and then you transform them'.[34] Paula du Val plays at places like the Dolce Vita in Smethwick – a reference to Victoria's *New Faces* audition, and Julie Walters' home town. The starchy young actress in the audition, who is prepared to go nude for a dandruff commercial, was modelled on a friend or two from Birmingham University who suffered the wandering hands of their lecturer Clive Barker. She joins Lorryload, 'an educational theatre group based in Canvey Island' inspired by Vanload, in which both Julie and Geoffrey toured Liverpool in 1974. A witless tour guide showing visitors round Haworth Parsonage, with only the sketchiest interest of the Brontës ('now alas no longer with us'), grew out of Victoria's memory of going there as a child. A desperately serious sixth-former participating in a debate about school uniform harked back to the swots of Bury Grammar School. The thread linking each character was that Victoria's script and delivery told the audience far more about the speakers than they knew about themselves. 'What interests me,' she explained, 'is trying to tune into the experience of every ordinary person's existence – what it is like to be alive in the 1980s, what is like to get up, watch television, go shopping, the things everybody does.'[35] Yet normal life was filtered through a prism that could alchemise it into something glitteringly surreal. She imagined knotting sheets together to make a moped, orgasms and how to knit them, making a model of the Forth Bridge from empty lager cans, smoking a Lil-Let, converting a mill chimney into an aspirational family home.

In time for the run, *Lucky Bag* was released as an album from a recording made in Edinburgh – Geoffrey was tasked with selecting the order and suggesting cuts to reduce it to an hour. The national critics were dazzled. 'Two hours of Miss Wood turns out to be twice as funny as one,' purred the *Observer*. 'Miss Wood's new prowess as a stand-up comic is the great feature of the show.'[36] Victoria could not entirely enjoy her success in Islington, thanks to the supper-club layout of the theatre. 'You're performing for a public who are just on the coffee stage of a meal and hardly bother to look up. You have to fight across them for the public at the back who have come in special-ly for the show.'[37] Still, it was better than the Stables, the theatre in Buckinghamshire built and run by Cleo Laine and John Dankworth, where the layout meant she 'had to do all the jokes continuously on the revolve like a fucking lighthouse'.[38]

While Victoria performed in the evening, in the daytime she had another stab at a film script. This time she'd been paired with *Not Quite Jerusalem*, a Royal Court play which won its author Paul Kember the *Evening Standard* most promising playwright award the year after Victoria. The story, about young idealists going to a kibbutz in Israel, was hardly home territory, but the goal of the producers was to unite Victoria as scriptwriter with Julie Walters as star. It was to be made by Lewis Gilbert, who had directed *Educating Rita*. Victoria found him a frustrating collaborator. 'I'd travel in, wait while he had a coffee and read the papers, then instead of working, he'd just give me a bit of script to read and say, "See you tomorrow." Obviously not heard of the postal system.'[39] At another meeting he asked for a couple of rewrites ('page 32 – insert comic scene on camels etc'), which she did on the spot while he went off for lunch 'since when I've heard nothing'.[40] She referred to the project as 'Not Quite Funny Enough'. 'Lewis was a gorgeous man,' says Julie, 'but he was probably not the right person for her. He was very easy, very laid back and old school. He'd say, "You're the writer, darling, you do it."' From a demoralising episode, Victoria salvaged one nugget for future use: Gilbert's com-pany was called Acorn Pictures.

Back in Silverdale she read a book which would have a more stim-ulating impact on her scriptwriting and shared her enthusiasm with Jane Wymark: 'This morning I finished 'Nella Last's War' which is a diary 1939–45, kept by a 50 year old woman, in Barrow, for Mass Observation. Really interesting – mainly concerned with food and price of it and how to cook it, and saving things up for Christmas. I love reading about the war, I suppose compared with nuclear war it seems almost cosy.'[41]

For the annual summons to Russell Harty's Christmas show, Victoria dashed off 'a hasty seasonal monologue a la Billy Bennett, which if not sophisticated, did get laughs'.[42] While busy reinventing the landscape of British comedy, it was typical of Victoria to be steeped in the monologues of Bennett, who died in 1930 and exerted a formative influence on the likes of Tommy Cooper and Eric Morecambe:

> It was Christmas Eve in the crescent
> All the children were in their pyjamas
> All the parents were snappy
> Tense and unhappy
> Except two who were in the Bahamas.

Father Christmas proceeds to get legless on sherry and is carted off by reindeer in the small hours. Julie and Victoria found themselves in a similar state at a knees-up in the hotel after the recording, singing deep into the night with half a dozen Liverpool businessmen. The morning after, following 'a light breakfast of vitamins and Crest toothpaste', Victoria had a meeting with Ray Cooney, who had the run of the Ambassadors Theatre in the West End and now offered her a fortnight's residency in the new year.[43] She found him 'v pleasant and jolly and I don't trust him any further than I could throw him'.[44] Her warinesss stemmed from his suggestion that she whisk through the show without an interval. 'That would make the change in Paula du Val a mite difficult,' she wrote, 'so I declined to agree. I'll probably find it's been re-cast with Miriam Margolyes.'[45] But she accepted his offer.

It was one thing to sell tickets at the King's Head, another to fill even a small house in the West End. She submitted to all manner of indignity in order to flog tickets – answering questions fired by children on a kids' TV show, talking about Valentine's Day merchandise on Gloria Hunniford's show, sitting next to Mr Universe on TV-am. 'If I don't get any full houses next week it won't be for want of trying.'[46] Among yet more glowing reviews, not every male critic was ready for a full-frontal tour of the unruly female anatomy. One groaned at songs 'about cellulite, varicose veins, bosom-droop and all the other ills that female flesh is heir to'.[47] Another sighed that 'we can be reminded too often that the sex is mammarian and bifurcated'.[48] Despite male squeamishness, the box office was healthy enough for Ray Cooney to offer a third week. Victoria turned it down. There was a new job calling her home.

# SEEN ON TV

'Sex always comes up at parties and it's never been a strong point with me. It's not that I don't like it; I just don't like things that stop you seeing the television properly.'
*Victoria Wood As Seen on TV*, 1985

'This week is week 1 of TV series. V nasty week as starting is v. hard and I hate it and feel I have lost the knack but no doubt it will be OK in the end.'[1] On the first day of 1984, after two years away, Victoria began sketching her return to television. The idea had crept up on her while she learned the craft of live solo performance. 'I was being asked by lots of television companies to sign up with them to do a series. And I eventually thought BBC Two would be the best thing. I just got a contract "to write six shows starring Victoria Wood". That's all it said.'[2]

The overture came from the BBC's head of variety, James Moir. His fondness for pinstripes and military metaphors gave him a traditional whiff of the Rotary Club, and yet he was an architect of change in light entertainment who had already brought in the likes of Lenny Henry and Tracey Ullman. Victoria, visiting his office to pitch, left TV Centre with a mandate never previously granted by the BBC: to be the sole writer of her own sketch show. 'She explained that this is what she wanted to do,' says Moir. 'What was I going to say? "Let's see a test page, some draft scripts." It would have been foolish to try it. The business was done really quite quickly.'

While Moir's strategy was to rejuvenate mainstream comedy, it remained common at the BBC for jobs to be doled out on seniority rather than suitability. As she wrote the material for the show, Victoria soon grew alarmed that she would be assigned an old-school producer such as was foisted on her at Granada. She shared her anxiety with Jenny Bialek and Greg Childs, who both recommended someone called Geoff Posner.

Geoff Posner was unlike anyone Victoria had yet encountered in television. In the late 1960s he had gone to some lengths to break into television: every time the BBC rejected him he did another media degree. He had three by the time he was recruited as a floor assistant in 1974. Slowly he graduated to directing *Not the Nine O'Clock News* and *The Young Ones*. Already an admirer of Victoria's work – he saw *Good Fun* twice at the King's Head – he was eager to produce her show and asked Vivienne Clore, her television agent at Richard Stone, to put in a good word. The machination worked. Exultant, he was keen to meet his new collaborator only to be told, 'She doesn't want to meet you yet. She wants to write the programme and then see what you think.' He would have a long wait.

'Have been working on TV series for 3 weeks now, and have amassed a few ill-written foolscap pages of extremely unamusing humour. We press on tho'.'[3] The recipient of this and many other bulletins was Victoria's university friend Jane Wymark, who had moved with her husband to Bangladesh. Victoria treated her to long and richly entertaining letters in which she talked about her life: dieting, exercise, improvements to the house and garden, mutual friends from Birmingham, Geoffrey's adventures in conjuring, and the creation of her new television series. 'If all else fails,' she added, 'I shall perform nude with a sanitary towel on my head.'[4]

Victoria's nocturnal regime was long over by now. She would rise at 6.45 a.m. and drive half an hour to Kendal, where she'd swim three quarters of a mile. Back at home she supplemented her breakfast with multivitamins – a new development as she committed to vegetarianism. ('I'm all for killing animals and turning them into shoes and handbags,' was the moral line she developed. 'I just don't want to have to eat them.')[5] Then she sat down to write all day, breaking off for homemade soup and a Jane Fonda workout. She described it as 'a very lonely life. I sit at my desk gazing out at the sheep and cows, talking to nobody.'[6] The solitude was compounded by the absence of Geoffrey, trapped in Nottingham in the longest run in pantomime history. For eighteen weeks he commuted home to find Victoria had written a little bit more. 'Another day thinking up side-splitting dialogue,' she reported at the start of February.[7]

The idea that took shape was a show which would hold up a distorting mirror to the world of television. It would spoof commercials and children's entertainment, contemporary and costume drama, daytime magazine shows and video vox pops. There would be fly-on-the-wall mock documentaries and a send-up of a terrible soap opera. Threaded through would be stand-up, songs and sketches. Victoria had a half-formed idea for an in-vision continuity announcer with virulent opinions about class, culture and hygiene. 'There are a lot of those girls around,' she explained. 'In the regions you get these awful condescending women in between programmes.'[8]

The task was vast: to write six half-hours without any collaborative input. Her only sounding board was Geoffrey, to whom, on one of his weekly visits, she said, 'I think I'm going to call this *Victoria Wood As Seen on TV*. What do you think?' This was her show and hers alone, with no shared billing for Julie Walters, about which she was 'quietly pleased and quietly guilty,' says Geoffrey. 'She was relieved that Julie appeared not to mind the change in their professional relationship.' In fact, Julie, whom Victoria told about the series as she was writing it, felt the same way. 'I was kind of relieved that I hadn't got my name on it,' she says. 'The prestige was great, but I felt I didn't write them so my name shouldn't be on them.'

It left Victoria free to explore her preoccupations. With affection laced with sometimes cruel honesty, she conjured up grim women and dim girls, explored entrenched working-class attitudes and middle-class pretensions. She set her sketches in shops, libraries and dry cleaners, cafés, restaurants and bus shelters. 'The best sketches are confrontations,' she explained, 'and that's where I come across confrontations.'[9] Among her characters she liberally distributed her favourite funny words (varicose veins, moped, quiche lorraine, raffia, theodolite, cystitis, grouting, shoplifting, mangling) and names (Dick Francis, Liberace, *Bunty*, the Isle of Man, Taurus, Mavis Nicholson, Marbella). All were put in the service of a worldview that was uniquely female and distinctly northern.

The mockumentaries took longest to write, being in such a specific register and requiring the invention of so wide an array of new characters. They were inspired by a life that she knew: the terraced streets of the north; the swings and roundabouts of theatrical life. 'On Campus', about an awkward girl who attempts suicide after being bullied in her first week at university, was 'drawn from all the terrible people I knew at university'.[10] Most autobiographically of all, in 'Swim the Channel', Victoria depicted a family home where the parents are so neglectful they'd rather catch a West End show than watch their teenage daughter Chrissie attempt to front crawl to France. They seem barely concerned when she disappears. 'I'm sure she'll turn up eventually,' says her father. 'Slow but sure, that's our Chrissie.' The mother has forgotten all about their other children too. (Victoria's own parents were not perturbed by the subtext when it was shown. 'They really loved that one,' says her sister Penelope. 'Dad said it was so moving he nearly cried.')

As Victoria accumulated material, she plotted it all onto a map. 'I'd write a sketch, and I'd write its name on a filing card, and I arranged the whole series on filing cards on my carpet so it went song, quickie, song, sketch.'[11] The opening slot was fixed: a three-minute burst of stand-up. This was the clearest way of identifying herself as the sole author of the show, but it was also part of a longer-term strategy: she understood that at least part of her future lay in touring, and it was a shrewd move to introduce herself as a stand-up comedian to a television audience.

She took a big chunk of time off to promote and perform *Lucky Bag* at the Ambassadors in February. In March, at the request of John Dowie, she took part in a benefit at the Donmar Warehouse to raise £1,000 for the defence of two publishers on trial for using drug references in comics (they were acquitted). Dowie could not help noticing that 'more people queued to see her after the show than I'd ever performed to'. Then in April, inspired by the idea of seeing the world 'after spending 15 unadventurous years going nowhere', she and Geoffrey went on a cheap package holiday to Marrakech.[12] 'Swimming a lot, very hot, done the Tombs,' she reported to Rosalind, 'have bought a rug to be shipped out – whether we ever get it remains to be seen.'[13] It did arrive and was given pride of place at the entrance to Stankelt Road.

After they were typed up locally, Victoria presented the sketches to Julie Walters. 'I just love the scripts – I want to do it all,' she replied. 'Do you know who the director's going to be?'[14] Finally, Geoff Posner was summoned to Silverdale. Full of apprehension, she went to Lancaster station to collect a short man who fizzed with energy and wore a lavish walrus moustache. According to Posner, Victoria sought reassurance that the material constituted a series. 'I said, "Vic, this is wonderful stuff. I also know how we're going to do this together."' One concrete proposal he made was that she write extra material to ensure there was room to cut anything that didn't quite land with audiences. After she put him back on the train several hours later, she shared her first impressions with Geoffrey: 'She said he was pitching himself during the conversations and she felt he was a little too clear-cut.' In due course he would prove to be a brilliant technical innovator, adept at providing a framework for her comic inventions.

As with *Talent* and *Good Fun*, Victoria was reluctant to push herself forward as a performer, telling her producer she'd do 'bits and pieces'. Her instinct to share out the parts dovetailed with anxiety about her acting abilities. 'The nearest thing we had to a row,' says Posner, 'was me saying to her, "You've got to be in it. You do it best and it's your show."' She also had grand ambitions for casting. 'I am sending off a sketch to Alan Bennett in the hope that he will want to do it in the show,' she told Jane Wymark in May.[15] Bennett declined. 'It is very funny,' he replied, 'especially the bit about the shuddering and the finish, only (and you are entitled to despise me for this) I can't face playing any more men with dusters . . . Miss R.,' he added, 'is highly delighted with her coming contribution.'[16] Miss R. was Patricia Routledge, whom Victoria hoped would play Kitty, a reincarnation of Betty and Dotty dispensing wisdom from an armchair. She wrote five

Kitty sketches in five days ('which is a very good way of seeing what your brains look like when they fall out of your nostrils').[17]

Eventually Victoria decamped to London, staying in a flat in Maida Vale lent to her by Roger Brierley. Working from Geoff Posner's office at Television Centre, they did without a casting director so were free to make their own running. They started on the six documentaries. 'All the parts are tiny, but must be very well done,' Victoria reported. 'So a lot of good people turned them down on sight, which was eggy to say the least.'[18] Peter Eckersley's widow Anne Reid was baffled by a script she had been sent. 'It was just simply a waitress or cook shouting this menu. I didn't get it and so I went to see her and Geoff in London and said, "I'm terribly sorry, I don't want to do this."' It was a slightly awkward moment. I think they were quite surprised. Victoria was a fan of the National Theatre of Brent, the comically overambitious am-dram troupe which staged epic stories with a cast of two, and booked both its members. Patrick Barlow was cast as a supercilious theatre director in 'Whither the Arts?', a merciless mockery of *The South Bank Show*. Jim Broadbent, who had been in *Talent* in 1979, was to play, among other roles, a plodding door-to-door evangelist who runs a telephone deodorising business in a film she called 'A Fairly Ordinary Man'.

Several other actors who had been in Victoria's plays and dramas came in. For a parody of *The Wednesday Play* in which a married couple argue spitefully, she hoped to cast an actual couple she and Geoffrey had stayed with: Gregory Floy and his wife Deborah Grant, the bewitching star of *A Bouquet of Barbed Wire*. But Floy was committed elsewhere, so Denis Lawson stepped in. Victoria also proposed northern actors Geoff Posner had never heard of. Mary Jo Randle, whom she knew from the Rochdale Theatre Workshop, was cast in 'To Be an Actress' to play an earnest young woman who can't get a break in the profession. 'I'd work anywhere,' she says. 'I'd even work in the north.' At the King's Head, Victoria came across Andrew Livingston, whose hangdog face was ideal for the unromantic halfwit Carl pondering life's big questions in a bus shelter with his girlfriend Gail.

While Julie had been booked in advance, Victoria needed to gather an ensemble of actors who would appear regularly. One New Year's Eve a couple of years earlier, she and Geoffrey caught a Scottish sketch show called *81 Take 2*, featuring a delicious turn as Lady Diana Spencer by Celia Imrie. 'She always said she was a terrible actress and I took her at her word,' said Victoria, who had seen less of Celia since moving to Lancashire. 'I thought she was really good and what on earth had she been going on about?'[19] 'She saw me in that,' says Celia, 'and it gave her the idea that I'd be OK as, to all intents and purposes, the straight girl.' Her marquee value had been boosted by a recent stint in *Bergerac* – 'It meant that I was sort of known on television and I'm sure that helped.' Duncan Preston was disgruntled at having to audition: 'You always had to audition for her. I thought, she knows what I do. I'm not quite sure what to do here. Is she asking for something different? I made a right pig's breakfast of it and thought, I've blown that.'

During auditions Victoria and Geoff Posner developed a system of nodding to each other when an actor was on the right track, or discreetly shaking heads if they weren't. There was a lot of head-shaking as actresses came in to read for the continuity announcer. The character's scripts were initially much longer, and Victoria had not yet formed the idea of having her cue up the next item. One night she went to the King's Head to see a series of one-act American plays and was so struck by a particular actress that she collared her afterwards and asked her to come in. 'I wasn't familiar with her work apart from having seen her sing at the piano a couple of times,' says Susie Blake. 'I sat on a chair in front of Geoff and Vic – both were behind a desk. And I started laughing. It was hysterical. There were two or three of these long speeches.' Her audition made it clear that she understood how to capture the character's daggered smiles and toxic snobbery. 'She came in and could do it, just like that,' said Victoria, who was so encouraged that she scrapped the longer speeches and started again with shorter, sharper segments.[20] Susie Blake grew to inhabit the character so thoroughly that, in private, she dreamed up a name for her: Pamela.

A decision was taken early on not to water down the impact of Susie Blake's powerful screen persona by putting her in other sketches. As a result, more actors had to be hired, pushing up the cost, although this didn't seem to be a consideration. 'BBC producers were delightfully cushioned from the realities of cost,' says Geoff Posner. 'I wasn't entirely sure how much the budget was.' Thus the production could afford to hire a coach and pair to canter up the drive of a grand old country manor – a splendid flourish Posner bolted onto the front of a sketch in which Duncan Preston's top-hatted Mr Wilde knocks on the door and asks if Mr Dickens is in. 'Oscar Wilde?' says Celia's pert housemaid. 'Well, I'm not bleedin' Marty Wilde, am I?' Placed high up in the first episode, it would act as a fanfare announcing the scale of the show's ambition.

Victoria was short on confidence about her stand-up spots, 'which are the hardest to do . . . I feel I can't do them at all, actually, but as I absolutely have to there's no point worrying about it.'[21] The traditional optics of stand-up didn't sit well with an intimate television studio. Viewers were used to Ronnie Corbett's chair, or Dave Allen and Jasper Carrott perching on stools, but Victoria, who would be sitting at the piano for her songs, decided to stand at the microphone, feet planted firmly apart. Rather than double the jeopardy with new material, she proposed to borrow liberally from *Lucky Bag*.

The songs, however, were mainly new. Victoria had written more than necessary and, taking soundings from Geoff Posner, picked one per episode to reflect a range of styles and moods. 'Seasons of Love' was a lilting ballad with a sting in the tail ('We made love in the firelight / You turned to me and said / Whatever made you think that you were good in bed?'). 'Pissed Off with Love' was a cheesy pop duet in which ex-lovers slag each other off – she sang it in matching suits with Denis Lawson. 'Go Away' was an angry experiment in jazz funk. The musical arranger chosen to supply the backing was David Firman, whom Victoria knew from *Good Fun*. Her habit was to record the songs at her own piano and then hand him the cassette. 'I'd try out a few vague ideas with her,' he says. 'Then people left me alone to write it.' For backing he enlisted principals from the leading orchestras or, for the soppy northern ballad 'Skellern in Love', an entire brass band.

Another composition to arrive by cassette was the theme tune, in which Victoria sang the melody and played the chords. David Firman scored it for a quartet of clarinets, a euphonium and a violin in the cheerful key of A major. 'I thought that would say something about her and the writing. The first run-through didn't go well at all, because A major is not a key that clarinets and euphoniums play in. What it actually has is an edge to it, because all those guys are right on the edge of what they can play. They're having to really work.' It was Victoria's idea to have the music play over a claymation sequence in which a pink-jacketed figurine twirled at a microphone, only for her arm to fall off and be replaced by the animator.

The trust and understanding between Victoria and her arranger is audible in a heart-melting demo version they made together of 'One Day', which was written as part of 'Whither the Arts?'. The film's wider aim was to skewer a ponderous arts documentary as it reports on rehearsals for a silly musical about fat schoolgirl Bessie Bunter. Absurdly, a wafer-thin actress, played by Deborah Grant, has been cast in the title role, and 'One Day' is her big number. It's a ridiculous parody of Marvin Hamlisch – or 'Hamly Marvisch' as the director calls him – and at the same time one of the most yearning songs Victoria ever composed. She followed it with her raunchiest: the thin actress is booted out and in comes Victoria as Bessie, whipping off her boater and school tunic to reveal a basque underneath:

> I'm gonna go bleach my hair
> Wear clothes that show my tits!
> At the Ritz!
> I'm Bessie the Blitz!
> I'm gonna make Dolly Parton look like Meryl Streep
> I mean cheap
> I mean bad
> Drive men mad to make this girl surrender
> Will they get to my pudenda?
> Don't answer that – dance!

Victoria's vocal prowess was also on display in 'Shopping', a raucous gospel-blues ensemble number set in a tea room packed with hollering ladies of a certain age. Victoria held her own as a soloist alongside some full-throttle larynxes David Firman recruited from musical theatre. She even stepped in to do the three-part whistling solo in

'Knock Knock', an Andrews Sisters spoof shot in black and white. It was sung by a cheerful trio of crack session singers who were also meant to whistle in tight harmony, but it proved beyond them. 'They can't whistle!' said an aghast Victoria.

Before the production got anywhere near a studio, in June Geoff Posner took cast and crew away to shoot the exteriors. Birmingham was chosen for its variety of locations, from back-to-back terraces to accessible countryside. The idea was also to create a pleasant and stimulating atmosphere as actors arrived the night before shooting and rehearsed in hotel bedrooms. Then they moved to Norfolk to film, among other things, Victoria's scenes on a shingle beach as Chrissie. 'Tomorrow I am being filmed Swimming the Channel,' she told Jane Wymark, 'which I know will be Fucking Freezing and I will have to be a Jolly Good Sport about it. It's a night shoot in the North Sea (yet again, who wrote this?).'[22] There followed a day shoot in which she had to swim further out to sea. As she set off with her satchel roped over her shoulder, Victoria couldn't hear anyone repeatedly shouting 'cut' and swam into the distance, far further than was required for the shot.

She was so busy on the shoot that when her parents drove down from Bury to visit she was unable to spend much time with them, while they couldn't be persuaded out of the car to greet her colleagues. The strain got to her. She overdid her morning swims, had palpitations and had to be given injections to stop her vomiting. Then when filming the dance sequence as Bessie Bunter, she was kicking some fluff out of shot and fell into the orchestra pit, cutting her head and bruising an arm.

There was a two-week gap before the company convened at the BBC's rehearsal space in North Acton, where the stresses continued. 'Was vomiting from germs, then nerves,' Victoria reported a month in.[23] She burst a blood vessel in her eye, which meant some of her duet with Denis Lawson had to be shot in profile. 'I do find it hard work,' she conceded in August, 'because most weeks I have my own bit or a new sketch to write and I'm writing slowly now having been at it since Jan 1.'[24]

The schedule began early in the week when scripts were read and

blocked out. On the third day the crew would arrive to plot lighting and camera angles; Geoff Posner warned the cast not to expect
the crew to laugh, 'though they always did'. By the fifth afternoon
they gained entry to the studio at TV Centre and set about filming
pre-recorded material. Without an audience to play to, the one piece
of direction Victoria gave Susie Blake, now dolled up in pussy-bow
blouses and a Thatcherite perm, was to pause: 'She said, "They'll be
a laugh here so just give us a smile."' On the sixth and last day of the
schedule, the dress run was at four o'clock before the audience arrived
at seven.

Although there were to be no cutaways to show them laughing, the
audience was as far as possible handpicked. Word was spread around
theatres by the BBC's audience department. Posner didn't want
anyone under thirty who might expect Victoria's comedy to be alternative: she didn't swear, nor, aside from a couple of barbs aimed at
the health secretary Norman Fowler, did she stray into politics. After
the debacle at Granada, he didn't want pensioners either. His guiding
principle was to avoid the errors that loaded so much pressure onto
Victoria in *Wood and Walters*. Rather than sprawl over several hours,
the recording was designed as an evening to last two hours, with
an extra half-hour if needed. There were no bookings for warm-up
comics who might detract from the impact of Victoria's own stand-
up. Instead there were musical acts to keep the audience entertained
in the breaks: an a cappella group; a yodeller in lederhosen – the only
misfire was a potty-mouthed accordionist. Above all Victoria was
given comfortable, colourful outfits and a set design that, in contrast
to shiny Granada studio, reflected the intimacy of the material.

When the audience arrived Geoff Posner went out to introduce
the show and explain what the evening would hold, then Victoria
sometimes came out to say a few words. She was often intimidated by the scale of her responsibility: 'She had this feeling that she'd
written rubbish and it would go down badly and all these people
would blame her. I would have to go in and coax her in the early
days.' She was so anxious before the audience was shown 'Whither
the Arts?' that she turned to Susie Blake and said, 'I'm so nervous.
Susie, do you hug?' But there was barely time to worry. The hectic

pace meant the principals were changing in and out of costumes at speed. After one stand-up routine Victoria dashed offstage so quickly, removing her jacket as she went, that it couldn't be edited out of the final cut.

The material was not recorded in the order it was later broadcast. Because the set wasn't configured the same every week, Victoria might do as many as three stand-up routines in one evening. These were finessed up to the last minute, and always run by Geoffrey first. To reduce the burden on her, for her songs she often mimed playing the piano to a pre-recorded track.

Her co-stars felt the intensity too. Posner's idea of making the show run as an evening put pressure on the actors to get their lines right first time. 'Very quickly,' says Susie Blake, 'we all realised that Vic wants this known before we all arrived.' Even Julie, a veteran of *Wood and Walters*, 'found the show quite nerve-racking. It was fun in rehearsal, but it built up to this Saturday night. It was quite tense-making, because Geoff didn't get what actors went through in order to learn lines. He and Vic were quite in tandem over that. We all felt the pressure.'

With her lone name in the title, Victoria felt mandated to assert herself. She insisted that her gags had to be delivered her way, as written, and she would remind ad-libbers of her long lone months chewing a biro. 'I probably tried to add bits,' says Celia. 'And you only needed to be told once.' There was a reason for her perfectionism. Victoria had waited many years for this validating break. She had spent those years sifting the alphabet for the right rhymes, honing rat-a-tat dialogue in plays and dramas, and learning how to land jokes in front of an audience and a camera crew. Every word had its place on the map. 'I go around kicking their ankles if they say it wrong,' she admitted.[25] Her dialogue was so precise that Duncan Preston initially found it 'not easy to say – it has its own rhythms'. When he played a salesman in a commercial for new homes designed to look horribly lived in, he had to claim, 'There's an old tissue under every pillow in a Bunbury Home!' 'She said, can you say it with stress on "every"? I did it like that and of course it got the laugh. You wanted it to be right for her and there was a pressure to get it right first time and if you didn't there was a kind of silence. It was a bit prickly. Eventually you learned how to say her stuff.'

All of her principals experienced an intense desire to do well for Victoria. But she had a Lancastrian parsimony when it came to doling out praise, so they would only know they'd got it right if she threw her head back and laughed. 'To get the approval of Victoria was always a thrill,' says Jim Broadbent, who earned it for his gawky turn in 'A Fairly Ordinary Man'. 'She always quietly let you know if you were missing a trick.' Celia Imrie grew to fear displeasing her. 'If Julie or I went wrong in front of the audience,' she says, 'Vic would turn to the audience and say, "Tracey Ullman wasn't free." It made us feel like shit.' 'That wasn't about Ceals, that was about me,' says Julie. 'People used to confuse Tracey Ullman and me all the time. Vic could be cutting in a very funny way.'

Most nervous of all was Patricia Routledge, who had never performed in front of a television audience before. 'Pat Routledge . . . wouldn't rehearse if anyone else in the room was moving, or blinking, or breathing,' Victoria told Jane Wymark.[26] Her anxiety centred on the lines – not knowing them 'was complete anathema,' says Susie Blake. 'She stood in the wings and would just cling on to me shaking.' Once in front of the camera, she disconcerted the audience by yelling 'Yes?' whenever she dried, which was a risk because Kitty's were much the longest speeches Victoria asked of any performer. Stuffed with gems, they were crafted with a precision that made great demands.

Kitty inherited elements of Stanley Wood's mother, who was hoity-toity and played bridge. 'My grandma used to talk about Cheadle,' Victoria explained. 'It's just one of those funny words like pudding that make you laugh. My grandma might have been from there, or lived there for a time. It's just a trace memory.'[27] Kitty's brand of homespun wisdom leapt from the specific to the surreal and back again. She introduced herself with a watertight three-part gag which set her up as a fastidious, do-gooding spinster: 'I could have married, I've given gallons of blood and I can't stomach whelks, so that's me for you.' (This was an improvement on the first draft – 'I've had a boob off and I can't stomach whelks' – which somehow made it into *Up to You, Porky*, the sketch book published a year later.) Kitty is proudly self-reliant and indifferent to adversity. 'I've had my share of gynaeco-logical gyp,' she confides. 'I still can't polka without wincing but we're spunky in Cheadle, we totter on.' A blinkered suburban Thatcherite who takes a dim view of sex, she knows her place in England's class system. Her lofty intolerance of the lower orders comes out when her TV gets mended. 'Well, I say mended – a shifty-looking youth in plimsolls came and waggled my aerial and wolfed my Gypsy Creams, but that's the comprehensive system for you.' At the end of the series, Kitty gaily celebrates with a bottle of sherry and is all set to pass on an old Didsbury saying 'given to me by a plumbing acquaintance of my father's' when suddenly she blanks and dries. The joke of Kitty forgetting her lines would not have been lost on anyone who had seen Patricia Routledge's battle to remember hers. For all the anxiety she generated, her performance turned out to be magnificent.

Geoff Posner was credited as producer and director of five episodes, and one was directed by Marcus Mortimer, a younger production manager hired to share the load – it fell to him to shoot 'Swim the Channel'. In fact, Victoria often ran proceedings from the studio floor while Posner occupied the control booth. 'She was always on Geoff's shoulder directing,' says Susie Blake. 'He didn't direct, certainly not the first series. At that point she was very much in charge. She knew exactly what she wanted.' Robert Howie corroborates this. Victoria asked her university friend to perform a skit, one of six she wrote spoofing a new vox-pop show on Channel 4. 'For my couple of days on *As Seen on TV*, Victoria effectively directed the performances,' he says. 'Any messages from Geoff Posner – about an eye line, say – were passed on by a floor manager.'

Robert Howie played a naff old-school comic who objects to Chan-nel 4 employing drug-addicted alternative comedians. At his costume fitting he saw a nametag inside his jacket: Roy Walker. 'Exactly the object of Victoria's satire,' he says. Like several of the 'Video Box' scripts, it didn't make the cut. 'It was a shame,' Victoria wrote to him. 'My fault for writing too many little bits and bobs we didn't have time for.'[28] Over the phone she added that the selection bias was in favour of sketches featuring herself and Julie. A whole series of short skits set in a dry cleaner, and more in a library, were recorded then dropped.

Also axed was a spoof of *Mr and Mrs* in the style of Noël Coward starring Celia Imrie. The omission did little to dispel Celia's perception that she had been hired as a feed to cue up laughs for Julie and Victoria. 'It was pretty clear. Often she'd say, "Play it straight, play it straight." Very often I'd like to put something on it and of course it doesn't work. You have to have a straight girl. There were times when Duncan and I got quite down in the mouth.' Celia inadvertently made a further contribution. In a cheesy ensemble song, Victoria and the gang are randomly joined by a nameless man in a tuxedo. 'He's with me,' explains an embarrassed Celia. 'It's very casual, we both see other people.' 'Is he married?' asks Victoria. 'Yes, but we haven't slept together for ages.' 'When I had an affair with a married man she put that in,' says Celia. 'I was thinking, oh my God. But she would do that.' When Victoria was casting about for names of two posh girls in 'Just an Ordinary School', set in a private boarding school, she plumped for Babs and Ceal.

Geoff Posner was successful in dissuading Victoria from handing out too many plum parts that felt rightfully hers, and she was cruelly unsentimental about the northern women she incarnated – a thick checkout girl in a scuzzy supermarket, or poor dim Gail trying to coax loving words from her plodding Carl. In a laundrette a gritty old shrew groans about hard times of yore: 'Clogs on cobbles – you could hardly hear yourself coughing up blood.' To Julie, meanwhile, went the characters with a hard streak – an overeager self-help guru, an insensitive local reporter, a cultureless amateur-theatre director. Victoria and Julie came together to play an array of old crones and spiky gossips in a series of indelible sketches: 'Shoe Shop', 'Turkish Bath', the snippy TV presenters Margery and Joan fronting an inane magazine show. With her fake tan and chirpy manner, Joan was widely assumed to refer to Judith Chalmers. 'I actually came out looking more like her than I intended,' Victoria conceded. 'I'd hate to think she minded. If she did, I'd stop.'[29]

Some of these sketches were shot in full view of the audience; others that contained a reveal were filmed out of sight and relayed on screens. One section was always filmed in an empty studio and only then relayed to the audience. 'And now it's time,' said the continuity announcer, 'for the first of our twelve visits to *Acorn Antiques*, Manchesterford's favourite antique shop. And after last week's exciting cliffhanger, let's see if they're any further on with mending that umbrella stand.' Over Victoria's plinky bossa nova-ish theme tune, recorded on her Casio stylophone, the show's title appeared in a dated daytime font. Beyond it, the camera hovered on an elderly couple intently inspecting a glass vase before it swivelled round to Celia, wearing thick blue eye shadow and a peroxide wig and seated in front of an ornate retro telephone. Behind her Julie in a pinny clutched a tray and hovered uncertainly in shot as if awaiting her cue to enter. The episode lasted less than four minutes. The studio audience, who had not been advised that this was a parody, emitted barely a titter. In their first ever sighting, Miss Babs, Mr Clifford and the hunchbacked Brummie char Mrs Overall were greeted by confused silence.

Victoria had been warned this might happen. 'I had an idea when I wrote it that it was going to be really, really funny. Other people said, "I don't get it." I said, "Just wait. It's like this. They won't get it till they see it."'[30] The first person not to get it was Geoffrey. 'She wrote *Acorn Antiques* very baldly and very barely. I said, "There's not a lot here; it's a bit thin." She said, "That's all right, we'll put in lots of clichés."' An auditioning actor voiced a strong doubt about how funny it was, not realising he was speaking to the author. Victoria was so confident it would get laughs that she insisted it be recorded without an audience. 'We knew we would never get through it. They would be laughing and it had to be done as a soap would be done in the daytime in a cold studio.'[31]

When the first episode didn't get laughs from the studio audience, Posner took the decision to screen the second straight after – he had three in the bank, all filmed the day before. The hope was that the penny might drop with more exposure. Something shifted when Julie was seen to enter with her mouth full of biscuit and, being unable to say her lines, collapse in giggles. When they shot the scene again, Posner decided to retain the old take, separating it from the new one with a brief blackout. This edit wasn't in the script and went far beyond the rules of the parody, but the audience twigged, started to laugh and didn't stop until after the cast credits had bumped diagonally across the screen. Victoria then went on to introduce the first episode again and clarify what they were watching. This time it was greeted with much more laughter, prominent among it Geoffrey's booming guffaws.

'*Acorn Antiques* . . . took all the worst things from television,' Victoria explained to Russell Harty soon after it was broadcast, 'like wobbly sets and people drying and people being seen before their entrances and the backcloth at the back swaying from side to side and the same two extras looking at a jug every week and then putting it down and moving to the back of the shop – all the things I love in television.'[32] Often asked about its inspiration, Victoria would never quite settle on a definitive answer. She cited 'the really abysmal dialogue' of *Waggoner's Walk*, a Radio 4 serial featuring three women leading racy lives in a flat in Hampstead, which ran through the 1970s – at one point Fidelis Morgan was in the cast.[33] She also nodded to *The Archers*, while television gave her *The Cedar Tree* with its sludgy plots about a grand country house between the wars. 'Vic used to collect examples of soapy phraseology with great delight,' says Geoffrey, 'and *The Cedar Tree* was particularly fruitful. One of the great pleasures for Vic was watching Joyce Carey dry stone dead and then savouring how she would painstakingly worm her way out of it. It happened a lot and showed how low the budget was.' Another inspiration was *Take the High Road*, the cult Scottish soap begun in 1980 and set in a Highland village. Victoria was particularly taken with the grumpy cleaning lady Mrs Mack, which gave her the name for Mrs Overall. Then there was *Crossroads*, which she had devoured so avidly as a student. She seized on the way the script sought to confer glamour on itself by dropping in references to international locations. In the first two episodes alone Miss Babs receives a phone call from a mysterious man from the Middle East, Mr Clifford (played by Duncan Preston) returns from Zurich and the father of Victoria's character Miss Berta is shot dead in Dhaka – the Bangladesh capital was on the airmail envelope of every letter Victoria addressed to Jane Wymark. She was also seduced by *Crossroads*' ridiculous plots: 'Everybody is related to everybody else and every week there is some sort of denouement wherever somebody turns out to be related or have amnesia.'[34] Babs has triplets who are heard of but not seen, while she and Berta are supposed to be identical. 'As they are played by me and Celia Imrie, of whom I am twice the size, we both wear the same suit but I have a wig that makes me look like Pat Phoenix.'[35]

Geoff Posner had a sharp scholarly eye for the look of things on television. He was meticulous about capturing the grammar of documentaries, right down to the way the title of a film would bloom on screen just after an interviewee had uttered the key phrase: 'Swim the Channel', 'Just an Ordinary School', 'A Fairly Ordinary Man'. When Victoria first introduced *Acorn Antiques* to him she read out the stage directions: 'This is a soap opera with shaky sets and extraordinary acting.' He launched into an intense study of *Crossroads* in order to identify and then exaggerate its tropes. It was his idea to introduce the ever-present couple who never say anything: they were inspired by the figures played by so called background artists who would check into the Crossroads motel without speaking, because if they had lines they'd have to be paid more. A scene would begin with a close-up of fingers pointing at a map before the camera pulled away. The set was designed in such a way that the actors found themselves moving like sardines around clutter, or blocking one another thanks to a badly positioned camera, or in one case walking so far forward they leave the set altogether. Props took on a life of their own: a lampshade impeded an actor's exit or obscured them from view; the telephone would not ring at the right moment. The main generator of technical errors was Mrs Overall, forcing other actors to cover for her. 'I'd look at the monitor and shove my tray into shot where it shouldn't be,' says Julie. 'Or be really late coming on. A lot of that we did on the day. With the lines there was no improvising. Vic would not have that, and I never wanted it. But in terms of who Mrs O was, I decided. She would enjoy me doing whatever I did with it. It was just unsaid.'

Apart from Julie choking on a biscuit, everything was painstakingly rehearsed. *Acorn Antiques* took so long to film because it required cast and, especially, crew to unlearn everything they knew about technical competence. Geoff Posner coached cameramen to hold still when a character stood up, rather than rise with them. In the second series, when Duncan Preston bangs his head on the boom microphone, it took several takes to persuade the boom operator to go against his instincts and not lift it. 'Everybody could jump in,' said Victoria, 'and the cameramen could bump into each other and all the things they try valiantly not to do most of the time they could do.'[36]

Others also consulted *Crossroads* for inspiration. Celia based Miss Babs on Noele Gordon's performance as Crossroads motel proprietor Meg Mortimer. 'Noele Gordon seemed to keep the whole thing together,' she says. 'Miss Babs was in charge and no matter what was going on around her she was going to keep the ball going.' Her appreciation for the actress's personal style was rooted in an outing she once took with Victoria and Fidelis Morgan to a charity football match in Stratford-upon-Avon: 'There was this magnificent moment when she wore this turquoise suit and brought out this turquoise handkerchief.' The sky-blue eyeshadow was Celia's idea; Babs's telephone manner she copied from her agent's. Duncan based the pinstriped Mr Clifford, with a silk handkerchief frothing from the breast pocket of his three-piece suit, on Ronnie Allen's performance as absurdly plummy motel shareholder David Hunter. 'I wasn't taking him off,' he insists. 'I had him in mind.' Julie felt Mrs O 'should be like Amy Turtle: she should have a Birmingham accent and she should be old.' A wig was prepared but then the moment came for Julie to put her long hair up in a net: 'Vic and I were being made up and we both looked at one another and went, "Don't need the wig."'

Three more characters helped Victoria to send the plot spinning out of control. Derek, a Scottish handyman, is found to be Miss Berta's twin and Mrs Overall's long-lost son. A pert young cockney called Trixie is discovered to be Babs's daughter and ends up entering a nunnery. The role of Spanish lothario Cousin Jerez was played by Peter Ellis, whom Victoria knew from the original cast of *Talent*. When he asked if the character was modelled on the Great Soprendo, she didn't deny it.

The attention to detail in *As Seen on TV* ran through to the closing credits, which needed to be different from the juddering, accidentally overlapping credits for *Acorn Antiques*. Geoff Posner took advantage of a recently invented gizmo: the digital video extender enabled him to make the screen bob and swirl through 360 degrees so that the credits could roll and flip. The idea was to hold the viewer through to the finish, when a short extra piece might be appended. 'And there'll be more attempts at fun from the overweight comedienne next week,' said a male announcer as the credits rolled. Victoria had not quite shed her habit of joking about her size. The first ever episode concluded with a weather check from the continuity announcer, who is relieved there is to be no heatwave: 'Whenever it's hot a lot of the girls here come to work in sleeveless tops and some of them are very overweight and I get quite depressed having to look at their enormous arms all day long. Of course obesity is a tremendous problem for a lot of people – a lot of weak-willed, self-indulgent guzzlers, that is. Anyway, the weather . . .'

In August, when it was still being recorded, *Victoria Wood As Seen on TV* was announced as part of the BBC's autumn schedule. The initial transmission date was October, which was then put back to November and finally January 1985. In the meantime, a collection of Victoria's songs was published by Methuen, titled *Lucky Bag* and stretching stylistically from the widower's lament 'Love Song' through to Paula du Val's salty ditty 'Nasty Things'. The cover image of a round-buttocked blonde at the piano, naked but for a blue corset, was supplied by Beryl Cook, whose images of big brassy women Victoria loved. The book was launched in Manchester. In a speech reflecting on her life as a songwriter, Victoria looked back to the mock ad for Cupid's Kiss Cornplasters she wrote at Bury Grammar and her early collaborations with her boyfriend Bob Mason. Her first book – and her first retrospective speech – felt like a milestone, even if at the same event the queue for Beryl Reid's memoir was much longer. Victoria competitively sized up the discrepancy and told her publisher Geoffrey Strachan, 'Next year I'll do you a sketch book.'

In an introduction entitled 'Playing the Piano the Victoria Wood Way' Victoria had no practical tips to pass on: 'I don't play with my left hand . . . You can if you want to. We've put some notes in for clever chaps who do want to go bashing away with both hands at the same time, boring everybody stupid.'[37] She had long since stopped practising the piano and blamed her deterioration on the logistics of performance, explaining the problem to Russell Harty: 'You're trying to pull funny faces, you've got to breathe in very hard to project your voice and you're doing something flashy with the hand they can see, and the hand they can't see you think, oh well, never mind.'[38] The better she sold her songs to audiences, the less she valued instrumental technique. The performance was all.

She now returned to performing on a tour originally timed to coincide with the broadcast that autumn. It was proposed by André Ptaszynski, whom Victoria knew from Sheffield Crucible. He had since capitalised on the boom in alternative comedy by presenting live tours by Rik Mayall and Ben Elton, and he introduced her to a Preston-based former music promoter called Phil McIntyre, who had valuable experience of touring acts on the regional circuit. The venues they booked were much larger than any Victoria had yet played – Leeds Grand, Plymouth Theatre Royal, Birmingham Rep. When the postponement of *Victoria Wood As Seen on TV* robbed the tour of marketing potential, these thousand-seater venues did not instantly sell. There was even talk of pulling the tour altogether, but McIntyre urged Ptaszynski to hold his nerve. 'We realised it could turn round late,' he says. 'We toughed it out. Vic always remembered that – that we had faith in her.' She sat through a gruelling round of interviews to plug the show and the book. No promotional opportunity was too small. 'I've been asked to unveil a pub sign in Telford by Graham Woodruff!!' she told Jane Wymark – her former drama lecturer at Birmingham had moved into hostelry. 'How could I refuse?'[39]

Lasting six weeks into mid-December, this was Victoria's longest stretch on the road yet. She had a quip ready for every venue. In Warwick she muddled Coventry Cathedral with Habitat. Plymouth was 'classy and yet seedy', a line she would use for a lot of theatres. New material was slipped into the existing set: a haiku about bangers and mash, a new song languidly spoofing Brecht and Weill ('I vill go to bed viz you if you pose as a Black & Decker drill'). Everywhere she went she was greeted by thunderous applause and ecstatic reviews, if not always full houses – Ramsgate was even cancelled. 'I'm enjoying it a lot more than I expected,' she reported. 'I have a stage manager Liz and she takes care of all the technical side, the ironing and the

chivvying up of large crews of sullen men, the part I always disliked.'[40]
She couldn't help noticing that she had acquired 'a following of overweight lesbians (can't think why ho ho) who cluster round the stage
door and ask me for Julie Walters' phone number'.[41]

As the year ended Victoria reintroduced herself to potential audiences for the forthcoming TV show. She sang 'Don't Get Cocky' on
Bob Monkhouse's Radio 2 show, while she and the Great Soprendo
once more guested on Russell Harty's Christmas special. 'Our Vicky,'
said Harty over the applause for 'Northerners'. 'Our Vicky Wood.'
The episode ended with the cassocked choir of New College Oxford
singing 'Ding Dong Merrily on High', joined by Victoria and various
celebrities. They included Terry Wogan, on whose chat show she had
once clammed up, and Tony Blackburn, who was part of her song
cycle for *The Camera and the Song*. Mainstream fame looked an ever
more comfortable fit.

*Victoria Wood As Seen on TV* was scheduled for Friday nights on
BBC Two starting in January. Readers who turned to the listings
were none the wiser about what to expect. '"Chipper" Patel,' went
the blurb for the first programme, 'arrived from New Delhi in 1962
with an artificial leg and five pounds in his pocket. He now controls
a multi-million pound vinyl flooring empire. He didn't want to be
filmed. So here's a tatty old comedy programme with some women in
it.' The entries for the following weeks were no less opaque. 'Would
Jane Austen have used a food processor?' 'Managing without Opera.
It's the third week of the experiment . . .' 'Two years ago a woman
from a North Lancashire village forgot to stoke her solid fuel boiler.
An award-winning camera crew follow her determined and often
heartbreaking attempts to light it.' Victoria wrote these billings at
the prompting of Geoff Posner, whose idea was to extend the flavour
of Susie Blake's continuity announcements into the show's publicity
material. Victoria even boldly slipped in capsule reviews from the
newspapers. 'Fairly amusing (DAILY TELEGRAPH).' 'I loved it
(DAILY MAIL).'

On the night of Friday 11 January some of the cast gathered in
the basement of a restaurant in Shepherd's Bush to see in the series.
The opening credits, depicting a woman with a feathercut wearing

pink and standing at a microphone on a colourful set, gave way to the real thing. Conscious that she hadn't been seen on TV much at all other than in cheap, cheerful game shows, Victoria used her first monologue to address this head on. A taxi driver arrives to take her to the television station: 'He says, "You're on the television tonight." I said, "I can't be on television because *The Pyramid Game*'s finished." The next thing I knew, here I am talking to you.'

The cast at the restaurant received a phone call advising that the show was a success. 'We all went home on a complete high,' says Susie Blake. But broadsheet newspapers which had often reviewed Victoria overlooked her return to television. This was partly because the BBC did not let reviewers see its light-entertainment programmes in advance, partly because the Saturday papers tended not to carry overnight reviews. The Sundays had more time. Russell Davies in the *Observer* professed instant addiction to *Acorn Antiques*. Astutely, he spotted a change: 'The shadow of self-pity used to lurk behind some of Miss Wood's material, but she has now abandoned this in favour of ruthlessness.'[42] Critics were also distracted by the simultaneous launch of *Dempsey and Makepeace*. 'You are currently missing the treat of the week on at the same time,' hollered Nina Myskow in the *News of the World*.[43] One columnist proposed a week's hard labour watching TV-am for anyone who missed the show. A Glasgow *Herald* leader on westernisation in China even cited Kitty: 'How can you really respect any nation that has never taken to cutlery?'[44] This line and others would seep into the collective consciousness of an audience which peaked at four and a half million. In Victoria's spectacular reinvention of the sketch show, there were many of them to memorise:

'I can't say this often enough – it may be *Hamlet*, but it's got to be fun, fun, fun!'

'We think we've got hens in the skirting board. We found droppings by the pop sox.'

'I thought what would the Queen Mum do? So I just smiled and said, "We shall have fog by tea time."'

'I were in meat packing before. Then an overall came free so I come here.'

'What is it muesli?'

'We'll have more needlework hints next week when Philippa will be showing us how to stitch up the mouth of a talkative friend or relative.'

'We stayed up for the *News at Ten*. Three bangles and a polo neck, thank you.'

'She'll never get 'ers clenched. Take two big lads and a wheelbarrow.'

'I don't do French, I do woodwork.'

# 12

# DOING IT

'Don't start with the clapping. It's a very long song, you know. You'll get repetitive strain injury.'
Advice to Manchester audience, 1996

While *Victoria Wood As Seen on TV* was showing in the first weeks of 1985, Victoria was in digs in Bristol, where Geoffrey was appearing in *Aladdin*. He went out to work for eight hours a day and, encouraged by the producer Michael Codron, she sat down at a desk to attempt to write a play. 'Finished the first draft of my play,' she told Jane Wymark. 'I suppose I had better take a deep breath and do a second draft, which I know will be the hard work.'[1]

Like all other efforts since *Good Fun*, Victoria's desire to break back into theatre did not bear fruit. Indeed, even after her triumphant TV show was instantly recommissioned – 'She was delighted,' says Geoffrey – she would spend a fallow year casting around for other challenges. The first job that came up was a piece of writing for children's television. The commission came from Greg Childs, now a fledgling producer. Of all the big-name writers he asked, 'Vic was the only one who said yes. She probably did it as a favour to me.' She was given a deadline of two months and dashed it off in March. 'I locked myself away in a hotel on the south coast for two days to write the story,' she said. 'Maybe it was the smell of seaweed that gave me the idea.'[2] *Molly and the Seaweed Hypermarket*, rooted in her experience of arriving in Morecambe, had much in common with her unproduced radio comedy *Sunny Side Up*. It tells of Molly Seathwaite's attempt to rescue her local variety theatre, which has no cash for jokes or a decent magician, and prevent her greedy uncle stealing her diamonds in order to build a Slimy Seaweed Hypermarket. A love letter to the stage which also touched on food fanaticism and child neglect, this was a playlet for children that bore Victoria's signature. 'I'm fed up with being a disappointment,' says Molly. Unusually Victoria consented to the script being cut and edited without her involvement. Greg Childs asked for another one, but she politely declined.

In March there was another tour. The promoters' idea of a manageable itinerary struck Victoria as strange. 'They keep sending me dates like Glasgow followed immediately by Barnstaple – they think as long as you don't have to cross water everywhere in the UK can be managed in one day.'[3] Her claim that the average journey was 200 miles was an exaggeration, says her tour promoter Phil McIntyre: 'Obviously an artist thinks we're idiots, we can't read a map. Well, we can. It's always venue availability. She never complained about it.' The Midas effect of being seen on TV meant that the tour sold out. 'Everywhere except Chatham,' Victoria remarked.[4] It left her feeling 'a bit worn out – it's the worry over what the piano will be like at each venue'.[5] When she arrived at the venue she spent a couple of hours running through all of the songs. 'I think if I don't play through them, I'll forget them. And this has proved to be the case.'[6] New songs were added from the TV show. Another was a pastiche of Marvin Hamlisch in the voice of a dim salon dogsbody called Karina ('I'm doing / shampooing / and I'm training to converse').

By now Victoria was so confident in her ability to entertain an audience on her own for two hours that she grew nervous – 'keyed up' as she called it – only an hour before performing: 'The more I work the more I know, and the more I know what I want to do. And the less frightened I am that people won't like me. I don't care really.'[7] A BBC documentary, programmed to run in an afternoon slot, captured the rhythm of her working life on tour. It was a BBC Schools commission, which perhaps explains why Victoria was happy to be filmed at Stankelt Road. Though eager, as she explained, not to be seen as one of those celebrities who 'enjoy having everything seen by the public, their toilet paper and their duvet covers and their marriage – I don't get any pleasure out of it', she was filmed arriving home from a gig and, in unstarlike fashion, stuffing the washing machine with dirty clothes.[8]

Increasingly, fame was something that had to be thought about and managed. At one party in the Lake District, Victoria stationed herself in the kitchen to mix cocktails and wash up. 'Of course the longer I stayed in there, the more difficult it became to make an entrance without looking poncey, so I stayed in there all night and didn't have to speak to anybody, which was great.'[9] Friends, both in Lancashire and London, would avoid asking her about her work; one old friend irked her by never saying anything about the show when coming backstage afterwards. 'I'm not very famous,' she insisted when commissioned to write about fame. 'When questioned, five out of ten people thought I had just played for the last time at Wimbledon, or committed suicide by walking into the sea with rocks in the pockets of my cardigan.' The two Virginias – Wade and Woolf – remained handy tools for deflecting her stardom.

To recuperate after the tour, in April she and Geoffrey embarked on their most exotic trip yet. 'In those digs in Bristol we both felt successful for the first time ever really,' says Geoffrey. 'And we deserved a holiday.' They booked a villa in St Lucia, where they enjoyed room service, swimming and sunbathing – or 'lying on my back, toasting my doo-dahs,' as Victoria put it on *The Late Clive James*.[10] They encountered steel bands and limbo-dancing contests, but they mainly tore through books. As voracious readers – Victoria would devour up to three titles a day – they stuffed novels into luggage and supplemented their stash at airports. 'Very sunny nice warm sea and the natives are friendly,' Victoria told Rosalind. 'We're in a little cottage near the beach and having a nice time.'[11]

She returned to Silverdale invigorated for the coming task. 'I man the Bic for another crack at VWASOTVII,' she told Robert Howie. 'All those wigs to think up!'[12] The BBC's plan was to broadcast the second series in January 1986. Then in mid-May Victoria's agent Vivienne Clore phoned with frustrating news: Geoff Posner was leaving the BBC and would not be available to make the series in time.

'This call came on a day when I was with difficulty just scratching out to the first few gags and it put the mockers on it, cos I couldn't write it without knowing when it would be done – so yesterday I packed up.'[13] All the ideas that swilled in her head had to put in the deep freeze: 'I'm writing them late November–April instead, otherwise they will go completely dead on me.'[14] To vent her frustration she went swimming for a mile and a quarter.

She now had to find something else to do instead. Earlier in the year she had been chuffed to be summoned to lunch with the veteran film director Clive Donner, who had shot scripts by Harold Pinter and Woody Allen, only to be underwhelmed by the film he wanted her to write: 'It's about a miserable fat person (can't think why he thought of me).'[15] Now, with nothing else on, Victoria overcame her objections and started on it in June, then after two days remembered 'it was really a rather lousy, mawkish kind of "lonely fat girl" idea and I felt I'd been here before (especially in real life ho ho) and decided the true artistic course would be to write exactly what I wanted'.[16] On one of her frequent trips to London she presented her outline to Donner and his producer and was pleased that they 'laffed heartily when they read it'.[17] But nothing came of it. In the same period she received a phone call from Vince Cross, who produced her *Lucky Bag* album and had composed a single to tie in with *Return to Oz*, Disney's sort-of sequel to *The Wizard of Oz*, which he invited Victoria to record. She turned up at his studio in Milton Keynes and soon intuited that 'he loathes my voice, my phrasing (and who knows probably my entire personality), and really wished he had been allowed to record the song himself . . . I have never thought of myself as possessing a great voice but I definitely can put a song over.'[18] The experience cured her of the desire to record other people's songs.

The success of *As Seen on TV* resonated in other unpredictable ways. She explored her musical enthusiasms in *Russell Harty's Musical Encounters* on Radio 4 in May and then on Andy Kershaw's BBC Two show *Off the Record* in June. Her tastes were eclectic, stretching from Peter Skellern via the Beatles to the music she encountered on her father's wind-up gramophone: dance-band leader Harry Roy, jazz trumpeter Bunny Berigan and stride pianist Winifred Atwell. (For her thirty-third birthday, which they spent wobbling in canoes on Windermere, Geoffrey gave her a cheque to buy herself a trumpet – 'tho' I'm not sure if I should get one – as I haven't anyone to play with'.[19]) That summer Victoria was asked by her university friend Bill Lloyd to join Jake Thackray and Melvyn Bragg as judges of a competition run by the Brewery Arts Centre in Kendal to find talented young songwriters. She was less enamoured than the other two by an endless flow of 'so many really banal anti-nuclear, Maggie T, pro-miners etc dirges'.[20] When the judges gathered to pick a winner, says Bill Lloyd, 'Melvyn was very snappy and Vic commented afterwards that he was unnecessarily rude.' She and Bragg met again the following month at the Edinburgh Television Festival, where the creator of *Acorn Antiques* was invited to take part in a session chaired by Bragg titled 'A Slippery Soap – is Soap Opera pulling drama down the drain?' The panel of grandees included Julia Smith, the fearsome producer of *EastEnders*. The chance to observe her at close quarters was to bear fruit.

With her autumn schedule messed up by the postponement of *As Seen on TV*, Victoria entered 'a very bleak time work-wise'.[21] It emerged that Geoff Posner would not now be able to produce the show until July the following year, so there was no point in starting on the scripts till January. She hoped to make another album, but the deal fell through. 'I've sort of hit a brick wall and can't come up with any ideas. I took to long walks to try and decide what I really wanted to do (7 miles is my record so far).'[22] She tried writing yet another play – 'no dice – duff idea' – scrapping it on the grounds that it was too derivative of Alan Ayckbourn. Then Michael Codron suggested she write a film. He had just dipped his toe in cinema by producing *Clockwise*, from a script by Michael Frayn. Being asked by a theatre producer to do a film, she admitted, 'confused me and I got stuck again'. She spent several weeks at her desk worrying that she was 'all washed up', changed tack and decided to 'stop giving myself such a bad time, and see if anything pops up into my brain while I'm not looking. I shouldn't complain anyway – I've had it very good the last few years, and I'm not broke, so fuck it.'[23]

The other frustration was that there were no live dates to focus on as she had turned many down in order to write the series: 'So now the calendar's all chopped up with the odd one here and there (two days in November say "Geneva Friday Belfast Saturday" which I'm pretending will never happen).'[24] It nearly didn't. When Victoria got to Manchester to fly to Geneva she discovered she'd left her passport at home. Her cleaner's husband drove at high speed to deliver it just in time; to her horror she learned only afterwards that he was banned from driving. Her friend Charlotte Scott acted as her tour manager: 'We had to run to the furthest departure point onto a plane that was full of people. They just glared at her and then they realised it was her. We just couldn't speak. It was terrible.' The cabaret 'went very well,' Victoria reported, 'considering the audience was 70 per cent male managing directors'.[25] Then, at Belfast the next day, her luggage didn't turn up till half an hour before the performance. The only other work Victoria had that autumn was recording some children's stories for the BBC, during which she was alarmed to discover that, among many other voices, she would have to do a Spanish pirate. She asked to be excused so she could phone Geoffrey and be coached in Spanish pronunciation. 'Thank heavens he was at home or I'd have been fucked. My parrot was a minor triumph, I feel.'[26]

The year concluded brightly with the publication of *Up to You, Porky*, a selection of sketches and monologues from *Lucky Bag, Wood and Walters* and *As Seen on TV*. It took its title from the self-lacerating sketch in which Julie's boutique salesgirl calls Victoria obese, ugly and a fatso. She dedicated it to Peter Eckersley, 'who liked a laugh', and introduced it with a short piece entitled 'Thigs I Like by Vicky Wood age 32' that riffed on her poor typing skills. 'I like as well wen the man from MEPHTHUN(cant spell it)pone up and say we have some lambnatid covers gong begging do you have any old skechs we will pay hansomly but not for ages.'[27] Geoffrey Strachan, a pioneer of humour publishing, was soon firing more ideas at her, among them 'a miscellany of hitherto unpublished songs, sketches, and short essays culled from newspaper and magazines',[28] then 'an autobiographical book, a discursive book, or a work of fiction'.[29] Methuen were the publishers of the *Clockwise* script, so he was all ears about her own screenplay, not to mention any play she may be working on.

Victoria went to London for the launch of *Up to You, Porky*, and sat through a day of interviews. One was down the line to Walter Love, a broadcaster in Belfast who tried to draw her on the title of the book. 'I suppose that's got to be some kind of comment on something,' he said. 'I suppose so,' she replied warily before taking advantage of a bit of interference on the line to pretend she'd been cut off. 'The interview closed with Walter bellowing into the ether "Hello? Hello? We seem to have lost Victoria Wood for the moment," as I was happily walking out of the studio.'[30] Unless her fans had gone to the trouble of videoing *As Seen on TV*, *Up to You, Porky* was the only way of reconnecting with the likes of Kitty, Margery and Joan, Carl and Gail, as well as stage characters such as Victoria's half-witted guide to Haworth Parsonage.

Then, early in 1986, the BBC repeated *Victoria Wood As Seen on TV*, where it gained a larger audience on BBC One. Victoria finally began to write the second series with a change to her writing regime. She had to give up her morning swim because the chlorine was affecting her eyes, replacing it with half an hour's brisk walking to supplement a burst of the Jane Fonda workout. 'Jane Fonda – go for the burn,' she scrawled in a notebook under a page headed 'Gags'. 'I thought that meant you could stop for a bit and have a fag.'[31]

She also opted for a new look, swapping her unruly feather cut for a trim blonde pudding-bowl crop. 'Have had all my hair cut off and bleached,' she informed Jane Wymark. 'I look like a very old fat skin head but who cares?'[32] She unveiled it at the Broadcasting Press Guild TV and Radio Awards, where *As Seen on TV* won best light entertainment. Three days later it was up in the same category at the BAFTAs. The ceremony was held in the Grosvenor House Ballroom, and she dressed up in a cream double-breasted suit. As her category was announced, a short clip from 'Turkish Bath' was shown: 'Now that's the blue of our Margaret's new shower curtain – them varicose veins there.' Nicholas Barrett, who was producing the broadcast for LWT, witnessed its impact: 'Seasoned elder statesmen of the TV industry were suddenly besieged by their own unanticipated laughter at this blast of fresh air from the north. They had never encountered anything like it before.' Victoria was not expecting to win – 'Will

probably lose to Two Ronnies or Spitting Image,' she predicted – and
her delight when she did was slightly dulled when the award for a
show she had entirely written was collected, according to protocol
and tradition, by its producer-director.[33] After sheepishly following
Geoff Posner up to the podium, she had her own moment in the
Best Performance in Light Entertainment category – her nomination,
she mused, 'must be for the stand-up spot as the rest is only different wigs'.[34] She collected her statuette from Clive James and seemed
reluctant to speak. 'Well, I only do one performance,' she said hastily,
'so it's very nice to get a prize for it.' She shook the hand of Ronnie
Barker, who had been nominated twice in the same category, on the
way back to her table, where there was exultation. 'You got used to
the BBC paying for one bottle of wine to be shared between ten,' says
Geoff Posner, 'but on this occasion everyone was so pleased for Vic
that a second bottle was ordered.'

Then, days after the BAFTAs, came another tour. There were new
costumes to be made by 'a very nice designer girl who doesn't seem
to mind that I have the same vital statistics as a walrus'.[35] Because
Victoria had been working on a play and the second series, and lost
a week to flu caught at a Blackpool magic convention, not much
new material had been written. To supplement 'Love Song' before
the interval, and 'Music and Movement' and 'Northerners' in the
encore, she frantically wrote four songs and two monologues: 'I was
terrified of people complaining that they'd seen it all before, but as
I had only had a day to learn it all I was in a bit of a state the first
few nights, and usually cocked up at least one song per show, but
no body minded.'[36] She dashed around London looking for a wig
and any kind of outfit that would work for a second-half opener
to replace Paula du Val, even though she hadn't yet written it. The
character she came up with was an usherette called Margaret, who
explained to the audience that she was filling in while Victoria Wood
nipped to the Happy Haddock Fish Bar to get a bag of chips and a
jumbo sausage for the stage-door keeper. She described a racy lifestyle
of wife-swapping and strip *Trivial Pursuit* and closed by drawing
attention to collection tins to raise money for knackered usherettes.
Another monologue, entitled 'It Was Party Time in the Crescent',

was a comic verse recited in the chummy style of Stanley Holloway:

> Mrs Smith had just come off of a cruise ship
> And showed thirty-two slides of old frescoes
> 'This white wine I discern, is it from the Auvergne?'
> 'No, it's two quid, it's from Tesco's.'

The new songs were complicated to learn. 'Lousy' was an up tempo patter song about counting your blessings: 'I could have nasty lodgers and never get them shifted / I could have famous bosoms and be forced to have them lifted'. 'Photo Booth' was a lilting reverie inspired by memories of Bob Mason:

> Found your picture the other day
> From that booth all those years away
> Chips and kisses and tears and joy
> What a lovely boy you were.

At the last minute another new composition joined the repertoire. It emerged one night after Geoffrey had gone to bed, leaving Victoria to come up with a much-needed show closer: 'I went down to her office at about eight the next morning to find her still at the desk. She said she'd written something quite long. She sang it and we both agreed it could turn out to be a corker.'

The song shattered a rule long planted in Victoria's head that songs should not outstay their welcome. This was much the longest she'd ever written. Its length made it impossible to learn in the few days before she opened, so she inscribed the lyrics in an exercise book, cut it into strips and sellotaped it to the inside of the lid of the grand piano at Harrogate Conference Centre, where, as an encore on Thursday 20 March 1986, Victoria for the first time in public sang

> Freda and Barry sat one night,
> The sky was clear, the stars were bright.
> The wind was soft, the moon was up,
> Freda drained her cocoa cup.

She licked her lips, she felt sublime,
She switched off Gardener's Question Time.
Barry cringed in fear and dread,
As Freda grabbed his tie and said . . .

It had been a fraught night. Thanks to a sudden spike in her fame,
Victoria was now playing to the biggest venues on the circuit. On the
first night of the tour more than 2,000 people had assembled to be
entertained by her. In his first day on the job was a green young tour
manager called Andrew Fell. He had been warned by his boss André
Ptaszynski that Victoria 'can be a little prickly but the only thing
she's worried about is the piano'. To him alone fell the task of lugging
costumes and merchandise, checking sound and lighting, and ironing
Victoria's costumes. 'I did a very bad job,' he says. 'What made it a
million times worse was I could tell it was piling so much anxiety on
Victoria when the last thing she needed was anxiety. The atmosphere
backstage was very tense, very cold, very self-contained.'

'We were more nervous than usual,' says Geoffrey. 'The first night
at Harrogate was dominated by the dual drama of Andrew losing
his nerve and Vic and I being aware that "Barry and Freda" could be
a big thing.' Its first performance seemed to go on for ever – eight
minutes – in the middle of which there was a hiccup. After looking
out to the audience Victoria turned back to her crib sheet and lost
her place. 'The whole thing ground to a halt for possibly three or four
seconds,' says Geoffrey. 'But she collected herself, picked it up again
and cruised through to the finish.' At his suggestion she had doubled
up the last verse to give Freda the triumphant final word. The idea
they'd discussed for years was that Victoria could induce a standing
ovation if she was clinical about it. From the side of the stage Andrew
Fell witnessed it: 'It stormed. They went absolutely crazy. It was the
absolute standout of what was a jaw-dropping two-hour set.'

As a piece of craftsmanship, 'The Ballad of Barry and Freda' was
a complete expression of Victoria's genius. Into the three syllables
by which the song would be popularly known, she compressed the
essence of her comedy. 'Let's do it' said everything: it included, it
enthused and it suggested sex in a brusque pronoun. The chorus was

a homage to both Cole Porter and Noël Coward, whose song 'Let's Do It' she'd praised on *Russell Harty's Musical Encounters*. And 'Let's Do It' was how she referred to her song at home. 'But she realised the song might have legs,' says Geoffrey, 'so she didn't want it confused with Porter or Coward and she changed it before it went public.' On the original typescript she crossed out 'LET'S DO IT' and wrote 'BARRY & FREDA'.

The names were plundered from *As Seen on TV*. In a black-and-white spoof of British New Wave cinema, two northern lovers meet in a dark rainy alley. 'By 'eck,' says Barry, played by Pete Postlethwaite. 'I never thought of myself as romantic, Freda, but you've got a cracking bust.' From the very start Victoria had been writing about what does or doesn't happen in the bedroom. She was far more preoccupied with sex, with 'it', than any other contemporary entertainer – its ins and outs and ups and downs, its dos and don'ts. In the beginning Victoria wrote songs about dreading sex. In stand-up she resented the way it blocked the view of the television. Only a few months earlier, spending a week with Geoffrey at a health farm, she tested a device where she sat in cold water and put her feet in hot water, then swapped. 'Well that was worse than sex,' said a woman in the next cubicle.

Now she turned the tables. She came at sex from a perspective of a wife in midlife fired by a romantic desire to seize the day and 'do it till our hearts go boom'. Freda's ever more lurid fantasies find saucy new uses for items from the kitchen – an oven glove, a hostess trolley, an avocado – while Barry, who can't or won't show his hot-to-trot missus a good time, seeks refuge in such essential household tasks as grouting, lagging and vinyl flooring. Victoria edited her portrait of a marriage as she went along. Initially the song ended with 'No pyjamas / Just dramas / You be Desmond Wilcox I'll be Judith Chalmers'. She soon improved it to 'Be mighty / Be flighty / Come and melt the buttons on my flame-proof nightie'. Then she flipped the last two verses to end with 'Not meekly / Not bleakly / Flick me hard all over with a *Woman's Weekly*'. Intuiting that this conjured up the wrong sort of image, she altered it to 'Beat me on the bottom with a *Woman's Weekly*'. What happens at the very end? The lyrics don't say, but the music does. No fewer than four key changes ramp up the tension towards an inevitable climax supplied by the audience's orgasmic applause.

'She was so happy with that song,' says Geoffrey. 'It was a massive breakthrough.' Gradually, over twenty-two nights passing through Barnstaple and Edinburgh, Ipswich and Lewisham – and a slip in Portsmouth when she pulled up after a key change glitch – Victoria learned to deliver 'The Ballad of Barry and Freda' with effortless confidence. Her feelings about her tour manager did not change. 'It's the only time I knew Vic to be irksome,' says Phil McIntyre. Back at the hotel after the final date in Halifax she gave Andrew Fell, in his words, 'a lovely present' and wished him well. With her exultant promoters she got drunk.

After the tour ended in April, Victoria was 'completely knackered'.[37] But the scripts for *As Seen on TV* needed completing. As she wrote she felt a fresh burden imposed by her BAFTA: 'Every time I looked at the award I kept thinking that people would be expecting so much more now and I just wouldn't be able to live up to it. In the end, I just had to put the thing away.'[38] With days to the deadline, she told Jane Wymark, 'half the scripts are with the typist, some are in a scribbled heap on my desk, and fifteen minutes of crud remain to be written . . . I have to work every day and most evenings to get the bloody thing done.'[39] She and Geoffrey had a day off as sole witnesses at the wedding of Roger Glossop and a very pregnant Charlotte Scott. Over lunch at a smart hotel in Derbyshire, a waiter asked, 'Will you be having the intercourse?' Victoria looked at the newly-weds and said, 'They've already had it.'

Her anxiety about *As Seen on TV* deepened at the potential unavailability of Julie Walters, whose agents had double-booked her to do a film with Mike Leigh. In the end she was pinned down to three weeks in the studio and, when the Leigh film collapsed, Victoria hurriedly wrote her the part of a hairdresser in one of the mockumentaries. But first they were booked to make a series of television commercials for the advertising agency Bartle Bogle Hegarty, who were tasked with broadening the appeal of the ASDA supermarket chain. The creatives came up with the idea of famous shoppers pushing trolleys through countries where their food was sourced. Julie and Victoria signed up to shoot four ads in five days in three countries: Spain, France and a glacier in the Austrian Alps. Julie played a confident middle-class woman who knows her international recipes while a less-clued-up Victoria tags along. As with the songs for her One-Cal commercials, Victoria ended up taking control of the words. As they push their trolleys Julie asks for her opinion of Wiener schnitzel. 'I don't follow the tennis,' she replies.

Back in London Victoria spent three weeks casting the second series with Geoff Posner. For the mini-documentaries the parts remained tiny, but the show's reputation now went before it. She had better luck than in the first series luring Anne Reid, who in 'Mr Right' played a drab single woman seeking a dull husband via a computer-dating agency. Victoria was delighted to secure two grand old actresses: Dora Bryan as her nymphomaniac mother, and Constance Chapman as a retiree living in a terrace who scoops a million pounds in a competition in 'Winnie's Lucky Day'. For 'A Very Funny Young Man Indeed', about a stand-up with a terrible perm who enters a talent contest, she invited Derek Hobson, who hosted her *New Faces* heat in 1974, to play himself. It was another mark of her growing clout that Victoria invited celebrities on. In a parody of the game show *Tell the Truth* three panelists, faced with three guests, had to identify the Labour politician from Dennis Healey, Claire Rayner and Frank Bruno.

When the production assembled out of town, Victoria found herself dangling halfway down a cliff in Dorset, which she hadn't bargained for when she sent Margery and Joan on an activity week for singles. 'I thought it would all be faked,' she wrote in some speech notes, 'and I'd stand on a biscuit tin and they'd shoot it in close up.'[40] Once more the documentaries were filmed in Birmingham, taking Victoria back to old student haunts. 'I am at the HAGLEY RD!' she told Jane Wymark. 'I have been filming in the ELGAR ROOM where I used to play the piano. I have just been to the LAUNDRETTE in HARBORNE where I lived in first yr! Can't cope. I feel I should have polo mint hairslides and be doing forward rolls . . .'[41] (In the Elgar Room she was filmed singing opera badly in a documentary about tragically single flatmates.)

The production came to London to record the rest of the show in late September. For the duration Victoria stayed in the Highgate flat of David Leland, who had found success as a screenwriter – *Mona Lisa*, which he wrote, was released that month. (At the end of her stay she left a thank-you note under the lid of the loo seat, where, she explained, only a man would find it; she also gave him a vintage banjo as a present.) Across the series Victoria cast herself as a tattooist, a nervous schoolgirl sitting an interview for medical school, a woman who goes mad with boredom after moving to the country and a cheerfully dim waitress serving pudding ('Can you see it on the trolley?'). She made the biggest impression with Kelly Marie Tunstall, who stood at the bus stop in a tight short skirt, fishnets, heels and a messy peroxide crop. The sight of her legs 'shocked the cameramen,' said Victoria.[42] Kelly Marie tells extravagantly tall stories while her friend stands by and gawps. (In the first typed draft, the roles were for 'Vic' and 'Julie', but the friend was played by Mary Jo Randle.) Words tumble out of her in an unstoppable torrent, blunt monosyllables punctuated by wildly unexpected references to Magnus Magnusson, the Limpopo or lychees.

Kelly:  So I come out of toilets, right, and he says hey scallop face your skirt's all caught up in your knickers at back, I said I pity you, do you know why, he says why, I says cos it happens to be the latest fashion, I read it in a book, he says what book, I said *Vogue*, that's what book, he said oh likely likely, when do you read *Vogue*, I said when I'm in the hospital having exploratory surgery, that's when. So he said oh.

Pal:  He didn't.

Kelly:  He did.

Kitty returned. So did Susie Blake's continuity announcer. Her smile still fixed in place, she grows ever more ratty at the indignities of working on television: wearing curlers for the breakfast slot, budging up to make room for a person doing sign language, having to make Wally the Wallaby hop for children on their birthdays. Victoria found *Acorn Antiques* trickier to write the second time round. 'Last time a lot of stuff, like people banging into cameras, was put in by the cast and crew as we went along, so I was at a bit of a loss how to carry on. In the end I did what I had done originally.'[43] She also shook things up. After two episodes the theme tune, previously played on Victoria's tinny stylophone, was rendered on a spookily echoing piano. There was a new opening sequence, shot on film, in which Miss Babs trips on the pavement as she enters the shop (whose signage contains a typo). Victoria sourced the idea from the closing sequence of the Sixties show *Dee Time* in which a girl leaps into presenter Simon Dee's sports car: 'As she got in she fell and trapped her leg – and they showed this quite happily week after week.'[44] One week the antique shop randomly reopens as a health club and leisure facility. In this episode the cast threatened to become almost as unprofessional as the actors they played. Mrs Overall enters into the spirit by wearing her own interpretation of work-out gear. 'She had this sagging leotard with a scrunched gusset and a headband,' says Julie. 'Vic said, "Don't show anybody till the actual sketch." Then they all started to shake as they weren't expecting her to be in anything like that.' Victoria, Celia Imrie and Duncan Preston were wedged into a two-person sofa. 'You could feel the vibration,' says Celia, who was furthest away from the camera. Take after take had to be cut as the actors corpsed when Julie entered clutching a tray. The clock ticked towards ten o'clock when overtime would kick in. 'We were doing our best, but it was extremely difficult,' says Duncan. 'There was a lot of anger upstairs.' In the control room Geoff Posner eventually exploded: 'I shouted, "If we don't get this in the can, we are going to lose this!"' In the final take all three kept their eyes off Julie, but even then Duncan struggled to control himself. The scene would become a defining image of the second series.

There were two others. One did not involve Victoria but achieved such comic perfection that she and Posner agreed to close the entire series with it. The sketch, which Victoria titled 'Waitress!' but grew to be known as 'Two Soups', was inspired by an encounter Julie and Victoria once had in Morecambe when they ducked into a tea room during a downpour. 'There was no one in there,' says Julie. 'It was huge and we sat and thought, where the fucking hell is anybody? And at the end of the room there was the double door with a porthole in it and eventually it opened and this ancient waitress took for ever to walk up to us. "Ready to order?" "What is the soup?" That was it.' When Vic wrote it up she confided to Julie, 'I don't know if this is going to work.' Geoff Posner had his doubts too: 'I was uncertain how it would look until I saw Julie do it.' The sketch might easily have ended up alongside others on the cutting-room floor – in one live-studio recording session in early October, no fewer than three scripts were shot but never seen, among them a long sketch for the four main stars, about a Tupperware party to shift Wendy Winters Marital Aids.

Victoria specified that 'Waitress!' would work only if there were sufficient distance between the swing doors and the diners. 'It's a *long way* to the couple's table,' she insisted in the script. Once more, Julie's performance as the deaf and tottering old waitress caused severe discomfort for her fellow actors. 'Duncan and I never got through it in rehearsal, ever,' says Celia. 'Then we had to do it live. We had to keep still. If we'd gone, we would have had to start all over again. It's a great feat of concentration. I got blood in my mouth from biting my cheek.'

Songs in a blazing array of styles were distributed among the cast. 'Counting Moonbeams' was a delicious spoof of a schmaltzy Broadway duet; the cheery composer discovers to his horror that his ambitious young muse can't carry a tune in a bucket. In a snippet of passionate opera in subtitled Spanish (translated from English by Geoffrey) a mezzo-soprano despairs that they've run out of trousers at Topshop. 'I'm pig sick, Dennis!' she sings with lung-bursting passion. Julie played a saucy star of Edwardian music hall giving sung advice to her daughter in the style of the BBC's *The Good Old Days*:

So please take this as your slogan,
Go on Aspel, go on Wogan
But for gawd's sake never work with Roland Raaat!

Victoria was one of three old Lancashire lasses – Marrie, Clarrie and Min – wearing big bloomers as they sing a rumpty-tumpty end-of-the-pier song. Her most touching song was 'Crush', sung in the voice of a lovelorn schoolgirl yearning to be noticed by a much older boy.

As the second series loomed, Victoria hesitated about including 'The Ballad of Barry and Freda', wondering whether it would be better kept back for live performances. Eventually she realised she was a song short and played it to David Firman. 'I thought it was terrific,' he says, 'but I also thought, what do I do that responds to the guts of the piece, and how do I try to indicate two different voices of Barry and Freda?' For backing he summoned a banjo, trumpet, trombone, clarinet, bass, drums and washboard plus tubular bells, while he played a tack piano with pins attached to the hammers. The idea was that his barroom sound would provide a counterpoint to Victoria's Steinway: 'I wanted to be the reluctant man – that's my texture. I'm doing something different that's saying I can't do it. To start with the band are keeping out the way and marking time. That was the idea so that as the temperature and the key got higher and higher, they should be part of that.' In the end the tack piano was subsumed by the wind's shrieks and howls until the tubular bells at the end mimic the sound of wedding bells, as if Barry and Freda's nuptial vows are about to be renewed.

The band did one run-through when the artists and crew were at lunch. Because Victoria was sitting away from the rest of the musicians there were problems with syncing. 'Christ, this is a disaster,' muttered the bass player. They went back to address technicalities, played it through again, then did a camera rehearsal. In all the song had been rehearsed three and a half times by the time the audience arrived.

The performance was kept back to the end of the evening, and the band's anxieties had not been allayed. 'This was quite a challenge for us,' says Firman. 'We were thinking, are we going to fall apart? It's probably secure, but we're all living on our nerves.' Then they played it. 'Because it's such a long song you can smell the climax is coming – will it come? It's coming . . . When Vic starts to stand up as she plays and sings the final verses with the big pay-off lines, she's on a high. She just lays into it with every fibre. It finally arrives and the whole thing has gone off like a bloody rocket. I thought people would enjoy it. I didn't realise that there would be this incredible tumult of ecstasy from a TV audience in a TV theatre. The audience went bananas. This was not processed applause that has been whipped. This was an audience going potty because of what they had just witnessed.'

Victoria, with one last bounce on her piano stool, remained seated to take the applause. 'I think she was pleased. I know she was,' says Firman. In his headphones he got a message from Geoff Posner suggesting they do another take. 'And I said, "I thought it was very good, Geoff, it's the best we've been. What's bothering you?"' The news that another take was needed was broken to Victoria by the floor manager Roy Gould, who had watched the performance from behind the camera crane: 'The energy coming off her was immense. Vic was very up and then I got Geoff in my ear saying, "Go and talk to her." I crouched down by Vic and said, "Geoff wants to do another take." She said, "Oh no, they won't laugh again! What's the matter with the first one, Geoff? I don't want to do it again." In the end I put my arm around her and said, "It'll be fine."'

The audience did laugh the second time round, but Victoria could not quite match the exuberance of the first take, which was chosen for broadcast. Years later she could still recall the glow of her achievement: 'The first time we ever did "Barry and Freda" in a studio, which is a very, very complicated song to learn, it's got lots of keys changes and hundreds of rhymes . . . I was looking from camera to camera and one of my eyes has wandered around I was so tired. I was happy. That was a happy song to do.'[45]

# 13

# AN AUDIENCE WITH GRACE

> 'BOSOMS
> ACNE
> PERIODS
> DIETING'
>
> Stand-up prompt note, 1987

After the long slow birth of the second series, Victoria was in a mood to move on. She told anyone who asked, from *Marxism Today* to *Woman's World*, that writing for television had exhausted her. 'I can't honestly believe anybody actually enjoys writing,' she groaned. 'It's an absolute agony.'[1] Nor was she disposed to field yet more gruellingly predictable questions from tabloids about body image and women in comedy. One radio host she spoke to in New Zealand began by describing her as fat and plain: 'I should have put the phone down but because it was live I didn't have the nerve. How fucking rude, though.'[2] Her main point was that, for the moment, she was no longer willing to endure the solitary confinement required to churn out sixty sketches at a time. 'I've done what I wanted to do,' she said, 'and it's time to go while people still want more.'[3] The decision was partly driven by economic necessity. 'I don't earn that much from television,' she explained, 'because it takes me so long to write the bloody things.'[4]

*Victoria Wood As Seen on TV* was moved to Mondays. This time round critics could view it in advance, and previewers all insisted that the show should on no account be missed. Yet there were dissent-ers. One fretted sourly that the first episode, which climaxed in 'The Ballad of Barry and Freda', 'leans too heavily – and, in the case of the closing ditty, too desperately – on the sex-orientated joke and song'.[5] Victoria avoided such critiques but heard one by accident one night after returning from a cabaret booking in Surrey: 'Drove home in blinding rain, absolutely wrecked, got home, switched on TV – it was Points of View – someone had written saying "VW is about as funny as a nuclear explosion . . ." At least they didn't say I was fat and plain . . .'[6] The nation begged to differ. The viewing figures rose above 8.5 million – double the number who watched the first series – to make it the most viewed programme on BBC Two.

During the run, Victoria, wearing a long silver coat, joined a vast cast of celebrities for the Royal Variety Performance at the Theatre Royal Drury Lane. She was on straight after the synchronised tum-blers of Peking Opera – 'I was worried they might nick some of my material,' she told the audience. In fact, she nicked some of her own and wove it in among jokes about the stars crammed backstage. The Queen Mother and the Duchess of York honked with laughter as she revived a long-serving punchline about her Playtex Discontinued, dating from 1982: 'If God had meant them to be lifted and separated, He'd have given us one on each shoulder.'

The evening reunited her with Marti Caine, who was now present-ing a rebooted New Faces. As with all celebrities, Victoria considered her fair game. In her speech notes she depicted her lanky pal backstage 'squeezing into one of those dresses – like clingfilm with buttons'.[7] In the end she didn't use it at Drury Lane and stored it up for a speech at a literary dinner held a few days later to launch the paperback edition of Up to You, Porky. Victoria's most meaningful encounter at the Royal Variety Performance was with Paul McCartney. Her favourite Beatle wandered over before she was due to go on and quietly engaged her in conversation. 'He clearly admired her but didn't acknowledge it openly,' says Geoffrey, who was a witness. 'His friendliness and confi-dence spoke volumes enough.' As for the evening itself, she privately found it 'excruciatingly boring and HOURS LONG, Queen Mother nearly died of exhaustion. I did pretty well – got thro' it with no mistakes which was the main thing.'[8]

Another ordeal she volunteered for before the close of the year was to be grilled on *Desert Island Discs*. Asking the questions was Michael Parkinson, whose TV chat show she had failed to get onto back in 1980. On the irritations of fame she remarked that 'mainly people want to know if you are who they think you are'. Who Victoria really was she instinctively shrouded from listeners – she gave nothing away about her solitary upbringing. 'It was just very ordinary,' she said of a childhood in which she had in effect already experienced life on a desert island. 'She was furious about it afterwards,' says Geoffrey. 'She thought Parkinson hadn't done the research, wasn't interested in her.' Her musical preferences were ones she'd expressed in public before – for Prokofiev, Gershwin, Eric Coates, Bunny Berigan and Noël Coward singing 'Let's Do It' in Las Vegas. Coward, she said, was one of only two songwriters whose lyrics she liked listening to. The other, also selected, was Ian Dury. Her eighth record was by the Weather Girls, helpful for yomping up fells. For her reading she chose the collected works of Arthur Marshall, the former headmaster she'd made friends with on *Call My Bluff*, and for a luxury to keep her busy a mighty Wurlitzer. It was broadcast early in 1987.

Victoria closed 1986 with three dates at St David's Hall, Cardiff, under the title *Victoria Wood As Seen at Christmas*. She then went back to Silverdale for some much-needed time off. Among the succession of visitors was her school friend Lesley Fitton, who was the latest of her chums to become a mother.

After years of cadging beds off London-based friends, at the start of 1987 Victoria and Geoffrey decided that the time had come to find a flat of their own. Victoria headed south so often that she was beginning to think of the motorway as her true home. 'Most of the real living I do these days seems to be in my car.'[9] After Geoffrey made all the arrangements over the phone, in January she had three days of 'intensive snow trudging' looking at flats 'then half a day for a diabolical radio commercial which did at least pay for the hotel'.[10] In the evenings she saw two friends in plays. One starred Julie Walters – 'I'm hoping it won't be anything like the play I have vaguely in mind to write,' she fretted.[11] Another evening she saw Alan Rickman in the sizzling hit she called 'can't spell it – Dangerouse'.[12] They had a boozy night out that ended up at the Limelight Club. 'All very café society and it seems rather a shame I wasn't snapped with Alan and splashed all over the Daily Mail.'[13]

Victoria eventually plumped for a flat in Maida Vale which she was shown by mistake – being on the second floor it was not convenient for lugging magician's clobber up and down. 'I cannot tell a lie, it is a very boring ordinary flat,' she told Jane Wymark, situated on 'a very boring road . . . But we only need somewhere to live while we work in London, it doesn't have to be Shangri La.'[14] The flat in Castellain Mansions, a red-brick block in the road where they'd rented in 1980, had a view over Paddington Bowls club. Geoffrey hadn't seen it when they made an offer – he was doing panto in Liverpool and dashed down between shows: 'I'm dreading throwing open the front door with an eager expression and him standing ashen faced saying "Oh no, Vic . . ." Tough shit, too late now.' They took possession in May. There were no curtains or furniture or phone, and when Victoria first tried to cook she found the oven and hob in the freshly fitted kitchen had not been connected.

In March she was back at the BAFTAs, where neither Victoria nor Julie won in the performance category, but for the second year running she and Geoff Posner collected the award for Best Light Entertainment Programme. There were other appointments in London – *Call My Bluff*, a recording of Allan Ahlberg's *Ten in a Bed* for *Jackanory*, a grand dinner at the Royal Academy of Arts. Victoria was on a guest list with all the nabobs of the gallery world, plus the Duke and Duchess of Gloucester, the Lord Chancellor, the Archbishop of Canterbury, Isaiah Berlin and Iris Murdoch. She went down to Barnes to meet Hilary Hayton, who had made the children's animation *Crystal Tipps and Alistair* and sought to interest Victoria in a cartoon about a dog called Rosie: 'I wasn't too bothered about this, except I thought there might be a few bob in it (in two years time, which is how long it takes to animate thirteen programmes) but I was very impressed with them.'[15] In the end it took a lot longer than two years.

Despite Victoria's announcement about *As Seen on TV*, the BBC persuaded her to have one last reunion. Thus she spent the spring of 1987 writing fifty-five minutes of material for a forty-minute show. Just as the second series was being repeated on BBC One in June, the *Victoria Wood As Seen on TV Special* was rehearsed and record-ed. 'Let's go out the same way we went in!' Geoff Posner wrote on her shooting script. Casting this time was simple. Jim Broadbent was cast as a gobbledygook-spouting Doctor Who, along with sev-eral lesser-known regulars whose gift for comedy across both series Victoria had come to value and rely on – actresses such as Lill Rough-ley, Deborah Grant, Meg Johnson, Sue Wallace, Kay Adshead and Georgia Allen.

The show opened with an announcement from Susie Blake's continuity announcer that she was hosting a small sherry party and expecting some new curtains from Laura Ashley: 'And at the end of the month I'm being fired.' Having created a show about TV, Victoria decided to portray the end of *As Seen on TV* as a brutal decision taken by management. 'We've been axed because we're not a soap opera,' she explained in her opening monologue, pretending to sound incensed.

Rather than revive *Acorn Antiques*, she subjected it to the docu-mentary treatment. The idea was inspired by a fly-on-the-wall film about the making of *EastEnders* shown the previous autumn. 'It came on the telly,' says Geoffrey, 'and we looked at each other and said, "That's a gift." Vic particularly enjoyed the contribution of Julia Smith and decided that *Acorn Antiques* had to have a similarly driven producer.' Julia Smith, the co-creator of *EastEnders*, was a formidable figure known as 'The Godmother', whom Victoria had met at the Edinburgh Television Festival in 1985. In *As Seen on TV* she became Marion Clune, the terrifying ogre at the helm of *Acorn Antiques* who has a weakness for nonsense lingo ('molto libre', 'nila problemo') and issues-led plots. 'Let's box a wee bit dangerous,' she says as she pro-poses a storyline about earwax. 'I'm talking off the top of my hairdo now.' The quaking scriptwriter who reckons AIDS is a better bet is sacked on the spot and threatened with kneecapping if he bleats to the press. To incarnate Marion Clune, Victoria cast Maggie Steed, who played a horribly unkind actress in *Happy Since I Met You*. In another nod to Victoria's past, the reporter visiting the set was played by Paul Heiney, one of Esther Rantzen's sidekicks on *That's Life!*

But the sketch was also about thespian grandeur. The actors playing Mrs Overall and Mr Clifford were first glimpsed when their characters were axed at the end of the second series. Now Victoria fleshed out them out further. The actress playing Miss Babs is a hoity-toity ice queen who, unlike her character, knows how to pronounce Kirkcudbright. Mr Clifford does knitting and seethes with suppressed rage. As for the actress who plays Mrs Overall, never had Victoria been so savage about the delusions of celebrity. Bo Beaumont is afflicted by a monstrous ego and haemorrhoids. 'I'm a huge, huge star – this is the price I pay,' she simpers when the reporter asks about rumours of cast feuds. 'Look how the press treated poor Yorky.' When she wrote this, Victoria had only recently met the Duchess of York.

The other highlight was a pitch-perfect recreation of *Coronation Street*, shot in grainy black and white. Victoria's ear for the rich rhythms of the show's dialogue came from years of study. She had been watching *Corrie* since childhood, her father had written an episode and now Bob Mason was a regular scriptwriter. The break-up of Ken and Deirdre would remain one of her favourite jokes in stand-up and song. In tribute, she cast herself as Ena Sharples, the sour-tongued battleaxe played by her grandmother's old bridge partner Violet Carson. With a twist of the dial Victoria turned heightened northern dialect into clotted gobbledygook. 'I've heard enough skriking in this bug hutch to last me from t'Weatherfield Viaduct to t'Whit Week Walk,' says Martha Longhurst (played by Julie) as she sups on her milk stout in the snug.

To round out the parody, it had to look right. Victoria's make-up artist was Chrissie Baker, who had joined the show in the second series. In her interview in TV Centre she had nervously dropped her things on the floor. 'You need to be better organised,' said Victoria, who recognised something in the accent and, as they were leaving, asked where she was from. 'I said, "You will never have heard of it. It's just outside a little place called Bury, called Ramsbottom." She shook me on my arm and said, "You're going to do this job!" I said, "I really want to do it, but I am breastfeeding." She said, "Bring them with you!" She stopped me dead. You were *never* offered that.' They became lifelong friends.

Chrissie soon learned that working with Victoria she had to be quick. *As Seen on TV* was recorded at a lick, and there was little time to switch from one character to the next. 'She would be running down the corridor and shout out, "Come on, Baker!" She'd rip a wig off and be on to the next one. She loved the speed of it.' But the task of transforming Victoria into Ena Sharples, and the application of prosthetic eye-bags, required time. 'I thought, Vic's not going to sit in the chair. She wanted to be out there watching what everybody was doing. We started really early in the morning and I said, "You can't move." "I won't." "But you will. Vic, I won't be able to do this job unless you sit there." "Oh for God's sake! I promise you." And she sat there for three and a half hours.' When she walked on set the audience gasped at her transformation. A quite different challenge for hair and make-up was the show's joyous finale, a northern homage to *Grease* in which the cast wore garish wigs and face paint to sing and dance through 'At the Chippie'.

After twelve episodes of mainly playing the feed, Celia Imrie was finally let off the leash to play a presenter of 'McOnomy', a thrifty Scottish version of Margery and Joan's consumer show, and a pleased-as-punch housewife who talks like a walking billboard for domestic products. As for Duncan Preston, Victoria conceded he 'hasn't been exploited properly in the show because I tend to write parts for women'.[16] As if to include him, in one sketch he modelled a new bra for men. It wasn't the only new bra in the show. In her monologue, Victoria explained that the show's status as a special meant she had splashed out on a new one.

Victoria's sketch-writing reached a new peak of brilliance in 'Self-Service'. Julie pulled on a maroon beret to play a ghastly serial complainer queuing with a tray at a crowded buffet counter. 'Never touch prawns,' she snaps. 'Do you know, they hang round sewage outlet pipes treading water with their mouths open – they love it!' Victoria played the feed (named Enid in the published text) who self-lessly set up gag after quotable gag for Julie to nail. The sketch owes some of its uniqueness to the unusual camera angle: to save building a whole canteen for the set, it had to be shot from behind, with Victoria and Julie gamely performing over their shoulders. For other characters it was the end of the line. There was no more Margery and Joan, or Kelly Marie Tunstall. 'I thought I'll do another one and I couldn't do it,' Victoria said. 'It's gone dead on me. I couldn't do any more Kittys with Pat Routledge. I couldn't think of anything else to say.'[17]

No sooner was the special in the can than Victoria put her television career on hold to go back on tour. A pattern for slowly feeding freshly written material into the act was now becoming established. 'I don't think you can start off with a totally new show,' she reasoned before she set off. 'You'd be all over the place. You wouldn't know what worked.'[18] So she started with the material from the Cardiff set at Christmas and over a series of summer festival appearances dropped in new sections. At one of them Geoffrey lurked and took notes 'which was extremely useful as there were apparently a lot of things I was doing wrong performance-wise'.[19] After the gig two women burst into her dressing room, threw on hats and she had to watch them 'Doing One Of My Own Sketches. I shall say no more, but Geoff's toes curled so much he had to have an operation.'[20] The final warm-up was in Edinburgh, before the official tour began in September with three nights in Dublin and two in one of her favourite theatres, the Grand Opera House Belfast. Everywhere she went she told her audience that 'this is the theatre where Sooty was heckled'.

The show retained a few old favourites, some of which went way back. A nervous woman trying to light a Lil-Let was recycled from *Lucky Bag* in 1983. The Dutch cap gag was first heard in *Wood and Walters* in 1982. Trustiest of all was her dedication of 'The Ballad of Barry and Freda' to 'my deep interest in the act of physical lovemaking – it's very short'. She'd said the same at *The Secret Policeman's Other Ball* in 1981. From the same era she also mentioned her Hollie Hobby vibrator ('it's better than the My Little Pony one'). These were all retained because she knew she could rely on them at junctures – coming on, moving to the piano, cueing up a song – when she absolutely needed a laugh.

But most of the material was brand new. There were thoughts that arose from personal experience – swimming, Christmas with relatives, donating blood, periods – all twisted and wrought into gags. One monologue was an extended riff inspired by Victoria's trip to Alicante with ASDA, only in this made-up story she travelled on a package holiday with a large posse of sex-mad girls from Derby and a starchy single woman called Betty Comstock. The set was peppered more liberally than ever with references to shops and brands from Benetton to Spud-U-Like (poshly pronounced 'Spudoolickay'). Her piano, she said, was supplied by MFI. Victoria depicted herself buying trendy condoms in Boots ('shall I wrap them up or will you wear them now?'). The most savage joke about a brand was in the character of a whiny-voiced department-store beautician attempting, ever more desperately, to flog the new autumn range from Sacherelle: 'We have a special offer on special offer, coming to you with any item worth £36 or more – this is a free gift comprising of suede-effect pochette packed to the drawstring with handy-size oddments totalling mouth blot, eye wipe and shimmering cleavage enhancer.'

Another new character was a marketing desperado who found sundry ways to mispronounce 'bona fide' as she pitches her tone-deaf questions: 'Given some type of structured post-nuclear society, do you think people are more likely or less likely to be eating Hellman's Mayonnaise?'

The most successful new character made an entrance at the start of the second half: 'I come through the audience, which confuses them. With the house lights up. They think there's been a terrible mistake.'[21] Though highly visible in a bright orange mac and a yellow beret, it was only when she drifted onto the stage that audiences twigged. 'I'm looking for me friend,' she announced in a dense Lancashire accent. 'Kimberley. Have you seen her? She's got right dangly earrings with sausages on them, only they're not on her ears. She's really, really tall and they just pierced as high as they could reach.' Victoria stretched her arms up towards two imaginary nipples.

The mac was Victoria's recent gift to herself, which she then decided she didn't like. Geoffrey bought the beret to go with it. The resulting outfit had a comic implausibility – the endearingly naive character would never put together such a zesty get-up – but a long coat and beret were practical for a quick backstage transformation and had a bright simplicity that became rapidly iconic. It never seemed to matter that Kimberley was merely described while her friend did all the talking. (In a rehearsal tape Victoria gave Kimberley the surname of Clark. Privately she and Geoffrey always referred to the character in the mac and beret as Kimberley.) Kimberley's imaginary bulk enabled Victoria to turn up the dial on her jokes about body image. In *Wood and Walters* she played a fat shopper who is offered the cubicle curtain; the only thing in the boutique to fit Kimberley is the cubicle itself – 'she's having the doors taken up'. In *Lucky Bag* Victoria imagined her class at school denting the viaduct when out cross-country running; when Kimberley sits down she makes the town hall steps sag.

As the strength of Victoria's stand-up material grew, there were fewer songs. 'One Day', composed as a spoof, was repurposed as a straight-faced break from comedy. She closed the first half with 'Litter Bin', about a depressed mother putting her newborn baby in the rubbish, which tended to confuse audiences. 'I would start off that song,' she recalled, 'and people would start to giggle and then you'd think, I'm just going to hold my nerve and do it, and then they would realise.'[22] There were new comic songs too. In 'Things Would Never Have Worked' Victoria tells a man why they're romantically incompatible:

> Rapport's a thing you just can't manufacture
> You had your pin-up girl, I couldn't match her
> I didn't want to – it was Mrs Thatcher
> Things would never have worked.

The punchline is he shares her taste for hunky men. 'The Ballad of Barry and Freda' was now cemented as the closer.

Victoria embarked on an intense schedule with a new tour manager. Carol Spraggs was suggested by her promoter André Ptaszynski, but Victoria insisted she see a performance so the job requirements were clear in advance. 'My new girl Carol seems to be very nice, tall and jolly,' she was pleased to note.[23] The tour party expanded to three with a new sound man. All three travelled in separate vehicles, then at the end of the night they would wind down with a drink in the hotel bar, where Victoria sometimes found herself targeted by strange men.

'They'll come knocking at my bedroom door, saying: Can I sleep with you? Then there's this conversation through the keyhole, me saying No you can't . . . go away. If they've bought you a drink, they think it's quite all right to pop round later.'[24] The experience made enough of an impression for Victoria to write up a monologue about over-confident men in a notebook: 'They're all milling about with the big plastic badges that say "Hi I'm Barry I'm facing the future", "Hi there I'm Ken I'm going for it". And they come lurching up to you, and you think I should wear the badge "Hi I'm Victoria I'm knackered and I'm going to bed."'[25]

She was insulated from male attention whenever Geoffrey was around. He joined her in Birmingham, where they discovered her old bedsit in Priory Road had been converted into a private hospital. She was recognised when she entered a newsagent in Selly Oak. 'It's not every day we get Victoria Wood coming into the shop,' said the paper-boy, before turning uncertainly to Geoffrey – 'or Colin Welland.'[26]

The centrepiece of the tour was a prestigious fortnight at the London Palladium, which smoked out dispersed relatives. Her mother came and was rewarded. 'Best show yet,' Victoria wrote in her tour itinerary. 'I've finally got the hang of it now.' Rosalind brought her son Mazda – Victoria had seen neither for four years and was pleased to find 'they were both extremely nice'.[27] Elsewhere a young woman Victoria didn't recognise was ushered into the dressing room who turned out to be her brother's daughter, whom she'd last seen as a toddler. It was quite common in Victoria's family for relatives to keep their distance from one another. Once at a book signing a woman reached the front of the queue, announced that their mothers were sisters and disappeared before Victoria could engage her in conversation.

National newspapers had not reviewed Victoria live for three and a half years, and critics now discerned a new aura of confident command. 'The unmistakable gloss of success is upon her,' said Jack Tinker in the *Daily Mail*.[28] 'At 34,' said the *Financial Times*, 'Victoria Wood is already an Institution and one that demands an instant conservation order.'[29] The *Guardian* talked of her 'spiked knuckledusters',[30] *The Times* of her 'lurking viciousness'.[31] The targets of that aggression were mainly celebrities. 'I don't usually pick on specific people,' Victoria claimed while still writing the show, but sometimes she couldn't resist. Anne Diamond, the daytime presenter who had a penchant for oversharing in the media, was 'so publicity mad that she went for a scan and wanted to turn it into a cartoon'. She imagined Andrew Lloyd-Webber and Richard Stilgoe collaborating on a musical called *Twats*.

By now Victoria was becoming a target too as other entertainers took to impersonating her. That summer in Edinburgh Jan Ravens performed a song in the style of Victoria, who nipped in to watch it from the back and was not amused. According to Geoffrey, it caused 'some rumblings in the business – a feeling that comedians shouldn't take the piss out of comedians'. Pauline Hannah reached a much wider audience on ITV's impersonation show *Copy Cats*. But the most thought-through take on Victoria was in a series of solo sketches scripted by Geoff Atkinson (who had written for *The Two Ronnies*) and performed by Kate Robbins. She and her brother Ted, Victoria's old warm-up man, had their own show that summer on ITV. At the piano she went close to the knuckle with a song about female jealousy: 'You're prettier than me, and I can't live with it. / That pretty face of yours – can't you give me it?' In 'Victoria Wood: A Very Funny Woman', also from *Kate and Ted's Show*, Kate Robbins's besuited Victoria explains how she gets all her sharpest ideas from looking at food labels in the pantry.

After the high of the Palladium the tour proceeded to less salubrious venues. There was a hairy return flight from Aberdeen to Newcastle on a tiny plane which 'looked like it had come out of a cereal packet'.[32] When exhaustion set in, she was given a driver to ferry her in and out of venues and back to London. At Brighton Dome, where the performance was recorded for future release, a man wandered into Victoria's dressing room and walked off with £10. Carol Spraggs ('who turned out to be a real trouper') chased him down the corridor.[33] At the police station the theatre management wanted Victoria to press charges, but she was reluctant. In November, after the last date in Liverpool, there was a champagne party where Victoria drank for the first time in weeks and her promoters presented her with a black cake in the shape of a piano marked MFI. To Jane Wymark she audited her epic odyssey: 'Nine and half weeks, 27 hotels, 51 shows and 5869 miles – as the song says – and I'm still here.'[34] She felt flush enough at the end of it to send her parents money to sink a borehole at Birtle Edge House in order to access their own water supply after thirty years. 'The size of the cheque made me think it must be an insurance premium,' wrote her mother gratefully.[35]

December brought a last chance to write a silly billing for the *As Seen on TV Special*: 'Anthropologist Kerry Askham gave chimpanzee Chester a typewriter and lots of paper. After three years he came up with an idea for a jeans commercial, a sonnet and a Victoria Wood Special. Sadly, after this programme was made, Chester contracted an infection and is now working for Channel 4.' Meanwhile, a new set of sketches was published under the title of *Barmy*. It included material from the Christmas special which had not yet been broadcast, and there was even room for one that would never been seen at all: 'Lady Police Serial' poked fun at *Juliet Bravo*, the pioneering police drama with a female inspector, but ended up on the cutting-room floor. Victoria dedicated *Barmy* 'to Susie, Ceal, Duncan and Julie – for the acting' and added a preface by Margery and Joan.

Margery and Joan were exhumed for the last time when, in February 1988, Victoria made her first appearance on Comic Relief. Live in the studio, the pair took passive-aggressive potshots at each other while offering their usual consumer advice. It was revealed by Joan that Margery, the more sexually active of the two, was expecting a baby after a chance encounter with a café waiter called Pedro. In the original script Joan asks Margery what she's going to call the baby. 'Something short and snappy,' says Margery. 'Anne Diamond?' says Joan.[36]

The sketch capitalised on the news that Julie was pregnant, visibly so when sitting at right angles to the camera. Motherhood was much on Victoria's mind too. When her nephew was born ten years earlier, she described herself to Rosalind as 'a baby freak'.[37] For years the task of building a career, rather than starting a family, remained her priority. There was also the problem of scheduling – she and Geoffrey spent so much time apart on the road. 'It is about the best contraceptive there is,' she said during her previous tour, and it would continue: through the whole of 1986 they barely saw each other.[38] Meanwhile, many of her contemporaries from school and university were having children. 'If I ever do get around to it,' she told Jane Wymark, who was one of them, 'I should be quite an expert.'[39] Media interest intensified when Victoria and Julie did a press call for the second series of *As Seen on TV* dressed as Margery and Joan: 'All they wanted to know was who Julie was living with and when I was going to have a baby!'[40] Another magazine asked the same question: 'We've practically given up on the idea of ever starting a family. It'll be 1988 at this rate before we even get the chance.'[41]

In 1988 Victoria would turn thirty-five. On the last day of 1987 her thoughts about what it meant to be in her thirties were published in the *Sunday Times Magazine*. Dashing the piece off while on tour, she cracked a couple of jokes about wrinkles gathering around her eyes and did not mention motherhood. 'We thought about it a lot over at least two years,' says Geoffrey. 'Vic always knew she wanted to do this. Her clock was ticking. It was very much a natural impulse of hers, that she was just acting upon.' As often happened with her preoccupations, the subject burrowed its way into her comedy. In her stand-up show she told of a (possibly invented) friend who had post-natal depression: 'She showed me the baby, then I had it as well.' It was as if she was laying a false trail. 'Why are children so horrible?' she asked her audience. 'I don't know how people can have them. I don't! I don't know how people can give birth apart from anything else. No, the more I hear about it the worse it sounds.' In her speech notes she imagined a conversation between a child and its mother. 'Am I adopted?' 'Course not.' 'Yeah but – can I be?'[42] But as she came round to the idea, she began to accept that she could afford to put her career on hold, that she 'could stop for a bit and it wouldn't all disappear'.[43]

Victoria's pregnancy, when it came, was meticulously planned to fit in with her schedule. She had a tour booked for April 1988, preced-ed by a benefit gig for the King's Head Theatre at Sadler's Wells. 'I didn't want to be newly pregnant then, yet I didn't want to be too pregnant when I went on tour either.'[44] Also she needed to dove-tail with Geoffrey's schedule, so, in mid-January, Victoria flew back from Dublin and drove late at night from Heathrow to a hotel they'd booked in order for the date-sensitive rendezvous to take place.

Though scarcely necessary, ticket sales for the tour were boosted by a swift repeat of the *As Seen on TV Special*, which also won its third consecutive BAFTA. Victoria added bits and pieces of new material to her set – a joke about the spotty back of Jeffrey Archer, topical after his recent libel trial. As she drove herself up and down the land, she made notes about the venues she visited in a ring-bound itinerary. Such was the perfectionism she asked of herself, her morale could be affected by something as seemingly minor as the quality of the piano stool. 'V nice warm friendly audience,' she said of Crawley. 'Dire leisure centre venue as per.' 'Peculiar venue,' she wrote of St Austell, 'but who cares?' She grumbled about Wolverhampton's '*terrible* venue – useless crew' and St Albans' 'terrible ushers in and out all the time – don't want to play it again'. The venue in Norwich was 'horridish', in Newcastle 'dumpish' and in Hull 'khaziish'. She wasn't a fan of the Steinway in Scarborough: 'too old and battered and tinny'. In Oxford she encountered a 'v dead piano, v alive audience, v damp dressing room'. The audiences were the clay she went to work on, and they varied greatly. Her favourites were 'jolly'; her least favourite 'snotty' or 'snottish'. She got both over two nights in Birmingham: the first was 'TV-bad', the second 'FAB'. On occasion she'd have to work hard to earn an 'extremely good reception at end' (Preston) or 'fantastic reception at end' (Bournemouth). In Derby she '*really* worked my arse off and got them in the end'. In Lincoln they were 'v jolly, v thick', in Carlisle 'v agricultural'. Coventry: 'worst yet'. Liverpool: 'excellent audience – really warm and jolly. One of the best receptions'. She loved Sunderland: 'extremely *nice* kind audience – a good feeling'. Manchester was 'VVVG'. She had a great night in Edinburgh: 'tore em up'.[45]

By the time she started the tour she was three months pregnant and could begin to plan. It occurred to her and Geoffrey that Stankelt Road would be too small to house a family. Their initial thought was that the time had come to spend less time on the M6 and M1 and move south. They did some house-hunting along the M4 corridor – 'G nearly died of exhaustion going to Wilts every weekend,' she told

Lesley Fitton – and had an offer accepted on a vicarage in Bradford-upon-Avon.[46] On the day of exchange the vendor withdrew, so the next day Victoria offered the asking price for a house at the other end of Silverdale. Cove Lea was a converted pair of cottages on a narrow lane leading down to a small sandy inlet, with a walled garden and fruit grove over the road and a one-up one-down cottage to house a nanny. After nearly seven years in Stankelt Road, they moved in over the summer. Though she wasn't a fan of the 'floor-length Liberty curtains – all v. dreary but too good to discard and I can't afford new ones at the moment',[47] she enthused that 'it is a v nice house, with room for visitors'. It was sufficiently roomy that they had an intercom installed so she and Geoffrey could communicate from each other's offices without shouting.

Somewhere in all this Victoria found time to plough through books as judge of the inaugural NCR Award for non-fiction. Also on the panel, chaired by general director of the Royal Opera House Jeremy Isaacs, were Oxford University professor of modern history Norman Stone and Baroness Blackstone, head of Birkbeck College. According to Geoffrey, she 'hated one or two of her fellow judges – and expressed her feelings vehemently at home. Norman Stone treated her like one of his students.' Whenever back at home, and perhaps to get her into a parental frame of mind, she wrote the scripts for *Puppydog Tales*, the children's series she'd first discussed with the animator Hilary Hayton eighteen months earlier. The commission called for thirteen four-minute stories, each containing a little moral lesson, about a sensible dog called Rosie and her pals Ruff, Scratch and Sniff. Though written for pre-school children, the scripts retained her distinctive flavour, with jokes about TV, magic, chocolate. 'Hello, Sniff, got any cash?' says Ruff. 'I'm saving my money – I've seen a luxury semi-detached dog kennel in the paper.' 'How long's that gonna take?' 'About seventy-two years.' There would be quite a gestation for *Puppydog Tales* – playing all the characters, Victoria would record the dialogue and sing her own theme tune the following summer, after which began the long hunt for a broadcaster.

As the pregnancy advanced, the challenge now was to keep the news private. This would be difficult because, the month after finishing the tour, Victoria would be more scrutinised than ever before by a television audience: she had agreed to record a stand-up performance for London Weekend Television's *An Audience with . . .* strand. Alan Yentob, the controller of BBC Two, soon caught wind of Victoria's potential defection and implored her to bring it to the BBC instead. Victoria replied that the decision had not yet been taken, adding a barb that was to reverberate through the BBC for years to come: 'I'm glad the BBC is interested too. Nobody has ever bothered about what other work I'm doing, or taken any notice of me while I was there, or acknowledged any awards that may have come the way of the programme – so it's nice to know.'[48] After she'd met the LWT producers she reported back to Yentob: 'As they all seem perfectly decent and professional, I can't really think of a way of getting out of it, especially as I think they would all notice if I nicked their formula and took it to Wood Lane. But I am busting to come back to the BBC – and will be there with you in 89.'[49]

The approach from LWT had come via Judith Holder, a producer whom Victoria met in 1984 when she was a junior researcher on Gloria Hunniford's *Sunday Sunday*. In mid-April Holder, executive producer Nicholas Barrett and Marcus Plantin, the head of entertainment at LWT, went to see Victoria perform in Guildford. After agreeing in principle, Victoria then asked the two men to leave the room. 'Listen, I'm pregnant,' she said to Judith Holder. 'I don't want anybody to know. It might be tricky because of costume fittings.'

By the time the show was recorded, on a Wednesday night at the end of June, Victoria would be nearly six months pregnant. '*An Audience with . . .* was a big deal,' says Geoffrey. 'She prepared for it meticulously – much of the prep focusing on hiding her pregnancy.' The outfit she chose to cover her bump was a long mid-blue satin coat over fuchsia trousers, affording no clue of her condition to an audience which included hawk-eyed journalists; only a single camera angle, shot from the side when she sat at the piano, offered the merest hint. Her clothes were designed, she said, 'by the famous couturier Maison Renée, or Renee Mason as we call her' – sharp-eared fans would have recognised the name from the 'Self-Service' sketch.

*An Audience with Victoria Wood* was Victoria's most exposing appearance on television yet, because she would be playing to an audience of celebrities, all of their faces visible. The fifty or so stars who said yes included a dozen actresses, plus broadcasters, controllers, presenters and comedians. 'Maidenhead and Barnes are like ghost towns this evening,' she told them. Some whose careers had intersected with Victoria's were invited to ask questions which were in effect cues for her to carry on with her regular act. She seized the opportunity to have a pop at Joan Bakewell, whom she'd met on the feminist discussion show *Pandora's Box* in 1977. 'Do you think large bosoms are a handicap?' Bakewell was asked to ask. 'I suppose Mensa was shut, was it?' replied Victoria. Celia Imrie and Julie Walters – 'the lady with the split ends' – gamely lobbed up questions. Jokes about being mistaken for Virginia Wade or Pam Ayres had become passé, so instead there was a running gag about being married to Lenny Henry, each prompting a cutaway to a beaming Dawn French. She sat between Jennifer Saunders and Adrian Edmondson, who afterwards told Victoria he felt the strain of having to maintain a broad rictus in case the cameras were watching.

Extraordinarily, ninety minutes were recorded without a single retake, later cut down to just under an hour for broadcast. For the second half Victoria launched into an extended narrative about being followed through town by a man she mistakes for a kidnapper. The chase takes her from a launderette through a department store and finally into a theatre where she finds herself taking part in a terrible farce called *Whoops! There Go My Bloomers*. The sequence, inspired by a real incident in which she escaped a stalker in London by ducking into a bad West End revue, enabled her to weave in her Sacherelle saleswoman. For an encore she pulled on her orange coat and yellow beret, clambered along a row containing the DJ Kid Jensen to walk onstage looking for her friend Kimberley. She finished with 'The Ballad of Barry and Freda'. Perhaps to apologise for Margery and Joan, she rewrote one of Barry's excuses for getting out of sex:

No dramas
Give me my pyjamas
The only girl I'm mad about is Judith Chalmers.

Despite the warmth of the reaction, at first Victoria wasn't convinced that the performance had worked. 'We were both a bit disappointed by it on the night,' says Geoffrey, 'and amazed afterwards when everyone had clearly been so bowled over – no one seemed quite able to believe it. Judi Dench was absolutely beside herself with enthusiasm.' He attributes their own despondency to the bright lights of the studio. 'The worst thing about doing *An Audience with . . .*,' Victoria would say, 'is not that the audience is famous, because it really doesn't make any difference, but that you can see them because it's a television show and they have to be lit. And I really never want to see my audience. That was the biggest trial for me. That and the fact that I was six months pregnant and my legs were aching standing up that long.'[50] At a packed afterparty she circulated in a glow, accepting praise and quietly breaking her news to an inner circle. Julie was already in the know, having had her daughter two months earlier – 'I thought I caught a whiff of Napisan,' Victoria said to her audience.

Her motive for keeping it secret was to avoid what she called an 'Anne Diamond media circus . . . I didn't think it was necessary to see me in the papers in the hospital with everything hanging out of my nightie.'[51] Eventually her pregnancy became public knowledge by accident when in late August she was spotted entering the Portland, the exclusive private hospital in central London which Julie had recommended. Victoria's antenatal check-up happened to fall on the day the Duchess of York was giving birth. 'Of course, I might just have been visiting – except someone in hospital let the cat out of the bag to the man from the *Sun*, so I had to admit it.'[52] She still contrived to keep the date of birth to herself by announcing that the baby wasn't expected until late November.

'At present it is upside down but there's plenty of time for it to flip over,' Victoria told Lesley Fitton as she entered her final trimester, which she spent doing Jane Fonda aerobics tailored to pregnant women and attending antenatal classes at the Portland alongside well-heeled women, none of whom recognised her.[53] 'It was like having your own comedy show,' she enthused. 'They were all really posh and very thin – very thick as well.'[54] Meanwhile, back at home she waited out her pregnancy by attempting another play for Michael Codron, this time set in 1969 and drawing on her own adolescence.

On the morning of the last day of September Victoria went in for an inducement only to find the delivery rooms all in use. That night she went into labour and, to while away the time, she and Geoffrey watched synchronised swimming from the Olympics in Seoul, which she deemed 'better than the epidural'. There were complications – high blood pressure, the cord wrapped round the baby's neck – but eventually, at 1.41 a.m. on 1 October, Victoria gave birth to a girl weighing 6 lb 3 oz. They called her Grace Eleanor.

As the new parents drove north with their precious cargo, Victoria's joy was instant and profound. 'She bathed in the glory of it,' says Geoffrey, 'the elation of it, the absolute delight, and she lived it day after day after day. It was just fantastic.' Indeed, Victoria would concede that Geoffrey 'really didn't get a look in to start with. My instinct was so strong. I might have excluded him at the beginning. She was very tuned into me. She just wanted me.'[55]

When Grace was two months old *An Audience with Victoria Wood* was broadcast and won her mother the most unanimous praise she had received for her work on television since *Talent* in 1979: 'There are no words good enough to describe Victoria's talent. She encapsulates everything we've ever thought about everyday life in Britain. And wish we'd said first.'[56] 'I was so weak with laughter that I could barely bother to be irritated by all those close-ups of second division celebrities grinning vacantly.'[57] One female reviewer reckoned the shots of famous men laughing had an influence on male viewers: 'Men have been telling me daily that Victoria Wood is the best thing to happen since zipped flies. And they feel safe saying it.'[58]

As for Victoria, the rhythm of her life was to change for good. She also had a new source of comedy. 'I'll probably get Grace a clean outfit for Christmas,' she said soon after the birth.[59] It was her first joke about motherhood.

# 14

# STAYING IN

'People come up and go, "Heh, heh, we know who you are!" And you want to go, "Yeah, I know who I am too, ta very much."'

Interview, 1989

At the start of 1989, Victoria held a new type of casting session. A nanny was sought to look after Grace. Help was required partly, says Geoffrey, because 'we knew we were going to get no support whatsoever from any of the four grandparents'. Two candidates were asked back to Cove Lea for a second interview, and during each conversation the parents contrived to be called away, leaving the applicant alone with Grace. Victoria and Geoffrey then listened through the door. One of them was a young woman called Amber who got the job when she was heard to say to her three-month-old charge, 'Well, Grace, what's your opinion?'

Grace's arrival did not keep Victoria away from her desk. A month after the birth Richard Stone promised Michael Codron she would deliver her play by Christmas, whereafter it quietly vanished. It was the last of her vain attempts to write a successor to *Good Fun*, whose publication with *Talent* drew a line under her career as a playwright. 'Somehow they just didn't work,' she mused. 'They just made me miserable.'[1]

Her first booking as a mother was to read Roald Dahl's newly published *Matilda* for *Jackanory*. For the recording, the party of four went to Newcastle, where a second dressing room was requested and the schedule was built around feeding times. The children's programme was moving away from static readings in chairs to something more dramatised, with sets and effects and an autocue. Victoria narrated in a bright and eager style and threw herself into the various voices. 'At the end of it there was a big sigh of relief,' says Geoffrey. 'Yes, that's worked. Vic can be a working mother.' When it was broadcast hundreds of children wrote in to say how much they'd enjoyed it.

In the meantime, the BBC awaited her. The successor to *Victoria Wood As Seen on TV* would be on BBC One and negotiations about how it would be presented got underway at the start of the year. Jonathan Powell, the controller of the channel, was so keen to announce Victoria's return to that autumn's schedule that he proposed to broadcast the start of the series when the end of it was still unfinished. Communicating through her agent, she put a stop to that. 'Victoria would be most unhappy,' her agent Vivienne Clore wrote to head of light entertainment James Moir, 'if the new series began to go out, while still in production.'[2] In March *An Audience with Victoria Wood* added two more awards – for best light entertainment programme and performance – to Victoria's haul of BAFTAs (she won ahead of *French and Saunders* and *The Lenny Henry Show*, both produced by Geoff Posner). The double win intensified the urgent need to bring her back to the BBC. 'I do hope that Victoria Wood is signed, sealed and delivered?' Powell wrote to Moir days afterwards.[3]

The series that Victoria wanted to write involved a longer narrative format. In six half-hour plays she would mulch together skills she had mastered in the last few years – sketch-writing and stand-up, character comedy and observational storytelling. She would sometimes cast herself as the feed, or as the commentator, then throw on a garish disguise and switch to grotesque caricature. The scripts would also draw on her aborted attempts at writing plots for theatre and film. The only element from her skill set that would be missing was music: for the first time in her fifteen-year career, Victoria would not compose or perform a single song.

Getting back into the swing was difficult. Victoria was habitually a slow starter, but now there was an extra distraction and she would take frequent breaks to dandle Grace on her knee. Confused by the trick of writing herself into comic dialogue, she got to the end of one first draft 'and I flicked through and found out I was only saying things like "yes" and "can I have my key?". I thought, this won't do, it's my show, I haven't got anything to say, so I scrapped that one and wrote it again and put some jokes in. It was hard to find a line.'⁴ As the deadline loomed, she finished one episode in only two days. She did at least have assistance from a secretary who lived in Silverdale and who was hired to type letters and help organise her diary.

The series had no fixed title. On one BBC draft typed out in July it was billed as *Victoria Wood Comedy Playhouse*. The title flirted with the idea that these plays were somehow connected to the theatre – Victoria called them 'playletinos'. It also evoked the pilot show *Comedy Playhouse* which gave birth to many popular BBC sitcoms, from *Steptoe and Son* to *The Liver Birds*. But the tag didn't quite fit. 'I can't call them sitcoms,' Victoria acknowledged, 'as there is no front door or a sofa.'⁵ There was also no continuity beyond the presence of Victoria in each episode. By September the title at the top of a studio rehearsal script had been reduced to *Victoria Wood*.

The boilerplate title was a simple reflection of her ever-increasing celebrity. In April *An Audience with Victoria Wood* was shown again to nearly ten million viewers. In May a second repeat of *Victoria Wood As Seen on TV Special* was seen by more than four million. In June a poll by *Punch* magazine asked readers to nominate Britain's funniest woman. Victoria accumulated 48 per cent of the vote; Julie Walters, Dawn French, Jennifer Saunders, Emma Thompson and Tracey Ullman all scored 5 per cent or less. Her mailbag included requests for interviews from students writing theses on women in comedy: 'I'm always first on the list. I just write back saying, "I have nothing to say. Sorry. Here's a signed photo."'⁶

Her unassailable popularity emboldened Victoria to have a go at something no one had quite attempted in British television comedy: she would play a version of herself. The idea is there in her pencilled draft to *The Library*, one of her new half-hour plays:

Interior. Edwardian library of largeish-town. <u>VW</u> is browsing round the shelves. She speaks quietly to camera.

VW: This is the dreariest library in the whole world. They haven't got anything new. I think they're waiting for the Domesday Book to come out in paperback. It's run by this terrible woman called Madge, awfully narrow-minded, makes Mary Whitehouse look like a topless waitress.

This was an experiment in comic storytelling. Victoria cast herself as 'Victoria' (now and then referred to by others as 'Vicki'). The scripts played on the idea that she was a famous entertainer. In *The Library*, about lonely hearts and computer matchmaking, Victoria offers to hold her friend's hand on a blind date, but the nervous friend urges her to keep her job a secret. 'As soon as he hears you're in television,' she says, 'he's not going to squint my way.' In one script Victoria describes herself, tongue in cheek, as 'a much loved and irreplaceable entertainer'. In another she is mistaken for one half of French and Saunders. At a drinks party she says she's a comedian. 'Call me old-fashioned,' drawls a guest, 'but I don't like to see a woman telling jokes. You name me a funny woman who's attractive with it.'

The format conferred freedom to delve deeper into her own pre-occupations. A stay in a health club with Geoffrey was the basis for *Mens Sana in Thingummy Doodah*, set in a terrible spa which trades in empty mantras and unscientific drivel. *Val de Ree (Ha Ha Ha Ha Ha)*, drawing on her love of fell walking, was inspired by a calamitous hike in the Lake District that was ruined by sudden rain and fog. 'Morale did get very low indeed,' says her walking companion Judith Holder. 'Vic started to sing "Val de Ree". At its lowest we walked into this field where these farmers were castrating lambs.' *Staying In* explored her horror of large social gatherings.

Victoria was not averse to seeking inspiration from her back cat-alogue. *The Library* was a longer version of 'Mr Right' – Anne Reid even reprised the role of a lonely spinster who has squandered her best years looking after an elderly mother. *We'd Quite Like to Apologise* revisited the theme of package holiday mishaps, described with such gusto in her recent live show. *Over to Pam* continued her project of satirising television with an angry broadside against daytime TV. 'It's so cheap and nasty,' Victoria explained. 'It's such an easy formula to get women in the studio and pay them virtually nothing to say a few words. We should instead put up a caption saying "We have no TV worth showing", and then leave the screen blank.'[7]

She didn't insert just herself into these dramas but also drew on her actual friendships. The friend she walks with in *Val De Ree* was partly based on Celia Imrie. 'There were three jokes in that,' says Celia. 'Me eating chocolate behind the bush, something about my tits and the fact that I was embarrassingly ill-read. These were quite sensitive things.' When the two hikers fail to erect their tent to its full height, Celia's character reasons that it won't matter as they'll be lying flat. 'And if you sleep chest down,' says Victoria, 'we can drop it another foot.' Victoria had been impressed by Celia's bust ever since borrowing her dress to appear on *That's Life!* in 1976.

Then in *Staying In* there is a bossy friend who parades Victoria at a cocktail party in order to boost her own career. 'Really let yourself go,' she says, 'jokes, routines – people will love it.' For some of her friends, the big glasses worn by Deborah Grant hinted ruthlessly at the character's inspiration. *We'd Quite Like to Apologise* even made a smutty reference to a boyfriend from her Birmingham years. Julie Walters, playing a manhunter called Joyanne, shows Victoria a snap of a potential holiday conquest: 'Nobby – you'll like him – he's very witty. I bet you've never seen a medallion hung round that before.'

As ever there were plenty of jagged little digs at celebrities – Alma Cogan, Felicity Kendal, former TV-am weather girl Wincey Willis, Harold Pinter and Elaine Paige, whose diminutive stature was irresistible. When *The Library* came up a couple of minutes short during rehearsals with Anne Reid, Victoria retreated to a table and wrote a speech about how Torvill and Dean never did it because they spent too much time lying down.

As she wrote, there were conversations with Geoff Posner about how to film them. Logistics helped force a decision: as they couldn't bring a studio audience with them to a moor in Yorkshire, they would do without one throughout. He was also keen to push boundaries by filming on video in order to erase the jarring switch in texture between exteriors and interiors common to all sitcoms whenever they ventured outdoors, which meant taking some unwieldy new equipment up onto Ilkley Moor.

As for casting, Victoria was loyal as ever to her troupe. 'It would be good if everyone was in at least 3 episodes,' she wrote in her casting notes. 'I think it would give it a nice Reppy feel.'[8] Thus Julie Walters played a dim beautician, a nymphomaniac holidaymaker and the horrendous presenter Pam. As well as Victoria's hiking partner, Celia became a ditzy travel rep, a silly socialite and an actress in a saucy television ad. For Jim Broadbent Victoria wrote the part of a bitter Yorkshire playwright. Another trophy guest in *Staying In*, he claims he can tell Victoria is from the north: 'There's a pain behind the eyes, a sob in the voice.' He deplores 'southern parasites licking the fat of the land while the north lies dying'. Victoria asks him where he lives. 'Chiswick,' he says. When Jim Broadbent received his script, it had a note attached in Victoria's hand: 'This is Colin Welland.'

The only absentee was Duncan Preston. He had just been cast in *Surgical Spirit*, a new hospital sitcom on Granada. His co-star was Nichola McAuliffe, who at the King's Head in 1980 had taken over the role Victoria wrote for herself in *Good Fun*. 'It doesn't look like the dates are going to work out for my next BBC thing,' Victoria wrote to him. 'I'm very sorry you won't be in it but as you have to have your rubber gloves up Nichola M for the next 20 years I hope you won't mind too much.'[9]

While Victoria stuck to her trusted company, with the help of a casting director the net was widened. Patricia Hodge and Joan Sims, both of them guests in *An Audience with Victoria Wood*, were cast. Such was the show's blur of reality and make-believe that Sims appeared alongside Victoria in *Val de Ree* and was namedropped by her in *Staying In*. 'I'm watching television,' she says while curled up on the sofa. 'It's a film with James Robertson Justice, Joan Sims, Hattie Jacques and Norman Wisdom.'

Joan Sims played a terrifying ogress who runs a youth hostel. The truth was that she was herself terrified when *Val de Ree* was filmed. 'Joan got very intimidated by Victoria,' says Celia. 'She was of an age where it becomes more and more difficult to learn. Victoria often wouldn't hide what she felt, and it made poor Joan get more and more nervous and in the end she had to have great big boards.' Celia herself, who had never worked on her own with Victoria before, found it 'a very daunting prospect knowing it was only going to be me and Vic'.

'I like people who learn the lines,' Victoria explained when asked if there was a special sort of Victoria Wood actress.[10] A lot of her lines were more difficult to deliver than usual, even for regulars. Much as she had in her stand-up monologues – the Brontë guide, the Sacharelle saleswoman – Victoria cocked an ear to quirky ways of mangling the language. The nervous woman running the health spa in *Mens Sana in Thingummy Doodah* coins gibberish in the hope it will make her sound more professional: 'I don't know everybody's name as yet,' she says in her welcome speech, 'and until me doing that, "everybody" as a sort of termitude will have to huffice.' She talks of 'intending to your needs' by 'intoxifying the body' before having to 'pronounce a change of itinament'. In *We'd Quite Like to Apologise* an airline employee uses befuddling jargon: 'To be explanatory you have ample minutage because your flight is carrying a small delay.' Susie Blake found it hard to get the scene right under pressure filming early one morning at Leeds Bradford Airport and was hurried along by a flustered Geoff Posner. 'Afterwards Vic told him off. He came over and said, "Thank you, that was really lovely." So she was in charge.'

Victoria placed no more pressure on others than she did on herself. She was in virtually every scene, in some of which she addressed the camera directly. Often the plot called on her to pretend to be someone else. In *The Library*, to make herself unattractive to her friend's blind date, she comes along as Miss Sapphire, 'an artiste in the entertainment business' who has a hygiene problem: 'I won't beat about the bungalow – I've been flatulating – and, boy, have I stunk!' When that doesn't work, she dresses up as Mrs Witherstrop, a grouchy old woman from Eccles who likes nothing better than a 'nice plate of brains and a ginger nut'. In *Over to Pam*, in order to expose the bullying daytime presenter who exploits her guests for entertainment, she dons a frizzy blonde wig and a plunging leopard-print top and presents herself as the product of a broken society. 'I had seven children before I were eighteen,' she tells Pam. 'But I couldn't cope. I were too stupid to cope. I kept leaving them in skips.'

Victoria's creative fixation with parental neglect was unaffected by becoming a parent herself. But there was a practical change to how she made television. The gang ethos fostered by Geoff Posner on the *As Seen on TV* location shoots was no more. Victoria no longer stayed in the same hotel as the cast and crew, while Grace was kept nearby with her nanny throughout rehearsals and production. 'I would never have put Vic down as maternal,' says Celia, 'but when we got to four o'clock she was absolutely yearning to see this little girl.' Victoria's mother turned up on the *Val de Ree* shoot – it was the only time Celia met her and recalls her as 'quite overpowering and not very warm'.

When Posner presented the finished versions to BBC executives the reaction was cool. 'Although we told the BBC we were shooting it without an audience,' he says, 'I got a very heavy director saying, "This doesn't feel warm enough for Victoria, and I suggest you put a laugh track on."' A pre-recorded laugh track was out of the question, so he showed individual episodes in the BBC Television Theatre in Shepherd's Bush to audiences who had come along to see a live recording of something else. One of the programmes was *Wogan*. Enthusiastic laughter was duly captured, but it was a fudge. Further warmth was supplied by Victoria's chirpy theme tune, arranged by David Firman and featuring a solo for harmonica.

There was little time for the whole package to be put together. The first episode was to be shown in mid-November, less than a month after filming on the last one wrapped. Victoria flung herself into promotion, going so far as to be grilled by *Hello!* She walked out after one broadsheet interviewer, seeming to assume hers had been a typical northern working-class childhood, asked if her parents had taken her to Blackpool. 'What do you take me for?' she huffed. 'We used to go to Vienna.'[11] The BBC publicist had to coax her back. As she had been out of the public eye for most of the year, interviewers could not help noticing that she had lost a great deal of weight. She also introduced a trim new bobbed pageboy haircut.

Once more Victoria's billings for the *Radio Times* gave nothing away. 'The Channel Tunnel – vital artery or alimentary canal?' she wrote of *Over to Pam*. 'Two experts and a French person thrash out the issues in a lively late-night debate. Song by Spinning Jenny.' For *We'd Quite Like to Apologise* she wrote, 'Ken Hope served a 16-year prison sentence for armed robbery and assault. Now he is one of Britain's top comedy script writers. Meredith Leazely asks if the law should be changed?' With *Val de Ree (Ha Ha Ha Ha Ha)* she supplied her own review: 'Patronising. D MAIL.' One or two of the actual reviews for the first episode weren't much different. *Mens Sans in Thingummy Doodah* had the best title but, with the most obvious target to aim at, it was the least ambitious of the six plays. 'If I explain that this comedy-let was set in a health farm,' grumbled the *Sunday Telegraph*, 'you really can guess most of the rest of it.'[12] Such critiques uncharitably overlooked the show's bold attempt to disrupt the traditions of half-hour comedy and Victoria's matchless ear for the absurdities of the dieting industry: women with 'underarm swoop' and 'runaway midriff', or the hard-boiled egg which 'kind of eats some of the meal for you'. The episode contained the first ever use of Volvo as a euphemism for vulva. For Alan Coren (another member of Victoria's LWT audience), there was more to savour in *We'd Quite Like to Apologise*: 'Wood triumphs over cliché not by ducking it but by meeting it head-on.'[13]

Victoria's foreword to the published scripts was an idiot's guide to creating a comedy series, from commission to casting to shooting. 'Now the fun really begins!' she repeated at every fresh stage of the process, right up to the moment 'the people who write for the newspapers are settling down to tell everybody just what they think of our "programme".'[14] But perhaps the fun never really began at all. Her audience at home grew and grew, peaking at over thirteen million, and there were as usual two BAFTA nominations in the light-entertainment categories. But Victoria would come to distance herself from *Victoria Wood*. She felt her ubiquity was a flaw: 'There was always that character that was always me except it wasn't me. I thought who's this person who looks a bit like me, who sounds like me who doesn't make any sense and has no part in the story?'[15] But mainly she attributed her dissatisfaction to the lack of a live audience:

'It was just so dull. We showed them to an audience afterwards, but it was just no buzz for me at all.'[16]

Making the series took her – and Grace and Amber – away from home for three months. While the show was running on BBC One, there were two significant events that brought her back to Lancashire. In November she could not resist the allure of an old girls' reunion, twenty-five years on, of the 1964 intake at Bury Grammar School. Victoria had always been a curious observer of others at school. 'I suppose they'll be looking at me now,' she sighed before she went.[17] For company she had her two oldest friends, Lesley Fitton and Anne Sweeney, who remembers 'when we went in the room there was a frisson of excitement'. It was not shared by their retired headmistress Dorothy Lester who was 'just so cold and made no reference to Vic's success'. Some contemporaries coolly kept their distance, while others gushed with admiration. One bounded up to announce that she had three degrees from London University but no job. 'Vic thought that was hysterically funny,' says Lesley. 'It became a catchphrase with her: three degrees and no job. In a faintly horrible way she and I were drifting around vaguely laughing at people we'd always vaguely laughed at.'

Less than a month later, on the day *We'd Quite Like to Apologise* was broadcast, Victoria was made an honorary doctor of letters by Lancaster University. The university's public orator praised her 'highly original investigations into contemporary anthropology' and, to her embarrassment, compared her voice to that of Samuel Beckett. After her pass degree in Birmingham in 1974, it was a pleasing accolade to be presented with her doctorate scroll by the university's chancellor Princess Alexandra. Her parents were in the audience to hear her muse in her acceptance speech on the recent school reunion she'd attended: 'I spent so much time in the corridor the only person who recognised me was the cleaner.' Afterwards local journalists gathered round for an impromptu press conference. 'When I was at school I was advised by an English teacher not to be a performer but to go into journalism,' she told them. 'You see, if I'd taken any notice of her, I could have been sitting round the back with the notebook, getting everybody's names wrong for the *Lancaster Guardian*.'[18] Dr Wood was chuffed, she added, that the university had accorded the same honour to Eric Morecambe.

It was a satisfying way to close the decade. Ten years on from the *Observer*'s nomination of eighty names to watch out for in the Eighties, at thirty-six Victoria was part of the national furniture, and an incomparable commentator on the British way of life. Plenty of reviews of the decade named her as one of its towering figures, while Victoria and Geoffrey were now established as a celebrity couple, in which capacity they were once again grilled by Mavis Nicholson, who had first interviewed them together at the King's Head in 1981. Sitting on a sofa in a Lake District hotel, Geoffrey talked about saying goodbye to the Great Soprendo. The new streamlined Victoria did not look down shyly even once.

# 15

# UP WEST

'God, it's hard work eating muesli. It's like having two jobs. Apparently in London you can phone up and somebody comes round and chews it for you but we don't have these facilities where I live in the north.'

*Victoria Wood Up West*, 1990

Victoria's first act of the 1990s was to fly to Ethiopia for a week to make a film catching up on Comic Relief's activities. She had done her share of pro bono good works. In recent months Pamela Stephenson had invited her to support her Parents for Safer Food campaign, although her phobia for socialising kicked in when she attended a dinner party to help launch it and she clammed up. Before Christmas, she appealed on Radio 4 for donations to a charity offering counselling and contraceptive advice to young people. She wasn't always careful about lending her name to a cause. Though just the right person to be on the board of trustees for a *Fame*-style academy planned for Croydon, she withdrew after a series of public spats about the venture.

Leaving Grace behind for the first time, Victoria boarded the plane the day after hosting an awards ceremony for the food industry at the Grosvenor House Hotel. 'I feel like a delicious combination of Kate Adie and Judith Chalmers, only paler and with less epaulettes,' she wrote in a cheerful article to promote the film, only to arrive in Addis Ababa looking 'like a cross between WH Auden and a self-assembly

Chesterfield'. The film was pitched as a plea to viewers not to give up on Ethiopia, to which they had donated five years earlier in response to Band Aid and Live Aid. 'Of course some of it was wasted – it was a crisis, people made mistakes,' she said in a piece to camera as she walked along a hot dusty road. 'It's a mess. I don't pretend to understand the half of it.' She used her humanising skills as a comedian to convey a message that the Ethiopians featured in her film were just ordinary people. 'Some of the children are absolutely horrible and are driving me nuts,' she said in front of a crowd of them. With the crew she travelled around the country for a week on buses and tiny planes. Her moment of greatest connection came when she was struggling with the language barrier in conversation with a shy birth attendant until a newborn baby urinated on her, which greatly entertained the surrounding throng: 'Years of being stuck in bus queues with comedy haters gives me a sound sense of the conversation. "Well I'm sorry she doesn't make me laugh." "What's that patch on her leg?" "A baby just weed on her." "Now that's funny."'[1] Back home she reported to Geoffrey that she had 'quite enjoyed the tough conditions in a masochistic sort of way. She definitely felt a strong sense of guilt and worried that she was being helicoptered in and out, bringing her privileged life with her, like a kind of Lady Bountiful.' Victoria responded to a quite different appeal a couple of months later when the novelist Rose Tremain asked in the *Independent* for funds to support Angus Wilson, who had fallen on hard times. She sent £1,000.

Her thoughts now turned back to what she considered to be her day job. Victoria had not toured in nearly two years but got back into the swing of performance with a couple of private cabaret bookings. One gig was at the Imperial War Museum, where she had the odd experience of 'trying to fit the piano between a tank and an anti-aircraft gun'.[2] These bookings were lucrative, and useful for introducing new material, but they could be precarious. 'They're full of drunken businessmen,' she said. 'When they're drunk they cannot concentrate. It's much better if their wives are there. They tend to behave better then.'[3]

A recording in Victoria's archive from 1989 reveals how meticulously she prepared for each performance. Taping herself on a cassette for Geoffrey to listen back to, she would sprint through the act and add her own notes and comments – such as where an extra gag was needed to cover a walk to the piano. Diligent about targeting the act at her audience, she crafted a boilerplate section into which she could drop the name of the client: 'I said, "Everybody will be drunk and they'll throw bread rolls at me." And they said, "Oh no, this is [name of company]." I said, "That'll be even worse. They'll all throw [name of product] at me."'

It was after finishing the scripts for *Victoria Wood* that Victoria got in touch with her tour promoters, who always hungered for her to do more live work. A tour was booked to start in May 1990. To whet the public appetite and stimulate ticket sales, *Victoria Wood Live*, recorded at Brighton Dome two years earlier, was released in January. This established a template that would continue for more than a decade. After double exposure on television and VHS, her live set would be dropped and replaced with a new show that in its turn would be released on video and broadcast on TV.

In April there were a few try-out gigs within driving distance of Silverdale. Victoria rehearsed right up to the afternoon of the performance, in each of which she dropped in more fresh material piece by piece. Then the tour proper started with three nights in Newcastle. While traces of *Lucky Bag* lingered on as a little package of gags about Dutch caps and the dyslexic boyfriend reading a sex manual – which she and Geoffrey referred to as 'Sex Chat' – she had plenty of new things to say about sex: 'I filled in one of those sex questionnaires. They sent it back marked, "very poor work – see me".' There was a section about British manners inhibiting suburban wife-swapping orgies. But Victoria was now more fascinated by the consequences of sex. The first-half setpiece was a brilliant narrative about ovulation ('one egg a month, like the war') and pregnancy testing kits ('have you tried weeing on a paddle? We've got the engine capacity but not the steering'). Motherhood had tilted Victoria's worldview and given her a new angle on things. 'I studied the symptoms for pregnancy,' she said. 'Moody, irritable, big bosoms. I have obviously been pregnant for twenty years.' Breast feeding, she reckoned, 'is like asking someone in a straitjacket to eat their lunch off of a beach ball'.

More than ever, this was a show about the female condition.

Women in the audience screeched with recognition at jokes about first seeing the diagram on a packet of Lil-Lets: 'I decided to put a ship in a bottle once a month instead – it was easier.' A lot of the material flew over the heads of the mystified men in the audience, and the pitch of the laughter coming back at her told her who found this stuff funny. Geoffrey, wandering the auditorium to check how the show looked from various angles in the venue, confirmed it: 'The men received the gags in stony silence and then stared at their wives, who were crying with laughter, and had not a clue what they were laughing about. They just sat there looking baffled and occasionally angry. There were sharp intakes of breath at the word "period" and delighted amazement at, say, "we've got the engine capacity but not the steering". The audiences couldn't quite believe it. At the beginning of her stand-up career she briefly billed herself as "The New Comic for Girls" and now it was coming true.' At one point, after a gag about the strip in her new bikini bottoms, Victoria said, 'Oh tell him what I mean, for heaven's sake. We'll be here all night.' She was rewarded with an even bigger wave of screams.

There was another unsisterly kicking for Anne Diamond (the answer to the question: 'what do you get if you cross Kylie Minogue and Mussolini?'). She expanded on the Bury Grammar reunion material she'd road tested in Lancaster, while the introduction of the unpopular poll tax tempted Victoria to make a rare foray into politics: 'We've had over a decade of Mrs Thatcher and they're only just now finding out about mad cow disease.' At the start of the second half Victoria came on as Susan, a grotesquely fat northern roadie who preferred to be referred to as obese, while in the character of an inept speaker she addressed a luncheon club on the subject of 'Life Begins at Forty'. These sections did not necessarily hit the heights but, says Geoffrey, 'they gave variety to the show, just in the way the songs did, and she could write those kinds of sketch in her sleep. She relied on performance technique to get the laughs with them, rather than the ingenuity of the writing.'

The other change was to the end of the first half. Hitherto Victoria had closed the set with a low-key song and a blackout. She now experimented with 'Carry on Regardless', a clap-along tune which had not worked as a show-closer and didn't quite land in its new slot either. The rest of the songs were scattered less liberally throughout the set. The highlight among the new ones was 'Saturday Night', which borrowed from 'Oh Dear What Can the Matter Be' to give a rambunctious account of two young women painting the town red. Tracey Clegg and Nicola Battersby were gaudy descendants of Julie and Maureen in *Nearly a Happy Ending*, or Kelly Marie Tunstall – out for a night on the tiles, and heedless of the consequences. To establish a sense of them Victoria harked back to the rhyme scheme of a song from *In at the Death* in 1978:

> They rendezvous in front of a pillar.
> Tracey's tall like Jonathan Miller.
> Nicola's more like Guy the Gorilla,
> If Guy the Gorilla were thick.

Her most lyrically inventive new song since 'Barry and Freda', it contained no fewer than seven clever rhymes for Battersby. 'This one is good fun to sing,' she said when the lyrics and music were published, 'and was no trouble to write as the tune is nicked.'[4]

No longer was there much in the way of single-night bookings necessitating daily stints on motorways. Victoria was now so vastly popular her promoters could book her for a week at a time at the Bristol Hippodrome, Manchester Opera House and Birmingham Hippodrome, where six shows sold out so quickly two more had to be tacked on in July. She greeted each venue with the same opening quip: 'All the glamour and glitter of show business is encapsulated in one venue. But not this one.' Amber and Grace – as well as her tour manager Carol Spraggs and her sound man – travelled with her in convoy wherever she went.

'I have done 30 shows now,' she told Jane Wymark in mid-June, 'and I'm *just* getting it the way I want.'[5] Grace adapted to life on tour, although she needed to be entertained when she woke up at six in the morning. The early start meant her mother would 'slap on a deal more panstick than usual to hide the baps by the time the half comes round'.[6] In a tour schedule Victoria meticulously listed

vital items, including Grace's cot toys, shoes, book basket, dolly, reins.
'It's like taking a chimp round with you really,' she quipped. 'You
really need a zookeeper to come with you.'[7] Whenever the schedule
allowed – Blackpool, Liverpool, Manchester – Grace would be kept
at home and Victoria would dash back to Cove Lea after each show.
For Nottingham and Sheffield, to both of which Victoria returned for
extra shows in July, they stayed in splendour at Hassop Hall in the
Peak District. Another measure of her enhanced status was the twenty
days off built into the itinerary. Now and then Grace came along to
the venue, from one of which she retains a very early memory. 'Mum
would put me in the wings,' she says. 'I was sat on a chair watching
her from the side and as she moved from the mic to go round and sit
at the piano, she gave me a little look, like a little smile.'

Everywhere, Victoria was greeted with crescendos of ecstasy as the
show built to its climax. The official closer was 'Reincarnation', an up
tempo number that looked at other lives she might try on for size.
Through a series of bravura rhymes she imagined being a traditional
housewife, a go-getting City trader, a timid singleton. It was, she later
said, 'a bugger to write. You try thinking up two rhymes for flip-flops.'
She went on and off stage left throughout the evening and, just as the
audience thought the night was over, she reappeared stage right in an
orange mac and yellow beret, triggering yells of delight. In an encore
of only two minutes, Kimberley's friend shared her enthusiasm for
penis colada – 'I made one myself out of a recipe in *The Watchtower*'
– and told of her efforts to teach herself Flemish 'in case I ever go to
Flem'. 'The Ballad of Barry and Freda', which remained the closer,
was now so popular that one night in Birmingham the audience tried
to join in the chorus. 'I wasn't aware it *was* a duet,' Victoria paused to
say, 'but we could try.'

Before the spring tour was over Victoria prepared for the announcement of the autumn dates. Having deferred to Phil McIntyre to
organise the national tour, André Ptaszynski took on the London leg.
'Vic had built up a fair head of steam for a decent London run,'
he says. 'The Palladium season had sold out so quickly and she was
considerably more famous than she had been three years earlier. She
was overdue for a meaty run in the capital.' To that end he persuaded

her to commit to ten daunting weeks at the Strand Theatre. The auditorium's capacity of 1,100 meant that there were more than 46,000 tickets to shift. The show was given a title – *Victoria Wood Up West* – and sold out so quickly that two weeks were added. Before it opened, the run was reported to have taken over a million pounds. Indefatigably, Victoria wrote the entire programme in the style of a celebrity magazine titled *Ooh Hello!* (whose exclamation mark kept moving). A spoof feature on 'The Remarkable Home Life of Victoria Wood as told in her own words exclusively to Ooh! Hello's Deborah Klepper' was a merciless attack on celebrities who do Faustian deals with lickspittle glossies. 'Earlier this year,' it chirruped, 'Victoria's trip to Ethiopia to poke gentle fun at starving people had made a very nice feature in "Ooh Hello!".' Pictures of Ethiopian children appeared alongside snaps of Priory Road, the ASDA shoot and Victoria with Dolly Parton, 'who flew over specially to advise her on diet and rib-removal'. The contents page offered more next week – 'Celia Imrie ex Bergerac star shares her cocoa-dependency problem . . . Linda Lusardi shows us her doorknobs . . . Morrissey. We share the secrets of his tumble-dryer.'

In preparation for the West End run the family all squeezed into the flat in Castellain Mansions, which Victoria nicknamed Gravy-stain Mansions. There wasn't really room and Geoffrey soon retreated north to prepare for his new post-Soprendo career as an after-dinner speaker – Victoria wrote some gags for him which he complained were too rude. She also wrote one for Grace: 'I taught Grace to say "hello you old baldy" to Geoff and of course she will not stop saying it and I am afraid we may now bump into Ned Sherrin with embarrassing consequences.'[8] As ever with a London run, she sent out invitations to her friends. 'Dear Dunc,' went a typical summons. 'My first night at the Strand is Oct 2 – same old crap but do you want to come?'[9]

In fact, before she took up residence Victoria worked on some site-specific material, readily supplied by the delicious news that Joan Collins was to open in *Private Lives* next door at the Aldwych. Victoria urged her audience not to make too much noise: 'It does annoy Joan.' Exactly ten years earlier their paths had crossed on the arts programme *On the Town*. In the interim *Dynasty* had happened, and Victoria could not resist taking aim: 'They wanted a soap star of similar stature to star alongside her in *Private Lives* – but Albert Tatlock from *Coronation Street* was dead.' Her audience wasn't to know the joke's private subtext, that the producer of *Private Lives* was Michael Codron.

'Wood is, now, the bigger star and the bigger draw,' said her avowed fan Alan Coren in *The Times*; 'you can still get seats for Collins.'[10] The show brought in more critics than had ever reviewed her work. Not all of them enthused, some resenting the fact that, as the run was sold out, their views were superfluous. The *Standard* grumbled about 'her transformation into a slick semi-pornographic entertainer'.[11] The *Observer* fretted that 'all her jokes about fat, once upholstered by the authority of her own bulk, now seem thin'.[12] The critic who profoundly understood Victoria's development as a stand-up was Jane Edwardes of *Time Out*, who had worked at the King's Head a decade earlier: 'Those far off times when she clung to the piano for support as she told a few jokes in between a programme of songs are now a distant memory.'[13]

The strain of performing night after night with barely any respite for months on end took its toll – even if, as one journalist noted, Victoria was earning enough to buy a bungalow each week. 'The Strand is knackering me,' she confided.[14] She was so exhausted that she declined when Morrissey, a devoted fan who had adapted the lyrics of 'Fourteen Again' in a song by the Smiths, asked her out for tea. Towards the end of the run Victoria offered comps to her sister Rosalind. 'You don't have to,' she said. 'Also if you'd like to come over and see Grace. She's a v nice girl I must say. Things have been hectic with only Sundays off.'[15] One afternoon she took Grace to a children's birthday party in Maida Vale, where the toast of the West End went into her shell. 'She wouldn't mix with the other mums very easily,' says Chris Beetles, who was her host. 'Her shyness would kick in again.' Privately she was shocked that the candles had to be blown out a second time for the video. 'That's W9 for you,' she told Jane Wymark.[16] Beetles was now an art dealer specialising in British cartoons, and Victoria was attracted to his collection of thirty works by the *Punch* cartoonist Pont, on sale for around £3,000 each. She and Geoffrey already had two Ponts: 'I treated us to 2 little ones as a cheer-up. Geoff of course thinks we should sell something like a flat and buy the other 28.'[17]

In fact, they were trying to sell a flat. Grace had turned two and Castellain Mansions was now deemed too small. Thanks to Victoria's earnings, she and Geoffrey could afford to make an offer on a third-floor flat in Lampard House, a mansion block on Maida Avenue which looked down on the long boats moored along Regent's Canal. There were no immediate plans to make it their permanent home, but that changed soon after *Up West* ended in early December and the family prepared to head back north. Victoria and Geoffrey set off in separate cars on a Saturday morning, she with Amber and Grace and a cargo of Christmas presents. Traffic ground to a halt south of Coventry, her car battery gave out and bladders started to burst. 'While I will bob down anywhere at the drop of a hat,' she told Jane Wymark, 'the middle of a stationary 3 lane traffic jam with not a tree in sight was a mite daunting, especially when one had a familiar face to the great British public (I didn't want any other parts to become familiar, particularly).' Further north the M6 was closed by snow. There was no means of getting to a hotel. It grew dark and cold, and the petrol nearly ran out so she couldn't run the heater. 'It was a long night . . . I was scared Grace would die of cold . . . At 5.00 someone said an ambulance was coming down the other carriageway with HOT SOUP so I rushed over for 2 lots of tomato but it was cold. Another low point.' Eventually, after twenty-two hours stuck on the motorway, they were allowed to turn through the barrier and drive south: 'The M6 must have been like Horse Guards Parade by morning.' In Rugby she asked the police if there was any chance of getting to Lancashire: 'They just laughed. (Ho ho. Oh look it's Victoria Wood ho ho).'[18] They headed back to Maida Vale, where they found the central heating had broken down. Geoffrey had a similarly eventful journey but made it to Silverdale. 'That was the decision,' he says. 'We're moving to London.'

The lure of London had been the subject of a marital debate ever since they moved to Morecambe in 1978. In public Victoria kept to the line throughout the 1980s that the north was the best place for her.

She maintained, a little fancifully, that she'd moved to Morecambe in pursuit of material for comedy. 'It's nice to be where everybody else isn't,' she said on *Desert Island Discs*. 'I do like to keep away from other comics. I don't want to end up doing the same as everyone else.'[19] The solitude aided productivity. She also relished being close to the source of northern rhythms. 'I'm just very attracted by construction of sentences, the vocabulary,' she would argue. 'Everything in the north is constructed back to front. Lancashire people, instead of saying, "haven't they sent your carpet?" they say, "Have they not sent it – your carpet?"'[20]

The snowstorm was the catalyst, but there were other factors. Grace was being left in the care of her nanny too often for comfort, and the layout of Cove Lea had an undermining effect too. 'It never worked,' Geoffrey adds. 'We were never happy there. Because it had been two houses it didn't have a hearth.' These misgivings were not mentioned by the estate agent when it was put on the market the following spring for £385,000.

They took possession of the Lampard House flat in mid-January 1991. The idea was to stop in Maida Avenue for a couple of years, and a Montessori school was found for Grace. As Amber chose to move to Winnipeg rather than live in London, a new nanny – Rebecca Wood, no relation – was employed. Geoffrey rented an office in the basement of Edwin Landseer's studio around the corner in St John's Wood, while Victoria took a room next door and spent a great deal to have a piano craned in over the roof although ended up rarely using it. The studios were run by Rita Birrane, the sister of the owner, and at Geoffrey's suggestion Victoria offered her a job as a PA.

In terms of work, the year began quietly. Victoria was 'not actually working my arse off for once'.[21] She was jolted into action when Comic Relief informed her that a song she'd written before Christmas for Red Nose Day would work as a single. She spent a weekend recording 'The Smile Song' and shooting a video in a north London studio with sixty musicians, dancers and crew. With high-velocity, densely rhyming lyrics, her medley of pop parodies called for her to dress up 'in a series of ever more ridiculous outfits (Kylie mini-dress, heavy metal-type leather studded corsets and thigh boots etc etc)'.[22] The song concluded with Victoria encrusted in jewels and singing in the style of 1930s cinema sweetheart Jessie Matthews. The weekend was, she said, 'good fun but knackering'.[23] While she thought of 'The Smile Song' as her first single, quietly ignoring her misadventure with *Return to Oz* in 1985, it was in fact released as a B-side to 'The Stonk' by Hale and Pace, a less subtly crafted rock'n'roller that reached number one in March.

Then she was back on tour, dashing for six weeks around the 2,000-seaters she'd not stopped in a year earlier. During the run she hurried up from Southampton to Tottenham Court Road, acting on a tip that the eminent designer Betty Jackson was a fan who would love Victoria to wear her clothes. 'I thought she was one of the funniest people on the planet,' she says. 'I used to watch her on television and think I could maybe make a difference somewhere. I always thought there was this huge feeling of insecurity and I could maybe take that lack of confidence away.' On this occasion, Victoria was not looking for an outfit to perform in – she needed something for the Olivier Awards, as *Victoria Wood Up West* had been nominated for Best Entertainment. 'They bundled me in and out of various outfits, told me which suited me, stuffed them into a carrier bag (*with* jewellery) and when I said – "er, how much" said it was all FREE and to come back any time. Funny old world. It was nice to feel I had the right gear on for once.'[24] Victoria presented herself at the National Theatre for the ceremony on the last Sunday of the tour. She had an inkling that she wouldn't be winning when she found her seat was in the middle of a row: 'A real bum-number of an evening. I could have been watching telly with G and getting pissed.'[25]

The Betty Jackson effect was instant. Having begun the tour in a garish outfit of blue-and-purple spotted trousers, orange shirt, green-and orange jacket and mauve desert boots, by the time Victoria recorded the show for video release at the Mayflower in Southampton she was wearing a loose white suit with forthright shoulder pads over a blue top from M&S. To jazz up the visuals, the upstage backdrop featured vast images of Victoria. The director Marcus Mortimer suggested she do an extra section for the video only, so Victoria wrote a sketch in which she was grilled in the interval by a journalist from Neighbourhood Watch, whose tape recorder doesn't work and who doesn't let her interviewee get a word in. It was a sly attack on all the sloppy interviewers who had ever poked a microphone at her.

The tour had a sunny postscript when Victoria was booked to do a cabaret in the Paradise Island resort off Nassau in the Bahamas, courtesy of the boiler manufacturers Glow-worm. There was just enough slack in the schedule to put her feet up. Back home, one of her last acts as a resident of Silverdale was to go with her university friend Alison Lloyd to see the Silverdale Village Players perform Alan Bennett's *Habeas Corpus*. Bennett's *Sunset Across the Bay* having lured her to the area fourteen years earlier, her Morecambe Bay story had come full circle. 'I know living in the flat we won't have the wide open spaces and the Smallbone fucking kitchen but at least every job won't mean 3 days away with 2 days on the motorway.'[26]

One of the last letters she received in Cove Lea was from Geoffrey Strachan asking her to update the title or subtitle for a new edition of her *Lucky Bag* songbook. She scrawled an image of the pianist's bare bottom by Beryl Cook and wrote 'EVEN BIGGER!'[27] At the age thirty-eight, Victoria became a Londoner.

# 16

# HENRY AND ALBERT, MARGARET AND PAT

**'I didn't know what love was till I bred my first Afghan.'**
*Pat and Margaret*, 1994

'I gather that Victoria Wood is making a video of her current tour,' Jonathan Powell, controller of BBC One, wrote to James Moir in April 1991. 'Are we in the market for this? Shouldn't you be bidding for it?'[1] As Victoria's year-long tour came to an end, the tug of war between the BBC and ITV resumed. In the battle to claim her for their network, London Weekend Television resorted to covert tactics. 'Marcus Plantin wanted to do another programme involving Victoria,' says Nicholas Barrett. 'I said, "She and Julie are so close, why don't we approach Julie and that would be a way of Victoria also appearing?" The idea for a showcase to be called *Julie Walters and Friends* was born.

The concept was similar to the *An Audience with . . .* format, with the wealth of the material to be written by Victoria, while Alan Bennett, Alan Bleasdale and Willy Russell submitted one monologue each. According to Barrett, 'Victoria jumped at it. She said to me, "I want you to know I've got lots of stuff and if you're running under let me know." Victoria wrote three sketches soon after the spring tour, and ended up doing three more, as well as a beautifully crafted ballad for Julie to sing. The show became, in effect, *Wood and Walters* a decade on.

Filming was delayed for some months owing to the illness of Julie's daughter, who had been diagnosed with leukaemia. It was eventually shot over two days in late September in a bare, shiny studio with minimal sets and props. If it had been postponed any further, it would have endangered one of the four sketches Victoria and Julie performed together. In '8 Around Me Breakfast Bar' they play two northern women going through the complicated arrangements for what sounds like some sort of sleepover. At the end, when they remove their dressing gowns, they are revealed to be wearing tarts' basques. At that point, after another meticulously planned conception, Victoria was two months pregnant.

The sketches Victoria wrote were designed to suit Julie's astonishing range as a character comedian. Julie played a little girl from Lancashire in 'Jayne Mansfield's Balls', sitting on a wall in around 1960 and trying to coax her friend into a rude word game. In 'Old Bag' she became a posh, bedridden crone who reminisces about the 'Roaring Twenties' before revealing that she didn't have sex till she was sixty-seven, 'and that was only because I couldn't find any small change for the window cleaner'. In 'Offensive Old Man Dancing' Julie wore a moustache and a combover as a revoltingly sexist Desert Rat. In 'Mary Brazzle' she was a glacially calm middle-aged woman who breaks down from the mounting stress of recording a video to promote her failsafe relaxation routine. The health guru secretly addicted to toxins was a favourite joke of Victoria's.

In her song for Julie she changed the mood. 'Between the Lines' was a downbeat flipside to 'The Ballad of Barry and Freda'. Another portrait of an ordinary marriage, from blind date to breastfeeding, it offered a piercingly sad glimpse inside the mind of a young woman straining for happiness:

They're stuck at the airport, a three-hour delay,
They sit in their new clothes with nothing to say,
He stubs out his fag in a throwaway cup,
She touches his hand but he doesn't look up.
A modern romance.

The pulsing melody unexpectedly surges towards optimism as the young couple pledge to keep going 'because love can struggle up between the lines'. Victoria never recorded or performed it, and yet 'Between the Lines' was the most profound expression of something she had been straining to say about the bumps and blessings of love and marriage in twenty years of songwriting.

At the recording the four writers all did a tribute to camera. Victoria chose to veer away from gushing sincerity. 'Julie Walters is a person,' she said, sounding nervy and Lancastrian, 'a woman type of person sort of effect. And, erm, she has hair and, um, some feet and, er, she does washing up . . . and drying. And that's really all . . . all I know about Julie.' Before the recording, writers and star all gathered for a publicity shot. 'It was awkward,' says Julie. 'Writers don't usually meet and there were all those egos. Vic was awkward too.' She was similarly reserved working with a new producer. 'There was never a moment where I looked into her eyes and she looked into mine and we had a conversation where we knew we were talking to each other,' says Nicholas Barrett. 'The reserve coloured everything.' In the same month as *Julie Walters and Friends* was broadcast, Victoria sent word through her agent that she wanted to return to the BBC to make a one-off special in just under a year's time.

While pregnant with Grace Victoria had accepted the most daunting challenge of her career. This time round she arranged to keep a clear schedule. Her tour video, titled *Victoria Wood – Sold Out*, in honour of the run at the Strand, was released near the start of her pregnancy. To promote it she made her first return to *Wogan* since the disastrous debut nine years earlier. Cued up by guest host Gloria Hunniford, she ran through some of the material in a polished metronomic performance that gave nothing away about herself. Towards the end of her pregnancy the video was shown on ITV.

Free from other obligations, Victoria decided to fulfil a long-held ambition and write her own original film script. Encouragement came from LWT, which had enjoyed modest success putting Mel Smith and Griff Rhys Jones on the big screen with a film of Tom Sharpe's crime farce *Wilt*. The idea she hit on was suggested by *Surprise Surprise*, the LWT show hosted by Cilla Black in which long-separated relatives were thrown together in front of a studio audience: 'I always wondered what happens when the lights go down. It's all very well to have a big kiss in front of the cameras. But what do you do then with this terrible relative you've not seen for so much time?'[2] Her interest in family estrangement had a more personal source. Her mother Helen had refused throughout her adult life to engage with any of her siblings and had long since broken off contact with her only son. While Victoria had occasional contact with her brother Chris, she had nieces and, via her mother, first cousins of whom she knew next to nothing. 'It was completely normal,' adds Geoffrey, no more intimate with his own family, 'for both of us not to see siblings for months or sometimes years on end.'

She worked on a script about the reunion of two sisters separated when young. One lives in a bedsit and works in a motorway café, the other is the glamorous star of a Hollywood soap who has suppressed the facts of her past on her rise to fame. In these mismatched women, Victoria saw a chance to act in a drama with Julie again for the first time since *Nearly a Happy Ending* in 1980. 'I rang Julie and said, "I'm writing a monstrous part for you. A horrible megalomaniac called Pat." She was thrilled.'[3] So was LWT, to which she submitted a draft with the working title of *Sisters*. Having read it, Julie's enthusiasm was tempered by an understanding it would require surgery. 'I thought I want to play that woman,' she says. 'I loved the character. The speeches were hilarious. But I felt it needed a lot of work on it. It was very early days and I thought, well, if they're going to make a film of it, it will be edited. I was worried that she might not want to do it.' But negotiations with LWT began with a view to signing contracts within weeks. Marcus Plantin, who had commissioned *An Audience with . . .* four years earlier, was now LWT director of programmes, in which capacity he announced the film at the Montreux Festival in April 1992. 'I have read the script and it is scorchingly funny,' he said, mentioning a prospective budget of £6 million. 'We could not have hoped to put our money into a better movie than this one.' The controller of drama Nick Elliot chimed that it was 'not just hilarious but very moving too'. Production was confidently predicted for 1993, LWT sent Victoria the CVs of potentials directors and within a few months she was corresponding with Geoffrey Strachan at Methuen about publishing the script for *Pat and Margaret*, as she was now calling it.

In the autumn of 1991 there was another project: to look for a new home to house a growing family. Thus the geography of London was on Victoria's mind when, in the middle of house-hunting, she appeared in Clive James's *Postcard from London*. Sitting in Gibson Square in Islington, where she had first kipped in the house of Rob Buckman in 1975, she reminisced about her scuzzy early experiences of the capital. 'I don't think *it's* changed,' she said. 'I think you change yourself and if you get more money you go to nicer bits of it.'[4] The nicer bit that she and Geoffrey plumped for was in Highgate in north London. They were familiar with the village, having first lodged there with Jane Wynn Owen in the 1970s. It bordered Hampstead Heath, giving Victoria hills to yomp up. The size of the house they eventually bought reflected the magnitude of Victoria's success. It was a Grade II listed early Georgian terrace in Highgate West Hill, with enough space for the family, a nanny and two offices. The purchase was not contingent upon selling the Lampard House flat – indeed their flat in Castellain Mansions was still on the market too, as was Cove Lea in Silverdale. They couldn't move in until the crazy DIY exploits of the previous owners had been corrected, which consumed several months, so they eventually took up occupation early in 1992. Grace, who was upset by so many changes of address, extracted a promise from her mother that there would be no more upheavals – Victoria went so far as to make a public pledge on their change of address card: 'Victoria Wood, Geoffrey Durham and Grace Durham are moving on January 22nd', it said. 'After that they are never moving again'.[5]

Victoria's desire for Grace to feel settled found her making friends on her behalf. One day after a step class in Marylebone she was in the changing room when a little girl started talking to Grace, then three. The child's mother had been in the same class. 'We were standing naked,' says Lizzi Kew Ross. 'I don't even know if I knew who she was. She said, "Do you want to come and have tea with us?"' She invited my daughter to go and have a playdate and that was it.' The children's friendship was outlasted by the mothers'. Lizzi, a choreographer and a vicar's wife, became her exercise-class friend. Victoria's celebrity was not always so easily bypassed. When Grace started at her new nursery school in Highgate, to help her overcome her shyness she was paired with a girl called Emma Wellbelove. Wanting to invite Grace on a playdate, her mother Norah asked the teacher if she could be introduced to Grace's mother: 'The teacher said, "She will be here in a minute, but I need to tell you who she is. Her mum is Victoria Wood." I said, "No, I can't talk to her!" All of a sudden Vic was there covered in paint. They must have just moved in because she was decorating.' The girls became friends, but so did the mothers. 'I had nothing to do with show business at all,' says Norah, who worked as an educational welfare officer. 'We were both northerners. I understood that she was quite a quiet person, and she understood I wasn't expecting her to make me laugh.'

Once established in London, Victoria was able to nurture friendships which had previously been conducted long distance, most regularly with Jane Wymark, who lived down the road in Stoke Newington and became another gym buddy. Though a regular visitor to the house, just as often they would meet somewhere in north London, says Jane, for 'a cup of tea, a bun and a laugh'. At the same time, motherhood and new proximity to a greater number of friends made Victoria a less assiduous letter writer, which was reversed only with the acquisition of a fax machine – and a more full-time assistant – later in the 1990s.

On Sunday 2 May, Victoria gave birth to a boy in the Portland. This time her labour was not induced, there was no epidural and she accompanied her contractions with 'yelling and screaming and letting myself go'. When a nurse warned her she'd get a sore throat she replied, 'I really don't care. I want to shout.'[6] The new arrival, weighing in at 8 lb 2 oz, was called Henry William.

It was in the months nursing him at home that Victoria found herself switching on the television in the mornings, where breakfast shows gave way to vapid hours of daytime entertainment hosted, in a relative novelty for British television, by paired presenters. The sheer badness of such programming was catnip to the creator of *As Seen on TV*. She found them 'unintentionally funny because they're on every day, and of course things are going to happen and things are going to sound banal. You can't interview people on a daily basis week after week after week after week.'7 The crowning absurdity for Victoria was the fact that Judy Finnigan presented *This Morning* every day on ITV in harness with her husband Richard Madeley: 'I just love the idea of them being married. I think that's so funny to be sitting next to your husband and having to be nice to him.'8

The idea for the special first mentioned to the BBC at the end of 1991 now crystallised into a Christmas special called *Victoria Wood's All Day Breakfast*, set partly in a daytime TV studio presided over by married co-presenters Sally Crossthwaite and Martin Cumbernauld. Victoria imagined petty aggravations simmering just below the surface. 'No, I love him,' says the domineering Sally after every laser-guided slapdown. Martin gets his own back when he pointedly trails an item on 'wonky wombs and faulty fallopians'. Their random roster of phone-in subjects includes tranvestites, split ends and the self-assembly coffin. The show has its own right-wing fitness instructor called Jolly Polly.

*This Morning*, and its new BBC competitor *Good Morning with Anne and Nick*, were not the only sitting ducks on television. Although she had fronted an advertisement for Maxwell House coffee a couple of years earlier, Victoria took aim at the Gold Blend commercials, which over five years had taken on the character of a long-running drama. She invented Romany Roast Fine Blend and put it at the heart of a slow-burning medical romance between two suave coffee fanciers. He is ill, but even on his deathbed he is fed fine coffee by intravenous drip. An unused instalment was set in a cemetery, where the deceased's gravestone reads, 'He really appreciated the true smokey flavour of Romany Roast'.

For the special there was a calamitous new soap to feast on as well. *Eldorado*, shot on the Costa del Sol, was born two months after Henry, and Victoria was much tickled by its cackhandedness: 'You couldn't hear it, or when you could hear it, it was in a foreign language, it looked awful, they had people called Bunny and Fizz, people who couldn't act, people who couldn't talk properly. Apart from that it was jolly good.'9 To lampoon it she created 'The Mall', which flits between three outlets in a shopping mall in Gloucesterford. Pippas Nix (the apostrophe was missing from the signage) is a lingerie boutique stocking aerobic girdles, flesh-tone cleavage grippers and fishnet groin enhancers. Pippa (played by Celia Imrie) is in the habit of making pointless interjections. 'You know I had that ludicrously irresponsible unprotected sex session in that remedial jacuzzi in Hove?' says her perky assistant. 'Near Brighton?' Opposite is a café owned by a rampantly camp barista and his much younger French boyfriend, enabling Victoria to play with gay clichés. 'In my day,' the jealous Roger tells young Pierre, 'cookery class meant breaking eggs with one hand, not licking melted chocolate off the pectorals of a Salvation Army trombonist!' Pam's Chox is a confectionary run by a toxic gossip and language vandal. 'It's all very que sera de brouhaha,' says Pam. Victoria, who earmarked this role for herself, delighted in giving Pam crass expository dialogue: 'This mall's been open – what? – eighteen months and she's – what? – the sixth business to go in there?' Pippa eventually sells the premises to a shady woman whose name she can't quite recall: 'Was it Mac or Gabardine? I'm sure it was some kind of garment.' Thus in the finale Bo Beaumont as Mrs Overall makes her wobbly re-entry, clutching a tray and still not knowing her lines. She reopens Acorn Antiques with the legacy left her after her employers died 'in a mysterious food poisoning accident on the M42'.

There were more alpha females for Julie Walters to play: a bossy pretentious shopkeeper; a self-pitying pensioner. Victoria visited her Bury Grammar days as Alison Smedley, a naughty schoolgirl in the Lower Fourth who comes up with ever more absurd excuses for her poor behaviour. Another ghost from her distant past was Alan Rickman, whom Victoria first met in *Gunslinger* in 1976. When he was starring in *Les Liaisons Dangereuses* she joked that she couldn't pronounce the name of the play. Sally Crossthwaite makes a great show of getting it right, only to introduce him in the studio as 'Alan Dickman'. Victoria wrote the sketch before she knew Rickman would do it.

The core cast and other regulars gathered to film some of the show, including 'The Mall', without an audience. New actors were blended in – it was specifically decided to use unfamiliar faces for the Romany

Roast ads. Then on a Saturday night in early December the rest of the sketches were shot before an audience. On the script for the Sally and Martin sections, Victoria wrote, 'See the set for "This Morning" and copy it'. The *All Day Breakfast* set was ludicrously littered with ancient maritime bric-a-brac. As with *As Seen on TV*, Geoff Posner filmed more sketches than were needed, and Victoria was not precious about culling her own performances – out went a patronising telethon presenter and a useless weather girl.

Posner advised holding her usual stand-up section and song back for the finale. 'That released a bit of a blockage in Vic,' he says. 'Previously she had supplied a load of sketches and I put them into an order, but this show came fully formed.' The stand-up was originally to be cued by Martin Crossthwaite (played by Duncan Preston) – 'if you like your comedy female-style, take a look at this!' – before the idea was dropped for lack of space. To perform as herself Victoria wore a double-breasted tuxedo and a longer version of her trademark crop. She joked about moving house, and low self-esteem, and how she and her husband used to leave messages to each other on the mirror in lipstick. This image was the product of a visit to Lizzi Kew Ross's home – when breastfeeding Henry in the bedroom Victoria was intrigued to see 'I love you' inscribed in lipstick on a mirror. She then walked over to white piano to sing 'Real Life', a new song with the same melody as the *All Day Breakfast* theme tune. The two sides of Victoria – the empathetic entertainer suffering ups and downs like everyone else – were neatly contained in the chorus:

Cos this is real life
Which is always such a mess,
Badly designed, under-rehearsed, no proper tunes.
We live in real life,
Which is not a nice address,
Needs doing up, needs some white paint, needs a few balloons.

The credits rolled over black-and-white footage of cast and crew backstage, inspired by the recent practice of adding behind-the-scenes extras to video releases. There was little time to stitch the show together, and it was only late in the day that it was granted a prime slot on BBC One on the evening of Christmas Day. Among the millions who watched were Judy Finnigan and Richard Madeley. Victoria heard word that 'they were thrilled by the attention'.

The income from television – and the release on video of an *Acorn Antiques* omnibus – could not be matched by the riches promised by touring. At the start of 1993, after two years spent giving birth to a boy and two television specials, Victoria once more prepared to return to the stage. In that period she had also acquired not one but two new homes. The second came about as a result of a visit from her sister Penelope, who voiced a worry about feeling unsafe in her area of Bradford. Victoria had an idea: to buy a house in the north that Penelope could look after. This would address Victoria's mounting nostalgia for the north, while quelling anxieties about leaving a second home empty. 'In particular,' says Geoffrey, 'she missed the voices and the language and the word order and the turns of phrase. All those things combined to help her write jokes. She had northern voices in her head all the time and she was hankering for them.' A few months on Penelope found a small ad for a converted barn with a granny flat in a village outside Skipton. It had a vast living room with ancient beams and a children's playroom. They made an offer in the early part of 1993 and gave it a new name. 'Just a brief note in the middle of this blur of bedwetting, nappies, shows and white wine,' Victoria wrote to Jane Wymark near the start of her tour. 'From Saturday I'll be at Mole Barn, Halton East. We are trying Mole Barn out to see how it looks on the envelope.'[10]

Not for the first time, the task of coming up with a new show brought on domestic strain. 'Geoff is the one who gets everything dumped on his head,' Victoria conceded. 'It's a bit of a strain for him. I can be hard to live with. If I get down about working I moan all the time. I have a huge insecure patch before I start something, but he's used to hearing me say, "Life is over, nobody wants me, my nose has got bigger and I cannot tell jokes any more."'[11] She relied on him not just to stiffen her spine. With two small children, she had to be more organised than ever about creating an entirely new show. Together they came up with an even more rigorous system for dropping in new material piece by piece in a series of weekly warm-up gigs. The venues were booked for Sunday nights in towns with biggish theatres not far from London. Scarcely publicised, shows in Swindon and High Wycombe sold out on word of mouth. Initially Victoria went on after a magician booked by Geoffrey whose act would not compete with her comedy. Working close to the wire, she spent a week on a new opening section and learned it with cue cards Blu-Tacked to the piano lid. In the first try-out she bolted it onto the front of forty minutes of old material.

'We'd come home and do a post-mortem,' says Geoffrey, 'some-times only deciding then what should follow the new opening. Next morning she'd make a start on that and she'd have another, say, fifteen minutes written by the following Friday. She'd learn it on the Satur-day. I'd sit with her exercise book of script, only chipping in when she dried completely – that was usually better for her than trying to learn what she'd written word for word. Little connecting gags could creep in unexpectedly that way, too. It was always a scramble having to keep more and more in her head as the weeks went by.' By the fourth week she had enough material to do without a support act, but the whole set wasn't yet complete. Three days before she opened in Sheffield, she dashed off a twenty-minute section and performed it without even rehearsing it. It went 'pretty well,' she reckoned. 'I thought I was doing well to know it let alone perform it.'[12]

She prepared for the tour by visiting the studio of Betty Jackson, who found their early consultations tricky: 'Vic was so private at the beginning that it was a bit like pulling teeth. She always said, "I'm nobody's fashion icon and I never care about the way I look." I wanted to do her justice because she was a genius.' Already a friend of Dawn French and Jennifer Saunders, she slowly earned Victoria's trust – it helped that she came from Bacup in the Rossendale Valley – and was able to sell her the idea of dressing androgynously: 'A boy's suit was always my starting point with her. She had great legs and really narrow hips. The rest of it I didn't ever want to draw attention to. I thought make her look more energetic and modern. Once that image walked onstage it reinforced everything: she was in control.' Unlike some celebrity clients, Victoria made a point of leaving enough time for the fitting session and for the suits to be made, and on paying her way. 'At the beginning she said, "I'm not here to get something for nothing." I said, "If you cover the cost, then that's fine. It was the pattern cutter's time and the seamstress's time and the fabric that I billed her for. There was a northern respect about that.' (Betty Jackson's other service was to send Victoria around the corner to Charles Worthington, whose salon took charge of her hair for the rest of her life.)

As Victoria wrote in her large eighteenth-century north London home – to downplay its grandeur she took to calling it a 'Georgian semi' – there was a new fear that she might become disconnected from the ordinary lives of those who paid to see her. 'You can fall out of favour very easily,' she acknowledged in the first week of the tour. 'I don't know if it's a side effect of being successful or having quite a lot of money – is that you're not in touch with people. I do worry about that slightly. I don't think it's happened yet.' Her solution was to visit 'the below-the-waist area' in more detail than any comedian had ever done before. She had strategically avoided the subject of childbirth on her previous tour: 'It's only now that I've got two and people aren't going, "Oh yes, she's just had a baby," I feel I can mention it.' But she was careful to ensure that her own children and their father remained out of focus – the only glimpse she afforded her audience was that her latest baby looked 'like something out of the *Beano*'.

To reassure the women in her audience that she was still one of them, she softened them up with a riff on the differences between super-thin celebrity mothers with model babies and their real-life counterparts. Real mummies, among whom she counted herself, 'carry their stomachs up to bed over one arm' and 'think sex is like full employment: it's a nice idea but it'll never happen in their lifetime'. This was a warm-up for a second-half section about antenatal classes, epidurals, pelvic-floor exercises and breastfeeding. Victoria had grown increasingly frank and unembarrassed about the female body, but now went further than ever: 'You know something nobody ever really told me about having a baby? When you're having a baby, as the baby pops out the front, a haemorrhoid pops out the back. Mine was massive. It weighed more than the baby. I phoned my mother up: "Knit two hats!"' Geoffrey reckons this 'may just have been her all-time best line'.

Among all these gynaecological close-ups, Victoria found a new use for one of her favourite comic words. A nurse tells her that labour is like passing a rubber dolly through a balaclava helmet: 'I remember looking down at myself and thinking, no, there's a design fault here. This is nothing like a balaclava.' As she worked her way through the mechanics of birth it was as if she was a conductor in control of a choir of 2,000, which with masterly manipulation she led towards an inexorable hysteria. Throughout the show she couldn't leave the subject alone – she imagined a car called the Vauxhall Placenta and reached a peak of graphic candour in 'Bum to the World', sung from the point of view of a baby surveying its new surroundings:

I'm terribly torn about being born
I mean what is the whole thing about?
Plop! Out you come
Very near someone's bum
It can't have been properly thought out.

Having a child of school age whom she could no longer bring with her, Victoria stipulated certain scheduling conditions to Phil McIntyre, who had now become her sole promoter. She would perform four nights a week, Monday to Thursday, go home on a Thursday night and stay until Monday morning when she would take Grace to school. For the spring leg she resumed the arrangement of touring with a baby and a nanny. Travelling with Henry, she said, was 'a bit like taking Keith Moon on tour except the damage is only two foot up the walls'.[13] One week in the north he came down with chicken pox – not a hazard encountered by any male comic on the circuit: 'I ended up wrapping him in a blanket and taking him to the bar to cheer him up.'[14] If the venue was anywhere near London, she'd travel alone and dash back every night.

Victoria had another travel companion in the shape of a new young stage manager. Amie Beamish, a New Zealander in her early twenties, was introduced to Victoria by Phil McIntyre and earned her instant approval. An intimate ritual soon developed when Victoria was about to go onstage. 'If she and I were alone, she'd give a little flash,' says Amie. 'Up with the shirt and down – and that would give her an adrenalin rush to build herself up. She'd take a big step onto the stage on the back of it.' A routine was established away from the theatre too: 'Part of my job was to sus out the best chippie between the venue and the hotel. Afterwards I would stop by the chippie while she waited in the car, and we would sit in the hotel bar with a bottle of champagne and chips and talk till two or three in the morning.' Victoria came to rely on what she identified as Amie's 'twinkly ruthlessness' which found her getting the job done 'without crews realising that metaphorically speaking, she's just mashed them in the groin with a mole wrench'.[15]

There was more to the show than baby talk, including much discussion about the real life of royalty. Among a new set of celebrities now placed in the firing line, tabloid fixation Camilla Parker-Bowles provided the punchline for a long, fantastical section about insomnia: when presented to Her Majesty at Buckingham Palace, Victoria finally remembers the name of a posh rebel with a double-barrelled name she was at school with. She invented a treacle-toned right-wing Radio 2 DJ called Charlene Dawson, 'putting the we into the wee small hours', based on Julie Dawn whom she used to be hooked on in the 1970s. A scathing attack on Weight Watchers found her giving vent to real political anger.

Victoria emerged after the interval to pumping music, dressed in big curly wig and padded leotard, to take an aerobics class. Madge, introducing her 'low-impact class for fatties with attitude – welcome to FATTITUDE!', was an experiment in physical comedy. It took courage to go out in body-hugging Lycra – earlier in the show she talked about squeezing herself into an exercise bra: 'like trying to fit two blancmanges inside an envelope'. But there was an instant reward: 'The first time I went out in that leotard the woof that went up I thought, oh thank God, this is going to be all right. I'm all right here for a few minutes. I'll just stand round wearing this leotard for a bit.'[16] Her many years doing Jane Fonda's workouts meant she knew how to devise a comic set of aerobic thrusts and jerks: 'I just worked it out as if I was an actual aerobics teacher and what would I do? And then I just tried to make the movements funny rather than real.'[17] On a weekly regime of four aerobic and body-conditioning classes, with an exercise step in her dressing room, she was also fit enough to carry it off. As Madge eggs on her plus-size class of amputees and lobotomees, she radiates can-do self-belief and medical savvy, talking up the importance of the 'glutonious maxitive muscle' and a vital hormone known as 'phenophonobarbametamorphomone'.

For her encore Victoria used an offcut from *All Day Breakfast*. 'Madeline' was a wordplay funfair, in which a hairstylist remembers how her ambition to model was quashed by her mother: '"Ooh, Madeline, you'd be very middling at modelling." I said, "Would I?" She said, "Yes, if you go muddling with modelling, you'll be middling, our Madeline." I said, "You're meddling."'

The set was less reliant than ever on music. The opener 'In the Mood Tonight' – a self-mocking portrait of life as a comedian – didn't arrive until fifteen minutes in:

> Comedians are tough and hard
> We've all been hurt, we've all been scarred
> We all do ads for Barclaycard
> I'm feeling in the mood tonight.

The previous year Rowan Atkinson had taken the Barclaycard shilling. According to Geoffrey, 'Vic was really beginning to doubt the songs – she found them hard to write and she often thought they were naff. But she knew she needed them.' She limited the supply of downbeat songs to just one. 'I've rooted that out,' she said as the tour started. 'I thought I don't want to be moving. I just want to get a lot of laughs.'[18] And yet the lone ballad was one of her very best. With a bittersweet, McCartneyesque melody, 'Go With It' urged anxious and fainthearted loners to seize the day:

> Just another life, it's true,
> But particularly yours, particularly you.

If you have a dream, go with it.
Feel the slightest hint, go with it.
What is there to lose?
Do you dare, dare to choose?

When the encore came around after two triumphant hours the audience greeted Barry and Freda and Kimberley as old friends.

Halfway through the spring tour, Victoria turned forty. The day fell on a Sunday, and she and Geoffrey threw an afternoon party with a children's entertainer. 'It's a sort of late housewarming/b'day do', she wrote on the back of one printed invitation.[19] The chippies and decorators who'd helped do up the house rubbed shoulders with Dawn French, Lenny Henry and Alan Rickman at the first proper party Victoria and Geoffrey had ever been able to host – and Victoria's first since she turned twenty in Richmond Hill Road. To make up for all their years of not hosting, they would soon start to throw Christmas parties that became an annual fixture. For the most part the house would remain a private sanctum – Victoria entertained friends and school mothers with afternoon tea and cake, but evening guests were rare. 'The truth is that not many people came to the house,' says Geoffrey. 'Vic expressed her love for people by writing to them, which in many ways was more important to her than face-to-face communication, because she was in charge of it. She needed control. And she used to fret that she couldn't talk about her life in ways that people not in show business could empathise with. That became more of an issue as an increasing number of her showbiz pals moved out of London and so weren't around to socialise with at weekends.'

Over the summer Victoria worked on a new draft of *Pat and Margaret*. Her film script about estranged sisters was duly approved by Marcus Plantin, whose background was in light entertainment, but was less welcomed by the drama department, whereupon the relationship with LWT rapidly broke down. Victoria felt aggrieved about the snub: 'They couldn't wait to do it. Six months later they couldn't wait not to do it.'[20] Informed that there were problems with the script, 'I said, "What are they?" She said, "Well, I haven't read it properly yet," and that was the last I heard from her.'[21] Sarah Wilson, LWT's

'I remember thinking the heavens had sent her to me,' says Julie Walters.

Meeting Geoffrey Durham
was 'a fantastic stroke of luck'.

The only wedding photo of
Victoria and Geoffrey.
1 March 1980. 'Five-minute
job then spaghetti on toast
and knickerbocker glory.'

In her album Victoria scrawled a caption over a photo of *Funny Turns* at the Duchess Theatre.

Victoria's early years as a stand-up involved a lot of sitting down. The setlist on cue cards is stuck to the piano.

After two weeks performing *Lucky Bag* at the Ambassador's in early 1984, Victoria went home to write *As Seen on TV.*

The stars of *Acorn Antiques* with Chrissie Baker, Victoria's hair and make-up designer for nearly thirty years.

'Nine and half weeks, 27 hotels, 51 shows and 5869 miles – as the song says – and I'm still here.' At the party to mark the end of her 1987 tour.

'I've heard enough skriking in this bug hutch to last me from t'Weatherfield Viaduct to t'Whit Week Walk.' Victoria and Julie as Ena Sharples and Martha Longhurst.

's quite cosy. It's a bit like a Jammy Dodger.' In 1993 Victoria performed at the Royal Albert Hall for the first time.

With Celia Imrie
recording *All Day Breakfast* in 1992.

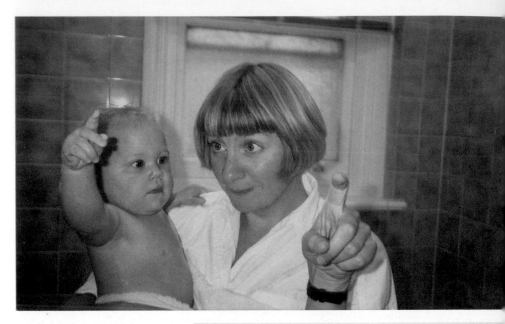

Victoria gave birth to Grace
in 1988. 'She bathed in the
glory of it,' says Geoffrey,
'and she lived it day after day
after day.'

Grace and Henry with
their mother during
the making of *Pat and
Margaret* in 1994.

In Zimbabwe for Comic
Relief with one of the
Masara family in 1995.

The family in the
garden at Mole Barn.

With Geoffrey after
his dramatic weight
loss, backstage on
tour in 1996.

The cast and crew of the first series of *dinnerladies* in the week they recorded 'Moods'. Producer-director Geoff Posner is to the right of Victoria.

'My daughter born Christmas Eve, so we called her Brenda.'

Polishing a *dinnerladies* script in her BBC dressing room.

controller of drama, clarified to Vivienne Clore that there were 'very serious concerns about the script . . . we cannot convince ourselves that the story in its present form will survive a theatrical release'.[22] Rank, the film distributors who were to put up some of the money for production, were no more than lukewarm. So, on her agent's advice, Victoria bought back the rights. She told Bob Monkhouse, who was about to feature in his own *An Audience with . . .* on LWT, that she wouldn't go near the building again.

The autumn brought a much-needed boost to her morale as her tour resumed. While there were ready-made large-capacity venues all over the UK, it was far harder to meet the demand for tickets in London. Three years earlier the solution was an extended West End residency, which had exhausted her. 'She hated the idea of being stuck in a thousand-seater for two months,' says Phil McIntyre, who proposed a shorter run at a much larger venue: the Royal Albert Hall. Victoria had joked about the imposing size of the old hall in *Talent*: having sex after a hysterectomy is 'like waving a woody in the Albert Hall'. Well aware that Billy Connolly had played there in 1987, she was eager to try it herself, so McIntyre took Victoria and Geoffrey for a recce. While she stood on the stage, the other two rambled all over the auditorium searching for poor sightlines. 'We found that there were only about ten bad seats in the house,' says Geoffrey, who then replaced Victoria onstage while she roamed herself. On one thing she was adamant: unlike Connolly, she would not use side-screens, insisting that she could play only to an audience that was looking at her.

Finding a space in the Albert Hall's clogged calendar was not simple. There was also the problem of wealthy debenture holders who, on about half the nights, had priority access to more than 2,000 of the best seats, exiling the majority of Victoria's fans to high up in the gods. For other performances McIntyre was able to sell all 5,600 tickets himself. 'She could tell the difference on those nights,' he says. 'But because Vic was every person's comedian, she didn't fare too bad.' Technical rehearsals took longer than usual. 'There was a lot of due diligence,' says Amie Beamish. 'She treated it with huge reverence. She felt it was an extraordinary magical place and it was really important to her to do well there.'

Victoria entered to a full house for the first time on 21 September 1993. 'When she walked out on stage,' says Geoffrey, 'I knew we'd got it right. She warmed to the place instantly and within five minutes she was playing it as if she'd never played anywhere smaller.' As she embraced the space, it embraced her back. 'It's quite cosy,' she said as she anticipated performing there. 'It's a bit like a Jammy Dodger.'[23] To make herself and her audience feel at home she wrote a new open-ing section welcoming everyone in. 'Have we got people at the top tonight? Hello! I've got a black suit and blue eyes, OK?' She was care-ful to bow and scrape and give the hall its royal prefix; otherwise 'it could be somewhere you play bingo in Widnes'. Quickly she learned that laughter travelled more gradually round the room, so she had to go more slowly, which she found tiring.

Friends who had known her since Birmingham or even Bury were given tickets for the first night and could only marvel that the shy, lonely teenager they had known now held nearly 6,000 people in the palm of her hand. Phil McIntyre booked fifteen nights in all, but shrewdly announced only twelve so that he could add extra shows by popular demand. Victoria, on a percentage of the box-office take, was immensely proud that every ticket went. 'Oh it was wonderful,' she said. 'Instant gratification.'[24] Now when it was put to her yet again that she was the new Alan Bennett, she had a fresh retort: 'He hasn't played the Albert Hall, has he?'[25] Methuen asked her to update her bio for the jacket of her next publication, and after the words 'She is one of Britain's top comedians' she biroed an insert: 'And the only one ever to have sold out fifteen consecutive nights at the Royal Albert Hall'.

After the Albert Hall, Victoria continued with her visits to English cities. Then, one weekend in November, Stanley Wood died at the age of eighty-two. Of her parents, her father had been the one who evinced pride in her remarkable achievements, so much so that Helen forbade him from talking about her when they were out and about. At a book fair where they would sell some of the thousands of volumes Helen had accumulated, she once rapped him on the knuckles having caught him showing someone a snap of Grace. 'My father used to talk about me to strangers at bus stops,' said Victoria the following year, 'and adored the fact I was on television. My mother won't discuss me with other people. If someone says, "You sound awfully like Victoria Wood," she might admit through gritted teeth we're related.'[26]

After retiring only a few years earlier, he gradually became dependent on Helen and lost interest in leaving home as he succumbed to dementia. Throughout, both parents kept their daughters at arm's length, fending off visits which, according to Geoffrey, did nothing to mitigate the sense that Victoria 'felt quite detached from Stanley's death'. Indeed, she decided to honour her commitments and carry on with four performances in Newcastle. The only event she postponed was a ceremony to receive an honorary doctorate of letters from Sunderland University – it fell on the same day as the funeral in Bury, which was sparsely attended by immediate family only, as Helen refused to invite anyone. Not long after, Victoria's newly widowed mother came to stay in Highgate and brought with her the recording she and Stanley had made together in the 1930s. Typically for this family who had all lived in separate rooms, its existence was a complete surprise to Victoria.

It was in the days before Stanley's death that Vivienne Clore sent Victoria's second draft of *Pat and Margaret* to the BBC, adding that Julie Walters liked it very much. Alan Yentob, now controller of BBC One, passed it on to the drama department without reading it: 'Luckily for us, she has fallen out with LWT . . . I have no idea what it's like.'[27] The script was given to Margaret Matheson, who had arrived only that month to run the single drama strand Screen One. She commissioned a detailed report by a script executive who ruefully concluded that 'it's far too linear & predictable to warrant the running time' and contained nothing new or original – it was 'a case of Victoria revisited'.[28] Despite these internal reservations, Yentob acted fast after an alert that Marcus Plantin's enthusiasm at LWT had been rekindled. 'I wanted to ensure we didn't lose it or Victoria Wood,' he told his colleagues in Drama.[29] Matheson passed the draft on to Ruth Caleb, a senior producer of hard-hitting dramas whose bafflement at being asked to work on a comedy was not assuaged by first sight of the script. 'It wasn't like a drama script,' she says. 'It didn't feel rooted in anything. It was a series of sketches which seemed to be quite superficial. It didn't have the depth I thought a script would need.' When they met for the first time over lunch at the BBC's waiter-service canteen, she gently probed Victoria: 'I said, "Why did you write it? What is it about?" She said, "It's about blood not being thicker than water." I thought, that's it, I'll do it.'

Victoria didn't mention that the story was rooted in her own experiences – she was so averse to examination of her family background that three times she flatly refused to appear on *This Is Your Life*. The only inspiration for *Pat and Margaret* that she would admit to was *Surprise Surprise*. Thus she imagined her two estranged sisters Pat Bedford and Margaret Mottershead being thrust together in front of a television audience. Once the show is over – Victoria called it *Magic Moments* – they are forced to confront the vast chasm that divides them. They get to know each other as Pat fends off press curiosity about the identity of their mother, a former prostitute called Vera.

The first draft was a loose and baggy container Victoria crammed with gags, some about Claire, the freelance publicist who promotes Pat's new book. Giving her two small children and an obese northern nanny enabled Victoria to mint more jokes about the travails of motherhood. ('I weaned the baby early because I have inverted nipples,' says Claire in early drafts. 'As long as you do the job properly,' replies Pat, 'I wouldn't care if you had a three-speed vagina with stabilisers.') Plotting, never Victoria's strongest suit, was a muddle. There were several flashbacks. Not one but two separate journalists scamper around Lancashire looking for the missing mother. Margaret's romance with her illiterate boyfriend Jim (who lodged with a woman called Mrs Constable) was not resolved.

'I knew it would be quite hard work,' says Ruth Caleb, 'that you would have to strip away absolutely everything to work out what the central theme is and start to build it up again. I knew I would need a really good script editor to help me do that.' So Victoria found herself working with a younger woman who was mandated to push her. 'It wasn't my job to make it funny,' says Robyn Slovo, who was in her early thirties. 'It was already terribly funny. It was my job to help her get to the mother.' The script was stripped back to twelve pages and built up again so the theme of maternal betrayal could swim into focus.

In the second draft, submitted to LWT in August 1993, Victoria had already come up with a fiery confrontation between mother and daughter:

> Pat: I'm like you . . . Brought up the Vera way, what could I know – housework stinks and black bras don't show the dirt. What else – don't be warm, don't be kind, look after number one, stuff any other bugger who does different – you made me, you stupid cow, and you fucked up.
>
> Vera: Did I? Did I? Would you have got out if I hadn't shoved you out? . . . You should be thanking me for making you hard inside, because that's what pushed you on, that's what's kept you going.

Aside from the f-word, the exchange survived more or less verbatim through three more drafts. Also in this second draft Victoria created another mother by changing Jim's landlady into an overbearing matriarch who thwarts his relationship with Margaret. She even blurts, 'I'm supposed to be the woman you love!' Victoria gave her one of the drama's finest zingers: 'They didn't have dyslexia in those days; you sat at the back with raffia.' Of Victoria's many raffia gags, this was the apex.

Victoria went to work on a third draft early in 1994, with a mission to zero in on the theme of maternal abandonment. At no point did she mention even to Geoffrey that, as with 'Swimming the Channel', she drew from her own well of loneliness and her mother's emotional remoteness. 'We both took Helen's tacit contribution for granted,' he says. 'Vic lived and breathed parental unavailability, so we didn't need to talk about it.' The unspoken source was apparent to Julie Walters, in whom Victoria confided during the intense early phase of their friendship: 'She said that her mum left when she was about eleven. When she left Victoria went into chaos. She felt abandoned and she couldn't function very well.' Where Helen resumed her education and left Victoria to fend for herself, Vera's abandonment of Margaret takes a more dramatic form: she goes to prison for a few months and on her release doesn't bother to reclaim Margaret from foster care. 'We're not a very family family are we?' Vera says in an early draft, by way of an excuse for her coldness. Victoria used this very line when promoting the eventual film. 'We're not a very family family,' she said of the Woods in one interview.[30] 'I am close to my sisters, but not my brother,' she explained in another. 'I was five when he went away to university and I didn't have much to do with him after that.'[31]

The drama explores how such a gulf can widen between family members. But the relationship between Pat and Margaret had more complex origins. Pat was a culmination of all the hard-hearted egotists Victoria had written for Julie. 'I'm fascinated by people who are blatantly horrible,' said Victoria. 'That sort of pushy, dominant, domineering person who screams "get me this!" "You give me that!"'[32] Pat angrily boasts that she 'came sixth in the world's Most Envied Bottom Poll, 1992, only two below Claudia Schiffer' but is now 'publicly linked with someone whose buttocks practically skim the carpet'.

Victoria gained a new perspective on her own celebrity when Grace, prompted by gossiping classmates, asked her, 'Mummy, are you famous?' For all her own fame, Victoria was not Pat – the rank-pulling tantrum was not in her armoury. Nor was she Margaret, who has no get-up-and-go. And yet between them they made up two halves of a self-portrait. In one character she explored the side of herself that had achieved fame and wealth, ate healthily, did aerobics, was pestered by fans wherever she went and had fled her northern roots. In the other she revisited the rented bedsit which, in another life, she might never have escaped. In her introduction to the published script Victoria wrote of how, as she turned forty, 'I had started to look back at my own youth . . . and think about the changes that had happened to me since I had become a television performer, and how easy celebrity makes it to distance oneself from the pre-famous self.'[33] She went further in a *South Bank Show* profile two years later: 'It was both me. It was that battle between the one who can never get on, the impotent person, and the one who is so determined to get on there's no room for anything else.'[34]

Victoria collected her honorary degree from Sunderland in February 1994. The same month, as she worked on the third draft, she went to see the first of several therapists. 'I felt I had everything I wanted,' she explained to Lesley Fitton, 'career, kids, nice house, enough money, but was still depressed. So I started to have counselling, some of which was good and some of which was really dreary and hopeless, and some of which was in Neasden.' The best of them, she concluded, 'was terribly helpful in that it helped me get my ideas straight about the past and the different ways I'd behaved and I began to see it was possible to behave in a different way from before, and that it didn't all have to stay the same for ever and ever.'[35] Writing for Pat was also a kind of therapy. 'I give her all these great putdowns that I would love to say to people myself,' she said. 'I suppose it's one way of working out my anger at always saying yes to people when I wanted to say no.'[36]

There was a significant change between drafts when Celia Imrie, for whom Victoria had written the role of Claire, told her she was three months pregnant. She swiftly rewrote the part so that Claire stopped being a neurotic mother with inverted nipples and became an expectant mother with a pressing bladder problem. Pat's lack of education, and tendency to get words wrong, was a new source of jokes: she says 'virago' meaning 'farrago', 'vagina' instead of 'Geneva' and claims to be travelling 'incognino'; ordering chicken she clicks her fingers at the foreign maid and asks for 'Pollet? Poulente?' Right at the end, when Jim tells his mother that he and Margaret have had sex on her bed, Victoria added a new line in biro which would be immortalised by Thora Hird: 'MUM: Not on the eiderdown.'

In mid-March, Victoria went back out on tour for three weeks. After 104 performances, in which she entertained 300,000 people, she finally put the show to bed in a studio performance recorded by Geoff Posner in front of an audience at TV Centre for later broadcast.

Meanwhile, *Pat and Margaret* was becoming a process of excavation. Pat was given a line that was possibly suggested by Victoria's sessions of therapy: 'You shove it all away, move on, grow up, cut your hair, and it's all there waiting, isn't it, waiting to be dealt with.' The rewriting continued into May. As Robyn Slovo sent over yet more pages of suggestions, at one point Victoria cracked: 'I phoned Vic on a Friday afternoon when we were just about to go into production and I gave her some notes and she burst into tears. She said, "You don't understand, I've got a whole life, I don't like being a writer, I don't like getting notes and I just can't." I thought, God, this is amazing, I made Victoria Wood cry.' In fact, Victoria did not resent being pushed and, according to Geoffrey, 'really rated Robyn Slovo – she thought she was brilliant'. The final draft resolved the ending. Her career revived by a tell-all interview, Pat takes Vera back to Los Angeles as a trophy mother and buys Swiss Cottage, the café where she was once a teenage waitress, for Margaret and Jim to run together.

By now the production had a director. Margaret Matheson originally thought of Stephen Frears, who said no. Instead Gavin Millar was recommended to Victoria by Julie, who had worked with him twice in the 1980s. 'I thought he would be the person who would knock it into shape,' she says. A second suggestion made by Julie was to give the role of Jim to Duncan Preston after Jim Broadbent, Victoria's original preference, turned it down. Other regulars, who were required to meet Millar before he would cast them, were Deborah Grant as the predatory journalist Stella Kincaid and Anne Reid as the presenter of *Magic Moments*. Shirley Stelfox was cast as Vera, the chilly whippet-thin mother who, in her daughters' memory, 'used to do it standing up for ten Bensons . . . and lying down for twenty'.

The BBC didn't announce the production until May, which is when the press first heard that LWT had dropped the film announced two years earlier. The four-week shoot began in mid-May, migrating in London between Elstree Studios, Heston Services near Heathrow and the Regent Hotel on Marylebone Road.

Margaret was described in the script as 'plumpish and fairish', while Pat deplores her 'perm you could go trick or treating in'. To put detail on this look, Victoria asked her make-up designer Chrissie Baker to create a tight frizzy wig. 'No naked flames near it, please,' she joked on set, 'all the budget went on it.'[37] The million-pound budget was sufficiently tight that in one scene Gavin Millar had to play the manager of an old people's home. Victoria quickly developed a high regard for her director. 'I kept my nosy, critical, interfering side away,' she claimed. 'After you've written a play, you should hand the actors their words and let them get their own performance. It's like a relay race.' Resolute self-denial proved harder than she made it sound. 'She'd be hanging around giving notes,' says Duncan Preston, 'and Gavin said, "Victoria, are you in this scene?" She said, "No." "Well go away then, let me do it." He didn't want her to tell us how to do it. To her credit she took it very well.' Millar was similarly emphatic with Anne Reid: 'At one point he said, "I want you to slow down on this speech." I said, "Oh my God, Vic won't like it." And he said, "She's not directing this, I'm directing this."'

After two weeks the shoot moved to Blackburn, attracting attention on the steep street where Duncan and Victoria filmed their climactic clinch. It was her first-ever screen kiss. 'I'm quite nervous,' she confided to Duncan. 'Are you all right with this?' But the star of the scene was Thora Hird. 'The whole bloody street turned out to watch her brush the privet with her feather duster,' says Duncan, 'and when she said, "Not on the eiderdown!" about a hundred people laughed and we had to do it again.'

The shoot was over in the middle of June. As if to draw a line under the story, Victoria went back to Birtle for the first time in several years to help her mother pack up the house and move to a bungalow in Skipton which she paid for. In the clear-out she and Penelope filled eight skips.

At a press screening of *Pat and Margaret* in Leicester Square, Victoria was finally offered a brief tantalising glimpse of how her work would look on a cinema screen. The television broadcast in early September was seen by ten and a half million viewers, and brought near unanimous praise, from the *Sun* ('The best thing Victoria Wood has written'[38]) to the *Guardian*. 'Victoria Wood has an ear for a manner of speaking that is akin to perfect pitch,' reckoned Nancy Banks-Smith.[39] The *Evening Standard*, berating LWT for dropping the ball, purred that 'the aroma of a Bafta nomination began wafting through the screen from the start'.[40]

The following year, in March 1995, *Pat and Margaret* was indeed up for Best Single Drama at the BAFTAs, while the vulnerability and guts of her revelatory performance found Victoria, rather than Julie, nominated for best actress. Both awards were to go elsewhere, despite a rumour that reached Ruth Caleb as she mingled before the ceremony: 'In my mind I thought, we'll get the Single Drama award. We're sitting there waiting for it and they said, "And the winner is . . ." and I started to get up. And I was really pissed off. Victoria would have loved to win, and she should have done.'

# 17

# JOURNEYS

'Party bags are a real nightmare where I live . . . This year
you can't really get away with less than one decent piece of
jewellery and some air tickets.'

Live show, 1996

After *Pat and Margaret*, Victoria experienced something new and
unfamiliar: a hiatus. The pause was of her own choosing. 'After years
of practically flogging myself to death,' she said, 'I have the need to go
on working, but only when I'm really enthusiastic about something.'[1]
Richard Eyre, the artistic director of the National Theatre, tried to
enthuse her about the idea of writing a play, possibly for children. 'I
don't think I could attempt a children's play,' she replied, 'but I am
taking a break at the moment for the specific reason that I want to
think about stage plays – I haven't written one for 14 years, and now
might be the time. I'll let you know.'[2] She had made no progress with
her own play when Eyre renewed the offer eighteen months later.

Victoria did express interest in a pitch to make a documentary
about food. Catherine Seddon, a young producer at the BBC, contacted her directly rather than through her agent. The series she
proposed would address the marketing of food, emotional responses
to food, body image issues and the development of eating disorders,
all under the working title of *Food, Glorious Food*. They duly met in
Highgate to map out half a dozen films. The approach was timely.
Geoffrey, having peaked at 20 stone, was near the start of a long quest

to eat more healthily and lose weight without officially dieting. He ate his last biscuit in May 1994 and threw himself into Canadian Air Force exercises, while the house acquired a rowing machine. With the proposal fleshed out, a lunch followed with more senior BBC figures, including Alan Yentob. 'Conversation began to veer away from what I had originally discussed with Victoria,' says Catherine Seddon, 'and I could tell that she had some reservations, but I wasn't in a strong position to remonstrate.' In due course Victoria felt the idea slipping through her fingers and wrote to Yentob to withdraw: 'It was a really good proposal, and I was very keen on it, but after the tour and the special and *Pat and Margaret*, I need some time off before I commit myself to a new project.'[3]

After the summer Geoffrey prepared to perform over Christmas 1994 back at the King's Head. Having relied on his involvement for all her live shows, Victoria now returned the compliment. The subtitle was hers: *One Man's Intrepid Journey Up His Own Sleeve*. 'Vic and I spent a lot of time discussing it, working out a sequence and giving it a reason to be there,' says Geoffrey. 'She wrote bits of script for it, too, but I ended up sounding like a carbon copy of her, so that side of the plan was abandoned quite quickly.'

As for herself, Victoria stuck to one-off commitments and good causes. In October she did a benefit at the Spa in Scarborough to raise money for the newly built Stephen Joseph Theatre at the request of Alan Ayckbourn, who witnessed for himself the transformation in real time between the two Victorias: 'When she arrived she was this very quiet person. She started on a walk that took her round the auditorium, and I gathered that this was a woman psyching herself up for a performance. She got increasingly nervous and focused. By the time she came on she was Victoria Wood. An amazing show.' Afterwards she chatted and laughed with the local ladies, all keen fans, who had organised the benefit before going back to his house for dinner: 'She was sitting there at one end of the table and was keeping us all in fits. She began to quieten down and by the time we finished she was back to her quiet monosyllabic self. The spell had worn off.' In the guestbook the next morning she wrote, 'Nice clean bath.'

In November, for the Sunday afternoon show *The Bookworm*, she went to Norwich to do a short piece about safeguarding libraries, so often a feature of her comedy. On Christmas Day, *Victoria Wood Live in Your Own Home* was shown on ITV to an audience of more than thirteen million.

Then she was invited, as an eleventh-hour substitute for Lenny Henry, to make another trip to Africa. According to Geoffrey, 'she had reservations about Comic Relief as an institution and got quite edgy about it if she suspected people of using it to enhance their reputations, which she was convinced they did. But she did love being the person to get someone out of a jam.' In February 1995 Victoria flew club class – the crew were upgraded to join her – to Zimbabwe to make a film about a family living with minimal access to water in a village several hours' drive from Harare. The children of the Masara family she met were called Scholastic, Besta, Apologise, Blessing, Forward, Before and Fortunate, which the director worried might be a source of amusement. 'I am hard put not to smile,' Victoria reported, 'when in the middle of filming she calls out, "Tell Forward to go backwards."'[4] On the first day she joined in the family's daily tasks, collecting water from half a mile away, milking the cow and digging trenches. 'I barely do one percent of what the family does every day, and by evening I am completely knackered.'[5] The plan for the night was for Victoria to share their mud hut with the four daughters before getting up with them at four in the morning – they were filmed cheerfully bidding one another good night. But there was no room for her inflatable mattress and mosquito net, so she was obliged to keep to her tent. On the second day, helping with irrigation and sanitation projects, she was delighted and moved when the children and then the village women sang to her in harmony. After a half-baked plan to detour to the Victoria Falls did not come to pass, she returned home 'very full of the family she'd been with,' says Geoffrey, 'and relieved that the rapport she had with them enabled her to be natural and unpatronising, though she found the culture shock of the whole experience pretty intense.'

*Living Without Water*, presented by Victoria at her most empathetic and practical, was broadcast the night before Red Nose Day, when Victoria made another contribution in the form of a sketch. Following her many assaults on bad television in *As Seen on TV* and *All Day Breakfast*, she now took aim at the rowdy daytime talk show. The genre was new to the UK – *Vanessa*, presented by Vanessa Feltz, began broadcasting in the same week that *Pat and Margaret* was screened. Victoria was quick off the mark. In her sketch a blowsy alpha-hostess in a peroxide wig and a figure-hugging pink two-piece was played by Dawn French.

Victoria's friendship with half of French and Saunders had been slowly growing over the years – long before she met them she sent a supportive note advising them to ignore a bad Edinburgh Festival review. She overcame her dislike of parties to go with Geoffrey and the children to the summer get-togethers thrown in the early 1990s by Dawn French and Lenny Henry at their home near Reading, attended by the cream of British comedy. Competing in the tennis tournament for the Double D Cup, Victoria wasn't a natural, but 'she gave it a bloody good go,' says Dawn. For a while theirs was an unequal friendship: 'Vic had a very big issue with trusting people and I certainly had to pass a lot of tests and I had to be persistent. I was aware that it was a bit one-sided for quite a long time.' Gradually they formed a bond over shared anxieties about motherhood: 'She was one of the few friends of mine who absolutely admitted she didn't know what she was up to. She was a real safe harbour for that. She listened for hours to me talking about my fears and worries. She was discreet and understanding and quite wise and said things that were helpful.'

It was a different story when they worked together on the Red Nose Day sketch. As 'Dawn', Dawn dashed about the set, perching on laps, faking outrage, thrusting her microphone in faces and flirting with the camera. Victoria cast herself as a soppy Brummie housewife, married to a ping-pong addict who believes in the power of love. 'Can I just say?' she simpers, 'If love's on the table, who needs gravy?' Many of Victoria's regulars were in the cast. Celia Imrie played a woman who tolerates her husband's serial attempts to poison her (reprising a similar figure played by Julie in *Wood and Walters*). In a loving dig at ITV's hospital sitcom *Surgical Spirit*, Duncan Preston appeared as a man wearing scrubs who has had seventeen operations to make him look exactly like Duncan Preston. Jim Broadbent played an angry transvestite in earrings ('thinks ban on importation of tortoises should be lifted' read the caption). A woman 'campaigning for leg waxing to become Olympic Event' was played by Anne Reid.

Dawn, who knew of Victoria's mousiness at social gatherings, was now exposed to her steely professionalism: 'She was absolutely directing it word for word. It wasn't like a relaxed collaboration where we threw some ideas around. Vic had written a little Rolls-Royce and I needed to get in and drive it. I went from feeling so delighted to not enjoying it much at all and feeling like I was getting it quite wrong. If you work with her, and I only did it for that tiny little moment, I could see what the cost would be. She wasn't humourless. Whenever you tripped up, she would forgive you once. Once. I felt like I had learnt my lines as well as anything I ever did. But it wasn't sufficient for a Victoria Wood sketch.' None of these lesions were visible when it was broadcast, but the hierarchy was clear from a caption that appeared at the end as Victoria tried to grab Dawn's autograph: 'Wants people to know she wrote this sketch, not Dawn'. According to Geoffrey, 'Vic came home having greatly enjoyed working with Dawn.'

Aside from the odd well-paid cabaret booking, much of the remainder of 1995 was a year of recuperation, childcare and grappling with a new computer. 'Just a short note to say thankyou [sic] very much for lunch today,' Victoria wrote to Jane Wymark in February, 'and I'm sorry one of us wet our pants . . . I'm learning to type in case this comedy thing doesn't work out.'[6] At the invitation of Eric Morecambe's family, which came partly because of her connection to his home town, one Sunday in May Victoria unveiled a commemorative blue plaque outside his home in Finchley before a hundred-strong gathering. 'The only thing Vic insisted on,' says Morecambe's son Gary, 'was that no one else was involved in unveiling the actual plaque or making any kind of speech. I got that completely – she was either chosen to do it or not do it, but nothing in between.' In her speech hailing a genius of comedy, she made supportive noises about plans for a new museum of comedy in the town and reminisced about the wax museum. Then, in July, Bolton University awarded Victoria her third honorary degree. There were no speeches at the ceremony, but a reporter from the *Bolton Evening News* asked if she had any advice for the students. To his bafflement she suggested doing a first-aid course, having just completed one herself.

Meanwhile, continuing in therapy, the main topic she wished to confront was her ceaseless perfectionism. The drive to pay attention in every area of her children's lives grew out of her own memories of childhood abandonment. Grace grew up with the story of Stanley Wood's lackadaisical approach to his daughter's music education: 'Mum told me that she wanted him to teach her the piano and he said, "That's middle C," and left.' When Grace started learning piano and violin, practice took place every morning at seven o'clock before school. 'It was a bit hectic,' says Grace, 'and I remember moaning to school friends that this was what I had to do. Sometimes she would get impatient.' The impatience was felt in other areas too: 'A lot of the time it was because she was so quick and intelligent and also quite hard on herself that she didn't extend any more patience to anyone else than she did to herself. She wanted to be as good a mother as she was a performer and she threw that energy at absolutely everything and that's a really tiring thing to do.'

The desire to provide her children with the detailed attention her own parents had not given to her meant that Victoria was in constant fear of failure. While she continued with therapy, another kind of spiritual guidance was available at the Hampstead Friends Meeting House of the Quakers, which Geoffrey started to attend regularly, sometimes accompanied by Victoria and the children. The clerk was Richenda Carey, an actress who was under no illusions about the extent of Victoria's commitment: 'She went because Geoffrey and the children went and because it was a real place that had real people in it. She never became a Quaker and wasn't a regular attender. But she was very much in sympathy with it and understood about letting your lives speak and there is that of God in every person.' For several years Richenda became a supportive local confidante of Victoria's, though the friendship would be conducted as much in the exchange of long faxes packed with detailed reports of ordinary home life. Victoria acquired her fax machine the following year and used it to communicate prolifically. She acquired a pen pal in Maureen Lipman, with whom she enjoyed jousting repartee about show business. With Jane

Wymark, soon to join the cast of *Midsomer Murders*, she traded in gossip, banter and book chat; both often wrote in the quaint style of the whimsical countryside novelist Dora Saint, in honour of whose pen name 'Miss Read' they signed themselves Miss Wood and Miss Wymark.

Victoria's main commitment for the year was a film for the BBC's *Great Railway Journeys*. Having agreed in principle to take part, Victoria rejected one potential producer-director who had just made an essay about art with Alan Bennett – she deemed him too intellectual. The second choice was Russell England, who had made several playful films with Jonathan Meades and a profile of Ernie Wise. When he asked her what kind of film she wanted to make she said, 'I don't want to go very far. I just want to watch people mostly.' Over a couple of meetings in Highgate, she alighted on a circular journey taking her clockwise from Crewe up to Thurso and back again, wherever possible on local branch lines. She didn't mention that the itinerary, which would enable her to film in five-day blocks and fit in two trips home, followed the path of a Wood family road trip around Scotland in her childhood.

As she made her debut as a factual presenter, Victoria was conscious of following in the footsteps of Michael Palin, the globetrotting Python who had done two films for the series. 'One of my biggest worries has come true,' she said to camera on the first day of filming, from a bench on a platform at Crewe as men went in and out of the gents behind her. 'That under the new-style BBC, if you're a comedian, once you hit forty you have to stop telling jokes and just be in documentaries.' Her commentary was dotted with familiar reference points – quips about Margaret Drabble, Esther Rantzen and Judith Chalmers – but Victoria was determined to steer away from regular terrain. She made a point of avoiding Morecambe and Edinburgh, and also Scarborough, which was so associated with a rival comic writer – though she did imagine buying Alan Ayckbourn a pair of water wings.

As they began their journey the crew had an ominous start when they were ushered into a first-class carriage. Against the wishes of a hovering Virgin Trains publicist, they stole into second class to look for people happy to be filmed. Victoria was soon collared by a sozzled Glaswegian who recognised her and asked her to hold his McEwan's while he fished out a fiver to donate to Comic Relief. This was telly gold on day one, but it was precisely the sort of encounter Victoria dreaded. 'I don't want to meet any more people,' she told Russell England. 'I don't really like talking to people and I would prefer it if you could just film people and film me watching people and I'll write something funny.' They reached a compromise. She went through with some pre-arranged set-ups, but others were cancelled. As it was her own idea, she was happy to meet a woman who'd been an extra in *Brief Encounter*, shot in a now dilapidated Carnforth station. A trainspotter in Carlisle gave tips on his mystifying hobby. She was most reluctant to hang out in Yorkshire with a collector who kept bits of train in his garden, having no soft spot for the age of steam – she also had to be persuaded to do picturesque sequences in the West Highlands and the North York Moors. There was no avoiding the public when a rowdy carriage full of teens on the school train to Whitby clamoured for her to autograph their exercise books.

A scene at the core of the film captured something of her essence. In a Glasgow tea room a beady Victoria sat alone in the middle at a table surrounded by chattering ladies. She listened and watched and quietly smiled, exactly as her father used to in cafés when she was a child. At her suggestion, the pianist played 'Strangers on a Train' so she could mime playing along at her table ('I can hardly play the piano at all. I've got grade eight tablecloth though'). Much of the time, as the crew filmed on trains and platforms, she would hide behind them pointing out faces worth capturing. She also hid from the crew in the evenings, apart from one night when she joined them to play darts. The one fixed point in the schedule arrived at 6.30 every evening, when Victoria would pull a book and a mobile phone from her bag, go to a quiet place, and read the children a bedtime story.

The railways were not close to Victoria's heart. She had driven everywhere from the moment she first acquired a car, and in the voiceover she fondly recalled holidays across Europe with her father spending days at the wheel. But the project of rail privatisation, embarked upon the year before, made her vocal. The production had to deal with a dozen different railway companies, some of whom wouldn't let the crew board certain trains. The last straw came back at Crewe when they were refused permission to film Victoria drinking tea in the café, so instead she resumed her place on the bench where the film started. A man supping McEwan's sat down and offered her shortbread. Insular to the last, she declined with a smile and dived into a paperback. Viewers – and reviewers who picked out this telling vignette – were not to know it was a set-up: the man with the shortbread was the production spark.

'The idea of it being a train journey before they closed the railways was not a fully formed idea when we set out,' says Russell England, who, when editing the film in Shepherd's Bush in September, was surprised to get a call from Victoria asking if she could come to the cutting room. She visited three times and wrote her commentary as she watched the beautifully captured footage assume a shape. Suddenly the film started to sing with jokes about tea, marriage and the war as her writing responded to the visual rhythms of the edit in a new kind of comic duet. Unpredictably, the voiceover also bloomed into a polemic. After years of keeping her left-leaning views out of the public domain, Victoria had seen enough to feel she could weigh in. As she passed Sellafield, she voiced a prejudice against nuclear power, picturing employees 'clutching their deformed reproductive organs in a jiffy bag'. With rising youth unemployment, she predicted a bleak homeless future for the children who asked for her autograph. She grumbled about traffic pollution, was angered by the grotesque discrepancy in pay between railway workers and company chairmen, and mourned the imminent demise of less lucrative branch lines. She finished with a modest but furious demand for 'good fast trains that connect with other trains, that are affordable, reliable, safe, with proper food on them, with clean toilets'. There wasn't room in the film for a sequence about a station announcer in York celebrated for her sing-song delivery. So over the credits, Victoria made her own station announcements: 'Bing-bong! Customers please notice the toilets on platform 3 are closed due to them not being open . . . Please do not ask for a ticket as a refusal often offends . . . We don't travel on your railways, please don't travel on ours.' The film would not be broadcast for another year.

The autumn brought another new foray when Victoria accepted an invitation to join most of the cast of Monty Python in Terry Jones's new take on *The Wind in the Willows*. Jones asked her to play a washerwoman, later changed to the tea lady, who is taken prisoner by a gang of evil rats. She had never appeared on the big screen before and, while she didn't particularly admire Jones's script, 'she loved big studios,' says Geoffrey. 'All that camaraderie, all that technical skill, and she thoroughly enjoyed the job.'

In September Victoria's publisher at Methuen announced his retirement from full-time work. It was a measure of her esteem for Geoffrey Strachan that, asked to pay tribute in a farewell volume, she composed an enchanting poem full of witty echoes of his surname. The verse, never published, concluded:

> Never was one's work received
> With apathy or scachan.
> Never was one forced to publish
> Cookery or pachan.
> But now he plans to bugger off
> And soon he will be gachan.
> And I for one am sad to see
> The back of Geoffrey Strawn.[7]

Not that this came to pass. Strachan offered to edit any further works of hers – 'not excluding,' he hopefully suggested, 'that novel you once alluded to in a rash moment'.[8] A couple of months later he and his successor Michael Earley proposed an omnibus edition collating everything in *Up to You, Porky, Barmy* and *Mens Sana in Thingummy Doodah*, and suggested including some character monologues from paststand-up shows. Thus 'Fattitude', 'Toupee Time' and 'Madeline' joined 'Brönteburgers' and 'This House Believes' as the only sections of Victoria's live act that she consented to have published. She called the new omnibus *Chunky* and, in a mockery of therapy speak, dedicated it 'to all those very special people who have assisted in my personal growth and helped me become the uniquely flowered human truth unit that is wholly "me"!'

One of the sketches had a fresh airing in the West End. *The Shakespeare Revue*, collating songs and skits on a Bardic theme, was originally devised for the Royal Shakespeare Company. Christopher Luscombe, who co-staged the show, asked her for permission to perform 'Giving Notes', the sketch from *As Seen on TV* in which Julie Walters bossily addresses an am-dram troupe rehearsing *Hamlet*. Having her work performed by the RSC proved irresistible, and Victoria happily consented to editorial tweaks. In November Michael Codron brought the show to the Vaudeville Theatre, inviting Victoria and Geoffrey to the opening night, and then to the Ivy for a post-show dinner. It was her second momentous visit to the West End that autumn – the previous month she and Geoffrey were at the Comedy Theatre to see Harold Pinter's *The Hothouse*, starring Celia Imrie alongside the playwright. Afterwards it was Celia's idea to take them to Pinter's dressing room. 'It was pretty momentous, and a fine mutual respect was marked,' says Celia. According to Geoffrey, Pinter 'gave no inkling whether he knew who Vic was or not. If he hadn't, he was very good at hiding it.' The night she saw *The Shakespeare Revue*, Pinter happened to be dining at the Ivy too, and Victoria split off from Codron's table to remake his acquaintance.

While the hiatus continued, she supported the BBC's latest plan to repeat her shows, although she by no means placed equal faith in them all. In June Vivienne Clore had told Alan Yentob that Victoria 'is fairly happy for the half hour "playlets" to go out round about the end of July as she thinks that fewer people will see them'.[9] *As Seen on TV* was exhumed either side of Christmas 1995, while *Pat and Margaret* would be shown again in March 1996. Sensing that she didn't seem to be up to much, the editor of the *Sun* Stuart Higgins even asked her if she fancied standing in for Garry Bushell as TV critic. 'Much as I feel at one with Mr Bushell in many ways,' she replied, 'I am unable to accept your kind offer to take over from him as TV critic while he's at Pontins. I am in the middle of writing my new stage show and I daren't leave off.'[10]

*

The decision to go back on tour in 1996 – taking her back to the Royal Albert Hall in a schedule that ran deep into 1997 – persuaded Victoria to participate in her first television profile in a decade. After an over-ture from Melvyn Bragg, her involvement with *The South Bank Show* had a rocky birth when a researcher and prospective director arrived late for their first meeting to discuss what shape the film might take. Victoria complained to Bragg that they didn't seem interested and threatened to pull out. A new director was assigned in the shape of Nigel Wattis, the head of arts at LWT. When he visited her at home 'it was quite a frosty reception,' he says. Nonetheless, a film schedule was drawn up.

'I have had three weeks of sorting out press, brochures, T shirts, backing tapes, costumes, black patent loafers as decreed by Betty Jackson,' Victoria told Charlotte Scott in January. 'Now all I have to do is write the bloody thing.'[11] Before she could sit down to write she threw herself into a ritual of mental cleansing, sorting the knicker drawer, buying socks, and tidying up the Duplo and Lego. 'My house has to be to be perfect for one day before I can start writing,' she said. 'It's like cleaning the windows before you have a baby.'[12]

By now the live formula she had been shaping for more than a decade was set in stone. After her traditional welcome ('We've made it! We're out the house!'), sections about motherhood, royalty and celebrity were all dropped into the grid. Some themes were revisited – terrible plastic-surgery clinics, assertiveness classes, awful marketing surveys, men buying erotic underwear for their wives, her posh neigh-bours. The second half opened with Kimberley's friend, promoted from her previous place in the encore. As before, Victoria made use of the long tall yarn about an imaginary friend to explore baffling areas of modern life – cellulite anxiety, faddy diets, invasive treatments, the nightmare of Christmas with someone else's family. Having imagined meeting the queen in her 1993 show, Victoria now became her, pre-senting her own version of the queen's Christmas message. Geoffrey resumed his role as an outside eye measuring the show's impact on audiences as it took shape. What he witnessed from the auditorium was her total command of the material: 'There were lines and phrases and moments in this show that always caused catatonic explosions of laughter. Seeing it night after night, I watched Vic continually pressing her nuclear button with deadly accuracy. It was a good feeling.'

Once more her audiences were treated to a frank access-all-areas tour of the female mind and body. Victoria imagined jamming an emergency Lil-Let up a stalker's nostril. She joked about pubic outcrops, bad bras, the inconvenient fashion for wearing a body ('Oh sod it, Angela, let's just wet ourselves'). At a high-impact gym class she pictured middle-aged mothers wearing Pampers. She talked about the little roll of fat concealed about every woman's person, indicating her own midriff: 'Sometimes I think if I fell into a canal, would anybody bother to throw me a lifebelt?' Cellulite, she explained, 'looks like you've got raw crumpets tacked to your thighs'. Kimberley had hair extensions in her armpits and her friend was off to have her legs done: 'For two quid you can keep your tights on, they just do what's poking out your ladders.' She mimed one friend having her first ever orgasm at the petrol pump.

As usual the show came together in a series of gigs in the Home Counties on Sunday nights in March and April (punctuated by a wet Easter holiday in Mallorca). New material gradually replaced the old, which lingered in her head from recent charity and cabaret gigs. For the first-night encore Victoria came on in a long blonde wig and Lycra, plonking down an exercise step that she had bought for personal use a few months earlier, and introduced herself as step-class instructor Hayley Bailey. The successor to Madge of Fattitude was on and off much more quickly and, by shunting the exercise routine to the encore, Victoria no longer had to perform an exhausting workout at the start of the second half. The comedy was mainly physical – she choreographed and refined funny lunges and jerks as the tour progressed. 'That's enough of that,' she said after one stretch. 'Take me knickers off me ovaries will have fell out.'

During the show's gestation, Victoria had her biggest crisis yet about her songs. 'She wanted them out,' says Geoffrey, 'but she couldn't see a way to do it, and regretted keeping them in.' When the *South Bank Show* researcher Simon Cherry proposed filming a sequence in which she would unpick her songwriting technique at the piano, she demurred. 'I don't have very much to say about them,' she replied.[13]

One new song about wannabe celebrities she dropped during the try-outs. The first song was now delayed until more than twenty minutes into the show. Yet for all her desire to expunge melancholy songs, she had not come up with a better solution for closing the first half. So she composed the hauntingly sad 'Andrea' about a seventeen-year-old girl whose sister has already left home and who hopes to 'fly away to a better day'. Although Victoria had watched her own older sisters fly the coop, she insisted the song was not autobiographical. 'It comes out of how I perceive people to be living at the moment,' she told Melvyn Bragg. 'It's not from my own life.'[14]

The other songs riffed mainly on sex. In 'Baby Boom', which she reprised with different lyrics at the end, Victoria sang of what she'd learned as she'd grown older:

> Spots, specs,
> Terrible at sex,
> Lay there like a stunned gazelle.
> I was thirty-three
> When it dawned on me
> That girls could move as well.

'Pam' was delivered in the clipped voice of an Englishwoman of a certain age who has proudly never had an orgasm ('Not me, not my scene / I prefer a game of Rummy and an Ovaltine'). The climax was a tango about masturbation. 'Wanker' was her response to the (perhaps apocryphal) news that the EEC was to ban the term 'speccy four eyes' among other pejorative terms. The rhyme scheme was ingeniously constructed to deliver the first laugh before she got anywhere near the punchline: 'But there's a term I'm rather fond of / And to use it I do hanker / It's not heard in *Casablanca* . . .' The song was a linguistic milestone for Victoria, who longed to say 'fuck' in her act as other comedians were now doing with impunity. 'It was a daily discussion,' says Geoffrey. 'She used that word and others in her ordinary life, but she thought that a big proportion of her audience would baulk at it, so she decided not to.' She voiced this frustration at a try-out date in St Albans when she was first filmed for *The South Bank Show*. 'Terrible strain having a film crew,' she confided. 'I haven't said bollocks since Tuesday.'

Having talked in detail about giving birth in the last tour, Victoria used the business of bringing up small children as a new way of connecting with her audience. There were hoots of recognition as she described the frantic explosion of activity at ten to nine on a school morning. Something about having a small boy provoked Victoria's unsentimental side: 'If I want to know how tall he is, I just check the snot mark on my trousers.' One morning, she said, her son wouldn't get dressed, 'so I overreacted. I've had him adopted.' Meanwhile, having a daughter brought Victoria face to face with her own shortcomings. A survey asked her what she'd discovered about herself since becoming a mother: 'I had to put that I am crap at plaits.'

The tour began in May and, in the main, stuck to the pattern of midweek residencies with long weekends at home. In every dressing room she plastered the mirror with snaps of the children. Her homing instinct was so great that she commuted to and from every performance as far away as Wolverhampton and Nottingham. During half-term week, she hooked up with the children at Mole Barn while doing shows at the Bradford Alhambra. Phil McIntyre laid on a driver who was instructed not to talk to her. 'On the way there I need to be quiet and calm,' she explained, 'and on the way home my head's still racing. Either way, I need a bit of silence.'[15] Once delivered back to Highgate, her habit was to check the fax machine, pick up socks and do the washing, then read in bed beside a slumbering Geoffrey until half past one. 'I'm getting a bit tired now,' she told Simon Cherry in early July. 'The show is not the problem at the moment, it's getting up at six thirty to listen to Grace doing the scale of E minor.'[16]

When the tour reached Blackpool, she was interviewed by Melvyn Bragg, who blindsided her by suggesting that *Pat and Margaret* represented two sides of her own personality. 'That's a bit perspicacious of you,' she muttered uncomfortably. (In fact, all the questions were written by Simon Cherry.) By now Victoria had developed a warm relationship with the director Nigel Wattis, who grew bolder. 'It was a friendly dance,' he says. 'She knew she had to give us enough to make a film.' Thus from Blackpool he chartered a helicopter to fly up the coast to Morecambe and Silverdale, where from a passenger seat she pointed down at her old homes.

Victoria had another chance to revisit the past when, between two shows in Southend, she collected yet another honorary degree. This was to be her fourth and last such honour and, as it came from her Birmingham University a quarter of a century on from her matriculation, the most meaningful. 'Of course,' she told an audience of graduating students and their families in a charming retrospective speech, 'in the autumn of 1971 I wasn't the glamorous, sophisticated figure that I never became.'[17] From her student years she recalled her feelings of social and intellectual inadequacy, her predatory lecturer, and her grim bedsits, and she reheated a faithful old gag about the Baby Belling that took half an hour to heat a tin of soup: 'I could never wait that long so I used to drink it cold and hang my stomach over the gas fire.'[18] Offered this platform, she once again touched on her new preoccupation with the narrowing life chances of the next generation. 'Thank you to the Government of 1971 who gave me a full grant,' she concluded. 'Will they ever catch on again, I wonder? I'm off now to do what my education has qualified me to do, which is to get laughs from 2,000 people at the Cliffs Pavilion, Southend.'[19] She didn't mention her pass degree, nor did she have time to stay for the luncheon.

The recollections continued when the first leg of the tour concluded with a dozen shows at the Palace Theatre in Manchester. *The South Bank Show* proposed visiting Victoria's childhood homes, and one morning they all drove over to Bury. She was nervous about being filmed in Tottington Road so, through the window of her gleaming black Subaru Forester, she pointed to the window of her first bedroom. It was a harder task to persuade her back to Birtle Edge House. With begrudging permission from its new owner, she was filmed walking on the lawn at the front of her teenage eyrie, now smartly restored. While up there, and without warning, Simon Cherry ambushed her with a copy of *A Swish of the Curtain*, her favourite book in childhood. As Victoria read from Pamela Brown's homage to the theatre a glowing smile spread across her face. Another old haunt they visited was the Granada studio where *Wood and Walters* was made. Not every encounter could be quite so well choreographed. Two excitable fans turned up at a post-show signing session wearing yellow berets. 'Oh Christ,' muttered Victoria as she saw them coming – the reaction was carefully excluded from the film. On another day a mother and daughter dashed up on the street and asked for an autograph. 'I don't understand what people think they're getting from that contact,' she told the crew.

Having much more power to say no than when she was profiled in the early 1980s, she refused to let the camera crew into her home. So the real meat of the film was caught backstage before, during and after performances, where she was ministered to by Amie Beamish and at her most intensely focused. When she saw an edit of the film she told Nigel Wattis she worried that she came across as 'gloomy'.[20]

As for the live show, in July a bomb planted by the Provisional IRA devastated the centre of Manchester, prompting Victoria to drop a reference into her act: 'I was walking round St Ann's Square – I was thinking, now why have all these shops got plywood curtains?' One day she jumped at a rare invitation to visit the usually closed set of *Coronation Street* to watch the show being recorded and have lunch with the cast in the Rovers Return. In the daytime she kept in shape in her hotel suite doing aerobics and 'some yoga-effect stuff called psychocalisthenics . . . it claims to revitalise your sexual organs,' she confided to Jane Wymark, 'but I won't be too bothered if it doesn't.'[21] Romance was not, however, entirely dead. The same month was the twentieth anniversary of Victoria and Geoffrey meeting at the Leicester Phoenix. 'We thought we'd do something about it,' he says, 'and get a couple of rings made. Vic asked around and discovered a jeweller who was a friend of a friend. We liked them and wore them a lot.' By now Geoffrey had lost seven stone and eight inches from his waistline.

September when it came looked very much like national Victoria Wood month. 'Crewe to Crewe' won an audience of five million viewers, the largest on BBC Two that week. Within days came the *South Bank Show* film, as well as the publication of *Chunky*. Though some weary critics found her railway journey less than great, the reception for both films was positive and brought unlooked-for consequences.

An invitation arrived from *The Cambridge Guide to Children's Books* to write its entry on *The Swish of the Curtain*, which Victoria submitted long before she'd even received her contract. A couple of months later Railtrack announced that it would stump up £1 million for the restoration of Carnforth station, which had been recently threatened with demolition. Victoria's advocacy had made the difference. 'You'd think Carnforth would be a gift for the nostalgia boom,' she argued in *Great Railway Journeys*. 'You could have a buffet with a spoon on a chain and people behind the counter going, "Don't you know there's a war on?" whenever you asked for anything.'

Meanwhile, there was a promotional blitz as the Royal Albert Hall dates loomed at the end of September. Victoria was never a fan of media chores, but one interview plumbed new depths. It took place, she told Maureen Lipman, 'in a super stretch limo with a woman from GMTV in snakeskin trousers with passers-by hurling abuse through the windows as we cruised the streets of Westminster. Her first question was "Now you're a very private person aren't you?"'[22] She was thrilled to be back at the Albert Hall for another sell-out fortnight, and it showed in an alteration to her routine. 'Vic was always an early arriver at theatres,' says Geoffrey, 'but never as early as there. She used to turn up in the afternoon, just to play the piano. And she used to concentrate harder on the show ahead at the Albert than at any other venue.' One day, while Grace ran around on the stage, she played the organ, and both were given a tour of the roof. At her invitation friends flocked to her dressing room, which was bedecked with well-wishing bouquets. One night she drove herself home via the house of her friend Norah Wellbelove, whose husband was chronically ill with cancer, and deposited a bunch of flowers for her to discover when she opened the front door in the morning. Many cultural eminences paid court. 'You must be the most adored woman in England,' said Michael Codron.[23] 'You were stupendous,' said Richard Eyre, who still couldn't persuade her to write a new play for the National Theatre.[24] His successor elect Trevor Nunn introduced himself, lavishly comparing her to Chekhov, Gogol and Molière. He too suggested she write a play, 'hopefully a big theatre play about living here in England, now'.[25] Another offer came in from a record company wishing to release 'Wanker' and 'The Ballad of Barry and Freda' as a double A-side for the Christmas market. They didn't have a plan for overcoming the problem that the lyrics of 'Wanker' would limit its air play, and the collaboration didn't come off.

In October at the Savoy Victoria addressed the Women of the Year lunch, which she'd first attended in 1980. 'Just what I need after 12 nights at the Albert,' she grumbled to Jane Wymark. 'Where is my "good" handbag, I wonder.'[26] Among the women listening were Anne Diamond and Margaret Drabble, who had often featured as punchlines in her stand-up. The same month brought the release of *The Wind in the Willows*, featuring Victoria's cinema debut, just as she waited to find out about another film. The director Peter Chelsom had been a guest of Gavin Millar at the Leicester Square screening of *Pat and Margaret* in 1994, and a few months later Victoria returned the compliment by attending the premiere of his film *Funny Bones*. On the back of its success Chelsom moved to Los Angeles, where he proposed adapting *Pat and Margaret* for the big screen and transplanting it to the American south. With Victoria's approval he acquired the rights and retitled it *Patty and Marge*. While content to remain at arm's length, Victoria warmed to the idea of seeing her name prominently displayed in a Hollywood film. 'MGM love it,' he confidently updated her over the summer. 'It looks like it will get made.'[27] A table reading took place with Lynn Redgrave in the role of Patty, and word of the script reached Cher, who arrived at a meeting at Chelsom's office in leathers on her motorbike. Then there was a regime change at MGM and the project was promptly dropped from the slate.

While Victoria's graduation to the big screen stalled yet again, on the small screen her regal status found her at the heart of BBC Television's sixtieth anniversary celebrations. The half a million viewers who cast their votes in the BBC's birthday poll chose her as their favourite comedy performer and *Victoria Wood As Seen on TV* as their favourite comedy. The awards were doled out at a ceremony broadcast in November as *Auntie's All Time Greats*. The seating planners made sure Alan Yentob was by Victoria's side. 'I was all ready with my good loser face, not needed,' she said, accepting her first award. Privately, to Dawn French, she pronounced it a 'dull evening on very hard seats'.[28]

The creative highlight of the broadcast was a new addition to the canon of *Acorn Antiques*, which Victoria used to spoof fresh fashions in television. Susie Blake reprised her continuity announcer, now languishing on cable as a nighthawk presenter. 'Asians, wheelchairs,' she grumbled, 'that's where the jobs are these days. But if you're from Camberley, forget it.' The two browsers in Acorn Antiques were now in wheelchairs which jammed at the exit like bumper cars, forcing the actors to rise up and walk off set. The episode was sponsored by a stairlift company. In the latest developments Miss Babs was on day release from open prison, Mr Clifford revealed himself as a transsexual whose real name is Fern, and Miss Berta had contracted a tropical disease from playing ping-pong. 'Yes, well,' said Mrs Overall, 'sometimes an incurable disease is God's way of sending you to Disneyland.' The most overt reference to new soap trends drew on recent lesbian storylines in *Brookside* and *Emmerdale*. The episode was meant to climax with Mrs O in a passionate clinch with Miss Babs. But Bo Beaumont simply refused to utter the key word. 'What I have to say is that I'm a l . . . a lll . . . a Lebanese!'

Victoria retreated over the winter as 1996 turned to 1997 to look after the children while Geoffrey was away doing panto. Sharing a home with the bookish Grace, now eight, and larky Henry, four, 'feels like living with AS Byatt and Benny Hill'.[29] Her one outing was to attend the inaugural South Bank Show Awards – Melvyn Bragg informed her she was nominated in the comedy category, but she didn't win. In February the family flew with their old Sheffield Crucible chums Roger Glossop, Charlotte Scott and children to Disneyland in Florida, where Victoria was embarrassed to be ushered to the front of every queue.

The first task of the new year was to bed in her new assistant. Rita Birrane had decided to leave, and Victoria asked the likes of Dawn French and Maureen Lipman to recommend someone local 'who might want to answer my phone crossly and mistype my letters'.[30] In the end it was Jane Wynn Owen who suggested a mother of three children who had worked in casting and lived nearby.

'I didn't think it would work out,' says Cathy Edis. 'My attitude was, I'm not sure if I want this, but it would be nice to meet Victoria Wood. I went to the house. The first thing that struck me was how slight and small she was. We had a quick interview, very business-like. She made out that she was seeing other people, but I don't think she was.' Cathy started in January 1997. Her routine was to visit two mornings a week, which soon became three five-hour days. 'I'm very pleased with her so far,' Victoria informed Geoffrey by fax. 'I think we can build a good thing, and I think she's very committed to making a good job out of it, and enjoying it.'[31] The job initially encompassed everything from typing to housekeeping, dealing with gardeners and builders, running Victoria's appointments diary and opening her post. One of the first letters Cathy opened was from Buckingham Palace announcing that in the forthcoming Queen's birthday honours list Victoria was to be made an Officer of the Order of the British Empire. 'Vic's first response to the letter was amazement,' says Geoffrey, 'and real uncertainty about whether to say yes. OBEs were the kind of thing given to other people, and she wasn't sure she wanted it. I was still in the mode of encouraging her to believe in herself and was quietly delighted that she'd achieved that kind of recognition. In the end she said she'd accept it, but she wouldn't be saying yes to anything else that might get offered in the future.'

When Comic Relief came around again in March, Victoria contributed an appeal on behalf of carers, making an affecting short film in the West Country about a woman looking after a husband suffering from Alzheimer's and Parkinson's. Then in April the tour resumed, taking in cities Victoria had missed the previous year. At the urging of Phil McIntyre's office, Victoria went into the studio to record new versions of her songs to be sold at the venue and through shops. *Real Life – The Songs* contained 'all the songs I can remember,' she told Geoff Posner, 'and I'm just going to do them with piano, keep it simple is my motto.'[32] Released from the need to sing over her right shoulder to an audience, her left-hand bass-playing acquired oomph. The selection was mainly from her three 1990s live shows, but she went back to the late 1970s for 'Love Song' and 'Music and Movement' and the mid-1980s for 'Crush' and 'The Ballad of Barry and Freda'. Geoffrey came up with the running order – 'They are

fairly well mixed as far as spreading the gloom around goes,' she told
McIntyre[33] – while she assembled the lyrics for the inner sleeve. It
didn't sell particularly well.

It was during the spring tour that Victoria took the momentous
decision to leave the Richard Stone Partnership. Stone's retirement
was the reason she cited to Phil McIntyre, whom she now asked to
represent her. 'We were walking along Oxford Street and she said, "I
want to move from Richard Stone because he's not involved any more.
Do you think you'd be interested?"' Vivienne Clore, who handled all
her television work, had first caught wind of the move as preparations were underway for a tour of Australia and New Zealand. This
was organised in haste at the suggestion of McIntyre's colleague Paul
Roberts, who was in Australia on a stand-up tour with the agency's
client Ben Elton. 'There was a question of her going to Australia,' says
Vivienne Clore, 'and Phil Mac was busy selling it out there without
us knowing about it. I said to Phil, "We don't know what's going on
here."'

By early May, Victoria had made up her mind and sent an ominous
fax to the Richard Stone office from her tour hotel in Birmingham:
'I would like to have a meeting with you all as soon as possible next
week. I have been thinking a lot about my future and I have taken
some decisions.'[34] After they met on the Monday morning, Victoria
described the scene to Maureen Lipman: 'On Monday I left my agents
after twenty years. You can imagine what that was like. There was so
much nervous tension in the room the Expelair was working and
it wasn't even switched on.'[35] 'She came in and just said she wanted
a different kind of management,' says Vivienne Clore. 'She sent a
hamper from Fortnum's and a nice note and went off into the sunset.'
In her handover instructions to McIntyre she concluded, 'I suppose
if it had to happen at all, I'm glad it's you – look after her . . .'[36] On
the day Victoria went in to sign her contract they made sure to get
the china cups out of the kitchen cupboard. In due course her agent
in effect became McIntyre's colleague Lucy Ansbro and her assistant
Adele Fowler, who handled all her needs and attended all her recordings. She came to refer to both as her lady bodyguards.

When the tour brought Victoria to Portsmouth, she took the ferry to the Isle of Wight to pay her respects to Richard Stone, who was able to congratulate her on her OBE, announced days earlier. *The Times* listed her as 'Miss V Wood (Mrs Durham) comedian, serv to entrtnmnt'.[37] Among many nabobs sending congratulations was the mayor of her home town: 'Bury really is very proud of you!'[38] The sentiment was echoed by Julie Walters. 'I feel very proud of you,' she wrote. 'Is that daft?'[39] When replying to Vivienne Clore, who was still handling any business relating to deals she'd originally negotiated, Victoria signed off 'love Vic OBE'.[40] She would not receive the award till the end of the year, when it was presented to her at Buckingham Palace by Prince Charles. 'Afterwards,' says Geoffrey, who sat and watched with the children, 'Vic couldn't really remember what was said – it was very much a something and nothing conversation.'

The trip Down Under was scheduled for the school holidays. Victoria's last act before getting on the plane was to work the tombola at Grace's end-of-term fête, honouring a promise from the previous year to keep the date free. In the parents' race she finished in the middle of the pack. 'I can't tell you what a thrill that was,' she confided to her audio diary the following year. 'It gave me a boost all the way to Australia, that did.'[41] She also worked up some new jokes specific to the Antipodes, did two days of Australian press and had a fitting with Betty Jackson. 'She is doing me a couple of pleated skirts for the trip,' she told Jane Wymark. 'We think beige and possibly even a muted lilac.'[42] Victoria, the children and Rebecca the nanny boarded a plane bound for Auckland at the end of the first week of July. Amie Beamish, though from New Zealand, could not accompany her as she was about to give birth – Victoria asked if she could be a godmother and was accepted.

Victoria was nervous about this leap into the unknown, and Julie Walters attempted to allay her anxiety. 'They will absolutely love you,' she wrote, adding that 'they are nothing like as foreign as the Americans'.[43] The first two weeks were given over to an intense schedule of promotion: 'A typical day has been – awake at 4, Grace in at 4.30, persuade Gr. back to bed at 5, Hen in at 5.30. for a big colouring session by Mummy of Popeye and Woody from Toy Story, Mummy in the shower, Rebecca in at 7 with a cold missing fiancé . . . Mummy down in the lobby by 7.50 for non-stop and I mean that day of interviews, Pebble Mill at One type TV shows, "madcap" radio shows etc etc. Interviews finish 7ish by which times kids are in bed, mummy is a complete zombie.'[44] Just before her first performance Geoffrey arrived in Auckland to share the strain. Grace remembers spending 'hours in the bathroom drawing because I didn't want to wake anybody else up'.

Victoria worried that she'd had little rehearsal time to bed in her new location-sensitive material: 'altering references to Curly Wurlys etc (replace with Dried Koala)'.[45] She was familiar with the process, having performed a similar surgery before recording the voiceover for the US version of 'Crewe to Crewe' (out went Sooty and Thora Hird; in came Roseanne and Bob Hope). There were ten dates in all. After some debate – because it would eat into family holiday time – a later show was dropped into the schedule at a larger venue in Auckland, which sold out. 'NZ was v. pro-me,' Victoria reported. 'They knew me and were quite thrilled I had come. Ozzies couldn't give a damn, never heard of me and don't want to know. So I am going out all guns blazing but it is being a tough few days.'[46] On one light-entertainment show she was allotted three minutes of stand-up to sell her wares: 'Whoo hoo. I seem to remember being in this position 20 years ago . . . Where are my platform shoes?'[47]

For much of the trip the family were based in a smart high-rise flat in Quay West overlooking Sydney Harbour, from which Victoria commuted in and out of different Australian cities, where the venues were smaller – in one theatre the capacity was only 500. The reception was still tumultuous. The gruelling itinerary meant she had plenty of reading time. After a quiet final show in Perth, where Victoria was joined by the family to go on holiday to Bali, she asked Paul Roberts – who was acting as tour manager – to take home some books for her that she'd bought while on tour. She handed over two heavy suitcases stuffed with paperbacks.

Roberts, from up the road in Preston, was McIntyre's more emollient sidekick, and over the years they had come as close to friendship as professional prudence allowed. One night, after a show, the two of them sat on the steps of the Sydney Opera House looking at the harbour and the skyscraper where Victoria's children slept.

'You've done all right for a girl from Bury,' he said.

'Yeah,' she replied. 'I never expected to make people laugh this far away from home.'

# 18

# DINNERLADY

**'Just sign it, Bren, I've got an itchy bum.'**
*dinnerladies*, 1998

Victoria first flirted with writing a sitcom during her 1987 tour. Two tours later, in 1993, she thought she'd missed the boat: 'When Jennifer Saunders wrote *Absolutely Fabulous* I thought that is what a sitcom should be and I can't do that now. I haven't got that edge now.'[1] But the idea for a mainstream sitcom continued to solidify until it came to the notice of Alan Yentob at the start of 1996. 'I don't mind taking it to another channel,' Victoria told her agent. 'I am not trying to do a Vicar of Dibley, I don't mind creeping in with a low key series.'[2] It remained just an idea until the summer of 1997 when she met up with Geoff Posner, who committed to booking studio space for a year hence. Before she flew to New Zealand Victoria sounded out Julie Walters. 'Vic I would love to be in your series – as regular as you want me to be,' she replied. 'Have you any idea when it will be? & have you written it yet?'[3]

She hadn't. But she had a notion of what it would be, and what it wouldn't. 'I didn't want to do a domestic comedy,' she later recalled. 'I don't like mother, father, grumpy teenage daughter – I don't like all those sitcoms. It was going to be a group of people and you only saw them in their work setting. So everything you had to find out about them you could only find out from what they said to each other in casual conversation.'[4] The setting she fixed on was a fictional factory

canteen in the north of England. To get a flavour she did a discreet
shift in a real one in Manchester and had lunch in her friend Lesley
Fitton's workplace canteen at the British Museum, while tapping into
memories of school lunches at Bury Grammar. She also commissioned
a researcher to supply her with technical information about toasters
and the minutiae of who in a canteen did what.

Meanwhile, she started to think about characters and who might
play them. On the first page of a notebook, Victoria listed and
described five women: 'Me – bit barmy, cheery – engaged for years
but never got around to it? – Up! 2nd in command.' There was a
female boss who is 'v much in charge, up for her rights and the rights
of the girls – husband, kids – everything a battle.' A younger woman
called Anita was 'only into really dim things . . . Tory. Much more old
fashioned than the older women.' The older women were called Annie
and Thelma, after the actresses Victoria hoped would play them. One
was 'v. vague, picking up tail ends of conversation – a widow? Married
to sex maniac? Not worked for years?' The other was 'Forever on a
diet? Some mythic 6lbs she has to lose?'

Knowing they were friends, Victoria approached the two actresses
separately. Her pitch to Anne Reid was 'How do you fancy working
with Thelma Barlow?' Victoria had met Thelma Barlow only once, at
a charity cabaret in Rochdale, but learned that after twenty-five years
in *Coronation Street* she itched to leave: 'I kept my ear to the ground
and as soon as she was out I was in there.'[5] She tried out pairs of
names for their characters, perming from Doreen, Noreen, Maureen,
Irene, Eileen, Nesta, Denise, Deirdre, Daph and Gilly before plumping for Dolly and Jean. They would be bickering friends – Dolly
morbidly obsessed with staying thin and inclined to draw attention
to the rounder dimensions and slovenly habits of Jean. 'Someone's
old mother to come in,' she scribbled on the next page. 'All having
completely unfocused discussions the whole time . . . Smokers go on
fire escape.' After a few more pages she relisted the characters, one
of whom was now Asian, another pregnant. One of the women, she
wasn't sure which, should be 'at it like knives'. In another list she added
the name Dunc. Duncan Preston was duly sounded out to play Stan,
a dour handyman given to irascible outbursts. She now mentioned

a manager called Tony and a character who might be named after Petula Clark, who would be mother to Sandra.

Sandra became Bren, a single woman in her middle years. Her mother was Petula Gordeno, a grotesque figure full of fantastical reminiscences of celebrities she claimed to have known. 'It just became apparent to me,' said Victoria, 'that she has this terrible mother who when she turns up Bren's heart just sinks because she knows something terrible is going to happen.'[6] Petula, to be played by Julie, was the last mother Victoria was to create while her own mother was still alive, and she once more returned to the theme of parental absenteeism. Petula says she has had 'post-natal disinterest for forty years', and actively boasts of having neglected Bren: 'I put her in the orphanage and lost the address.' Bren for her part is asked if she wants to spill the beans in an episode of *Kilroy* on 'mothers who have let their daughters down'. The only other cast member Victoria rounded up before she started writing was Celia Imrie. 'She described it as a very northern setting,' says Celia, 'which made me nervous, as I knew I couldn't attempt to be one of them. So I suggested, how about I am simply zooming in and out all the time?'

These preparations unfolded over several months, but the writing would have to wait. Straight after returning from Australia, the show Victoria had been living with since the beginning of the previous year was captured in a live recording. The theatre she chose was the Swan in High Wycombe, a favourite of hers which provided both capacity and intimacy. As the rights to the performance were being negotiated, Alan Yentob proposed broadcasting the two-hour set over two nights at Christmas. Victoria, after discussing it with Geoffrey, preferred to mulch the show down to an hour. Although it would involve sacrificing a more generous advance, she also favoured keeping the video release till after transmission. 'I am aware I am not likely to sell a large number of copies doing it this way,' she told Vivienne Clore, then still her agent, 'but I am more interested in making a big impact on TV, after a long time away.'[7] In the end it was sold to ITV, who had to be persuaded to include an anatomically frank section on pubic clumping. As Victoria was nervous about nailing a new one-hour version of the show, her performance was recorded by Geoff Posner over two nights, which turned out to be a wise precaution: she told Maureen Lipman that on the first night 'an entire step routine which had seemed hilarious in my office was received in stunned silence'.[8]

The intense gestation of her sitcom caused Victoria to reject a wide array of job offers: to act in a play by Jack Rosenthal, script an episode of *Murder Most Horrid*, be grilled by Jeremy Isaacs for the prestigious interview series *Face to Face*, doctor the script of Aardman's forthcoming animation *Chicken Run*, play lead in *At Home with the Braithwaites*, adapt a novel by Mavis Cheek, write a memoir. But at the start of 1998 one extracurricular task Victoria could not resist came about as a result of an impending tour of *Talent*, twenty years on from its premiere in Sheffield. To provide a full evening of entertainment, the producer David Graham suggested stringing together the five Kitty monologues. Re-reading the scripts 'gave me a good laugh after all this time,' Victoria told him.[9] Although she had not written in Kitty's voice since 1986, she slipped seamlessly back into it to compose a new stage ending:

> Anyway, I must go. Hopefully (name of actress in cast) will have finished her so-called Yoga by now. We're sharing a dressing room and she's at it the day long. I pop in to buff up my knack knacks and she's there with her knee up behind her hair do. I mean Helen Murchison has her weak points but you can pass the time of day without getting a face full of groin.

Writing in the voice of Kitty was a cinch. Finding the voices of a large ensemble of new characters, then stitching them into their surroundings and six half-hour plots, was much tougher. One day Victoria concentrated so hard during a 'script brainstorm' that she left the car unlocked, allowing a burglar to make off with the stereo.[10] Her social life and exercise routine shrank 'owing to joke commitments. I have twenty pages to do before nightfall,' she told Jane Wymark, 'and Cathy is upstairs frantically typing so we have something to show Geoff Posner when he arrives on Friday, eager to know all about it. I don't know much about it myself yet.'[11] Her schedule had been further compromised by the departure of the nanny after six years to get married.

The first conversations with Geoff Posner centred on the feel of the recordings. Victoria was adamant that a live audience would force her to deliver a high rate of gags. An obvious influence for a gang comedy was *Dad's Army*, but she also had two American templates in mind. The unlikelier of them was *ER*, with its long immersive takes and uncut movement around a workplace set. She even wanted to mimic the lower-case title that appeared in the opening credits – her show, she insisted, should be called *dinnerladies*, not *Dinnerladies*. The second was *Cheers* for the theatrical playing space visited by a random set of characters. She was also curious about a standard procedure in US comedy – to tape the final dress rehearsal so it could be studied before the evening recording. 'I said to Geoff Posner, "I would really like to do this because I think until you've done it once in front of an audience, you don't really know where the laughs come or where it sits and what you could improve. And he said, which was a very clever idea, "Well, let's just do it twice."'[12] This had never been done before in British television and, at around £400,000 per episode, would render *dinnerladies* a third more expensive than any other sitcom.

'It was hard for my finance guys to swallow,' says Peter Salmon, who had taken over as BBC One controller the previous year. 'Sitcoms were failing everywhere. You were starting to think, should I continue to invest in the genre? I felt it was a price worth paying.' In fact, he green-lit *dinnerladies* before he'd even met Victoria. Three years her junior, and from Burnley, Peter Salmon was the first channel head to work out that she had trust issues with television management which needed to be assuaged: 'She's a genius, she's the funniest person in Britain, but she comes in, she's more nervous than her status might have suggested. I knew what she liked, which was enough reassurance but not too much interference. I had comedy experts who worked for me, but Victoria was bigger and better than any of them and what would they have to contribute?'

As if to re-establish her status as the funniest person in Britain, *Victoria Wood – Still Standing* was broadcast one Sunday night in April. The following week Victoria was on the guest list at a celebration of culture at Windsor Castle. 'Word is there will be about 600 of us, so I will probably just skulk near the Kettle chips,' she told Jane Wymark, affecting nonchalance.[13] 'I have painted my toenails blue and trimmed my fringe with the kitchen scissors.'[14] To make a day of it she and Betty Jackson had tea at Cliveden before travelling on to their royal assignation, where Victoria made an impression on the staff. 'This footman with a tray of warm gin and tonics was a huge fan and couldn't get over meeting Victoria,' says Betty. 'Then this person shoved the footman out the way and said, "She's on her route."' Joanna Lumley, who was standing with them, introduced the group to Her Majesty as 'three natural blondes'. On the drive back to London, the two natives of the Rossendale valley talked about Bury and Bacup and the vast journey they had travelled. 'Who would have thought?' they said to each other in exaggerated accents. 'I know! Who would have *thought*?'

The next month Victoria was herself treated like royalty when she and Geoffrey went to Woking to see the Kitty monologues and *Talent*. While she gave advice afterwards to the actress playing Kitty, she concluded that the experiment 'didn't really work as it was too rich a mix to have so many all at once, and it didn't have anything to do with the play'.[15]

With new representation, and a supportive controller at BBC One, Victoria was well placed to assume tighter control of her new show than she had ever enjoyed before. There was 'the most unbelievable palaver over the deal over the series with the production company who are making it,' she told Lesley Fitton.[16] Phil McIntyre did a deal to ensure she would own the television rights to *dinnerladies*, rather than – as felt outrageous to her – Geoff Posner's company Pozzitive, and for the first time she took a full producing credit so she could be consulted on such matters as hats, overalls and tabards. She composed the theme tune, for which David Firman submitted a couple of arrangements – the one she plumped for she found 'very sweet, rather like the character I play'.[17] Meanwhile, she, Posner and a casting director sat through hours and days of auditions. To play a grumpy Mancunian girl known as Twinkle they saw 'about 40 nervous girls, all in the same black bootleg trousers and huge trainers' before they alighted on a recent RADA graduate with a loamy Bolton accent called Maxine Peake.[18] Looking for someone to play the dim-witted Anita, she found 'Asian girls are thin on the ground' – the role went to Shobna Gulati, a young actress from a Hindu background in Oldham.[19] Geoff Posner wasn't there the day Andrew Dunn, a jobbing actor from Yorkshire in his late thirties, came in. Victoria was smitten: 'I thought, oh what a great smile. I was very taken with the way he took the dialogue and made it sound very real.'[20] (Off camera he would also provide the sound of Petula's flatulence by blowing raspberries.)

Actors from way back answered the summons. Lill Roughley was cast as a protective mother whose teenage boy Clint is seduced by Petula. Sue Wallace was asked to play a charmless harridan brought in to run the canteen in Tony's absence. Bernard Wrigley, who backed Victoria and Julie in 'Northerners' on *Wood and Walters*, was a factory worker. Andrew Livingston, Carl in the bus-shelter sketches, returned as Norman, a breadman afflicted by phobias.

Eventually, in early June, the cast met at the Groucho Club in Soho. For Victoria it was 'a bit like a day long Northern cocktail party. At one point Eric Sykes was chatting with Dora Bryan, with Elspet Gray coming up on the rails and I thought, "What have I done?"'[21] To act as stage manager Posner hired Jane Cotton, who had worked with Victoria at the Mermaid Theatre in 1975. There was a read-through of the six tightly plotted scripts, each of which had its own one-word title. 'Monday' introduced the characters. 'Royals' featured a visit to the canteen from a minor duke and duchess (the latter played by Victoria's friend Richenda Carey). In 'Scandal' Petula's engagement to Clint provokes outrage and ends up being featured on a *Kilroy*-type talk show. In 'Moods' the staff all bring a parent to work – Dolly's plain-speaking mother (played by Thora Hird) boasts, like Helen Wood, of having no sense of humour. In 'Party' the factory's Christmas celebrations shine a light on the staff's romantic lives. For 'Nightshift' the canteen struggles under draconian new management when Tony is off having chemotherapy treatment. The Groucho readings reverberated with laughter, fuelled by regular deliveries of toast and chips. Victoria discovered that she'd overwritten every episode by seven minutes, obliging her to go home and trim.

On a Monday morning in June the company convened at the BBC's rehearsal room in North Acton for a week of preparations. Theirs was to be one of the last productions to enter the building before it was converted to offices. There was a training day when the dinnerladies were taught how to chop vegetables and wrap sandwiches. Victoria was wary of the sharp knives: 'The idea that we will come out with high class comedy dialogue while pulverising parsley in a high speed professional manner (ie not looking at it) is I think a little optimistic and may lead to a few missing fingers.'[22] In the end they mainly spread marge.

As production began, a problem arose in the shape of a BBC radio comedy called *Dinner Ladies*. Victoria did think of appealing directly to the other show's makers but was advised against it by Geoff Posner. They discovered that it was impossible to copyright a title, so it was down to the BBC to decide. Victoria was unflustered and in early July came up with an alternative in case: 'What I've settled on just for today is *Gravy Days* for the title. Which I like as well in a different sort of a way.'[23]

At the start of rehearsals she began to keep an audio diary. Her thought was to make notes for a future memoir, so while describing the days of rehearsal and recording, she also called up memories, often suggested by addresses she drove past on the way to and from west London – the Bush Theatre, hers and Geoffrey's first rental in Maida Vale in 1980, the home of the woman who made the dungarees she wore on *New Faces*. But she was much more focused on the six days it took to rehearse and record twenty-eight minutes of comedy. The first episode they worked on, 'Royals', was not the first scheduled for broadcast – a standard practice to ensure there would be no hint of actors finding their feet. The precaution was especially needed because, as they familiarised themselves with the script, Victoria felt an urge to improve it.

She went home and came in on the Tuesday with changes: 'Although I'd done lots of drafts, when I'd bring the script in on a Monday morning and I'd hear it read, I'd always think, that isn't right, I'm sure I can do something to change that.'[24] She still expected the cast to know their lines by the Wednesday when she deputed Jane Cotton to underline every word that any actor got wrong. 'If you've written an F sharp,' she reasoned, 'you don't want people to play an E flat. It drives you mad. And if you've written that word you've written it for a reason.'[25] In a coffee break those underlinings would then be circulated. The actors grew used to the idea that their lines were to be performed with no improvisations or variations. Victoria knew Julie so well she felt able to read her face like a book. 'Her R eyelid flickers when she's about to dry,' she privately noted.[26] The rigorous discipline was a shock to Thelma Barlow, even though she had been forewarned by her producer friend Nicholas Barrett that 'suggestions for even the slightest script modification were unwelcome'. 'You just thought this is the way Vic works and it's tough,' she says. 'It's very hard on actors to have to keep on learning and learning in a short period of time.' But Victoria asked nothing of the cast that she wouldn't do herself. In her audio diary she confessed that she struggled to ingest Bren's lines. It didn't show. 'I don't remember underlining Brenda,' says Jane Cotton.

On the Thursday the crew came in to do a tech run. Geoff Posner assembled the pick of the BBC's sound and camera crews to solve issues which didn't usually come up in sitcoms: how to film on several cameras and capture sound fluidly on a complex set. On the Friday they moved into the studio at TV Centre and Victoria was allowed to park at the front, 'which I absolutely adore'.[27] The audience reflected the breadth of her fanbase. 'Sometimes you get a load of screaming queens,' she said, 'and sometimes you'll get a load of OAPs from Purley.'[28] Almost always there were friends in, and Geoffrey whenever he could make it. One night an overzealous woman on the door excluded anyone with a blue rinse. Rather than farm the job out to a warm-up act, Victoria welcomed the audience herself, opening with patter she'd been using onstage since 1983: 'We're out the house. We've said, "That's it . . . we're coming out!"' After explaining the plot she presented the actors, gently ribbing Maxine Peake's RADA credentials, and introducing Duncan as the tall one from the Beverley Sisters who now drives a Vauxhall Viagra. 'I did Ceal's nostrils, which is always good for a laugh,' Victoria told her diary one night.

After the episode was recorded Victoria took the tape home, then on Saturday morning watched the VHS with Posner, who lived nearby, before going in to the studio to make more changes. These were first passed on to the script supervisor in charge of the camera script and then distributed to the actors. She soon grew wary of their reaction. 'If we make too many cuts,' she said in a diary entry late one Friday, 'everyone will have the vapours and have to lie down frothing at the mouth with damp cloths over their eyes so we didn't change very much.'[29]

'It was quite tense,' says Andrew Dunn. 'Everyone sat round in a circle thinking, what's coming up here? There was a look of fear and dread on some faces in case they were the ones that had to relearn things.' Victoria sometimes asked Jane Cotton to pass on the cuts for her. According to Posner, the Saturday rewrites were 'the source of about 50 per cent of fluffs'. While he took charge of the cameras, Victoria was effectively the actors' director. 'She was very much in control,' says Anne Reid. 'Geoff Posner was a brilliant editor, but she knew what the joke should be. She was terribly strict. She had no bedside manner at all. She would say, "It's not funny like that." She couldn't bear it if it wasn't perfect. She could be very unnerving because you could see she wasn't really concentrating on the scene when she rehearsed. It is quite hard to act with somebody if you know that they're judging you.' Her quilted dialogue, with the characters chattering at cross-purposes, was so technically hard to master that even battle-hardened veterans felt the pressure. 'If you saw behind the flat of *dinnerladies*,' says Celia Imrie, 'you'd see Julie and me taking Rescue remedies. It was like being on a skating rink.' Duncan Preston grew disgruntled: 'I said to Julie, "This is ridiculous, the pressure we feel on this. I'm sick to death of it." And it's not a happy atmosphere when you do that. Although it turned out all right the process was not.' Victoria's gang were so associated with one another in the public mind that such tensions would have been unimaginable to her audience. In fact, they didn't often meet outside a television studio. The only regular at Victoria's Christmas parties was Duncan, who lived nearby, while Julie did not visit her house for the first time till later that year, seven years after its purchase. 'We were probably more the best of friends at the very beginning,' says Julie. 'But it was more a work relationship, if I'm honest – partly that I lived in West Sussex and she lived in Highgate.'

From the very start Victoria was running the show on depleted reserves of energy. It was at a read-through of the opening episode that she noticed a flaw. 'I thought, no, I can't get away with this,' she recorded in her diary that evening. 'I'm just not in it. It's the first episode and I've got to establish my character. I've got to take my right place in the middle of the ensemble. I'm on the edges and it isn't right.' She had a photoshoot in the afternoon and came home, according to Geoffrey, 'saying she had misconceived it completely and she needed to work on it then and there. This was at about seven in the evening. I popped my head round the door at eleven to ask how things were going. She said there was more to do. I woke up alone the next morning and thought she must be sleeping in the spare room. I went down to her office and there she was, still writing and completely knackered. But she did a great show for Grace and Henry at breakfast-time, merry and bright and cracking gags.' In fact, she did snatch a little sleep before Duncan gave her a lift in: 'I was really glad because with two hours' sleep I don't think I was fit to drive really. I don't know if I'm fit to act but I managed.'[30] Overnight, even in the depths of exhaustion, she had triumphantly slipped a line into the script that caught everyone unawares and triggered a deeply gratifying chorus of laughter. The next night she stayed up writing till one and got up at six. And so her routine continued. She was envious of the naps that Duncan and Julie took on the rehearsal-room sofa. 'If I didn't have Celia to catch an eye with I think I'd go barmy,' she said at the start of the third week.[31] That night, at two in the morning after a seven-hour shift at her desk, she reported that 'I've just kicked the crap out of the ending of "Scandal"'.[32] The audio diary is peppered with sniffs and yawns. 'I am getting very tired,' she confided to Jane Wynn Owen. 'I am trying to be very up and team leader but I have to say once I get home I flag severely . . . But it is being the most fantastic job, and I love it.'[33]

Across six weeks and twelve recordings, audiences were royally entertained with character comedy – and an avalanche of jokes – that could have emerged from no other source. The structure of each episode established Bren as the canteen's mother hen. Jean and Dolly would be bickering as they came in together. Twinkle was forever sullen and Anita sweetly naive. Victoria was aiming, she said, for 'non-eventfulness', the sense of a workplace where nothing much happened and the vacuum was filled with conversation.[34] Writing for a largely female set of characters enabled her to revisit areas covered in her live show. The canteen thrummed with talk of mood swings, thrush, bras, cystitis, insemination by turkey baster, visible nipples, periods, irritable bowel syndrome, yeast infections, HRT patches, Fallopian tubes, orgasms. 'I've worked on my pelvic floor,' says Dolly. 'Jean's more or less let hers dangle.' 'And where's it got you,' retorts Jean, 'having a pelvic floor like a bulldog clip?' In the character of Tony Victoria created a sex pest with a porn habit and no understanding of women but somehow managed to make him loveable. 'I'm not a dinosaur,' he declares. 'I quite like women in a sad baffled sort of way.' Victoria stayed true to her comic credo – that sex was no more exciting than any other domestic task. 'Did you get any?' Tony asks Bren at the start of 'Monday'. 'What?' 'At the weekend, did you get any?' 'Any sex? 'No, I had to go to t'launderette.' She was loyal to another of her instincts. While the dictates of sitcom found Victoria's writing at its most radiantly cheerful, even here she threw in a shadow of sadness by giving Tony cancer. 'She never made a big thing of it,' says Andrew Dunn. 'I asked her, "How come you've given Tony cancer?" She just said, "Cos he has."'

Meanwhile, Stan the jobsworth handyman galumphed around the canteen, attending to the toilets and the toaster, reminding everyone his dad was a Desert Rat. Petula stole in and out, a disruptive whirlwind dropping names and spreading havoc. The odd one out was Philippa in human resources, whose southern wishy-washiness gave the rest of the staff something to unite against. Victoria wanted the many minor characters she included to have their share of jokes rather than be used as feeds. 'Have you never seen *Vertigo*?' Bren asks Norman the hypochondriac breadman. 'Seen it? I've got it!' Led by Bren, there was a lot of knowledgeable chat about popular culture – films, sitcoms, soaps, TV drama. Victoria's characters found themselves referring to the same celebrities who had populated her comedy for years: Pam Ayres, the Nolan Sisters, Mia Farrow, Richard Clayderman, Sarah Ferguson, Fatima Whitbread, Judith Chalmers. She gave a peculiar form of colour-blindness to Petula, who recalls encounters with people who looked 'like a black Frankie Vaughan' or 'like a black Mary Hopkin' or 'like a white Nina Simone'. Victoria couldn't resist yet another private joke about Celia's anatomy. 'They can gape, can't they, the overalls,' says Dolly to Philippa, 'if you're heavy-busted.' Threaded into the workplace banter was plenty of old-school innuendo. 'Bren, can you spread them for Tony?' 'Answer me one question, luv. Where's my Clint?' 'Can you smell my Charlie?' asks Jean, drunkenly hitting on Tony. 'Vic did write some filthy lines,' says Anne Reid. 'I didn't like saying 'can you smell my Charlie?', but you wouldn't argue with her.' It caused such an eruption that the audience had to be asked to laugh less in a second take. A viewer would write to complain that the loud laughter spoiled her enjoyment. 'That's how loud they laughed!' Victoria replied. 'I agree with you – it's a bit too loud!'[35]

Some of the wordplay was fiendishly complex. Tony accuses Jean of 'teetering on the thrush threshold, threatening to thrash'. Bren, searching for a word just beyond reach, would come at it from a surreal angle. 'What are them things like cucumbers? Suffragettes.' One short speech contained most of the essential ingredients in Victoria's comedy: 'His auntie Dot from Cockermouth ate a raffia drinks coaster. She thought it was a high-fibre biscuit. She had to be held back from moving down the table and buttering two more.' But there was also fresh fun to be had with feng shui and the internet and a new prime minister. 'Tony Blair,' sniffs Dolly. 'Stick two poems up in a bus shelter and call it a university.' It was in Bren's nature to be cheerful, but Victoria barely had to act as she heard her jokes being delivered with such finesse. 'Julie is giving a very good performance,' she told her diary. 'I can't look at her because she's so funny. I knew she would be.' One day Andrew Dunn asked Julie how she and Victoria had met, and she told the story of that day at Manchester Poly when she did her an impression of a nurse wheeling a commode. 'How wonderful,' said Victoria on tape, 'that I'm sitting with her at a table having first heard her talk about this when I was seventeen.'[36]

After the last episode was recorded in mid-July, several months before broadcast, Victoria hosted a company party at home. They were ferried there by a Routemaster bus decorated with balloons and a banner reading 'HWD Components Canteen Closing Down Event' – Thora Hird was cheerfully carried up to the top deck. Victoria presented everyone with a bespoke *dinnerladies* plate with a ceramic egg and chips and their name daubed on the side, which had been sourced by Cathy Edis.

Then she had an unsettled summer: 'I have never worked so hard on anything, some days right through the night, and by the end of it I felt I'd used up all my sociability, jollity, energy etc.'[37] As well as a holiday in Mallorca, the family were weekend guests of Phil McIntyre, who took them out on his boat into the Solent – Victoria had no sea legs and caught the train back to his house in Lymington. The family went up to stay at Mole Barn, where an old revolving summerhouse in green and white she'd bought at Sotheby's had been installed in the garden. She visited her mother, who was now bedridden having undergone three hip replacements. But *dinnerladies* was never far from Victoria's mind as she awaited the series edits anxiously. 'I hope they are OK,' she fretted, 'because disagreeing with Posner is so hard.'[38] After watching all six episodes, Peter Salmon declared himself happy enough to hope for more. Victoria started on promotional tasks, which ranged from being photographed next to giant vats of baked beans to doing her bit for the BBC's *dinnerladies* website. 'I can see a day,' she prophesied, 'when we don't make programmes at all, we just describe them on the internet.'[39]

Victoria prepared to reappear on BBC One after a long absence – *Pat and Margaret* was four years in the past, *All Day Breakfast* six and her last comedy series was broadcast nine years earlier. At the heart of the campaign to reintroduce her was a profile for *Best of British*, a BBC series of tributes to popular stars. Victoria duly submitted to an interview in the Palladium, scene of her first major London triumph in 1987, and was filmed being interviewed on *Woman's Hour* by Jenni Murray. She ticked Murray off on air for calling her a southerner. 'No I'm not,' she said. 'I carry my heart with me wherever I go. I carry my language with me.'[40] Murray then asked why she had accepted an OBE but never done *This Is Your Life*, prompting a less than complimentary retort about the ITV show. Victoria sent a pre-emptive apology to its presenter Michael Aspel. 'I did ask them to take it out,' she wrote, 'but they then acted as if I had requested that Jenni Murray give the Pope a blow job . . . and told me to get lost. So that'll learn me. Or not.'[41] He wrote back to say he wouldn't be upset, even if she'd meant it. The usual suspects were interviewed for the profile, while original perspectives were provided by David Morton of the Rochdale Youth Theatre Workshop and Lesley Fitton from Bury Grammar.

The most intriguing choice of interviewee was Caroline Aherne, who acknowledged Victoria as an inspiration. While the programme was being made, the first episode of *The Royle Family* was broadcast, starring and co-written by Aherne. Its characters barely moved around a set shot on a single camera without an audience, forcing a down-in-the-mouth Victoria to fret that she was out of step. 'When I saw *The Royle Family* I thought my sort of sitcom is dead. It's just been blown out of the water because they'd established the new style and mine suddenly looked like *My Wife Next Door* from twenty years ago.'[42]

*Best of British* and the first episode of *dinnerladies* were shown on consecutive nights in November. 'I do feel nervous about the old dinnerladies going out,' Victoria confessed to Richenda Carey, 'even though heaven knows I've given it my best shot.'[43] To help it along Peter Salmon loaded the Thursday night schedule with his most bankable comedies, and 'Monday' duly reached an audience of over twelve million.

The next day Victoria and Geoffrey flew to Barcelona for a restorative weekend away, where they 'rambled very happily in the Ramblas, gawped at the Gaudis, peered at the Picassos'.[44] As the series continued, with audiences hovering either side of ten million, she was called back to her writing desk. Richard Curtis asked if she had thoughts up her sleeve for Comic Relief in the new year. A sly idea occurred to Victoria to spoof *Hetty Wainthrop Investigates*, the gentle BBC crime drama starring Patricia Routledge as a retired housewife sleuth which had just completed its final series. *Wetty Hainthrop Investigates* was written in haste in early December. Victoria cast herself as the gumshoe who tackles various types of crime – 'nothing upsetting' – and is hired to solve a case of stolen fish fingers and disappearing celebrities. To send up the original character, she asked her regular costume designer Anna Stubley to supply her with an ever-changing array of woolly berets. For Julie Walters she wrote the part of an old woman who keeps tripping over the carpet, Celia Imrie was cast as a husky femme fatale in a nightclub and Duncan Preston played Wetty's sidekick Sopwith Heckmondwyke, who is obsessed with naked gameshows on cable TV. She had fun writing cameos for Judith Chalmers, Alan Titchmarsh as his jealous younger twin Adam, and, to top off a long ticklist of northern clichés, the cast of *Coronation Street* filing out of the Rovers Return. Harriet Thorpe, a north London friend of Victoria's, played a chanteuse called Carol Singer. To add authenticity, Geoff Posner filmed it on badly lit sets which cast distracting shadows. *Wetty Hainthrop* was to have one significant side-effect. Victoria composed a theme tune, and at the recording sessions she was much taken by the sound of the soloist's cornet. 'It really set me off,' she confessed. 'I will have to buy a trumpet now.'[45]

Victoria greeted 1999 'hoping for world peace and the chance to snap Woody Allen's clarinet in two' (Allen's jazz odyssey *Wild Man Blues* was released a few months earlier).[46] She also had a sitcom to write and threw herself into meetings to 'decide if, when, how many, with whom, rehearsed where . . .'[47] Peter Salmon professed a wish to get a second series of *dinnerladies* on by the autumn, culminating in a Christmas special. 'Can't quite see how we would do this without recording them before they have been written, which would be a first,' she mused. 'Once I get going it will not be too hard to do. I just know, however easy it is creatively, it is still a huge commitment and work load and effort and all those things for which I am paid so handsomely, and sometimes balk at the toll it takes of the family and the marriage and all that malarkey. But maybe I will manage it better this year.'[48] She now trusted Salmon, who had made sure to show up at rehearsals and recordings and keep the door to his inner sanctum open to her. 'This is the first one I think I can deal with face to face like normal people,' she told Richenda Carey.[49] She outlined a plan for the second series to start in late November, with episodes pegged to Christmas and the millennium and possibly three more in the new year. Salmon agreed to repeat series one beforehand.

In January Victoria went to up to Bolton to see a stage version of *Pat and Margaret* at the Octagon, having advised the theatre's artistic director Lawrence Till on adapting it. His first draft included songs plucked from her back catalogue. To Margaret he had given 'Bessie Bunter', Pat got 'Fourteen Again' and they united at the end to duet on 'Saturday Night'. Victoria firmly discouraged this archival rummage. 'Take it by the scruff of the neck more,' she counselled.[50] When she saw the production she privately judged it 'a bit of a curate's bumhole but not too dreadful in parts'.[51] She was surprised to hear little snippets of *dinnerladies* crop up in the script and expressed her displeasure to the director Joanna Read when she wrote to her about reviving *Talent* at Watford Palace. Read asked Victoria if she might append an actual talent contest to make a full evening of Victoria's short debut play. 'Is it for the bar receipts?' Victoria asked tartly, suggesting she instead couple it with a one-act play by a young female playwright the same age she had been in 1978.[52] It was paired instead with an Ayckbourn.

While in Lancashire she paid a rare visit to Bury, which she found 'ripped to shreds by developers of course, and I can't say I felt very at home, but it was by way of researching for dinnerladies so it was worth it'.[53] It may have been this visit to her home town which prompted an act of contrition. Victoria found a Bury Library label inside a book on her shelves. 'I have a feeling I must have stolen this from your library!' she wrote as she belatedly returned it, adding that she'd walked off with many more as a young teenager. 'I'm very sorry – here's a small donation to help replace a few.'[54] She enclosed a cheque for £100.

As was her habit Victoria turned down Richard Curtis's invitation to be live in the studio on Red Nose Day, but she did agree to act as guest editor of the *Radio Times* for their Comic Relief issue. Rather than merely lend her name as a figurehead, she drove to a meeting at the magazine's office in west London, where she signed up to write several features. She 'interviewed' 'Julia Walters' ('the actress most men would like to discuss hernias with'[55]), questioned the Chancellor Gordon Brown about Third World debt, wrote about celebrity ailments (including her own bunion), surfed through the desert wastes of digital TV and had a pop at *The Archers*, 'expressing my wish that the entire cast would fall into the slurry'.[56] The cover portrait, shot by her regular photographer Brian Moody, required her to look editorial. 'I don't really know how editors act,' she wrote for the magazine. 'I settle on an expression of paranoid smugness, which I think will cover most jobs in the media.'[57] She enjoyed the experience but found it exhausting – 'I'm too tired to do capitals,' she told her commissioning editor – and went with the family to a Belgian Center Parc to recover.[58] The advantage of slipping across the Channel was anonymity. 'I cannot bear being pestered when I'm with the children,' she confided to Richenda Carey, 'and neither can they. It's a bit inhibiting when one is in one's cossy to be accosted by beaming couples wielding cameras . . . But then how can I complain after shoving my features in front of the Great British P for 25 years?'[59]

Victoria started on the second series just as *dinnerladies* and Julie Walters were up for BAFTAs. *Father Ted* and its recently deceased star Dermot Morgan won in both categories, but a few days later she fared better at the Montreux Festival, where the 'Party' episode was shortlisted for the press prize. She flew to Switzerland with Paul Roberts. 'I didn't cry,' she reported, 'but felt a bit gulpy and ooer when the woman said the jury had been unanimous but mainly I was trying to get to the stage without losing a bosom.'[60] At her table she was approached by a young northerner introducing himself as Steve Pemberton of *The League of Gentlemen*. 'She had quite a startled look on her face that I bowled up to her without any of the niceties,' he says. 'I said, "How are you? Good to see you." It was as if she was a friend of my mum's.' Afterwards the two parties stayed up talking in the hotel bar and paid a late-night visit to the lakeside statue of Freddie Mercury. The League frankly admitted that they were devotees of her sketch collections and that Pauline from the Royston Vasey job centre was a straight lift from *Mens Sana in Thingummy Doodah*. It was to be the start of an occasional relationship.

The day Victoria got back, her work ethic forced her to write through to the morning to make up for lost time. She was ambivalent about embarking on another regime of all-nighters – 'it just buggers up the next day so I'm not sure it's worth it' – but simply couldn't stay away from her desk.[61] A month on from Montreux she reported that 'eps have been going very well, even though Geoff was away and I had more domestics to do, but on the other hand I didn't have to be married all evening, I could just work, so it evened out'.[62] According to Geoffrey, 'We thought the children never twigged that she'd had no sleep, but as the weekly pressure of her hair-shirt regime began to take its toll she found it harder to keep family life together.' In fact, her nocturnal writing sessions earned the disapproval of Grace, now ten. 'She did it enough for me to notice and think, you shouldn't be doing this,' says Grace. 'There was one specific time when I told her not to stay up all night. She went, "Yeah, yeah, yeah." I said, "No, I really don't want you to stay up all night." And I made her snacks. I said, "You have to eat this at one, you have to eat this at two, and you have to go to bed." It was things like toast that wasn't going to last six hours. I hadn't really thought this through.'

Rather than heed such pleas, Victoria now created a rod for her own back. It became apparent as she mapped out plotlines on a magnetic wall chart that the new *dinnerladies* would need to stretch to ten episodes. She started to work on a more thought-through story for her characters. Having given Tony a non-specific cancer in the first series, she consulted Rob Buckman, nowadays an oncologist in Toronto: 'What could he have that makes him feel he has got away with it to a certain extent, but that next time he could die?'[63] He suggested a diagnosis of stage B bowel cancer. She also commissioned a researcher to look into the finer points of divorce, food poisoning and how to fire a canteen worker. In the end, none of this research was used but, as she plotted, an idea was floated from on high that Tony Blair should appear in the millennium episode. Instead of falling in with this idea, Victoria upped the rate of jokes at his expense. Dolly now complained about him every other episode. ('Tony Blair! It used to be the police taking these criminals from place to place – now it's anyone with three rear seat belts and a driving licence.')

For several months, with only the most necessary distractions, Victoria retreated to her office to come up with five hours of comedy. The process proved more exacting than anything she had yet attempted. Each first draft might take twelve hours 'when I'm working at speed. That's when I know what I'm doing.'[64] But every draft spawned rewrites. Some scripts were thrown away; others she asked Geoff Posner to bin. 'The trouble with doing ten episodes,' she told him, 'is that the first draft is fine and you feel really pleased with yourself, but by the time you have clocked up the second and third lots, it's knackering. But I am steaming ahead as fast as I can.'[65] The process was lonely too. She found herself wishing for 'one other person that knew everything I was doing that I could talk to about it. I can't imagine sharing the writing. Just the sharing of the burden of the thinking it through.'[66] After she voiced her gathering despair at one meeting, it was put to her by someone who should have known better that she farm out some of the work to co-writers. 'Vic did a face that looked down and smiled and said, "I don't think so,"' says Geoff Posner. Her crisis of confidence lingered for so long 'that I left it past the point where I could jack it in. It's a horrible situation to be in.'[67] As she wrote she kept the episodes to herself – Posner had to ask for a plot outline of the millennium episode to take to the BBC's press launch. When she did send him scripts she forbade him to share them with the cast, as she said they would only start learning what might later be changed.

Victoria stopped for a week at the end of April to prepare for a couple of fundraiser shows at the Millfield Theatre in Edmonton for the children's primary school. It would be hers and Geoffrey's first appearance on the same bill since 1983. 'Back together by unpopular demand,' she told Jane Wymark.[68] Between scripts, Victoria organised a fiftieth birthday party for Geoffrey, marred somewhat by the caterer ignoring the order for wholefood only. The mishap was retooled as a joke for *dinnerladies* when the pittas delivered to the canteen are wholemeal. 'What do you think this is,' says Tony, 'the Labour Party Conference?' As a present she booked a weekend in August at the Oslo Jazz Festival, only for the headliner to be indisposed. They spent the evening in their hotel room watching films on TV.

In August the casting process began while the scripts were still being written, pushing the family holiday to Mallorca back to the very end of the summer. So Victoria approached recording in September in a state of extreme fatigue. The night before the first rehearsal she told

David Firman that she needed to rewrite an episode to accommodate a vocal version of the theme tune: 'When I am going to write "millennium" I'm not quite sure. But this totally serves me right for being a smartarse and trying to do ten episodes in the time normally needed for six.'[69]

It was a sign of her exhaustion that she started to complain about Geoff Posner. 'Geoff I'm sure does like me and thinks I'm very good at what I do,' she told Richenda Carey, 'but there has been no acknowledgment since January that I am working on a huge project, at times very difficult.'[70] In auditions, and as decisions were made about shooting, she felt like an underling and eventually sent off a fax saying so: 'It is EXTREMELY rare for me to kick up about anything, and I did feel wobbly about it . . . My big fear, and this is an old childhood thing, is that people will shout at me when I say what I mean and tell me they don't like me. But I cannot go on getting upset with Mr Posner, moaning to G, and then carrying on smiling and going along with it. It's not honest.'[71] Posner, who in her lighter moments she referred to as Poz, treated these stresses as a mark of her perfectionism. 'I was in the firing line but that's my job,' he says. 'The grumbling was because she felt under much more pressure to get it all right.'

Victoria's workload increased even further by a request from the BBC to write a sketch for their millennium celebrations. For a comedy compendium titled *The Nearly Complete and Utter History of Everything* they wanted a two-hander for her and Thora Hird, the only stipulation that it be set during the last thousand years. Victoria was worried about doing a sketch on film 'having only ever done them in front of coach parties'.[72] She dashed it off and sent it to her agent after she got home from the first *dinnerladies* rehearsal: 'I hope they like it, if they don't we'll just have to forget it because I don't have time to do another one, strangely enough.'[73] Then she stayed up and made more adjustments to the first episode.

'Catering' was a cluttered episode in which decorators cause the canteen to close when they accidentally wedge a ladder across it. 'If you feel you are standing around with not much to do,' Victoria warned the principals, 'then don't worry.' She promised good exposure for each character in six of the ten episodes, 'and four where they do the equivalent of Emily standing in the Rovers asking for a medium sherry'.[74]

After six months at her desk, Victoria felt 'excited about starting at last, and a bit disappointed I haven't totally finished the writing'.[75] When they met at the LWT rehearsal rooms in south London she was shocked, even angry, to discover that Maxine Peake had quietly shed five stone. For this Victoria had only herself to blame. 'You are going to get typecast,' she had advised the young actress. 'You're big, you're northern.'[76] A fat suit was ordered to restore Twinkle's frame to previous proportions, and references to her fluctuating weight were added to the script, but there was no hiding the change: in one early episode Twink appeared in a crop top baring a svelte midriff.

The new episodes had titles, but also dates. 'Catering' was set on Friday 9 April 1999. It opened with Bren and Tony poring over a staff rota wall plan, as if Victoria's meticulous plotting had bled across into the script itself. There were complications in the staffing rota for the cast too. Julie had other commitments, so Petula Gordeno was written into only half the episodes. Celia was in all of them, but Philippa's affair in the first series had proved so underpowered that Victoria wrote her love interest out of the script. As usual Celia had to put up with teasing. 'I liked you in glasses,' Dolly says to Philippa after a makeover. 'They diminished your nostrils.' When Celia arrived late at rehearsal in a fiery state thanks to Tube chaos one day, she found her wild rant all but transcribed into the script for the millennium episode 'Minnellium'. Anne Reid and Duncan Preston were kept much busier, with ructions in the private lives of Jean and Stan which would end with them joined together in romance. ('I can't say either of them looked best pleased,' Victoria told Richenda Carey. 'Actors!'[77]) Meanwhile, Anita grows attached to a blow-up male companion she calls Malcolm. Minor characters who had sparkled in the first series were brought back for more – among them Kate Robbins as gormless Babs who comes from Urmston, and Sue Devaney as the bouncy, beaming secretary Jane, always ordering twelve rounds of white, low-fat spread. New characters were brought in for the dinnerladies to bounce off. A

burly breadwoman called Glenda overshares information about her
bladder-stapling surgery – there were hints that she may be a transsexual, prompting one viewer to send Victoria a reprimand. In an
episode titled 'Christine', a new dinnerlady insults all her colleagues
with her plain speaking. (She was played by Kay Adshead, a trusty
veteran of *As Seen on TV* and *Over to Pam*.) This was Victoria venting
her anger with infuriating passive-aggressive New Age types. 'I might
have to smash you in the face with a tin of beans,' Bren tells Christine.
'I'm not joking.'

Bren wasn't joking for much of the second series, and sometimes
seemed to be visiting from another sort of show altogether thanks
to a will-they/won't-they plotline about her romance with Tony. The
rest of the cast have a bet on about how soon they'll kiss and have
sex, while Victoria put Bren through agonies of doubt, misery and
low self-esteem. At the very moment Bren and Tony smooch under
the mistletoe, Victoria even had an ex-husband walk in. There were
several such bombshells: Tony's cancer, Anita's secret pregnancy, an
unwanted Christmas baby left on the fire escape, Stan's grief at his
father's death, Dolly revealing her son lives with a marine biologist
called Marcus, Jean's rage at her husband abandoning her for a dental
hygienist in Cardiff. The series sometimes threatened to turn into an
explosive issues-led soap.

Victoria had touched on melancholy themes in her bleaker songs
and sketches. The logical outcome, even though this was a sitcom,
was that she now actually had to cry on camera. On the day of recording the Christmas episode she sought advice from Julie. 'I remember
Vic rushing up to me and saying, "How do you cry? I want to cry
at the end of it. How do I do that?" I said, "You have to kind of
feel it. If you can't feel it through the words, you've got to psych
yourself up in some way and produce it, but you have to feel it in
the moment."' Meanwhile, in another episode Bren is blisteringly
rude about Juliet Stevenson's snot crying in *Truly Madly Deeply*.
Among other namedrops were various comedians – Ben Elton, Billy
Connolly, Rory Bremner. To Twinkle she gave a sarcastic put-down
– 'Oh ha ha, Alan Partridge' or 'Oh ha ha, League of Gentleman'.
On one level these were public jokes about public figures; on another

they were private nods to friends and acquaintances or, in the case of Juliet Stevenson, a fellow parent at Grace and Henry's primary school.

Other elements of the show were more familiar – jokes about More-cambe Bay and Pam Ayres, Woody Allen and Kiri Te Kanawa. The talk of babies and birth meant a reprise for favourites from Victoria's stand-up show. 'I've got a haemorrhoid but it's quite a dinky one,' says Anita after giving birth. 'My cousin had three big ones, sort of in a cluster.' There were lashings of sex gags, and they were growing filthier. 'You want to pump that Malcolm up a bit,' Stan says to Anita. 'You don't want him going down on you.' There was a double en-tendre about what George Michael, another Highgate neighbour, might get up to in a public convenience.

The shoot took the whole of the autumn. Halfway through, rehearsals moved to the National Youth Theatre's premises in north London. There were moments of strain. Victoria felt bruised when Geoff Posner suggested the first episode was 'undirectable'. She wor-ried there was not a single close-up of Bren. 'No I am not queeny really in that respect,' she confided to Jane Wymark, 'but I do think when one has the main part, albeit in an ensemble piece, one should be top of the pecking order when it comes to being favoured by the camera. So I had to say that to him.'[78] After the second episode she felt stung on hearing that Duncan Preston thought he was being underused and sent him a three-page letter explaining 'how no one can have a huge share, and it is after all focused on Bren and Tony'.[79] She told Paul Roberts that sending the fax, 'for me, was a bit like invading Poland' but that since doing so 'I have felt fine'.[80] She then sent a load of tongue twisters Duncan's way to keep him occupied. The stresses were not helped by yet more sleep deprivation, despite which Victoria did not stint on the morning routine of breakfast, musical-instrument practice and the school run. One week she was cheered that Steps were rehearsing in the next room and secured their autographs for Grace. 'It's a lovely job and I'm glad to do it,' she reminded herself. 'I'll be even more glad when I can just be Bren and not the poor writer.'[81]

The writing never really stopped. One night she took the children up to stay with their old nanny then went home to write from 10 p.m. to 3 a.m., then got up for two full days' recording of 'Gamble', the pre-Christmas episode. The episode included her kiss with Andrew Dunn 'which I found very difficult to do for real, and Celia had to take us in a corner and direct us'.[82] After the recording she and Geoff Posner drove up to Manchester to meet the Black Dyke Band, who were booked to play the theme tune, arranged by David Firman, live in the studio for the Christmas episode. The celebrated ensemble was led by the trumpeter James Watson, whom Victoria took to instantly: 'I told him I used to play the trumpet but that I hadn't played since I was seventeen, and he held out his trumpet and he said, "If you can play a scale on that I'll give you a pound." So I did, and he did.'[83] For 'Christmas', after the cast reading on the Monday, she stayed up all night to fix the script, did two more pages for Wednesday, then found it was too long and 'just cut my own lines to save moaning'.[84] She also wrote lyrics for a sung version of the theme tune to play over the credits of 'Minnellium'.

The company said goodbye to Julie in mid-November just as the second series started broadcasting on BBC One. Victoria saved the biggest rewrite for this final episode, which was recorded out of sequence owing to Julie's availability. 'Toast' was set on 29 February. As the canteen is threatened with cuts and then closure, Bren puts her film knowledge to good use by entering a quiz show called *Totally Trivial* (hosted by Henry Kelly, who had also played himself in 'Winnie's Lucky Day' in *As Seen on TV*). Then she is diverted to the deathbed of her mother, who reveals her real name is the same as her daughter's – Brenda Furlong. In a touching finale of pure wish fulfilment, Victoria laid to rest the theme of maternal abandonment. 'I'm sorry I've not been a very good mother,' says Petula as she dictates her last will and testament on video and leaves a jiffy bag of cash, enabling Bren and Tony to begin a new life in Scotland as the canteen closes. Once more she stayed up all night after the Monday rehearsal. 'But something was bugging me, couldn't tell what,' she told Richenda Carey.[85] On the Thursday the cast and crew gathered at Victoria's home to drink champagne and watch that night's episode broadcast live. It was, she said, 'an acknowledgement of all we'd done together'.[86] She was unhappy with the Friday recording and, after watching a tape of the episode with Geoffrey, rewrote it on Saturday morning before the company gathered to shoot *dinnerladies* for the thirty-second and last time. 'When the cast assembled for notes I told them I thought it was bad last night, and that we could really pull it off tonight if they got themselves together. Which they did.'[87] After this final demonstration of her implacably high standards, at the wrap party she presented her co-workers with another bespoke plate, this time with tart and custard. There was a nice extra bauble for Victoria that month, as *dinnerladies* won the Comedy Award for Best New Comedy Programme.

Despite feeling physically and mentally 'wrecked', and out of condition having had so little time for exercise, she had only a day to learn the vast amount of words she'd written for *The Nearly Complete and Utter History of Everything*.[88] Unlike much of the rest of the show, in which male comics did sketches about the deep past, Victoria set hers in a salon. It was 'chosen for ease and simplicity. Thora can sit down and not learn any lines, and I can make it up as I go along and wear a wig.'[89] As the customer, Thora Hird read her few lines very slowly off cue cards. As the hairdresser, Victoria prattled about her three gay husbands and her cat Robert De Niro. They had to do three takes, and 'died on our arses,' she told Michael Parkinson. 'The whole thing was received in baffled silence . . . but the wig was bloody marvellous.'[90] It was shown on the second day of 2000.

Victoria's true greeting to the new millennium was seen on BBC One on 30 December. 'Minnellium' closed with fireworks exploding through the window at the back of the canteen and the sound of Victoria singing along to the *dinnerladies* theme tune – her first new song for television since *All Day Breakfast* in 1992. In counterpoint to the fireworks, the low-key lyrics painted a wistful picture:

All the dreams that you had when it all lay before you
All the plans that you made, all the things you would do
All the schemes that you knew time would bring to fruition
Did they happen? Not so far, at least not to you.

The episode, instantly repeated, reached a spectacularly large audience of fifteen million, putting the cap on another mighty feat in Victoria's career as an entertainer: to try her hand at sitcom and conjure up an instant classic. But the personal cost was high. At the peak of her triumph, she was thousands of miles away at a luxury resort hotel in Kenya, where she performed in the open air on a stage adorned with a spectacular sail. The fee for the booking was a ten-day stay for the family, including five days on safari in the Masai Mara, on one of which they rose at four in the morning to go up in a hot-air balloon. The year, the century and the millennium ended with yet another all-night vigil as Victoria and Geoffrey stayed up to see the sun rise over the Indian Ocean.

'Next year,' she predicted, 'will be easy compared with this.'[91]

# 19

# TRIMMING

'I feel sorry for poor old Debbie McGee. What has she done wrong in this world really? She fell in love with a bald magician. We've all done that.'

*Victoria Wood At It Again*, 2001

'For the first time – the bare bosoms of . . . Celia Imrie, Victoria Wood, Julie Walters (all hidden by tea urns, sieves and pianos but they don't need to know that).'[1] Early in the new century, Victoria felt a craving. The previous April, the Rylstone and District branch of the Women's Institute released a calendar to raise money for leukaemia research. Eleven Yorkshirewomen allowed themselves to be photographed wearing no clothes and soon became an international news story. Victoria still yearned to make a feature film and, when she read that the ladies were being romanced by a film company, decided to see if she could persuade them to entrust her with their story.

Rylstone was barely any distance from Mole Barn. A local builder she employed spread the word along the dale and she was soon declaring herself a fan to Moyra Livesey, aka Miss May: 'It's a gift of an idea for a writer, especially a Northern female writer, and believe me, I wouldn't treat it casually: done properly it would be moving and funny, hopefully. And with bosoms thrown in for added value!'[2] Victoria enthused to her agents that they were in a fairly strong position 'because I am (I think) so obviously the ideal person to write the screenplay and take one of the parts . . .'[3] Victoria wrote to all the

calendar girls, blaming her absorption in *dinnerladies* for not having
had 'such a blindingly wonderful idea' sooner.[4] Her serious pitch
reminded them that 'my best work has always had that combination
of humour and sadness. I don't think really you can do anything true
to life without both . . . Sometimes,' she concluded, 'you feel a project
has your name on it. I feel it has everything as a story . . . and I want
to do it!'[5] While Victoria waited to meet them, she could not help
tipping off her friends. 'It is something you just might want to do,'
she told Julie Walters.[6] She was giddy at the prospect of baring her 'la
las', she told Celia Imrie. 'It would be funny to have them up on the
silver screen after all this time, wouldn't it?'[7]

It soon became apparent that there was a schism within the calendar girls. Some had no idea that others had been negotiating with
a film company for far longer than they initially suspected. The
excluded group welcomed Victoria's interest. 'They thought she was
absolutely ideal,' says Moyra Livesey, who invited all eleven ladies
to meet Victoria and Phil McIntyre in her kitchen. 'She spoke for
about half an hour. She mentioned people she hoped to be involved.
It really sounded good.' Phil McIntyre added that the women would
be co-owners of the film. The same evening Victoria had a pricklier
encounter with the other group. One of them brought their son, a
solicitor who, Victoria reported, 'needs to look to his manners'.

A few days later, fearing the rival company backed by Disney's
international distributor Buena Vista had the upper hand, Phil McIntyre offered £75,000 for the rights, plus a third share of profits and a
third ownership of the film. Victoria could write quickly, so the film
could be in production by the autumn, and without any American
interference. But the core group led by Angela Baker, whose husband's illness and death was the catalyst for the calendar, could not be
lured. Victoria was 'bitterly disappointed,' wrote her manager. 'In the
eighteen years I've known her, no other project has overwhelmed her
as this one has done.'[8] He made a final offer of a non-returnable fixed
fee of £250,000 whether the film was made or not. A media lawyer
advised the calendar girls that this was the most generous offer he had
seen for a British film of this scale. Six weeks after first having the
idea, Victoria gave up the chase. 'I pulled out because it was dragging

on,' she told Julie. 'So I'm not doing much at the moment, which makes a lovely change.'[9]

The focus in the household was on navigating secondary-school entrance for Grace. No sooner did she get into her preferred choice, a state girls' grammar in Hampstead Garden Suburb, than they were apologetically asking Victoria about a possible fundraiser. There were other claims on her. She turned down an invitation from Sam Mendes to do a summer residency in the intimate Donmar Warehouse. One request she could not resist was a plea for help from the Masara family she had filmed in Zimbabwe in 1995. A forlorn letter from Forward Masara broke the news that his father had died. She sent £1,500 via Comic Relief, who cheekily requested another sketch.

In March Victoria made her belated debut on *Parkinson*. It was a chance to lay a nagging memory to rest from twenty years earlier, when a researcher from the talk show went to Morecambe to pump Victoria for anecdotes and she had clammed up. Now, with the entire programme given over to her, she was full of stories about the dysfunctional world of Birtle Edge House, her feelings of failure until she met Julie, plus peeing in pint glasses backstage at the Bush. 'I feel I'm not coming out of this very well,' she said after telling another yarn against herself. The memories were polished into glinting gems which Victoria delivered as a kind of sit-down stand-up routine. To project a sense that this wasn't another stage performance, Geoffrey suggested a switch from her regulation Betty Jackson suit. Instead she bought a black leather jacket and had 'a few extra blonde bits put into my fringe for luck'.[10]

The show called for her to perform three songs at the piano. Having barely written any in several years, she chose 'Andrea', quirkily arranged by David Firman, and the bittersweet theme tune to *dinnerladies*, which, lacking a second verse, was slightly exposed as a full-length song, before finishing on 'The Ballad of Barry and Freda'. 'It was quite a strain,' she told Richenda Carey, 'not just the interview, which had to cover so much ground, and not having any umming or erring, but the songs, two of which were with the band, and I hardly ever sing with a band.'[11] Broadcast a day later, it reached an audience of seven million. Victoria and Geoffrey were not among them as they dashed away for a weekend in Paris where, to avoid compatriots, they froze on the top deck of a river-cruise boat. Soon after she got back there was a letter from the Bush Theatre, chuffed at their mention and asking if she'd put in a good word with their landlords Bass the brewery, who were planning refurbishments. 'I personally didn't mind weeing into pint pots,' she duly wrote, 'but no doubt most performers would prefer a lavatory. Any chance?'[12]

Then the *Radio Times* asked for a list of her favourite sitcom scenes for its survey of great comedy moments. The only show from which she made two selections was *Dad's Army*. The classic sitcom was at the forefront of Victoria's mind because she had agreed to front a documentary about it. 'She was very hard to convince,' says the producer Gerard Barry, 'but I eventually got her to accept lunch, and there received a grilling about my own knowledge of *Dad's Army*. Hers was, of course, encyclopaedic.' Having prepped by watching forty episodes, in April she reported for duty in Thetford in Norfolk, where the sitcom's exterior scenes were filmed. On the first night they had dinner with the writers David Croft and Jimmy Perry, and Victoria was thrilled to josh and share stories about the history of sitcom. During the three-day shoot she togged up in Home Guard khaki and got behind the wheel of Jones the butcher's delivery van, which she drove jerkily onto the A11. 'Now I have to warn you,' she said from the driving seat, 'this could be the only documentary entirely made in second gear.' In her pieces to camera, delivered as if off the cuff, she praised *Dad's Army*'s vanishing virtues. 'It's celebratory and it's positive and it's innocent,' she argued, and 'full of wit, pathos, character, slapstick, farce, overplaying, underplaying.' And because it was set in the past, it could never age. 'Wish I'd thought of that,' she concluded. In hymning *Dad's Army* she was making a case for *dinnerladies* without once mentioning it.

A couple of weeks later her sitcom was up for two BAFTAs. 'I really don't want to go,' she moaned. 'Geoff is doing a barmitzvah, and I haven't got any clothes, and we won't win, and whinge whinge . . .'[13] *Dinnerladies* didn't win. Having guest-edited the magazine only a year earlier, and just submitted her list of sitcom scenes, she shared her dismay with Richenda Carey at seeing her show described in the

*Radio Times* as 'not a sit com, just a load of people doing stand up'.[14] That month nine million watched *Don't Panic! The Dad's Army Story*.

Peter Salmon at BBC One had made it clear at the start of the year that he was eager for more comedy from her pen – 'series, mini-series, specials. Whatever! Even a Christmas 2000 treat would be welcome.'[15] In May Victoria went in to discuss making her first Christmas special in eight years, though she was not yet certain what it would be. 'I know it will have music and sketches in it,' she mused, 'but the finer details escape me at the present.'[16] All she knew for certain was that she wanted to do without a stand-up monologue and an audience – 'the days of the studio audience and the big expanse of lit floor have gone for ever,' she argued in a confidential outline – and to work with a new producer.[17] She wrote to tell Geoff Posner of her choice and met several candidates in June: 'One I liked a lot, though she was very nervous, and a bit gauche.'[18] Jemma Rodgers, who had produced two series with the League of Gentlemen, learned that Victoria picked her because 'she wanted to change what people perceived her as. She definitely wanted to go darker.' As they began to discuss the show, she had to get used to Victoria's method of circling round an idea. 'Once it's written we'll all know what it's about,' Victoria explained. 'Something will happen when I start writing, and till then we'll both be in the dark to a certain extent.' Mainly what she was aiming for was 'something that hadn't been done before'.[19]

Plenty of new television tropes and styles presented themselves as targets. Adaptations of novels by Jane Austen and Charles Dickens abounded in the 1990s, so Victoria set about scripting note-perfect parodies of *A Christmas Carol* and *Pride and Prejudice*. The new cruise-ship superstar Jane McDonald was a sitting duck, prompting Victoria to write a mini-docusoap about sea-borne crooner Stacey Jane Leigh, a massive egotist who boasts of having 'a good big dose of plain Lancashire humility'. Later she renamed her Stacey Leanne Paige.

There was a more personal inspiration for other sketches. Having helped to restore the fortunes of Carnforth station in *Great Railway Journeys*, Victoria wrote a loving treatment of *Brief Encounter*. 'I'm Celia Johnson (I'm so like her as you know),' she informed Celia

Imrie, 'and you are the friend Dolly, and you get your skirt ripped off by a train and come in in just your furs, jacket hat and underskirt (don't worry, no bloomer work).'[20] In order to salvage something from the calendar-girls debacle, she imagined the WI going about their business, but with a twist. Her handwritten draft said it should be 'based totally on ER . . . The accents and acting styles are American. The look is authentic English middle class.' She had originally wanted *dinnerladies* to be filmed like the high-octane medical drama. As an ailing tea urn was given emergency resuscitation by WI ladies speaking in wobbly American accents, the bizarre clash of styles would belatedly come to fruition.

As for music, there was a period piano duet for Hilary and Valerie Malory, both dressed to the nines and shot in the style of *The Billy Cotton Band Show*. Victoria wrote the sketch – and the tune in the style of Winifred Atwell she called 'Keyboard Collywobbles' – to perform with Anne Reid, who in some trepidation went to Highgate to practise timing the dialogue to the music. 'Brassed Up', which took the mickey out of stubbornly sexist northerners, enabled her to revisit her youth as a trumpeter in Bury's military band. She had taken up the trumpet again in recent months – Jim Watson of the Black Dyke Band had been giving her lessons and in due course they took to playing 'very hard duets . . . what I don't know is if after I've gone he reels out of the room going "Fucking hell I could hardly keep a straight face."'[21] The sketch told of the Associated Fettlers and Warp and Weft Adjusters Silver Band, facing extinction thanks to the demise of the fettling industry. Victoria cast herself as a fettler's daughter made good, who proposes to save band and town if only she can join. The role required plenty of trumpet practice. 'They play the second eight bars,' she wrote in the script. 'Woman joins in, plays to the end, duetting with first trumpet – all very beautiful and moving. The men are quietly impressed.' She gave her character the surname of Eckerslike – her nickname for Peter Eckersley.

It was to be the most expensive show of its type the BBC had ever made, in which Victoria's hope was to flood the screen with big names. 'I have a long list of people I would love to use in this special,' she told Richenda Carey, who yearned to be one of them. 'All I can do is write a load of stuff and then put the best people in it, and hopefully there will something that only you can do.'²² As ever, first on the list was Julie Walters, who was free for one day only and was put down for two decrepit crones: Scrooge's housekeeper Mrs Humbletypop and a cockney pensioner smiling pluckily through the Blitz on a 1940 newsreel. Victoria played her daughter; in the same sketch Henry Durham would make his screen debut as a capering urchin in a gas mask. Not to be upstaged, Grace Durham dressed up as a bonneted extra in the Austen spoof 'Plots and Proposals'.

Such was Victoria's status that she could dream of approaching almost anyone. 'We are on full actor alert on Monday, Alana Rickman and Ricardo E Grant,' she wrote before shooting 'Plots and Proposals' at Squerryes Court, a stately home in Kent.²³ They were joined by Imelda Staunton, whom Victoria had befriended in Kenya at the turn of the millennium. Victoria didn't quite reel in everyone she wanted. Early cast lists had Michael Gambon as Scrooge. Judi Dench had to pull out. The withdrawals were often caused by the logistical headache of assembling so many busy stars when budgetary constraints called for constant changes of date and location. When Frances de la Tour was suddenly unavailable, Victoria reluctantly cast herself as a Regency sexpot. As Geoff Posner once had, Jemma Rodgers was forever persuading Victoria to be in more sketches. 'It's all very well to give the best parts to the Dames and Sirs,' she told her, 'but people want to see you.' Popular celebrities made up the numbers. A mobcapped Delia Smith bangs on about recipes, while Alan Titchmarsh plays a mutton-chopped gardener.

This gathering needed an unflappable director. Jemma Rodgers suggested John Birkin, who had experience wrangling stars on *French and Saunders* and was highly organised, insisting on plotting out scenes with storyboards. 'Working with a new director is very jolly,' Victoria enthused.²⁴

Her biggest coup – and placed as a statement at the top of the show – was to lure 007 onto the London Eye. Victoria cast herself as a silent temptress, all arched eyebrows and sultry moues under a white fur hat. As she headed for her assignation in the pod, a tall figure lowered his copy of the *Beano* to reveal the face of Roger Moore. 'We want it to look glamorous and sophisticated (that's your job, I'm not much help there),' she told him beforehand.[25] Moore donned a smart overcoat and black leather gloves to send himself up as an ageing Lothario. 'Do you like Roger the Dodger,' he purrs, 'or do you prefer Minnie the Minx?' The camera cut to the skyline as the two prepare to get down to business. 'Can I just warn you, Roger?' says a hitherto silent Victoria in flat northern vowels, 'I've got really complicated pants on.' She enjoyed her half-dozen revolutions in the pod with a former Bond more than she had anticipated. 'He was so lovely, and he knew his words, which I didn't expect. And he was staring down out of the window and there was a pod below us of children, and he said, "If I wasn't in UNICEF I would flash those children." It made me laugh.'[26]

The original idea was that Victoria would be a Russian assassin seducing her way through 007s. Pierce Brosnan was approached: 'I wondered if you fancied making any sort of a brief guest appearance. (I nearly typed "gusset" then, which wasn't the sort of appearance I had in mind at all.) I've written a Bond sketch, which I don't imagine for a moment you would be allowed to be in . . .'[27] His swift agreement came through while they were filming 'Plots and Proposals' – he even asked if he and Victoria would smooch. 'Whoo hoo is what I have to say,' she replied. 'Your fax has caused untold excitement here, everyone has rushed out to buy vitamin B and new bras, even John the director.'[28] There was talk of flying to Los Angeles to film his bit. All she could tell him was that their scene would be set 'probably in a hotel room' and that the money 'is weeny, so small I don't have a key on the computer to type it with'.[29] In the end her original hunch proved correct. Brosnan's agent intervened to adjudge that the serving Bond could not be seen to mock the franchise.

As usual, Victoria wrote more than would fit into the fifty minutes on offer. But where she and Geoff Posner used to ditch the sketches that earned the fewest laughs, with no studio audience she now had to choose before filming. The choice was based partly on her desire for the show to look cinematic. So the contemporary TV parodies, which tended to look cheaper, were culled, among them some of the sharpest and wittiest material Victoria ever discarded. 'Where the North Is', a spoof of heart-warming northern medical dramas like *Peak Practice*, would have starred Victoria as Winnie Bago, a much-loved district nurse who turns out to have no empathy. 'A Bit of Spam', written for Michael Gambon, had a laugh at the expense of maverick TV detectives who live miserably alone – Derek Spam's quirk is that he is an extremely messy eater. There was no room for 'Delia's Back to Basics', featuring advice on how to heat up cheap baked beans and eat them from the tin while gawping out of the window. Bob Monkhouse was to have presented a mock ad for coffins: 'Hi! I'm Bob Monkhouse and I'm ordering my coffin now, while I'm still alive.' The most impractical script was a potted history of British women in the twentieth century: 'And now, a new fifty-two part drama – Bella Taylor Cookson's – *The House of Lolly Goggins*.' On length alone, it was the easiest to drop – thwarting Victoria's plan to cast Daryl Hannah as Farrah Fawcett Majors. At the last minute a ninety-second song-and-dance number based on *The Sound of Music* which attacked politically correct casting was painfully axed to save £20,000. 'With hindsight not the right decision,' Victoria concluded.[30]

It was only in the weeks before filming began that a postmodern framing device emerged. Victoria would arrive to rehearse her Christmas special in a community hall, to discover she was being filmed for a new digital channel called BBC Backstage. The idea rose out of the recent proliferation of branded channels. She imagined a slew of digital channels called things like BBC Knitwear, BBC Upmarket, BBC Wartime, BBC Good Old Days and BBC Braindead. In the community hall the head of digital, played by Hugh Laurie, introduces himself as John Malkovich ('no relation'). *Being John Malkovich* having just opened, this was Victoria's joke about the interchangeability of faceless managers in suits. And because *Big Brother* aired for the first time over the summer, cameras lurk behind a mirror in the ladies. Nichola Holt, one of the show's first contestants, is seen peering into it.

There was another source of her rage against the corporation. In June, just as she started writing, Peter Salmon faced criticism from the board of governors and the media, prompting Victoria to write bluntly to Greg Dyke, the new director general: 'In seventeen years of working for the BBC [Peter Salmon] is the only executive who has ever bothered to make personal contact with me, to take an interest in what I was doing and how I felt about it . . . I don't have to stay if I don't feel appreciated. (And God knows appreciation has been very thin on the ground) . . . I think it's worth saying that my loyalty to Peter has been a huge factor in me attempting to deliver you something special for Christmas night on BBC1.'[31] (She was the only person to write such a letter. 'Greg showed it me,' says Salmon. 'It was very touching.') In a climactic snarl Victoria wrote a scene in which Bob Monkhouse asks for a cup of tea in the rehearsal-room canteen. 'Do you have a BBC loyalty card?' asks John Malkovich, who has been demoted to assistant head of tea-bar purchasing. Monkhouse looks puzzled. 'Has anyone?'

To populate the rehearsal room, there was an eleventh-hour casting offensive. The idea was to evoke the memory of *The Morecambe and Wise Christmas Show*, with its array of surprise guests. In the most overt nod, Angela Rippon aims a high dance kick at a surveillance camera in the ladies' loo. Betty Boothroyd, former Tiller Girl and outgoing speaker of the House of Commons, rubs shoulders with Lou Beale from *EastEnders* and Nora Batty from *Last of the Summer Wine*, *The Royle Family* creators Caroline Aherne and Craig Cash, and 'H' from Steps. Even Victoria couldn't reel in the biggest fish of all. She asked Paul McCartney to be a 'glimpse' in the special, but he politely said no. 'I know what you mean about not wanting to be on television too much,' she replied, 'in fact I'm thinking of not being in it myself.'[32]

The show came together in November. It was 'like doing five different films in a week,' she reported, 'good fun, but the pressure is on to deliver the minutage, with no chance of picking up the next day.'[33] To match the look of so many different film styles, the originals were meticulously studied for reference. Victoria's make-up designer Chrissie Baker was joined by production designer Grenville Horner and costume designer Yves Barre, who had both worked on *The League of Gentlemen*, and cinematographer Alastair Meux, who John Birkin knew from shooting commercials. Together they became experts in black and white cinema, studying *Brief Encounter* and *A*

*Christmas Carol* for hours, and had several long meetings going over storyboards.

The footage shot in the community hall also called for precision. 'This fly on the wall stuff has to be so carefully plotted to look on the hoof and still catch all the dialogue,' Victoria told Jane Wymark.[34] The old guard, including several familiars from *dinnerladies*, were used to her exacting standards. Some guests weren't. In 'Brief Encounter' Michael Parkinson – another link to Morecambe and Wise – was cast as Joe Buggersthorpe, a saucy railwayman inspired by Stanley Holloway. He told his co-stars that there was no need to run the lines as he knew them more or less. 'Celia and I went white,' says Richenda Carey, who had spent days learning to mimic the film's sour station barmaid played by Joyce Carey. 'We looked at him and said, "Oh, I don't think that's going to do."' Imelda Staunton, to whom Victoria gave exquisitely tailored dialogue as a hysterical Regency matriarch ('Suppose? Suppose? You are very suppository, miss!'), knew instinctively what was needed. 'The most important thing was delivering Vic's lines absolutely to the nth degree. She knew she couldn't tell every actor how to say the lines; she knew that she had that battle with herself. But she was always right. What can you add to what she's written? Not a lot.'

Another old habit of Victoria's was to be painfully shy around her guests, especially if it involved schmoozing over a meal. One night, dinner in the hotel was attended by Alan Rickman, Geraldine McEwan, Pete Postlethwaite, Derek Jacobi, Bill Paterson and Imelda Staunton. Jemma Rodgers begged not to be left to hold the fort: 'I said, "You have to stay till at least the main course is through." She literally finished her plate and off she went to bed.' At the same time Victoria enjoyed using Jemma to play a trick on her co-stars in the make-up truck. 'I'd come while Vic was being done alongside some huge Dame or Sir and ask if she wanted a tea then when the others assumed I was the runner, they asked for tea as well, she'd say, "Can I introduce you to my new producer?" It worked every time.'

The trickiest part of the shoot in the community hall was a sparkly Yuletide anthem, reprising the tune from the 'Brassed Up' sketch. It featured dancers, a children's choir, two sexist northern comics and a singing quartet of Robbins siblings in Christmas woollies – Ted, Kate and two of their sisters. Victoria popped out of a giant Christmas pudding in the guise of Ann Widdecombe singing her own praises:

Ann Widdecombe, Ann Widdecombe,
I'm woman through and through. (This is true.)
Exuberant, protuberant,
I inspire lust with my bust.

In September Victoria wrote to the shadow home secretary to seek her blessing. 'The joke hopefully is in the incongruity of the situation, rather than poking fun at you,' she explained. 'I only thought of it because you have such a wonderful name, and the tune I was working on had a four note phrase to which, try as I might, I could only put the words, "Ann Widdecombe" . . . I won't do it you would prefer I didn't.'[35] Mo Mowlam, she added, 'doesn't scan'. In early November Jemma Rodgers wrote to the MP even suggesting she do a walk-on part at the end. Instead Victoria closes the piano lid. 'What d'you think?' she says. 'Dunno,' shrugs the youthful new head of BBC, Maxine Peake. 'Don't really watch telly at Christmas.'

Once edited together the show was screened to an audience in the BBC radio theatre whose laughter was recorded and added in. Finally, a title was needed. Throughout production there was no name for the show beyond 'Victoria Wood Christmas Special'. It was only in early December that it became *Victoria Wood with All the Trimmings*. On Christmas evening her unsurpassable blend of savage satire, loving parody and celebrity cavalcade was shown to the nation. Julie Walters spoke for an audience of more than eight million when, before Victoria went to bed that night, she sent a fax. 'Brilliant! Brilliant! And I say again – Brilliant!'[36] Victoria, who watched it with the family plus Geoffrey's brother and sister-in-law, wasn't so sure. 'When I saw it myself on the night,' she told Peter Salmon, 'I thought then it could have been packaged up better and been a bit friendlier, but it's awfully hard to tell what's best when you're in the middle of it.'[37] She had anxiety dreams about the viewing figures and, up at Mole Barn after Christmas, 'couldn't shake off that feeling that I had somehow let the

BBC down by not denting Coro's figures'.[38] Phil McIntyre drove over for tea and assured her 'you can't beat the Street etc, and I felt a bit better'.[39] Such was her state of worry that she broke her self-imposed embargo to read a positive review and a gossip-column item suggesting Ann Widdecombe had enjoyed it.

Early in 2001 the BBC were soon in touch to point out that the production had gone over budget. Though a demoralising coda, it didn't dampen Victoria's desire to get straight back into bed with them. There was some talk of 'another dose of Trimmings on Xmas Day', which thanks to all the unfilmed scripts was already half-written.[40] She duly met the new BBC One controller Lorraine Heggessey – 'she seemed a very nice woman and it was a mile away from being patronised by men in suits' – but didn't leap at her suggestion of two half-hours in lieu of a special.[41] Instead a proposal came in to front a history of sketch comedy. Victoria decided to say yes because, she explained, 'I get fed up with people presenting programmes on subjects they know nothing about. I think I know about sketches.'[42] There was a pattern here. A year earlier she fronted a documentary about a sitcom soon after finishing her own. Now she was to repeat the process with sketch comedy. It was as if she itched to explain herself after the event.

To stamp her signature on the programme, Victoria could not resist writing more sketches, to be directed by John Birkin. One was a canny meta-sketch in which she dressed up as a working-class housewife from yesteryear who answers the door to a middle-class couple, played by Celia Imrie and Duncan Preston, asking her to perform an old-school sketch with them. 'I don't do subtleties, nuances of character or anything intellectual,' Victoria says. 'Or spam.' 'Any Proust gags?' asks Celia. 'Ooh no, you want Mrs Monty Python for that, at 33 Smartarse University Humour Avenue for Proust.' Her other sketch was inspired by the recent return of *Crossroads*, which she disembowelled all over again with another episode of *Acorn Antiques*. In this version the soap is more of a calamity than ever – every cue missed, most lines forgotten, actors nakedly angry, non-actors flagrantly in shot. And the plot is more extreme. Mrs Overall dispenses tequila and crack and is shot by a burglar. As she lies on the floor an irate Bo Beaumont hollers, 'I'm sorry! Am I acting with anybody at all? It wasn't my idea to come back. Sir Peter Trevor [is] all panting for a glimpse of my Gertrude.'

In her introduction Victoria argued that one of the joys of the sketch is that it's not stand-up: 'You're not standing there by yourself, running the risk of alcoholism, loneliness, depression and varicose veins.' Notwithstanding, after four years away, in 2001 she was to go back on tour. She spent much of January at the gym 'trying to get myself fit after the filming and Christmas,' she told Amie Beamish, 'but I'll start writing it soon.'[43] They met up a few days later in Birmingham, where Victoria got back in the swing with a cabaret booking. Another cabaret was booked for Harrogate in March.

As the date approached, Victoria could no longer ignore mounting pain and tiredness, which impaired a half-term trip to Florida, not helped by Brits in waterparks forever saying 'hello, Bren'. She started to feel ill on the plane home but 'thought I had just picked up a virus in Mickey Mouse land (foot and mouse disease)'.[44] On a visit to Phil McIntyre's office he summoned his doctor who diagnosed a chest infection and suggested she have a scan on a lump in her stomach. Two days later she struggled down to Geoffrey's office in Kentish Town. 'There was an insistent knock on the front door. She was bent double and said, "You've got to take me to hospital – I can't walk, I can't move."' They hurried to their GP, who sent her in an ambulance to the Whittington Hospital, where she was given a scan. 'I had this huge fibroid,' she explained, 'but I didn't notice it because I just thought I'd got bigger, because I've got such an odd body image because of having an eating disorder.'[45] She had never been in hospital before other than to give birth and, once the pain-killer had done its work, her comic instinct asserted itself: 'When I was sitting waiting for a scan next to a woman who had come from Holloway prison, between two policemen, I thought this is quite funny.'[46] Advised to stay in overnight, she was put on a drip, which she accidentally wrenched out while tidying her cubicle. She asked for it to be reinserted – 'but they never connected it to anything, so for the next 24 hours I had the thing that hurt but not the thing that was supposed to help. I thought, this is really mad.'[47] Without asking for one she was given a private room, but she soon panicked that on an NHS ward she remained a sitting duck for the press. Geoffrey contacted Marcus Setchell, who had delivered Henry, and she was soon moved to the Portland, where she had an emergency hysterectomy. After five nights she went home to continue her convalescence, while Victoria's publicist Neil Reading issued a short statement, triggering an avalanche of get-well-soon cards. 'Don't forget to be kind to yourself,' wrote Julie Walters before leaving for the Academy Awards – she was nominated for her performance in *Billy Elliot*.[48]

Recovery was supposed to take six weeks – her doctor addressed a letter to her insurers to that effect. Victoria gave herself three. By mid-March she was 'feeling much better, possibly because I have been reading Endurance, about Shackleton's doomed trip around Antarctica . . . Made me feel the odd operation was neither here nor there.'[49] A week later when her management arrived to discuss rearranging her tour, the meeting was 'v jolly in that they had expected me to be bent double in a nightie, they were pleasantly relieved to see me quite nimble and clothed and compos'.[50] Most of the original dates were cancelled and others were moved to July and early September, when Victoria had hoped to take the children on another adventure Down Under. That tour was regretfully sacrificed.

By early April Victoria was trying to write stand-up, though not always succeeding. She distracted herself by clearing green algae from her roof terrace and garden: 'Every day when I was writing the show I'd think, 'Just do a bit more and then you can get out the water blaster.''[51] She happily ducked out of the BAFTAs when *All the Trimmings* was nominated, encouraging Jemma Rodgers and John Birkin to accept the award if the show won (which it didn't). Rehearsals for the new show were attended by Betty Jackson, who clothed Victoria more stylishly than ever with knee-length coats in navy gabardine and red leather. 'They have three sets of measurements for me,' she told Richenda Carey, 'a less bosomy set from when I was doing the allnight dinnerladies run, the fibroid set when I was bigger round the middle, and my usuals.'[52] She hired a new tour manager – Emma Cope had just finished touring with the League of Gentlemen. Her first warm-up, postponed from April to May, was a charity performance at the Stables in Buckinghamshire. More practice gigs followed within striking distance of London, and fresh material was dropped in piece by piece which she wrote on the fly between costume shopping, song-writing and Henry's trumpet exam. One day she drove to Ealing for a wig fitting and saw a huge poster of herself: 'I thought oh give us a break, I've not even collected the bloody wig yet.'[53] The image, shot back in February, was a straight close-up at her behest – 'I am tired of standing up trying to look like a comedian,' she reasoned. 'If people don't know by now what I do then let's just forget the whole thing, I will just run tombolas.'[54]

For the summer half term, Victoria was looking forward to a family holiday in Barbados, despite the knowledge that her mother was close to death. Helen Wood had long since elected to stay in bed after a couple of falls and spent her last years devouring hundreds of books – in Victoria's phrase, she avoided 'books that had the temerity to be written post 1867'.[55] Towards the end she had a form of dementia which caused her spiky personality to soften. She tried to remember poems she'd learned as a child and even read hymns, though she rejected Rosalind's suggestion that she see a priest. 'I just like the words,' she replied. 'I don't believe there's an afterlife.' She duly died at the age of eighty-one on the last Sunday in May. Victoria had a show in Wellingborough that night and was due to fly on the Monday. According to Rosalind, she was reluctant to deny the children their holiday, though, in a fax dashed off by hand, she told Richenda Carey that she travelled with her sisters' blessing. 'Sisters say go on holiday – so I am – show went well . . . she died in her bed at least and peacefully.'[56]

The day after returning home, Victoria flew to Leeds Bradford Airport to make it to the funeral at the crematorium in Skipton. Her brother Chris, who had barely seen his mother for forty years, was invited by his sisters to read out an article of hers for the Costume Society magazine. The songs recorded by Stanley and Helen were played. There was a surprise deputation from the Mape family, none of whom the Wood sisters had ever met. 'The funeral went very well,' Victoria reported. 'We ignored my mother's request to have no one but family at funeral.'[57] Privately she confided to Geoffrey, who was unable to attend, that 'she felt slightly guilty and embarrassed about how little she felt emotionally about her mother's death', while she conceded to Rosalind that she wished she'd been there to help organise the funeral. Helen's death sparked a conversation between Rosalind and her younger sister that would continue for years: 'I felt that Vic was too hard on our mother and tried to suggest that her behaviour was because of her own harsh upbringing in a big family. She was probably a bit neglected herself. While Vic did soften, she still felt strongly that Mother loved having babies but didn't like children very much.'

Helen may not have believed in an afterlife, but she was granted one anyway when Victoria paid instant tribute to her by writing her into her set as an eccentric and stoical figure:

> She said you should put up with everything, which is a very north-ern thing, it's a very Lancashire thing. And that's how she was brought up, to put up with everything. Because she was brought up in the 1920s, very poor, little tiny house in Moss Side. She said to me one year they were so poor they didn't have a coat. None of them had coats. She didn't have shoes. None of them had shoes. She didn't have sense of humour. That was just her.

She called the show *Victoria Wood At It Again*. The title came from *Sunny Side Up*, the radio sitcom she wrote in 1977. ('I had a marvel-lous catchphrase,' says an ex-ventriloquist. 'He's at it again.') Anyone reading the tour programme beforehand might have sensed that Vic-toria was preparing to be autobiographical. There were no joke ads or fake articles, just the transcript of an illuminating conversation with Richard E. Grant, an ardent fan who knew much of *As Seen on TV* by heart. They occasionally met for lunch at the Crypt café under St Martin-in-the-Fields in Trafalgar Square, where he would quote her lines at her or imitate her signature gesture of pushing up her sleeves. 'She asked me to officially interview her,' he says, 'having pre-viously shared and compared our oddball childhoods, the common denominator of which was a profound sense of loneliness within our

families. Being an outsider, looking in, was something we unexpectedly shared.' She thanked him by baking a sugar-free fruitcake and
sending it in the post.

The through-line of Victoria's career in stand-up demanded that
she draw on her recent medical history. 'I've been asked to take over
in the Vagina Monologues,' she wrote in an early draft. 'I don't know
if I've got enough material.' She had barely walked onstage before she
was mentioning her menopause and, for the first time in public, her
eating disorder. 'The madness of women is what a lot of it's about,'
she explained several weeks into the tour. 'It's nice to say, "Yes, we are
barmy and poor old men have to live with us."'[58] She moved on to
describe the discovery of her lump and the array of indignities visited
on her once she was in hospital – suppositories, undressing in front of
others, internal inspections. Her surgeon recommended a bikini-line
incision. 'Do you wear a bikini?' 'Oh, come on,' she replied. The line
was greeted by a rush of knowing laughter – by now Victoria's audience were almost as familiar with her body, and her ongoing issues
with it, as she was. They were less prepared for a frank description of
her pubic arrangements. The lights came down on the first half before
she could go the whole hog and bare her scar.

It was not exactly her own hysterectomy Victoria was describing,
and yet it wasn't not hers. 'I've never let it get so near to my own
experience before,' she said. 'This is very based on what actually happened to me. I wasn't scared to do it any more. I wasn't trying to hide
behind something. I've got nothing to prove, and I wanted to grant
myself the freedom to talk about what I wanted to talk about. It's not
a confessional, and it's not therapy; it is just jokes, but it is very rooted
in what I've just been doing.'[59] Gone, as a result, were the capering
yarns featuring made-up friends, and gags about royalty, although
some regular riffs survived. Her convalescence gave her a way in to
describe the latest developments in terrible daytime television. There
was some recycling from *All the Trimmings* – namechecks for *ER* and
Ann Widdecombe (other targets included Vanessa Feltz, Oprah Win-
frey, Charlie Dimmock, Elaine Paige and, one final time, Pam Ayres).

The big change was the absence of a grand piano – 'a total anachron-
ism,' Victoria had decided.[60] She finally achieved her long-cherished

ambition not to pepper the show with songs. This meant she was less reliant on Geoffrey's help. 'She thought my skill had been getting her on and off,' he explains, 'getting her to the piano and back. She was sick of it and wanted a change.' He did end up being her outside eye in the early performances, and nor could she do without songs altogether. Stacey Leanne Paige, unabashed in her vulgarity, tottered onstage at either end of the second half to love-bomb the audience with unfiltered Lancashire patter about shopping and shagging. The last of Victoria's straight-talking northern grotesques, she sang a couple of songs, for which Victoria decided to hire an accompanist. She found Nick Skilbeck through the Royal Academy of Music and chose to make a feature of him. Entering for her encore, Stacey Leanne and her pianist hurried on adjusting their clothes, as if just interrupted backstage. In a final burst of energy, Victoria staggered back on in a puce wig and gym gear to close out the show with another of her clowning exercise routines given by flame-haired Pat, trainee instructor at Body Conscious Fitness Facility. Nick Skilbeck wrote the plinky music to go with it.

Victoria had often struggled with the loneliness of solo touring, so it was a novel sensation to have another performer join her. As the tour continued, he took on a secondary role offstage. 'We'd arrive at the theatre at four,' he says, 'and we'd find a piano somewhere and we would play duets. It was great fun. She had a lot of the music. Then during the tour we would try and fish out other stuff from music shops. "The Arrival of the Queen of Sheba" was one of our party pieces.'

She found a second companion in the stage designer Lez Brotherston. Another *As Seen on TV* aficionado, he first met Victoria as a guest of Anne Reid at a *dinnerladies* recording and was invited to an early try-out to discuss designing a simple, colourful set for the tour, having recently done something similar for *French and Saunders*. He quickly became a sympathetic companion on shopping expeditions. Victoria always found talking to assistants excruciating, so he did it for her. On one trip they were in a Bond Street boutique looking for something to go under her Betty Jackson coats: 'She said, "They won't have anything to fit me." I went in and said, "Do you have this in a large?" The girl was quite sniffy and said, "Of course we wouldn't have." My instant reaction was, "Don't be so rude. It's a yes-or-no question." Vic was utterly gobsmacked. She would have run out of the shop mortified.'

Victoria embarked on the tour thinking it would be her last, and jotted her initial feelings in a notepad: 'I don't want to stop being a comedian – it makes me very happy – and occasionally I do suffer from depression – it's par for the course with comedians – it could've been worse – could've been golf.'

Underlying this train of thought was a fear of becoming irrelevant. 'I don't want to get totally out of date,' she said just as she set off on tour. 'Which you just wouldn't know. That's the sad thing. I'd be going on doing jokes about Sanatogen. I don't want to be like that. I want to leave when I want to leave.'[61] She reassured her disappointed audience she wouldn't retire till they'd gone home. But there was another disincentive to carry on. 'Obviously the richest vein of comedy is living with children,' she said, 'and I can't use it. Grace has said, "I don't want you to talk about me."'[62] Grace was now twelve and, she says, 'well old enough to pay attention. There were jokes about "my kids" that felt a bit hard to listen to. I'd asked her something like, "Did you mean that? Was that really about us?" and she would say, "No, of course it wasn't. It was a joke; it wasn't real," and I think I wasn't totally sure where that line was, so I probably drew one of my own. It wasn't about us, but I think twelve-year-old me was more sensitive and worried.' Henry, only just nine, found it easier to make the distinction. 'I knew it wasn't connected,' he says. 'I knew it was a joke.' 'I could do a whole act about Henry,' his mother said, 'and he wouldn't mind a bit.'[63]

Mainly the show was a portrait of a middle-aged marriage. Geoffrey, or a fictionalised 'Geoffrey', cropped up again and again – his *Countdown* jackets, his vasectomy ('Didn't tell me, the bloody liar! Said he was going to the garden centre'). She even imagined the psychological impact of her hysterectomy on his libido: 'Does your husband's penis panic and say, "Go back! It's too big, too big, it's too big!"?'

In her initial notes Victoria went further than she would onstage: 'We were both really busy, so I didn't really see him and then I got very depressed – and I decided it was his fault. I had read one of those books – Men Are from Mars and Women Are Bloody Marvellous.' She described visiting a therapist to 'have a good moan once a week – my husband does this, my husband does that'. Victoria had not actually seen a therapist in several years, but this fictional therapist suggests a trial separation:

> I can't – because it would be in the papers – and I'd have to be photographed coming out of the house like this – (grin) – or to stop it being in the papers I'd have to do an exclusive deal with Hello magazine – northern comedian bravely faces life of solitude and discusses plans for back garden, and I can't be separated in Hello because I haven't got enough rooms in house or enough outfits.

None of this made it into the show. Instead it closed with Victoria's description of their attempts to restore romance to the bedroom, thwarted by physical ailments – his hernia, her bunion and bad back, his dismal eyesight, her incontinence. She wrote it at the end of the first week of the tour – 'it virtually wrote itself,' she said.[64] 'I knew it wasn't about me,' says Geoffrey. 'And it never really occurred to her that her audiences would think it was me.'

Victoria travelled up and down England throughout July. In Manchester there was an alarming incident at the Palace when a cage on one of the lamps in the lighting rig broke and a glass bulb skimmed her body as it fell. After that the entourage gained a pair of lighting men, increasing to six the party who, at Victoria's insistence, convened in the hotel afterwards for sandwiches and drinks. In August the Wood family gathered again for the wedding of Rosalind's son Mazda. In September, as Victoria prepared for five nights in Nottingham, terrorists flew two planes into the World Trade Center. 'I feel weighted down by it,' she told Richenda Carey two days later. 'I'm trying to put it out of my mind some of the time otherwise I couldn't do the show which is after all what people have paid to see.'[65] It was at one of these cathartic dates that Nick Skilbeck discovered how it felt to be alone onstage with Victoria and on the receiving end of her public's tumultuous love and gratitude. 'The audience as one rose and cheered,' he says, 'and she had to take a few steps backwards because it was just such a wave. The most instant, unanimous standing ovation was like a force of energy coming at you. She turned round to me and went "Whoa!".' When they came offstage they were both tearful.

Six days after 9/11 Victoria was back the Royal Albert Hall. She was given another tour of the building, clambered onto the roof and wrote in the venue's guestbook: 'This will be the nearest I ever get to working with Vladimir Ashkenazy. Back for the 3rd (and last?) time.'[66] One of her many guests was her surgeon Marcus Setchell, who wrote to applaud her gynaecological frankness: 'Your de-mystifying of the whole operation etc does a great deal of service for other women'.[67] Some of these women made themselves known to Victoria afterwards when she went down to sign merchandise. 'I've had at least one hysterectomy a night coming to me at the stage door, offer to show me her scars,' she said mid-run. 'And they all say, "You've made us feel really good because you're on stage jumping about and looking fit."'[68]

During the Albert Hall run she appeared on *Parkinson* alongside Ann Widdecombe. Always meticulously prepared for such appearances, she was expecting to be asked about *The Sketch Show Story*, shortly to be broadcast, but thanks to crossed wires Michael Parkinson focused on her live show. Caught on the hop, she found herself awkwardly trailing snippets from her act – 'I was saying in my show . . . I was doing this thing in my show' – and was annoyed in hospitality afterwards. Already going through another of her cooler phases with the BBC, she had no qualms about offering the option on her live show to ITV, whose controller of comedy Sioned Wiliam she met over a cup of tea and liked. Her performance was captured over two nights by John Birkin.

After fourteen shows at the Albert Hall, Victoria permitted herself a drink or two at a small celebration. While the set was being dismantled, she joined Phil McIntyre staffers and some younger guests as they raced on office chairs around the corridor encircling the basement of the auditorium. Even as they shrieked hysterically, Victoria's competitive instinct asserted itself. 'I think that might be the happiest I've ever seen her,' says Paul Roberts. 'We took it really

seriously. We let her win. First rule of promoting: the act always wins.'
After the tour ended, there were charity performances for old friends:
one at the Old Laundry Theatre in Bowness run by the Glossops,
then in Harrogate for Jessie's Fund, founded by her old school friend
Lesley Schatzberger, to help children in hospices express themselves
through music. It was named after Lesley's daughter, who had died of
an inoperable brain tumour, and for two years Victoria had been its
patron. The performance, along with a Lifeline appeal by Victoria on
BBC One, raised £40,000.

While she joked about a fictional marriage onstage, Victoria tipped
off friends about fissures in her real marriage. To Richenda Carey she
mentioned 'frostinesses which don't go on for long but while they do
it's Ugly Mouths all over the shop'.[69] She admitted to feeling 'very
tired, and these last few weeks of me being away have put a strain
on the old marriage . . . complicated . . . I just need to catch up with
myself (photos still not in albums, that will tell you the measure of
my exhaustion) and sit with myself.'[70] It was a frequent topic in her
nightly conversations on tour with Nick Skilbeck: 'She was sad about
it. She spoke a fair bit about it. I felt she was really trying to figure
out what to do to make it work. I think that's why the duets were
useful – it was just a great distraction.'

To some extent Victoria and Geoffrey had had the idea of a successful marriage projected onto them. 'We didn't find it particularly easy,'
he says, 'that the press had canonised us as a golden couple for whom
everything was marvellous. We never denied it, because that would
have been foolish, but we certainly didn't present ourselves as that.
On both sides there was some unthinking cruelty.' Victoria hinted as
much when Duncan Preston's marriage ended in 1990. 'How Geoff
and I have never murdered each other over the last 14 years I don't
know,' she wrote to him. 'Apathy probably.'[71] In the 1990s she and
Geoffrey twice attempted marital counselling. They lasted longer the
second time, until the counsellor started saying to Victoria, 'Now
*you'll* understand this.' 'We've got to stop this,' she told Geoffrey after
one session. 'She thinks I'm the woman off the telly.' At the root of
their difficulties was work and the absences it imposed. The two-year

ordeal of *dinnerladies* placed immense strain on Victoria and those around her. Other than relishing the adrenalin surge of audience laughter, she admitted at the start of the tour to being 'puritanical about almost everything else – working and getting up and filling every minute, always on at my children. I'm very hard to live with.'[72] Over the years the subject of a trial separation, hinted at in Victoria's draft script, had certainly come up. The squalls increased in frequency, and it became more difficult to recover from them. There was talk of Geoffrey moving round the corner in order to protect the children from domestic tempests but, whenever the subject came up, such a solution felt too radical. 'I know from personal experience that marriages are hugely elastic, flexible changeable things, they can survive a huge amount if the will is there,' she told Richenda Carey when recovering from her operation earlier in the year. 'We have left off taking the final drastic step because of the children, and that has given us enough valuable breathing space to re trench, re group, have a bloody rest from all the aggro, and have another bash.'[73]

In November Victoria was full of optimism as she decided to resume therapy – 'going to the Bonkers man', as she called it, where she was able to work through marital tensions. Her new therapist was recommended by a friend in show business with similar issues. 'Some,' she said, 'are very deep rooted, and some are of the sort any couple would have when one person is overstretched and feels resentful and unsupported (and I have to say Geoff feels overstretched and unsupported as well, which he is . . .).'[74] The process was helpful to her in normalising her agony. 'I found it very comforting to talk to a therapist who had talked to lots and lots of people,' she later said.[75]

Over Christmas there was a climactic crisis. They had one of their stormiest rows yet at the culmination of which Victoria and Geoffrey found such a void opening up between them that, to at least one of them, only one solution seemed feasible. Geoffrey announced that he would move out of the house and find somewhere to live nearby. In the new year, at the suggestion of her therapist, they tried marital counselling again and stuck with it for several months. 'Things have been extremely difficult here,' Victoria told Jane Wymark in January, alluding to 'a backlog of ancient deepseated problems with a top-dressing of overwork, operations – lots of things – but anyway – it has all been v painful though it is a bit calmer now.'[76] In order to protect the children from disruption, they agreed to buy a flat locally and found one in the mansion block where, in the 1970s, they used to rent a room off Jane Wynn Owen, only for it to fall through. Geoffrey moved out of the marital bed and into the spare room, but some routines remained intact. When Victoria needed an eye cast over the rushes of her stage show, as ever she trusted his judgement, while he in turn asked her to write a joke for his magic show. She gave nothing away in a Radio 4 interview with BBC head of entertainment Paul Jackson recorded before an audience in Manchester at the end of January. She even told a story about how, straight after her hysterectomy, she moved a piece of furniture that had defeated Geoffrey: 'I thought, I bet I can bloody get it through the door . . . I'd only just come out of hospital and I thought, he's going to be so mad when he sees it's gone through, I had to push it back. He doesn't know that. He's going to go mad now.'[77]

A few days later the tour resumed in Newcastle, from where Victoria wrote to Jane Wymark: 'It was never a perfect marriage. But there was always a Huge Bond, however dysfunctional.'[78] She was hopeful that Geoffrey might come to see her as 'just a barmy middle-aged over-achiever who's willing to have a go at changing, then maybe we can re-structure the whole thing and move on together'.[79] Later that month, as she was about to drive off to Margate, Victoria found herself 'veering madly between self blame "If only I'd had therapy earlier, been nicer . . . blah blah" and self justification "but he never did this, that . . .", all so pointless'.[80] Citing the problems caused by 'mutual busyness, unintentional neglect, years old stuff about the children, whatever . . .', she was more inclined to try again than Geoffrey, while very understanding of his writhing agonies. 'Of course he is terribly miserable as well, but feels he has no choice,' she added, then confessed that she herself felt 'pretty shredded, and am just hoping the old Great Healer does its job, and sometimes I can count my blessings which are many, we are certainly buffered (why did I just type buggered . . .) in all this by dosh, jobs, no extra marital hanky panky'.[81] When Geoffrey voiced his fear of being alone for ever, she predicted he'd soon meet a Quaker. She took up this theme with her therapist, imagining Geoffrey with 'some peaceful but fun loving Quaker with whom he finds the true love previously denied him by angry pants Woody'.[82]

As the tour took her round Britain, she found no difficulty in continuing to talk about her marriage – or her scripted version of it – on stage. 'She made up a marriage and talked about it,' says Geoffrey. 'The fact that her marriage was in desperate trouble didn't affect the jokes she was telling about a marriage. They really were separate. She could do it because it was a *show*.' Her misery was evident to Julie Walters, who, in March, caught the show in Brighton. 'Vic didn't really talk too much about feelings,' she says, 'but I could see that things were really not good. There was a feeling of bemusement and sadness. She was clearly devastated by it. She seemed reduced when we sat down after. She seemed in some ways a lot softer and more vulnerable.'

Victoria pasted photographs of the tour into an album – the children backstage in Edinburgh, Nick Skilbeck paddling in the sea at Bournemouth, her in a vast empty auditorium in Cardiff. The very last performance was a Sunday night in mid-April which brought Victoria back to the Albert Hall to do a benefit, yet again, in aid of the King's Head Theatre, of which she was now life president. 'When I stood on the stage of the Albert Hall for the last time,' she said, 'I had a good look round and thought, that's it. I just said to myself, I don't think I'll be doing this again.'[83]

Back at home there was only confusion. 'I have no idea what's going to happen,' she told Jane Wymark. 'I realised that none of my brilliant disaster avoidance techniques were working.'[84] In their final session of marital therapy she and Geoffrey agreed to part, but there was still no certainty if or when he would leave. 'I am not counting on anything,' Victoria told Jane. 'Over the months I have had to develop a sense of self-preservation.' She rehearsed the now familiar themes of overworking and operations while stressing that the marriage had had its good parts – 'there have been tons of those, there really have'.[85] They made an offer on another flat a short walk away which was eventually accepted.

One weekend in June Victoria flew to Manchester and took a taxi to the Lake District to join her sisters at a hotel in Grasmere. She paid for three rooms, with a suite for herself so they had somewhere private to talk. Penelope collected Helen's ashes from Skipton and had Stanley's couriered from Bury and then transported the two urns in the boot of her van. A footpath led west from the hotel up onto the Langdale Pikes, where their parents had fond memories of camping as young courting communists. Victoria carried her father's ashes in a rucksack; Penelope took Helen's. 'There was a lot of gallows humour,' says Rosalind. 'Vic sped ahead, leaving us behind. She was annoyed that we were so slow, but she was at peak fitness. When we reached the top of the hill we lit some candles and incense and threw the ashes into the air. The wind immediately blew them back in our faces, which caused much hilarity all round.' They took a picture of the three of them grinning broadly in cagoules.

One day in July Victoria and Geoffrey joined the children in their basement playroom and broke the news that he was to move out of the spare bedroom and around the corner, but that as parents they would play as equal a part as possible. 'I don't think I saw it coming particularly,' says Grace. 'I was aware of problems. It was short-fuse type stuff, being impatient with each other, losing their temper with each other. I was not aware of any kind of escalation and to an extent that was present when I was a little child as well. They were quite calm. I think they handled it really well. Despite not having anticipated it I also wasn't wholly surprised.' Henry by contrast 'was pretty unaware. I never had a conscious thought about it at all. I think we both cried. It was a sad atmosphere. Dad was just going to move down the road and they'd already figured that out, which is very them.'

Victoria took Grace and Henry to stay with the Glossops, who had a place in Villars-sur-Ollon in the Swiss Alps. While they were away, Geoffrey vacated the spare room in Highgate and moved out. The only witness was Victoria's assistant Cathy Edis. 'I can't believe I'm doing this,' he confided to her as his relationship with Victoria came to an end after twenty-six years. Victoria started to spread the news among friends, who wrote kind, commiserating letters back. At some point the rest of the world had to be informed too. In August the newspapers were full of the murder in Soham of two ten-year-old girls, and Geoffrey worried that their news would be fallen on as light relief, so they waited. In late October the tabloids were feasting on the private antics of Angus Deayton, who duly lost his job as the host of *Have I Got News for You*. 'I rang Victoria,' says Geoffrey, 'and said, "I think today's the day."' She agreed.' They informed Neil Reading, who issued a press release. 'The separation is entirely amicable,' it advised. 'There are no other parties involved. They have asked for their privacy to be respected.'

The next month *Victoria at the Albert* was released in time for the Christmas market. Whether it was truly a portrait of Victoria's marriage or not, it was the only testimony her fans had to go on. 'I think I said I loved him,' she would say. 'I said that, that I didn't want to be with other people. I mean I absolutely meant it.'[86]

# 20

# ACORNS

**'It's a musical. It isn't about anything.'**
*Acorn Antiques: The Musical!*, 2005

'Dear Victoria Wood. I am a fan.'[1] Victoria received many such letters from devotees. Only one of them ran the National Theatre of Great Britain. Trevor Nunn first made contact in 1996 when about to take over as artistic director at the National. His was a name to revere: Victoria had seen his Royal Shakespeare Company productions as a schoolgirl. Nunn urged her to write a play about England, but *dinnerladies* intervened. Then, in December 2001, they finally met when Victoria went to the South Bank armed with a pitch. 'I was delighted to see you at the National,' he wrote early in 2002 'and even more thrilled that you came to talk about a new musical piece based on the sublime Acorn Antiques characters.'[2]

The idea came to Victoria when she passed a poster for the ABBA musical *Mamma Mia!* 'I wanted to do a musical and I thought on and off, how could it be? How could I do it? And then suddenly, I just thought, *Acorn Antiques*, is that my *Mamma Mia!*? It's my thing. And it's very dear to my heart. I thought it would look so nice on the posters.'[3] Her spoof daytime soap was the one creation of Victoria's that she could never quite lay to rest. Its most recent exhumation, on *The Sketch Show Story*, was broadcast only two months before Victoria met Nunn. During the tour she started mentioning it to her pianist Nick Skilbeck: 'She was quite guarded about it at the beginning. She said she was thinking of doing a musical version of, as she said, "a sketch that I used to do". Then she asked me who she should approach. I said, "Trevor Nunn is probably the best person to speak to."'

Nunn was the world's preeminent director of musical theatre – his long-running productions of *Cats* and *Les Misérables* had broken records in the West End and on Broadway – but Victoria couldn't be sure he was steeped in *Acorn Antiques*: 'He seemed to have seen it. He went, "Ooh, fantastic idea." I know he is very, very charming, but I didn't think that he was completely lying to me.'⁴ At the meeting Victoria floated the names of Julie Walters, Celia Imrie and Duncan Preston, hoping they might wish to take part, though, after her arduous experience of writing and performing in *dinnerladies*, she had no desire to be in it herself. 'I don't want to be onstage at the moment,' she told him, and suggested Imelda Staunton for Miss Berta. Schedule permitting, it was agreed that Nunn might direct it in the Cottesloe, the smallest of the National's three theatres. 'But whoever ends up trying to keep those girls in order,' she wrote, 'I hope we can meet and discuss it all along the way.'⁵

Victoria proposed a deadline for delivery of nine months hence, soon loosened to a year, and managed to negotiate a promotion to the much larger Lyttelton Theatre. But with her spring tour schedule for *At It Again* vastly expanded, she realised she would have in effect only six months to write a full-scale musical. She didn't tell Nunn about the deepening crisis at home. 'Although I could really push and have the whole thing written in time,' she explained in February 2002, 'I feel I shouldn't. I have overloaded myself with work for about the last three years . . . So for once I'm trying to be sensible and not just crash about, pushing myself to the limit, and trying to be with my family at the same time.'⁶ Instead she would work on the musical under her own steam, aware that in doing so she would probably sacrifice the chance of working with Nunn at the National, which he was due to leave in April 2003.

A Victoria Wood musical had occurred to others too. Days after she postponed *Acorn Antiques*, Victoria heard from the Belgrade Theatre in Coventry, which suggested a musical version of *Pat and Margaret* (another new adaptation was about to open at the Salisbury

Playhouse). 'I have cleared the next few months because I really want to have a good think about what to do next,' she replied.[7] In fact, for the rest of 2002 she put all serious work to one side as the marriage breathed its last. She was in no mood to write: 'I didn't feel very funny.'[8] Her main commitment for the autumn was to perform at a fundraiser for the women's health charity Wellbeing of Women. The booking came about when, in the green room after seeing her perform at the Albert Hall a year earlier, her gynaecologist Marcus Setchell joked, 'I ought to have 10 per cent of the takings – there wouldn't have been a first half of the show!' She promptly offered to do something for a charity of his choice. Her set at a Savoy Hotel dinner for 400, featuring much talk of hysterectomies and ending with Pat the trainee fitness instructor, raised over £35,000.

After Geoffrey's departure, the atmosphere in the house tended to be sombre. 'Stating the obvious,' says Grace, 'she was really unhappy that it had happened. She didn't filter that much, she didn't overly protect us, and also I was quite angry about it all in a very normal thirteen-year-old way. We'd talk about it, and occasionally she'd open up as well. I did get a sense aged fifteen and beyond that she wanted me to be her friend and be another adult as well as being her kid.' Henry was ten when the separation came and had a feeling of being insulated from tensions going on over his head but picked up on his mother and father keeping things civil: 'They were both very vigilant about going to every parents' evening. It could be awkward, but also not, depending. There was also a rapport as well. It wasn't buddy-buddy, but it was different shades of polite.' Victoria had no need to protect friends, who now assumed ever greater importance for her, from the true extent of her rawness. 'Vic told me that just before Geoff left,' says Jane Wymark, 'they were standing together in the kitchen and he made a joke about the dire state of their tea towels which made them both laugh out loud. She said she couldn't believe that he was going to go. When he did she was very unhappy, but her focus was on making the situation stable for the children.'

On Tuesdays and Thursdays and every other weekend the children would be with their father. When she was on her own, Victoria booked to see every musical on in London and beyond. Then, while the children were with Geoffrey after Christmas, she made her first ever pilgrimage to New York. Her guide was Catherine Ashmore, her university friend who now did all her production photography: 'Vic wanted to do her meticulous homework and see as much variety of stage musicals as possible. New York was the place. We had great fun and adventures. One clanger of a show made us rush for the exit at the end and run a couple of blocks before we felt free.' Sitting through bad shows was not necessarily a waste of Victoria's time. She bought tickets to an ill-fated *Romeo and Juliet* which blundered into the West End in the autumn of 2002. 'It was just awful,' she said, 'but it was very inspirational in a way. It was instructive the way they'd constructed their lyrics and the pompousness of the music.'[9] As she sat down to compose, it would provide her with opening lines for Miss Babs and Miss Berta:

Two sisters both alike in dignity,
Manchesterford is where we lay our scene.
Their trade was knick-knacks of antiquity,
No squabbles marked their day-to-day routine.

When Trevor Nunn had only weeks left at the National, Victoria went to see him again. 'I still want to do it,' she said. 'Should I do it here?' He advised her to think of doing it as a commercial production. Thus, with no commission from a producer, for much of 2003 Victoria worked on her first musical since *Good Fun* nearly a quarter of a century earlier. Having parodied a soap in which everything goes wrong in a television studio, she decided to explore the ways in which things malfunction in a theatre. What she came up with was an ambitious hybrid. 'It's two musicals in one,' she explained. 'It's a rep musical and then it's a West End musical. There's a musical where it goes wrong and a musical where it goes right.'[10]

In the earliest handwritten draft, three of the original cast have reassembled in Sutton Coldfield to work on a dystopian version of the soap. This is the concept of a pretentious small-time director called John, somewhat based on her old tutor Clive Barker. 'As a clever joke he's called it *Acorn Antiques*,' Victoria explained during the writing process, 'so he can get the middle classes into the building to show them his terrible vision.'[11] His plans are thrown into disarray when Bo Beaumont barges uninvited into the first rehearsal and proposes jollying things up by importing songs and tap from a Fifties musical she was once in called *Café Continental*. Her artistic vision and the director's do battle in a chaotic dress rehearsal attended by members of the Enoch Powell Society and an underwhelmed producer who flatly refuses to take it to West End. But Bo wins the lottery, enabling her to bring it in herself. The second half was to be Bo's musical. In this more benign plot, Acorn Antiques is threatened with closure when the whole of Manchesterford's high street is put up for sale. A coffee chain called The Guilty Bean threatens to buy up the shop in a takeover led by a Miss Bonnie, who turns out to be the long-lost sister of Miss Babs and Miss Berta. 'It's about that balance between fear of things changing but things having to change,' Victoria said of this early draft. 'It's done in a very light way, but that's what it's about.'[12]

As well as the script she composed a dozen songs. As a next step Nunn introduced her to his regular collaborator Gareth Valentine, who had recently worked on musical scores by Cole Porter, Stephen Sondheim and John Kander. When he went to Highgate to hear what she'd written he was warned by Lez Brotherston that she was 'terribly nervous "because you're Mr Music". We had a cup of tea and she played some rudimentary chords and a melody and sang some lyrics. The lyrics were second to none. The music was pretty derivative.' The derivations were intentional: Victoria's idea was to create a chocolate box of pastiches and parodies in an array of styles – from *Annie* to Sondheim, *Les Mis* to Bob Fosse, Sandy Wilson to the terrible *Romeo and Juliet*.

Victoria's writing routine was accompanied by a strict exercise regime. In the gap left by Geoffrey's departure, another friend to assume a central place in her new single life and become a regular visitor to the house, was the actress Harriet Thorpe. Their former marriages became a topic on long walks over Hampstead Heath. Then, early in 2003, they decided to take part in the MoonWalk, an overnight marathon dedicated to raising money for breast cancer charities. Their training sessions lengthened till eventually they were doing eleven-milers three times a week. On one walk they were near Kenwood House when Victoria spotted an acorn. 'It was a rapturous moment,' says Harriet. 'She picked it up and took it home.' For the marathon itself they donned pink bras and joined the throng walking through the night.

The following week, on 19 May 2003, Harriet was among the women with whom Victoria marked her fiftieth birthday. The lunch was held in a balloon-adorned private dining room at the Charlotte Street Hotel in Fitzrovia. 'I invited all the friends that had helped me in the year. I decided it would be a celebration of ladies too.'[13] She coyly said as much to her guests. 'She made a brief speech,' says Lizzi Kew Ross, 'saying, "Thank you for being my friend and this has not been an easy year." It was very warm. It felt a significant party, almost like a public moment where she could allude to something so private.' Also in attendance were Lesley Fitton from Bury Grammar, Catherine Ashmore and Jane Wymark from Birmingham University, her hair and make-up designer Chrissie Baker, her PA Cathy Edis, her tour manager Amie Beamish, her friend in the north Charlotte Scott, Richenda Carey from the Quakers, plus Harriet Thorpe, Imelda Staunton, Kate Robbins and Julie Walters. Not every one of these friendships was to remain on the same level of intense familiarity, but for now each in her own way was a confidante on whose loyalty Victoria felt able to rely.

During the lunch Victoria seized the opportunity to sound Julie out about *Acorn Antiques*. 'I thought, oh what a hoot,' says Julie. 'And then I thought, I probably won't be able to do that because it's West End. I may as well go to the moon and do it. And Vic knew that.' There were mixed messages from the other originals. Duncan Preston, to whom Victoria mentioned it in the back of a cab, was sceptical: 'My first reaction was that will not happen. I didn't say it, I just thought it. But I said, "Yes, of course."' Celia Imrie was more vocal: 'I said, "Vic, are you sure you want to make it into a whole musical?" I didn't think it was a good idea and said so. Her reply was, "I'll just look elsewhere."' But as Victoria carried on writing, and the prospect loomed of a get-together, Celia's reservations were overcome: 'I didn't want anyone else to play Miss Babs.'

A wary feeling that Victoria could no longer simply click her fingers and summon the gang was fed by the opening in September of *Calendar Girls*. The film was shot on her doorstep in the Yorkshire Dales, and the rival company had employed Julie, Celia, Chrissie Baker, Harriet Thorpe and Ted Robbins. 'Some of them were in *Calendar Girls* because I had actually mentioned my cast to them when I was pitching to get the idea,' she said soon after the film opened. 'I was a bit wishing I was with them when they were making it. I just thought, my girls are making a film when I'm not there. I wanted to be at the party.'[14] She wrote to wish Celia well as she prepared, in Victoria's phrase, to parade her la-las. 'It probably doesn't help,' Celia replied, 'and maybe even make you cross – but I've got to express my sadness that you're not with us.'[15] In Julie's view Victoria would not have openly communicated her anguish. 'That would be demeaning for her,' she says. 'She didn't think it was much cop, I don't think.'

Victoria would have her own party whenever the gang got back together for the workshop. Trevor Nunn offered a week in October but counselled holding off until February 2004 when he had a fortnight to devote to overseeing a semi-staged version. 'We probably need another meeting,' he wrote, 'when you could give me the privilege of a command performance of the last two or three songs.'[16] Thus, in a rehearsal room in the Sadler's Wells Theatre, Victoria performed a suite of songs from the show to Nunn and Gareth Valentine. It was the largest collection of her own songs she had played to an audience in twenty years.

With the workshop postponed until the following year, Victoria was free to turn her attention to a job that, in its own way, felt just as personal. At the start of the year she heard from Judith Holder, the television producer who was instrumental in bringing her to LWT in 1988. She was now with an independent production company and, emboldened by many tête-à-têtes about body image and food problems, proposed a documentary fronted by Victoria on the slimming industry. As friends with children of the same age, that summer they went on a canoeing holiday in France, which was not an ideal prelude for a working partnership. Victoria pronounced it 'one of the best holidays we've ever had. It was on the Dordogne. On it? Some of us were *in* it.'[17] Judith capsized her canoe on the first morning 'and became a basket case. I don't think Vic found it easy, but she took it upon herself to be strong. She would say, "OK, white water coming up here. I'll go down it first." She fell in too, but not that much.'

Dieting, which her mother first thrust upon her when she was twelve, had been a leitmotif of Victoria's creative life for thirty years. She sang about it as a gloomy student in 'Nobody Loves You When You're Down and Fat', and it was a preoccupation in the early dramas and sketches she wrote for herself and Julie. 'This is a boutique not the elephant house,' says Julie's sales assistant in *Wood and Walters*, aiming a sub-machine gun at Victoria. Not long before the series was broadcast, Victoria gave her measurements to a fashion editor who wanted to do a feature. 'Do you wear kaftans?' came the reply. It cut her deeply when at a fitting in a West End costumier a woman said to her, 'If you'd only lose two stone, you could wear all these of Anna Massey's.' Her tactic in her early stand-up shows was to mention it before anyone else could. 'You could dial my measurements,' she said in *As Seen on TV*, 'and get through to the Midland Bank, Bulawayo.'

This running theme was co-opted by the advertisers who made her the face of the low-calorie drink One-Cal. In the early Eighties the press kept landing on the same word to describe her. She was like 'a plump and bashful schoolgirl',[18] exuded 'plump placidity',[19] was 'the plump, dimpled, dumpling one',[20] 'plump and homely',[21] 'dumpy and plump',[22] 'a plump blue-suited Andy Pandy',[23] 'comfortably and pleasantly plump',[24] 'pert and plump'.[25] It amounted to a form of group bullying. As Victoria's fame grew, a pattern set in: she would declare that she was eating better than she used to and no longer worrying about her weight while continuing to obsess about it privately. 'In interviews I always had to say I was quite happy,' she said during the *At It Again* tour. 'I wasn't at all happy, but I felt that that was a good party line to take.'[26] She began to watch herself after one journalist, who'd consumed far more than her over lunch, wrote down what Victoria ate. 'After that I stopped eating when the press were around. Drank black tea.'[27] Then she started to fight back. In her mid-thirties a magazine put her on their cover as slimmer of the year, and she forced them to publish a retraction. In 1989 *Mens Sana in Thingummy Doo dah* attacked the vapid despotism of health spas. A section in her 1993 stand-up show angrily confronted the slimming industry. Through Dolly and Jean in *dinnerladies* she poked fun at women bickering about weight. The exercise routines in her last three shows made light of high-energy gym classes.

It was not until *At It Again* that Victoria was able publicly to admit to an eating disorder. 'If you've got an eating disorder,' she elaborated, 'then eating replaces almost any need that you have. It covers up your feelings. While you're eating, you're totally blanked out, you're not feeling anything. It puts up a barrier between you and people because people are scary but food's not scary, you know exactly where you are with it, whereas a person is unpredictable. When you're with somebody you're thinking, well, I won't have to talk to them much longer and then I can go and eat something. You are in a state of high tension that is only relieved by eating. It isolates you socially. You have to do it privately.'[28]

All of this went into the mix when she came to make *Victoria Wood's Big Fat Documentary.* 'I think I can do the programme,' she said as she embarked on filming, 'because it's something that I've come to see doesn't really go away. Whereas before I was always trying to find the thing that would solve it, so that I would no longer have any problem with food or eating, now I think I probably will always and that's all right as well. I know what I think about certain things, but I'm willing to change my mind.'[29]

As she and Judith Holder worked on the two-part series, Victoria acquired another ally in the shape of Ben Warwick, who had created the look of Nigella Lawson's first cookery series *Nigella Bites* and was suggested as a director. In her vulnerable state after the break-up he found her quick to confide. On his first visit to Highgate he spotted the BAFTAs on the bookshelves: 'And yet I was talking to this very normal woman. I was overweight and I could identify with the subject matter. We immediately found ourselves able to be very comfortable and very honest with each other. When I saw her particularly crestfallen I'd give her a cuddle and hold her hand.' He mentioned that once, as a floor manager, he had met Geoffrey and been let into the secret of a handkerchief trick. 'My God, he must have liked you,' she said. 'He never showed anyone anything.'

To establish that this was a personal journey, the series opened with a piece to camera shot in Victoria's home – the last such intrusion had happened in Stankelt Road in 1985. She imagined the pitch she would make to St Peter at the pearly gates: 'I was on British television for thirty years, quite fat, a bit fat, not so fat, and in all that time I never brought out a diet book, a detox plan or an exercise video.' The two films grew into something more than an attack on the profiteers of the slimming industry as Victoria investigated the epidemic of obesity caused by fatty fast food and sedentary lives, and contrasted it to the unnerving lack of flesh on celebrity role models. The pressures put on skeletal actresses was something she was determined to expose: 'I'm interested in who's writing these pieces in *Heat* and *Now* and all those magazines, doing twelve worst bottoms and twelve worst cleavages. I think big ugly girls are writing those articles probably.'[30] In the event, none of those titles accepted the invitation to be interrogated by Victoria.

Many of the interviews were set up at her suggestion, among them with celebrities who had felt the lash of her tongue – Vanessa Feltz, Anne Diamond, Ann Widdecombe and the Duchess of York (who was a good hour late to their interview at the Berkeley Hotel). Victoria resisted the proposal to mock them behind their backs. One of the most powerful contributions came from Nina Myskow, whom she first met at the Edinburgh Festival in 1975 when they compared notes on food addiction. Nearly three decades on, Victoria wrote to request an interview. 'I had never been asked to talk about it,' says Myskow. 'When the letter arrived I was utterly thrilled. I knew Victoria would understand on a literally visceral level. I felt I was having a conversation with somebody who understood completely what I was saying.' On camera she told Victoria about the time she made a dozen scones in the middle of the night, wolfed down seven of them, hurled the rest in the bin, then fished four out in the morning and polished them off, leaving only a scone soiled by a tea bag. After the interview Victoria thanked her for her honesty. 'I didn't want to tell Nina,' she added on the voiceover, 'that in my most compulsive days I would have eaten all the scones, and then eaten the tea bag.'

In mid-November the production flew to Los Angeles. It was Victoria's first visit. She had zero cachet as a celebrity to call in interviewees and, with less than a week to shoot in, the stressful schedule was subject to short-term changes – they were late for one appointment with a visibly cross author. But it yielded some eye-opening television. Victoria donned leggings to do high kicks at an exercise class for overweight women. The extrovert exercise guru licked the sweat off her bare shoulder – no one back home would have countenanced such an impertinence. To interview two belly dancers from Pasadena in a jacuzzi, Victoria consented to wear a swimsuit on camera for the first time since 'Swim the Channel' in 1984.

Victoria was determined that the programme would project good cheer. Near the production hotel in Santa Monica, she marched along the beach in pastel aerobics gear looking like a glam Californian native. 'Hello, I'm Victoria Wood,' she said in a mid-Atlantic drawl. 'When I lived in England and was the star of such hit comedies as *Wood and Waters* and *The Lunch Ladies*, I was overweight, and could not even look in a mirror.' Then she hawked her colon-removal kit ColonToGO! Back in the UK Victoria enlisted actor chums, among them Harriet Thorpe and Andrew Dunn, to lighten the mood with chat and sketches about body image. Kate Robbins joined her in a black-and-white mockumentary about how women stayed thin in the war by digging, scrubbing, carpet-beating and, at the local fleapit, snacking on raw sprouts from a paper bag (just as Stanley and Helen munched on carrot squares when courting). She concluded with an inspirational two-minute rallying cry, delivered from the steps of St Martin-in-the-Fields in Trafalgar Square as the traffic roared in the background:

> I'm not saying people shouldn't lose weight if they want to do it
> . . . What I'm saying is find out about yourself first. You decide
> . . . You have to be able to face yourself in the mirror. If you think
> you're all right, it doesn't matter what anybody else thinks . . . And
> if life deals you a pile of manure, they say you should grow roses.
> So I say, if life gives you a belly, go dancing.

*Victoria Wood's Big Fat Documentary*, finished in early December, was edited together at speed and broadcast in early January 2004. The sight of Victoria committing to a serious exercise in campaigning journalism prompted many viewers to express gratitude and share their own stories with her.

One Sunday night during filming Victoria went to the BAFTA tribute to Julie Walters, filmed at the BBC, taking Lez Brotherston as her guest. Her citation was the finale of the show broadcast on BBC One. 'Before she went up to do her bit,' says Julie, 'she handed me a bit of paper and it said on it, "We're missing *Brideshead* for this."' The private message looped them all the way back to grumbling pensioners at the *Wood and Walters* recordings. After everyone else had gushed, as ever Victoria saluted Julie by underpraising her for always learning her lines. 'It's kind of flattering really,' says Julie. 'It's like the opposite of what she feels, and she can't say it – that's what I always felt.'

The BAFTA tributes, first made as one-offs, were now being done biannually – Victoria agreed to take part in another dedicated to Bob Monkhouse. The offer inevitably came to be the subject of one herself, but she baulked at the prospect. The reason she cited was recent personal turmoil. And yet, more than a year after Geoffrey's departure, Victoria was beginning to recover. 'Her spirit lightened,' says her neighbourhood friend Norah Wellbelove. 'It was a slow process. You could see it getting lighter and lighter. I think she was feeling free. She went back to having the odd glass, which she had stopped for a long time. She changed furnishings in the house. It was just like she was trying to reclaim her life. A lot of fun came back into her.'

Victoria's feeling of well-being was underpinned by regular visits to a new therapist whom she saw as 'somebody to accompany you on the journey. It sounds ludicrous, but when you're separating from your husband you haven't got a husband to help you go through it so the person that was in your corner that helped you along the way is suddenly not in your corner.'[31] One of the issues she took with her into the sessions was a profound feeling of guilt about the end of the marriage: 'I felt a failure, completely. That's quite hard to live with. If you're quite a punishing sort of person anyway, then, whoa, you've suddenly got the biggest mallet to whack yourself over the head with.'[32] On the rare occasions she met up with Geoffrey to talk about the children, she would voice this thought to him too. 'She told me more than once,' he says, 'that her distress and frequent tearfulness were caused by her sense of guilt and responsibility for the break-up, rather than feelings of abandonment.'

In February 2004 Victoria's gang convened at the LWT rehearsal studio in Kennington, where some of the second series of *dinnerladies* was rehearsed. A small ensemble was drawn from the casts of *My Fair Lady* and *Anything Goes* – one Nunn-directed musical had recently succeeded the other at Theatre Royal Drury Lane. Thus Trevor Nunn entered the physical world of *Acorn Antiques*. 'I thought it was a hilarious combination,' says Julie, who had first met him when rehearsing *Educating Rita* with the Royal Shakespeare Company. 'But I thought he will do it really well. I couldn't wait for Mrs Overall to be able to sing.' Another interested observer at the workshop was Lez Brotherston. In a sign that Victoria didn't play by the conventions of theatre she insisted he be the designer before she'd even approached Nunn, in whose hands such a decision would normally lie. The workshop was the first time he had worked with Nunn too, so he and Victoria were less prepared than others for the duration of his welcoming speech. He talked about comedy and television and seemed to imply that the musical had been his suggestion. 'Vic did her funny boss-eyed thing at me,' says Lez. After a script-read round the table, director and principals began to work on scenes while the ensemble learned dance routines with Stephen Mear, whom Victoria asked for after seeing his witty choreography on *Anything Goes*. The songs were taught to the cast by Gareth Valentine. With Victoria taking notes and sticking to Nunn's side throughout the workshop, her old role of Berta was taken by Janie Dee, who, acting alongside Julie and Celia, suffered from impostor syndrome: 'I said to Vic, "Why don't *you* play Berta? That's what's missing. It should be you." She said, "I can't. I've got to oversee it."'

At the end of the fortnight there was a performance for an invited audience of fifty or so friends and colleagues. With no set beyond the odd antique lamp, Nunn differentiated between the two musicals by placing the guests in the middle of the room and playing each half from opposite ends. They laughed and laughed from the opening lines of Mrs Overall in a song called 'Residents' Parking':

Oh! Miss Berta and Miss Babs!
Has one of you got crabs?
I said you should get jabs.

They were treated to plenty of theatrical in-jokes that would not make it to the West End – one about the producer Michael Codron, another in which Bo touted her stage credentials. 'Joan Littlewood? That was my cap actually. Samuel Beckett? I wasn't born a telly star – I did eight weeks in a bin for him at Pitlochry. Metal too, none of your lovely big wheelies.'

Victoria came away from Kennington aware that there was work to do: 'The numbers came out really well, and the first half had a good shape to it, but the second half didn't quite come off as a story. It was a verbal idea about acorns turning into oak trees, and it didn't happen onstage.'[33] A climactic song called 'Little Acorns', sung by Mrs Overall, did not survive beyond the workshop ('This acorn's only tiny, nature's own trainee / Not whingy though, or whiny').

The musical had other hurdles to overcome. 'I absolutely loved doing the workshop,' Julie told Victoria. 'Considering how much we got done it was very relaxed and unpressured. That's where old Trevor is so good. He understands how to deal with actors.'[34] Celia concurred: 'You have written something quite magical, unique, uplifting, touching, mad, fun and hilarious and songs to set the Thames on fire.'[35] Even though the original stars were full of praise, Victoria was aware that they would commit to a limited West End run only, and she briefly considered an out-of-town try-out with a less starry cast. In addition, Mrs Overall was too energy-sapping a role to do eight times a week, and Julie had the option of reprising her role in a new stage-musical version of Billy Elliot. Rather than go through agents, two months after the workshop Victoria wrote to her: 'From our point of view, it's your part, you're brilliant in it, you would bring in the punters and obviously you're worth every penny . . .' But she accepted Julie might not end up doing it: 'We're all in this to make a living and have a good time: as long as you're in the front stalls for the first night waving a macaroon I'm happy.'[36] Victoria had certainly anticipated Julie's presence in a stage direction in the workshop draft: 'Enter Mrs O – to entrance round which she acknowledges.' There could be no applause on Mrs O's first entrance without Julie, who replied: 'My feeling is – either we'll thrash out a deal that's good for both of us or we won't – and there will be no hard feeling. Whichever route you choose I'll be there on the 1st night with my macaroon.'[37]

A solution had already suggested itself to Victoria the previous autumn when she saw a flyer for *Thoroughly Modern Millie* with Maureen Lipman and Marti Webb alternating in one of the roles. 'I could do the Monday nights nobody wants to do,' she said. 'Or if Julie didn't want to do her matinees. Also, there's a bit of a groan moment when they say so and so will not appear at the matinee. If you can put someone in who's fantastic, they could collect Mrs Overalls.'[38] The answer which emerged was to do both Monday nights and Wednesday matinees herself. Meanwhile Celia, who had always avoided long West End runs, weighed up options. 'Julie and I talked,' she says, 'and she said, "I'll do it if you do it."'

A break from writing came with an invitation from the League of Gentlemen, who were transplanting Royston Vasey to the big screen and, in a historical section of the script, had written cameo roles for a northern King William and Queen Mary. To play them they approached Alan Bennett and Victoria Wood. 'We thought these are our king and queen of comedy,' says Steve Pemberton. 'This will be a little treat for us. Alan said his acting days were behind him. Victoria didn't do that much outside of her own writing. She was delighted to be asked.' She flew to Dublin for a couple of days and found herself magnificently togged up with a towering wig, rouged cheeks and a fat beauty spot. As a sweetener they encouraged her to change her lines. She found just the right royal words to receive a line of beggars: 'Have you staggered far?'

Back in London, Victoria and Harriet Thorpe pledged to stagger far for a second year running with the MoonWalk. This time Victoria was commissioned by Sioned Wiliam at ITV to make a half-hour film to raise awareness of the charity 'Walk the Walk'. One night in mid-May Victoria and Harriet followed by two film crews walked for 26.2 miles through central London. 'We're doing this for our breasts,' she told an excitable crowd in bras at the start. 'It's doing fuck all for our bunions, but never mind.' She and Harriet got round in eight hours, pumping arms, singing, playing word games and inventorying their aches. Among hers Victoria listed 'blisters the size of Dutch caps'. 'I'm so glad we did it,' she wrote to her various sponsors, 'but to be surrounded by fifteen thousand women in bras, all whooping, did make it feel like a huge rather nightmarish hen party.'[39] *Victoria Wood: Moonwalking*, a moving gem assembled artfully by Ben Warwick, was shown in October. In her voiceover Victoria summarised the mission: 'Everyone who has cancer has to go through it on their own. All you can do is walk alongside. And that's what we're doing. We're just putting one foot in front of the other walking alongside the ones who aren't here, the ones taking their own harder, longer journey.'

Victoria spent the middle months of 2004 attempting to fashion a plot for the second half of the musical. 'Your second act outline made me laugh,' wrote Trevor Nunn in May after reading a draft, 'but I think I have given you a bum steer.'[40] He gave her a forensic set of notes. 'I really want to know what you think,' she replied, 'and am quite prepared to get stuck in again and take it in another direction.'[41] The second half now opened with 'Manchesterford', a cheerful welcome by a streetful of right-wing shopkeepers who smugly sing of a world unvisited by modernity:

> Our water's sweet, our bread is full of bran
> No drunks or beggars mar the civic plan
> We've shipped them all to Douglas, Isle of Man
> By gum by golly it's jolly nice round here.

The town's peace is threatened when the Countess of Manchesterford decides to sell off the high street to the likes of the PashminasToGo, the Hong Kong Thong and Panty Hut, and the Drop-In Silicone Breast Centre. Acorn Antiques can be saved from an aggressive takeover by

The Guilty Bean only if the money left by the father of Mrs Overall's triplets can be found. In an idea lifted from *dinnerladies*, he appears on video to deliver his living will. In a rousing finale, the Manchesterford Players' perform 'Oh! Oh! Oh! Mrs O!' in the style of the finale of *A Chorus Line*.

There were interruptions to the writing process. That summer Victoria took the children to Canada on their most adventurous holiday yet. After a happy first leg spent on Vancouver Island, canoeing and jumping off bridges into freezing water, they had a highly stressful transfer to Calgary. After landing late, they drove into the night looking for their hotel and realised they'd gone wrong. Tempers flared. 'At about one in the morning,' says Grace, 'we said we are going to knock on the door of the first house we see. We didn't see another house for two hours.' Eventually they headed towards some distant lights, which turned out to be Calgary, where all the motels were block-booked for a Christian conference. 'We ended up sleeping in the car. The silver lining was that we set off at six o'clock in the morning and saw the sun rise over the Rockies.' On her return there was jolting news for Victoria: at the age of fifty-three Bob Mason had died of cancer of the oesophagus. He had become a successful character actor who also scripted three dozen episodes of *Coronation Street*. At a handover Victoria asked Geoffrey in and told him: 'She knew more or less what he was working on most of the time, and his death came out of the blue. She was quite shocked.'

Long before rehearsals were due to begin, Victoria started to have lessons to master Mrs Overall's comedy tap routine in the act-one closer 'Tip Top Tap'. 'I've never danced before,' she said. 'I've never even danced socially.'[42] Her coach at Pineapple Studios, giving her two private sessions a week for six weeks, was Stephen Mear's assistant Sammy Murray, a cheerful former dancer from Yorkshire. 'When she first came in she was terrified of looking herself in the mirror, her head was down and she barely said a word to the point I used to go back to Stephen and say, "She hates me." It got quite upsetting. After about three weeks, half the session was just sitting down getting a coffee and talking things through. For me that was a turning point. Not only did her tap get better but also the trust started happening.

She used to send me messages: "Practising my tap as I'm doing my soup."'

Victoria was distracted as she learned tap because the production still had no home. The task of finding a theatre was in the hands of Phil McIntyre, but competition for a West End house with an orchestra pit was intense. The Cambridge Theatre and Shaftesbury Theatre were tried. In July there was a rush to tie down the London Palladium, despite Trevor Nunn's practical objection that its wide acres would simply swallow up the first half of the show. They turned their attention to the Piccadilly Theatre, where *Jailhouse Rock* was struggling but had to go below its break-even threshold for three consecutive weeks before the landlords could give it its notice. 'We had one week to wait,' said Victoria. 'By the Tuesday of that week their figures started to climb up. I felt terrible about it. I didn't want them to fail. I just wanted to be able to go somewhere.'[43] Her distress increased when it looked as if a theatre would not come free at a time when Trevor Nunn and Julie Walters were available: 'I was so upset that it was being taken away from me. I just felt this was the time. And I just felt robbed. I was so depressed.'[44]

Eventually the Theatre Royal Haymarket was booked. Julie's determination to do no more than sixteen weeks, plus the 900-seat capacity, meant that an expensive production could not recoup its costs unless ticket prices were pushed to unprecedented heights of £65 for a seat in the stalls. Despite grumbles in the theatre press, tickets for *Acorn Antiques: The Musical!* sold fast after Victoria and Julie posed in Marigolds at the launch.

The cast which assembled for rehearsals at the Jerwood Space in Southwark included new faces. Josie Lawrence was cast as a Brummie wardrobe mistress in the first half and Miss Bonnie in the second. Neil Morrissey was John the saturnine director in the first half, then a ruthless loan shark called Tony who unleashes Miss Babs's repressed nymphomania. Several of the workshop ensemble returned – at Victoria's suggestion, they weren't all sleek athletes but a cross-section in varying shapes and sizes with charismatic faces. The role of Berta went to Sally Ann Triplett, twice a Eurovision contestant in the early 1980s but more recently a star of *Anything Goes*. To her fell the task of singing a ballad called 'Remind Him', which Victoria composed to provide Berta with a romantic hinterland. The song tells of her secret crush on Mr Clifford, who has lost his memory, but it was apparent to those around Victoria that the sweetly generic lyrics about pining for a lost love drew on her own lingering sorrows:

> Once we were together and I didn't see an end
> Didn't see what changes could arise
> Now he's not a stranger but you couldn't call him friend
> Still my dreams survive.

At one point, when Victoria was not in the room, Trevor Nunn shared his suspicions with the company. 'It's astonishing,' Gareth Valentine remembers him saying, 'she has recently parted with her husband and it was a very dark time for her and this ballad I'm convinced is a love letter.' She flatly denied any such connection to Ben Warwick, who hovered during rehearsals while making a behind-the-scenes documentary for ITV: 'She played me the song on the piano. I said, "I certainly know who that's about." "Who? No, that's not about Geoffrey." She was adamant.' Still, it would make her weep when it was sung in rehearsal.

Before rehearsals started, Victoria shared her worries with Gareth Valentine that the rehearsal draft was too long. 'Trevor is known for not cutting stuff,' he advised. 'If you want to cut any fat out of it, now is the time to do it. Don't get it into that rehearsal room domain, because he won't cut.' The show had grown bloated partly because Victoria felt she had to dole out songs to the principals. 'They all wanted their moment,' she said during rehearsals, 'and in the heat of the moment you bung in as many numbers as people want.'[45] There was one critical omission: Miss Babs was alone in not having her own song. Celia had always self-effacingly accepted her status as a butt of jokes, which did not relent in *Acorn Antiques*. When Mrs Overall takes a truth drug, she calls Miss Babs a 'snotty thick-ankled cow' and a 'dozy big-breasted pillock'. Now she plucked up the courage: 'Victoria was very good about saying, "If anybody has got something they want to talk to me about, then I'm here." I thought, I've got to say something. At the eleventh hour I went to her one lunchtime. She said, "Oh, it never occurred to me. I can't really now. There's no room."' In fact, it had occurred to Victoria. A draft completed since the workshop even had a number titled 'Babs' Song'. Though grouchy about shouldering the extra work, over the weekend she bashed out a short, brash fantasy number. She recorded 'Have You Met Miss Babs?' at her piano, handed the tape to Gareth Valentine on Monday morning and it was swiftly dropped into the show.

While it took all Trevor Nunn's formidable stagecraft to wrestle Victoria's two-headed hydra onto the stage, the one area where Victoria did not defer to him was comedy. He revealed his unfamiliarity with her work one lunch at the Jerwood Space. 'There was Trevor, Victoria and me and the rest of the cast behind us,' says Gareth Valentine. 'And Trevor said to the women, "Two soups, please." And the entire cast broke into laughter and Trevor was the only one not in on the gag.' Later, during a technical rehearsal, a set of magnetic letters fixed to an upstage window clattered to the floor when a door slammed. 'Vic and I hit the floor laughing,' says Lez Brotherston. 'Trevor was going, "Oh my God, what are we going to do?" Vic went, "We'll keep it, Trevor. It's funny."' Julie quietly deferred to Victoria in this area: 'Occasionally Vic would come up and say, "Do that note now but don't do it on the night." And I'd go, "No, I know." It would be comedy stuff which just wouldn't work the way Trevor said.' But her director was fiercely protective of the production. At one point Phil McIntyre was looking to cut costs and zeroed in on an expensive arcade that was part of Lez Brotherston's set design. Nunn insisted on keeping it and said that, if need be, he'd pay for it himself.

Unusually for a West End rehearsal schedule, the company took a week's break over Christmas so Victoria could be with the children. It was during this period that she somehow found time to spoof another soap, courtesy of an invitation from Vanessa Whitburn, the editor of *The Archers*, who wanted her to write an episode for Comic Relief. Victoria threw herself into a plot about prize marmalade, a pigsty conversion and a mystery celebrity who turned out to be Stephen Fry. While stuffing in one-liners that gently twitted the show's conventions, she smuggled in some of her own signature words too – Vimto, mangle, *Crossroads*. Victoria asked if she could come to the recording a few weeks later, where she helped the studio manager with sound effects and signed the cast's scripts.

When rehearsals resumed Victoria started to fret that Julie wasn't sleeping as she attempted to learn Mrs Overall's dance routines. 'I was so engrossed in it I had terrible insomnia,' says Julie. 'I had to go and get sleeping tablets. She came into the dressing room once and I saw there was a look of worry on her face.' A second concern was the length of the show. 'Oh God, it's so fucking long,' she told Gareth Valentine. 'I know exactly what to do and he won't cut it.' 'People have got to catch buses,' she told Trevor Nunn. According to Stephen Mear, her director 'absolutely adored her and that's why he didn't want to cut anything. Vic said, "Cut anything you like." But he said, "You're a genius."' A song called 'Gravy Train' did eventually bite the dust.

To whet public appetite, the original sketches were released on DVD in January, while Victoria eventually accepted that BAFTA could help sell tickets by offering viewers a foretaste of the show. *Victoria Wood: A BAFTA Tribute* was broadcast a week before the first preview. To open and close it, David Firman arranged a cheerful brass version of 'Feeling in the Mood Tonight', her 1993 show opener. Recorded at the Prince of Wales Theatre, it attracted a guest list from all walks of Victoria's life – the stars of *dinnerladies* and *All the Trimmings*, the Robbins siblings, her favourite channel controller Peter Salmon. Opening the evening, Susie Blake revived her caustic continuity announcer to introduce some of the forthcoming guests, including 'Julie Walters, star of *Calendar Girls*. She was the one behind the sink plunger. But first, a word from the star of some other films I haven't liked: Richard E. Grant.' Some stars paying tribute got their facts wrong or, to Victoria's frustration, misread from the malfunctioning autocue. Not every mistake was accidental. Steve Pemberton paid tribute to 'Victoria Woods' and 'heard this tutting and muttering in the audience. Ronnie Corbett was most offended. I'd like to think mega-fans would have understood the reference.' The evening climaxed with Victoria's entry, to a standing ovation, to accept her BAFTA from Jim Broadbent and Boadicea Overall. Then she introduced the new version of *Acorn Antiques*. The soap, she said, had been cruelly axed after losing a ratings battle with *When Celebrity Breast Enlargements Go Wrong* but had now become a musical. With a performance of 'Tip Top Tap', viewers were offered a first glimpse of Miss Babs, Miss Berta and Mrs Overall singing and dancing (Mr Clifford was exempted as Duncan Preston couldn't dance). The act-one showstopper, boosted by Chris Walker's riotous orchestration, was one of Victoria's favourite moments in the entire musical. 'Watching it in rehearsal,' says Gareth Valentine, 'she would glow and tap her feet. She really enjoyed the sound. It was the only time I ever saw her content.'

At the very first performance at the end of the month some of Victoria's anxieties were calmed by the reaction of the audience – 'They went absolutely mad,' says Julie. 'People were throwing Marigolds on at the end' – and the previews continued in that vein. One night Victoria stood at the back of the dress circle behind a glass panel with Lez Brotherston, looking down on row upon row of middle-aged men with crewcuts roaring with laughter. 'Old Compton Street must be a wasteland,' she said.

Five days later came the first night. The grandees of musical theatre – Andrew Lloyd Webber, Cameron Mackintosh, Elaine Paige – presented themselves. So did Ronnie Corbett, who had a video cameo as the father of Mrs Overall's triplets. The celebrities were intermingled with what Julie calls 'a dead belly of critics in the centre downstairs – people with pens'. Victoria watched in horror from the dress circle with Stephen Mear. 'It was nothing compared to the previews or any show after that,' he says. 'It was the worst show. She just grabbed me in disbelief and said, "Why have we got this audience tonight?" It was so sad to see. She stood at the back in the second half. She didn't want to hear anybody's opinion.'

In the very first draft of the show, after the cast take their bows the assistant stage manager brings news that the first review is already online. 'Any good?' says Bo. This hostage to fortune was cut before the workshop. In commercial terms, Victoria had been invulnerable to reviews for nearly twenty years but nonetheless hoped for favour as they came in over the weekend. 'It's the supreme cheek of the endeavour that will irritate some and exhilarate the rest of us,' predicted the *Independent*.[46] Most reviewers fell somewhere in between. 'Mischievous, good-natured, charming,' said *The Times*. 'But a comic masterpiece? Not really.'[47] The *Observer* relished 'some ridiculously enjoyable moments' but found it 'a muddle and a mess, and at least a third too long'.[48] There was a consensus that the show couldn't decide if it was a love letter to theatre – with its flying scenery, jokes about Stephen Baldry and Sir Trevor Eve, and spoofs of Brecht and Fosse – or a ruthless mugging. The most crushing verdict came from Michael Billington of the *Guardian*, who professed ignorance of the original sketches and awarded the production one star.

'The reaction wasn't good,' says Julie. 'We didn't hear anything from Vic, and we all thought she's going to be feeling down. I texted her and said, "Look, there are queues around the block, that's all you need to know."' Victoria had to show her face on the Monday evening, as she was due to understudy Julie.

Playing Mrs Overall was another source of apprehension. In the rush to get the show on, her access to rehearsal time was limited. Aside from blocking calls and a dress rehearsal with the band, she had barely any preparation before she acted in a theatre for the first time since *Good Fun* in 1980. She gradually emerged from her shell as Mrs Overall but never quite escaped the shadow of Julie. A *Radio Times* cover shot by Patrick Lichfield depicted Julie as Mrs Overall proffering a flute of champagne on a tray to Victoria on a throne wearing a crown and ermine. Onstage that hierarchy was reversed. She shared her anxiety to Duncan Preston: 'Vic said to me, "Blimey, people are going away if they hear that Julie's not doing it. They're asking for their money back." I said, "Well, she is the heart of the show really." She was never a patch on Julie, and she did know it.' After one performance she asked Sammy Murray, to whom she had grown close and who visited her dressing room following every performance, if there were empty seats: 'I said, "Yes, Vic, there were." She had a bit of a meltdown. She said, "I didn't need to know that." I said, "Vic, you asked me the question. Even if I lie, you'll be looking at the box-office figures." The next morning at half past seven she rang and said, "Sammy, I could see all the people weren't there. I'm really upset and I took it all out on you. I felt really shitty."' Victoria gave twenty-nine performances as Mrs Overall and received a steady flow of friends in her dressing room afterwards. Geoffrey Strachan, her old publisher, lavished praise. 'What a shame you don't do the reviews for the Guardian!' she replied. 'It's lovely to play – which I hadn't expected!'[49]

Every single one of the £65 tickets was sold. No one spotted the irony when Mrs O pointed to the stalls and told them to 'behave in the cheap seats'. While Celia's Miss Babs was a sizzling portrayal of midlife sexuality, Julie pulled focus every second she was on the stage and attracted the lion's share of the one-liners:

> You had a difficult birth – you had your nose wedged right up against my pubic bone.
>     I was giving the postman a mouthful of something tasty by the scullery door and he filled me in very thoroughly.
>     There was a rubber shortage. We tried painting condoms on with gravy browning but the thing is they wasn't a hundred per cent effective.

'They are the funniest lines I think I've ever had the privilege to say,' says Julie. 'Some nights it was utterly uproarious. I felt I had free rein and I could see the joy Vic took in anything new I got in, and that made me feel really happy.' Her big moment was 'Macaroons', in which Mrs Overall argues that men should drop their various vices and instead consume more biscuits. Her tip for Ozzy Osbourne, always uproariously received, was to 'have a custard fucking cream and shut the fuck up!'

For fans who couldn't see the show Victoria hoped to capture it on DVD. 'That became an absolute frigging nightmare,' says her agent Lucy Ansbro. 'One actor got greedy, and he was winding everybody else up about it. Vic became the negotiator for everybody. She was saying, "Come on, we can't afford it at that level. You've got to do it on this basis if you want to film it."' A deal was eventually struck. Ben Warwick watched the dress rehearsal, filmed an early performance on a wide angle then plotted a camera script with over 3,000 different shots filmed by seven cameras. The crew came back for another performance to capture Victoria's Mrs Overall, which was one of the DVD's extras.

Victoria gave her last performance the day before her fifty-second birthday. There had been talk of continuing after Julie and Celia's contracts came to an end, but she soon saw this would be folly. 'I thought it would suffer very badly if we recast it while we were in the West End.'[50] As the production approached a natural terminus, there was a sense that Victoria's company was also coming to the end of the line: 'I was very appreciative of the fact that Celia and Duncan and Julie were prepared to tip up eight times a week on the stage to bring this to fruition. It felt like a great glorious conclusion to something. I don't know if they felt the same way.'[51] Julie agrees that 'there was a feeling of that somewhere – I didn't feel sad because I'd come to the end of a great massive run and it was good to be finishing'. 'There was an unspoken agreement that this was sort of it,' says Duncan, who made the best of slim pickings in the role of Mr Clifford. As for Celia, 'I'm glad I did it,' she says. 'I'm extremely proud to have got the Olivier award. But after that time Vic and I never worked together again.'

# 21

# HISTORIAN, 53

**'I was always roaring with laughter when I wasn't sobbing on camera.'**

Interview, 2007

There were to be more endings. In the summer of 2005 Dan Crawford, the artistic director of the King's Head Theatre with whom Victoria had such a long association, was terminally ill in hospital. On the day she hoped to say goodbye, the 7/7 bombings happened. He died two days later, and at his funeral in Islington she admonished Janie Dee for crying as she sang 'Spread a Little Happiness'. Mole Barn went on the market and the sale was completed in September. Victoria bought a flat for her sister Penelope in Hebden Bridge, but her own residential link with the north was once again severed. While she witnessed her other sister Rosalind remarry at a registry office, that summer Victoria and Geoffrey sought advice from a solicitor about how to get a DIY divorce which would attract no attention from the press.

These sunderings had one happier by-product: Victoria felt free to succumb to her work ethic without guilt. 'I am just flexing my muscles a bit,' was how she would put it, 'and doing what I want, rather than trying not to rock the marital boat.'[1] She started to push herself harder than at any time since creating *dinnerladies*, and in drastically new directions. For the next two years, her schedule would be densely latticed with overlapping projects. None would involve live performance. Although the question of whether she might tour again refused to go away, Victoria was clear in her mind that she could not. 'I did not have an amiable separation from my husband,' she explained to a television producer. 'It was all very painful and horrible, and that's one reason why I'm not doing stand-up, because I don't want to talk about it onstage, and I don't know how to do any stuff about myself without talking about it.'[2] Yet she was aware that her personal circumstances could not be entirely suppressed. 'It's unimaginable that something big like that would happen to you and it wouldn't in the end be assimilated into your work,' she said. 'It will come in in some guise.'[3] So it proved.

Victoria was always receiving approaches from hopeful broadcasters. One that pricked her interest had come at the end of 2003 from Michele Buck, the controller of drama at LWT, who pitched a drama for Victoria to write and star in. It would feature a quiet but clever office cleaner working the night shift at a police station where, in partnership with a sweet young cop, she would solve crimes. Victoria was unseduced but did not discourage further overtures. There were all new young people at LWT since she had fallen out with the drama department over *Pat and Margaret* a decade earlier. In particular, the young head of development Piers Wenger was, in his own description, 'a real hardcore fan in my teens' who had seen Victoria perform live several times. In March 2004 he and the head of drama Damien Timmer, who also knew her sketches inside out, sent out another pair of offers. One was a guest role in the new Miss Marple, the other an invitation to adapt and complete Jane Austen's unfinished novel *The Watsons*. Victoria, allergic to going back over old ground, had already parodied cosy crime with *Wetty Hainthrop Investigates*, and Regency costume drama in 'Plots and Proposals'. Yet LWT's persistence was rewarded. 'We got a very short letter back which was handwritten,' says Piers Wenger. 'It said, "I am busy writing my musical at the moment but I have got an idea which I might be more able to talk about in six months or a year's time." There was an incredibly long wait and it was very tantalising.'

As for Victoria, it made for a pleasant change to be courted by younger people – Piers Wenger was twenty years her junior. 'They were sort of pestering me for ages and ages,' she said, 'and they were so nice and such big fans.'[4] Eventually she and the LWT three met at J. Sheekey, the swish West End fish restaurant. The lunch was interrupted when the sociable novelist Kathy Lette approached the table. 'Vic just fixed her with one of her Paddington Bear stares,' says Piers, 'and said, "I'm sorry, I don't think we have met." She was completely deadpan. In a very quiet way she dealt with this interruption.' Piers, finally meeting his idol, was granted a glimpse of her steeliness. She confirmed she had an idea in mind. 'I'm interested in writing about a marriage,' she said. As she left she announced that she was off to buy a clock at Selfridges. 'It felt like a coded way of saying that we might get to know her,' says Damien Timmer. 'We really wanted to be in her gang.'

The diary of Nella Last, which had been in Victoria's possession for more than twenty years, was written for Mass-Observation, a research project set up in 1937 to 'record the voice of the people'. Of the 500 volunteers, Mrs Last, a housewife from Barrow-in-Furness, became the most prolific contributor – by the end of the war she had submitted two million words, detailing the life of a middle-aged woman trapped in a stifling marriage. Her husband William Last was a master carpenter with an antisocial streak who discouraged visitors and refused to let her leave the house without him. Instead she poured her love into her two sons Arthur and Clifford, until the Second World War forced her to let go of them. At the same time, war liberated her to escape the house and join the Women's Voluntary Service, where she was much valued. She also opened a shop for the Red Cross which raised money to send parcels to prisoners of war. Most of all, she found a release in her Mass-Observation diary entries, which reveal the aptitude of a born writer.

Mrs Last died in 1968. *The War Diaries of Nella Last* was published in 1981, to the consternation of Barrow residents about whom she had been bracingly frank. Victoria came across them a year later, when *Funny Turns* was on in the West End during the Falklands War: 'I went out on the piss one night with Keith Waterhouse. We walked up the Strand towards the offices of the *Daily Mirror*, and he took a book off the shelf and gave it to me. It was Nella Last's diaries.'[5]

Much as her mother had accumulated books about Queen Victoria,

Victoria became an obsessive collector of Second World War literature. Two of her siblings had been born during the war, and her
stand-up was suffused with imagery of the conflict. ('It was quite an
old plane – I was sitting next to the rear gunner.' 'You only get one
egg a month, like the war.' 'They probably don't know the war is
over in Morecambe.') Several *All the Trimmings* sketches, including
some unused ones, were set on the home front. At first the diary fed
her thirst for wartime detail – coal fires, rationing, the bombing. But
Mrs Last, frustrated by limited life chances available to intelligent
women of her generation, felt familiar. 'Nella was really a bit like
my mother,' Victoria said. 'She was an intellectual from a working-
class background. My mother couldn't be doing with neighbours and
gossip and suburban life.'[6]

Helen Wood's talent as a lively writer was on Victoria's mind. Her
brother Chris had edited their mother's unfinished childhood memoir
for publication and, towards the end of the *Acorn Antiques* run in the
West End, Victoria was asked if she would write a foreword and let
her name be on the cover. She was reluctant to be a promotional
pawn. 'I just think it's so NAF,' she grumbled to Rosalind, 'to have a
book about a Manchester childhood and have to say on the cover "Oh
by the way, one of her daughters ended up on the telly . . ."'[7] But she
was persuaded to relent, and the following year *Nellie's Book: The Early
Life of Victoria Wood's Mother* came out with a short introduction in
which Victoria described Helen as a woman born in the wrong era.

As Victoria reached the age at which Nella started writing, the
diary began to speak to her more personally. Nella grappled with
depression – she had suffered a nervous breakdown before the war
and feared a recurrence. Victoria recognised her coping mechanism
– the drive to be bustlingly busy – as similar to her own: 'When you
have depressive tendencies, adrenalin works really well. She seemed
to get a whole boost of energy from dashing about and doing lots of
things. People were always telling her how marvellous she was which
must have given her a great boost.'[8] In Nella Last, a northern woman
from an ordinary background who used her unique voice to describe
the world around her with a lively clarity, Victoria had found a kind
of twin. As a statement of her intention to adapt them, she sent copies

of the diaries to Damien Timmer and Piers Wenger, who gave her a box of macaroons for Christmas. But it was only once *Acorn Antiques* ended, more than eighteen months after LWT first made contact, that Victoria was free to start talking to them about Nella Last. 'She was very tentative,' says Damien Timmer, 'partly because she didn't know if she wanted to do it with us and partly because she was trying to make sense of it in her mind, feeling her way into something that was a departure for her.'

As her relationship with ITV resumed, Victoria accepted an invitation to take part in *What Did ITV Do For Me?*, a series marking fifty years of independent television – she was the only woman among six profiles celebrating the likes of Roger Moore and Bruce Forsyth. Victoria was by now extremely practised at finding a fresh route through much-told tales of school, university and her early steps as a performer, and took the opportunity to pay tribute once again to Peter Eckersley. 'Without ITV I'd have to strip away half my career,' she concluded.[9] When it was broadcast in September she received a corrective email from Rosalind: 'Mother did watch you in New Faces. I saw it with her and she was very proud of you!'[10]

The chance for a more profound retrospective arose from a less expected quarter when Dawn French asked Victoria for an interview as part of a series about female comedians she was planning for BBC Four. To her surprise, Victoria said yes, and in doing so helped to greenlight the entire project. The interview, in November, took place at a house near Victoria's home.

'What I totally expected from Vic,' says Dawn, 'was that our friendship would be respected as outside the door and what was inside the room was the professional Vic, guarded and self-editing at all times. I did not expect what then happened, which was that Vic answered pretty much every question utterly openly.' Friendship, and professional parity, enabled Victoria to be more honest and natural than she had ever been on television. The conversation covered ground she'd been over many times before: her relationship with her audience; her place in the comedy firmament. But also on display was her emotional intelligence, yielding hard-won insights into herself that were truly familiar only to Victoria's most trusted friends. She surprised Dawn by suggesting her withdrawal from the stage might not be permanent after all: 'If I want to do it, then I think it will be the right thing to do, and bollocks to anybody who thinks I'm too old to do it.' Her interviewer was alarmed enough by her frankness to offer her a final say on what went in: 'I thought she'd been far too open for her own good, and I didn't want to risk our friendship for that. I said, "If you don't like anything, just let me know and it'll be gone." She didn't ask to see it.'

Victoria was far too preoccupied with Mrs Last. Having begun on the first draft in July, she submitted it in October, provisionally titling it *Nella's War*. 'I was completely bowled over by it,' says Piers Wenger. 'As a fan it had everything I had dreamt of. Reading it was like sitting down to watch the Christmas special but only you would be allowed to see it.' Many of the scenes which made it into the final drama were already there, but there was a lot of clutter, faithfully carried over from the diary. What was already in place was a sense of Nella as a woman struggling with depression, or 'nerves', and her fear of the petty snobs and casual racists who run the WVS, led by the kindly but patronising Mrs Waite. As her confidence grows, Nella's seething rage at her husband intensifies. Victoria also revelled in Nella's humour, which was encouraged by Mrs Waite to boost morale. None of her jokes being recorded in the diary, Victoria made some up: 'What's the difference between the dog that does you know what on the front steps here and Hitler? No? Hitler lifts his arm up!' This didn't reach the final script, while comic dialogue more clearly in Victoria's style did. 'God help any plane you're flying,' someone says to a young RAF recruit. 'You can't aim a forkful of mash to your mouth without an accident.'

As she handed in the draft, Victoria made it clear that she wanted to work once more with Gavin Millar, with whom she had remained in contact since he directed *Pat and Margaret*. 'Piers and I were a little bit dismayed, because he was very old school,' says Damien Timmer. 'We would test the waters, but it was clear she wanted Gavin.' Further drafts – the second was completed by early November – were forwarded to Millar for comment. Although it wasn't his official job title, for the next nine months Piers Wenger became Victoria's script editor: 'I was desperate to be that person to her. She was amazingly trusting of me, given that we had never worked together before. I don't think she ever actually asked me what my job was.' The role he performed was similar to that played by Robyn Slovo in *Pat and Margaret*: to conduct an unstinting search for the emotional heart of the story. Sometimes with Damien Timmer, he started going to Highgate, where Victoria got on her hands and knees to spread pages from the various drafts on the floor of her office as they sought a viable structure.

A professional relationship flowered into a friendship. It deepened as they set off on a series of cold wintry field trips to Barrow, which, despite having lived nearby in Morecambe, Victoria had never previously visited. Her first period drama now allowed her to channel a passion for historical research. Staying in a hotel in the Lake District, they visited the local records library to find out more about the Last family and knocked on the doors of people who remembered Nella. Among them was Nella's old neighbour, now in her eighties. Victoria quizzed her about an incident in the diary in which Nella's GP asked her to take in a newborn baby whose mother was ill. 'I said to her next-door neighbour, "What about that baby?" She said, "That never happened." I thought, well, if that never happened, what else never happened? So I just had to pick my own story of my own version of what happened. In the end you're trying to keep the essence of what you felt when you read it.'[11] Victoria took this as permission to make up diary entries rather than quote verbatim. They also visited the pebble-dashed semi where Nella lived during the war: 'I said to the rather baffled man who let me in, "Did you know this house was bombed?" He said, "Yes, I did, because one day I came in and shut the door and the ceiling fell in."'[12] Their moment of highest excitement came when locating the Lasts' first marital home, where they found a sign, painted over, in which the words 'E Last and Son' could be faintly discerned. 'That was such an electrifying moment,' says Piers. 'We went back to the hotel and talked and talked and talked.'

Meanwhile, for background Victoria pored over the minutes of Barrow WVS meetings, old newspapers, wartime radio bulletins and 1940s editions of the *Radio Times*, which advised her what the Lasts would have been listening to. Much of it she knew from her father's collection of 78s. 'I didn't want to just say, "Get me some Glenn Miller and Vera Lynn." Actually Nella Last couldn't stand Vera Lynn. She couldn't stand Gracie Fields or George Formby.' These aversions made their way into the script. So, for a while, did an in-joke about Arthur Askey, the wartime comic who was a judge on *New Faces*. Partly to seek their informal blessing, Piers tracked down Nella's three grandsons, one of whom confirmed Victoria's hunch that Clifford Last was homosexual.

As with *Pat and Margaret*, the demands of rewriting tested Victoria. 'She got a bit tired and fed up with it at one point,' says Piers, 'and I had to have a bit of a conversation about that. She was very hungry for rigorous and detailed feedback. She said, "I just know if I rewrite it ten times, it will be ten times better when we make it."' In fact, there were nine drafts, to work on which she resumed her old habit of sometimes writing all night. In the early hours she would drive the two miles from Highgate to Primrose Hill and post a disc through her producer's letterbox. By March 2006 the drama's title had changed to *Housewife, 49*.

While she was preoccupied by the Second World War, another approach captured Victoria's attention, this time from the production company Tiger Aspect, who were keen to collaborate on a documentary. Victoria had her mother's obsession to thank for the initial pitch, which seemed underdeveloped. 'They said, "Do you want to go all round the world to places called Victoria?" I said, "Oh yeah!" And then I thought, that's not a programme; that's just a holiday. I said, "It'll have to be about something."'[13] That something turned out to be the British Empire. Thus far her knowledge of it was confined to what she'd learned at primary school – 'that we were the hub and lots of "darkies" were proffering goods to us. That was how I was taught about the empire. And so I thought, what is the empire? That became the nub of it.'[14] She started on her own reading while being fed research by Ben Warwick, who at her request was hired as director and producer. 'I'm not interested in dates or statistics,' she told him. 'I'm interested in people.'

Their fifth collaboration was to be their most ambitious, and gruelling: over half of the entire shoot would be spent travelling. With
*Housewife, 49* in pre-production, in April 2006 Victoria flew to
Ghana to join the crew in Accra. For company she had her friend and
make-up artist Chrissie Baker, whose task was to make her look pre-
sentable in the sapping humidity of the mosquito season. 'I wouldn't
advise anyone planning a menopause to come here,' Victoria joked
on the voiceover. 'I feel like a complimentary hand towel in an Indian
restaurant.' Ben Warwick soon discovered something that Victoria
had known since making her *Great Railway Journeys* film in 1995:
even as the focal point of a travel documentary she was much happier
observing than mingling and engaging.

The theme of this first journey took Victoria further than she'd
ever strayed from her comfort zone. She visited an inland river where
chained captives were washed before they were sold into slavery, then
looked round a coastal fort where they were held in dungeons. She
conducted interviews with local curators and met two New Yorkers
who had severed family ties to move to Ghana to reclaim their roots.
More cheerfully she had dinner with a smiling Ghanaian comedian
and watched a game of football on a patch of scrubland named Victoria Park, over which a bust of the other Victoria presided. After
two days in Ghana and a night in Heathrow, the crew flew on to
Jamaica, where they all fell ill. One day, filming in a rainforest at the
site where rebel slaves signed a peace treaty with the British, the only
umbrella was held over the sound equipment and a stoical Victoria
got a soaking. According to Ben Warwick it was here that 'she realised
what was going to be needed to get through this series with respect
for those who'd suffered under the Brits'. The production experienced
its third different climate within a week in St John's in Newfound-
land, where the thinness of the original concept was exposed when
Victoria stopped at another Victoria Park which had nothing to
recommend it. But in Canada she enjoyed a welcome respite from
the theme of British guilt. 'It's cold, it's wet, I can't see anything, I'm
in the car,' she said in the back of a taxi. 'All I need is my parents
arguing in the front seat and it would be like every holiday I've ever
been on.'

Nine days after leaving it she was back in London, where casting for *Housewife, 49* began. Some auditions took place in her home, others at LWT on the south bank of the Thames. Victoria was joined by Piers Wenger, Gavin Millar and a casting director who was briefed to bring in a clean slate of talent. 'Victoria was pretty clear about that,' says Piers. 'She wanted to work with some lesser-known people and some new people.' She had particular actresses in mind. For the strident Mrs Waite she was eager to get Stephanie Cole, who had once been on the shortlist for her 1989 series of half-hour plays. She also wanted someone specific to play the invented character of Nella's waspish sister-in-law Dot. 'There's this actress, I can't think of her name,' she kept saying to Piers. Her frustration mounted until suddenly she remembered in time for Lorraine Ashbourne to be cast. Only one role went to an actor Victoria had worked with before: Sue Wallace, a veteran of *Good Fun*, *As Seen on TV* and *dinnerladies*, played one of the WVS ladies.

The most important search was for an actor to incarnate Nella's joyless husband, only ever known as 'Daddy' in the script. David Threlfall, who came in during a break from *Shameless*, had seen Victoria in *In at the Death* in 1978 but didn't know her personally. 'She was quite quiet,' he recalls. 'Gavin did a lot of the chatting. I thought, Is she going to turn out to be one of those comedians with problems?' The audition went well enough for him to be called back – his agent told him they wanted 'to "see if you've got a range". That set me in a rage.' His rage deepened as he was kept waiting in the foyer and spotted Victoria arrive and enter the lift. He detoured to the gents where he put on a pair of grandad's glasses and a fake moustache. 'I looked in the mirror and I was shaking. I was saying, "I'll give you range, Woody." We read all the scenes. My moustache came loose. I put it back on. She started laughing. She told me later, "I think we should cast Threlly because I don't know what we're going to get with him."' Victoria also admitted to him that she didn't quite have the measure of Nella's husband, having found on her research trips that the real William Last was by no means the cold fish portrayed in the diary: 'They said he was lovely and that she browbeat him and that she nagged. I thought, well, I don't care. I didn't want him to be a villain. I wanted him to be one of those buttoned-up people who can't behave any differently from how they behave.'[15]

While it was emphatically not her marriage that she was writing about, in the story of the Lasts Victoria was able to explore some of her own feelings. During a bombing raid, crammed into a Morrison shelter, Daddy makes a begrudging declaration of love. 'You're everything to me,' he says. 'I didn't want to die and not tell you – you're everything to me.' On a train Nella bumps into her GP, who has escaped his marriage and encourages her to follow suit. 'You can't just ditch people,' Nella says quietly but firmly. (Victoria named him Dr Brierley in memory of her friend Roger Brierley, who had died as she worked on the first draft.) Towards the end, when the Lasts have long since stopped sharing a bed, Nella says, 'I felt my whole married life had been a dream.' In the aftershock of separation Victoria sometimes had comparable doubts about her own marriage. 'You look back at the good bits and the bad bits,' she said the previous year, 'and you think, were the good bits that good?'[16]

In June the cast and crew met for a read-through, followed by two days of rehearsal. They then went north. Most of the filming was done in Huddersfield, mainly because the only way for ITV to meet the costs of a single drama was to piggyback the production facilities of the Granada drama series *Where the Heart Is*. 'That was quite challenging for Victoria,' says Piers. 'But we all wanted the most money we could get on screen.' Where she could exercise influence, she did. No one on set policed the production for authenticity with a beadier eye. When a Christmas cake was brought on set encased in icing she reminded the art department that sugar was rationed in the war. Wardrobe was summoned when an actor was wearing the wrong sleeveless pullover.

She asserted herself in other ways. When shooting *Pat and Margaret* Gavin Millar had politely asked Victoria to stop co-directing behind his back. Now, nearing seventy, he was happy to tolerate it. According to David Threlfall, 'Vic directed it. Gavin had got older and wasn't quite as sharp as he was before.' Victoria and Piers often had hushed conversations on set and continued them every evening on the balcony of a cottage they rented. The unconventional hierarchy was a source of confusion for Christopher Harper, the young actor playing Nella's son Cliff: 'She was in charge of everything. It did strike me as strange that I was receiving four different batches of direction. Gavin's advice was the one that made most sense, but he was third or fourth in command – that's how it felt. If he told me to do something and Vic told me to do something, I'd have to do what Vic said. She was quite a hard taskmaster. I never really knew when she approved; I just knew when she didn't approve.'

The one performance Victoria could not direct was her own. The role of Nella Last required the most serious acting she had yet attempted. When making *dinnerladies* she had had to ask Julie Walters how to produce tears for one scene, but now she was required to cry often. There was some technical assistance from a tear stick smeared in Vicks VapoRub and dabbed under the eyes. 'But she understood the emotions and the unhappiness,' insists Christopher Harper. 'There was no level at which you thought she's performing – you felt that wave of loss and waste.' David Threlfall took it upon himself to offer her practical advice: 'I said to her, "You blink too much." It's reflective of an inner state – she's not quite settled on what she's doing and I thought I bet I can get her settled a bit more. She just listened and took it.' With the mobile camera often hovering intrusively near her make-up-free face, it was as if Victoria was acting with one less layer of skin.

Through all this Victoria's bond with her co-star was warm and light. In one of the most sombre scenes the Lasts visit an angry, invalided Cliff in a rehabilitation home. Before the take Victoria had David Threlfall in hysterics when two nuns walked on set. 'Oh, hey up,' she said. 'Our Lady of the Tea Urns.' They practised dancing for a scene Victoria inserted at the end to provide some hope and redemption for the Lasts' marriage. 'Every so often we'd be filming,' he says, 'and I'd just grab her.' Eventually Victoria summoned Sammy Murray to choreograph something with a little more shape – she taught the pair of them one evening in the car park outside the hotel.

The shoot fetched up in Barrow. The street where Nella lived was filmed, but the more important exterior was the beach on Walney Island which was so bathed in hot July sunshine for a scene set on

Boxing Day that no amount of grading to dim the colours in the edit suite quite worked. The density of the heat was captured by a film crew from *The South Bank Show*. Ten years on from her last profile, to support *Housewife, 49* Victoria had agreed to be the subject of a second. On their first day of filming, they found her sweltering in a bun-style wig, lumpy tweed and wraparound shades.

Filming was completed towards the end of July. Victoria went home to recuperate with the children for a week, then flew to India for the second leg of her series about empire. She briefly stopped in Delhi for breakfast, then travelled on to Darjeeling, where she much enjoyed filming a sequence about the tea industry. After Kolkata, there were two days in the bling of Hong Kong, where Victoria asked a fortune teller if she could foresee a relationship for her. Then it was on to Borneo to tell the story of headhunters, orang-utans and bird's nest soup, which she sampled under duress. Aware that she was exhausted, Ben Warwick fed her information before each section was filmed rather than inundate her with piles of research. 'I can't underestimate the impact of just having shot *Housewife, 49*, where it's all scripted and you know the shots,' he says, 'and then to go to something completely unknown – her professionalism was like nothing I've ever seen before.'

But there was no guarding against things going wrong. The shoot concluded, anticlimactically, with a bumpy three-hour drive into the jungle at the end of which all there was to film was a shop selling Vim and Cadbury's. In this wilderness a weary Victoria concluded the episode with a piece to camera that sat defiantly on the fence: 'It's not for me to say whether it's a good thing or a bad thing that the British should take over these places like India and Hong Kong and Borneo. But I think you have to admire the courage and the tenacity of the people who first arrived here, all those public-school boys hacking their way through the jungle. Because it is jungle still. You feel if you sat here long enough something would grow up your trousers.'

As she raced between projects, nothing could be less likely to happen to Victoria. Her first task back at home was to view an edit of *Housewife, 49*, which Gavin Millar furtively sent behind the back of the producers. 'Dear Vic(tim),' he wrote, 'let's say there's a certain amount of disagreement about what should be in and what should be out . . . What we'd really like is you to say what you'd really like. Welcome home. I dare say you'd rather be back in bloody Borneo.'[17] Twenty-five minutes needed to be excised. In the process, the director himself was edited out of the process. For the next fortnight the drama's original progenitors more or less moved into the edit suite in Soho. 'We have had lots of hoo hah on the WW2 drama,' Victoria told Richard E. Grant, 'and now the lunatics have taken over the asylum and me and the producer and another editor have been editing it ourselves, and the director and his editor haven't been.'[18] It was highly unusual for the writer and lead actor to participate in the edit but, according to Damien Timmer, 'she had no ego at all. She just wanted it to be good. She rolled her sleeves up and she really enjoyed it.'

At the same time Victoria grew concerned that *The South Bank Show*'s film should not be based wholly around *Housewife, 49*. At her prompting the director Daniel Wiles, an LWT veteran, approached Tiger Aspect to ask if the empire documentary might also be featured. 'Confidentially,' came the reply, 'it turns out we're having some tricky moments on Victoria and we don't want them to take their eye off the boil [sic].'[19] Instead Victoria suggested including yet another project that she had crammed into her schedule.

Ever since the end of the run at the Theatre Royal Haymarket, Victoria had not given up on *Acorn Antiques: The Musical!* Earlier in the year, when Julie Walters and Celia Imrie were both nominated for Olivier Awards and the latter won, Victoria was already thinking ahead and hoping 'to see if it's got a life away from its connections'.[20] In its original form the show was far too unwieldy to send out on tour, so she formed a radical plan: to amputate the first half. 'It's the cleanest cut that you can do. I couldn't bear it that it was too long. I really wanted to make it shorter.'[21] She asked Trevor Nunn if he minded, and he didn't. So in rare spare moments in the first half of 2006, Victoria took the second half of the show and started to refashion it. Without anyone to stop her, she grew ruthless. 'In the cold light of day I was able to deconstruct it and take out the numbers I didn't want in. I don't have to give a song to Neil Morrissey.'[22] Among the casualties was 'Have You Met Miss Babs?'

Her other big idea was to take the next logical step and, rather than sit behind someone else's shoulder, direct it herself. 'I haven't directed anything before. Not officially,' she said as she embarked.[23] To ease herself into the role, with Nunn's blessing she decided to base her production on the original and enlisted its assistant choreographer Sammy Murray to co-direct. The musical director she selected to work with was a bright young protégé of Gareth Valentine's called Nigel Lilley. At the end of August the three of them, with the choreographer Stephen Mear, assembled to hold auditions. Nigel, who 'sort of knew Vic's stuff', was taken aback by the impact of her gigawattage on actors: 'What you quickly realised is people tended to act slightly weirdly around Vic and she wouldn't always make it easier for them. People in auditions are nervous anyway and then they've got their ultimate icon sat there.' One actress took the biscuit by announcing she would sing the words of 'Macaroons' to a tune she'd made up herself.

They saw actors of all ages, shapes and sizes. The most critical search was for an actress who could pin on Julie's overall. An idea pinged into Victoria's head when Ria Jones, auditioning for Miss Bonnie, asked if she could take her heels off: it was the kind of spontaneous thing Julie would do. 'Welsh,' Victoria wrote in her casting notes as a reminder. 'Mrs O?'[24] 'Half of it is if Vic likes you,' says Sammy Murray. 'She liked Ria.'

Once the rest of the roles were doled out, Victoria's relentless schedule found her boarding a plane to New Zealand, where, in the series' oddest sequence, she sat in an Auckland radio studio, a witness in headphones as a shock jock argued with a Maori. 'The British betrayed us, Victoria!' said the Maori. 'You should be ashamed of yourself!' She said nothing because, as she travelled around the globe, she came to an understanding that there was no one thing she could say about the British Empire. The last leg of the documentary was the most demanding of all. After two days filming in Auckland and the Bay of Islands, the crew took off at three in the morning, arriving eighteen hours later in Alice Springs, where, that evening in the middle of the outback, Victoria conducted a sensitive interview about the Aborigines' relationship with the British. The following morning they travelled to Melbourne. There was just enough slack in the schedule for Victoria to pay a flying visit to the house of Clifford Last, who emigrated to Australia and became a respected sculptor: 'The taxi driver jumped out of the car and knocked on the door for me. This guy came out and I said, "I'm not really a mad person, I just want to take a photograph of this house because it belonged to a sculptor called Clifford Last." And he said, "I bought this house from him." He didn't know anything about his mother.'[25]

After Hobart, which was the final stop in Australia, there was a long flight via Johannesburg to Zambia, where the film fetched up at the Victoria Falls, which she had nearly visited when filming for Comic Relief in 1995. Behind her right shoulder the body of water with which she shared a name was reduced to a seasonal, bathetic trickle. 'The more I've gone from country to country,' she said to camera, 'the less I feel able to do some clever end-of-documentary smarty-pants summing up.' Then, drawing on her last reserves of intellectual energy, she did just that in a compact monologue that deftly mulched the history of the British Empire and its aftermath into two and a half minutes. 'All these threads come together, and they're knitted into a big sort of shapeless moth-eaten old woolly that is the empire,' she concluded. 'And some people are very fond of it, and some people want to chuck it in the bin. I don't know. I'm done. I'm going home.' Back in London the opening section of the entire series was shot in Victoria Station.

'Have just got back from the third leg of my Empire documentary filming – v full on,' she told Rosalind. 'I feel I've been away a bit too much from the children this year, not that they complain, but I feel it myself.'[26] Although Victoria moaned about it, the tightness of the schedule was created by the competing demands of *Housewife, 49* and *Acorn Antiques* and her desire to be away from the children for no longer than a fortnight. 'We had to tell a big enough story to warrant us going to these places,' says Ben Warwick. 'A lot of the time we had to shoot more sequences than we needed. I couldn't lighten the load for her, and I could see her getting more and more tired. She really was on her last legs. It was incredibly difficult to keep our relationship as buoyant as it had been before. The stresses accelerated the realisation that we'd done what we could do together.'

As the edits came through across the autumn, Victoria got down to writing the voiceover for the documentary, using as her template the responsive observational style she'd established on *Great Railway Journeys*. In October she returned to *The South Bank Show* with an interview filmed in the Novello Theatre. A good proportion of the questions put to her by Melvyn Bragg went over areas dealt with in the previous profile a decade earlier, including her early encounter with Joyce Grenfell. She was even asked the same question as last time – if Pat and Margaret were two halves of a self-portrait. The following night her episode of *More Dawn French's Girls Who Do: Comedy* was broadcast. Recorded nearly a year earlier, it covered the same ground but with a much more intuitive line of questioning. Privately Victoria grumbled about Bragg's inflexibility as an interviewer and was soon in touch with Daniel Wiles to request another go at it. 'I felt very depressed after the interview,' she wrote. 'Pat and Margaret is 12 years ago – I've got nothing to say about it. Same with stand up comedy, and working with Julie . . . I'm so excited about what I'm doing . . . and I've got so many plans for next year – and I just felt I didn't really express myself well in the interview.'[27] Another encounter was scheduled for her lunchbreak in a pub round the corner from *Acorn Antiques* rehearsals, which the *South Bank Show* crew also filmed.

At the age of fifty-three, in the American Church in Tottenham Court Road, Victoria took charge of a rehearsal room for the first time. She made a short speech in which she impressed on the cast – full of unfamiliar faces who tended to look upon her with reverence – that she had one golden rule. 'I spent hours writing the script,' she told them, 'and if you put another word in, I'll get really annoyed.' Ria Jones, like everyone hoping to bond with her, was struck by her shyness and seriousness: 'I thought we'd be cracking lines from *As Seen on TV*. But no. She was quite nervous.' Victoria's nerves manifested themselves again a few weeks later when the company did their first run-through in front of a small audience of invitees. 'Halfway through act one,' says Nigel, 'Vic ran up to the piano and said, "Why is everything so slow?" I was mortified. It was her composition and she probably felt exposed about it.'

There were seventeen numbers in all, three of them new, including a touching duet for a pair of middle-aged gay shopkeepers. The big new showstopper was 'Manchesterford'. Like the cheerful song of the same name from the West End show, it welcomed the audience to the cosy vintage setting of the musical, but everything else was different. The clue was in the opening lines:

> Come on boys we're going to paint the town
> We're going to take you to . . . Manchesterford.
> Come on ladies won't you come on down
> Well here's another clue . . . Manchesterford.
> It's not Chicago but there's no embargo on the va va voom
> It's the spot that's got the lot and it's twinned with Cheadle Hulme.

Stephen Mear and Sammy Murray were tasked with coming up with a dance parody of *Chicago*, the hit Kander and Ebb musical. Picked out by a spotlight, Ria Jones came on in fishnets and a single Marigold, limbs gyrating raunchily, to be joined by a podgy troupe in sheer black. Victoria encouraged her new leading lady, who was a more natural showgirl than Julie, to play to those strengths, while advising her not to go hunting for laughs. 'You're a natural at comedy timing,' she told her, 'but let the audience decide you're funny, not you.'

In early December the production moved up to the Lowry Theatre in Salford. When the band played with the company for the first time the moment came for the actor playing Miss Berta to sing 'Remind Him'. 'It was all going really well,' says Nigel Lilley, who was unaware of the song's provenance, 'and then Vic lost it during that song.' She lost it again, this time in frustration, when bluntly lecturing the cast after a disappointing dress rehearsal. For the most part she bonded with the company in the hotel bar. 'She'd start telling the stories,' says Ria Jones. 'We'd all be gathered around her and hanging on her every word.'

*Housewife, 49* was broadcast on ITV on a Sunday night in December. Victoria was pleased with the slot – 'I didn't want it to get swallowed up in Christmas,' she told Rosalind.[28] Despite competing against *BBC*

*Sports Personality of the Year*, it was seen by eight million, which was a lot for the multichannel age. 'It really mattered to her that it got a big audience,' says Piers. 'It was thrilling when those figures came through.' Emailing that night, Richard E. Grant put a finger on what the success must mean to her. 'CONGRATULATIONS VIC!' he wrote at midnight. 'Your Calendar Girls really showed 'em.'[29] His was the first of many raves. She emailed back to thank him at three in the morning from her hotel in Manchester. The following evening brought the first preview of *Acorn Antiques*, when Victoria began to relax only when she heard the audience start to laugh. She had launched two hits – one featuring her first serious acting role, the other her debut as a director – on two consecutive nights. She had become much more than the nation's favourite funny lady.

Just before Christmas, Victoria performed her final duty for *The South Bank Show* with a tour of Nella Last's Barrow. When Daniel Wiles and his researcher were travelling the three miles from the station to the hotel they happened to spot Victoria pulling her suitcase along the road: 'We stopped the taxi and said, "Hi, Vic, climb in." And she said, "Oh no, I like the walk."' Despite the national spotlight she had directed onto the town, she went largely unrecognised apart from that evening in the hotel where she and the crew were having dinner. A party of thirty women from the WI twigged that she was in the restaurant and asked if she'd say hello to them. 'She just went to pieces,' says Wiles. 'She said, "If you come in with me, I'll go."'

*Acorn Antiques* stayed at the Lowry for four weeks. In January 2007 it embarked on a vast tour, Nigel Lilley and Sammy Murray travelling with the production to bed it in each week. Not every venue it was booked into was equally well set up to house it, but the DNA of *Acorn Antiques*, where things not working is in the fabric of the comedy, meant solutions could be improvised. The cast sometimes grumbled. 'It was quite a challenge sometimes to say, "This is what it is,"' says Sammy. 'I would always go, "Victoria's fine with it. End of story."' After each performance Victoria was sent a show report which she zealously policed for any sign of overrunning. 'She wanted act one to be an hour fifteen,' says Nigel. 'If it went up to one seventeen, she'd ring.' A frequent visitor as the show travelled up and down and across England, she was thrilled to witness a riotous reaction at the Hippodrome in Birmingham. There was a special guest at the Saturday matinee in Richmond. 'Vic was really excited that someone was going to be in,' says Nigel. 'We thought it was going to be Julie. In fact, it was Trevor Nunn. She really wanted him to see her work as a director. He was incredibly generous and that meant an awful lot.' One night when the show was in Brighton she went out with Stephen Mear: 'When you got to know her you'd forget how famous she was,' he says. 'I stupidly took her to a gay bar, and she leant over to me and said, "Stephen, I think I'm going to have to go home now. I feel like Cilla Black."'

It was her status as a national treasure which ASDA sought to exploit when, twenty years after she and Julie appeared in an advertising campaign for the supermarket, they asked Victoria back to front another. The pitch of the agency was that ASDA's bread is as authentic as the people who bake it on site, and they conceived the idea of Victoria working as an ASDA baker. Manchester was considered as a location before a branch near Gateshead was chosen. The original plan was for Victoria to clock in at seven each morning and do a ten-hour shift, and she'd be filmed on two cameras by director Patrick Collerton. 'What I quickly realised,' he says, 'was she was working ferociously hard and she was giving a show, more or less. About an hour and half in she was starting to flag.' The performance she gave was as 'Victoria Wood', cheekily interacting with the staff and the customers. After four days there were twenty hours of film from which eight adverts of varying length were made. The first was launched immediately. The last showed Victoria scraping flour off the work surface as the other bakers knocked off for the day. As she looked around and noticed everyone had left, a caption appeared on the screen: 'Thank you Victoria from all of us at ASDA.' The supermarket's bread sales enjoyed an instant boost. Not long after, Victoria's sister Rosalind was between jobs. 'If dosh would help please let me know,' she wrote. 'I got a lot for my ASDA ads and what's it for if not to help family . . .'[30]

Victoria's final duties as a historian of the empire was to write and submit several thousand words to the publishers Hodder &

Stoughton for the book to accompany *Victoria's Empire*, as the series was now called. It was published concurrently with the series, which was broadcast in May and prompted a flow of letters, she told Lesley Fitton, 'from ancient men typed wonkily saying v fussily that the Brits were not the first to use slavery etc to which I can only say "I KNOW! I SAID THAT IN THE FRIGGING PROGRAMME!"'[31]

Of her exhausting forays into the past, Victoria remained prouder of *Housewife, 49*, which that month was up for BAFTAs. Betty Jackson, consulted about what to wear, managed to persuade her into a navy-blue frock with a plunging neckline and yards of chiffon. Victoria travelled to the ceremony with David Threlfall, who had not been nominated: 'I said on the way there, "You've got two BAFTAs, haven't you?" She went, "Five." I said, "There's no need to brag about it, old boy!"' She had two more by the end of the evening: one for best single drama, the other, to her genuine surprise, for best actress. The judges put her performance ahead of Anne-Marie Duff, Samantha Morton and Ruth Wilson. 'It's a relief to win,' she said in her acceptance speech, 'because I was engaged on a no-win no-fee basis.' At the afterparty at the Natural History Museum, Victoria carried her awards around in a plastic bag. 'She stayed for a bit,' says Piers Wenger, 'but she really wanted to get home. On some level, although she massively played it down, she was really thrilled. It was the one achievement that right up until the end of her life she would say, "God, that was a good night, wasn't it?"' Her assistant Cathy Edis had a different perspective when she came in to work the next morning and found two BAFTAs on the kitchen table. She asked how the celebrations went: 'Vic said, "Oh, I just came home and went to bed." She had no one to really applaud what she'd done.' Later, Victoria expressed a debt of gratitude she felt she owed to David Threlfall by giving him one of the awards. 'You're what it says on the front of this,' she wrote in the card as she presented it to him. When he turned it over it said 'bee's knees'.

The following month Victoria accepted another less public award at the Royal Academy of Music, where she was presented with an honorary fellowship – a rare accolade for a non-musician. She sat bashfully among the graduates who, along with her proud trumpet tutor Jim Watson, cheered as her citation was read by John Suchet. 'When she ambled up to deliver a brief vote of thanks on behalf of those honoured at the close,' says the principal Jonathan Freeman-Attwood, 'she delivered a part-piece of supreme virtuosity. It was so funny and affectionate and perfect, we all felt we were in heaven.'

At the same time, after more than six months on the road, *Acorn Antiques* fetched up at its final destination in Cardiff. Victoria watched the show on the Friday night at the Wales Millennium Centre and was there for the warm-up before the Saturday matinee to speak to the company. They were expecting to be patted on the back for a triumphant tour, but she stayed true to the exacting standards she'd set at the dress rehearsal. 'She laid into us big time,' says Ria Jones. 'She suddenly gave us a notes session from hell. We all walked away terrified and a bit upset. Afterwards she came to my dressing room and gave me the biggest hug. I wanted to say, "Why did you just do that?" It was maybe for us not to rest on our laurels for the last two shows. She didn't want them to be all schmaltzy. It worked.'

For the matinee Victoria delighted the company and the audience by coming on as a barista in a cap. Then, for the very final perfor-mance, Ria Jones persuaded her to take a bow at the end wearing a T-shirt with the Welsh flag, sending the audience into a frenzied ecstasy. It was the last hurrah for the musical Victoria wrote to cheer herself up after the end of her marriage. 'It was just the happiest thing I've ever done,' she would reflect, 'from writing the music, working with Trevor, rewriting it, directing it. The whole thing.'[32]

## 22

# MID LIFE

'I'm not any younger just because I'm squashed into a big beige condom.'

Untitled script, 2008

Straight after *Acorn Antiques* closed Victoria took the children to Montreal. She and Grace were canoeing over rapids when they capsized and were swept out of the boat, which floated off down river along with the bag containing her money, cards and phone. 'Was a bit scary for a few minutes,' she told Rosalind.[1] It was their last family holiday before an inevitable rite of passage. Having won a choral scholarship to study French and Italian at Cambridge University, on returning home Grace left to spend the next year in Lille, where she had a job as an usher in the opera house.

If Victoria dreaded this moment, she didn't let it show. 'I think Mum was excited for me,' says Grace. 'She did really nice things. We packed all my stuff, and when I got to Lille I found she'd hidden all sorts of sweets and notes.' She visited twice that autumn, first with Henry to see Grace sing in a concert on Armistice Day weekend. 'She has a lovely voice,' Victoria proudly informed David Firman – 'very big – she tries valiantly to blend in when in a choir.'[2] In December she took Cathy Edis and her daughter on a day trip to the Christmas market. As they wandered a woman spotted Victoria, ran over and flung her arms round her.

With her first child gone, that autumn Victoria revisited the world of her own childhood. Piers Wenger, now firmly established as a friend and confidant, had moved to the BBC, where he was producing an adaptation of *Ballet Shoes*, Noel Streatfeild's tale of three orphans attending an academy of dance and drama in London. As a favour to Piers, and as it was her next best children's book after *The Swish of the Curtain*, she agreed to take the role of the matronly Nana. To get into character, she asked if she could be fitted with a sizeable bottom: 'I wanted it to be vast, like a Titanic in tweed. You just know in the meeting when you make a suggestion and people don't really answer you, you think, all right then, that's not going to happen. It wasn't my show so I couldn't call the tune.'[3] The experience of not being in charge on the shoot in locations around London was salutary. She had no fondness for spending long fallow hours in a Winnebago: 'I really would prefer to be a bit busier. You could go off and do other things and then come back, but because you've got a grey wig and a fat arse you can't go anywhere.'[4] She made it her business to come in and support Sammy Murray, whom she recommended as choreographer, even when not needed on set herself, and particularly enjoyed the company of Eileen Atkins. 'It was worth it just to meet her,' she told Rosalind. 'I think it will be okay if you like that sort of holiday telly (which I do normally but not when I'm in it).'[5]

There was another task to keep her mind occupied on set. In November BAFTA was to mark its sixtieth anniversary with a gala night filmed by ITV at the New London Theatre. As the entertainer with the biggest tally of award nominations – twelve in twenty-one years – Victoria was top of the list of invitees and was asked to close the evening with a stand-up set. 'I felt there's something missing in my life if I don't do it ever,' she explained. 'I don't want to do another big tour, and I don't want to go out and talk for two hours, but I thought perhaps I could just do a little bit just to put my toe in the water.'[6] It had been more than six years since she wrote the material for *Victoria Wood At It Again*, and the question of what area of experience she could spin into comedy needed addressing. Joking about divorce was not an option, so instead she worked up a set based on the seven signs of ageing. At the sound check she encountered a familiar face in Alasdair Macmillan, who had directed *An Audience with Victoria*

*Wood* in 1988. Her one request to him was that, unlike everyone else throughout the evening, she enter from stage left – as she always had. 'My only real worry was that I wouldn't be able to remember it because I hadn't been able to try it out anywhere. I thought, I'm not going to be nervous. I've been doing this for thirty years and it's only a telly show.'⁷ Shallow breaths, and the cribsheet she produced from the pocket of her grey Betty Jackson suit, told another story. Her chosen theme enabled her to come at familiar territory – catalogues, body image, brand names – from a fresh angle. The first sign of age, she said, was when 'you don't really know who anybody is' and thus confuse Kerry Katona with Kiri Te Kanawa. The fifth sign was when 'all your respectable married friends go completely off the rails . . . Suddenly they're losing four stone, zipping themselves into suede trousers and going, "This is my time, Derek."' In twenty minutes she offered a glimpse of the live show about the next stage in a woman's life that she would never perform. She was resigned to the fact that, for broadcast, it would be cut to a mere eight minutes. Aside from the cribsheet, her other insurance was 'to put a couple of old gags in so I can get off with a big laugh'. Both were about grooming and the proliferation of body hair: 'Honestly, if you leave it, you look like you should be sitting cross-legged in a forest playing the pan pipes. And apparently these days it has to go into a shape. You can't do what I do, which is just chop the odd chunk off with the nail scissors.'

'I don't mind people knowing that about me,' she told Kirsty Young when she was interviewed that month for *Desert Island Discs*. 'But I would hate anyone seeing my tea towels.' Victoria's second stint as a castaway was very different from her encounter with Michael Parkinson twenty years earlier. Much less shuttered, she dwelled more openly on the travails of her childhood and, when pressed, said she felt sorry for the neglected little girl she had once been. The recording got off to a haphazard start when, after a few minutes, a fire alarm sounded and Broadcasting House had to be evacuated. The throng of radio staffers didn't bat an eyelid as Victoria stood on the pavement. 'Then an open-top London bus goes past,' says Kirsty Young, 'and the commentator on the bus says, "On your left-hand side is the Langham Hotel, where blah blah blah during the war. And on your right" – and we can hear he's about to say "is the BBC" and he turns and says, "is one of Britain's greatest comedians." And give her her due, she did look up, she gave a little smile and a wave.'

Back in the studio, the end of Victoria's long marriage could not be ducked. 'I felt like one of those cartoon people that steps over a cliff,' she said. 'Your legs are moving but there's nothing underneath.' As she talked about Geoffrey, says Kirsty Young, 'she was staring absolutely across the table at me and her eyes were brimful of emotion without her crying. And in her eyes at one point I felt – and it was very, very poignant and very moving – a look of "please don't ask me any more – this is as far as I can go". Then when we got into the music, she didn't say anything, she was just in her own thoughts. It was a very difficult moment for her and was clearly still raw for her.' Victoria articulated her melancholy by choosing music by Arvo Pärt and Randy Newman. In twenty years her musical palate had veered away from the pre-war tastes inherited from her father. Three of her picks – songs by Weather Report, Tom Waits and Mr Scruff – were made in concert with Henry, while she selected a John Rutter carol sung by the choir of Clare College Cambridge, which Grace was soon to join. Afterwards her anxiety focused on how much she had unexpectedly let slip about her childhood. 'I wonder whether I said too much,' she said to Piers Wenger.

In November Victoria flew back across the Atlantic with Piers to attend the International Emmy Awards in New York. There for several days, she enjoyed the rare sensation of anonymity: 'I could just go barging about gawping at people. On the red carpet this woman called Cognac Wetherspoon or something like that with false eyelashes – she was very, very bizarre-looking – asked, "Why are you here?" I said, "I've been nominated for best actress." She said, "Oh, that's marvellous. What else do you do?" I said, "I've done documentaries; I've written a musical," and she said, "That's *right*, you have!"[8] The ceremony was 'incredibly long and boring,' says Piers. 'We were falling asleep at the table with the jet lag.' She was the only British nominee not to prosper – 'but it was still great to be there and be nominated,' she told Rosalind.[9] Her greatest pleasure was watching Robert De Niro attempt to read a citation from the autocue: 'A treat

I will long remember. I thought, put your glasses on! It was excruciating. He was doing a word at a time. It was like a sight test.'[10]

*Desert Island Discs* was broadcast just before Christmas. 'I had been a bit anxious about the transmission,' she told Richard E. Grant. 'In fact I drove to Southwark I felt so twitchy and had to get out of the house.'[11] After Christmas, she, Grace and Henry travelled by train with the Glossop family to wander around a misty Venice.

Victoria was soon back in the radio recording studio thanks to David Threlfall, who had a commission from Radio 4 to write a short story as part of a Valentine's week series: 'Along the way I remembered what she'd said: if I can hear someone in my head, then write for them. "Victoria," I said. "Got you a little present. If you don't want to do it, say so." She said, "No, I'll do it."' After more than twenty drafts he'd produced something that sounded very like her. 'Stupid Cupid' was a galloping short story about Joyce, a housewife who takes explosive revenge on her husband James for the sin of being dull. There was less than an hour's studio time booked in Shepherd's Bush to record and edit the fourteen-minute story. Victoria had prepared thoroughly and, reading in the same brisk, vibrant style as her *Jackanory* recordings, made barely a fluff.

After 2007, 2008 was to be much quieter. 'Slavery and the Empire nearly did me in, and Ballet Shoes finished me off,' she told Lesley Fitton, 'but next year I am just doing GCSEs (well Hen is but you know how it is) and writing.'[12] With Grace away, Victoria and Henry were now thrown upon each other as the only permanent occupants of the house. She put a lot of energy into gearing him up for exams that, at the same stage in her life, she had mainly failed. A keen instrumentalist and a natural comedian, Henry felt aware that he had inherited another of his mother's traits. 'There's a lot of similar internal wiring,' he says. 'I was smart but lazy, and it was a fundamental problem getting stuff done. I would say to her, "You always told me you were lazy at school and then found this work ethic later on, and I always knew that it would be the same." There was a common understanding about a lot of stuff.'

For the first time in many years, Victoria had nothing planned and

no conversations on the go with broadcasters about potential projects. Her ambition instead was to work in the one medium which,
despite several attempts, she had not yet conquered. 'I think I've got
a story that is for cinema,' she volunteered at the end of 2007. 'I'm
not overconfident about being able to write a film and getting it done
at the end of it, but I can give it a go.'[13] She referred to a new writing
project on *Desert Island Discs* – 'It's just about life now really . . .
of a middle-aged person,' she said – but could be tempted to reveal
no more. There was a reason for her coyness. Far less obliquely than
in *Housewife, 49*, the untitled script she began writing in January
2008 was a portrait of a failed marriage. Her two protagonists have
been married for years, and their children have left home, but rather
than stencil the precise circumstances of her own break-up onto the
script, she created a more dramatic scenario. In the first scene Sally
is blindsided when she learns that her husband Tony is abandoning
her for a much younger woman at work. His new girlfriend insists
Tony clears the air by going with Sally to a couple's counsellor, who
in turn advises them to meet on neutral ground once a week. As
Sally bravely navigates the indignities of midlife singledom, it's put
to her that she should try speed dating. 'I'm too old!' she says. 'It
would be more like carbon dating.' Meanwhile, Tony comes to realise
that, beyond sex, there's not much fun to be had with a younger
woman who understands none of his cultural reference points. In the
redemptive final scene, the marriage, with its long history of shared
jokes and memories, is resumed.

Victoria made an effort to distance herself from the story. Sally
bakes cakes for a living, while it's her faithless husband who is the
celebrity – he presents a popular history series on TV. She has a joyless and hoity-toity neighbour whose children (Clemency, Lysander
and Perdita) are not allowed sugar. Victoria set it in Harpenden, the
commuter-belt village in Hertfordshire, which she knew from visits to
Lesley Fitton. 'Need to go to Harpers,' she told her, 'as I think film I
am writing is set in some place like it, if not it . . . I need a place that's
commutable, has a mix of people not just posh.'[14] There were new
targets and old to aim at: the petty Home Counties mindset, vacuous
spas, dogging. Tony's girlfriend gets a job on a callous TV show called

*Fat Chavs* in which overweight working-class people are trained up in boot camp to pass themselves off as toffs. But for all the camouflage, the story was deeply rooted in autobiography. In a flashback to 1961 a neglected young Sally watches television on her own in a silent house. The ghost of Bob Mason is evoked in another flashback: a teenage Sally poses in a photobooth with a poet boyfriend who goes off to art college where he is won over by a lithe new girlfriend – Victoria had attempted a play on this theme when pregnant with Grace. Sally's surname is Bedford, like Pat's in *Pat and Margaret*.

At the core of the comedy is the simmering rage of a woman left to navigate middle age on her own. 'You tore our whole marriage to bits week by week – just to justify you following your cock!' Sally shouts at Tony. But Victoria did attempt to be even-handed. At the end Sally apologises for her own failures:

> You did do lots to try and help me feel better and I never said thank you . . . And I'm sorry I didn't help you with your pro-gramme and didn't have exciting pubic hair and forgot to have sex and all that. And you were great to be married to a lot of the time really, and you're a great dad . . . sorry for all my bits.

Victoria moved on to a second draft but felt unable to develop it any further. 'It just wasn't any good,' she said the following year. 'It was about a marriage. I think I couldn't really do it. I literally threw it away.'[15] She didn't, as a copy survived, but she dropped all thought of developing it further.

Meanwhile, another idea loitered: to tell the little-known story of the Guinea Pig Club. Its members consisted of RAF pilots who had been shot down in the Second World War, surviving with horrific burns that were treated by pioneering surgeon Archibald McIndoe. Early in 2008 Victoria and Piers Wenger visited the hospital in East Grinstead in Sussex, now a museum, where they had been treated. Afterwards she and Piers met some surviving Guinea Pigs in a pub. 'They clearly adored her,' says Piers. 'They loved the fact that she was funny and clever and yet terribly down to earth.' The secretary of the Guinea Pig Club sent DVDs to aid her further research, and Victoria

With the cast of her *Brief Encounter* spoof for *Victoria Wood with All the Trimmings* in 2000. From the left: Michael Parkinson, Bill Paterson, Celia Imrie and Richenda Carey.

The 'Keyboard Collywobbles' sketch with Anne Reid was filmed in black and white, diminishing the impact of Victoria's crimson gown.

With Rosalind and their mother Helen, whose spiky personality softened in old age.

The three sisters walked up Langdale Pikes in the summer of 2002 to scatter their parents' ashes.

Oh! Oh! Oh! Mrs O. At the Theatre Royal Haymarket in 2005, Victoria understudied the lead role of *Acorn Antiques: The Musical!* on Mondays and Wednesday matinees.

A director at last. With Nigel Lilley and Sammy Murray in rehearsal for *Acorn Antiques: The Musical!* on tour in 2006.

'Couldn't have liked it more': at her sixtieth birthday with Sammy Murray, Nigel Lilley (behind), Stephen Mear (right) and his partner Mark Smith.

Victoria's recital at the wedding of Beth Willis and Jonny Campbell at Wiltons Music Hall in December 2013 was her final performance.

Oh! Oh! Oh! Mrs O. At the Theatre Royal Haymarket in 2005, Victoria understudied the lead role of *Acorn Antiques: The Musical!* on Mondays and Wednesday matinees.

A director at last. With Nigel Lilley and Sammy Murray in rehearsal for *Acorn Antiques: The Musical!* on tour in 2006.

On the set of *Housewife, 49* with producer Piers Wenger, 'a hardcore fan' who became her closest companion after her divorce.

With old friends (from left) Jane Wymark, Catherine Ashmore and Jane's husband Paul Howson.

Grace, Henry and Victoria in Venice to see in 2008 with regular holiday companions Charlotte Scott and Roger Glossop.

Vegetarian Christmas
lunch in Highgate with
Grace and Henry.

With some Barrys and
a Freda filming *Victoria
Wood's Mid Life Christmas*
in 2009.

On the set of *Eric & Ernie* with (from
left) Daniel Rigby, Jim Moir and Bryan
Dick. Victoria is wearing a hairclip
between takes.

'Couldn't have liked it more': at her sixtieth birthday with Sammy Murray, Nigel Lilley (behind), Stephen Mear (right) and his partner Mark Smith.

Victoria's recital at the wedding of Beth Willis and Jonny Campbell at Wiltons Music Hall in December 2013 was her final performance.

In Huddersfield Town Hall in 2014, the director-composer listens as her music for *That Day We Sang* is performed by the Hallé Orchestra.

In the Swiss Cottage garden on the edge of Esthwaite Water with Beth Willis and her baby daughter.

At it again at the Royal Albert Hall.

asked Cathy Edis to find out more about the life of RAF pilots and more information about the Guinea Pigs. 'One day,' wrote McIndoe when the hospital ward was closed down in 1948, 'someone will tell the complete story of Ward II.' It was not to be Victoria. The bawdiness of the Guinea Pigs' banter soon persuaded her the story was safer in the hands of a male writer.

In March, just as Victoria nursed the desire to write a film, she was celebrated with a month-long season of her work at the BFI Southbank. All of her greatest hits, and the odd lesser-known curio, were shown on a big screen: *Talent, Nearly a Happy Ending, Wood and Walters, Victoria Wood As Seen on TV, Over to Pam, Pat and Margaret, dinnerladies* and *Housewife, 49*. Amid the screenings Victoria was interviewed in front of a packed auditorium. The same month *Talent* was revived in the small theatre over the road in Highgate. Formerly an old music hall, the Gatehouse Theatre had set up as a fringe venue in 1997 and Victoria had become its first patron. One revival begat another. Victoria had no musical recordings of *Talent* they could work from so contacted David Graham, the producer who had toured it ten years earlier. He agreed to share his recordings if she would grant his company the stage rights to *dinnerladies*. She accepted the bargain, and Graham set to composting the first series down into a single play and booking venues for a tour to begin the following year. She took on a supervisory role, with final approval of the script and publicity material.

In this slack period Victoria pondered creating a website, then thought better of it. 'I don't have anything to flog and I don't particularly want a bigger fan base,' she told Rosalind, to whom she also mentioned buying a rural bolthole for all the family to use. When her sister offered to hunt for cottages, Victoria laid out her parameters – she didn't want anywhere in Sussex, being too close to an oast house Geoffrey had bought with his girlfriend. 'I don't find the seaside very appealing in this country,' she added. 'I'm more of a lakes and woods type person.'[16]

She celebrated her fifty-fifth birthday in May by rendezvousing with Grace in Paris and hosting a small party at home in the garden – guests huddled under blankets and round braziers. In June

the Queen's Birthday Honours list brought a CBE. 'For serv Entertainment,' read the citation. A year earlier Betty Jackson had been
made a CBE and when Victoria wrote to her she took to addressing
the envelope 'Commander Betty Jackson'. Now she was able to sign
herself, 'from one commander to another, love Vic.'

After popping up as a guest on *The Apprentice: You're Fired!*, Victoria
had nothing much else on for the rest of the year and decided to have
an operation on a bunion. 'You have to have your foot up for two
weeks,' she told Rosalind, 'and then hopping about four weeks but I
think it's worth it, as I want to be filming next year.'[17] Penelope came
south to look after her and Henry while she recuperated by watching
the Olympic Games from Beijing. She sprang up sooner than she was
meant to when she learned that Sammy Murray, and one of the twin
boys to whom she had just given birth, had been severely ill – though
still in plaster, she drove to visit them in Stoke Mandeville hospital.
For a while Victoria wore a built-up shoe, and for the rest of the year
was not allowed to wear anything but Uggs and Birkenstocks. The
only exception was her day out at the palace in October, accompanied
by Grace, Henry and Catherine Ashmore, who snapped her with a
row of Beefeaters. The queen of England asked the queen of entertainment if she'd been doing the job for a long time: 'I said, "Yes, a
very long time!"'[18]

By now Grace was in her first year at Cambridge. After waiting a few
weeks before visiting – 'or she will feel I'm breathing down her neck' –
Victoria began driving up to attend evensong and concerts.[19] She thus
found herself a tourist in a culture which, what with its conveyor belt
of Oxbridge comedians, she had always held at arm's length. 'She was
in the nicest possible way bemused by it,' says Grace. 'She had the sense
of how the hell did I produce a kid who can do this?'

The year had already yielded one semi-autobiographical film script.
In the autumn Victoria hoped for more success with a second. Once
more her protagonist was an isolated woman in her fifties. Eunice lives
on a remote farm in the Lake District with an unloving father who
fills the house with clutter. 'They've got no phone and no television
and no connection with the outside world,' Victoria explained, 'and
it's about what happens to her from the day he dies and how she has

to reconnect back with the world.'[20] She researched the psychology of compulsive hoarders, while drawing too on memories of Birtle Edge House and her mother, who had devoted her life to shedding family while accumulating junk. 'It's a much exaggerated version of how we lived, I suppose,' she said. 'It's about television as well. If you live with no telly, you're quite disconnected from ordinary conversation. The first thing this woman does when her father dies is she buys a big telly. And then she starts to try and make her house look like houses look on the telly. But she doesn't know how to communicate with people, so she gets all the exterior things right and it's about how you've got to sort yourself out.'[21]

She called it *The Giddy Kipper*. The title came from a speech by an irate teacher who, in a flashback to the early 1960s, throws out young Eunice for telling jokes in class: 'Do you know who's going to heaven – the clean little girls – the ones who do as they're told – not the grubby ones, not the giddy kippers – god doesn't like giddy kippers – giddy kippers go to hell.'

Most autobiographically of all, Eunice feels nothing at the death of a parent. 'My dad's dead,' she tells the surgery matter-of-factly. 'Well, you know he was dying? And she said just like call [the doctor] if there was any change. There wasn't any change, so I didn't call her. But he's dead now, which is a change, so I'm calling.' Later the undertakers come to take the body. 'Not getting the broken-hearted trophy, is she?' one of them mutters. At her father's funeral, attended solely by Eunice, she picks a medley of party tunes by Winifred Atwell.

When the first draft was finished in November, Victoria gave it to Piers Wenger in the hope that he would want to produce it. 'We had better then talk about how to get the money,' she wrote to Lucy Ansbro. 'Do we lob Phil [McIntyre] at people or do I have to do it myself?'[22] She produced a plot summary for the sales pitch concluding, at Piers's suggestion, with a statement of her intentions. These were 'to play Eunice and to direct the film . . . I'm shining a light on the ordinary people we don't always see on screen, and telling the story of one person's difficult, awkward, but ultimately uplifting journey towards happiness.'[23] By the following summer no money had been raised and her desire to break into cinema was no further on.

\*

Uniquely for Victoria, 2008 was an unproductive year. Then in December the seeds were sown for three projects that would occupy her for the next three years. The one that would have the very longest gestation came, unusually, from elsewhere. The film production company Left Bank Pictures had optioned an article in the *New Yorker* about the notorious English pianist Joyce Hatto, who had died in 2006 having enjoyed a remarkable late-flourishing renown. A series of over a hundred recordings released in her seventies had generated acclaim from chat-room fans and flabbergasted critics. Soon after her death it was established by digital detection that almost all recordings issued in her name in fact featured the work of other pianists. Andy Harries of Left Bank, casting around for someone to write the script, showed the article to Piers Wenger, who, thinking a story of musical oddballs set in the commuter belt would appeal to Victoria, recommended her. When they met, Harries found her 'quite wary of men, and I had been warned that she could be prickly. Because I had been at Granada in my youth, I had seen her very earliest performances. It helped break the ice a bit.' The project did indeed enthuse Victoria, so he put a researcher onto the task of fleshing out the human story of Hatto and her husband William Barrington-Coupe. The latter, still alive, was chiefly – and perhaps solely – responsible for the breathtaking deception perpetrated upon the classical-music industry. Left Bank's researcher Kerry Gill-Pryde was soon joined by Cathy Edis, who spent the next few months sleuthing on Victoria's behalf.

In the same week as she met Andy Harries Victoria had lunch with Janice Hadlow, the new controller of BBC Two, to pitch a long-cherished idea to tell the story of when Eric Morecambe met Ernie Wise. She had read several biographies of the pair and was particularly taken with a story in which, on a train during the Blitz, Eric's mother told the two hyperactive young boys to channel their energy by writing some material together. The more Victoria thought about it in the coming months the more she understood that, like her Guinea Pig Club idea, the script would better flourish in the hands of a male writer. Piers Wenger suggested they sound out Peter Bowker, best known for his seedy, rollicking 2004 drama *Blackpool*, which she admired. They met at her private-members club in Shaftesbury Avenue.

'I might be doing myself out of a job here,' Bowker said to her, 'but why aren't you writing this? The obvious line in British comedy travels through Morecambe and Wise to you.' 'I don't think I can write men,' she told him. 'And I wanted somebody who clearly gets that northern material.' He was from Stockport, the other side of Manchester from Bury, and quickly found a way past her defensive force field. When they moved on to the Ivy restaurant, Victoria confided that one of her pet hates was being Masonically nodded at by celebrities she had never met. A very famous actor promptly nodded at her. She turned and said, 'See what I mean?'

Peter Bowker soon joined Victoria and Piers on a pilgrimage to seek the blessing of Eric Morecambe's widow and son. Over tea and biscuits Victoria's shyness threatened to undermine the encounter. 'She was a bit off,' says Gary Morecambe. 'Almost cold. Piers Wenger said, "Gary, you must understand she's so nervous to be here talking to you!" I couldn't believe it: my mother and I were both in awe of her.' When Victoria said she ought to be off, Joan Morecambe said, 'Why, have you got another meeting to get to?' 'Well, no,' said Victoria. 'I just didn't want to take up any more of your time' 'My mother laughed,' says Gary, 'and told her to have another cup of tea. Vic visibly relaxed and that was it – from then on we were on the same page.' A comparable visit to Ernie Wise's widow Doreen was a little more fraught. 'She was quite cagey and defensive and a bit prickly,' says Bowker.

At the same time the BBC's controller of comedy commissioning was interested in putting together an archival package of Victoria's sketches. This got her thinking about 'a sort of Trimmings 2 where the old stuff would be woven in with a lot of new,' she told Lucy Ansbro. 'Next year will be 25 years since I recorded As Seen on TV so that could furnish a good enough reason? . . . Am quite keen to do something and if we can grab Walters for a few filming days – and Celia – don't know who else yet.'[24] By the start of 2009 she had refined her thinking: 'I have a list of old stuff which I love, but there is something self congratulatory about weaving it in amongst new stuff . . . would it be better to do a whacking great compilation of archive stuff – with bits from celeb fans who could pick their faves etc and just be very unapologetic about it and it would be a celebration. AND THEN DO AS WELL. A brand new special that has a different look.'[25] She imagined a mini-documentary following Bo Beaumont 'as she attempts to revive her career – going on Strictly etc etc', as well as a where-are-they-now follow-up on Jim Broadbent's character from 'A Fairly Ordinary Man'.[26] Her change of stance partly arose from talking to Piers, who advised that mixing old sketches and new would set the latter at a disadvantage. She added that the archive package should be shown months earlier: 'What we want to avoid is VW overload.'[27]

In February 2009 *dinnerladies* went into rehearsal and Victoria's role became more than supervisory as she was asked to solve problems in knitting up the script. 'I'd come back from rehearsal at nine at night,' says David Graham, 'and send her an email saying I couldn't think of an ending for a particular scene and I needed twenty lines. Six thirty the next morning I got the scene.' Victoria found the process a little more frustrating that she let on. 'Aaargh have spent all day trying to make mini amendments to make the ending work a bit better without being there at rehearsals,' she told Lucy Ansbro. 'I don't think I can do much that is effective.'[28] The next month the show opened in Eastbourne and Victoria caught it in Cardiff. Thus she met up again with Andrew Dunn and Shobna Gulati, who had returned as Tony and Anita: 'I plied them with champers and let them have a moan and wrote to the producer suggesting he lets them have a bit more of a free rein.'[29] Over the next two and a half years there were four tours, the second two with a new script based on the second series in which Victoria was less involved.

There was more nostalgia that spring when she returned to the Theatre Royal Haymarket, home of *Acorn Antiques: The Musical!*, to record her debut in *I'm Sorry I Haven't a Clue*, 'which is supposed to be improvised but of course is all worked out v carefully in advance,' she told Sammy Murray – 'rehearsed most of the day with that but it was quite nice to be on stage again.'[30] Victoria kept her comedy hat on as she returned to her desk to write a sketch show for the first time in nine years. Drawing inspiration from the prevailing spate of Sunday-night costume dramas that fed an appetite for cosy rural escapism, Victoria decided to take *Cranford* and *Lark Rise to Candleford* and mulch them into 'Lark Pies to Cranchesterford'. The plot featured the squalidly poor Halibut and Catheter Finch of Donkeyfield, whose pretty daughter Araminty goes to work in the Cranchesterford Post and Potato Office run by Miss Finch. At the top of the social ladder is Lord Cranborne, to whom Miss Finch would gladly give herself if only she could rip off her undergarments in less than twenty minutes. Victoria was to play Miss Finch and narrate the story in the voice of the older Araminty. 'I'm not parodying any of the characters,' she insisted when seeking permission to film on the *Lark Rise* set in Wilt-shire. 'It's more like Acorn Antiques with bonnets than a parody.'[31]

Victoria's fortnight ingesting the action from Beijing was put to good use as she imagined Olympic competition for middle-aged contestants – the men's pedalo race, ladies' outdoor reversing, a pen-tathlon with shopping trolleys – although the real joy for her was in aping the language of the pundits in the studio. She scripted rather more for her Midlife Olympics than was eventually included and, as usual, wrote plenty of extra material. A selection of filler sketches expressed her impatience with modern trends: an ad for a language-learning tool for up-to-date banal banter; a fatuous sermon by a gay vicar. Others were shot but eventually sacrificed: 'Coffee Palaver' about ethical coffee chains; 'Swatch Team' about a detective squad policing the streets for mismatched colours and fabrics. In 'Fragile Tissue' an American woman walking along a beach confides to the camera that 'after menopause a woman's intimate tissue can lose its elasticity'; the scene then cuts to two teenage boys dumbstruck with horror as they watch this on TV, for which Henry and a friend of his were enlisted.

The working title was *Victoria Wood's Credit Crunch Christmas*. Her hope was that Piers Wenger might produce it, but he was unavail-able, so Phil McIntyre's office introduced her to John Rushton, who had produced *The Royle Family* for their client Caroline Aherne. His unflappable good cheer would be needed, as Victoria's relationship with the BBC grew choppier than ever. She was already aware that a culture of top-down interference now predominated. On *Desert Island Discs* she had disparaged the labyrinthine structures of modern comedy commissioning – 'You have to battle with about twenty-two ladies in nice suits telling you what they think comedy is about.'[32] Her fears were confirmed when she presented what she had written to the BBC. The encounter left her 'reeling', she told Sammy Murray. 'It was a meeting with the "creatives" but was run by the head of finance who would not budge.'[33] Cuts were suggested. 'They in their own fashion wanted to have some editorial input,' says John Rushton. 'Vic found that slightly difficult. An email saying "we do want this and we don't want that" she found brusque and abrupt.' It was unfair, she told Jane Wymark, that *The Royle Family*'s most recent Christmas special had cost £1 million despite having one set, a small cast and no CGI: 'We want to do all singing, all dancing, period, set pieces the whole caboodle, we want 1.4 and they won't give us anything like that. Back to the chopping board.'[34]

A production office was rented in Islington. Victoria interviewed four directors before plumping for Tony Dow, who had directed *Nighty Night* and two dozen episodes of *Only Fools and Horses*. She found him 'a normal middle aged very experienced director, very positive and I'm hoping with not too much ego to chuck around'.[35] As they started casting 'Lark Pies' Victoria made it clear to him that, despite initially thinking of Celia Imrie and Jim Broadbent, 'she was very keen not to use her usual suspects. She wanted to get away from that and be doing something slightly different.' Instead she crammed the screen with half a dozen actors from *Housewife, 49*. For the role of the smouldering Lord Cranborne, she went back to Richard Lintern, who had played a young rock star in *Staying In* in 1989. Her friend Harriet Thorpe returned for the first time since *Wetty Hainthrop Investigates*. Reece Shearsmith was cast as the fatuous vicar.

The idea to flood the special with dance grew out of Victoria's friendship with Stephen Mear: 'She said, "Do you fancy doing a dance duet with me? Let's do Nick and Margaret on *The Apprentice*." I said, "Will it be funny?" She looked at me like, seriously? I knew how she moved so I knew how far to push it.' He choreographed a routine in which Alan Sugar's two sidekicks ease up out of their seats and throw themselves into a perky dance that is blissfully at odds with their hatchet-faced roles on the show. Once more, as when learning to tap, Victoria had to overcome her self-consciousness and watch herself train in the mirror. 'Everyone at Pineapple is weeny,' she told Rosalind, 'and the corridors are very narrow – about the same width as me, so all these tiny bony ballet girls shrink back when they see me coming.'[36] It was Victoria's idea to have Stephen Mear rip her skirt off mid-dance to reveal another identical skirt.

There was a second and more spectacular piece of choreography that grew out of Victoria's dream to revisit 'The Ballad of Barry and Freda'. 'I thought, don't piss about with a new song,' went her rationale, 'when you could do the song that everybody knows and likes. Just whizz it up with a big band and twenty dancers. I probably won't do any more specials. Finish with that.'[37] The song was to be subjected to a grand conceptual reboot. On the piano would be a little snow globe, inside which Barry in a beige zip-up cardie and Freda in her dressing gown sit on the sofa watching television. As the song heats up, they would leap up and lead a joyous tap routine with a multiplying chorus line of Barry and Freda lookalikes. 'I want the girls to take off their dressing gowns to reveal lovely Christmassy cossies under,' she told Sammy Murray.[38] Nigel Lilley worked out a musical bridge in which Victoria's singing would make way for the dancing, while Stephen Mear suggested shooting from an overhead camera in the style of Busby Berkeley. The dancers, many of them *Acorn Antiques* veterans, rehearsed in the Dominion Theatre and moved to a studio for a complicated green-screen shoot in which Victoria recorded the song at a piano.

As for the song itself, she updated the lyrics with new references to Fearne Cotton, Philip Schofield and Russell Brand, and provided Barry with a fresh set of excuses for avoiding sex. Gone are all the domestic chores that want doing; his body is now no longer up to the task:

Can't do it, can't do it
I must refuse to get unzipped
I'm tearful, I'm fearful, worried that I'm ill-equipped

Don't bully, I can't fully
Guarantee to cope without a rope and pulley.

When Freda proposes sex as a seasonal celebration, she mentions two
of Victoria's favourite comestibles:

Get festive, get restive
Dunk me in the duvet like a big digestive
Just humour a late bloomer
Stuff my Christmas stocking with a big satsuma.

The song was recorded in a studio with a big-band orchestration by
Steve Sidwell, who had composed the soundtrack for *Victoria's Empire*.
At first they tried recording it to a steady click track to make it easier
to sync up with the camera shots further down the line. 'It just didn't
work; it wasn't funny,' says Nigel Lilley, who was supervising. 'So we
had a quick crisis meeting and then started at one tempo and every
verse we bumped it up by two or three. Suddenly it was hilarious. Vic
was happy.'

In July the production spent an unsunny week shooting 'Lark Pies'
in Wiltshire. To bond the cast and crew, John Rushton organised a
quiz night in the pub – Victoria was so eager for her team to win
she urged one ignorant actress to desist from answering questions.
The village was populated with more extras than had ever crowded
into a Victoria Wood sketch, and there were even more when the
production moved to the ground of Brentford FC, the only football club they could find who would allow them to film the Midlife
Olympics on the pitch. Victoria was disappointed that the stands
could not be filled with cheering crowds, but she and her colleagues
spent most of the shoot in hysterics as they tried to wrangle locally
sourced participants in national tracksuits to compete in made-up
events.

In August work on the Christmas special was suspended while
Victoria plunged once more into her past. *Talent* was to be revived
at the Old Laundry Theatre in Bowness-on-Windermere, run by her
friends Roger Glossop and Charlotte Scott. Their annual arts festival

had been running since 1992, and normally they welcomed shows from outside, but this year they wanted to mount their own production and came to Victoria, who was persuaded by the successful revival at the Gatehouse Theatre: 'The audience really liked it, and I thought, oh, it seems to hold up in some strange, naive way.'[39]

Initially Victoria decreed that she wasn't the right person to direct it, but her involvement deepened after an approach from the Menier Chocolate Factory, the fringe theatre near London Bridge with a track record of hit transfers to the West End and Broadway. She proposed the theatre come in on a co-production that would take the show from Windermere to Southwark. Both theatres put it to her that the original play was too short at only seventy-five minutes. Whereas previous attempts to persuade Victoria to lengthen *Talent* had fallen on deaf ears, now she was more amenable: 'I said, "If I can get the running time to one hour thirty, do you consider that reasonable for your ticket price?' They were happy with that. So then I got really interested because it was new material. Then I did want to direct it. You get what's in your head and on the page onto the stage without filtering it through somebody else. It's just easier.'[40]

Victoria composed new songs to bookend the show and beefed up the male roles. The play now began with a compère welcoming the audience to Bunter's Piccadilly, 'three times winner of the North West Clubland Middle Size Club of the Year'. He introduces a long-haired male vocal trio in lurid frills and platforms called Triple Velvet – exactly the kind of act Victoria competed against on *New Faces*. Then Julie enters, now a star in a bell-bottomed catsuit, but as she sings it becomes clear that this is a fantasy sequence and she hasn't made it at all. The lights change and on comes a gnarled manageress to prepare the house for the evening's entertainment. To her Victoria gave the best joke in the rewrite as she remembers dancing at Bunters in the war with a Yank stationed at Bury. 'We won a talent night here, funnily enough,' she says. 'They weren't giving cups out, cos the metal was going for Spitfires.'

Victoria left the body of the play untouched: 'I was a bit tempted. But I thought it's not fair. If that play was written by somebody who was twenty-five, then that's what it's like. So I decided not to mess

with it.'[41] At the very end, Julie's shy, fat friend Maureen comes out
from her shadow to lead the company in a Sondheim-esque song
about nursing ambition and overcoming social awkwardness. Its
catchy final chorus collapsed the distance between Maureen and the
teenage Victoria:

> Your life – just give it some welly
> Don't just slump with the telly
> Take a tip from Minnelli
> And never sit alone in your room!

The show ran for two weeks at the Old Laundry from late August.
'Our show is up and running and doing good business in Bowness,'
Victoria told Jane Wymark. 'It will go differently I'm sure in Southwark, as I don't think mentions of Douglas (Isle of Man) and Kendal's
(dept store in Manchester) will be greeted with the same shrieks of
delight.'[42] To plug the London run Victoria reluctantly consented to
appear on television. 'Oh my lord the One show,' she exclaimed to
Rosalind. 'I thought that sort of telly had gone out years ago – I did
it as it has 7m viewers.'[43] At the Chocolate Factory the production
was met by ho-hum reviews – the consensus was that, while the performances were pleasing and many gags still landed, the play would
have been best left unexhumed. Victoria instructed Lucy Ansbro to
call the minute ticket sales dipped in case she needed to do extra
publicity but heard that 'everyone was v happy and no one needed to
do anything'.[44]

The highlight of the run for Victoria came when Julie Walters
attended as her guest and, for the very first time, watched the stage
play written for her in 1978. 'That should perk them up a bit,' she
told Jane Wymark.[45] They went at the end of a week filming for the
Christmas special. Victoria called the sketch 'Beyond the Marigolds:
What Mrs Overall Did Next . . .' Framed as the portrait of a 'busy
working actress', Bo Beaumont spends a week looking for opportunities to work in one of the new TV formats, which were lined up
like bottles on a wall for Victoria to shoot at. Bo's encounters with
Anton du Beke, Delia Smith and Torvill and Dean find her unsuited

to the indignities of celebrity participation. 'The thought of this awful pompous actress that plays Mrs Overall,' says Julie, 'I found it very funny as ever and I said, "Yeah, I'm there."'

It was her first meaningful appearance on screen with Victoria since *dinnerladies* ten years earlier. The deal was complicated by Julie's commitment to the Harry Potter films. By the time it was shot, Tony Dow had lost his director of photography: 'So I got two lightweight cameras, got rid of most of the crew and said, "We are going to have a week of following around two of the great women in show business."' Victoria cast herself as Bo Beaumont's dowdy, doting helpmeet Wendy. No more than a voiceless figure at the end of the phone line in *Acorn Antiques: The Musical!*, now she is seen sharing a bedroom if not a bed in Bo's apartment 'on the borders of Paddington'. The intriguing relationship between two middle-aged women was partly inspired by a visit to Kirkcudbright in 1976 with Victoria's university friend Robert Howie, whose aunt depended on a female companion. To Julie the set-up felt 'utterly believable. I think there probably was a bit of fiddling a long time ago, but it's long gone is what I imagine.' Eventually the docile Wendy shows her cards. 'She's my life!!' she screams after one probing question too far from Colin, a discreet reporter played by Jason Watkins.

Most of the film was shot in the fly-on-the-wall style of the *As Seen on TV* documentaries, but Tony Dow took inspiration from *Georgy Girl* to film Bo as she sashayed through a street market in her signature white suit. At one point he suggested Julie big up her performance. 'You're the first director who's ever said that to me,' she replied. She had a rare attack of nerves when they arrived at the ice rink in Queensway but, once assured that Torvill and Dean would keep her safe, she improvised new ways to fail on ice and Victoria struggled not to corpse in her reaction shot. 'The mutual respect was enormous,' says Tony Dow. 'Vic thought Julie was amazing, but Julie went, "This is the one person who's made me funny."'

To Victoria's chagrin, Julie's agent would not let her appear without a fee in a behind-the-scenes documentary about the making of the show. The idea of the film was 'to screw extra wig and costume money out of the BBC', which meant there was a second camera crew watching Victoria at work throughout the shoot.[46] She called it *What Larks!* and, with Tony Dow, cobbled it together with hastily shot pieces to camera and a spry commentary. The last piece of footage for both programmes was captured in October at the Bloomsbury Theatre, which was booked when it became clear that the finale would work best if Victoria performed 'The Ballad of Barry and Freda' to a live audience. For an extra treat, they would be shown the rest of the special. At the insistence of the BBC, and much to Dow's annoyance, their laughter was recorded for use in the broadcast.

For two days at home Victoria practised to the big-band arrangement. To get her audience in the mood she asked Ted Robbins to do a warm-up and told her well-worn story of Ted flashing his bum at a recording of *Wood and Walters* in 1981. Then, after an introductory spiel about all the Barrys and Fredas who would be watching at home, she sat down to perform her iconic anthem to an audience for the first time since *Parkinson* in 2000. The song was some way beyond her vocal range now, so for the rousing finale she spoke the lines rather than sang them. In the first take she had to stop two thirds of the way in for a technical issue. 'I thought this going to go one of two ways,' says Nigel Lilley, watching nervously on a monitor backstage. 'It was one of those moments where I saw her drill down into wherever she went, that place she went. The massive focus. And she was just astonishing. She went back and she nailed it. It was quite a high-wire act.' At the end, Victoria swivelled round and slammed both feet on the floor to bounce up and take a deep bow from the waist as the audience, as ever, went nuts.

The disagreements were not over. As early as June John Rushton had told the BBC that 'Victoria has invested all her efforts into a programme specifically dedicated to a Christmas day transmission'.[47] Confirmation now came that it would go out on Christmas Eve. The final decision rested with BBC One controller Jay Hunt, who had already annoyed Victoria by suggesting 'Beyond the Marigolds' be extracted and lashed together as a separate programme. An emissary explained the decision to Victoria, who reacted 'really terribly', according to Lucy Ansbro. It was not so much the decision itself that grated – 'Xmas Eve is not what I was promised but actually it's a good slot,' she told Sammy Murray – so much as the distant manner of the communication.[48] 'I've still not met the person in question,' she told the *Guardian* some months later. 'If somebody's got a problem with something I'm doing I think they should step into the same room or email me or telephone me, and not send a winged monkey to talk to me about it.'[49] Although *The Royle Family*, preferred for the Christmas evening slot, was also produced by John Rushton, Victoria's personal relationship with him did not suffer – on New Year's Day she drove down to Hastings to celebrate his birthday with his family.

Meanwhile, her vexations continued back at the Menier Chocolate Factory, where in November Victoria joined the cast to take a bow on the final night of the run. Afterwards she emailed the theatre's artistic director David Babani. Her hope was for the production to tour and, while she was aware he had explained the position to Lucy Ansbro, she was annoyed not to hear back from him directly. It soon emerged that the set had been destroyed after the last night. 'We're all busy,' she grumbled to Nigel Lilley. 'I'm trying to make a programme out of bits of left over pastry, am still finishing the main programme, am script editing someone else's drama and planning about eight other things, when I'm not busy falling downstairs – how come he's the one who can't answer an email?'[50] (The fall happened at home. She bashed two ribs and took herself to Ireland for three days to recover.) At a subsequent opening night party Babani approached and asked Victoria how she was. 'Still waiting for your phone call,' she said, and turned away.

Such was her toxified wariness of decision makers in high places that her defences were up when the only BBC controller she had fully trusted got in touch. Peter Salmon was now based in Manchester as the BBC prepared to move much of its operation to Media City in Salford, where he was also on the board of the newly created Manchester International Festival. Its dynamic Scottish director Alex Poots was eager to commission a piece of work from Victoria. When Salmon provided the introduction over lunch in Kensington Place she vented about BBC management. In its short life – there had been only two programmes so far – MIF had ventured to blur the distinction between high and low art. 'Why would you bother wanting me to make a piece?' she said to Poots. 'Why would you take lunch with me?' he replied. 'You could work with anyone.' 'There is this thing,' she did eventually concede, 'but I'm sure you won't be interested.' And she mentioned a documentary about a children's choir she had seen as a student: 'I've always wondered what happened to them.' But for now she felt no urge to fall under the sway of this new suitor or take the conversation any further.

Christmas approached. The annual invitation went out by email. 'Mince pies at my house Tuesday 22nd from seven . . . friends, kids, mothers in law all welcome . . .'[51] While the Christmas party for friends and neighbours was set in stone, since the divorce the day itself had taken on a different flavour. Some years Victoria made an effort to gather all four Wood siblings. On Christmas evening Harriet Thorpe would visit with her children and they indulged in an annual viewing ritual. First up was Harry Secombe on ITV's religious series *Highway* introducing a bevy of female amateur choristers in Eighties fashions singing 'Who Will Buy?' from *Oliver!* as they march around a newly opened shopping centre in Ipswich. After that came *Fanny Cradock Cooks for Christmas*. Both were rich in unintended comedy, and Victoria never, ever tired of feasting on them.

Having wanted to avoid 'VW overload', that Christmas she was on television more than ever before. *Victoria Wood's Mid Life Christmas* on Christmas Eve was followed by *What Larks!* on 30 December, which ended with a shot, recycled from an unused sketch, of Henry and his mate on the sofa staring nonplussed at the screen. But four nights before Christmas there was *Victoria Wood Seen On TV*, a ninety-minute trawl through her career in which friends, collaborators and celebrities paid tribute to her genius. It included quotation from an exhaustive and analytical interview Victoria gave about her career, filmed in a library on the South Bank earlier in the autumn. At home on the sofa she watched her career flash in front of her with Nigel Lilley for company. 'That felt very special,' he says. 'I got to watch the original *Acorn Antiques* with her and she'd point out the bits where they were corpsing. She said she'd never watched 'Swim the Channel'. I remember her being very proud of it. And she was howling at everything.'

# 23

# LOVING ERIC, ERNIE, EUNICE, TUBBY, ENID, JOYCE AND BARRIE

'Well, you can smile, but that's how people go to hell unfortunately.'

*The Giddy Kipper*, 2010

The prospect loomed of Victoria's second child leaving the nest. Early in 2010 she drove Henry north for his interview at Leeds College of Music. 'I thought in my biased motherly way he did look a bit more on the ball than all the other shambling depressed looking hunched hooded figures,' she concluded. 'At least Hen cracks a smile once in a while.'[1]

It was a season of farewells. When Victoria sang at a concert to mark the fortieth anniversary of the Stables Cleo Laine revealed in the green room beforehand that John Dankworth had died earlier that day. Victoria performed 'The Ballad of Barry and Freda', backed by Dankworth's band playing Steve Sidwell's arrangement. She was asked to take part in a Melvyn Bragg tribute as *The South Bank Show* ended its run on LWT. By way of valediction to *Talent*, the Glossops invited her for a week in the hills above Malaga. They took the sleeper from Paris and stayed in a hotel run by an old friend who had been prop maker at the Crucible, but their plan to go walking was thwarted by February rain.

Soon after returning Victoria flew to New York for a week. Her goal was to supplement the information on Joyce Hatto which had been amassed over the previous year on her behalf. The research looked into every peculiarity of the Hatto story, eventually filling two ring-bound folders with facts about her career, her husband's fiendish deception and its sensational discovery. Kerry Gill-Pryde of Left Bank Pictures had already visited William Barrington-Coupe, better known as Barrie, at his home in Royston, and eventually Cathy Edis went too. A morally evasive figure who had once been in prison for tax fraud and had a history of lying with breathtaking ease, he was now keen to be involved in the musical side of the drama. Meanwhile, whenever she had a moment Victoria pursued the story too, interviewing the novelist Rose Tremain, who was taught by Hatto as a schoolgirl, and Jeremy Nicholas, a music journalist who became bound up in the story. When directing *Talent* she invited two women to the Menier Chocolate Factory who as girls in Royston had known Joyce Hatto well.

Her objective in New York was to meet those who had participated in the exposé, as well as the author of the optioned *New Yorker* article, the idea being to give the story an American dimension and curry finance from HBO. It was 'quite scary trotting round the city, sitting in cafes to meet people I had never spoken to and had no idea what they looked like – people who didn't have a clue who I was either . . .'[2] She was ready to get going when she got home: 'I have been thinking terribly hard about what I want the story to say – the plot itself is easy – she gets famous, she dies, she gets found out – but when the protagonist dies before the end of the story that's not so great dramatically so I need to take another line on it, which I think I've got now.'[3] A month later, on the way to visit Grace in Cambridge, she passed through Royston and drove into the road where Barrington-Coupe still lived: 'And stone me he was on the frigging pavement giving me a very sharp look as I hastily but casually drove past.' She tailed him as far as she could by car but 'didn't dare pursue on foot as he would have recognised me'.[4] Her quarry wormed his way so far into her consciousness that one day when making notes she accidentally called the script 'Barrie and Freda'.

While Victoria wrote her own script, that spring she simultaneously acted as script editor for Peter Bowker, who began working through drafts of *Morecambe and Wise*, as the drama was initially titled. (It was later provisionally changed to *When Eric Met Ernie*.) They had long since agreed that the origin story of Morecambe and Wise did not have a dark side such as was explored in recent BBC biopics of Kenneth Williams and Frankie Howerd. The worst thing that happened to them, apart from the Blitz, was their poor treatment by the patrician nabobs at the BBC who foisted bad scripts upon them. *Running Wild*, their variety show recorded at the Shepherd's Bush Empire in 1954, was an infamous flop. 'Definition of the Week,' wrote one critic. 'TV set: the box in which they buried Morecambe and Wise.'[5] Victoria's notes were concisely focused on structure and comedy. 'Come out of the line earlier, that's funnier,' she'd say. While resisting the urge to volunteer her own dialogue, she also offered a line or two gleaned from her early experience of grim hotels on tour. 'Don't piss in the sink' was one of hers.

Peter Bowker followed his hunch that the kernel of the story lay in Eric's relationship with Sadie Bartholomew, the driven mother who shoved him into talent contests and soon took young Ernie under her wing too – precisely the kind of enabling parent who had been absent from Victoria's childhood. 'I always knew that Vic was going to play Sadie,' he says, 'so you start to write to her rhythm.' Thus, in her dialogue with Eric, his Sadie started to sound a lot like Victoria: 'You make people laugh, you're a lovely dancer and you can hold a tune . . . but more than that – and I mean this as the mother that carried you and bore you and raised you – you aren't any good at anything else.'

The drafts were overseen by a newly hired director. Jonny Campbell came on the recommendation of Piers Wenger, for whom he had shot a couple of episodes of *Doctor Who*; also on his CV was the first series of *Phoenix Nights*. His first encounter with Victoria was at Broadcasting House. 'She was a daunting presence,' he says. 'What was important in that meeting was the subtext: are we going to have a laugh on this journey?' It was to his advantage that, like Bowker, he was from Stockport. For the first time Victoria chose to collaborate with a much younger director. (He happened to be the partner of the drama's other executive producer Beth Willis.) One of his early interventions was to suggest the story required not two Erics and two Ernies, but three. He also threw himself into his own research and unearthed a quotation from Eric Morecambe that more or less summed up the plot: 'I'm grateful to my mother now. She pushed me into showbusiness and kept me there until she knew I was safely in Ernie's hands; he's been doing the pushing ever since.' Victoria was thrilled. 'Thanks for the quote,' she said. 'Am having it embroidered on to a set of table napkins for Doreen.'[6]

Having visited both the widows to conduct archival research, as a courtesy Victoria shared the final draft with them. Doreen Wise, who nursed a grievance that the nation loved Eric more than Ernie, was the tougher nut to crack, so she was invited to Claridge's to be cajoled and charmed. 'Well, it's another fairy tale,' she said of the script, 'but it's a fairy tale I can live with.' To celebrate Victoria ordered champagne which, in the new culture that prevailed at the BBC, had to be itemised as an expense. 'The *Daily Mail* will implode,' she told Peter Bowker, 'because on the one hand it's Claridge's; on the other it's Ernie Wise's widow, so they won't know which way to jump.'

In April she was dragged away from her writing desk to prepare for a charity night in Hendon organised by Maureen Lipman. Victoria enlisted Harriet Thorpe to do 'Coffee Palaver', the sketch that had not made the cut for *Mid Life Christmas*. She was wary of becoming an old turn to be wheeled out past her prime. In one week that spring she caught demoralising live performances by Julie Andrews and Debbie Reynolds, and treated the spectacle as a warning. 'In twenty years' time,' she wrote to Nigel Lilley, who had booked the tickets, 'please don't let us be on the stage of some small half empty theatre with an audience of old gay men – you on the piano/bontempi and me in a red sequinned trouser suit . . . I want to quit while I'm ahead.'[7] Nigel and his Spanish partner Luis were to become Victoria's regular theatregoing companions – his habit was to book three tickets and only then tell her what they were going to see. 'Every couple of weeks we'd go and see a show,' he says, 'and then go and have a good bitch about it. It was a way of getting her out house. When she was writing she would just not leave the house.'

While she continued with Hatto-related field trips, six months on from their first meeting Victoria received a visit at home from Alex Poots, who wanted to follow up on his quest to commission a play from her for the Manchester International Festival. Still bruised from recent battles with the BBC, she lacked faith that any producer would leave her to her own devices. 'You wouldn't let me do what I want,' she told him warily. It took a third meeting, and offers to introduce her to artists who had had a happy time at the festival, to tempt her into saying yes.

The idea she proposed was inspired by an episode of *This Week*, a Thames TV documentary she remembered watching in her Birmingham bedsit in 1975, which told of the million-selling 78rpm made in 1929 of Purcell's 'Nymphs and Shepherds'. Under the baton of Sir Hamilton Harty it was recorded in the city's Free Trade Hall by the Hallé Orchestra and the 250-strong Manchester Children's Choir. Victoria anticipated that a play requiring a vast choir of children would be unattractive to the festival. What convinced her of Poots's good faith was the discovery that MIF had a department whose role was to reach out to the community: 'At that point she realised we were serious and she might have an opportunity to do something she couldn't in the commercial sector. The choir got her over the line.'

Armed with the commission, Victoria duly rewatched the programme and was dismayed to find that her recollection was almost wholly inaccurate. 'Lordy what a disappointment,' she confessed. 'I'd made up a whole documentary out of my head.'[8] But she did have one kernel to work with. A manual labourer was asked what singing meant to him. 'It's been an expression of joy,' he replied. 'It's a really wonderful thing to be able to sing.'

As she thought further about what this production might be, Victoria was already certain she wanted to direct it, though less sure about how to proceed with the musical element. 'It would involve them starting up new children's choirs,' she told Nigel Lilley in June. 'I find that rather a great thought tho not sure if I can write anything for them to sing . . . will have to talk to you about it.'[9] A few weeks later she was no closer: 'Music is a bit thin on the ground with me at present.'[10] There was a timely reminder of her fecundity as a songwriter with the first ever am-dram production of *Acorn Antiques: The Musical!*, which she attended in Leighton Buzzard. 'A really good effort,' she enthused, 'and so nice to hear the music!'[11]

In early summer Victoria submitted a first draft of her Joyce Hatto script as Henry sat his A levels. Just as he was leaving school, his mother concluded her two-year off-and-on hunt for a rural bolthole. Initially she worried about getting somewhere in the Lakes – 'It's so far away and I don't think the kids would ever come there,' she told Sammy Murray, whom she had enlisted to help search – but via an estate agent she found a place on the shore of Esthwaite Water.[12] By happy coincidence it was called Swiss Cottage, the same name as the café Pat buys for her long-lost sister Margaret. Having asked the Glossops and Piers Wenger to inspect it for their thoughts, she made an offer.

In the midst of all this, at the invitation of the Manchester-based Mines Advisory Group (MAG), Victoria flew to Laos to make a short film for BBC Lifeline. She first heard from the explosive ordnance removal charity when asked to donate to an auction of celebrity footwear – it was no trouble to hand over an uncomfortable pair of Prada shoes bought for the BAFTAs. When MAG secured a prestigious fundraising slot on the BBC they emailed Lucy Ansbro asking if Victoria would consider fronting a film about the lingering devastation caused by US cluster bombs dropped during the Vietnam War. Victoria replied directly with a series of questions, which were duly answered. 'Well I suppose I'd better do it then,' she said. The charity arranged for her to spend four days in Xieng Khouang province in the north of the country. A rickety plane delivered her, a producer, a cameraman and the MAG representative to their billet – a set of wooden hilltop chalets with spectacular views of tropical forest. In the corner of the dining room there was a piano. 'Do you play?' the producer asked Victoria. There were long drives in intense heat. One morning at breakfast she reported she'd been pooed on by a gecko, she was bitten by a leech which had to be burned off, and on a visit to a scrap metal dealer the local MAG guide spotted a live cluster bomb and instructed the group to back away. Victoria visited a boy recently hospitalised by a cluster-bomb explosion and spent time on a farm where an all-female team were clearing unexploded cluster bombs dropped on one farmer's land. The detonation was deafening.

Back home after a twenty-six-hour journey, Victoria was soon taking Grace and Henry on a trip to Iceland to look at whales and geysers, then she joined the search for six actors to play Eric Morecambe and Ernie Wise. Word was spread through dance groups and drama clubs in the north, and she made a call for young talent via the *Yorkshire Post*. But the most reliable source was via *Billy Elliot*, whose casting director Jessica Ronane oversaw a rolling trawl for young singers and dancers. For long days in London, Manchester and Leeds, well over a hundred actors were seen. 'Vic brought out the best in the children,' says Sammy Murray, who was to oversee the dance scenes. 'She put them at ease in a motherly way. Even the ones that couldn't say their name because they were so shy, she would give the same time as anyone else.' As part of her casting duties Victoria stood up to read scenes with them. 'I must say my reading of Eric is luminous and touching and my interpretation of Ernie a triumph,' she told Jane Wymark. 'My reading of my own part however is sub Carry on Northern with unsubtle touches of late Peggy Mount.'[13]

It was only once the quartet of child actors to play Eric and Ernie had been cast that the hunt for the adult actors could begin. There were plenty of halfway decent Erics. Then a gangly, awkward actor walked in lugging a heavy rucksack. Daniel Rigby had been pulling pints in a Baker Street pub, had just vacated his digs in Hackney and was on his way to perform stand-up at the Edinburgh Festival. 'You just knew,' says Jonny Campbell. 'It was like Eric was in the room. He organically fused Eric's personality and material to the point where it was just mesmerising to watch him. Vic was very, very positive. As soon as he left with his knapsack it was "Let's book him."' He came back from Edinburgh to read with prospective Ernies: the best chemical reaction was with Bryan Dick, who had a far longer CV and could dance. As for the rest of the cast, Victoria pushed for Jim Moir, one half of Reeves and Mortimer, to play Eric's quiet, long-suffering father George Bartholomew and Ted Robbins to be cast as the children's impresario Jack Hylton.

By late August, with a press release imminent, no actual title had yet been settled on. 'I like Eric and Ernie because that's what it's about – they were 2 little boys called Eric and Ernie,' she argued to her director, signing herself 'Vic (ex dumb blonde)'.[14] She got her way. While she threw herself into such producing tasks, Victoria had not done any serious acting in four years and confided to Charlotte Scott that she was 'not that interested in playing this part – the bit of filming I like is the being outdoors and the hustle and bustle – the putting the costume part on I find a bit tedious . . . but of course I will give it my best shot'.[15] The company met in King's Cross to read through the script and rehearse, then decamped to Morecambe for a September shoot. Thanks to last-minute problems with the train Victoria decided to drive up three of the younger cast members herself, arriving late at night before a very early start.

She felt odd about returning to Morecambe for the first time in a quarter of a century. Staying at the 1930s art-deco Midland Hotel, formerly a symbol of the town's decline but now refurbished, she got up early every morning when it was still dark to walk along the prom. When it was lighter she rambled round the town on what she called a 'memory walk'. One day Jonny Campbell was out with her when they were approached by a woman who introduced herself as a former pupil of Helen Wood. 'Your mum was lovely,' she said. 'The way Vic reacted said it all . . .'

Throughout the shoot Victoria took up where she'd left off on *Housewife, 49*. While playing her role of wife and mother, as executive producer she also kept an eye on the bigger picture, nitpicking about period design details when she felt something had been missed. Some of this was captured by a crew there to film a behind-the-scenes documentary which brought more money into the budget. She wasn't entirely in charge. To protect her wig on set, Chrissie Baker made her wear a hairnet with a hairdryer contraption affixed to it at all times. 'Chrissie would come down on her like a ton of bricks if she wasn't wearing it,' says Beth Willis. 'But she was keen to get back out there, sucking it all up, taking it all in.' When not producing Victoria gave a detailed performance as a big-hearted and proactive mother who makes it her life's work to see her son fulfil his potential. In her most moving scene the camera held on her face as Eric and Ernie, flush with hope for the future, put Sadie on the train and send her back to the exile of home.

Much of the filming took place in charismatic old theatres, requiring shots of laughing extras in the stalls. Ted Robbins reverted to his day job as a warm-up man to entertain them: 'I stood up and did twenty minutes of stuff that I knew Vic loved. A lot of comics are very mean-spirited, and they can't bear to see someone else getting laughs. She was stood at the side, and she would throw her head back and roar with laughter.' For the culminating scene of the drama, in which Morecambe and Wise find their feet as a double act, Victoria as Sadie had to come in late and shuffle along a row. It was filmed at the Stockport Plaza and the stalls were stuffed with locally sourced volunteers from the families and friends of Peter Bowker and Jonny Campbell. Victoria sat down next to Piers Wenger, looking profoundly ill at ease in Fifties mufti, while beside him Beth Willis chuckled obligingly.

At the very end of the shoot the explosive interview with the *Guardian* appeared. Victoria gave it to publicise her work in Laos, but the headline told another story: 'I feel at the BBC I'm not trusted, not valued, not needed.' She criticised the vast salaries for individual stars which meant cheese-paring when it came to costumes and wigs and complained that 'there are great hierarchies and you can't have a personal relationship. So it's just defeating because it becomes faceless.'[16] 'It was pretty blunt,' says Piers Wenger, 'but then again she had felt very wounded by that experience. I had a conversation with Lucy [Ansbro] saying "It's a bit awkward." But it was fine really.' Geoff Posner and Jon Plowman both wrote to high-five her for saying the unsayable, while a higher-up at ITV cannily invited her to abandon the BBC and come back to them. The irony was that Piers, then head of drama at BBC Wales, had become her most trusted friend, while his colleague Beth Willis with her partner Jonny Campbell were being adopted into her inner circle. 'She just decided that we were going to be her friends,' says Beth, 'which is what she did with people, and then was incredibly loyal to them.' (In the interview her trip to Laos went undiscussed and, when it was aired, her MAG appeal brought in a surprisingly low yield of only £6,000 in donations.)

Another bond was formed on set with Daniel Rigby. 'It took a long time for the sheen of her status to make you stop being so over-whelmed,' he says. 'By the end of the shoot we knew that we got on. Once she really made me laugh: we were walking to set and there was cable everywhere and the lady says, "Watch yourself on the cables," and she proceeds to pretend to trip over every single one of them. It was really daft and for her surprisingly slapstick.' After the shoot was over, Victoria made him an offer. 'I'm sure you have lots of places to stay,' she wrote in a congratulatory card, 'but I do have a spare room in my (empty) house and it would be lovely to see you . . . Or there's the shed.'[17] It was not an entirely selfless gesture. During the shoot Victoria took a day off to drive Henry to Leeds for the start of his course, while Grace was to spend the academic year in Verona. She was fearful of becoming 'Miss Havisham in big empty house', as she explained to Lesley Fitton. 'He is broke and I wanted to help him out, he's a stand up comic so I had a fellow feeling for him. He's very shy and only makes toast.'[18]

A surrogate version of the mother–son relationship they had played on film slowly developed in Highgate as Victoria's shy lodger quiet-ly slunk to and from the kitchen trying not to disturb his landlady. 'What was really remarkable was hearing her discipline through other rooms,' he says. 'She'd be up at dawn and would exercise, spend the morning in the study. In the afternoon, if she'd done enough work, she would treat herself to a bit of telly – that's how she put it.' The television they watched together was mainly recorded episodes of *MasterChef* – Victoria delighted in cracking jokes at the expense of its presenter Gregg Wallace. Her invitation to stay till Christmas was soon extended to the summer.

Aside from post-production on *Eric & Ernie*, and then press duties, Victoria had plenty to keep herself busy. The Manchester Internation-al Festival pressed her for a title and a synopsis for next year's show. While in emails she kept referring to it as 'Nymphs', she alighted on *That Day We Sang*. Although she had not yet written a word, she sent very particular instructions about the image she had in her mind for the marketing: a photograph of a boy in the 1920s running along an alleyway in working-class Manchester. It was announced at the start of October. A week later she took possession of Swiss Cottage and pondered improvements. 'Though the house needs quite a bit doing to it,' she told Rosalind, 'the view was so lovely it made up for it all.' She anticipated a long haul for the builders, 'but I'm really busy so they can just get on with it hopefully'.[19]

After a quick visit to Grace in Verona, in November she was back in the north-west thanks to an approach from BSkyB. In a bid to lure household names to the network, it conceived *Little Crackers*, an anthology series in which comedians would script a short film chronicling an incident from childhood. Victoria was happy to take part on two conditions: she wanted to direct her own film and, despite the specificity of the brief, had no interest in writing overtly about her own childhood. Such was the channel's eagerness to brandish her name that they agreed to bend the rules.

Initially Victoria thought of salvaging a flashback scene from her untitled 2008 script in which two teenage friends on a bus go to meet a boy, who was somewhat based on Bob Mason. While shooting *Eric & Ernie* she talked about this idea with Beth Willis: 'She had a whole story which she'd planned in massive detail, and then when she went to write it she just hated it.' The ten-minute script she submitted instead was all that was left of *The Giddy Kipper*, also from 2008. Again, Victoria repurposed a flashback scene which showed her protagonist Eunice at primary school in the early 1960s getting into trouble for being funny in class. She now built a story around that lonely little girl, living with her father on a remote hill in Lancashire, while down in the village the nasty girls taunt her. 'You're a giddy kipper and you can't behave!' they sneer, parroting the hatchet-faced Sunday-school teacher who berates Eunice for her individualism: 'I don't have giddy kippers in my class, do I? We don't push chairs away when people are about to sit down, do we?' Briefly, when delivering eggs to the big smart house in the village, Eunice enters a wonderland of warmth, comfort and Christmas cheer. Later, as she trudges home in the gloaming, she imagines the dancers she's seen on the big house's black-and-white television capering in colour alongside her and her parents in the sunlit fields.

Having always hoped to shoot the longer script herself, Victoria now had ten minutes and £100,000 with which to make her debut as a film director. There was more casting of child actors to be done in Manchester, while the adult actors she drew from *Housewife, 49* and *Mid Life Christmas*. Lorraine Ashbourne played the unkind teacher. Sammy Murray was enlisted to play Eunice's mother in the fantasy dance sequence, which she choreographed and presented to Victoria at Pineapple Studios. The shoot was done over four days in the Ribble Valley 'where they did Whistle down the Wind which I'm taking as a good omen,' Victoria told Rosalind.[20] She was characteristically obsessive about buying the best warm wet-weather gear which, as a cosseted actor, she had never needed. As for the basics on directing, over a drink in her local she pumped Jonny Campbell for tips. 'But she knew,' he says. 'She didn't need me to give her any steers. Taking creative control was the next inevitable stage for her.' She also asked Tony Slater-Ling, the director of photography on *Eric & Ernie*, to shoot the film and show her the ropes. 'She told me she was quite nervous about the technical aspect,' he says, 'but she had a natural instinct in terms of the visual. She just adapted quickly. I got the feeling that it just became another string to her bow.' Sky's head of comedy Lucy Lumsden visited on the second day and found Victoria in clover: 'I sat next to her in a muddy field in the freezing cold. There was a definite feeling that she couldn't be happier.'

There was as much joy creating a deliciously sentimental soundtrack inspired by the American composer Leroy Anderson, whose 'Forgotten Dreams' was arranged and recorded in Angel Studios by Nigel Lilley with Jim Watson on trumpet. A disproportionate amount of the session was taken up with giggling as Victoria tried to nail a short whistling solo. 'Film . . . went very well for me,' she reported. 'Four day shoot, 2 day edit, half a day to record music, day to put it on, a few hours to grade pictures . . . A steep learning curve!'[21] A couple of months later Victoria was distressed when Watson, her much-loved former trumpet tutor, died suddenly of a heart attack aged only fifty-nine.

While on set Victoria insisted on filming a short piece to camera explaining that the film was 'not exactly my story but it is my world and it is my landscape and it is, in a lot of ways, my childhood'. To Rosalind, who was best placed to spot the clues, she said 'it's about a little girl in a farmhouse on the moors in 61 delivering eggs in a village'.[22] While not directly autobiographical, *The Giddy Kipper* was emotionally true to her formative memories – the absent mother, the distracted father, the solitary house on the hill, an unkempt girl saved from unbearable solitude by *Bunty* and the spirit of her imagination. Aglow with nostalgia and shaded by melancholy, with bright glints of observational wit, *The Giddy Kipper* was fathoms deep, and it was very beautifully filmed. Although the reach was modest, its audience witnessed Victoria's conquest of yet another discipline. After this short apprenticeship, she looked forward to a bigger challenge: to direct *Loving Miss Hatto*.

Broadcast a week before Christmas, *The Giddy Kipper* was her second appearance on Sky that month. Victoria also emceed for a night of comedy featuring female comedians and performers she selected herself, among them Jo Brand, Joanna Scanlan, Vicki Pepperdine, Julia Davis, Jessica Hynes and Harriet Thorpe, with whom she presented 'Coffee Palaver'. Broadcast live to cinemas, *The Angina Monologues* was put together with the British Heart Foundation, who asked her to help spread the word that women are vulnerable to coronary heart disease. The Theatre Royal Haymarket was secured and thus one Sunday night Victoria returned to the first home of *Acorn Antiques: The Musical!* She began writing the material on the set of *Eric & Ernie* and, more than a decade on from *dinnerladies*, invited Geoff Posner to direct and edit it, and trade sly winks with her in rehearsals.

The all-female bill, Victoria said in her opening remarks, was a sign of progress: 'If we'd tried that twenty years ago, we'd have been over by an about quarter to eight. It would have been me, Jo Brand and Danny La Rue.' Off and on several times throughout, she made reference to her son leaving school, being single, taking in a lodger, and the recent pairing on *Strictly* of Anton du Beke and Ann Widdecombe. One joke, about what happens when a woman puts on beige body-shaping underwear ('it makes you look like a big old dog chew'), was purloined from her untitled 2008 script. Because she knew she could rely on it as a set closer, Victoria finished with the only joke she and Geoffrey wrote together, about the dyslexic boyfriend with a sex manual looking for her vinegar. At the end she cued up 'The Ballad of Barry and Freda' to a tremendous roar. 'If I lose track, could you join in?' she told the audience after a few bars. 'I have lost track now saying that.' It was her intention to make this the song's final farewell.

Before Christmas Victoria nipped back to Morecambe to shoot her bits for the making-of documentary that doubled as a tribute to Morecambe and Wise. Thanks to *Eric & Ernie*, she had a new set of firm friends to invite to mince pies and carols round the piano in Highgate. She spent the holiday 'mooching, doing jigsaws and watching crap telly (some with me in it tee hee)'.[23] For the third Christmas in a row, the BBC deployed her as a seasonal treat. Christmas Day brought out a new Radio 4 version of *Pat and Margaret*, involving many friends and collaborators – Andrew Dunn, Thelma Barlow and Imelda Staunton were in it, and it was adapted by Richenda Carey's husband John Foley. Other than giving her permission, and signing off on the script, Victoria kept her distance. Then, to glowing reviews, *Eric & Ernie* and its companion documentary were shown back to back on the first day of 2011, to round off a fulfilling year in which, as performing in her own work grew ever less important to her, she honed new skills as a director and as a producer.

Victoria returned to her desk in January to write her play with songs – she insisted it wasn't a musical – for Manchester International Festival. After half a year away from it, she also had another pass at Joyce Hatto. 'So I have to run two projects at the same time,' she told Lesley Fitton, 'which should at least fill the gap left by Henry.'[24] There was time somewhere in all this to join the cast of a Comic Relief spoof of *Downton Abbey*. The sketch united Victoria with other great practitioners of sketch comedy – Harry Enfield as the Earl of Grantham and, as the Dowager Countess, Jennifer Saunders, who wrote the script and allowed Victoria the odd ad-lib in the starchy Penelope Wilton role. 'Don't I know you from Lark Pies to Cranchesterford?' she said to the limping footman. In all her contributions to the charity since 1987, this was the first time she appeared in someone else's script.

She kept Nigel Lilley updated with progress reports on the new play. 'Just so you know I have had a very brain aching time working on the first draft,' she wrote in early February. 'I THINK I know what I'm doing now, but that only happened the day before yesterday – so I don't have much useful to say about the music.'[25] With the press launch due in mid-March she hurtled towards the end of the draft.

The plot Victoria fashioned from the Thames TV documentary was about Tubby and Enid, a shepherd and a nymph for whom one shining moment in childhood has been succeeded by a lifetime of anti-climax. They meet when a crass local magazine programme rounds up some old choristers for the fortieth anniversary of the recording. Tubby Baker, who (like Stanley Wood) sells insurance, is all chortles and nerves; Enid Sutcliffe, a PA, is reserved and dowdy. Via the broadcast they are reunited with fellow choristers Frank and Dorothy Brierley, whose bickering and petit-bourgeois status anxiety are no great advertisement for matrimony. Tubby makes awkward overtures to Enid only to discover she nurses a confident hope that her boss, with whom she has been having secret trysts for years, will leave his wife one day soon. Meanwhile, there were flashbacks to 1929 and the formation of the choir when the enthusiastic young Jimmy Baker, the only son of a destitute single mother, is not yet tubby nor worn down by disappointment. Tubby communes with his self as his young life is transformed by membership of a children's choir. The play ends with the climactic recording when Tubby and Enid declare themselves to each other.

As Victoria wrote she came to understand that, as well as the children's choir, the adult characters should also sing. So at speed she wrote half a dozen songs, calling once more on all her compositional skills. In 'The Berni Inn' the Brierleys reveal the absurdity of their pretensions. 'Was That Me?' was a yearning memory song in the style of Sondheim, 'If We Were Ginger and Fred' a lilting romantic fantasy about the life not lived. In 'Come Away with Me' Tubby and Enid croon in romantic harmony. Chris Walker, who had orchestrated *Acorn Antiques: The Musical!*, was once again sent demos of Victoria singing them.

In May she and Piers Wenger spent four days in La Gazelle d'Or near Taroudant – her first visit to Morocco since her trip with Geoffrey in 1984. Her platonic friendship with Piers was the closest Victoria would come to replacing that relationship. 'Despite the depth and intensity of the friendship,' he says, 'I don't think I ever got over the thrill of getting to know her. We shared many of each other's ups and downs, but the friendship was also predicated on a lot of laughs – getting to share jokes in person with the person whose jokes you had loved on TV became a lifeline to me. I felt like the luckiest person alive a lot of the time. I had spent a lot of my life feeling a bit lonely, and I think that to some degree Vic had been the same and we filled that space for each other. So I just felt grateful to her. I really, really wanted to make her happy, for her to thrive and for her talent to be appreciated as much as I did.'

Even in one of the most exclusive hotels in Africa, Victoria did not entirely down tools. 'V peaceful hotel in huge gardens,' she told Rosalind. 'Worked in the mornings and lay about the rest of the time.'[26] She readied the next draft of Joyce Hatto so it could be sent out by Left Bank Pictures to hook a commission from a broadcaster. As with every draft, her first reader was Piers, even though he was now at Channel 4 and had no professional stake in the script. 'Piers gives brill notes and has v good ideas about story,' she reported to Jane Wymark.[27] Back home she checked up on the builders' progress at Swiss Cottage, then visited Grace in Verona, taking Henry who had progressed from long hair to a mohawk to no hair at all. 'Shaved head and glasses give him look of eighties lesbian in some lights,' his mother informed Lesley Fitton.[28] The month also brought two visits to BAFTA ceremonies. *Eric & Ernie* was nominated for several craft awards, from which Peter Bowker's script emerged victorious. Then came the main event. 'We have two nominations,' Victoria told Amie Beamish, 'but we're not very hopeful.'[29] Denied the prize for Best Single Drama, Victoria and her fellow producers barely dared to dream in the Best Actor category. Daniel Rigby, who nine months earlier had been lugging his life around in a rucksack, was up against Jim Broadbent, Benedict Cumberbatch and Matt Smith, the new Doctor. As producers of *Doctor Who*, Victoria's colleagues felt less able to leap up when her lodger's win was announced. His accept-ance speech trawled through a long list of names before alighting on a visibly moved Victoria, who, he said, 'has shown me a thousand kindnesses she never needed to'. 'She was like a proud mum,' says Beth Willis, 'and it was the best night.' They all stayed in Highgate, and for the next couple of days Jonny Campbell haunted the house in a borrowed dressing gown, losing to his hostess at Scrabble as his hangover slowly wore off. 'Vic was very competitive,' he says. 'If I ever did win, she'd want to play again.'

A couple of weeks later the month-long rehearsals for *That Day We Sang* began in London at Copperfield Studios near Borough Market. The night before, the cast were all invited to a party in Highgate, including the young boy cast as Jimmy, whom Victoria remembered liking in the *Eric & Ernie* auditions. Soon other children were coming down from Manchester to join in as Victoria wrote little bits for individual choristers to perform. With a large choir to accommodate it was a complicated show to stage, limiting the scope of Lez Brotherston's designs, so, to add another dimension, film was to be projected onto an upstage screen. She reported on her progress to Jane Wymark: 'I am doing a lot of very confident blocking "yes you go off there . . ." and stage management are doing a lot of correcting. "Actually Vic that's a wall . . ."' That was not the impression of Vincent Franklin, who was cast as Tubby. 'She knew exactly what she wanted,' he says, 'had a really clear idea of how this is going to work. She could lose it if people weren't working hard: she works hard and you better work hard.'

The tight-knit triumvirate from the *Acorn Antiques* tour was reconstituted as Nigel Lilley oversaw the music and Sammy Murray, who had much more experience of running rehearsals than Victoria, co-directed. Once the company moved to Manchester Opera House for the technical rehearsals, she also became Victoria's voice on the 'god mic', with which the director addresses all on stage from the stalls. 'She never wanted to pick it up and speak loudly into it,' says Sammy. 'I saw a side of Vic I hadn't seen before. She would worry what the company thought of her.' This didn't stop her bossing the rehearsal room when she wanted to. Alex Poots was torn off a strip for doing his emails at the back during the final run-through, which she thought the height of bad manners. Nor had she outgrown her habit of instructing actors how to speak her dialogue, which was an alarming surprise for cast members not used to her ways. 'If you weren't getting the musicality the way she heard in her head,' says Jenna Russell, cast as Enid, 'she let you know. She was a hard nut to crack. But once you were playing by the rules of her writing, that's when she opened up.'

As with other leading actors whom she had befriended and confided in – David Threlfall, Ria Jones, Daniel Rigby – Victoria locked on to her two leads. To Vincent Franklin one afternoon she suggested a visit to the Imperial War Museum in Salford, followed by chips at Harry Ramsden's. On another they sat in their separate flats and watched *Ironside* while dissecting it over the phone. She sat in Jenna Russell's dressing room during the run and often urged her to 'look after your marriage and make sure you spend a lot of time with your kids'. To her fell the job of singing the show's comic showstopper, an angry tango in which Enid throws off the dull image conferred by her lifeless name:

> For Enids never get seduced,
> Your inner Enid rules the roost
> Your sex life will not be your claim to fame.
> You won't inspire a Byron, be a temptress or a siren
> A courtesan, a diva or a dame.
> You won't have a stock of sex tricks
> You won't hum like a Scalextrix
> When Enid is your name.

'Enid' was Victoria's most brilliant song about female desire since 'The Ballad of Barry and Freda'. Twenty-five years after its composition, she now brought her signature tune out of retirement. The occasion was a concert in tribute to Jim Watson at the Royal Academy of Music, which she was to host, and she rehearsed one day after lunch with only her principal actors listening. 'She said, "I've got to practise something to play this weekend,"' says Vincent Franklin. 'Jenna and I sat on the edge of the set with our legs dangling and just looked at each other as we had a private performance.'

Victoria, who had loyally attended many concerts at the Academy, confided to its principal Jonathan Freeman-Attwood that 'she'd never been more terrified. There was something about Vic,' he says. 'Her jaw used to drop when she heard young talented musicians from the Academy – she was really emotional about it.' As she prepared to compère a gathering of the world's greatest trumpeters she fretted about adopting the right tone. 'I knew I shouldn't really do much stand up as then the gig would have been about me,' she told Jane Wymark, who was in the audience with Henry, 'but I knew people would be disappointed if I didn't crack the odd joke.'[30] So she crafted a series of comic in-fills. She introduced the trumpeter who played the solo line on *Goldfinger* at nineteen. 'Which is great,' she said. 'To a mother of a nineteen-year-old boy I would be more impressed if you'd emptied the dishwasher.' For her valediction to Barry and Freda she was accompanied by a small brass ensemble of dazzling sassiness from the Academy playing Steve Sidwell's *Mid Life Christmas* arrangement. Rehearsing with the band, she told the audience, 'was a bit like being mugged in rhythm from behind'. Then she cued up the song with a couple of her old sex gags. Edited down to four minutes, it turned into a technical challenge, as she couldn't hear herself on the foldback speaker, but the audience's joyous applause – as she said farewell to a beloved musician and a beloved song – told its own story.

Manchester audiences were also on Victoria's side as they welcomed her home when *That Day We Sang* opened at the Opera House. There were only ten performances, with two children's choirs doing five shows each, so Victoria chose to stick around for the whole run. 'Have to be there with cattle prods,' she said.[31] At the rare sight of unsold house seats in the stalls she was straight on to the resident producer. Many of her friends – including Imelda Staunton – travelled to see it.

'It is lovely to know people like the show here,' she enthused. 'They are very warm towards it and after the grind of Nymphing and Joycing it's a relief.'[32] Jenna Russell had to pause in the middle of 'Enid' when the rhyme of 'sex tricks' with 'Scalextrix' triggered applause (to achieve the rhyme Victoria happily misspelled the brand name). After two performances Vincent Franklin wasn't getting a laugh on a particular line, so Victoria told him to restore the H that he was dropping from the word 'handsome'. 'The next night,' he says, 'we nearly

had to stop the show.' The most reliable ovation was for Victoria herself, who would wait until the lights were about to go down and slip
into her seat, only to be applauded by the whole theatre as she came
back in after the interval. She was 'very upset when people clapped,'
according to Alex Poots. 'It would be "don't make so much fuss".
Deep down she was thrilled.' Afterwards fans waited at the stage door
in huge numbers.

'It was a really happy time,' says Nigel Lilley. 'She was firing on all
cylinders.' The joy was briefly interrupted when Victoria learned of
plans for Radio 4 to record the show live which, fearing the sound of
clunking sets and thumping feet, she swiftly blocked. Towards the end
of the run she went to a party at the Mint Hotel thrown for Snoop
Dogg, who had just performed as part of the festival. At one point
she nipped outside and was snapped by paparazzi. 'You don't want
me,' she told them. One of Snoop's bulky bouncers manning the door
begged to differ. 'Lady,' he said, 'we heard that you're the shit.'

After the run the festival expressed enthusiasm for sending *That Day
We Sang* out on a tour. 'I can't see how the logistics would work with
the choirs,' she told Alex Poots. 'I also feel it would lose something of
its appeal.' But she didn't rule out a future for the show: 'I would love
it to have a further life . . . but I think we should be looking at finding
TDWS a home.'[33]

For the moment she put these considerations aside as, the day after
the run ended, she flew to Cape Town to be in a BBC adaptation of
Mary Norton's book for children *The Borrowers*. Having accepted the
job at short notice, she received her schedule only a week before her
departure. She was cast as Granny Driver, who is obsessed with flush-
ing out the little people that live under her floorboards and borrow
her possessions. After the intensity of Manchester, she was attracted
by a compressed schedule of only six days on set and splendid accom-
modation. The Nelson Hotel, she told Lesley Fitton, was 'like the one
where Agatha Christie escaped to . . . but the cocktails are cheap!'[34]
Her drinking companion was Shaun Dooley, who played her son-
in-law and, on their one day off, accompanied her on a trip down to
the very bottom of the continent. When they came to the Cape of
Good Hope they found that every other visitor had fled a howling

sandstorm: 'She looked at me and went, "Shall we go on the beach?" We could barely see anything, the waves were going crazy and we just played like kids, lifting our coats above our arms to lay into the wind. We were falling over and giggling. It took us hours to get cleaned up.'

Back in the UK Victoria went to Stoke-on-Trent for the final performance of *dinnerladies* after two and a half years of sporadic touring. Though it was a commercial success, she itched to get another version commissioned that would be a romantic comedy centred on the relationship between Bren and Tony. Having already tried a couple of writers who were too busy, she approached Peter James, whom she knew from her early days at the Sheffield Crucible. He proposed setting the play on the plane as Tony and Bren fly off on their honeymoon, with flashbacks to the canteen, but the problem of compressing all their dialogue into a coherent play proved 'an impossible mission,' he says. 'There was too much material there and she really didn't want to cut anything. We never got down to a script.'

In August Victoria was a guest of Richenda Carey and John Foley in Languedoc, went to Salzburg with Grace, then worked on a sixth draft of the Hatto script. 'Trying to please everyone at the BBC as usual who all have different ideas about what the story should be,' she told John Rushton, 'but I'm hoping this will be the draft that gets things moving and hopefully then it might shoot next spring.'[35] As draft followed draft, Victoria narrowed in on the relationship between Joyce and Barrie. In early versions of the story she had focused on the sudden inflation of Joyce's fame via internet chat rooms and the exposure of the scam through digital sleuthing. She deployed her New York research by adding in a couple of American characters. But these were all stripped out. 'In the end,' she said during the shoot, 'it took away from what the basic thing is which was two people in a co-dependent relationship and the effect they have on each other – that's the story.'[36] The key question she asked herself arose from William Barrington-Coupe's claim, when visited during the research, that 'Joyce knew nothing, nothing about it'. Victoria decided that, on the balance of the evidence and for the purposes of her drama, this could not be true and set about imagining the circumstances in which the hoax might have happened: 'They have expectations that are bigger than they can manage and then they become disillusioned. The feeling that they were owed something at the end of their lives – that's the motivation for the scam in my story. They invented the Joyce Hatto that she should have been.'[37]

Victoria looked forward to 2012. *Loving Miss Hatto* was to be her next adventure. 'It looks like I will be directing my drama about a mad lady pianist,' she told Amie Beamish. 'I have been working on it for ages on and off and the BBC have just given us the money.'[38] Meanwhile, a year after purchasing it, she hoped to get Swiss Cottage finished. Then in late October a shadow fell across the future with the discovery of a cyst that proved cancerous, causing a series of operations under general anaesthetic to remove potential growths in her lymph node. Yet she wasn't entirely immobilised. One procedure she delayed in order to compère the opening night of the London Jazz Festival at the Barbican, which involved much boning up on the performers. She felt robust enough to record the voiceover for *The Talent Show Story*, a five-part series for ITV, and go up to Sheffield to see Nigel Lilley conduct a production of Stephen Sondheim's *Company*. 'It didn't feel that ominous,' says Henry, who was back at home having suspended his music course to take up an internship with a music producer in Muswell Hill. 'It was like, uh-oh, it's cancer. It looks like it's going to be OK, but we just have to get through it.' Grace, who was in Cambridge for her final year and applying for music colleges, sensed that her mother found the ordeal 'very hard. She shared what she had to but given the choice I think she would have shared absolutely none of it.' Victoria took Grace to the Comedy Awards in December – having had to skip two other awards ceremonies, 'I don't want rumours spreading that I'm at death's door,' she explained to Sammy Murray.[39] Victoria's sisters were informed, and very few friends. At the Christmas party she drew aside Norah Wellbelove, who assumed she was going to announce she had a man. 'I've got something but it's not a man,' Victoria replied, and asked her to help keep Henry fed as she embarked on a daily course of radiotherapy. 'It's all fine really but effing boring,' she told Lesley Fitton, with whom she saw in the new year in Harpenden, 'so could do with some distractions.'[40]

The distraction was *Loving Joyce Hatto* which, for budgetary reasons, was to be shot in Dublin. In mid-December Victoria was still intending to direct it and sent out a lengthy planning memo to Andy Harries of Left Bank Pictures. They started to talk about casting. 'I don't think we should move on Joyce till we have our Barrie,' she argued.[41] When Jim Broadbent turned it down, she was happy to turn to Alfred Molina and was pleased that Left Bank liked her idea of Francesca Annis for the title role, which came to her having seen her in *Company* at the Crucible. Victoria packed plenty of production meetings into her first week of radiotherapy in the new year. But as she started on a low dose of chemotherapy she asked to meet Harries: 'She was sitting in my office waiting for me early. She said, "I've got cancer and it's serious. I don't want to not direct this but I'm not sure I'll be able to." It was deeply shocking.' At a meeting she also notified Radford Neville, who had been producer on *The Borrowers* and whom she recommended for *Loving Miss Hatto*: 'I thought we'd be talking about casting, suggestions for director of photography. She pointed towards her tummy area and said that she was ill.'

When the BBC's head of drama announced a new Victoria Wood project the details were kept vague. Within days she had withdrawn and as a replacement proposed Jonny Campbell who, with a baby on the way, had to rule himself out. 'I don't really know any other directors that well,' she confessed.[42] Eventually Andy Harries suggested Aisling Walsh, who had shot an episode of *Wallander* for Left Bank. Victoria decided against viewing her previous work: 'Better not send me any – might hate it! I'll take her as I find her!'[43] Before handing over the reins, she promised both her leads she would work with them before the shoot. That proved impossible.

She went alone to her many hospital appointments. 'I can't be bothered to put a good face on it and be jolly,' she admitted to Peter Bowker. 'The big blessing is that Henry is at home and is very sweet and that is a comfort.'[44] Luckily he was at home when, with only a week of radiotherapy left, Victoria felt sudden pain and swelling in her leg. An ambulance took her to the Whittington Hospital, a blood clot was diagnosed and she was sent to the Royal Free for yet another operation.

As she convalesced at the London Clinic Victoria received several visits from Chris Beetles. They had met some months earlier to toast his old comedy partner Rob Buckman, who had died from unknown causes on a transatlantic flight. Beetles's medical background now inclined Victoria to open up: 'She liked my visits because she could moan about having to go on blood thinners. She hated the intrusion and indignity of it all in a why-me way and talked very frankly. One time she broke down and cried. What triggered the tears was the idea she'd be on warfarin for the rest of her life. I moved to hug her and she waved me away and composed herself. She wasn't going to have my paternalism make her feel less strong and independent.' Geoffrey, now in the loop, was among those who arranged deliveries of books for her to read. She described her hospitalisation to Amie Beamish as 'a hellish 3 wks the last week of which was me being wheeled about to finish my treatment which is daily . . . the treatment flattens and has various tedious side effects'.[45] She was delighted at least to have not lost any hair to chemo, but mostly she found lying in bed very boring, according to Henry, who cheered her up with daily visits: 'She never seemed comfortable, physically, mentally, from not having anything to do, but she was always trusting of the process and determined to see it through.'

While she recuperated Piers Wenger kept an eye on *Hatto* casting decisions on her behalf. By the end of February Victoria was back at home and reluctantly reinserted herself into pre-production. 'I'm not sure how sharp my brain is,'[46] she warned Radford Neville, then a fortnight later: 'I can't work many hours in a day but doing as much as I can.'[47] She managed to do some late rewrites, which she found draining. 'I can only walk really slowly,' she told Sammy Murray in mid-March, 'and I waver like an old lady when groups of school children come barrelling along the pavement.'[48] By the end of March she had enough energy to go to Dublin for the cast read-through, before flying home to attend the Broadcast Press Guild awards at the Theatre Royal Drury Lane, where she was thrilled to hook up with the *Eric & Ernie* gang. 'We already knew we'd won,' says Beth Willis, 'so we were very relaxed and celebratory. I was on maternity leave and it was one of my first days out – Vic blissfully and gigglingly pointed out I had lactated on my dress . . . She was on great form.' She had another fillip that month when, as the culmination of a long series of conversations about adapting the 'Miss Read' books for television, Damien Timmer of Mammoth Screen optioned them.

Victoria was in Dublin for most of the *Hatto* shoot and sat by a monitor to watch the action unfold. 'I'm not sure if I even should have been there or not,' she mused. 'It was odd not really having a job but I felt I wanted to have some sort of relationship with Rad the producer who had only come on board cos I was directing – as had Francesca and Fred – so I did have to turn up.'[49] In fact, her presence obliged Radford Neville to sit next to her and act as a permanent firewall between the writer and her replacement as director. 'I became a diplomat,' he says. 'It was frustrating for Victoria because she was expecting to be completely at the helm and had to take a backseat. Sometimes she got a little bit grumpy.' Victoria as ever was policing not only her dialogue but the accuracy of the period design, though she made an effort wherever possible to bite her lip. 'Producer and I are in tune,' she reported mid-shoot, 'and when I see or hear something that's just plain wrong he nips in – but we try to keep those to the really important things.'[50] She loved the two older leads: 'Fran is playing a blinder – really clever and moving – and Molina is great too – they are both so nice to be with.'[51] Both gave sparkling and charismatic performances that drew out the subtle and intriguing flavours of Victoria's script, as did Rory Kinnear and Maimie McCoy as the young Barrie and Joyce.

Two days after her fifty-ninth birthday, Victoria was back in Dublin to see the first cut. As edit succeeded edit, she offered notes and thoughts but generally hovered in the background like any other executive producer. The story she had chosen to tell grew from her empathetic interest in human foibles. The only script she ever wrote from someone else's idea, with much the longest gestation, was perhaps her most intricately crafted drama. It was also the least overtly personal, yet even here there were chimes from the hinterland of her own past. The image of the widowed Barrie pouring out two drinks, then returning one to the decanter, evoked the opening lines of 'Love Song', composed in 1978 ('Made your breakfast this morning, just like

any old day / And then I remembered, and I threw it away'). Revered
by her pupils but antisocial and probably depressive, the older Joyce
Hatto was not dissimilar to Helen Wood. As for the younger Joyce
and Barrie – she ambitious but riddled with nerves; he constantly
there to stiffen her spine – they shared something with the young
Victoria and Geoffrey, the Start-Rite kids who once upon a time had
bravely taken on the world.

# 24

# THAT DAY SHE DIRECTED

'And then you have a choice
To dare to find your voice
And sing.'

*That Day We Sang*, 2011

When she was still recovering from her illness, Victoria went to the West End to see a production of *Sweeney Todd* that had originated in Chichester. As she enjoyed catching up with the conductor Nick Skilbeck, their shared past caught up with her. A decade earlier he was her accompanist when she transformed herself into the monstrous Stacey Leanne Paige, who was somewhat based on the cruise ship crooner Jane McDonald. Victoria was in the dressing room of Michael Ball after the show when word came through from the stage door that the real Jane McDonald was approaching.

Victoria swiftly concealed herself in Imelda Staunton's adjoining room, where she overheard a speech that she may as well have written for Stacey Leanne: 'What can I tell you?' McDonald told Ball. 'You were absolutely marvellous! This is Sue, hair and make-up, she goes everywhere with me. You, you are just like me – you gerrit. Yeah, you gerrit.' Michael Ball could not resist the temptation to introduce them. Victoria awkwardly asked McDonald if she'd taken offence at Stacey Leanne. 'No, no, I've not seen it!' she replied cheerfully. 'She was very nice about it!' Victoria reported to Sammy Murray.[1] The memory of the encounter would be a building block as she formed a new friendship. 'That would be our little catchphrase together,' says Michael Ball. 'You're like me, you just *gerrit*.'

After the *Loving Miss Hatto* shoot, and with no work of her own planned, Victoria looked for opportunities to be active. One soon arrived courtesy of Harry Enfield, who with Paul Whitehouse was making a fourth series of *Harry & Paul*. He had written three sketches featuring an irksome pair of minor royals who are patronisingly out of touch with the real world. He thought of Victoria, after working with her for the first time on Comic Relief the year before. 'She was just so funny in it and just so on the ball,' he says. 'Even when the camera wasn't on her she was totally in character all the time and observing everyone. I thought, well, I wonder if she'd be interested? I went to see her at home and she said, "Yeah, I'm up for doing anything at the moment. I've just recovered from cancer."' 'Minor Royals', three sketches filmed in north London one day in late spring, united the two major royals of British sketch comedy. Harry Enfield suffered from 'this huge bag of nerves working properly with her and kept on fluffing up my lines. She didn't need any notes and never fluffed a single thing.' Victoria's royal spring continued. With Harriet Thorpe, Jonny Campbell and Beth Willis she watched the Thames Diamond Jubilee Pageant from a riverside restaurant, then on the day of the jubilee she had friends round to drink Earl Grey-infused London gin with rhubarb and strawberry syrup topped up with champagne.

An offer to front a documentary about the history of tea came in. Victoria went to Claridge's to listen to the pitch from Paula Trafford of KEO Films, who explained her goal was to explore the geopolitical back story of the humble cuppa. With fond memories of visiting Darjeeling for *Victoria's Empire*, Victoria said yes. 'I feel I missed the last twelve months of my life I had so many hospital palavers,' she told Peter Bowker, 'which is why I'm doing this doco. It meant going to China and India and getting out of the house.'[2]

In June she went up to Swiss Cottage to keep up with the decoration. It was now two years since she had made an offer on it. 'Can't wait for the day I just go up to lounge about,' she said, 'and not worry about pan rails or dressing gown hooks.'[3] The summer house from Mole Barn that had been in storage since 2005 was installed. Grace sat her finals at Cambridge. Henry resigned from his job in order to tour Ireland with a band he was in. 'I think this is a good time for him to give it a punt,' his mother reasoned. 'You don't know till you try if these things will work out or not.'[4]

Throughout all this Victoria was getting used to self-medicating. 'Could really do with an extra leg Rolf Harris style to stick the needle in,' she joked to Jane Wymark.[5] Instead she was soon reduced to the use of one leg when she tore a muscle at the top of her thigh. Immobilised for three weeks, and finding it difficult to get up from her seat, she had to cancel an appearance on *QI* and an outing to see Julie Walters at the National Theatre. She managed to make it to Grace's graduation. 'I am limping in ludicrous fashion,' she warned Lesley Fitton as they prepared to meet, 'but before you see me and go OMG it's not as bad as it looks but I can't walk fast.'[6] In fact, it was worse than it looked. The healing process was slowed by the anti-coagulant, and she discovered only a year later when she went for a scan that, despite the initial diagnosis of her GP, it was not a tear but a break: 'So that's why it hurt so much!'[7]

As she started moving again, Victoria made her way to Dublin to see the final *Hatto* cut. She treated herself to a stay in a spa in Lake Garda, moved on to Switzerland to see the Glossops, then took Grace to Swiss Cottage for the first time. In August she went to a cold and wet Edinburgh for the unveiling of *Loving Miss Hatto* at the television festival, followed by a Q&A. She spent a few spare days in tiny venues seeing young stand-ups represented by Phil McIntyre Entertainment. 'She sat right at the front bold as brass,' says Jonny Campbell, who went with her to one show. 'Have seen a lot of terrible shows at the Fringe the last couple of days,' she told Rosalind. 'It's all a lot more fancy than when I played here but same old crap shows.'[8]

Her other reason for being in Edinburgh was to play a small part in *Case Histories*, adapted from the Jackson Brodie private-detective novels by Kate Atkinson. After a first series, shown the previous year, the author was keen to tempt Victoria and over tea at the Savoy they quietly expressed their fondness for each other's work. The part on offer in *Started Early, Took My Dog* – a shopping-mall security guard who, prompted by events in her past, takes possession of an abused child – called for crying, light running and other physical exertion. 'She was in pain, her leg was bad, and was entertainingly stoic about the fact she had to stomp across a shopping mall the whole time,' says Jason Isaacs, the show's star. It was not the sort of work she was used to. 'Spent today smacking a crackhead around in a car park,' she reported to Rosalind.[9] For her big emotional scene with Isaacs in which her character came clean, Victoria had to be dissuaded from wearing sunglasses. 'I think she was slightly off piste acting in someone else's script,' he says. 'We did the scene and it was fine and then we turned the camera round for me and off camera she broke down completely. It was incredibly moving.' Kate Atkinson was sufficiently impressed to start writing a screenplay about a female detective for Victoria to play and in the interim sent her a proof copy of her latest novel. 'Thought it was brill,' Victoria enthused to Jane Wymark, whom she nonetheless urged to stay away from *Case Histories* when it was broadcast:[10] 'Don't watch me on the telly – I look like Hitler's fat limping sister.'[11]

To prepare for the documentary Victoria read several histories of tea, which she confessed to finding 'a bit dull'.[12] As usual she asked to vet the director proposed by KEO Films. John Moulson passed muster, and in early September filming began in Harrogate and London, where she hung out with cabbies and visited noted tea-guzzler Tony Benn (although they got on well, their conversation did not make the final cut). She and Chrissie Baker then joined the crew to fly to Kolkata, where Victoria saw a tea-bag machine being blessed and was served by a chai wallah on the banks of the Hooghly. They went on to Assam on the border with Myanmar to watch elephant-mounted tea-pickers at work. An elephant calf 'went a bit haywire,' she told Richenda Carey, 'which was scary for a few secs. Have sat with chaps smoking opium and then watched other chaps in cere-monial dress make tea in bamboo tubes over an open fire which did make me want to say have you never heard of a kettle and teabags.'[13] When they were filming in a tea plantation she slipped and tumbled out of sight. She got up laughing and, although the director walked into shot to check if she was unharmed, the footage was too good not to use. They spent two nights in an eco-lodge, where everyone had to wash in hot water delivered in a bucket. 'Very good for bonding,' suggested Victoria, who didn't complain.[14] More comfortably, they stayed in a tea-planter's bungalow decorated, she suggested in a piece to camera, 'in a style that I would say is 1950s Chorlton – it reminds me a bit of my grandmother's house'.

After the crew flew overnight from Mumbai to Shanghai, Victoria listened mischievously as a beautifully dressed tea lady in a tea restaurant presented a ceremonial beverage with an extremely long introduction in Cantonese. 'Minestrone's off,' she translated for the camera. In a museum she was mobbed by schoolchildren demanding her autograph. When not filming she shopped for presents, but the schedule was stressfully dense. 'Oh my lord we are right in the thick of it now,' Victoria told Jane Wymark. 'Director is wilting under pressure and has gone from chewing Nicorette to chain smoking Coke drinking and chewing Nicorette.'[15]

It was on the next foreign leg of the trip – after outings to Woburn Abbey and Blackpool – that the director pulled off the programme's greatest coup. John Moulson knew that Morrissey was a fan of both tea and Victoria Wood so proposed they meet on camera. Victoria was vaguely aware that 'Rushholme Ruffians' from the Smiths' 1985 album *Meat Is Murder* contained a lyrical homage to 'Fourteen Again'. Morrissey had attempted to have tea with her in 1990 when she was at the Strand Theatre, but she had been too tired and said no. Now he was pinned down to New York. At the prompting of Piers Wenger, Victoria emailed Peter Bowker to ask for a Morrissey tutorial and received a playlist by return: 'I guess the fact that he's agreed to do the interview must mean he's reasonably well disposed towards me. I can imagine him refusing to disclose where he stands on loose leaf versus teabags though.'[16] The night before the interview she and her director went to see him perform at Terminal 5, where in the middle of a song, the music stopped, the venue sank into darkness and Morrissey sonorously intoned the bleak finale of 'Northerners':

Cobbles in the morning mist,
Park Drive,
Dead at forty-five
From a backstreet abortionist.

'He's doing one of my songs!' Victoria hollered. Afterwards they went backstage, where Morrissey shyly presented her with a mixtape full of Patti Smith, Nico and other singers she had barely heard of. 'They really seemed to hit it off,' says John Moulson. 'They chatted for about forty minutes about *Coronation Street*, Jimmy Clitheroe, Alan Bennett. It was quite touching and very funny. He was teasing her. She showed him a picture of something we'd shot in China. "Ooh, someone's been on their travels."' In the interview itself Victoria presented him with a black-and-white tea cosy made by Norah Wellbelove. Back in London she soon met him for a drink with Chrissie Hynde. 'Any tips on her?' she asked Peter Bowker.[17] 'I wouldn't try and compete on the eye liner front,' he advised.[18]

Aside from Morrissey, the highlight for Victoria was going to York to make tea in a NAAFI van for Second World War veterans, who were as thrilled to meet her. The same day she went to Preston to do *I'm Sorry I Haven't a Clue*. Her appearance had an unexpected outcome when Graeme Garden asked her to step in at short notice to act as emcee at a festival of slapstick in Bristol. 'I thought well why the heck not,' she said. After steeping herself in the material, she declared Buster Keaton 'my new heart throb'.[19]

Four years after she was first approached about the idea, the BBC confirmed *Loving Miss Hatto* would go out two days before Christmas. 'I have to say if I had directed it, it wouldn't look so classy,' she told Richenda Carey, 'though it would have more laughs in it!'[20] The date of transmission, somewhere in the annual avalanche of new dramas, reflected the anxiety of the BBC's Editorial Policy department. The script was on solid ground legally, but there were fears that William Barrington-Coupe might sue or that they might be seen to be picking on an old man. Despite widespread critical praise, 'it somewhat got lost,' concludes Andy Harries. 'I don't know why that was. *Housewife, 49* had gone through the roof. Ours just didn't and I couldn't work out why.'

Victoria and Piers Wenger began 2013 with a week in St Lucia, where on New Year's Day they decided to treat themselves to a glamorous cruise aboard a skippered yacht. 'When we got there the boat was this really tiny ramshackle thing,' says Piers. 'We were supposed to have lunch on the boat, and the guy had brought two mangos from his garden and sliced them up with a rusty penknife that he took out of his pocket. That became a highlight of the holiday.'

Back in London Victoria had two more shootings days on *Victoria Wood's Nice Cup of Tea*, as it was now titled, then wrote and recorded the voiceover. 'The tea stuff is quite a challenge,' she confessed. 'I feel it's now on my shoulders to come up with some sort of overall theme (done it before with the Empire prog but was hoping not to have to do it again).'[21] The job wasn't completed till late February, which frustrated her desire to push on with her next venture: a television version of *That Day We Sang* which she would direct herself.

The previous summer she had first taken the idea to Ben Stephenson, the head of drama commissioning at the BBC, and he now organised for her to choose from a selection of producers. The one she warmed to was Hilary Bevan Jones, whose formidable CV included *Cracker* and *State of Play*. 'Hilary has been dead keen on the script from day one,' she enthused to Nigel Lilley and Sammy Murray, once again enlisted as musical director and choreographer.[22] Her ambition was for Vincent Franklin and Jenna Russell to resume as Tubby and Enid, though she was aware that the BBC might insist on bigger names to justify the budget. 'Of course I will fight for them both but not to the extent that it jeopardises the project.'[23] 'Is it worth mentioning Michael Ball?' Nigel Lilley replied.[24]

In the hope that it might be shot in the summer, Victoria committed herself to rushing out a ninety-minute first draft in only three weeks. She went to Swiss Cottage to start whittling away at her original script, trimming out most of the scenes involving choir rehearsals that were integral to the MIF production. She renamed her new script *Tubby and Enid* for the pragmatic reason that a chamber production of *That Day We Sang* was now in the pipeline at the Royal Exchange in Manchester. The idea was suggested by Alex Poots to the theatre's artistic director Sarah Frankcom, who was looking for a Christmas show. Galvanised by the prospect of a revival, Victoria took the train to Manchester the very next day. 'You seem you know what you're doing,' she told Frankcom. 'I think you would need to work with Sammy and with Nigel. If you work with them then great.'

The recycling of her back catalogue was to become a theme of Victoria's year. While she was at Swiss Cottage converting *That Day We Sang* into a drama she met up with Charlotte Scott, and between them they cooked up the idea of a stage version of *Housewife, 49* for the Old Laundry Theatre in Bowness-on-Windermere. The Radio 3 broadcaster Paul Allen was asked to adapt it – as a young journalist he had been the first critic to review *Talent* at the Crucible, where twenty years later he had his own stage hit adapting *Brassed Off*. Peter James would direct it. Both sat on the Old Laundry's board of trustees with Victoria. She saw yet another of her old titles revived when *Acorn Antiques: The Musical!* was staged by an amateur troupe in Sheffield. Though chuffed to hear the songs once more, from a distance of five years she 'found the plot a bit hard to follow – and I'd written it, so don't know what the others made of it'.[25] The retrospective mood continued that month as she presented Julie Walters with an outstanding-achievement award at the South Bank Sky Arts Awards. Having paid tribute in her speech, Victoria used the presence of press microphones to vent her fury at the viral spread of enhanced reality shows such as *The Only Way Is Essex*: 'They put a bunch of real people into situations and get them to act something out. To me that is taking the bread out of the actors' mouths.'[26]

*Victoria Wood's Nice Cup of Tea* was broadcast in April, but she had moved on. 'Let the cards fall where they may,' she told Richenda Carey. 'I did my best and it's just a trivial bit of telly.'[27] Meanwhile, there were signs of an impending commission for *Tubby and Enid*, and even some money for pre-production. Victoria was begrudgingly aware that her script must make its way through the sundry strata of managerial decision makers at the BBC. Having dashed off the first draft, once more she found herself 'madly racing on with my next draft as I need to get it in to the Big Cheese for the thumbs up – implementing the Small Cheese's notes'.[28]

On 19 May, Victoria marked her sixtieth birthday with the biggest party she had ever thrown. Normally she would drive down to M&S in Finchley at seven in the morning to get her party food and gather a few friends around a brazier in the garden. This time, urged by Piers

Wenger to splash out, she booked a Moroccan marquee bedecked with cushions, Indian catering and a young jazz trio sourced by Henry. Guests from all walks of her life were there, including the new circle of younger friends she had acquired on *Housewife, 49*, the *Acorn Antiques* tour, *Eric & Ernie* and *That Day We Sang*. One abiding image in the throng was of Wood and French and Saunders in a huddle. 'Couldn't have liked it more,' the hostess concluded. 'And so nice not to have to spend the aftermath clearing up as I do at Christmas. I wish I could have kept the tent.'[29]

As Victoria waited for someone at the BBC to read her script she went to Garsington Opera to witness Grace's professional debut in the chorus and felt huge pride when, subsequently, a casting director approached her and said, 'You must be Grace's mum,' then showered her daughter with praise. 'Whenever that happened, and it happened a handful of times,' says Grace, 'she said that was the nicest thing for her: that people were coming up to her not for her and turning the tables. She loved it.' That summer Victoria also caught Anne Reid's cabaret at The Stables. With no wingman to protect her from admirers, 'it was like being at the petting zoo,'[30] she told Nigel Lilley, to whom she soon confided that she was 'creeping round to the idea of writing another one at some point so want to see what everyone's up to . . .'[31] She went to Sheffield to see a new musical by Tim Firth, who had written the *Calendar Girls* film script, and went so far as to tell the Crucible's artistic director Daniel Evans that she had an idea for a musical, but the conversation went no further. Project ideas continued to bubble up. With Stephen Mear she talked about making a documentary on the history of dance troupes featuring the Bluebells, the Rockettes and the Tiller Girls – they accumulated a stack of books to do research.

By early August the cheeses at BBC Drama had all read and approved the latest draft of *Tubby and Enid* and thoughts turned to casting. One of their provisos was that it be cast to the hilt, so Victoria wrote apologetically to inform Jenna Russell that the part of Enid would not be hers. The BBC insisted the script be sent to Emma Thompson to try and engender American interest. 'I didn't feel I could go against that as an idea,' she told her colleagues, but her preference was for

Imelda Staunton.[32] 'If she said yes I would work round her availability as I don't think we can do better.'[33] Imelda had for a time been a close friend of Victoria's, but aside from occasional encounters the connection had lapsed. 'I was so shocked to get the script,' she says. 'I thought, that's weird, we haven't been in touch for years.' The first she learned of Victoria's illness was when she visited her garden to talk about Enid. She was back a few days later to work on the songs but was not available for the whole of the autumn, which at least gave the production time to locate a Tubby and some funding.

Victoria then spent a couple of days back at the Edinburgh Fringe, partly to see her brother's twenty-year-old granddaughter have a crack at stand-up, partly to catch a play starring Daniel Rigby, who was once again lodging with her for a few months. At the television festival she was taken aback to discover that the controller of the channel *That Day We Sang* was destined for knew nothing about it. 'I pounced on Janice Hadlow,' she reported to Nigel Lilley, 'and when she opened the conversation with "Victoria – HOW can I persuade you to do something for BBC2?" I realised she wasn't quite up to speed on the whole Tubby sitch. So I did a bit of gulping and explained there was a script which I was waiting for her to read.'[34] Victoria also took the opportunity to pitch the dance documentary: 'She went mad for that too.'[35]

In early September Victoria was in the Lakes to help usher *Housewife, 49* onto the stage. The cast, whom she invited to tea at Swiss Cottage during the run, included Andrew Dunn as Nella Last's husband and Richenda Carey as Mrs Waite. She had no qualms about handing over her own role to another actress. 'I didn't feel weird about it,' she told Richenda. 'My attachment is to the whole thing rather than the part of Nella. I just love that she is having a further life.'[36] In the hope that its life might extend beyond Windermere, Phil McIntyre invested in the production and turned up to the read-through. Once it was in preview Victoria suggested a succession of cuts to Paul Allen, whose adaptation was more faithful to Nella Last's diary than she had been. 'She was much more ruthless with material that didn't always directly lead the narrative to the next plot point or the resolution of a particular scene,' he says. While praising its 'quiet cumulative power,' the *Stage* found the production 'never quite overcomes its screen origins'.[37] It attracted a strong audience from Barrow-in-Furness, including many who remembered the real Nella, but the play was to have no further life.

By now Victoria's focus was narrowing onto her musical as it forged separate paths towards stage and screen. To Nigel Lilley, who would work on each of them, she declared herself 'very excited about both versions now!'[38] Hilary Bevan Jones introduced her to an experienced cinematographer, and she went to Manchester to inspect the model of the Royal Exchange set. She had casting approval for the theatre production but mainly kept her distance as she concentrated on casting the television drama. Victoria's first thought for Tubby was Conleth Hill, the sinuous Northern Irish actor she had admired since seeing the West End hit *Stones in His Pockets* in 2000. The BBC held out for a bigger name so instead he was cast as the puffed-up Frank Brierley, with Sophie Thompson as his wife. As for Tubby, eventually Victoria fell in with Nigel Lilley's idea from six months earlier and the most popular male lead in musical theatre was sounded out.

'They sent me some script and the songs, and I really worked my arse off,' says Michael Ball. 'I was so nervous, but I just knew this character and I was desperate to do it.' As they worked on dialogue, Victoria impressed upon him her abhorrence of paraphrasing: 'I got the words wrong and she said, "I don't think that's what I wrote." She almost had a physical reaction.' According to Nigel Lilley, it was 'an audition that wasn't an audition. They needed to suss each other out. Afterwards she was walking down the street going, "Michael Ball is singing my songs!"' 'He's v lovely,' she wrote glowingly later that day. 'Not starry.'[39]

As for the rest of the cast, Victoria stayed loyal to actors she trusted. Vincent Franklin, the original Tubby, returned as Enid's unpleasant boss/lover. Dorothy Atkinson, from *Housewife, 49* and *Mid Life Christmas*, was the kindly choir mistress Gertrude Riall. Daniel Rigby was cast as Mr Kirkby, a wounded veteran of the trenches who gruffly takes young Jimmy under his wing. In her most sentimental coup Victoria found a role for Ian Lavender, the last survivor of the *Dad's Army* Home Guard, as the commissionaire who turns a blind eye when Tubby, like a midlife Romeo, climbs up a ladder to declare his love to Enid.

The production required a budget of £2 million, only some of it to be supplied by the BBC, so Victoria and the producers travelled to Manchester, where she was 'to be pimped out as truly northern'.[40] The trip bore fruit when Peter Salmon, having been there at the show's conception, dipped into a discretionary fund for such projects on the proviso that the production have a Mancunian footprint. A distributor gave them an advance, and they received some private equity. 'Getting that last couple of hundred grand together was really hard and frustrating for us,' says Hilary Bevan Jones, who by now was so emotionally invested in the project that she agreed, with Victoria, to reduce her own fee.

Victoria spent the autumn haring between London and the north. She made a hectic overnight visit to Scarborough to see Vincent Franklin in a play. One evening in October she did two charity events – one speaking about her schoolfriend Lesley Schatzberger's charity Jessie's Fund at a privately held auction, the other a short stand-up set as the headliner in aid of Breakthrough Breast Cancer at the Roundhouse. The latter, she told Jane Wymark, was '40 yrs on from John Cage and his music circus!'[41] She was whisked on the back of a motorbike between the two. She couldn't resist an invitation to record two episodes of *I'm Sorry I Haven't a Clue* at the Theatre Royal Drury Lane. 'Such an exhausting day,' she said. 'A mixture of being in the writer's room for Sid Caesar and an old folks' home. Was there from 10 30 till midnight.'[42] She sang 'Bob the Builder' to the tune of 'I Dreamed a Dream', provoking a raucous ovation before she'd even finished. In the game of changing a title by the addition of one word, she namechecked an old *New Faces* contestant by suggesting 'Les Dennis Miserables'. Asked to propose a film to be enjoyed by senior citizens, she nominated 'Cakes on a Train'.

There was more singing the next day at the read-through of *That Day We Sang* at the Royal Exchange. Being the only person in attendance who knew the songs, Victoria tentatively volunteered herself. 'None of them in my key,' she told Jane Wymark. 'It was like a horrid mixture of Molesworth and Susan Boyle.'[43] At short notice she stepped

in to host another opening night at the London Jazz Festival and had
a fun evening out at a Russell Brand gig in Hammersmith Apollo,
where after the show she ran into Morrissey in hospitality: 'Morrissey
insisted on getting in my car and I had to drive him to Claridge's and
then apparently (Lucy was watching from upstairs window) Russell
ran after the car begging us to stop but we never heard him . . . celebs
eh!'[44] Her own celebrity was wielded as a big blunt instrument at
Broadcasting House when, to increase the pot of funding, she and
Hilary Bevan Jones pitched a documentary about making *Tubby and
Enid*. When they got to the meeting the person who could greenlight the project was not in the room: 'Hils went and whispered to
someone that if they didn't get the head of Docs in the room NOW
then I was going to go mad. (I was quite innocently sitting there not
knowing she was using me in this way).'[45]

In regular commutes to Manchester Victoria met up with the
Hallé Children's Choir and its choir mistress, and once more sat
through hours of children's auditions. She chose a young actor
called Harvey Chaisty to play Jimmy, the junior incarnation of
Tubby, while another boy tickled her by doing a bit of Kimberley
and won a part. Locations were scouted in Manchester, Liverpool
and Huddersfield, whose town hall with splendid organ pipes was
deemed the closest facsimile to the Free Trade Hall where 'Nymphs
and Shepherds' was recorded in 1929. 'It's all a bit bonkers trying
to prep this musical, and rehearse dancers, and choose urchins and
find musicians who have to come from outside the M25,' Victoria
reported to Richard E. Grant.[46]

In this hectic timetable she stole one day off, dashing to and from
Paris on Eurostar as a belated sixtieth birthday treat courtesy of Nigel
Lilley and his partner. They visited a museum, took a trip on the
Seine, had lunch and drank champagne. 'J'aime beaucoup la Musee
D'Orsay,' she wrote gratefully. 'Je ne trouve pas la punctuation fran-
caise sur mon keyboard. Je ne regrette riens. Victoire.'[47]

In December the cast and musicians of *Tubby and Enid* recorded
the songs in a London studio, where Michael Ball found her an open-
minded collaborator. 'It wasn't a difficult sing,' he says. 'When we
started doing it, there were only a couple of musical things where I

would say, "Could I go up a third and try a harmony here?" Nigel would go, "You can ask her. I'm not going to." She said, "Let's hear it." If something didn't work and she didn't like it, she'd absolutely say no. If you could contribute something and she loved it . . . you wanted to please her. You wanted that smile.' Then song and dance rehearsals began on a sound stage in Salford. While in Media City Victoria was invited by Radio 4's *Front Row* to choose a single word to be illuminated in giant neon above a building there. She thought about picking 'Chips' but eventually alighted on 'Happy'. 'It relates to what I try to be,' she explained to the presenter John Wilson as she hit the switch, 'and what I try to convey in my work and what I think my job is. It's to do with my responsibility to the audience.'

Victoria's own moment of personal happiness came at the December wedding of Jonny Campbell and Beth Willis at Wiltons Music Hall in east London. Invited to give an address in the ceremony, somewhere in her schedule she found time to adapt Marriott Edgar's comic poem 'The Lion and Albert', popularised by Stanley Holloway in the 1930s. She repurposed the story of a boy coming to an unfortunate end at the zoo as a nuptial narrative called 'Whitney's Wedding':

There's a famous seaside place called Blackpool.
You'll have the next line on your lips –
It's noted for fresh air, and also for fun
And mugging, and drag acts. and chips.

And Blackpool's the scene for my story,
A wedding, one morning in May,
When Mr and Mrs Ramsbottom
Gave their only child Whitney away.

They'd worried she'd never get married,
That the way to her heart would stay barred.
Cos she only liked sitting ont sofa,
And Strictly, and Bake Off, and lard.

A few days later she was at the press night of *That Day We Sang* at the Royal Exchange, where she had been an ever more frequent visitor. Having already consented to various cuts and edits, as she saw the production take shape Victoria offered some notes 'that were like keyhole surgery,' says Sarah Frankcom. 'At the dress rehearsal she was very serious, at the preview she'd thawed a bit and at the press night she sat in the first gallery and just smiled the whole way through.' It became one of the theatre's most successful Christmas productions.

By Christmas Victoria was exhausted. 'Have just had a meeting about a doco I might do,' she told Nigel Lilley on the 23rd. 'I'm so tired I could barely listen or look interested.'[48] After Christmas she took off to New York for a few days with Grace and Henry.

In January 2014, after many years of waiting, Victoria began at last to direct a full-length television drama. She was all too aware that it was going to be a challenge. 'I don't have the experience with cameras,' she told Sammy Murray, 'but we will all work together and that's what I like about filming anyway – the collaboration.'[49] On the first day of the shoot Imelda Staunton as Enid marched determinedly up a residential street in Liverpool singing along to playback as the camera followed her on tracks. The song, 'Do It', was composed especially for the drama. They didn't quite finish the schedule that day, but the producer Paul Frift called a halt. 'Vic hadn't been slow and we only needed one more shot,' says Hilary Bevan Jones, 'and Paul quite rightly said, "Stop, show the crew that we're not going over every day." Other directors might have had a complete fit, but she could see the logic. She was a total team player.'

Filming six days a week with early starts, Victoria was kept extremely busy. Every day she would get back to her rented flat near Canal Street at eight o'clock and pore over the rushes from the day before. 'Not much time to lift weights,' she told Jane Wymark.[50] On a relatively small budget the production had to capture the look of the 1920s and the 1960s and incorporate colourful fantasy song-and-dance sequences. It was extremely cold filming the exteriors. 'Happiness Street', the other new song she composed especially for the drama, featured a cheery quartet of singing and dancing urchins – to dress the Liverpool alley where it was shot an art department trainee was on his hands and knees obscuring yellow lines under freezing mud. There was a positive sign of things going well: when 'The Berni Inn' was filmed on the sound stage in Salford one of the sparks, baring his builder's bottom on the floor as he prepared for the next shot, was singing the tune. 'Vic was so chuffed,' says Hilary. 'The whole crew were in love with this show.' Victoria had another high when the production moved to Huddersfield Town Hall to record the finale with the Hallé Orchestra and the Hallé Children's Choir. It was 'quite a scary day as we only had the Hallé for that day and they knock off prompt after so many hours! But we got it all.'[51] By habit an energetic texter, afterwards she made a rare phone call to Nigel Lilley. 'She was strangely emotional for Vic,' he says, 'and on a bit of a high. She never thought she'd get her music recorded by a symphony orchestra.'

The shoot for *That Day We Sang*, as it was once more titled, was a culmination enfolding everything she'd learned in the forty years since a *New Faces* judge told her she had no future. Having always hankered to call all the shots, Victoria was now directing her own feature-length script, set and mainly filmed in Manchester, for which she had written the jokes, the lyrics and the music. The result was bliss. 'Vic was just doing the job really, really well,' says Imelda Staunton. 'This was her stuff, she knew how she wanted it to look, how it was going to sound. She knew exactly how she was going to shoot everything. She was so, so happy because every element seemed to work, and she knew we could all deliver it.'

Throughout the shoot Victoria got on extremely well with Michael Ball, who, she reported, 'has enthusiastically embraced his inner and outer Tubby and has 2 puds every lunchtime. We may have to put a piece in his trousers by week 3.'[52] He had even less experience as a TV actor than she did as a TV director. 'We just clicked,' he says. 'We were very, very tight on set. I would pick up quite quickly on when she would need a hug or be made to laugh. She would say how hard it is sometimes to be the one everybody comes to, to make sure everyone's got respect for you. She would feel intimidated. Hilary was very, very good at guiding and calming her.' As well as the catchphrase conferred by Jane McDonald, they had a running joke about an extra who furtively snuck into every shot. They nicknamed her Rosemary West.

An intense schedule landed Victoria with a chest infection on the last day, which made for an uncomfortable journey home. 'Have totally run out of steam,' she told Nigel Lilley a week later. 'Could not have kept up that pace much longer but am missing charging about in the cold having a laugh.'[53] She spent her recovery period watching films as part of her BAFTA-judging duties. In early March, at a lunch at the Park Lane Hilton Hotel to mark the retirement of Sir Marcus Setchell, she made a short speech on a gynaecological theme in tribute to the doctor who had delivered Henry Durham and Prince George. (The latter's mother was also in attendance, though Victoria held back from the throng pushing to meet her at a small reception beforehand.) 'She made some very hilarious observations about what it is to be a woman,' says Kirsty Young, who found herself sitting next to Victoria. The connection they had struck up on *Desert Island Discs* seven years earlier was not to be revived: 'It was almost as though we hadn't had that very intimate exchange. She was pretty closed, and I thought, that's interesting – that just happened at the moment it happened.'

For much of the rest of the year Victoria was in an edit suite. Every day she made her way to Wardour Street in Soho to sift laboriously through all the takes on huge high-definition screens and assemble them into a ninety-minute film. She soon found herself having meetings with audio techies about the arcana of dubbing, mixing and smoothing out the sound. 'Some of these gents deal only with music,' she marvelled, 'some with vocals, some only with sound that has been pre mixed, and some can only be sent bits of sound that have nothing to do with each other. All these things have to be sent to the right person in the right order at the right stage in the editing process or lord knows what will occur.'[54] She'd come a long way from *Happy Since I Met You*, her first drama shot on film in 1982. After six weeks of editing she watched everything they'd put together on a television and was sufficiently underwhelmed to ask for costly tweaks – 'though how expensive can it be for someone to turn up the brightness – it's very quick when you do it at home'.[55]

She then turned to composing the score. 'Normally,' she conceded to her musical supervisor, 'the director wouldn't be writing the
music!'⁵⁶ In April the score was orchestrated by Chris Walker and
recorded with lashings of luscious brass. 'I am slightly dreading the
end of the film,' she admitted to Richenda Carey, 'as up to now I've
been able to keep working on it and improving it – with the titles and
the music and the grade and the sound mix and after Wednesday it
will just be in its box – done.'⁵⁷ The following month she went to the
Serpentine Gallery for a party thrown by one of the film's investors,
where 'If We Were Fred and Ginger' was shown in a silent loop. 'Can
you lip read?' said someone who spotted Victoria with her eyes glued
to the screen. 'I don't have to,' she replied. 'I wrote it.'

With the drama in the can, next up was the documentary about
the making of the drama. A film crew had been there to record
Victoria as she met the Hallé Children's Choir, attended recordings
and dance rehearsals, and captured some of the actual shoot. She now
found herself sifting through eighteen hours of footage. 'Crikey it's
so hard to watch,' she told Jane Wymark. 'I hate watching myself
anyway (none of me will go in the finished film I have at least that
privilege).'⁵⁸ Then came the business of choosing a producer-director.
Having enjoyed total control as a director of the drama, she was
reluctant to cede it and specifically sought someone 'who can get on
board with how I want it to be and not try and be creative on their
own behalf'.⁵⁹

In July there was an invitation to be an onstage guest of Monty
Python, promoted and produced by Phil McIntyre as they reformed
for a run at the O2 Arena. As it involved being in a sketch with a bag
on her head Victoria turned it down. David Walliams gladly depu-
tised. She went along to the show and, while enjoying the spectacle,
found the principals 'curiously disengaged I thought – not warm –
only Palin and Idle really gave it any performing welly'.⁶⁰ She also
declined an invitation to return to the stage from Michael Codron,
who was making his swansong as a West End producer and dangled
a role in *Mr Foote's Other Leg* about an eighteenth-century actor. 'I
don't really like acting!' she replied. 'I much prefer running about in
my own clothes bossing people about. I have so many things I want

to write and produce, and it feels like time is short as every project takes so long to get off the ground.'[61]

There were two holidays that summer. To the Glossops she expressed a specific desire to go to an island, so they took a train to the south of France. When they disembarked and made their way onto a peninsula Victoria became suspicious. 'It is an island, isn't it?' she asked nervously, and was only reassured when they boarded a ferry to Porquerolles, one of the Îles d'Hyères. There was another island retreat when she took Grace and Henry with his new girlfriend Steph to Zanzibar, where they stayed by the beach and mooched around the town before moving on to the mainland. 'Had a fantastic time,' she told Sammy Murray, 'just swimming and lying around and had a mini safari in the middle – really good to be together with them all.'[62]

She carried memories of Tanzania into her next assignment: for Comic Relief Victoria volunteered to take part in a celebrity instalment of *The Great British Bake Off*. Michael Ball, who had done it the previous year, encouraged her to sign up and lent her his lemon zester. She spent several days practising a tray bake inspired by the spices of Zanzibar. Her friend Norah Wellbelove, who was staying in the spare room, proposed making rice-paper palm trees: 'I don't think she has quite grasped that I have to do it myself on the day.'[63] After forty years on television, Victoria found the prospect of being filmed while cooking 'so stressful . . . I have a great fear that with cameras etc I will drop my reading glasses into my tray bake and Mary Berry will be rushed to A and E after ingesting my one point fives and die on a trolley in a corridor.'[64] The producers also asked for a cake in the form of a self-portrait, so she opted for Kimberley in a yellow beret. When she turned up for filming she was so attuned to the programme's rhythms that 'I tried to assist the Bake Off MasterChef style drum and bass edit by making all my moves in a four four beat,' she told Daniel Rigby. 'At one point I did actually shout "Cue the music!" which made me and the cameraman laugh.'[65] With her competitive streak trumping her instinct to entertain, she took to her tasks with a straight face. 'I know you're supposed to say no, no, no, it's all about Comic Relief,' she said on camera, 'but, yeah, desperate to win is the sad truth.' She gleefully sucked up every compliment and, thanks to her triumphant Kimberley cake, emerged a very chuffed winner, qualifying her for the final, six months hence.

The bulk of the autumn was once more devoted to promoting *That Day We Sang*. The Royal Variety Performance was considered, but with Imelda Staunton unavailable it was mooted that Victoria deputise to duet with Michael Ball. She discouraged the idea. 'There's something so terribly showy offy,' she told Nigel Lilley, 'about directing and writing something and then stepping on to the stage in a frock and saying "Guess what folks – I could have played Enid as well!"'[66] Instead she and Michael Ball went on *Weekend Wogan* to petition Radio 2 listeners for memories of 'Nymphs and Shepherds'. It was her first professional encounter with Terry Wogan since her ill-fated appearance on his chat show in 1982.

The footage ended up on the documentary about the making of the musical. Much of the film was about the business of rehearsing and shooting the drama, but woven into it was a portrait of the world in which the musical was set and the story of the Manchester Children's Choir. Victoria visited the city's central library to pore over documents and dropped in on Forsyth's music shop, where as a child she bought her first piano book, written by the choir's founder. She met the three makers of Thames TV's *This Week* film, and for a couple of days she took Michael Ball on a ramble around the Manchester of her youth. The sight of two famous faces touring the city in tandem attracted ecstatic gawpers. 'We took it in turns to be recognised,' he says. 'You realised just what an effect she had on people. They just bloody loved the bones of her, and she was absolutely brilliant with them.'

While Victoria had long experience of writing a voiceover to footage, she had never been so involved in every pernickety stage of piecing together a documentary before and found the task of sitting in a room with a director and an editor in Salford, latterly in Soho, 'a bit like folding gravy'.[67] She and her co-workers developed a habit of having egg and chips every Friday lunchtime, even on the day in late November when *That Day We Sang* was shown to the press at the Covent Garden Hotel. She was due to have lunch with Michael Ball and Imelda Staunton afterwards, only to have to respond to a plaintive text and go and buy them their lunch in the Berwick Street chippie. By now she was working to the wire: 'The time pressure is horrendous, and twice I have had to write commentary and record it just as the commissioning editor is making his way up three flights of stairs to view the doco. Am very glad there's no lift.'[68]

They didn't finish till ten days before broadcast. Relentlessly Victoria carried on plugging the drama – at a press screening in Manchester, and on breakfast television, *The One Show* and *The Graham Norton Show* on which the previous week she 'watched Julie utterly baffle Nicole Kidman by coming on as Mrs O').[69] At her Christmas party Michael Ball added his voice to the carol singing until he was finally asked to give someone else a chance. *Victoria Wood with All the Trimmings* was repeated on Christmas Eve. On Boxing Day *That Musical We Made* and *That Day We Sang* were broadcast on BBC Two. Victoria was delighted to receive many congratulatory texts from friends and colleagues. The rave she savoured the most was from the conductor John Wilson, who praised the music. 'Meant a lot to me,' she told Nigel Lilley, 'as no one ever much mentions it and he was comparing me to Sondheim which is a great compliment.'[70] Rashly she then decided to google *That Day We Sang* 'and was hoist on my own petard as a headline from Telegraph popped up – Sweet but Saggy . . . so that served me right.'[71]

Victoria's most local review happened when she was talking outside the front door to her neighbour, who was expecting a visit from her son. He happened to be the Hollywood director Christopher Nolan: 'He came up the drive and she said "oh this is Victoria she's just directed something for TV . . ." at which a look of utter horror and disdain came over his face – he felt obliged to say "how did you get on" and I said "They've offered me the next Bond film" which he did manage to crack a smile at.'[72]

# 25

# THE BOGEYMAN

'The wig is only itchy cos of being bald as normally of course one would have it gripped to one's own hair or a stocking cap ... would go bald if not for press/anyone with a phone outing me.'

Email to Jane Wymark, 2 October 2015

Victoria began 2015 with a cleansing weekend in Budapest, where she and Norah Wellbelove soaked in the city's healing thermal waters. January brought the ritual of decluttering. Filing cabinets were reorganised, bookshelves and cupboards rationalised. Gleefully she responded to a request for an item to auction in support of the Duke's Playhouse in Lancaster, where in 1980 she made some of her earliest appearances as a comedian. She filled two boxes with memorabilia and sent them off. 'I don't suppose Tom Stoppard nips to the Oxfam before he sharpens his pencils,' she told Jane Wymark, 'but then he's an intellectual.'[1]

Then came the final of *The Great Comic Relief Bake Off*, recorded in front of an audience of amateur bakers. Victoria brought in 'a cake I spent many hours faffing over' which would be submitted to a blind tasting by Mary Berry.[2] She planted a clue as to her sponge cake's authorship by decorating it with an image of a hunched elderly waitress carrying two soups and was unabashedly thrilled to be anointed the winner. The heats were shown during Comic Relief week a month later, and even in victory she stayed competitive. 'Celeb Bake Off has been a bit rubbish so far,' she told Daniel Rigby. 'Very low standard of baking and comedy – I have a feeling that when mine is shown next week they will have edited us to look like we couldn't do anything when actually everyone was trying very hard.'[3]

She watched the shows in between stints back at her desk. 'Am at the bin staring despairing stage of trying to write something new,' she told Nigel Lilley in mid-February.[4] Victoria's last unfulfilled ambition was to make a feature film, and she now had an idea which grew out of the tiniest acorn – a joke she had cracked at the Theatre Royal Drury Lane when recording *I'm Sorry I Haven't a Clue* in 2012. Asked to nominate film titles suitable for the elderly, she had suggested 'Cakes on a Train', which conjured up something cosier than the action thriller *Snakes on a Plane*. Her stint as a *Bake Off* contestant was also among the list of ingredients, but as she started to write she mainly drew on a lifetime spent devouring cheap and mediocre television. She imagined a Sunday-night show called *Chuffed!* which would mulch together several of the British viewer's obsessions into one truly naff package. In each episode a steam train would travel through a historically resonant part of the countryside, while on board a cook would be filmed preparing a dish. Meanwhile, members of the public would make their own version of the dish, which would be judged once the train pulled up at the station platform. There would also be live entertainment from local troupes – trampolining, brass bands, a Segway display. 'It's a little round Britain travel programme,' says the jaded producer. 'We'll edit it into nice little pieces, we'll chuck music all over it like a bucket of potato peelings off the back of a cross channel ferry.'

Victoria peopled this world with types she knew well from her years making documentaries: a commissioner of factual entertainment who under her pashmina is as hard as nails; a male director who would far rather shoot a history of firearms called *All Guns Blazing*; a seen-it-all make-up artist who can think of nothing beyond her own working needs. At the heart of the drama is Pam Pickles, a decent but utterly humourless woman in her fifties who accidentally becomes the break-out star of *Chuffed!* She runs cookery courses and is looking forward to a happy retirement with her globetrotting husband Tim. When

*Chuffed!*'s original cook departs in a hurry after a viral sex-video scandal, the producers urgently need to unearth the next Delia. Pam is talent-scouted at short notice and, despite her early awkwardness on camera, the viewers warm to her straight-talking authenticity. 'Praise is a lovely warm bath I know,' she tells one amateur chef, 'but in the end that water cools off and we all have to get out and stand shivering in a cold bathroom.' For all the absurdity of the mangled concept, the show is a huge hit. Overnight Pam becomes a celebrity who is asked for autographs everywhere she goes, causing her grumpy husband to feel like a spare part. To stave off his jealousy, Tim is invited to take photographs for the book accompanying the series but is soon caught smooching with the food stylist. The live finale of *Chuffed!* descends into chaos with two of Pam's fellow presenters coming to blows while Pam calmly announces her husband's betrayal and, with her co-presenter, sings 'I Am What I Am' from *La Cage aux Folles*.

Once before Victoria had tried to dramatise the end of a long marriage. Her untitled script, written in 2008, was shown to no one and deposited in the bottom drawer, but she now salvaged several elements from it. Like Sally and Tony from the previous script, Pam and Tim live in a Hertfordshire village, have two grown-up sons in North America and neighbours who bestow ludicrous names on their children – in this case Fabian and Salome. Pam like Sally works in home catering; Tim like Tony seduces a younger woman. Whereas in the previous script Victoria engineered a reconciliation between the sundered couple, this time she took a different path. In the end Pam calmly accepts that she and Tim have long since stopped caring for each other and the marriage cannot be salvaged. In the final moments Pam's career continues with a new show called *Steaming Ahead*, while Tim miserably trudges around the shops with his new wife and baby.

Victoria used the script to satirise various irritants of the world around her. The television channel rates Pam according to consolidated audience appreciation figures measured out in pie charts and diagrams: 'Her performance in week one was eighty one percent nervous, with eleven percent wooden, three percent boring and five percent could not categorise her performance.'

'Writing goes on,' Victoria reported after a month at her desk.

'Dead slow but I have to put everything in a first draft just to see what the story is . . . same old but I know it will be OK in the end.'[5] Among the things she lobbed into the pot was a colourful gallery of characters. Her co-presenters included a disgraced Tory MP, a professional northerner who likes real ale and jug bands (a nod to her university friend Bill Lloyd), and someone clearly modelled on Michael Ball. Simply known as the Talent, he is 'Mr Musical Theatre, the unthinking woman's crumpet' who is often mobbed by middle-aged female fans and has a tubbiness issue. Victoria hoped that Michael Ball would play him and told him about it as she wrote.

By now 'Little Mickey Ball', as she dubbed him, had joined the smallish throng of intimate friends in whose company Victoria felt safe and comfortable and even daring. He persuaded her to do the ice-bucket challenge. One weekday afternoon they caught up over lunch at the Ivy. 'We came out,' he says, 'and said, "What shall we do? Let's go and see something." We looked across the road and went, "Have you ever seen *The Mousetrap*?" We got two tickets and just wet ourselves. By the second half word had got in because the performances certainly rose.' A much more outgoing celebrity, he peppered her with invitations. In March he asked her along to a pop-up production of *Sweeney Todd*, where he promised to introduce her to Stephen Sondheim. She was double-booked so had to say no. 'And he wouldn't know who I was anyway,' she told Nigel Lilley.[6] As Michael Ball's guest she attended a reception at Buckingham Palace hosted by Princess Anne for the Motor Neurone Association. She found it 'a lot jollier than I thought it would be and we could wander about and look at the Canalettos'.[7]

Victoria took a break from writing to pay a visit to Dawn French and her husband Mark Bignell at their home in Fowey. It proved to be a little test of their long friendship, as she was soon asking to move bedrooms and, having just won *Bake Off*, disparaged the cake in the local tea room. 'This is Vic at her most lovely, most loving, very happy to be with you,' says Dawn. 'But honestly quite demanding!' They laughed and had late nights and, as Victoria had only ever been to Cornwall once to perform in St Austell, Dawn drove her up to the rugged north coast to walk on one of the big surfing beaches. She soon noticed that Victoria, who normally strode ahead, was hanging behind. 'She was a bit grumpy, had a hat on. I said, "What is your problem?" She said, "I don't like beaches." I just laughed and laughed and I knew I was risking her temper and then she laughed and then we were all laughing, so much so that I did this impression of her to her several times after that. I said, "I don't like beaches? What the fuck are you talking about? There's no such thing, is there? I've never met anyone like you, Vic."'

On her final day in Cornwall Victoria spotted Dawn's husband brandishing a metal detector. 'I'm going to find some doubloons,' he told her. She asked if she could come too, so he lent her a spare, trained her how to use it and they disappeared for hours. She boasted to Nigel Lilley of finding 'a 50p piece and a 1921 penny and a sewage outlet pipe' and inserted a reference to metal detecting into *Cakes on a Train*.[8] Days after her return both Victoria and French and Saunders were included in the Royal Mail's celebration of comedy greats, issued on April Fool's Day. There were ten stamps. On hers Victoria was depicted twice, looking for her friend Kimberley in the foreground and, behind, singing at the piano in *The Angina Monologues*. A set of postcards was sent by the Royal Mail, which she stuck up in the kitchen.

By mid-April she was far enough ahead with *Cakes on a Train* to think about casting with Hilary Bevan Jones, who was to produce it. Aside from Michael Ball, roles were earmarked for Daniel Rigby and Conleth Hill, and Victoria hoped Julie Walters could be tempted to play Pam. She pitched it when Julie made a very rare visit to Highgate. 'Julie liked the idea,' she enthused, 'so I got very excited.'[9] 'She just told me the story,' says Julie, 'a mad caper about a Delia Smith-type woman. I didn't know whether I could do it.'

Meanwhile, as she plotted her new drama, Victoria was drawn back into the world of *That Day We Sang* when invited by Manchester International Festival to speak on its behalf at a fundraiser hosted by the Chancellor of the Exchequer George Osborne at 11 Downing Street. It prompted her to think of developing a third stage production, after MIF and the Royal Exchange, that would fold in elements of the television drama – to Nigel Lilley she pledged to 'have a think about how to combine the best of both versions'.[10] As for the drama, after copiously promoting the DVD release on radio and daytime television, she was hopeful of BAFTA nominations for *That Day We Sang* that, when they came, were confined to sound and production design. Victoria concluded ruefully that 'people just didn't count it as serious drama . . . I'm sad for Michael and Imelda but it's just how it goes. Onward and upward.'[11]

Onward and upward meant appearing in a new Sky One expanded version of *Fungus the Bogeyman*. She took it on as 'a little get out of the house break', and she liked the idea of working with Timothy Spall, fresh from his Oscar nomination for *Mr Turner*.[12] But she was not encouraged by the read-through of a three-part script which greatly expanded Raymond Briggs's story of a green monster whose job is to scare humans. Nor did she warm to the scriptwriter who 'came up to me and said "it's so great to be able to give gags to someone like you and know they will land" to which I was very tempted to reply – "Yes, when I am getting those gags?"'[13] In fact, they were supplied by a new writer hastily drafted in to revamp the scripts. Victoria, who was to play Bactoria Snotsoup – the name was a sort of fungal compliment – was offered the chance to have her say by the director Catherine Morshead. 'I'm hoping I don't turn nice,' she replied, adding a few notes on some of her dialogue.[14] The shoot felt chaotic and dragged on longer than she anticipated: 'I beg and plead every day for a schedule . . . Producer has taken to avoiding me as the problem seems to lie above his head.'[15] At least she bonded with her co-star: 'Tim Spall and I entertain ourselves talking about old telly . . . in silent moments one of us will suddenly go "Arthur Haynes!" or "Mr Pastry!"'[16] To play a rich suburban villainess who assumes human form, she put on a thick Birmingham accent, and spent ninety minutes in make-up having her hair teased into extravagant ringlets by Chrissie Baker. Her fate at the end of the drama, as her wicked schemes are thwarted, was to have her mouth glued up.

The shoot had finished by the end of June and Victoria's thoughts returned to *Cakes on a Train*. Although she had plenty of experience of filming on steam trains, she sounded out Amie Beamish, who lived in Dartmoor, about visiting a steam railway in Devon and invited

Jane Wymark on a research trip to the west coast of Scotland to ride along the famous railway between Fort William and Mallaig. Flights were booked for the end of August. But at the start of the month it was no longer certain if it would go ahead.

There had been signs that all that was not well. During the filming of *Fungus the Bogeyman* Victoria developed what she thought was a sore throat which inhibited her appetite. The visible impact was evident to Sammy Murray when she showed her a photo of herself in costume: 'My first impression was she'd lost a lot of weight.' After the *Fungus* shoot she went on a holiday in Turkey with Piers Wenger, who when he got back to his desk at Channel 4 reported to his colleague Beth Willis that Victoria had not been herself. 'We both knew,' says Beth, 'and we were desperate for her to go and get checked, and there was a slight delay as she wanted to go to the Lakes with Henry and we were frustrated she was not going to the doctor.' Victoria was reluctant to put off the trip north because it was the first time Henry and his girlfriend would stay in Swiss Cottage. Henry noticed that 'she was definitely uncomfortable, and just wasn't in a good space. I didn't wonder what it was consciously, probably for not wanting to. She was still willing to be gung-ho. We did a zipline near the cottage. We went on a canoe on the lake. But she was very tired and seemed like she was struggling a bit.' While there she met the Glossops in Bowness. 'There's something really wrong,' she told Charlotte Scott. 'I've got to go back and see the specialist. It's nothing good.'

Back in London Victoria met Harriet Thorpe, who insisted on ringing a doctor friend. Over the next few days she underwent a series of tests that grew ever gloomier. She was initially encouraged that it might be a hiatus hernia, but by early August she was reporting otherwise to her sisters: 'Don't be too upset but it turns out that I have a lump outside my gullet and it's malignant . . . I am sure it will be fine but of course I am pissed off having thought my cancer was behind me.'[17] Her trip to Scotland now looked doubtful. 'Tricks not good,' she told Jane Wymark as she was 'swept back into that world of backless gowns and injections . . . Oh well just have to get on with it.'[18] Even a short overnight in Chichester to see Michael Ball in *Mack and Mabel*, choreographed by Stephen Mear, was cancelled.

She kept the brutal news to a small circle of her closest friends. Damien Timmer, whose family were frequent visitors to Victoria's home, texted the good news that they were buying a house two minutes away. She texted back: 'I've just today found out the cancer's returned.' The shock of its return was intensified by disquiet about its location. 'She had spent a couple of months wondering if there was something wrong and not knowing what,' says Grace. 'What was completely surprising was that it was in a completely new place in the body.' Grace, who was once more singing in the chorus at Glyndebourne, was not surprised to find her mother reluctant to communicate with her children: 'It was not just to shield us but because it was painful to talk about. She just didn't want to be dealing with it at all.'

In mid-August Victoria readied herself for a course of chemotherapy in Harley Street. 'She was being very positive and practical about it,' says Beth Willis, who sat with her in the garden before the treatment started. Her attitude was 'just have to get head round it and get on with it'.[19]

Her agent Lucy Ansbro's job now was to fend off offers and enquiries. The trickiest came from BAFTA, which was keen to award Victoria a fellowship. Eventually Hilary Bevan Jones, who was on the BAFTA committee, was enlisted to explain to the chief executive that 'as much as Victoria would love to accept a BAFTA Fellowship, this wasn't the right year for her as she was juggling a number of things and didn't know where she'd be at the time of the awards but to please ask her another time'. Even with her circle of friends, Victoria's desire was to keep the news of her illness to a small and manageable group. She talked to Nigel Lilley about 'slightly stripping down the friend group as things progressed. I don't think she felt that she could maintain the levels of friendship that she'd had with everyone.'

Victoria's main mode of communication was texting, but Jane Wymark became an outlet for chatty updates about programmes she was watching, books she was reading as well as medical travails she was undergoing. She visited her hairdresser to prepare for the impact of chemo, then at the end of August Chrissie Baker, who for thirty years had crimped and primped Victoria for public appearances, came

494 LET'S DO IT

to Highgate for a different sort of commission: 'Very exciting day yesterday . . . got Chrissie to shave my head which feels quite chilly so am wearing Last of Summer Wine style woolly hat.'[20] A couple of days later she had her second course of treatment, which left her sense of humour unimpaired: 'Left chemo at 8 45 last night . . . I was the last baldy standing – I thought they would tell me to turn out the lights and pop the keys back through the letter box.'[21] Her morale was not always so invulnerable. Before the third course she insisted that 'I don't really have much fortitude – I feel very weedy and wimpy most of the time.'[22] The wig she had was too itchy to wear for long and she awaited colder weather when she could go out in a hat.

She was cheered in September when Grace took part in a competition at the Avignon Opera House and from a field of over 150 singers won a couple of prizes. For the next five months Grace would return to Highgate most weekends while resuming her studies at the Royal Conservatoire of Scotland in Glasgow, where she had been for the previous year. Henry, who was a self-employed songwriter, was a more constant presence. 'Because we'd been through it before,' he says, 'there was a feeling of, right let's just get back to it then. Let's do everything we can.' His mother was glad when he and Steph, who had moved in, managed to get away for a weekend: 'It must be a bit oppressive here at the moment tho he seems to deal with it very well.'[23]

While the chemotherapy continued there was no chance of working, 'as at least a week after each chemo I feel pretty bad and then slowly recover . . . but never totally bounce back before the next lot'.[24] Victoria's reading grew ever more escapist. From Agatha Christie she progressed to *The Wind in the Willows* and Mapp and Lucia: 'Just want a cosy world as opposed to grim reality.'[25] The television offered *Strictly*, *Bake Off* and *Downton*, for which she delighted in supplying alternative dialogue. In October Daniel Rigby came over to watch a stock of *MasterChef*s she'd recorded. Other methods of filling the time, such as learning Spanish or taking on a complicated jigsaw, proved too challenging.

In late October Victoria received a visit from Sir Marcus Setchell, her retired former gynaecologist, who lived nearby. 'He heard on the

Prof grapevine I was sick again and offered himself for a cuppa – very sweet . . . it was all a bit best behaviour – but he's said I can text him any time and he will tell me what questions to ask my consultant – which could be very handy.'[26] By now she was off not only alcohol but even tea 'which makes most trips to tea shops a bit pointless'.[27] A round of chemo in early November made her anxious and tearful: 'And then I feel a wimp and think there is probably someone in the next room who is having their leg cut off with just a slug of gin and a rag to chew on and I should just shut the fuck up.'[28] A week later she regretfully had to forego a singing competition at the Wigmore Hall, where Grace was to sing. She asked Cathy Edis to go for her and, ever keen on evidence that her children's talents might bring an income, was pleased that Grace came second and won £1,000. Spending so much time reading or in front of the television, she decided to replace her sofa cushions, which, she told Jane Wymark, were 'so old they give no support and every time you plump them it's like you sacrificed a chicken'.[29] She continued to watch DVDs as a BAFTA judge and compared notes on some of the new releases with Jonny Campbell. Still the jokes came: 'Hen is a tower of strength and may even tackle his first Horlicks later for me.'[30] But there were days, increasingly, when she stayed in bed: 'Too much work to get dressed and what am I trying to prove? . . . am running out of patience with the whole sorry saga.'[31]

This was a rare glimpse of deeper fears as Victoria courageously submitted to invasion by medical science. Stephen Mear had a portent one day that autumn when she agreed to leave the house to meet him: 'She had a wig on, not a particularly great wig. The first time she'd ever done this to me – she gave me a hug and said, "Love you loads," and she's so not like that. She gives you a quick hug and that's it. I rang Sammy and said, "I think that's the last time I'm going to see her."' When friends got in touch she had to decide whether or not to loop them in. 'I'm glad you emailed as I didn't really want to text my news,' she told her favourite tour manager Amie Beamish. 'I wouldn't have told you out of the blue – just letting people know as and when and trying to keep it quiet.'[32] Friends not in the know approached about potential work. Shaun Dooley and Radford Neville, who in

May had asked her to write up their drama idea about a disparate group on a long walk across Britain, came back to her in December. In her reply she admitted to 'a few health problems lately' which had impacted on her own project: 'I don't think I can stack anything else up behind it – I only want to be thinking about one thing at a time.'[33]

Christmas approached, and friends looking forward to the annual invitation to mince pies and carols started to notice that Victoria had gone quiet. Two days before Christmas she received an anxious letter from Richenda Carey and felt the need to reassure her by return: 'I suppose I have just changed myself over the years and I don't seem to have the same energy or enthusiasm for being social as I did before I was ill three years ago. I was diagnosed with another cancer earlier in the year and have just gone through a lot of chemotherapy and am just starting to get over it. Not many people know and I find it easier that way and now I'm on a breather I'm trying to forget about it over Christmas.'[34] This could easily have been sent to any number of old friends. Norah Wellbelove, whom Victoria had informed by email the day after her result in August, was kept at arm's length having lost her husband to cancer after many years of illness. 'I don't want you to get back on the cancer bus,' Victoria told her.

Grace and Henry bought a Christmas tree and decorated it. As for the day itself, 'in some ways it was difficult and in some ways it was really nice,' says Grace. 'Henry and I made the Christmas dinner and she ate as much of it as she could and said she was satisfied.' She was exhausted for the next two days. Over the holiday they were visited by Piers Wenger, Daniel Rigby, Jonny Campbell and Beth Willis. Victoria was too unwell to join in a charades-type game they called In the Bag. 'She was absolutely weeping with laughter,' says Beth. 'I remember her sitting on the sofa and just saying, "I can cope with the pain, it's the dying I'm not OK with." That's the only time she acknowledged that she may not come out of this.'

A couple of days after Christmas, Victoria, Grace and Henry sat down to *Fungus the Bogeyman*, then she spent New Year's Eve feasting on the original *Crossroads* with Piers. In the Christmas episode they watched, Noele Gordon turned to the camera to sing a show tune while the cast had to look on. In Victoria this bizarre breach of the fourth wall provoked delight that could barely be contained.

Very early in January Victoria was in the Princess Grace hospital for a small operation to insert a stent which would help her swallow. She was meant to go home that day but severe chest pain kept her in. Then she moved to the London Clinic to begin having radiotherapy as an in-patient. 'It's all been a bit of palaver,' she told Rosalind, 'so I am glad to be looked after here and not have to monitor my own symptoms.'[35] She was happy too to give Henry a rest from responsibility. Two weeks on she was confident of going home soon. In fact, she stayed until beyond Easter.

The room Victoria was given was on the first floor with a view over the Marylebone Road to the Royal Academy of Music, where she was an honorary fellow. She felt positive about her new surroundings. 'It's quite nice to have a change of scene,' she told Jane Wymark. 'I was getting utterly sick of the bed/sofa/radio 4 extra ground hog existence and the food thing became very depressing. So actually I feel quite peaceful here.'[36] For the first month, as she underwent invasive treatments and procedures, she was reluctant to receive any visitors. At one point she lost her voice thanks to the radiotherapy and when she tried to explain to a member of staff that she had to be off anti-coagulants for two days it 'was a struggle as I don't think Jane Winearls ever taught me the international sign for Riveroxaban'.[37] (Jane Winearls was the dance teacher at Birmingham University.) Ten days later her voice returned 'in a Fenella Fielding kind of a way'.[38] While Henry was there often, her tireless conduit to the outside world was Cathy Edis. 'You are a huge help to me,' she emailed in the midst of it all, 'and we will have a jaunt when this is over. Love Vic.'[39] Those friends who knew of her illness didn't know who else knew – Victoria's assistant for nearly twenty years kept them updated. Several supplied reading material: 'Of course I keep getting books I've already read but there's a misspent youth for you.'[40] As she devoured book after book in a room on her own, it was as if the conditions of her solitary teenage existence in Birtle Edge House had been reconstructed fifty years on.

By the end of January Victoria was open to the idea of a visit from

Geoffrey, who scored a bullseye by introducing her to the novels of Tana French. 'Geoff coming in this aft . . . should be OK I guess.'[41] His presence tacitly acknowledged that the situation was now grave and that Grace and Henry needed parental support. Prompted by Cathy, who felt strongly that Victoria should have company, a trickle of visitors arrived. Rosalind was let in. Penelope came down from Yorkshire. Imelda Staunton was encouraged to go soon after returning from a long holiday. 'I kept it fairly light,' she says. 'I wanted to say hello but was of course saying goodbye, but I don't think she felt that at all. She was sitting by the window looking at the Royal Academy of Music across the road. She said, "It's very good to see life going on." She also said how wonderful Geoffrey was at that time. She said, "He has so stepped up. He has been absolutely brilliant." Vic, whatever the circumstances, would give credit where credit was due.'

Aside from Cathy and Henry, the most constant presence from February was Piers Wenger, who for ten years had been Victoria's bulwark against loneliness: 'To begin with she didn't let me see her. I basically in the end managed to create a reason to go and went. Once I'd been once I was allowed to go quite a lot.' Beth Willis arrived pregnant and loaded with books: 'She went through each of them going "read it, read it", this most random pile, and there were only about two she hadn't read.' She tired easily. Sometimes with her visitors she wanted to sit in silence, other times to read. Daniel Rigby, who was practically family, was aware that 'if someone came in actively trying to buoy her up it didn't feel genuine to her'.

Mostly she could not bear to be seen by some of her dearest friends. 'I don't want a big gay crying at the end of my bed,' she told Stephen Mear. Sammy Murray, who was down from Yorkshire for a meeting, was walking past the London Clinic and asked if she could come up. 'She said, "Henry's here. I think I'll be a bit tired. Can we leave it to another day?" That's how she used to fob us off. I said, "OK, but I'm going to tap dance across the street outside your hospital window. You better be watching because I'm going to make a tit of myself." And I did it. I tap danced across the lights outside just in case she was looking through those net curtains. And she didn't text me, so I don't know.'

In early March Victoria took the decision to have a second stent inserted. 'They were saying it's a 50–50 operation,' says Henry. 'She was really suffering up until that point. It was me, Steph and my dad in the hospital waiting room. It was late and the surgeon came down to say it was a success. I sat with her in intensive care after and we talked about how relieved we both were. She got through it and it was the best thing ever.' The next day Grace came down from Glasgow to visit and, with a job at Glyndebourne that month, soon moved back to Highgate. Victoria's desire to go home now deepened. 'I can't bear to be here much longer,' she told Cathy.[42] One of her last visitors in hospital was Julie Walters, who found Victoria in a state of determined denial: 'Vic said, "I just need to get this managed – the pain. And then I'm going to write something." They were sending her home to die in fact, but she wasn't going home to die. It was her way of dealing with it. Otherwise you have to face, OK this is the end. She didn't want to do that.'

Victoria, wearing jeans and a jumper and sitting on the edge of her bed, chaired a discussion about her return to Highgate with Henry, Piers, Geoffrey, Cathy, Rosalind and various doctors. Piers asked detailed questions about nursing care and took notes. On Easter Saturday, when she was permitted to go home for an hour as a trial run for a permanent return, he drove her back to Highgate through Regent's Park: 'I was going really slow and she was going, "Oh my God, don't drive so fast!" Having been in hospital for so long it was quite overwhelming to her.' Grace and Henry were there to greet her. The house was full of daffodils and scented candles. It was a happy hour and four days later Victoria came home for good.

'Feel a bit nervous leaving hosp,' she admitted to Jane Wymark, and yet she was determined to treat her return as a chance to recover.[43] She decided to order some novels by Trollope. Paul Roberts, who sat on the steps of Sydney Opera House with her in 1997, visited and found that 'she clearly wasn't accepting how ill she was. Because she didn't suffer fools gladly you didn't want to bullshit her and I said, "Vic, you do not look well." She said, "I don't want to hear that." We spent a lovely afternoon once I had cottoned on to the fact that Vic was happy denying the inevitable.' When Nigel Lilley paid a visit she was full of plans. 'I'm going to kick this thing,' she told him, 'get better and get back in the rehearsal room with you and Sammy.'

By now emails were growing shorter and some weren't ever sent. The gaps between her texts grew longer. Apart from Victoria herself, the last person to admit that she would not recover was Piers: 'Maybe I just couldn't really accept the truth because she couldn't. Victoria said to me days before she died, "I might not get rid of it, but if I can just get on my feet and just get back to work . . ."' The problem of who would care for her arose. She didn't want a stranger in the house and was keen not to burden Grace and Henry, so Piers volunteered and moved in for two weeks. 'Piers is being brilliant with the drugs and the feeding machine,' she said soon after returning home, 'and am ordering a small posh telly for the bedroom as my teeny one is 15 years old and they seem really cheap now . . .'[44] It was on her new television, Piers lying next to her on her bed, that they spent his second week watching episodes of *MasterChef* in batches of three.

At the end of the fortnight he handed over to Rosalind, who found her sister 'in very good nick emotionally'. When she wasn't listening to Radio 3, Victoria would ask for her bedroom window to be opened so she could hear the birdsong. Once, lying in bed, she set off on a comic routine about tidying her sock drawer: 'It was as if I was the audience and I was cursing that I couldn't record it. It was absolutely hilarious.' This was the longest that the two sisters had spent together in decades, and Rosalind saw a chance for both of them to find closure about the long shadow cast by their childhood: 'I said to Vic, "It would be nice to talk some time about how we were neglected as kids." She said, "We must have a conversation about that some time. Maybe later."'

By now a pair of Twilight Nurses were visiting nightly to manage Victoria's pain and help her sleep. She would welcome them with a spooky greeting: 'Woooo, the Twilight Nurses!' Palliative-care nurses arrived too. One in particular, whom she liked very much, tried to engage her in conversations about end of life. 'She was quite freaked out by that,' says Piers. 'She said to me, "Why have I got a palliative-care nurse? Isn't that for someone who's terminal?" And I totally fudged it and said, "They're sort of cancer nurses and deal with people who are suffering in the way that you are."'

On Thursday 14 April Victoria texted Daniel Rigby about him coming to stay the following week. On Friday evening she was too tired to manage more than one episode of *MasterChef* with Piers. On Monday, after Cathy Edis had finished work, Victoria texted her: 'you know more than you think'. 'I'm with you all the way,' Cathy replied. In these last days Grace and Henry came in and out, knowing that their mother was eager for them to go about their regular lives for as long as possible. 'Although she didn't say this explicitly,' says Grace, 'she wanted me to keep working. It helped me to have a professional life and I think she wanted me to have one.' But where before Victoria had been at least stable, her condition now took a sudden turn for the worse and it became clear that she did not have long to live. On the Tuesday Henry worked into the evening and when he got home went up to his mother's bedroom where he found Grace and Rosalind and the Twilight Nurses already there. 'She was doolally on the morphine. She said, "What have you been up to?" I said, "I've been working." She said, "Do you like work?" And I said, "Yeah, I loved it," and she smiled.'

The advice of the palliative-care nurse was to check on Victoria every two hours through the night. But Rosalind and Grace decided to stay and sit quietly with her. At four in the morning Rosalind took two hours' sleep then resumed her vigil at six as Grace went to bed. Rosalind, who welcomed her baby sister home to Tottington Road nearly sixty-three years earlier, spoke to Victoria in the hope that she could still hear. 'Everybody loves you,' she said, and she kept talking until, at a quarter to seven on the morning of Wednesday 20 April 2016, the greatest entertainer of the television age took her last breath.

## 26

# UNFORGOTTEN DREAMS

'Seventy-two baps, Connie. You slice, I'll spread.'
*An Audience with Victoria Wood*, 1988

Victoria's children woke up to the news that their mother had died. Their father, who walked up the hill from his home, and their aunt were there to comfort them. Piers Wenger and Cathy Edis were soon in the house too. The question of how to spread the word was discussed. Henry produced his mother's laptop containing all her contacts. Piers went into producer mode and organised for everyone to take a list of names, go into a separate room and disseminate the sad tidings. Grace and Henry called neighbours and family friends. Geoffrey rang the friends he and Victoria had known from their years together. Piers spoke to professional friends and Cathy to work associates. At five minutes to three Geoffrey informed Victoria's brother Chris. Then at three o'clock Neil Reading, who had handled Victoria's press since the early 1990s, issued a short statement: 'Victoria Wood has sadly passed away, after a short but brave battle with cancer. The multi-Bafta-award-winning writer, director, actor and comedian died peacefully at her north London home with family this morning.'

The thunderclap triggered an avalanche of tributes from those who had known her and worked with her, comedians who had followed in the trail she had cut for them, from innumerable fans who had grown up on her and knew by heart her every deathless gag. The year had already claimed other cultural grandees, some of whom had crossed paths with Victoria – Alan Rickman, Terry Wogan, Ronnie Corbett. She was the youngest, whose death was widely felt to be the cruellest. There was a consensus among Victoria's devotees that there would have been so much more to come. While her performing days were done, her first film for cinema may well have followed, and perhaps she would have gone on to adapt 'Miss Read' for television.

She died on the first day of Taurus, the punchline for the joke that changed her life. The following day was the ninetieth birthday of Elizabeth II, whose coronation tour through Bury Victoria had attended as a tiny baby. One face and name dominated the front pages of the national newspapers.

A fortnight later, on 4 May, the funeral took place at Golders Green crematorium. Seventy of Victoria's family and friends were invited to say farewell in a private ceremony conducted by a humanist celebrant whom Victoria had seen and greatly liked at the wedding of Beth Willis and Jonny Campbell. In July there was a much bigger public memorial at St James's Piccadilly, organised by Victoria's lady body-guards Lucy Ansbro and Adele Fowler in concert with Grace, Henry, Cathy and Nigel Lilley. Hundreds from all walks of Victoria's life and career were invited. Ria Jones sang 'Fourteen Again' and Michael Ball performed 'Go With It', both accompanied by Nigel. Julie Walters recited 'Giving Notes' from *Victoria Wood As Seen on TV*. Grace sang an aria from a Bach cantata, selected because her mother loved Bach and because its message invoked a sense of peace and rest. All held it together – Victoria, who was against performers crying at such gatherings, would have approved. Grace and Henry invited friends from various phases of their mother's life to pay tribute: Jane Wymark, Harriet Thorpe, Lesley Schatzberger and Daniel Rigby, who painted a picture of life under the same roof as an inexhaustible talent: 'She was rehearsing "Barry and Freda" for a benefit gig. She was on a break and we'd had a cuppa in the kitchen and then time was up and she got back to it, updating lyrics and tweaking. From the office "Let's Do It" stuttered through the air and I leant back against the warmth of the oven and thought, how lucky am I? How lucky I am. How lucky we were.'

The memorial ended with the sound of her beloved brass. The Royal

Academy of Music Brass, with whom she had performed in tribute to Jim Watson, now did the same for Victoria. Led by Nigel Lilley at the piano, they played a medley arranged by Victoria's orchestrator Chris Walker. First came Leroy Anderson's 'Forgotten Dreams', the lovely, haunting elegy she chose to close *The Giddy Kipper*. It was followed by 'Happiness Street', the effervescent anthem from *That Day We Sang* that was one of the very last songs Victoria ever composed. In two tunes the primary colours of her work – pathos and joy – were twinned one last time.

She lives on in sundry ways. Victoria was delighted when two members of the *Acorn Antiques: The Musical!* company met, fell in love and started a family. A few years later, on their day trip to the very bottom of Africa, Shaun Dooley told her of his crippling indecisiveness. Back in Cape Town, out shopping for presents to distribute when *The Borrowers* wrapped, she bought him a coin that had yes on one side and no on the other. A couple of months later, when he and his wife were uncertain about having another child, he produced the coin. 'Let Vic decide,' he said. They nicknamed their unborn baby Woody.

There would be other legacies. In her will Victoria left Swiss Cottage to be used by her family and friends, and a fund of £4 million to be distributed to charities nominated by the Victoria Wood Foundation. Bury Art Museum was granted access to Victoria's archive to mount, in 2018, the most popular exhibition in its history. A statue to stand in the heart of her hometown was proposed and initially crowdfunded by her brother before the Foundation assumed control. The sculptor Graham Ibbotson, whose statue of Eric Morecambe adorns the sea front of the town after which the comic took his name, accepted the commission. It was unveiled on a sunny afternoon in May 2019. Before he yanked off the shroud, Victoria's old warm-up man Ted Robbins told the crowd that, of all the people who were asked to do the honours, he must have been the only one who wasn't working that day. She would have loved that gag. Her likeness, installed opposite the library from which she used to pinch books, suggests how hard it is to capture in bronze the bounce of her hair and the glow of her smile.

Finally, and overwhelmingly, Victoria Wood lives on in the work which pulses through the British bloodstream. She more than any contemporary found a way to tell us about the slings and arrows and stumbles of all our lives, to incarnate them in Barry and Freda, Pat and Margaret, Margery and Joan, Kelly Marie Tunstall and Stacey Leanne Paige and Betty Comstock, all those Connies and Pams, dreaming Andrea and lovelorn Miss Berta, Kitty and Kimberley and her friend, Maureen and Julie, Mrs O and Bo, Tony and Bren and Tubby and Enid and all the other giddy kippers.

Those who knew Victoria have their own intimate memories and private correspondence, now generously shared in this, the story of her life. Let's end it with one such letter, written to Jane Wymark in the style of their beloved 'Miss Read' in the summer of 1995. It accompanied a book Victoria sent in the post, and at the memorial was read out by her friend:

Dear 'Miss Wymark'
I was opening my mail this morning, worn capable hands caressing God's good notepaper, thriftily rolling up pieces of string and brown paper against a day of need, when I saw this amongst the bounty.

I immediately thought of you, all those miles away in the little village of Stoke Newington and how your faded but still beautiful eyes would light up at the sight of it, and how your toil-worn digits would eagerly unwrap the parcel . . .

I suppressed the ignoble thought that this book might after all be as funny as a hand-reared squirrel's bowel movement, with all the wit and charm of the discarded underpants of a trainee osteopath, but no matter: tis the idea behind the gift which counts.

Now I am thankfully surveying my own little kingdom, and happy I am to do so. A rare hour of solitude awaits me, and how to fill it is the only blob on the escutcheon. I could stroll in the woods, taking in the view of the rookery, the new born lambs, the white sheets flapping on the line . . . or I could go and pick up 258 pieces of Duplo, 29 stuffed toys, 357 bits of Lego, and take the 36 plastic dinosaurs out of the paddling pool.

You know what I have to do.

With love, a gnarled hand waving from the vegetable garden, an invisibly darned apron, a floury bap and a large joint.

'Miss Wood'

# SOURCES

Sources have been dated as accurately as possible. Some of Victoria's undated letters and cards can, from their contents, be pinned down to a month; where they cannot, only the year is given. Unless otherwise stated, all correspondence cited is written by or sent to Victoria Wood. Wherever interview transcripts are used as a source of quotation, the date of the interview is given, rather than the date of any subsequent publication or broadcast. All notes, manuscripts and notebooks are from the Victoria Wood archive.

**Introduction: Victoria Woods**

1  *Dinnerladies* tapes, 11 July 1998
2  Interview with the author, 6 June 2001
3  Clive James, *Observer*, 8 June 1980
4  Antony Thorncroft, *Financial Times*, 22 October 1980
5  Philip Purser, *Sunday Telegraph*, 24 January 1982
6  'Victoria's Plums', interview with James Rampton, *Radio Times*, 18 October 2001
7  Email to Richenda Carey, 16 September 2012
8  Fax from Richenda Carey, 8 May 1998
9  Letter to Tom Weldon, 13 November 1998
10 Interview with the author, December 2007
11 Postcard to Rosalind Wood, 10 July 1957
12 Letter to Alan Samson, 7 April 2016
13 Email to Daniel Rigby, February 2015

**Chapter 1: Faces**

1  Stanley Wood diary, 19 May 1953, quoted in *Victoria Wood: Comedy Genius – Her Life and Work* by Chris Foote Wood, 2016
2  Interview with the author, 10 November 2006

3 Ibid.

4 Interview with the author, 6 June 2001

5 *The South Bank Show*, ITV, 15 September 1996

6 *Scene – Personal View: Victoria Wood*, BBC Two, 9 May 1985

7 *Parkinson*, BBC One, 24 March 2000

8 Stanley Wood's diary, 15 April 1958, quoted in *Victoria Wood: Comedy Genius – Her Life and Work* by Chris Foote Wood, 2016

## Chapter 2: House on the Edge

1 *Parkinson*, BBC One, 24 March 2000

2 Interview with the author, 10 November 2006

3 *The South Bank Show*, ITV, 15 September 1996

4 *Desert Island Discs*, BBC Radio 4, 23 December 2007

5 *Victoria Wood At It Again*, programme interview with Richard E. Grant, 2001

6 Interview with the author, 10 November 2006

7 Interview with the author, December 2007

8 *In Conversation with . . .*, BBC Radio 4, 14 March 2002

9 Interview with the author, December 2007

10 Ibid.

11 'If I'd been thin as a teenager and gone out with boys I wouldn't have had anything to write about', interview with Ray Connolly, *The Times*, 28 October 1989

12 *The Cambridge Guide to Children's Books*, Cambridge University Press, 2001

13 Interview with the author, December 2007

14 *The Swish of the Curtain*, BBC Radio 4, 4 January 2007

15 Fax to Richenda Carey, 16 May 2001

16 *Victoria Wood At It Again*, programme interview with Richard E. Grant, 2001

17 *More Dawn French's Girls Who Do: Comedy*, BBC Four, 11 October 2006

18 *Parkinson*, BBC One, 24 March 2000

19 'Seriously funny', interview with Allison Pearson, *Daily Telegraph*, 7 November 1998

20 Interview with the author, 4 January 2005

21 *Great Railway Journeys*, BBC Two, 4 September 1996

22 Stanley Wood's diary, 19 August 1961, quoted in *Victoria Wood: Comedy Genius – Her Life and Work* by Chris Foote Wood, 2016

23 'If I'd been thin as a teenager and gone out with boys I wouldn't have had anything to write about', interview with Ray Connolly, *The Times*, 28 October 1989

24 *In Conversation with . . .*, BBC Radio 4, 14 March 2002

25  *Desert Island Discs*, BBC Radio 4, 23 December 2007

26  Interview with the author, 10 November 2006

27  *Desert Island Discs*, BBC Radio 4, 23 December 2007

28  Stanley Wood's diary, 18 December 1960, quoted in *Victoria Wood: Comedy Genius – Her Life and Work* by Chris Foote Wood, 2016

29  'If I'd been thin as a teenager and gone out with boys I wouldn't have had anything to write about', interview with Ray Connolly, *The Times*, 28 October 1989

30  *Parkinson*, BBC One, 24 March 2000

31  Fairfield Country Primary School report, July 1959

32  Fairfield Country Primary School report, July 1960

33  *Parkinson*, BBC One, 24 March 2000

34  Ibid.

35  *Victoria Wood At It Again*, programme interview with Richard E. Grant, 2001

36  Ibid.

37  *Junkin's Jokers*, BBC Radio 2, 12 June 1991

38  Stanley Wood's diary, 14 April 1962, quoted in *Victoria Wood: Comedy Genius – Her Life and Work* by Chris Foote Wood, 2016

39  Fairfield Country Primary School report, December 1962

40  Fairfield Country Primary School report, July 1963

41  Fairfield Country Primary School report, July 1964

**Chapter 3:  Buried**

1  'Mum passes A levels – now she seeks degree', unidentified newspaper report, 1968

2  'A-level Mum, 48, is off to university', *Bolton Evening News*, 1968

3  *Best of British*, BBC One, 1 November 1998

4  Bury Grammar School report, December 1964

5  Ibid.

6  *Parkinson*, BBC One, 24 March 2000

7  Bury Grammar School report, July 1965

8  Bury Grammar School report, July 1966

9  *More Dawn French's Girls Who Do: Comedy*, BBC Four, 11 October 2006

10  *Parkinson*, BBC One, 24 March 2000

11  Letter to Stanley and Helen Wood, 24 July 1966

12  Ibid.

13  Letter to Rosalind Wood, July 1966

14  Ibid.

15  Ibid.

16  Interview with the author, 6 June 2001

17  *Desert Island Discs*, BBC Radio 4, 23 December 2007

18  'Seriously funny', interview with Allison Pearson, *Daily Telegraph*, 7 November 1998

19  'I feel at the BBC I'm not trusted, not valued, not needed', interview with Decca Aitkenhead, *Guardian*, 27 September 2010

20  *Russell Harty's Musical Encounters*, BBC Radio 4, 25 May 1985

21  *Dinnerladies* tapes, 3 July 1998

22  *Desert Island Discs*, BBC Radio 4, 8 February 1987

23  Bury Grammar School report, December 1966

24  'Porky's revenge', interview with David Hepworth, *Q* magazine, October 1987

25  Piano report, July 1967

26  *Russell Harty's Musical Encounters*, BBC Radio 4, 25 May 1985

27  'Victoria's plums', interview with James Rampton, *Radio Times*, 18 October 2001

28  '*Cygnus*, Bury Grammar School (Girls) magazine, 1967

29  'A magic combination', interview with Avril Deane, *Newcastle Journal*, 10 February 1982

30  Speech at the memorial concert for James Watson, 18 June 2011

31  *Russell Harty's Musical Encounters*, BBC Radio 4, 25 May 1985

32  *Parkinson*, BBC One, 24 March 2000

33  'If I'd been thin as a teenager and gone out with boys I wouldn't have had anything to write about', interview with Ray Connolly, *The Times*, 28 October 1989


## Chapter 4: Workshop

1   *In Conversation with . . .*, BBC Radio 4, 14 March 2002

2   *Parkinson*, BBC One, 24 March 2000

3   *More Dawn French's Girls Who Do: Comedy*, BBC Four, 11 October 2006

4   'Weird', interview with Paul Morley, *Blitz*, October 1987

5   *The English Programme*, Thames TV, 4 March 1981

6   Interview with Roger Wilmut, 9 July 1987

7   *Cygnus*, Bury Grammar School (Girls) Magazine, 1970–71

8   'Porky's revenge', interview with David Hepworth, *Q* magazine, October 1987

9   Interview with Roger Wilmut, 9 July 1987

10  School notebook, 1970

11  Fax to Richenda Carey, 11 January 2001

12  *More Dawn French's Girls Who Do: Comedy*, BBC Four, 11 October 2006
13  'Weird', interview with Paul Morley, *Blitz*, October 1987
14  *Desert Island Discs*, BBC Radio 4, 8 February 1987
15  *More Dawn French's Girls Who Do: Comedy*, BBC Four, 11 October 2006
16  *Dinnerladies* tapes, 25 June 1998
17  Interview with Roger Wilmut, 9 July 1987
18  *Dinnerladies* tapes, 25 June 1998
19  Ibid.
20  *Dinnerladies* tapes, 2 July 1998
21  Stanley Wood diary, 7 September 1971, quoted in *Victoria Wood: Comedy Genius – Her Life and Work* by Chris Foote Wood, 2016

## Chapter 5: The Green Room

1   *Scene – Personal View: Victoria Wood*, BBC Two, 9 May 1985
2   *Parkinson*, BBC One, 24 March 2000
3   Letter to Robert Howie, 19 April 1978
4   *Clive James – Postcard from London*, BBC One, 31 July 1991
5   *Saturday Night Clive*, BBC Two, 2 December 1989
6   Stanley Wood letter to Rosalind Wood, 23 October 1972
7   *The Late Clive James*, ITV, 22 June 1985
8   *Desert Island Discs*, BBC Radio 4, 8 February 1987
9   Ibid.
10  Letter to Rosalind, 14 February 1973
11  Letter to Rosalind Wood, June 1973
12  Letter from Leslie Lowe, 10 July 1973
13  Letter to Rosalind Wood, July 1973
14  Letter to Robert Howie, 15 July 1973
15  Letter to Bill Lloyd, 17 August 1973
16  'My first job', interview with Louise Roddon, *Company*, October 1987
17  'Porky's revenge', interview with David Hepworth, *Q* magazine, October 1987
18  *Parkinson*, BBC One, 24 March 2000
19  Letter to Rosalind Wood, September 1973
20  Letter from Jane Wymark, 6 September 1973
21  Letter to Rosalind Wood, September 1973
22  *Desert Island Discs*, BBC Radio 4, 8 February 1987
23  Letter to Bill Lloyd, 17 August 1973
24  Letter to Rosalind Wood, September 1973
25  Letter to Rosalind Wood, September 1973

26  Email to Jane Wymark, 27 September 2015

27  Letter to Robert Howie, 15 July 1973

28  Ibid.

29  Letter to Rosalind Wood, September 193

30  Letter to Bill Lloyd, 1973

31  *Desert Island Discs*, BBC Radio 4, 8 February 1987

32  Letter to Bill Lloyd, October 1973

33  Letter to Bill Lloyd, 1973

34  Ibid

35  Letter to Jane Wymark, 21 July 1983

36  *Sounds Local*, BBC Radio Blackburn, 1 January 1978

37  Interview with Roger Wilmut, 9 July 1987

38  Letter to Bill Lloyd, 1973

39  Ibid.

40  Letter to Rosalind Wood, September 1973

41  Letter to Rosalind Wood, April 1974

42  Notes for a speech to launch *Lucky Bag: The Victoria Wood Song Book*, 1984

43  Letter to Rosalind Wood, May 1974

44  Interview with Roger Wilmut, 9 July 1987

45  Letter to Rosalind Wood, 1974

46  Letter to Rosalind Wood, May 1974

47  Letter to Rosalind Wood, June 1974

48  Bob Phillips, *Coventry Evening Telegraph*, 15 May 1974

49  Letter to Lesley Fitton, 22 April 1974

50  Ibid.

51  'Things I Don't Like About Fame by Victoria Wood age 32', manuscript

52  *Parkinson*, BBC One, 24 March 2000

53  Interview with the author, 19 August 2009

54  Letter to Rosalind Wood, 1974

55  Letter from Lesley Fitton, 20 April 1974

56  Letter from Alison Sabourin, 3 May 1974

57  Letter from Anne Sweeney, 3 May 1974

58  Letter to Rosalind Wood, June 1974


## Chapter 6: New Face

1   Letter to Rosalind Wood, September 1974

2   Letter to Rosalind Wood, June 1974

3   Letter to Rosalind Wood, September 1974

4   Interview with the author, 19 August 2009

5   Ibid.

6   Letter to Rosalind Wood, October 1974

7   'The "New Face" of stardom for Victoria', *Evening Mail*, October 1974

8   Preface to *Chunky*, Methuen, 1996

9   Letter to Rosalind Watson, October 1974

10  Interview with Roger Wilmut, 9 July 1987

11  *Dinnerladies* tapes, 26 June 1998

12  Interview with Roger Wilmut, 9 July 1987

13  Interview with the author, 19 August 2009

14  'Introducing Victoria Wood', interview with Eileen Totten, *Warwickshire & Worcestershire Life*, May 1975

15  'Glorious good Wood', interview with Louise Gannon, *Daily Express*, 25 April 1992

16  *John Dunn*, BBC Radio 2, 8 June 1982

17  John Bird internal memo, BBC Written Archives Centre RCONT21 – Wood, Victoria, 23 January 1975

18  Letter to Roger McGough, March 1975

19  Ibid.

20  Letter to Robert Howie, 28 January 1975

21  Letter to Roger McGough, 1975

22  Letter from Bernard Miles to Beetles and Buckman, 11 April 1975

23  Scrapbook, 1973-1976

24  *Clive James – Postcard from London*, BBC One, 31 July 1991

25  Letter to Roger McGough, 1975

26  Ibid.

27  'Original, gentle, rather rude', interview with Andrew Crofts, *She*, 1979

28  Letter to Roger McGough, 1975

29  *Desert Island Discs*, BBC Radio 4, 8 February 1987

30  Interview with the author, 19 August 2009

31  Interview with Roger Wilmut, 9 July 1987

32  'The determined new face of Victoria Wood', interview with Ken Roche, *TV Times*, 23 August 1975

33  Letter to Lesley Fitton, September 1975

34  Letter to Roger McGough, September 1975

35  Letter to Lesley Fitton, September 1975

36  Letter to Andy Roberts, 1975

37  Ibid.

38  Letter to Roger McGough, c. October 1975

39  'Victoria would', interview with Hilary Bonner, *Sunday Mirror Magazine*, 4 September 1994

40  Ibid.

41  B.A. Young, *Financial Times*, 12 December 1975

42  Interview with Roger Wilmut, 9 July 1987

43  Letter to Andy Roberts, 1976

44  Letter to Roger McGough, 1976

45  'The rhyme and reason of what makes girls break into verse', interview with Eithne Power, *Woman's Realm*, 1 January 1977

46  *Sunday Times*, 8 February 1976

47  Letter to Roger McGough, 1976

48  Interview with BBC Radio Blackburn, 1 January 1978

49  Interview with John Dunn, BBC Radio 2, 8 June 1982

50  Interview with Wendy Howard, BBC Radio Blackburn, 1 January 1978

51  'I love fashion, but it doesn't love me', *Woman's Own*, December 1979

52  Letter to Rosalind Wood, 1976

53  Letter to Roger McGough, March 1976

54  Ibid.

55  *Celebration*, Granada TV, 26 March 1980

56  Ibid.

57  'Victoria's show is on the road at last', interview with Arthur Steele, *Evening Mail*, 10 May 1976

58  Sheridan Morley, *Radio Times*, 6 May 1976

59  *Sunday Times*, 9 May 1976

60  Interview with Lucy Kenwright, BBC Additional Programmes Unit, 2009


## Chapter 7:  Soprendo

1   *Best of British*, BBC One, 1 November 1998

2   Letter to Robert Howie, 15 July 1976

3   Letter to Roger McGough, 1976

4   *Best of British*, BBC One, 1 November 1998

5   *Desert Island Discs*, BBC Radio 4, 1987

6   'Song spots not so easy', *The Journal*, 31 March 1977

7   Letter to Robert Howie, August 1976

8   Ibid.

9   Letter to BBC Copyright Department, BBC Written Archives Centre, September 1976

10  Interview with the author, 19 August 2009

11  Letter to Rosalind Wood, April 1977

12  Interview with Roger Wilmut, 9 July 1987

13  Letter to Rosalind Wood, April 1977

14  Letter to Robert Howie, October 1976
15  Letter to Rosalind Wood, April 1977
16  Letter to Rosalind Wood, April 1977
17  Letter to Robert Howie, 8 November 1976
18  Helen Wood letter to Rosalind Wood, 6 November 1976
19  Stanley Wood letter to Rosalind Wood, 7 December 1976
20  Letter to Robert Howie, 8 November 1976
21  Ibid.
22  *Sunday Times Magazine*, 23 March 1980
23  *The Stage*, 23 September 1976
24  Letter to Robert Howie, 8 November 1976
25  Stanley Wood letter to Rosalind Wood, 15 November 1976
26  Stanley Wood letter to Rosalind Wood, 7 December 1976
27  Ibid.
28  Helen Wood letter to Rosalind Wood, 15 December 1976
29  Letter to Robert Howie, 8 November 1976
30  Letter to Robert Howie, 15 January 1977
31  Letter to Robert Howie, February 1977
32  Interview with Lucy Kenwright, BBC Additional Programmes Unit, 2009
33  Letter to Robert Howie, 15 January 1977
34  Robert Low, *Birmingham Post*, 24 March 1977
35  Ibid.
36  Brian Glover, *Birmingham Evening Mail*, 24 March 1977
37  Helen Wood letter to Rosalind Wood, 23 March 1977
38  'Song spots not so easy', *The Journal*, 31 March 1977
39  Letter to Rosalind Wood, 1977
40  Letter to Robert Howie, 5 May 1977
41  *Sunday Times*, 8 May 1977
42  Card to Robert Howie, May 1977
43  Steve Grant, *Time Out*, 13 May 1977
44  Interview with Roger Wilmut, 9 July 1987
45  'A talent to amuse', interview with Deborah Moggach, *Over 21*, February
    1979
46  Letter to Robert Howie, 5 July 1977
47  Letter to Rosalind Wood, May 1977
48  Letter to Roger McGough, 1977
49  Ibid.
50  Ibid.
51  Ibid.
52  *Celebration*, Granada TV, 26 March 1980

53  Interview with BBC Radio Blackburn, 1 January 1978
54  'Victoria Wood rising on a gale of laughter', interview with Jeremy Pascall, *Company*, January 1981
55  Letter to Robert Howie, 12 November 1977
56  Stanley Wood letter to Rosalind Wood, 11 April 1978
57  *Best of British*, BBC One, 1 November 1998
58  Interview with BBC Radio Blackburn, 1 January 1978
59  Letter to Robert Howie, 19 April 1978
60  Letter to Chrissie Poulter, February 1978
61  *Desert Island Discs*, BBC Radio 4, 8 February 1987
62  Letter to Rosalind Wood, May 1977
63  'Victoria Wood rising on a gale of laughter', interview with Jeremy Pascall, *Company*, January 1981
64  'Funny girl', interview with David Robson, *Sunday Times Magazine*, 23 March 1980
65  Interview with BBC Radio Blackburn, 1 January 1978
66  Ibid.
67  *Dinnerladies* tapes, 3 July 1998
68  Interview with BBC Radio Blackburn, 1 January 1978
69  Letter to Robert Howie, 19 April 1978
70  Ibid.

## Chapter 8: Talents

1  Interview with Roger Wilmut, 9 July 1987
2  *Dinnerladies* tapes, 27 June 1998
3  Notes for a speech to launch *Lucky Bag: The Victoria Wood Song Book*, 1984
4  Ibid.
5  *Dinnerladies* tapes, 27 June 1998
6  Ibid.
7  Ibid.
8  Ibid.
9  Interview with the author, 19 August 2009
10  'How We Met', *Independent on Sunday*, 27 December 1992
11  *Dinnerladies* tapes, 3 July 1998
12  'Tales from the Bush', *New Statesman*, 12 November 1997
13  John Barber, *Daily Telegraph*, 18 July 1978
14  Francis King, *Sunday Telegraph*, 23 July 1978
15  Michael Coveney, *Financial Times*, 22 July 1978

16 Irving Wardle, *The Times*, 18 July 1978

17 Steve Grant, *Plays and Players*, September 1978

18 *Round Midnight*, BBC Radio 2, 6 February 1979

19 Letter to Robert Howie, September 1978

20 'Original, gentle, rather rude', interview with Andrew Crofts, *She*, 1979

21 Interview with the author, 19 August 2009

22 *Celebration*, Granada TV, 26 March 1980

23 Interview with the author, 19 August 2009

24 *Celebration*, Granada TV, 26 March 1980

25 Interview with the author, 19 August 2009

26 'Talent gets top billing', interview with Douglas Orgill, *Daily Express*, February 1979

27 *Round Midnight*, BBC Radio 2, 6 February 1979

28 Paul Allen, *Guardian*, 10 November 1978

29 Stanley Wood letter to Rosalind Wood, 22 September 1978

30 *Desert Island Discs*, BBC Radio 4, 8 February 1987

31 Letter to James Eckersley, 13 November 1985

32 *Celebration*, Granada TV, 26 March 1980

33 'Victoria Wood, by the woman across the road', programme to *Lucky Bag* at the King's Head, 1983

34 Jim Hiley, *Kaleidoscope*, BBC Radio 4, 8 February 1979

35 Nicholas de Jongh, *Guardian*, 10 February 1979

36 Robert Cushman, *Observer*, 11 February 1979

37 'The girl who made a fat friend the most unlikely heroine', interview with Michael Briscoe, *Daily Mail*, 7 August 1979

38 'How We Met', *Independent on Sunday*, 27 December 1992

39 Ibid.

40 Letter to Robert Howie, 12 April 1979

41 Stanley Wood letter to Rosalind Wood, 13 April 1979

42 Letter to Lesley Fitton, 21 August 1979

43 'The girl who made a fat friend the most unlikely heroine', interview with Michael Briscoe, *Daily Mail*, 7 August 1979

44 Letter to Robert Howie, 3 September 1979

45 Ibid.

46 Introduction to *Victoria Wood Plays: 1*, Methuen, 1998

47 'Queen Vic', interview with Vicki Woods, *Evening Standard*, 12 September 1996

48 Nancy Banks-Smith, *Guardian*, 6 August 1979

49 Sheridan Morley, *Evening Standard*, 6 August 1979

50 Peter Buckman, *Listener*, 16 August 1979

51  'Funny girl', interview with David Robson, *Sunday Times Magazine*, 23 March 1980

52  Letter to Chrissie Poulter, 21 August 1979

53  Letter to Robert Howie, 29 August 1979

54  Ibid.

55  Ibid.

56  Ibid.

57  'A Certain Style', BBC Radio 4, extract in *Listener*, 20 December 1979

58  Letter to Robert Howie, 29 August 1979

59  Letter to Robert Howie, 19 November 1979

60  'The girl who made a fat friend the most unlikely heroine', interview with Michael Briscoe, *Daily Mail*, 7 August 1979

61  *Afternoon Plus*, Thames TV, 21 October 1980

62  Benedict Nightingale, *New Statesman*, 28 July 1978

63  'Talent gets top billing', interview with Douglas Orgill, *Daily Express*, February 1979

64  Patrick O'Neill, *Daily Mail*, 4 August 1979

65  'Funny girl', interview with David Robson, *Sunday Times Magazine*, 23 March 1980

66  'Victoria plumps for quiet fame', interview with Elizabeth Griffin, *Daily Post*, 11 August 1979

67  'The girl who made a fat friend the most unlikely heroine', interview with Michael Briscoe, *Daily Mail*, 7 August 1979

68  *Afternoon Plus*, Thames TV, 21 October 1980

69  Letter to Rosalind Wood, 1979

70  'Wood makes a splash', interview with Richard North, *Observer*, 30 March 1980

71  Memorandum from Peter Eckersley, 29 February 1980

72  Letter to Chrissie Poulter, 29 May 1980

73  'Great Soprendo's greatest trick', *Daily Mail*, 31 May 1980

74  'Victoria, Julie and happy beginnings at the swimming baths', *TV Times*, 28 May 1980

75  Letter to Robert Howie, 3 September 1979

76  Letter to Robert Howie, March 1980

77  Letter to Chrissie Poulter, 29 May 1980

78  *Arena*, BBC Two, 26 March 1980

79  Foreword to *Good Fun & Talent*, Methuen, 1988

80  James Fenton, *Sunday Times*, 6 April 1980

81  B.A. Young, *Financial Times*, 8 April 1980

82  Letter to Robert Howie, April 1980

**Chapter 9: And Walters**

1  'Eighty for the Eighties', *Observer*, 30 December 1979

2  Notes for a speech to launch *Lucky Bag: The Victoria Wood Song Book*, 1983

3  Ibid.

4  'Hilarious end to City's festival', *Lancashire Evening Post*, 26 May 1980

5  Notebook, 1980

6  'This Victoria is amused', interview with Judi Goodwin, *Radio Times*, 29 May 1980

7  'Victoria swims to her happy ending', *Daily Record*, 13 May 1980

8  'Victoria Wood rising on a gale of laughter', interview with Jeremy Pascall, *Company*, January 1981

9  Letter from Julie Walters, 15 July 1980

10  Interview with Roger Wilmut, 9 July 1987

11  'Game for a laugh', interview with John Cunningham, *Guardian*, 12 October 1983

12  Charles Spencer, *Evening Standard*, 30 September 1980

13  Irving Wardle, *The Times*, 30 September 1980

14  R.B. Marriott, *Stage*, 9 October 1980

15  Michael Billington, *Guardian*, 30 September 1980

16  Stanley Wood letter to Rosalind Wood, 20 October 1980

17  Letter to Roger McGough, 1980

18  *Afternoon Plus*, Thames TV, 21 October 1980

19  Ibid.

20  'The girl who knows how to say no', interview with Pauline Peters, *Sunday Express Magazine*, 24 January 1982

21  Notes for a speech to launch *Lucky Bag: The Victoria Wood Song Book*, 1983

22  Nicholas de Jongh, *Guardian*, 22 October 1980

23  John Barber, *Daily Telegraph*, 21 October 1980

24  Russell Davies, *Sunday Times*, 8 June 1980

25  Herbert Kretzmer, *Daily Mail*, 2 June 1980

26  'Victoria Wood rising on a gale of laughter', interview with Jeremy Pascall, *Company*, January 1981

27  Ibid.

28  *Victoria Wood Seen on TV*, BBC One, 21 December 2009

29  Letter to Robert Howie, December 1980

30  Letter to Robert Howie, 13 January 1980

31  Letter to Roger McGough, 1980

32  Interview with John Dunn, BBC Radio 2, 8 July 1982

33  Letter to Robert Howie, 15 August 1981

34  Letter to Robert Howie, May 1981

35  'The sex-war traitor', by Chris Greenwood, *Sun*, 8 August 1981

36  Letter to Rosalind Wood, March 1981

37  Postcard to Rosalind Wood, 2 May 1981

38  'Victoria Wood: leaving the one-liners behind', interview with Bryan Apple-
    yard, *The Times*, 20 January 1982

39  Letter to Robert Howie, May 1981

40  Letter to Rosalind Wood, 1981

41  Interview with Roger Wilmut, 9 July 1987

42  Letter from Peter Eckersley, 6 July 1981

43  Letter from Peter Eckersley, July 1981

44  Letter from Peter Eckersley, 13 July 1981

45  Letter to Robert Howie, 15 August 1981

46  Scrapbook, 1977–1981

47  *The Times*, 28 August 1981

48  Letter to James Eckersley, 13 November 1985

49  Interview with Roger Wilmut, 9 July 1987

50  David Wade, *The Times*, 31 October 1981

51  'The girl who knows how to say no', interview with Pauline Peters, *Sunday
    Express Magazine*, 24 January 1982

52  Letter from Roger Brierley, 16 April 2002

53  Interview with Lucy Kenwright, BBC Additional Programmes Unit, 2009

54  Interview with Roger Wilmut, 9 July 1987

55  Letter to Lesley Fitton, October 1981

56  Ibid.

57  Interview with Roger Wilmut, July 1987

58  'Victor, Victoria', interview with Tom Hibbert, *Options*, December 1989

59  Review by Stanley Reynolds, *Guardian*, 10 August 1981

60  Letter to Rosalind Wood, 1982

61  'Tile though your heart is aching', manuscript, 1982

62  'Girls are a laugh!', interview with Hilary Kingsley, *Daily Mirror*, 15 February
    1982

63  *The South Bank Show*, ITV, 15 September 1996

64  Michael Church, *The Times*, 18 January 1982

65  Chris Dunkley, *Financial Times*, 3 February 1982

66  Interview with Lucy Kenwright, BBC Additional Programmes Unit, 2009

67  'A magic combination', interview with Avril Deane, *Journal*, 10 February
    1982

## Chapter 10: Funny How Things Turn

1   Letter from Julie Walters, 27 February 1982
2   Interview with Avril Deane, *Journal*, 10 February 1982
3   Pamela Gardner, *Belfast Telegraph*, 13 March 1982
4   *Reporting London*, Thames Television, March 1982
5   'Funny turn', Christopher Montagu, *Sunday Times Magazine*, 9 May 1982
6   Letter to Robert Howie, May 1982
7   Tom Sutcliffe, *Guardian*, 14 May 1982
8   Michael Coveney, *Financial Times*, 13 May 1982
9   Robert Cushman, *Observer*, 16 May 1982
10  Jack Tinker, *Daily Mail*, 14 May 1982
11  Postcard to Robert Howie, 25 May 1982
12  'Funny turn', Christopher Montagu, *Sunday Times Magazine*, 9 May 1982
13  'A talent to amuse', interview with Bruce Jones, *Outlook*, October/November 1989
14  *Dinnerladies* tapes, 27 June 1998
15  'Sweating in the wild West End', *The Times*, 9 June 1982
16  Interview with Lucy Kenwright, BBC Additional Programmes Unit, 2009
17  Philip Purser, *Sunday Telegraph*, 5 September 1982
18  Letter to Jane Wymark, 28 July 1982
19  'It's funny how Wood warms up with slick Spick', interview with Jasmine Profit, *Bath Evening Chronicle*, 25 January 1983
20  Letter to Jane Wymark, 21 July 1983
21  Letter to Jane Wymark, 16 August 1983
22  Letter to Jane Wymark, 21 July 1983
23  Letter to Jane Wymark, 8 July 1983
24  Letter to Jane Wymark, 21 July 1983
25  Ibid.
26  Letter to Jane Wymark, 8 July 1983
27  Letter to Jane Wymark, 21 July 1983
28  'Game for a laugh' interview with John Cunningham, *Guardian*, 12 October 1983
29  Notes for a speech to launch *Lucky Bag: The Victoria Wood Song Book*, 1983
30  Letter to Jane Wymark, 16 August 1983
31  Ibid.
32  Paul Barker, *New Society*, 1 September 1983
33  *Best of British*, BBC One, 1 November 1998
34  Interview with Lucy Kenwright, BBC Additional Programmes Unit, 2009
35  Interview, *Plays*, March 1984

36 'Good Wood', Robert Cushman, *Observer*, 6 November 1983
37 Interview, *Plays*, March 1984
38 Letter to Jane Wymark, 7 December 1983
39 Ibid.
40 Ibid.
41 Ibid.
42 Ibid.
43 Ibid.
44 Letter to Jane Wymark, January 1984
45 Letter to Jane Wymark, 7 December 1983
46 Letter to Jane Wymark, 2 February 1984
47 Francis King, *Sunday Telegraph*, 19 February 1984
48 John Barber, *Daily Telegraph*, 14 February 1984

## Chapter 11:  Seen on TV

1   Letter to Jane Wymark, 6 January 1984
2   Interview with Roger Wilmut, 9 July 1987
3   Letter to Jane Wymark, 21 January 1984
4   Ibid
5   'Victoria: we are amused', interview with Adam Mars-Jones, *Independent*,
    7 October 1987
6   'Victoria's values', interview with Ann Steele, *Sunday Telegraph*, 6 January
    1985
7   Letter to Jane Wymark, 2 February 1984
8   'Porky's revenge', interview with David Hepworth, *Q* magazine, October
    1987
9   Ibid.
10  'Porky's revenge', interview with David Hepworth, *Q* magazine, October
    1987
11  *Best of British*, BBC One, 11 November 1998
12  Letter to Jane Wymark, 2 February 1984
13  Postcard to Rosalind Wood, 12 April 1984
14  Letter from Julie Walters, 1 April 1984
15  Letter to Jane Wymark, 3 May 1984
16  Letter from Alan Bennett, May 1984
17  Letter to Jane Wymark, 3 May 1984
18  Letter to Jane Wymark, 29 July 1984
19  'Wood on Walters on Imrie on Preston on Blake', interview with Sue Ted-
    dern, *Radio Times*, 10 December 1987

20  Ibid.

21  Letter to Jane Wymark, 25 June 1984

22  Letter to Jane Wymark, 29 July 1984

23  Letter to Jane Wymark, 30 August 1984

24  Ibid.

25  'Wood on Walters on Imrie on Preston on Blake', interview with Sue Teddern, *Radio Times*, 10 December 1987

26  Letter to Jane Wymark, 30 August 1984

27  'Victoria rules as queen of comedy', interview with Philip Young, *Newcastle Journal*, 20 March 1995

28  Letter to Robert Howie, 12 April 1985

29  'Don't I remind you of Jane Fonda?' interview with Jo Weedon, *Woman's Own*, October 1987

30  Interview with the author, 4 January 2005

31  Ibid.

32  *Russell Harty's Musical Encounters*, BBC Radio 4, 25 May 1985

33  *Parkinson's Sunday Supplement*, BBC Radio 2, 26 March 2006

34  *Russell Harty's Musical Encounters*, BBC Radio 4, 25 May 1985

35  Ibid.

36  Interview with the author, 4 January 2005

37  'Playing the Piano the Victoria Wood Way', *Lucky Bag: The Victoria Wood Songbook,* Methuen, 1984

38  *Russell Harty's Musical Encounters*, BBC Radio 4, 25 May 1985

39  Letter to Jane Wymark, 21 November 1984

40  Ibid.

41  Ibid.

42  Russell Davies, *Observer*, 27 January 1985

43  Nina Myskow, *News of the World*, 3 February 1985

44  'A thousand weeds', Glasgow *Herald*, 9 March 1985

## Chapter 12:  Doing It

1   Letter to Jane Wymark, 21 January 1985

2   *Radio Times*, 20 June 1985

3   Letter to Jane Wymark, 21 January 1985

4   Letter to Robert Howie, 12 April 1985

5   Ibid.

6   *Scene – Personal View: Victoria Wood*, BBC Two, 9 May 1985

7   Ibid.

8   Ibid.

9   Letter to Jane Wymark, 21 January 1985

10  *The Late Clive James*, BBC Two, 22 June 1985

11  Postcard to Rosalind Wood, 29 April 1985

12  Letter to Robert Howie, 12 April 1985

13  Letter to Jane Wymark, 28 May 1985

14  Ibid.

15  Ibid.

16  Letter to Jane Wymark, 24 June 1985

17  Ibid.

18  Ibid.

19  Letter to Jane Wymark, 28 May 1985

20  Letter to Jane Wymark, July 1985

21  Letter to Jane Wymark, 7 October 1985

22  Ibid.

23  Ibid.

24  Letter to Jane Wymark, July 1985

25  Letter to Jane Wymark, November 1985

26  Ibid.

27  Introduction to *Up to You, Porky*, Methuen, 1985

28  Letter from Geoffrey Strachan, 7 February 1986

29  Letter from Geoffrey Strachan, 21 April 1986

30  Letter to Jane Wymark, November 1985

31  Notebook, 1986

32  Card to Jane Wymark, 1984

33  Letter to Jane Wymark, 22 February 1986

34  Ibid.

35  Ibid.

36  Letter to Jane Wymark, May 1986

37  Ibid.

38  'Woodwork', interview with Gay Search, *Radio Times*, 6 November 1986

39  Letter to Jane Wymark, May 1986

40  Speech notes, 1986

41  Letter to Jane Wymark, 22 August 1986

42  *Marxism Today*, November 1986

43  'Woodwork', interview with Gay Search, *Radio Times*, 6 November 1986

44  Notes, 1986

45  *Dinnerladies* tapes, 25 June 1998

## Chapter 13: An Audience with Grace

1  Interview with Mervyn Edgecombe, *Woman*, 15 November 1986
2  Letter to Jane Wymark, 20 December 1986
3  'Farewell Victoria', Maureen Paton, *Daily Express*, 26 October 1986
4  'Porky's revenge', interview with David Hepworth, *Q* magazine, October 1987
5  Peter Davelle, *The Times*, 10 November 1986
6  Letter to Jane Wymark, 20 December 1986
7  Speech notes, 1986
8  Postcard to Jane Wymark, 1986
9  'Let's face it, I just love showing off!', interview with Gabrielle Donnelly, *Woman's World*, February 1987
10 Letter to Jane Wymark, 24 January 1987
11 Ibid.
12 Ibid.
13 Ibid.
14 Ibid.
15 Letter to Jane Wymark, 12 May 1987
16 'Wood on Walters on Imrie on Preston on Blake', interview with Sue Teddern, *Radio Times*, 10 December 1987
17 Interview with Roger Wilmut, 9 July 1987
18 Ibid.
19 Letter to Jane Wymark, 8 July 1987
20 Ibid.
21 Interview with Roger Wilmut, 9 July 1987
22 Interview with Lucy Kenwright, BBC Additional Programmes Unit, 2009
23 Ibid.
24 'Touch Wood', interview with Paddy Burt, *Home & Gardens*, October 1987
25 Notebook, 1987
26 Ibid.
27 Letter to Jane Wymark, 6 November 1987
28 Jack Tinker, *Daily Mail*, 13 October 1987
29 Anthony Thorncroft, *Financial Times*, 14 October 1987
30 Adam Sweeting, *Guardian*, 14 October 1987
31 Catherine Bennett, *The Times*, 16 October 1987
32 Notebook, 1987
33 Letter to Jane Wymark, 5 December 1987
34 Ibid.
35 Letter from Helen Wood, 20 December 1987

36 'Margery and Joan' manuscript, 1988

37 Letter to Rosalind Wood, 1978

38 'No-one is spared in Vic's comic cuts', interview with Jane Peel, *Lincolnshire Echo*, 22 November 1984

39 Letter to Jane Wymark, 21 January 1985

40 Interview with Gay Search, *Radio Times*, 10 November 1986

41 Interview with Mervyn Edgecombe, *Woman*, 15 November 1986

42 Speech notes, 1987

43 'Babe and the Wood', interview with Andrea Kon, *NZ Listener*, 13 August 1988

44 Ibid.

45 Tour itinerary notebooks, 1987 and 1988

46 Letter to Lesley Fitton, 22 July 1988

47 Ibid.

48 Card to Alan Yentob, BBC Written Archives Centre File ID 10175665 – Wood, Victoria, 13 April 1988

49 Letter to Alan Yentob, BBC Written Archives Centre File ID 10175665 – Wood, Victoria, 26 April 1988

50 *What Did ITV Do For Me?*, ITV, 20 September 2005

51 'Victor, Victoria', interview with Tom Hibbert, *Options*, December 1989

52 'Babe and the Wood – yes, Victoria's a mum!', interview with Andrea Kon, *TV Times*, 10–16 December 1988

53 Letter to Lesley Fitton, 22 July 1988

54 *Mavis Catches Up With . . .*, Thames TV, 13 December 1989

55 Ibid.

56 'That will teach you, Thompson', Margaret Forwood, *People*, 11 December 1988

57 Charles Catchpole, *News of the World*, 11 December 1988

58 'Funny girls', Hilary Kingsley, *Daily Mirror*, 15 December 1988

59 'Babe and the Wood – yes, Victoria's a mum!', interview with Andrea Kon, *TV Times*, 10–16 December 1988

**Chapter 14: Staying In**

1 'Wood craft', interview with Philip Oakes, *7 Days* magazine, *Sunday Telegraph*, 8 October 1989

2 Vivienne Clore letter to James Moir, BBC Written Archives Centre File ID 10175665 – Wood, Victoria, 31 January 1989

3 Jonathan Powell internal memo to James Moir, BBC Written Archives Centre File ID 10175665 – Wood, Victoria, 20 March 1989

4   *Mavis Catches Up With . . .*, Thames TV, 13 December 1989
5   'Growing out of Acorn', interview with Richard Brooks, *Observer*, 12 November 1989
6   'Victor, Victoria', interview with Thom Hibbert, *Options*, December 1989
7   'Growing out of Acorn', interview with Richard Brooks, *Observer*, 12 November 1989
8   Casting suggestion notes, 1989
9   Postcard to Duncan Preston, 1989
10  'Pitching for laughs', interview with Julie Welch, *Radio Times*, 9 November 1989
11  'Growing out of Acorn', interview with Richard Brooks, *Observer*, 12 November 1989
12  Noel Malcolm, *Sunday Telegraph*, 19 November 1989
13  Alan Coren, *Mail on Sunday*, 10 December 1989
14  'How a television series is made', *Mens Sana in Thingummy Doodah and Five Other Nuggets of Homely Fun*, Methuen, 1990
15  'On Tour with Victoria Wood', *Kaleidoscope*, BBC Radio 4, 15 May 1993
16  Interview with the author, 21 October 1999
17  'If I'd been thin as a teenager and gone out with boys I wouldn't have had anything to write about', interview with Ray Connolly, *The Times*, 28 October 1989
18  Speech notes

## Chapter 15: Up West

1   'Broken ice in Africa', *Independent on Sunday*, 18 March 1990
2   Notes for speech delivered at Lancaster University, 1989
3   'Growing out of Acorn', interview with Richard Brooks, *Observer*, 12 November 1989
4   *Lucky Bang: The Victoria Wood Songbook*, Methuen, 1991
5   Letter to Jane Wymark, 13 June 1990
6   Ibid.
7   *Wogan*, BBC One, 16 April 1992
8   Letter to Jane Wymark, 1989
9   Card to Duncan Preston, 1990
10  Alan Coren, *The Times*, 3 October 1990
11  Milton Shulman, *Evening Standard*, 3 October 1990
12  Kate Kellaway, *Observer*, 7 October 1990
13  Jane Edwardes, *Time Out*, 9 October 1990
14  Letter to Jane Wymark, autumn 1990

15 Letter to Rosalind Wood, autumn 1990

16 Ibid.

17 Ibid.

18 Letter to Jane Wymark, 12 December 1989

19 *Desert Island Discs*, BBC Radio 4, 8 February 1987

20 'Porky's revenge', interview with David Hepworth, *Q* magazine, October 1987

21 Letter to Jane Wymark, 7 January 1991

22 Postcard to Jane Wymark, 5 February 1991

23 Ibid.

24 Letter to Jane Wymark, 23 April 1991

25 Ibid.

26 Ibid.

27 Letter from Geoffrey Strachan, with handwriting by V.W., 5 June 1991

## Chapter 16: Henry and Albert, Margaret and Pat

1 Jonathan Powell internal memo to James Moir, BBC Written Archives Centre File ID 10175665 – Wood, Victoria, 3 April 1991

2 'Victoria Wood talks funny', interview with Jayne Dowle, *She*, September 1994

3 'A lump of wood? Not any more she isn't', interview with Hilary Kingsley, *Today*, 8 September 1994

4 *Clive James – Postcard from London*, BBC One, 31 July 1991

5 Change of address card, 1992

6 'A lump of Wood? Not any more she isn't', interview with Hilary Kingsley, *Today*, 8 September 1994

7 'On tour with Victoria Wood', *Kaleidoscope*, BBC Radio 4, 15 May 1993

8 Ibid.

9 *Aspel and Company*, ITV, 20 June 1993

10 Letter to Jane Wymark, June 1993

11 'Don't make me laugh', interview with Angela Levin, *You* magazine, *Mail on Sunday*, 27 June 1993

12 'On Tour with Victoria Wood', *Kaleidoscope*, BBC Radio 4, 15 May 1993

13 *Aspel and Company*, ITV, 20 June 1993

14 'Victoria Wood talks funny', interview with Jayne Dowle, *She*, September 1994

15 Victoria Wood on Tour, programme note, 1996

16 'On Tour with Victoria Wood', *Kaleidoscope*, BBC Radio 4, 15 May 1993

17 Ibid.

18  Ibid.

19  Card to Robert Howie, May 1993

20  'Pat and Margaret: this is your life', interview with Hilary Kingsley, *The Times*, 16 September 1994

21  'Sister act', interview with Alkarim Jivani, *Time Out*, 7 September 1994

22  Sarah Wilson letter to Vivienne Clore, 26 October 1993

23  *Aspel and Company*, ITV, 20 June 1993

24  'Victoria's plum role', interview with E. Jane Dickson, *Daily Telegraph*, 8 September 1994

25  'Victoria would', interview with Hilary Bonner, *Sunday Mirror Magazine*, 4 September 1994

26  'I used to think being fat was a criminal offence', interview with Andrew Duncan, *Radio Times*, 8 September 1994

27  Alan Yentob internal memo to George Faber, BBC Written Archives, 11 November 1993

28  Script report, BBC Written Archives, 19 November 1993

29  Alan Yentob letter to George Faber and Margaret Matheson, BBC Written Archives, 1 December 1993

30  'I used to think being fat was a criminal offence', interview with Andrew Duncan, *Radio Times*, 8 September 1994

31  'Victoria would', interview with Hilary Bonner, *Sunday Mirror Magazine*, 4 September 1994

32  'Sister act', interview with Alkarim Jivani, *Time Out*, 7 September 1994

33  Foreword to *Pat and Margaret*, Methuen, 1994

34  *South Bank Show*, ITV, 15 September 1996

35  Letter to Lesley Fitton, September 1996

36  'Doubling up with laughter', interview with David Weigert and Louise Gannon, *Daily Express*, 2 September 1994

37  'Ooo, it's that woman off telly', interview with James Rampton, *Independent*, 13 July 1994

38  Gary Leboff, *Sun*, 12 September 1994

39  Nancy Banks-Smith, *Guardian*, 12 September 1994

40  Matthew Norman, *Evening Standard*, 12 September 1994

## Chapter 17:  Journeys

1  'Sister act', interview with Alkarim Jivani, *Time Out*, 7 September 1994

2  Letter to Richard Eyre, 27 September 1994

3  Letter to Alan Yentob, BBC Written Archives, 15 August 1994

4  'My Comic Relief diary from Africa', *Daily Mirror*, 10 March 1995

5   Ibid.
6   Letter to Jane Wymark and Paul Howson, 12 February 1995
7   Poem for Geoffrey Strachan, 1995
8   Letter from Geoffrey Strachan, 30 September 1995
9   Vivienne Clore letter to Alan Yentob, BBC Written Archives Centre File ID
    10175665 – Wood, Victoria, 30 June 1995
10  Letter to Stuart Higgins, 5 February 1996
11  Letter to Charlotte Scott, 29 January 1996
12  'Getting down to the real Wood,' interview p.159, with Elizabeth Grice, *Daily
    Telegraph*, 12 September 1996
13  Letter to Simon Cherry, 3 July 1996
14  *The South Bank Show*, ITV, 15 September 1996
15  'A Life in the Day of Victoria Wood', interview with Sue Fox, *Sunday Times
    Magazine*, 8 September 1996
16  Letter to Simon Cherry, 3 July 1996
17  Speech in acceptance of Honorary Doctorate of Letters, University of Bir-
    mingham, 4 July 1996
18  Ibid.
19  Ibid.
20  Letter from Nigel Wattis, 19 July 1996
21  Letter to Jane Wymark, July 1996
22  Fax to Maureen Lipman, September 1996
23  Letter from Michael Codron, 7 October 1996
24  Card from Richard Eyre, 9 October 1996
25  Letter from Trevor Nunn, 18 September 1996
26  Fax to Jane Wymark, 7 October 1996
27  Fax from Peter Chelsom, 19 August 1996
28  Fax to Dawn French, November 1996
29  'A Life in the Day of Victoria Wood', interview with Sue Fox, *Sunday Times
    Magazine*, 8 September 1996
30  Fax to Maureen Lipman, late October 1996
31  Fax to Geoffrey Durham, 1997
32  Fax to Geoff Posner, 22 April 1997
33  Fax to Phil McIntyre, 1997
34  Fax to the Richard Stone Agency, 8 May 1997
35  Fax to Maureen Lipman, 1997
36  Vivienne Clore letter to Phil McIntyre, 13 May 1997
37  *The Times*, 14 June 1997
38  Letter from Roy-Edward Walker, Major of Bury, 17 June 1997
39  Fax from Julie Walters, 19 June 1997

40  Letter from Vivienne Clore, 19 June 1997
41  *Dinnerladies* tapes, 7 July 1998
42  Fax to Jane Wymark, 13 June 1997
43  Fax from Julie Walters, 19 June 1997
44  Fax to Jane Wymark, 19 July 1997
45  Fax to Jane Wymark, 13 June 1997
46  Fax to Jane Wymark, 19 July 1997
47  Ibid.

## Chapter 18:  Dinnerlady

1   'On Tour with Victoria Wood', *Kaleidoscope*, BBC Radio 4, 15 May 1993
2   Fax to Vivienne Clore, February 1996
3   Fax from Julie Walters, 19 June 1997
4   Interview with Lucy Kenwright, BBC Additional Programmes Unit, 2009
5   Interview with the author, 22 October 1999
6   *Dinnerladies Diaries*, Gold, 14 March 2018
7   Fax to Vivienne Clore, 1997
8   Fax to Maureen Lipman, 18 September 1997
9   Letter to David Graham, 9 January 1998
10  Fax to Jane Wymark, 30 January 1998
11  Fax to Jane Wymark, 21 January 1998
12  Interview with Lucy Kenwright, BBC Additional Programmes Unit, 2009
13  Fax to Jane Wymark, 29 April 1998
14  Ibid.
15  Letter to Joanna Read, 20 April 1999
16  Letter to Lesley Fitton, May 1998
17  Fax to David Firman, 22 May 1998
18  Card to Jane Wymark, 1998
19  Ibid.
20  *Dinnerladies Diaries*, Gold, 14 March 2018
21  Fax to Jane Wymark, 3 June 1998
22  Fax to Jane Wymark, June 1998
23  *Dinnerladies* tapes, 8 July 1998
24  Interview with the author, 21 October 1999
25  Ibid.
26  *Dinnerladies* notebook, 1998
27  *Dinnerladies* tapes, 26 June 1998
28  Interview with the author, 21 October 1999
29  *Dinnerladies* tapes, 27 June 1998

30  *Dinnerladies* tapes, 30 June, 1998

31  *Dinnerladies* tapes, 6 July 1998

32  *Dinnerladies* tapes, 7 July 1998

33  Fax to Jane Wynn Owen, 1998

34  *Dinnerladies Diaries*, Gold, 14 March 2018

35  Letter to Joan Hood, 23 November 1998

36  *Dinnerladies* tapes, 1 July 1998

37  *Dinnerladies* tapes, 27 June 1998

38  Fax to Jane Wymark, August 1998

39  Fax to Jane Wymark, 14 September 1998

40  *Best of British*, BBC One, 11 November 1998

41  Letter to Michael Aspel, 30 October 1998

42  *In Conversation with . . .*, interview with Paul Jackson, BBC Radio 4, 14 March 2002

43  Fax to Richenda Carey, 6 November 1998

44  Fax to Jane Wymark, 17 November 1998

45  Fax to Richenda Carey, 22 February 1999

46  Fax to Maureen Lipman, January 1999

47  Fax to Jane Wymark, 11 January 1999

48  Fax to Richenda Carey, 11 January 1999

49  Fax to Richenda Carey, 12 January 1999

50  Letter to Lawrence Till, 9 November 1998

51  Fax to Jane Wymark, 17 February 1999

52  Letter to Joanna Read, 20 April 1999

53  Fax to Jane Wymark, 17 February 1999

54  Letter to Bury Library

55  'If I had my time over, I wouldn't be so amazingly talented!', interview with Julia Walters by Andrea Duncan, *Radio Times*, 4 March 1999

56  Fax to Richenda Carey, 24 February 1999

57  'AbFab was never like this. . .', *Radio Times*, 4 March 1999

58  Fax to Ruth Huntman, February 1999

59  Fax to Richenda Carey, 12 January 1999

60  Fax to Richenda Carey, 30 April 1999

61  Fax to Jane Wymark, 9 May 1999

62  Fax to Richenda Carey, 14 June 1999

63  Fax to Rob Buckman, March 1999

64  Interview with the author, 21 October 1999

65  Fax to Geoff Posner, 20 July 1999

66  Interview with the author, 21 October 1999

67  Ibid.

68  Fax to Jane Wymark, 23 April 1999

69  Fax to David Firman, 1999

70  Fax to Richenda Carey, 13 September 1999

71  Ibid.

72  Letter to Jon Plowman, February 1999

73  Fax to Lucy Ansbro, 20 September 1999

74  Letter to the *dinnerladies* cast, 10 September 1999

75  Fax to Jane Wymark, 20 September 1999

76  Interview with the author, 4 January 2005

77  Fax to Richenda Carey, 26 July 1999

78  Fax to Jane Wymark, 30 September 1999

79  Fax to Richenda Carey, 4 October 1999

80  Fax to Paul Roberts, 5 October 1999

81  Fax to Jane Wymark, 1 October 1999

82  Fax to Richenda Carey, 1 November 1999

83  Speech at the memorial concert for James Watson, 18 June 2011

84  Fax to Richenda Carey, 4 November 1999

85  Fax to Richenda Carey, December 1999

86  Ibid.

87  Ibid.

88  Ibid.

89  Fax to Lucy Ansbro, 20 September 1999

90  Letter to Michael Parkinson, December 1999

91  Fax to Jane Wymark, 30 September 1999


## Chapter 19:  Trimming

1   Fax to Celia Imrie, February 2000

2   Letter to Moyra Livesey, 7 February 2000

3   Fax to Phil McIntyre and Lucy Ansbro, 7 February 2000

4   Letter to the calendar girls, 14 February 2000

5   Ibid.

6   Fax to Julie Walters, February 2000

7   Fax to Celia Imrie, February 2000

8   Phil McIntyre letter to Moyra Livesey, 6 March 2000

9   Fax to Julie Walters, March 2000

10  Fax to Richenda Carey, 27 March 2000

11  Fax to Richenda Carey, 27 March 2000

12  Letter to Bass, March 2000

13  Fax to Richenda Carey, 3 May 2000

14 Ibid.
15 Letter from Peter Salmon, 4 January 2000
16 Fax to Richenda Carey, 9 May 2000
17 Outline for Victoria Wood Xmas Special, 30 July 2000
18 Fax to Richenda Carey, 19 June 2000
19 Fax to Jemma Rodgers, July 2002
20 Fax to Celia Imrie, 2000
21 Fax to Richenda Carey, 30 January 2001
22 Fax to Richenda Carey, 6 September 2000
23 Fax to Jane Wymark, 17 November 2000
24 Fax to Celia Imrie, September 2000
25 Letter to Roger Moore, 3 November 2000
26 Interview with Lucy Kenwright, BBC Additional Programmes Unit, 2009
27 Letter to Pierce Brosnan, 9 October 2000
28 Letter to Pierce Brosnan, 3 November 2000
29 Ibid.
30 Letter to Peter Salmon, 13 January 2001
31 Letter to Greg Dyke, 22 June 2000
32 Letter to Paul McCartney, 15 October 2000
33 Fax to Jane Wymark, 17 November 2000
34 Ibid.
35 Letter to Ann Widdecombe, 28 September 2000
36 Fax from Julie Walters, 25 December 2000
37 Letter to Peter Salmon, 13 January 2001
38 Fax to Richenda Carey, 10 January 2001
39 Ibid.
40 Fax to Richenda Carey, 26 January 2001
41 Fax to Richenda Carey, 30 January 2001
42 'Victoria's plums', interview with James Rampton, *Radio Times*, 18 October 2001
43 Fax to Amie Beamish, 5 February 2001
44 Fax to Richenda Carey, 4 March 2001
45 Interview with the author, 6 June 2001
46 Ibid.
47 Ibid.
48 Fax from Julie Walters, 17 March 2001
49 Fax to Richenda Carey, 15 March 2001
50 Fax to Richenda Carey, 22 March 2001
51 Fax to Jane Wymark, 2001
52 Fax to Richenda Carey, 17 May 2001

53 Fax to Richenda Carey, 25 May 2001
54 Fax to Richenda Carey, 6 February 2001
55 Fax to Jane Wymark, 21 January 1999
56 Fax to Richenda Carey, 29 May 2001
57 Fax to Richenda Carey, 6 June 2001
58 Interview with the author, 10 September 2001
59 Ibid.
60 Ibid.
61 Interview with the author, 6 June 2001
62 Ibid.
63 Ibid.
64 Ibid.
65 Email to Richenda Carey, 13 September 2009
66 Royal Albert Hall guestbook, 2001
67 Letter from Marcus Setchell, 14 October 2001
68 'I used to binge on strawberry jam and a loaf of bread . . . at least it was cheaper than drugs', interview with Sue Carroll, *Mirror*, 8 September 2001
69 Fax to Richenda Carey, 12 October 2001
70 Fax to Richenda Carcy, 5 November 2001
71 Card to Duncan Preston, 1990
72 Interview with the author, 6 June 2001
73 Fax to Richenda Carey, 18 March 2001
74 Fax to Richenda Carey, 30 November 2001
75 *Desert Island Discs*, BBC Radio 4, 23 December 2007
76 Card to Jane Wymark, January 2001
77 *In Conversation with . . .*, BBC Radio 4, 14 March 2002
78 Card to Jane Wymark, 2 February 2002
79 Ibid.
80 Fax to Jane Wymark, 22 February 2002
81 Ibid.
82 Fax to Jane Wymark, 28 February 2002
83 Interview with the author, 16 October 2003
84 Fax to Jane Wymark, April 2002
85 Ibid.
86 Interview with the author, 16 October 2003

## Chapter 20: Acorns

1 Letter from Trevor Nunn, 18 September 1996
2 Letter from Trevor Nunn, 4 January 2002

3   Interview with the author, 16 October 2003
4   Interview with the author, 4 January 2005
5   Letter to Trevor Nunn, 14 January 2002
6   Letter to Trevor Nunn, 25 February 2002
7   Letter to Bob Eaton, March 2002
8   'I am much happier now I'm near 50', interview with Cassandra Jardine, *Daily Telegraph*, 9 May 2003
9   Interview with the author, 16 October 2003
10  Ibid.
11  Ibid.
12  Ibid.
13  Ibid.
14  Ibid.
15  Letter from Celia Imrie, 2002
16  Letter from Trevor Nunn, 5 September 2003
17  Interview with the author, 16 October 2003
18  Charles Spencer, *Evening Standard*, 30 September 1980
19  'Whether she's making you laugh or making you cry – Julie Walters is a natural', interview with Tessa Parun, 19 January 1981
20  Philip Purser, *Sunday Telegraph*, 24 January 1982
21  Francis King, *Sunday Telegraph*, 19 February 1984
22  Michael Rowberry, *Coventry Evening Telegraph*, August 1983
23  Paul Barker, *New Society*, 1 September 1983
24  Peter Hepple, *Stage*, 10 November 1983
25  Interview with Mervyn Edgecombe, *Woman*, 15 November 1986
26  Interview with the author, 6 June 2001
27  'Touch Wood', interview with Paddy Burt, *Home & Gardens*, October 1987
28  Interview with the author, 6 June 2001
29  Interview with the author, 16 October 2003
30  Ibid.
31  Ibid.
32  'Victoria's secrets', interview with Harriet Lane, *Guardian*, 9 January 2005
33  Interview with the author, 4 January 2005
34  Fax from Julie Walters, 9 March 2004
35  Fax from Celia Imrie, 28 February 2004
36  Fax to Julie Walters, April 2004
37  Fax from Julie Walters, 23 April 2004
38  Interview with the author, 16 October 2003
39  Letter to various recipients, May 2004
40  Fax from Trevor Nunn, 24 May 2004

41 Fax to Trevor Nunn, May 2004
42 'Victoria reigns', interview with E. Jane Dickson, *Radio Times*, 5 February 2005
43 Interview with the author, 4 January 2005
44 Ibid.
45 Ibid.
46 Paul Taylor, *Independent*, 11 February 2005
47 Benedict Nightingale, *The Times*, 11 February 2005
48 Susannah Clapp, *Observer*, 13 February 2005
49 Card to Geoffrey Strachan, 2005
50 Interview with the author, 10 November 2006
51 Ibid.

## Chapter 21: Historian, 53

1 Interview with the author, 10 November 2006
2 Email to Daniel Wiles, 25 October 2006
3 Interview with the author, 16 October 2003
4 Interview with Ben Lawrence, 12 April 2012
5 Interview with the author, 10 November 2006
6 Ibid.
7 Email to Rosalind Wood, 16 May 2005
8 Interview with the author, 10 November 2006
9 *What Did ITV Do For Me?*, ITV, September 2005
10 Email from Rosalind Wood, 20 September 2005
11 Interview with the author, 10 November 2006
12 Ibid.
13 Ibid.
14 Ibid.
15 Ibid.
16 'Victoria's secrets', interview with Harriet Lane, *Guardian*, 9 January 2005
17 Letter from Gavin Millar, 11 August 2006
18 Email to Richard E. Grant, 10 September 2006
19 Email from Paul Sommers to Daniel Wiles, 22 August 2006
20 Interview with the author, 10 November 2006
21 Ibid.
22 Ibid.
23 Ibid.
24 *Acorn Antiques: The Musical!* casting notes, 2006
25 Ibid.

26  Email to Rosalind Wood, 9 October 2006
27  Email to Daniel Wiles, 25 October 2006
28  Email to Rosalind Wood, 19 October 2006
29  Email from Richard E. Grant, 11 December 2006
30  Email to Rosalind Wood, 7 April 2008
31  Email to Lesley Fitton, 4 March 2008
32  Interview with the author, 19 August 2009

## Chapter 22:  Mid Life

1   Email to Rosalind Wood, 28 July 2007
2   Email to David Firman, 21 December 2007
3   Interview with the author, December 2007
4   Ibid.
5   Email to Rosalind Wood, 26 November 2007
6   Interview with the author, December 2007
7   Ibid.
8   Ibid.
9   Email to Rosalind Wood, 26 November 2007
10  Interview with the author, December 2007
11  Email to Richard E. Grant, 24 December 2007
12  Email to Lesley Fitton, 27 December 2007
13  Interview with the author, December 2007
14  Email to Lesley Fitton, 8 March 2008
15  Interview with the author, 19 August 2009
16  Email to Rosalind Wood, 5 May 2008
17  Email to Rosalind Wood, 20 March 2008
18  'Who's laughing now? Victoria Wood shows off slimline figure as she picks
    up CBE', *Daily Mail*, 30 October 2008
19  Email to Rosalind Wood, 29 September 2008
20  Interview with the author, 19 August 2009
21  Ibid.
22  Email to Lucy Ansbro, 24 November 2008
23  Plot outline for *The Giddy Kipper*, 23 January 2009
24  Email to Lucy Ansbro, 24 November 2008
25  Email to Lucy Ansbro, 21 January 2009
26  Ibid.
27  Email to Lucy Ansbro, 22 January 2009
28  Email to Lucy Ansbro, 3 March 2009
29  Email to Sammy Murray, 28 April 2009

30  Ibid

31  Email to Annie Tricklebank, 30 April 2009

32  *Desert Island Discs*, BBC Radio 4, 2 December 2007

33  Email to Sammy Murray, 30 April 3009

34  Email to Jane Wymark, 30 April 2009

35  Email to Rosalind Wood, 9 May 2009

36  Ibid.

37  Interview with the author, 19 August 2009

38  Email to Sammy Murray, 20 April 2009

39  Interview with the author, 19 August 2009

40  Ibid.

41  Ibid.

42  Email to Jane Wymark, 7 September 2009

43  Email to Rosalind Wood, 20 September 2009

44  Email to Nigel Lilley, 24 November 2009

45  Email to Jane Wymark, 7 September 2009

46  Email to Jane Wymark, 29 October, 2009

47  John Rushton email to Rebecca Papworth and Simon Wilson, 25 June 2009

48  Email to Sammy Murray, 11 December 2009

49  'I feel at the BBC I'm not trusted, not valued, not needed', interview with Decca Aitkenhead, *Guardian*, 27 September 2010

50  Email to Nigel Lilley, 24 November 2009

51  Email, 2 December 2009

## Chapter 23:  Loving Eric, Ernie, Eunice, Tubby, Enid, Joyce and Barrie

1   Email to Nigel Lilley, 21 January 2010

2   Email to John Rushton, 8 March 2010

3   Email to Nigel Lilley, 28 April 2010

4   Ibid.

5   Kenneth Bailey, *People*, 25 April 1954

6   Email to Jonny Campbell, 6 July 2010

7   Email to Nigel Lilley, 10 May 2010

8   *That Day We Sang* programme note, July 2011

9   Email to Nigel Lilley, 28 April 2010

10  Email to Nigel Lilley, 16 June 2010

11  Ibid.

12  Email to Sammy Murray, 20 April 2009

13  Email to Jane Wymark, 16 August 2010

14  Email to Jonny Campbell, 26 August 2010

15  Email to Charlotte Scott, 2 September 2010
16  'I feel at the BBC I'm not trusted, not valued, not needed', interview with Decca Aitkenhead, *Guardian*, 27 September 2010
17  Card to Daniel Rigby, October 2010
18  Email to Lesley Fitton, 5 January 2011
19  Email to Rosalind Wood, 16 October 2010
20  Email to Rosalind Wood, 18 October 2010
21  Email to Rosalind Wood, 24 November 2010
22  Email to Rosalind Wood, 18 October 2010
23  Email to Lesley Fitton, 5 January 2011
24  Ibid.
25  Email to Nigel Lilley, 2 February 2011
26  Email to Rosalind Wood, 24 May 2011
27  Email to Jane Wymark, 17 May 2011
28  Email to Lesley Fitton, 24 December 2010
29  Email to Amie Beamish, 21 May 2011
30  Email to Jane Wymark, 19 June 2011
31  Email to Lesley Fitton, 1 June 2011
32  Email to Jane Wymark, 10 July 2011
33  Email to Alex Poots, 26 September 2011
34  Email to Lesley Fitton, 22 July 2011
35  Email to John Rushton, 2011
36  Interview with Ben Lawrence, 12 April 2012
37  Ibid.
38  Email to Amie Beamish, 4 November 2011
39  Email to Sammy Murray, 28 November 2011
40  Email to Lesley Fitton, 21 December 2011
41  Email to Andy Harries and Matthew Read, 16 December 2001
42  Email to Radford Neville, 16 January 2012
43  Email to Radford Neville, 1 February 2012
44  Email to Peter Bowker, 6 February 2012
45  Email to Amie Beamish, 20 March 2012
46  Email to Radford Neville, 27 February 2012
47  Email to Radford Neville, 12 March2012
48  Email to Sammy Murray, 15 March 2012
49  Email to Sammy Murray, 2 May 2012
50  Email to Richenda Carey, 14 April 2012
51  Email to Nigel Lilley, 14 April 2012

## Chapter 24: That Day She Directed

1 Email to Sammy Murray, 2 May 2012
2 Email to Peter Bowker, 9 October 2012
3 Email to Richenda Carey, 6 June 2012
4 Email to Richenda Carey, 22 June 2012
5 Email to Jane Wymark, 17 May 2012
6 Email to Lesley Fitton, 2 July 2012
7 Email to Jane Wymark, 17 June 2013
8 Email to Rosalind Wood, 27 August 2012
9 Email to Rosalind Wood, 29 August 2012
10 Email to Jane Wymark, 21 March 2013
11 Email to Jane Wymark, 18 May 2013
12 Email to Jane Wymark, 22 August 2012
13 Email to Richenda Carey, 22 September 2012
14 Ibid.
15 Email to Jane Wymark, 29 September 2012
16 Email to Peter Bowker, 9 October 2012
17 Email to Peter Bowker, 29 November 2012
18 Email from Peter Bowker, 30 November 2012
19 Email to Jane Wymark, 24 January 2013
20 Email to Richenda Carey, 1 December 2012
21 Email to Nigel Lilley, 22 October 2012
22 Email to Nigel Lilley and Sammy Murray, 18 February 2013
23 Ibid.
24 Email from Nigel Lilley, 24 September 2013
25 Email to Nigel Lilley, 27 March 2013
26 'Julie Walters attacks arts cuts', Jason Deans, *Guardian*, 12 March 2013
27 Email to Richenda Carey, 10 April 2013
28 Email to Jane Wymark, 15 May 2013
29 Email to Richenda Carey, 31 May 2013
30 Email to Nigel Lilley, 17 June 2013
31 Email to Nigel Lilley, 3 July 2013
32 Email to Nigel Lilley and Sammy Murray, 3 June 2013
33 Email to Nigel Lilley, 5 August 2013
34 Email to Nigel Lilley, 25 August 2013
35 Ibid.
36 Email to Richenda Carey, 19 August 2013
37 Natasha Tripney, *Stage*, 16 September 2013
38 Email to Nigel Lilley, 10 September 2013

39  Email to Sammy Murray, 1 November 2013
40  Email to Nigel Lilley, 12 October 2013
41  Email to Jane Wymark, 15 October 2013
42  Ibid.
43  Email to Jane Wymark, 6 November 2013
44  Email to Nigel Lilley, 16 October 2013
45  Email to Nigel Lilley, 21 November 2013
46  Email to Richard E. Grant, 9 December 2013
47  Email to Nigel Lilley, 21 November 2013
48  Email to Nigel Lilley, 23 December 2013
49  Email to Sammy Murray, 3 September 2013
50  Email to Jane Wymark, 16 January 2014
51  Email to Rosalind Wood, 20 January 2014
52  Ibid.
53  Email to Nigel Lilley, 10 February 2014
54  Email to Jane Wymark, 14 February 2014
55  Email to Jane Wymark, 26 February 2014
56  Email to Nigel Lilley, 12 March 2014
57  Email to Richenda Carey, 12 May 2014
58  Email to Jane Wymark, 22 June 2014
59  Email to Nigel Lilley, 27 June 2014
60  Email to Nigel Lilley, 19 July 2014
61  Email to Michael Codron, 26 July 2014
62  Email to Sammy Murray, September 2014
63  Email to Nigel Lilley, 20 September 2014
64  Ibid.
65  Email to Daniel Rigby, March 2015
66  Email to Nigel Lilley, 2 October 2014
67  Email to Jane Wymark, 15 November 2014
68  Email to Jane Wymark, 22 November 2014
69  Email to Nigel Lilley, 2 December 2014
70  Email to Nigel Lilley, 29 December 2014
71  Ibid.
72  Ibid.

## Chapter 25:  The Bogeyman

1   Email to Jane Wymark, 30 January 2015
2   Email to Jane Wymark, 8 February 2015
3   Email to Daniel Rigby, March 2015

4   Email to Nigel Lilley, 12 February 2015
5   Email to Nigel Lilley, 18 March 2015
6   Email to Nigel Lilley, 30 March 2015
7   Email to Jane Wymark, 15 March 2015
8   Email to Nigel Lilley, 23 March 2015
9   Email to Nigel Lilley, 28 April 2015
10  Email to Nigel Lilley, 20 February 2015
11  Email to Nigel Lilley, 26 April 2015
12  Email to Rosalind Wood, 7 July 2015
13  Email to Nigel Lilley, 8 April 2015
14  Email to Catherine Morshead, 6 May 2015
15  Email to Jane Wymark, 26 May 2015
16  Email to Jane Wymark, 15 June 2015
17  Email to Penelope Wood and Rosalind Wood, 3 August 2015
18  Emails to Jane Wymark, 7 August 2015
19  Email to Rosalind Wood, 3 August 2015
20  Email to Jane Wymark, 28 August 2015
21  Email to Jane Wymark, 2 September 2015
22  Email to Jane Wymark, 20 September 2015
23  Email to Jane Wymark, 23 October 2015
24  Email to Amie Beamish, 20 October 2015
25  Email to Jane Wymark, 19 October 2015
26  Email to Jane Wymark, 24 October 2015
27  Email to Jane Wymark, 26 October 2015
28  Email to Jane Wymark, 3 November 2015
29  Email to Jane Wymark, 10 November 2015
30  Email to Jane Wymark, 28 November 2015
31  Ibid.
32  Email to Amie Beamish, 20 October 2015
33  Email to Radcliffe Neville, 8 December 2015
34  Email to Richenda Carey, 23 December 2015
35  Email to Rosalind Wood, 12 January 2016
36  Email to Jane Wymark, 7 January 2016
37  Email to Jane Wymark, 16 January 2016
38  Email to Jane Wymark, 25 January 2016
39  Email to Cathy Edis, 17 February 2016
40  Ibid.
41  Email to Jane Wymark, 30 January 2016
42  Email to Cathy Edis, 7 March 2016
43  Email to Jane Wymark, 29 March 2016
44  Email to Jane Wymark, 1 April 2016

# ACKNOWLEDGEMENTS

I am indebted, first and foremost, to Grace Durham and Henry Durham for granting me permission to write their mother's biography, also to Victoria's literary executor Lucy Ansbro and her colleague Adele Fowler for their unstinting generosity and support, and to Neil Reading for introducing me to Victoria in the first place and ensuring that we continued to meet. My profound thanks to them all.

I am deeply grateful to Geoffrey Durham, who selflessly gave up much time to answer questions and resolve uncertainties. His was the most extreme version of an experience undergone by those who knew and worked with Victoria over many years: Cathy Edis, David Firman, Celia Imrie, Nigel Lilley, Phil McIntyre, Sammy Murray, Geoff Posner, Duncan Preston, Paul Roberts, Julie Walters and Piers Wenger. My thanks to each of them for their kindness.

My first interviewee was Rosalind Watson, whom I thank for her ceaseless encouragement, as well as for handing over a horde of her sister's correspondence. My thanks also to Penelope Wood for conjuring up the world of Victoria's childhood. Many others, including some listed above, generously shared letters, faxes, emails and other unpublished writings by Victoria: Amie Beamish, Peter Bowker, Jonny Campbell, Michael Codron, Lesley Fitton, Richard E. Grant, Robert Howie, Alison Lloyd, Bill Lloyd, Roger McGough, Catherine Morshead, Radford Neville, Chrissie Poulter, Anne Reid, Daniel Rigby, Andy Roberts, John Rushton, Charlotte Scott, Imelda Staunton, Geoffrey Strachan, Daniel Wiles and Beth Willis. For sharing their collection of correspondence I am most indebted to Richenda Carey and above all to Jane Wymark. Special thanks, too, to Sahlan Diver for retrieving and digitising the earliest recordings of Victoria in performance, and to John Carnegie for sharing Victoria's trumpet alarums. I also thank Chris Foote Wood for permission to quote

Stanley Wood's letters published in *Victoria Wood: Comedy Genius – Her Life and Work*, Roger Wilmut for sharing the tape of his conversation with Victoria from 1987, and Ben Lawrence for donating the transcript of his 2012 interview with Victoria for the *Daily Telegraph*. My thanks to those who allowed their own correspondence to be quoted, and to those who gave permission for use of their image in photographs.

Many people I spoke to were close to Victoria for decades; for others, their path crossed hers only briefly. To all I am grateful for sharing their memories, often supported by photographs and documents: Paul Allen, Gareth Armstrong, Rachel Ashdown, Catherine Ashmore, Alan Ayckbourn, Chrissie Baker, Michael Ball, Thelma Barlow, Nina Barough, Nicholas Barrett, Gerard Barry, Chris Beetles, Alan Bennett, Graham Benson, Hilary Bevan Jones, Jenny Bialek, Susie Blake, Jim Broadbent, Lez Brotherston, Gaye Brown, Ruth Caleb, Jasper Carrott, Trevor Chance, Peter Chelsom, Simon Cherry, Greg Childs, Jack Chissick, John Clarke, Vivienne Clore, Patrick Collerton, Emma Cope, Jane Cotton, Aidan J. Crawley, Joe Dawson, Martin Davey, Janet Davies, Janie Dee, Les Dennis, Shaun Dooley, Nigel Douglas, Tony Dow, John Dowie, Andrew Dunn, Peter Ellis, Harry Enfield, Russell England, Daniel Evans, Nigel Everett, Louise Fisher, Gregory Floy, John Foley, Sarah Frankcom, Vincent Franklin, Stephen Frears, Jonathan Freeman-Attwood, Dawn French, Ian Gardhouse, Kerry Gill-Pryde, Roger Glossop, Stephen Glynn, John Gorman, Roy Gould, David Graham, Deborah Grant, Helen Gregory, Chris Harper, Andy Harries, Chris Haydon, Lenny Henry, Judith Holder, Graham Howarth, Wendy Howard, Dusty Hughes, Ron Hutchinson, George Irving, Jason Isaacs, Betty Jackson, Gerald Jackson, Peter James, Ria Jones, Steve Joyce, Lucy Kenwright, Lizzi Kew Ross, Claire Lachowicz, David Leland, Moyra Livesey, John Lloyd, Philip Lowrie, Lucy Lumsden, Christopher Luscombe, Kate Mackonochie, Mary McMurray, Nicky Martyn, Margaret Matheson, Sean Mathias, Billy Mawhinney, Stephen Mear, Alastair Meux, Deborah Moggach, Gary Morecambe, James Moir, Fidelis Morgan, Pieter Morpurgo, Marcus Mortimer, David Morton, John Moulson, Nina Myskow, Stuart Orme, Jim Parker, Steve Pemberton, Alex

Poots, Esther Rantzen, Dave Richmond, Kate Robbins, Ted Robbins, Jemma Rodgers, Lynda Ronan, Jessica Ronane, Jenna Russell, Peter Salmon, Lesley Schatzberger, Catherine Seddon, Marcus Setchell, Nick Skilbeck, Tony Slater-Ling, Roger Sloman, Robyn Slovo, Bob Smith, Russell Smith, Paul Sommers, Carol Spraggs, John Stacey, Anne Sweeney, Baz Taylor, Harriet Thorpe, David Threlfall, Lawrence Till, Damien Timmer, Paula Trafford, Steve Trow, Gareth Valentine, Sue Wallace, Ben Warwick, Jason Watkins, Nigel Wattis, Norah Wellbelove, Vanessa Whitburn, Sioned Wiliam, Charles Worthington, Jane Wynn Owen and Kirsty Young. I would like to pay my respects to the memory of Eddie Large and André Ptaszynski.

I was offered practical support by James Alexander, Will Awdry, Ian Birch, James Bromet, Miles Chapman, Jo Collins, Tim de Lisle, Ruth Huntman, Liz Keegan, Maya Kemp, Bertie Leigh, Don Maclean, Joy Wood and Caroline Wright. My thanks to them, and to the BBC Written Archives Centre, and to Susan Lord of Bury Art Museum and Libby Gregory, to whom I am particularly indebted for helping me gain access to the Victoria Wood archive.

I would like to extend deep gratitude to all at Orion who have brought this book to fruition with inspiring warmth and calm professionalism in the trying circumstances thrown at them by coronavirus: Anna Valentine, Lucinda McNeile, Virginia Woolstencroft, Helen Ewing and Natalie Dawkins. I am grateful also to Paul Murphy for his sensitive copy-editing, and to Paul Stark of Orion and Elspeth McPherson of Strathmore Publishing for overseeing production of the audiobook. I owe a second round of thanks to those of Victoria's family, friends and associates – as well as Chris Harvey and Veronica Lee – who read the first draft and provided valuable comments.

Finally, I would like to express my thanks to James Gill – no author could hope for a sturdier or more resourceful agent.

My most personal debt is to Emily Maitland for the years she spent living with this other life.

# INDEX

# PHOTO CREDITS

All photographs are the property of the Victoria Wood archive unless otherwise stated.

Stanley and Helen Wood. Courtesy of Rosalind Watson.

Penelope, Rosalind, and Victoria as a baby. Courtesy of Rosalind Watson.

Stanley with Victoria. Courtesy of Rosalind Watson.

Birtle Edge House. Courtesy of Rosalind Watson.

With Rosalind in the photobooth. Courtesy of Rosalind Watson.

With Rosalind and Penelope. Courtesy of Rosalind Watson.

An early performance in Birmingham. Photograph by Steve Glynn.

Victoria reading. Courtesy of Fidelis Morgan.

With Celia Imrie. Courtesy of Fidelis Morgan.

Austerity party. Courtesy of Fidelis Morgan.

With John Dowie. Photograph by Nigel Iskander. Courtesy of John Dowie.

Outside the Royal Albert Hall. Photograph by Chris Christodoulou.

With Helen and Rosalind. Courtesy of Rosalind Watson.

As Mrs Overall. Photograph by Catherine Ashmore.

With Nigel Lilley and Sammy Murray. Photograph by Catherine Ashmore.

With Piers Wenger. Photograph by Catherine Ashmore.

With Jane Wymark, Catherine Ashmore and Paul Howson. Courtesy of Jane Wymark.

With Grace and Henry at Christmas. Photograph by Penelope Wood. Courtesy of Rosalind Watson.

With some Barrys and a Freda. Photograph by Catherine Ashmore.

With the cast of *Eric & Ernie*. Courtesy of Daniel Rigby.

At her sixtieth birthday party. Courtesy of Sammy Murray.

Performing at the wedding of Beth Willis and Jonny Campbell. Photograph by Debs Alexander Photography. Courtesy of Beth Willis and Jonny Campbell.

Listening to the Hallé Orchestra. Photograph by Luis Cortes.

With Beth Willis by Esthwaite Water. Photograph by Jonny Campbell. Courtesy of Beth Willis and Jonny Campbell.

At it again. Photograph by Catherine Ashmore.